MATTHEW J. BRUCCOLI AND

JUDITH S. BAUGHMAN, EDITORS

CRUX

THE LETTERS OF
JAMES DICKEY

ALFRED A. KNOPF   NEW YORK   1999

THIS IS A BORZOI BOOK

PUBLISHED BY ALFRED A. KNOPF

Letters copyright © 1999 by the Estate of James L. Dickey III;
Matthew J. Bruccoli, Literary Personal Representative
Introduction and chronology copyright © 1999
by Matthew J. Bruccoli and Judith S. Baughman

Library of Congress Cataloging-in-Publication Data
Dickey, James.
    Crux : the letters of James Dickey / Matthew J. Bruccoli and
Judith S. Baughman, editors. — 1st ed.
        p.   cm.
    ISBN 0-375-40419-8 (alk. paper)
    1. Dickey, James—Correspondence.   2. Authors, American—20th
century Correspondence.   I. Bruccoli, Matthew Joseph, [date].
II. Baughman, Judith.   III. Title.
PS3554.I32Z48   1999
811'.54—dc21   99-15608
    [B]   CIP

Manufactured in the United States of America
First Edition

This book is dedicated to James Dickey's friend,

STANLEY BURNSHAW.

Crux n. A constellation in the Southern Hemisphere near Centaurus and Musca. Also called the *Southern Cross.*

A difficult problem or unanswered question.

The title of the unfinished novel James Dickey was writing at his death.

CONTENTS

ILLUSTRATIONS

ACKNOWLEDGMENTS

THE FOLLOWING PEOPLE answered letters, offered their advice, or made their James Dickey correspondence available: Dannie Abse; Michael Allin; Shaye Areheart; Jennifer Austin; Ronald Baughman; Ben Belitt; Wendell Berry; Robert Bly; John Boorman; Philip Booth; Alvin Boretz; David Bottoms; Brian Boyd; Al Braselton; Van K. Brock; Ashley Brown; William F. Buckley Jr.; Jean Burden; Stanley Burnshaw; Chris Byrne; Hortense Calisher; Mary Cantwell; Hayden Carruth; R. V. Cassill; Robert Conquest; Robert Cowley; Robert Creeley; Christopher Dickey; Patsy Dickey; Kate Donahue; Denis Donoghue; Nicholas Fargnoli; Paula Feldman; Sally Fitzgerald; Robert A. Geckle Jr.; Matthew K. Gwinn; Lloyd Hackl; Donald Hall; James Hardin; Joseph Heller; Jerome Hellman; Nat Hentoff; John Hollander; Richard Howard; David Ignatow; Marc Jaffe; Michael B. Jasper; Gary Kerley; Jascha Kessler; E. Lewis King; John L'Heureux; James Laughlin; Richard Layman; Robert Lescher; Denise Levertov; Laurence Lieberman; Gordon Lish; Jay Losey; Edward Madden; John Maloney; Inman Mays; Walter McDonald; Terry Miller; Willie Morris; Lance Morrow; Susan Brind Morrow; Dmitri Nabokov; John Frederick Nims; Joyce Carol Oates; Joyce M. Pair; William Pratt; Reynolds Price; Theron Raines (Agent for the Estate of James Dickey); David Ray; Thomas J. Rice; Stewart Richardson; Karen L. Rood; Ned Rorem; Louis D. Rubin Jr.; Thomas R. Smith; William Jay Smith; Monroe Spears; Elizabeth Spencer; Jacques de Spoelberch; Ernest Suarez; Henry Taylor; William Thesing; Brenda Tomlinson; Charles Tomlinson; Robert W. Trogdon; Mona Van Duyn; Peter Viereck; Anne G. Walsh; Gwendolyn Leege Walti; Theodore Weiss; Richard Wilbur; Miller Williams; Greg Wilsbacher; Herman Wouk; and Anne Wright.

The editors owe extraordinary debts to Dean George Terry, Patrick Scott, Jamie Hansen, Paul Schultz, Tom McNally, and Mary Anyomi of the Special Collections Department, Thomas Cooper Library, University of South Carolina; to Stephen Enniss, Department of Special Collections, Robert W. Woodruff Library, Emory University; and to Anne Posega, Modern Literature Collection, Olin Library System, Washington University in St. Louis.

The following librarians, publishers, booksellers, and officers of foundations and associations also provided valuable help: David C. Waters, Cemetery Committee, All Saints' Parish Church, Waccamaw, Pawleys Island, South Carolina; Virginia Dajoni, American Academy of Arts and Letters; John Lancaster, Archives and Special Collections, Amherst College Library; Nancy Saunders, University of Arkansas Press; Alison John, British Broadcasting Corporation; Gary Nargi, Bookfinder; Mark N. Brown, Manuscripts Division, John Hay Library, Brown University; Anthony S. Bliss, Rare Books and Literary Manuscripts, Bancroft Library, University of California, Berkeley; Bradley D. Westbrook, Mandeville Special Collections Library, University of California, San Diego; Ken Losey, Copperfield's Annex; Philip Cronenwett, Rauner Special Collections Library, Dartmouth College; L. Rebecca Johnson Melvin, Special Collections, University of Delaware Library; Janie C. Morris, Rare Book, Manuscript, and Special Collections Library, Duke University; Richard Higgins and Beth Rainey, Basil Bunting Collection, Durham University Library, Durham, UK; Idelle Missila-Stone, Archives Department, Ford Foundation; Nancy Davis Bray, Special Collections, Ina Dillard Russell Library, Georgia College and State University; Leslie A. Morris and Jennie Rathbun, Houghton Library, Harvard University; Gayle M. Barkley, Department of Manuscripts, Huntington Library, San Marino, California; William J. Maher, University Archives, University of Illinois at Urbana-Champaign; William Cagle and Saundra Taylor, Manuscripts Division, Lilly Library, Indiana University; Claire McCann, Special Collections and Archives, Margaret I. King Library, University of Kentucky; Alice Birney and William H. Mobley, Manuscripts Division, Library of Congress; L. E. Phillabaum and Erica Bossier, Louisiana State University Press; Linda Seidman, Special Collections, University Library, University of Massachusetts, Amherst; Andrea R. Beauchamp, Hopwood Program, University of Michigan, Ann Arbor; Kathryn L. Beam, Special Collections, Harlan Hatcher Graduate Library, University of Michigan, Ann Arbor; Alan K. Lathrop and Barbara Bezat, Manuscripts Division, University of Minnesota Libraries; Jim Baird, Monolithos; Jodi L. Allison-Bunnell, K. Ross Toole Archives, Maureen and Mike Mansfield Library, University of Montana; Mary Crittendon, Nanine Hutchinson, and Cynthia S. Thompson, University Press of New England; Roland Goodbody, Special Collections and University Archives, University of New Hampshire; Jo Ellen M. Dickie, Special Collections, Newberry Library, Chicago; Sandra J. Slater, Special Collections, Chester Fritz Library, University of North Dakota; Richard A. Shrader and Alice R. Cotten, Manuscripts Department, Wilson Library, University of North Carolina, Chapel Hill; Wayne Furman and Rodney Phillips, The Henry W. and Albert A. Berg Collection of English and American Literature, New York Public Library, Astor, Lenox and Tilden Foundations; Charles E. Moore, Mary Flannery O'Connor Charitable Trust; Don C. Skemer, John

Delaney, and AnnaLee Pauls, Manuscripts Division, Princeton University Libraries; Gerrianne Schaad, Department of Special Collections, Fondren Library, Rice University; Edward Skipworth, Special Collections and Archives, Rutgers University Libraries; Bill Blackbeard, San Francisco Academy of Comic Art; Catherine Fry and Barry Blose, University of South Carolina Press; Tim Noakes, Department of Special Collections, Stanford University Library; Robert J. Bertholf, The Poetry/Rare Books Collection, University Libraries, State University of New York at Buffalo; Kathleen Manwaring, Department of Special Collections, George Arents Research Library, Syracuse University; Thomas S. Staley and Bill Fagelson, Harry Ransom Humanities Research Center, University of Texas at Austin; J. Michalan, Department of Special Collections, Tufts University Libraries; Kathleen I. Smith, Special Collections, Jean and Alexander Heard Library, Vanderbilt University; Jeffrey D. Marshall, Special Collections, Bailey/Howe Library, University of Vermont; Edmund Berkeley Jr., Special Collections Department, Alderman Library, University of Virginia; John R. Turner, Division of Library Services, University of Wales; Gary A. Lundell, Manuscripts and University Archives, University of Washington Libraries; Vaughan Stanley and Lisa McCown, Special Collections, James G. Leyburn Library, Washington and Lee University; Suzanna Tamminen, Wesleyan University Press; Robert Turner, Tim Ericson, and Christel Maass, Department of Special Collections, Golda Meir Library, University of Wisconsin, Milwaukee; Jim Baird, Wordplay; Carol Bowers, American Heritage Center, University of Wyoming; Patricia C. Willis, Lynn Braunsdorf, and Maureen D. Heher, Yale Collection of American Literature, Beinecke Rare Book and Manuscript Library, Yale University; Richard Miller and Brooke Conti, Yale Series of Younger Poets, Yale University Press.

Arlyn Bruccoli and Ward W. Briggs provided excellent advice on the inclusion or exclusion of letters. Henry Hart shared substantial biographical information. Park Bucker, Lisa Damiano, and Barbara Brown, graduate students at the University of South Carolina, supplied exemplary research assistance.

M.J.B. and J.S.B.

EDITORIAL PLAN

ALL LETTERS are complete, except for rare instances in which a few words have been omitted on the grounds of privacy; these omissions are represented by empty brackets. When words appear within brackets, they are inferential readings from unclear carbon copies or manuscripts. James Dickey's deletions on his letters are not transcribed or noted. There are no editorial emendations—except for corrections of strikeovers or transpositions in typed letters, most of which were typed by secretaries after 1968. Dickey variously provided his secretaries with manuscript drafts and dictated to them. He characteristically corrected and revised the typescripts, having them retyped when his revisions were extensive. Uncorrected carbon copies were usually filed, as were—beginning in the early 1990s—Xeroxes of drafts or of final signed copies of letters. The letters in this volume have been transcribed from the best texts available: the mailed ribbon copies when located, otherwise the latest carbon or Xerox copy.

The heading for each letter provides four categories of information:

RECIPIENT
Date (if not on letter)   *Description and location of document*
              Place of writing (if not on letter)

These abbreviations are used to describe the documents that have been transcribed:

ALS (autograph letter signed)
AL (autograph letter unsigned)
CC (carbon copy)
MS (manuscript)
TLS (typed letter signed)
TL (typed letter unsigned)
RTLS (revised typed letter signed)
RTL (revised typed letter unsigned)
RCC (revised carbon copy)

The following designators are used to identify locations for Dickey letters:

Amherst College = Archives and Special Collections, Amherst College Library
Bancroft Library = Rare Books and Literary Manuscripts, Bancroft Library, University of California, Berkeley
Berg Collection, NYPL = Henry W. and Albert A. Berg Collection of English and American Literature, New York Public Library, Astor, Lenox and Tilden Foundations
Brown University = Manuscripts Division, John Hay Library, Brown University
Dartmouth College = Rauner Special Collections Library, Dartmouth College
Emory = Department of Special Collections, Robert W. Woodruff Library, Emory University
Harvard = Houghton Library, Harvard University
HRHRC = Harry Ransom Humanities Research Center, University of Texas at Austin
Library of Congress = Manuscripts Division, Library of Congress
Lilly Library = Lilly Library, Indiana University
LSU Press = Louisiana State University Press, Baton Rouge
University of Michigan = Special Collections, Harlan Hatcher Graduate Library, University of Michigan, Ann Arbor
University of Minnesota = Manuscripts Division, University of Minnesota Libraries
University of New Hampshire = Special Collections and University Archives, University of New Hampshire
University of North Carolina, Chapel Hill = Manuscripts Department, Wilson Library, University of North Carolina, Chapel Hill
Princeton = Manuscripts Division, Princeton University Library
Rice University = Department of Special Collections, Fondren Library, Rice University
University of South Carolina = Special Collections Department, Thomas Cooper Library, University of South Carolina
Stanford University = Department of Special Collections, Stanford University Library
SUNY Buffalo = The Poetry/Rare Book Collection, University Libraries, State University of New York at Buffalo

Syracuse University = Department of Special Collections, George Arents Research Library, Syracuse University

Vanderbilt = Special Collections, Jean and Alexander Heard Library, Vanderbilt University

University of Vermont = Special Collections, Bailey/Howe Library, University of Vermont

University of Washington = Manuscripts and University Archives, University of Washington Libraries

Washington and Lee = Special Collections, James G. Leyburn Library, Washington and Lee University

Washington University = Modern Literature Collection, Olin Library System, Washington University in St. Louis

Yale = Yale Collection of American Literature, Beinecke Rare Book and Manuscript Library, Yale University

INTRODUCTION

I make no real distinction between fact, fiction, history, reminiscence and fantasy, for the imagination inhabits them all.

—JAMES DICKEY

JAMES DICKEY AND I agreed that great writers are more important than everybody else. This conviction was the basis for our friendship while we were colleagues at the University of South Carolina from 1969 to his death in 1997. I disapproved of his conduct and celebrated his genius. On that basis we grew close, and his will appointed me his literary personal representative.

Jim's commitment to literature was authentic and convincing. Great writing—his own and other writers'—was a cherished thing for him. His literary taste and critical judgment were impeccable. Jim was the best book-talker I have known. Anything he said about literature—drunk or sober—merited careful attention. He was not unnecessarily truthful about himself, but he was trustworthy on literature.

Jim had the most retentive literary mind I have known. His literary memory is a characteristic of his epistolary technique. The true biography of a writer is a list of the books he read and how he used them. One afternoon when he was at my house drunk, and I was trying to take his car keys away from him, he noticed a copy of Perry Lentz's *The Falling Hills,* which Jim had read twenty or more years previously. He proceeded to discuss the novel in precise recall. On this same occasion he dictated, from memory, revisions for a statement on F. Scott Fitzgerald he had written several days earlier—thereby improving it. That was when I clearly understood my responsibility to serve Jim, because I would never find a better literary mind. The payoff for me was our sessions of book talk, usually on Sunday afternoons when his groupies weren't around.

The letters assembled in this volume represent perhaps twenty percent of James Dickey's located correspondence. The double rationale for selection was first to document the growth of a major writer—how a scarcely educated jock discovered that he possessed genius and that writing was the only thing that counted—then, second, to document the ways he fulfilled his genius and advanced his career. Jim was unabashedly a careerist. He had a clear understanding of the odds against any poet, no matter how gifted, and he recognized that his poetry did not exist if it was not read. He deliberately promoted and exaggerated his several reputations—genius, drinker, woodsman, athlete—until the legends took over after *Deliverance.* The best letters here are the ones about writing and the profession of authorship; his correspondence documents the accuracy of his critical judgments.

The decision to focus on the development of Jim's career obviated the life-in-letters biographical approach. These letters do not provide a systematic biography of James Dickey in his own words. His conduct as husband and father is only indirectly revealed. I regret that this volume does not establish the role of Jim's first wife, Maxine, in his success. She was my friend before he was; I greatly respected her. Nor do these letters adequately cover Jim's highly effective teaching of writing and poetry at the University of South Carolina. When he was running out of breath and unable to leave his chair where he lived in an igloo of books, Jim continued teaching his poetry composition course at home. In his final class James Dickey testified to the value of his craft:

> When we get started, I want you to fight this thing through. Fight the thing through that we start with your own unconscious and your own dreams and see where it comes out. That's the excitement and the fun of it. Deep discovery, deep adventure. It's the most dangerous game and the best. Flaubert says somewhere that "The life of a poet is a hell of a life. It's a dog's life. But it's the only one worth living." You suffer more, you're frustrated more. All the things that don't bother other people. But you also live so much more. You live so much more intensely and so much more vitally and with so much more of a sense of meaning, of consequentiality. Of things mattering instead of nothing mattering. This is what's driving our whole civilization into suicide. The fear that we are living an existence in which nothing matters very much or at

all. . . . A sense of non-consequence, a sense of nothing, nothing matters. No matter which way we turn it's the same thing. The poet is free of that. He's free of it. To the poet everything matters, and it matters a lot, and that's the realm where we work and once you're there you are hooked. If you're a real poet you're hooked more deeply than any narcotics addict could possibly be hooked on heroin. You're hooked on something that is life-giving instead of destructive. Something that is a process which cannot be too far from the process that created everything. God's process. . . . What this universe indubitably is is a poet's universe. Nothing but a poetic kind of consciousness could have conceived of anything like this. That's where the truth of the matter lies. You are in some way in line with the creative genesis of the universe in some way, in a much lesser way of course, because we can't create those trees or that water or anything that's out there. We can't do it but we can recreate it. We are secondary creators. We take God's universe and we make it over our way and it's different from his. It's similar in some ways, but it's different in some ways. The difference lies in the slant. The slant that we individually put on it and that only we can put on it. That's the difference and that's where our value lies. Not only for ourselves but for the other people who read us. The other people who read us. There's some increment there that we make possible that would not otherwise be there. I don't mean to sell the poet so long or to such great length, but I do this principally because the world doesn't esteem the poet very much. They don't really understand where we're coming from. They don't understand the use for us or if there is any use. They don't really value us very much. We are the masters of a superior secret, not they. Not they. Remember that when you write. You are at the top level and they are down there with Elvis and Marilyn Monroe and the general idols of the schlock culture we live in. We're the elitists. I don't mind saying that at all. Quality is what we strive for. The best standards. My grandmother was born in Germany and she used to quote from Goethe a lot and one of her favorite sayings was, "Whoever strives upward, him can we save." . . . we must find some way to write as though our hands were the hands of someone miraculously superior to ourselves. This is what we aim for. So when you begin to say things you didn't know you knew or you had never had any idea that you had any notion that you knew, then maybe you're getting somewhere you should be as a poet. Not invariably, but it's possible under those conditions. It's possible. . . .

M.J.B.

CHRONOLOGY

1923 2 February: James Lafayette Dickey, the second son and third child of lawyer Eugene Dickey and of Maibelle Swift Dickey, is born in Buckhead, a suburb of Atlanta, Georgia

1941 Spring: graduates from North Fulton High School in Buckhead

Fall: enrolls at Darlington School, Rome, Georgia, from which he receives a certificate in Spring 1942; wins award from Society of Colonial Daughters for his "Essay on Patriotism"

1942 Fall: enrolls at Clemson A & M College, where he majors in civil engineering and plays on the freshman football team

3 December: leaves Clemson and begins thirteen months as an aviation cadet in Army Air Corps pilot training: stationed successively at Miami; High Point, North Carolina; Nashville, Tennessee; Maxwell Field, Alabama; and Camden, South Carolina, where he washes out as a pilot

1944 7 January–11 December: trains as night-fighter radar observer; stationed successively at Ft. Myers and Boca Raton, Florida; and Hammer Field, Fresno, California

1945 30 January: joins 418th Night Fighter Squadron in the Philippines; subsequently serves on Okinawa and in Japan; earns five bronze stars and is promoted to second lieutenant

1946   1 March: separates from military service

Summer: enrolls on the GI Bill at Vanderbilt University as an English major; between 1947 and 1949 publishes four poems in the Vanderbilt student literary magazine, *The Gadfly*

1948   4 November: marries Maxine Syerson; shortly thereafter his poem "The Shark at the Window" is accepted by *The Sewanee Review* (appears in April–June 1951 issue)

1949   Receives B.A. in English, magna cum laude, from Vanderbilt

1950   Receives M.A. in English from Vanderbilt

September–December: instructor of English at Rice Institute, Houston, Texas, until he is recalled to service during Korean War

1951   10 March–9 August 1952: stateside service in training command of air force; stationed in Alabama, Mississippi, and Texas

31 August: son, Christopher, is born

1952   Fall: returns to Rice where he teaches until summer 1954

1954   August–June 1955: in Europe on Sewanee Review Fellowship; he and his family live primarily at Cap d'Antibes on the French Riviera

1955   September: joins English faculty at the University of Florida, Gainesville

1956   April: resigns University of Florida teaching position because of dispute over his reading of his poem "The Father's Body" and his dissatisfaction with his salary; takes job as advertising copywriter for McCann-Erickson in Atlanta and for five years builds a successful career in Atlanta advertising agencies

1958   18 August: second son, Kevin, is born

September: wins Union League Civic and Arts Foundation Prize from Union League of Chicago for "Dover: Believing in Kings"

1959   Fall: wins Longview Foundation Award; also wins Vachel Lindsay Prize for eight poems published in the July issue of *Poetry*

1960   23 August: publication of *Into the Stone and Other Poems*, in *Poets of Today VII* (New York: Scribners)

1961   10 July: resigns from his advertising position; during his five years in business, he publishes ten reviews and more than sixty poems in magazines and literary journals

Fall: "barnstorms" for poetry

1962   15 February: publication of *Drowning with Others* (Middletown, Conn.: Wesleyan University Press)

February: travels with his family to Europe on Guggenheim Fellowship; spends from 6 April to 20 June in Positano, Italy

Fall: lives in Atlanta

1963   January: becomes poet-in-residence at Reed College in Portland, Oregon, where he remains until May 1964

1964   27 February: publication of *Helmets* (Middletown, Conn.: Wesleyan University Press)

       10 July?: publication of *The Suspect in Poetry* (Madison, Minn: Sixties Press)

       September?: publication of *Two Poems of the Air* (Portland, Ore.: Centicore Press)

       September: becomes poet-in-residence at San Fernando Valley State College, Northridge, California, where he remains until June 1965

1965   Summer: teaches at the University of Wisconsin, Milwaukee

       23 September: publication of *Buckdancer's Choice* (Middletown, Conn.: Wesleyan University Press)

       Fall: "barnstorms" for poetry

1966   January: receives Melville Cane Award from the Poetry Society of America for *Buckdancer's Choice*

       February–March: serves as poet-in-residence at the University of Wisconsin, Madison

       15 March: presented the National Book Award for *Buckdancer's Choice*

       May: receives grant of $2,500 for creative work in literature by the National Institute of Arts and Letters

       July: teaches at the University of Wisconsin, Milwaukee

       August: becomes Consultant in Poetry at the Library of Congress; serves two terms ending in June 1968

1967   24 April: publication of *Poems 1957–1967* (Middletown, Conn.: Wesleyan University Press)

1968   9 February?: publication of *Spinning the Crystal Ball* (Washington, D.C.: The Library of Congress [dated 1967])

       1 May: publication of *Babel to Byzantium: Poets and Poetry Now* (New York: Farrar, Straus and Giroux)

       Summer: publication of *Metaphor as Pure Adventure* (Washington, D.C.: Library of Congress)

       Summer: named poet-in-residence and professor of English at the University of South Carolina, Columbia; because of contractual obligations with other schools, he does not begin teaching at the university until January 1969 but then remains on staff there until his death in 1997

1969   July: covers Apollo 11 liftoff for *Life*

1970   13 February: publication of *The Eye-Beaters, Blood, Victory, Madness, Buckhead and Mercy* (Garden City, N.Y.: Doubleday)

23 March: publication of *Deliverance* (Boston: Houghton Mifflin)

6 November: publication of *Self-Interviews* (Garden City, N.Y.: Doubleday)

1971   January: named poetry editor for *Esquire;* fills position until August 1977

May: production begins on the movie version of *Deliverance,* for which Dickey writes the screenplay and plays the role of Sheriff Bullard

14 July: publication of *Exchanges* (Bloomfield Hills, Mich.: Bruccoli Clark)

November: *Deliverance* wins Prix Medicis for best foreign-language book published in France

10 December: publication of *Sorties* (Garden City, N.Y.: Doubleday)

1972   18 May: is inducted into the National Institute of Arts and Letters

1974   10 October?: publication of *Jericho: The South Beheld,* text by Dickey, illustrations by Hubert Shuptrine (Birmingham, Ala.: Oxmoor House)

1976   May: television broadcast of Jack London's *The Call of the Wild,* from script by Dickey

21 September: publication of limited edition of *The Zodiac* (Bloomfield Hills, Mich. and Columbia, S.C.: Bruccoli Clark)

28 October: Maxine Dickey dies

5 November: publication of the trade edition of *The Zodiac* (Garden City, N.Y.: Doubleday)

30 December: marries Deborah Dodson

1977   19 January: reads his poem "The Strength of Fields" at President Jimmy Carter's inauguration celebration

1 February: publication of *The Strength of Fields* (single poem) (Bloomfield Hills, Mich. and Columbia, S.C.: Bruccoli Clark)

15 October: publication of *God's Images: The Bible, a New Vision,* text by Dickey, etchings by Marvin Hayes (Birmingham, Ala.: Oxmoor House)

1978   27 May?: publication of *The Enemy from Eden,* text by Dickey, illustrations by Ron Sauter (Northridge, Calif.: Lord John Press)

11 October: publication of *Tucky the Hunter,* text by Dickey, illustrations by Marie Angel (New York: Crown)

16 October: publication of *Veteran Birth: The Gadfly Poems, 1947–1949,* text by Dickey, illustrations by Robert Dance (Winston-Salem, N.C.: Palaemon Press)

4 December: publication of *In Pursuit of the Grey Soul* (Bloomfield Hills, Mich. and Columbia, S.C.: Bruccoli Clark)

1979   5 May: publication of *Head-Deep in Strange Sounds: Free-flight Improvisations from the UnEnglish* (Winston-Salem, N.C.: Palaemon Press)

July: publication of *The Water-Bug's Mittens: Ezra Pound: What We Can Use* (Moscow: University of Idaho)

14 December: publication of *The Strength of Fields* (collection) (Garden City, N.Y.: Doubleday)

1980   1 March: publication of limited edition of *The Water-Bug's Mittens: Ezra Pound: What We Can Use* (Bloomfield Hills, Mich. and Columbia, S.C.: Bruccoli Clark)

December: publication of *Scion* (Deerfield, Mass./Dublin, Ireland: Deerfield Press/Gallery Press)

1981   15 March: publication of *The Starry Place Between the Antlers: Why I Live in South Carolina* (Bloomfield Hills, Mich. and Columbia, S.C.: Bruccoli Clark)

17 May: birth of daughter, Bronwen

?: publication of *The Early Motion* (Middletown, Conn.: Wesleyan University Press)

?: publication of *Falling, May Day Sermon, and Other Poems* (Middletown, Conn.: Wesleyan University Press)

Fall: receives the Levinson Prize for five *Puella* poems that had appeared in *Poetry*

1982   4 January: publication of *Deliverance,* the screenplay (Carbondale and Edwardsville: Southern Illinois University Press)

29 April: publication of *Puella* (Garden City, N.Y.: Doubleday)

December: publication of *Värmland* (Winston-Salem, N.C.: Palaemon Press)

1983   March: publication of *False Youth: Four Seasons* (Dallas, Tex.: Pressworks)

?: publication of *The Central Motion: Poems, 1968–1979* (Middletown, Conn.: Wesleyan University Press)

15 October: publication of *Night Hurdling: Poems, Essays, Conversations, Commencements, and Afterwords* (Bloomfield Hills, Mich. and Columbia, S.C.: Bruccoli Clark)

1985   October: publication of limited edition of *Puella* (Tempe, Ariz.: Pyracantha Press)

1986   10 September: publication of *Bronwen, the Traw, and the Shape-Shifter,* text by Dickey, illustrations by Richard Jesse Watson (San Diego, New York, and London: Bruccoli Clark/Harcourt Brace Jovanovich)

1987   5 June: publication of *Alnilam* (Garden City, N.Y.: Doubleday)

1988   18 May: induction into the American Academy of Arts and Letters

October: publication of *Wayfarer: A Voice from the Southern Mountains,* text by Dickey, photographs by William A. Bake (Birmingham, Ala.: Oxmoor House)

1989   28 July: accepts appointment as judge for Yale Series of Younger Poets competition; serves as judge through 1996

       November: publication of *The Voiced Connections of James Dickey: Interviews and Conversations,* edited by Ronald Baughman (Columbia: University of South Carolina Press)

1990   November: publication of *The Eagle's Mile* (Hanover, N.H. and London: Wesleyan University Press/University Press of New England)

1991   ?: publication of *Southern Light,* text by Dickey, photographs by James Valentine (Birmingham, Ala.: Oxmoor House)

1992   July: publication of *The Whole Motion: Collected Poems, 1945–1992* (Hanover, N.H. and London: Wesleyan University Press/University Press of New England)

1993   September: publication of *To the White Sea* (Boston and New York: Houghton Mifflin)

1994   October: hospitalized with acute hepatitis

1996   ?: publication of *Striking In: The Early Notebooks of James Dickey,* edited by Gordon Van Ness (Columbia and London: University of Missouri Press)

       Spring: afflicted with fibrosis of the lungs

       June: receives Harriet Monroe Prize for lifetime achievement in poetry

1997   14 January: teaches last class for the University of South Carolina

       19 January: dies

PART ONE

BEGINNINGS: AIR FORCE AND VANDERBILT

May 1943–October 1951

Air Cadet Dickey in 1943

Postmarked 31 May 1943   *ALS, 2 pp & MS, 6 pp; Emory*
                                            High Point College[2]

Dear Mom,

Well, only three more weeks to go in dear old H.P.C. I am no longer afraid of Nashville.[3] I know I'll be o.k., and I know I'll be commissioned as a pilot. For something wonderful has happened. I know I am good for something. First I can run. The coach here clocked me in ten flat yesterday. While not altogether accurate, it must have been pretty close. But that is secondary. I can write. Always before I have had some doubt as to my ability, but not anymore. The English teacher here says my themes are the best he's ever read. Inclosed is a rough draft of an essay I was writing on Bix, but abandoned at the last moment in favor of a more conservative theme. Parts of it are good, some is rotten, and it is not at all the type of thing I intend to do in the future. But I think you'll admit it has some merit, and is interesting in a feverish, breathless, sort of way. There are no revisions on it, so naturally there are some grammatical errors, but, as "Down-Beat" would say, "the stuff's there, and it is mellow!!"

I've been having a pretty fair time here. I've had a fearful headache for the last two or three days, and last night got sick and had 99.6 fever. But all is well today. All is o.k., but the headache. It's still with me, I'm sorry to say, but not as bad as originally. I've got a tremendous appetite and am well on the road to recovery.

Take care of yourself, Mom, and here's hoping I'll see you in a month, as a bona fide aviation cadet!!

Love,

Jim

The Rebel Soul—1931

Most of us are cut from the same pattern, and, with minor variations, have practically the same interests and aims in life. But there are some, yes, many, who by the very nature of their own being, and by their particular talents, are destined to be singled out from the many and live brilliant but somehow strangely distorted and out-of-focus lives.

These men, for most of them are men, can only be likened to the oft-repeated and hackneyed metaphor of the comet flashing across the heavens— scintillating while it lasts, but fading quickly and then forever engulfed by inky blackness, which may be either oblivion or death, one of which is as certain, unrelenting and unconquerable as the other.

Such a "Rebel Soul" was Napoleon, as was Alexander the Great. Beethoven was another, Byron another and Shelley still another. Some were militarists, some musicians, some writers; but they all had that same indefinable "something" that made them great, and, make no mistake about it, it was not altogether the stamp of their particular genius, either. Call it incentive, will power, ambition, or what you will. It is the spark, the spark of greatness, that pulls them from obscurity to the heights and back again. But after they have gone, everything is not quite the same. Things have been altered. Sometimes big things, sometimes small things, but everything is not as it was.

The spark of greatness has been mistaken in some, and in others it has burned brightly, but to no avail. There is no sadder story in all mankind than that of genius unrecognized. Poe had the spark, undoubtedly, but he died a drunkard and in poverty. "Bix" Beiderbecke, the great jazz cornetist, whose improvisations have been likened to Debussy and Wagner, had it perhaps more than any musician within the last century, and, in some opinions, among them my own, more than any instrumentalist who ever lived.

The case of Beiderbecke, unknown to all but a hand-full of musicians, record collectors, and jazz critics, is of particular interest to us here, for it serves to illustrate two of the principles involved in what I have been writing:

1. That a man may have the mark of genius upon him, and, through his own weaknesses or the unwillingness of the public to recognize his talents, remain unknown.

2. That men of genius, real genius, are not all dead, that they exist here among us, if we would but recognize them.

"Bix" Beiderbecke was a musical phenomenon. Born in Davenport, Iowa, he could play simple tunes on the family piano at the age of three. He first came under the influence of jazz, when he heard "King" Oliver and Louis Armstrong on the riverboats that ply the Mississippi from New Orleans, cradle of hot jazz, to Chicago, which was to become, largely through the influence of Beiderbecke and his compatriots, the Mecca for disciples of the hottest, purest kind of jazz.

From the first, "Bix" was absorbed in his music, and his family, becoming worried over the boy's lack of attention to his studies, sent him to Lake Forest Academy in Chicago.

At that time there was an abundance of hot music in Chicago, almost all of which was the rough, unpolished but nevertheless potent "stomps" and "blues" of the riverboat negroes, of whom Louis Armstrong was beginning to become undisputed monarch. "Bix" spent more time in the speak-easies and clip joints of south Chicago, than in the classroom, and as a result, fell far behind in his studies. Even during his short stay at Lake Forest, "Bix" played in small bands at every opportunity for one night stands and club dates. In 1923, when only 19, he left school entirely and took the first trumpet chair in Jean Goldkette's band. Goldkette, perhaps more than any of his contemporary leaders, recognized some of the far reaching possibilities of hot music, and consequently gathered about him the outstanding hot musicians of the day; a list that today would read like a "who's who in popular music:" Bix, Jimmy and Tommy Dorsey, Russ Morgan and Joe Venuti, to mention a few, and there were others from time to time.

Due to the difficulty in paying all the musical "stars," Goldkette was forced to disband in 1930, and Bix, aiming only at the highest, achieved his pinnacle. Paul Whiteman took him on as first trumpet.

Bix played with Whiteman for two years, then left. The beauty of his playing during this period is attested to by the many records he made while with "The King of Jazz." Whiteman himself called him the "greatest instrumentalist and most profound influence in all American contemporary music." There are many more indications of his virtuosity, imagination, and wealth of original musical ideas, too many more to enumerate here.

After leaving Whiteman, Beiderbecke played with a few other bands, among them Glen Gray's. That was in 1930. On August 7, 1931, Bix died. He is buried in Davenport, Iowa, the place of his birth.

These are the cold, hard facts, such as historians and biographers thrive on. But who would write such a biography as this? "Bix" was a drunkard. He whored. He led the dissipated and irregular life that jazz musicians have always led. He lived ingloriously, and died as a result of his own weakness and folly. Which is as it should be. And yet?—he had one redeeming feature—one that stamps him in the minds, souls, and bodies of a very few as a genius, the greatest of the great,—his music.

Bix was a paradox. Music to him was a passion. Perhaps he himself could not have explained how or why. But the music was in him, and he had to get it out. Get it out or perish. His music never satisfied him. He was always striving, seeking new notes, combinations of notes, chord sequences; many of which were not possible to render upon his instrument. His only interest was music; when he was not occupied with his cornet he played piano, and very good piano, too. He was one of the originators of the "tenth-style" bass, and his Okeh recording of "In a Mist," perhaps his most original composition, carried out this conviction. It has an eerie quality, a searching, questing, haunting melody, with beautiful thirteenth chord progressions. One who hears it will never forget. It was Bix's only piano solo, though he composed several others, all in the same vein as "In a Mist."

The influence of Debussy was very strong in Bix's piano compositions. One has only to play "In a Mist" once to recognize the similarity.

TO: EUGENE DICKEY[4]

Postmarked 8 June 1943   *ALS, 2 pp; Emory*

A/S Jim Dickey
Flight "E"
326th C.F.D.
High Point Col.
H.P., N.C.

Dear Pop,

I've just gotten back from my first flight, and it was fine. I learned how to do all the elementary maneuvers, and also tried a loop, which didn't turn out so hot. My instructor is a fellow named Whitley, who is not too educated, but knows his airplanes thoroughly. You ought to see me up there, with those earphones clamped over my head and my parachute on. I feel almost ready to go after a Zero. My instructor said I was doing fine.

Since you seem to be interested in my writing I am inclosing a description of a day's football practice at Clemson.[5] While writing this I kept in mind not a single day's performance but a composite of all the days when we scrimmaged the varsity. I used as my model Remarque's "All Quiet on the Western Front" to lend reality to the picture. I tried to make the reader experience what I did. In this I did not entirely succeed, being considerably disheartened at the complete piece, for it did not convey the impression I intended to give. However I got a fairly good grade. Since then I have written several other short selections, which I will send to you from time to time.

Congratulate Tom[6] for me, and tell him he owes me a letter. He hasn't written me in 2½ months.

                                        All my love,
                                        Jim

P.S. I am drawing flight pay now—$75 a month. I don't get paid again until I hit Nashville.

                                                              J

TO: TOM DICKEY

Postmarked 8? October 1943   *ALS, 2 pp;[7] Emory*

A/C Jim Dickey
14175259
Southern Aviation School
Camden, S.C.

Dear Tom,

Excuse this writing, but I busted my thumb in a "crack-up" Saturday and have to write left handed. It will be all right in a couple of weeks and I can fly o.k. with it now. The way it happened was this—I was flying with my instructor Saturday and we came in and landed and taxied up to where you parked the planes and my instructor got out and I started to, but he said "Oh no you don't, you &&**~@@!! You have been trying to kill me for three weeks now, and so you can take it up yourself and bust your own ass."

"No, no," I said, "you can't do this to me," but he was gone by then, so I taxied out to the line and took off. I made the shakiest takeoff ever seen around these parts, and circled the field. I was shaking so bad the plane was vibrating like Pop's '34 on the road to What-cha-know-Joe's. I was afraid the engine would fall out, so I cut the motor and came in. I made the prettiest landing I ever made—the plane only bounced 30 ft. in the air four times. By the time I had it on the ground and was congratulating myself I noticed a very peculiar thing—one of the wings was dragging in the dirt. The plane went 'round and 'round and finally stopped, but not before I banged my thumb up against the instrument panel. When I got out I expected St. Peter to greet me at the Pearly Gates, but it was only the mechanics with a hose to clean the <u>shit</u> out of the cockpit. "Nothing lost, Mr. Christian."[8]

Anyway, I made a terrific effort to get away from my instructor, but after chasing me around the field three or four times he finally ran me down.

Every thing is o.k. now, though. I am still the hottest pilot around here, but I am quite a bit behind, with only 5 <u>minutes</u> solo time. Oh well. They have washed out about half our class, but I am still holding my own.

I went to High Point last week. All the boys thought I was Joe Foss[9] or somebody. I told them that I had not been in combat <u>yet</u>.

I will not get home for quite a while, but I might could get to Chattanooga some week-end. I'll call you next Monday nite.

Be good, and keep showing them your ass (in track I mean)

I am rooming with the "Dead End Kids."

                                                            Jim

TO: MAIBELLE SWIFT DICKEY

Postmarked 25 February 1944   *ALS, 2 pp;[10] Emory*

14175259
Cadet Det.
Bks. 219
B.A.A.F.F.G.S.
Fort Myers, Fla.

Dearest Mom,

Well, we graduate Tuesday.[11] I finally got through. This is pretty interesting work, but I'm glad it's over. Buy some gunner's wings and wear them. I'm sure it would cause a furor among your friends, not to mention the Browards. If you want them I can send you a pair of mine.

Now, before I forget it, see if you can get me a few books. If you get them, keep them at home.

Man with the Bull-Tongue Plow—Jesse Stuart
Selected poems of Conrad Aiken—Aiken
A Farewell to Arms—Ernest Hemingway
An American Tragedy—Theodore Drieser
The Sun also rises—Ernest Hemingway
The Ox-Bow Incident—Walter Van Tilburg Clark
Ulysses—James Joyce
{ Life and Poetry of James Thomson—H.S. Salt
{ Poetical Works—James Thomson {2 Vol}

Cash in some of my bonds and get these. The last two will be impossible to get in town, but there is a possibility that you may be able to order them from Millers or some other book dealer. The others should be fairly easy.

Things look pretty good, Mom, from where I sit. I will be with you again this time next year.

I love you,
Jim

P.S. I almost forgot:
Studs Lonigan—James T. Farrell

TO: EUGENE AND MAIBELLE SWIFT DICKEY

Postmarked 29 June 1944   *ALS, 2 pp; Emory*

F/O James L. Dickey
T-180270
450th AAFBU
Sq T-1
Hammer Fld.
Fresno, Calif.

Dear Folks,

I suppose you will be surprised to hear me say something good about the army for a change, but I am leading the best life I ever have (away from home, at least) and getting paid almost $300 a month for it. All we do is fly every night and go to a few lectures and classes, and the rest of the time is off. I just got back from San Francisco where I stayed for a week. I was not able to get a train ticket, or I would have come home. As it is I don't think I'll be back for a while.

When I was in San Francisco I was the guest of a girl (and what a girl) I met on the train coming out here. I'll tell you, Mom, they treated me like a king. They have a tremendous country estate, a swimming pool, and everything that I have always thought of very rich people having. The girl's name is Gwen Leege; her mother has married again, she is a Mrs. Stien, a very nice old <u>German</u> lady, and you'd love her, if only for that.[12] They wouldn't let me spend a cent of my own; all I had to do was casually drop a hint about "over seas" and they couldn't do enough for the "poor boy."

Gwen and I went to Chinatown, the zoo, the aquarium, night clubs, bars, millions of places, all of them wonderful. I had on my night fighter flying jacket most of the time (with appropriate insignia; a buzzard sitting on a new moon with "radar" shooting out of his eyes and a cannon under his wing) and one kid even asked me for my autograph.

Here, at last is one who can take Peg's[13] place. Gwen and I are in love, Mom. And it's the real thing this time. Don't worry about us marrying, though. She wants to finish two more years at Bryn Mawr and I have the war to fight.

I am in no danger at all. Flying at night is not dangerous, and I have foolproof instruments that do all my thinking for me. I am flying all kind of planes now. I may go into P-70's, P-61's, P-38's, Beaufighters, Mosquitos or even the new jet job. Mostly we are flying P-70's and P-61's.

My love to all

Jim

P.S. I sure am glad Tom got turned down.[14] Congratulations

TO: EUGENE AND MAIBELLE SWIFT DICKEY

Postmarked 16 August 1944   *ALS, 2 pp; Emory*
                                               Hammer Field
                                               Fresno, California

Dear Folks,

Hope you like the pictures. I thought they were pretty fair myself, but of course, I'm prejudiced.

Well, Mom, I guess you saw that spread in Life about the ten leading novelists of the last two decades, with my boy Thomas Wolfe in <u>fifth</u> place behind such <u>outstanding</u> (??!!*) "artistes" as Willa Cather, Ernest Hemingway and (the last straw) Sinclair (Arrowsmith) Lewis. What a laugh that is!

They grounded all our Advanced Stage aircraft for a month, so I hit the boys for a leave. I'll know in a couple or three days, and as soon as I know you'll know.

I have been reading enormously lately. I have a gigantic array of ponderous books in my room that instantly awes any suspicious Night Fighter who innocently strays into my "sanctum sanctoruum." When I get out of the army I'm going someplace where I can really get a good education in letters, whether it be L.S.U. the University of Virginia, Harvard, or Oxford. I am convinced that the only thing I will ever have any interest in as a career is authorship, or something akin to it. Though I have not blossomed out as a John Keats, I <u>have</u> shown an infinitessimal scrap of talent and originality in my writing, which is more than I have done in any other line of educational endeavor.

Be that as it may, first the war must be successfully concluded, and Tom and I must have a big time around home.

No need to tell you how much I miss you all, even Chow-chow and Andrew, the toothless 4-F.

Please Mom, make with some more of your delightfully garralous letters. I need them.

<u>All</u> my love

Jim

TO: MAIBELLE SWIFT DICKEY

Postmarked 20 October 1944   *ALS, 2 pp; Emory*
                                                                      Hammer Field
                                                                      Fresno, California

Dear Mom,

I do not mean to worry you unduly with my so-trivial problems. My theories are but theories at best. Better than to say I am an atheist, agnostic or what have you, were to confess, wearily, that I do not know. Perhaps faith is the answer. Of this I have little of late. My room-mate was killed last night. But of more cheerful things. Jane, my "wife!!"??[15] and I have been having quite a gay time. She is quite a student of poetry (my first love in literature) and thinks she can get a few of my better pastoral lyrics published. One has already come out in a little-known monthly (desperate for contributions) for which I received a tremendous endowment of three dollars ($3).[16] I am vainly attempting to obtain a copy of the magazine, which by now undoubtedly has surrendered to bankruptcy. I'll send it to you post-haste if I am lucky enough to track down a sample of the wayward publication.

Mom, you'd better not let Pop read this, in all seriousness. He would think I am out of my mind, or something.

As for the poem, it is written in blank unrhymed verse, in a rather involved metrical pattern, stemming no doubt from several of my favorites (Robert Bridges' "London Snow" was perhaps the unknowing godfather of this unworthy piece, which I call "Rain in Darkness"). As to my own inspiration, I've lain on the side porch listening to rain enough times to be fully aware of it's significance and meaning in the minds of most people. Please don't show this to anyone, as I am sure I shall do better in the future, and am frankly ashamed of such an obviously amateurish bit of fantasy.

Rain in Darkness

The rain fills us all, stemming our laboring hearts
To quiet passion. We see it falling softly, loosly,
Hear it hammering lightly with a multitudinous wet sound
Upon trees and towers and men. The roof tops and streets
Gleam brightly beneath it; down dark walls it cooly slips
Into leafed green ivy, while drops wave forlornly
From bare boughs. The limp clouds are wrung and brood
Incessantly over the land.
This is the time for weariness; and [thus?] the sound

Of warm clean beds and quiet talk, of soft lips and rustling sheets,
Of white, slow-stirring limbs and gentle contemplation
Over the wan night-ridden streets the rain beats out its life
Upon the stony structures, balanced slanting for an instant
Fenced within golden-glowing headlights, as dust
In a fugitive sunbeam. Running sideways into gutters,
Streaming downward past lank awnings. Pouring always
From dim heaven—O rain
Take not your love from us, we who need you——

TO: EUGENE AND MAIBELLE SWIFT DICKEY

Postmarked 6 February 1945   *ALS, 2 pp; Emory*
                                                            Philippines

Dear Folks,

We moved from the last place we were[17] (thank God) and now we are somewhere in the Phillipines. I can't tell you where but I <u>can</u> say that we are really in
the big time now. We are in the 418th Night Fighter Squadron. It is the hottest in
the world. This outfit has more victories than all the others in the Pacific put
together. I already have a couple of missions in and we are doing fine. We can take
care of things o.k., just like I said. All the old boys are really good fellows; they
were glad to see us because it means that some of them can go home. I think I will
be able to come home myself in about a year.

We have a fine insignia; a green background, with a very vicious looking wild-
cat head, and two sharp paws beside it. We live in tents on top of a hill. The breeze
comes through pretty strong. The weather here is about like Hawkinsville, Ga in
August. We have Filipinos to do our laundry and anything else we want done. I
have my personal boy, named Tony, a likely lad, aged 15.

Before I forget it send me some T-shirts and undershorts. I am sadly lacking.
See if you can find my Darlington "winged foot" shirt.

See if you can get hold of any of Roy Campbell's[18] books of Poetry for me.
"Adamastor" "Flowering Reeds," "The Flaming Terrapin" or "The Georgiad."

My pilot[19] wants to name our plane after his wife and child, but I am holding
out for the "Flaming Terrapin" (after Campbell).

"But when the winds have ceased their ghostly speech
And the long waves roll moaning from the beach,
The Flaming Terrapin that towed the Ark
Rears up his hump of thunder on the dark"—   Jim

TO: EUGENE AND MAIBELLE SWIFT DICKEY

Postmarked 22 February 1945   *ALS, 2 pp; Emory*
                                                  Philippines

Dear Mom and Pop,

I'm sorry I can't write you both a letter, but we're flying almost every night, and what few hours of sleep we can snatch between flights are quite welcome. I can't tell you where we go on our missions, but they are all at night, and last about 3½ or 4 hours. We are really knocking hell out of the Nips around here. I haven't shot down any enemy aircraft yet, but we haven't seen very many, and on the other hand they haven't shot me down either, so I guess we're even so far. I've got about 25 combat hours so far.

In three or four months I'll get to go down to Sydney, Australia, on rest leave. They say it is a fine town. My pilot has proved to be a little leery of the Nip, so he was made assistant personal equipment officer, and doesn't do much combat flying. Now I am flying with another boy who is really a hell-cat, and a fine pilot to boot.[20] He and I expect to get decorated in two or three months.

I hope Tom has a good track season this year. All the time I am not flying or sleeping I exercise with some weights I made, so I ought to be in pretty good shape when I get back.

Now Mom, don't think I am in mortal danger all the time, because it is not that way at all. It is just two or 3 hours a night, and even then I am flying with one of the best pilots over here. So don't worry. Everything looks fine now and I know I will be home this time next year.

Pop, you would really like these Philipinos. They are all crazy about cock fights. I bought a chicken from one of them and entered him in the weekly Sunday fights. He won in five pittings and I won fifty Pesos, but during the fight his left eye was cut up pretty bad. He seems to be getting along better now, though. I would welcome any suggestions on training him. I might come home a millionaire! His name is Max.

That's all for now. I am writing this just prior to take-off. Here we go again.

All my love to everybody, and
write soon.
Jim

TO: MAIBELLE SWIFT DICKEY

Postmarked 2 April 1945   *ALS, 8 pp; Emory*
                                                              Philippines

Dear Mom,

Everything is still very quiet here, as usual for the past month. My pilot is grounded for a couple of days with a cold, so I'll rest on my sixty hours awhile.

Henry Howe, a Harvard graduate who is our Special Services (movies, records) officer, wrote a letter to the Harvard faculty board inquiring as to the possibility of my "matriculating" there under the G.I. (loathsome term) Bill of rights upon the cessation of hostilities. I don't think my Clemson scholastic record, such as it is, will be too much in my favor, but perhaps they'll take pity on me, a poor uneducated soldier. Otherwise I'll be out of luck, for apparently others <u>cann</u>ot see the obvious brilliance which you and Maibelle[21] accord me. Be that as it may, I can see no reason for consigning my rather dubious talents again to a backwoods South Carolina agricultural school.

The pursuit of the ordinary (home, wife, children) leaves me quite cold if not horrifying me outright. I would attribute this to my youth if it were not for the fact that at this very minute my pilot and two young (20 and 21) flight officers, all married, were not planning homes and discussing the most odious names conceivable for their children, real and prospective. Ye Gods!! In a rut already! You have always had the most wonderful ideas concerning marriage, especially my own.

I am not in the least averse to marrying Peg Roney or some other equally attractive (and hot) young woman, were the ultimate consequences not quite so apparant. Young love is all well and good enough, but habit and monetary worries as a natural conclusion is strictly <u>out</u> as far as I am concerned; though it may be suitable for drudges. All the married mediocrities drone "You'll see, there's nothing like it." To which I can only reply (silently) "You poor damned fools!!"

If there is anything I despise it is mediocrity, which composes 99⁴⁴/₁₀₀ (apologies to Ivory Soap) of the armed forces. O for the days when I could choose my own company.

The trouble with the majority of people is, they don't want fiercely enough to accomplish things. The average Joe wants security and some poor woman, as defeated as he, to tell him that he is wonderful and all the rest of the post-marital baloney that is the stock-in-trade of wives. Men marry when they are sick of struggling with the world and acknowledge defeat. They want a hole to crawl home to every night, and love paid for by countless bills, rents and endless trivialities.

As for me I can see nothing but a battle stretching on before me, but let it be a glorious fight, unhinered, not a gangrenous battle of self sacrifice and day to day bickering.

Enough of this!

Have any of my books come in yet?

I have no other interest (as a profession) than writing. If there were more money in poetry I should quite naturally turn to it, but I fear I am not the genius that Shelley was.

Here's a short unrhymed cadence I wrote today on clouds

> Now hanging marble, wind-chiseled
> Now piling, shapeless
> Swiftly flowing
> Lit with the laughter of suns
> Shifting—
> Always the silent radiant tumult
> Above our leaden wings——

Heres a sonnet I wrote on death, since almost every other poet has had a try at it.

> Death comes not downward as a friend,
> Nor stretches his cloak for us to hide beneath
> Nor cautions us in virtue's steps to bend
> Before he frees us from this leaden sheath
> And flings us far beyond our mortal stars
> To golden realms of serenity and high peace
> Spurning the dirty corpse below which mars
> The earthly spirit; he spurns not the greatest or least—
> With careless tread he walks
> Among the worlds and whosoever happens upon
> Him forever again knows nothing; he talks
> With some, with others argues, is never done
> But when we chance upon him suddenly, he
> Is probably more surprised than we.

Did all my uniforms and books get home o.k. from Hamilton Field? I hope so. Take care of everybody, Mom. Tell Tom to be good.

All my love,
Jim

p.s. Here's a portrait of Life "On the Dickey Plantation" as portrayed by one of our boys. I thought it might amuse you. It did me.[22]

p.p.s. The picture (negative) I sent you was taken in New Guinea.

TO: MAIBELLE SWIFT DICKEY

Postmarked 11 May 1945   *ALS, 2 pp; Emory*
                                                           Philippines

Dear Mom,

I am writing this in the dead of night, so if you read it in daylight it will probably sound peculiar, but I know you will understand, as always.

As the time draws closer to my inevitable marriage, I find myself debating the merits of this girl or that girl, and am finally and always driven back to the only yardstick I ever had, my own mother. What little I know of your and Pop's courtship is (you probably never knew this) one of the most cherished memories I have. Your love for Pop must have been very great, greater than your entire world. I do not think I could ever love any girl more than I love you, Mom, so I know you loved Pop much more than I do Peg. I have never heard anything more moving than your defiance of your mother, who undoubtedly wanted you to "marry well," and subsequent marriage to Pop, regardless of his financial and social status, public opinion and all the rest of the pettiness that men occupy themselves with. In spite of all this you married him. God, how beautiful. And how wonderfully it has turned out. I don't think anyone had a more wonderful childhood than I, and it was all due to you and Pop. It brings tears to my eyes when I think of how wonderful you have always been to me.

I don't think I could write another letter like this.

I don't think you could have married a better man than Pop. Richer, yes, smarter, yes, but none better. If I ever have a son I want him to be like Pop, and I'm going to name him Eugene. I want him to be like Pop; a great man who never loses sight of the real joys of life in fruitless struggle for those phantoms, wealth and position.

God, how I love you both.

Jim

TO: MAIBELLE SWIFT DICKEY

Postmarked 29 May 1945   *ALS, 4 pp; Emory*
                                                           Philippines

Dear Mom,

I have been in Manila for the last couple of days. It is in pretty bad shape. I had my picture taken there and bought a few souvenirs. I wish you'd have fifteen or twenty prints made from this negative and send them over to me. We had a pretty good time in Manila. Nothing like the States, though.

I am looking forward to being with you again in from 7 to 9 months. I sure hope so. I am getting mighty tired of this over here. I wish I could see you soon.

If I didn't have a lot of books over here I might get pretty lonesome. As it is, it's not so bad.

Mom, look in my Ernest Dowson[23] book and copy out the poem which ends "Mother of God, O Misericord, look down in pity upon us, the weak and the blind who stand in our light and wreak ourselves such ill." I think that one is called "Breton Afternoon"[24] and also the one called "Ultima Impenithula"[25] or something like that. The last of it is

> Before the running waters fall and my life be carried under
> And thine anger cleave me through as a child cuts down a flower
> I will praise thee, Lord, in hell, while my limbs are racked asunder
> For the last sad sight of her face and the little grace of an hour.

I really like Ernest Dowson.
I wrote this one

> I having found in you more than dreams
> more sunlight than pride or wine
> kindles in the heart, now sanction,
> before diaphanous memories bequeath us
> to nothingness effete——
>
> the sun, sinking
> the slow radiance
> fading
> dissolving the lean shadows——
> all glorious things
> in utter loveliness stand
> held in an instant fleeting to darkness.

Don't worry about me over here, Mom; everything is o.k.

All my love,
Jim

P.S. Tell Maibelle I heard from Sybil. This other picture is my pilot. I think it would be nice to have them framed together. You can have the one of me enlarged if you like it.

TO: EUGENE DICKEY

Postmarked 5 June 1945   *ALS, 6 pp; Emory*
                                                                          Philippines

Dear Pop,

I am sure glad to hear Tom did so well in the S.E.C.

Over here we are doing o.k. too. It seems like we might get some pretty stiff going from now on out. I think every thing will be all right; but things like that are so uncertain it is hard to tell. It seems incredible that men should wish to behave this way toward other men. The things I have seen would not be conceivable to anyone who has not seen them with his own eyes. Nothing is good enough for the men who have fought in this war.

The Hollywood patriots have made it such a cheap thing it is a bit hard for some of the men to realize what the war is about and why they are in it. Strangely enough, the same reactions the movies have sentimentalized (and capitalized upon) are the actual feelings (perhaps underplayed, as compared to Robert Taylor) of the men in battle, flying, etc. Also none of the men over here, I daresay, could give a more eloquent and searching analysis of the issues, as well as the individual reasons for our being in this war than are given in the poem "My Country," written by Russell Davenport,[26] who has never been near the war and is not even in the army.

There are those who can put noble words into our mouths. We are grateful, for we could never say them. There are those who can dramatize our actions, until people who know nothing of the conflict can make a pretense of understanding us.

But no one but the men out here can realize the price our country is paying for its heritage. A combat report can tell of a life, a hundred, a thousand lives lost, but cannot show the individual deaths, some quick and some infinitely slow and painful. And for every one some persons will bear a life of grief. Whether we live or die is not the difference. The difference is whether America lives. Do not think I am working myself into a paroxysm of patriotic fervor and losing myself in a lather of words, for such is not the case. America is the hope of the world. There has never been anything like us and never will again. And when we fight for America, there is something bigger than a country, bigger than men banded together against each other. And that is the freedom of the individual. Men have struggled toward it for many thousands of years. The right of a man to live according to his own lights and to maintain harmony and tranquillity between himself and his fellows, without force. It is the basis of all religions. Of the Mohammedan, the Hindu, the Buddhist, and above all the Christian. When Jefferson wrote: "We hold these truths to be self-evident; that all men are endowed by their Creator with certain inalienable rights, among them life, liberty and the pursuit of happiness," he was sounding a chord barely touched by the English Magna Charta.

This war is a thing surpassing the Crusades, and the Saracen wars, and all the great religious wars and political wars and social wars ever waged. On its outcome will hinge the entire future of civilization. It is a struggle so fraught with gigantic implications that the poor guys who are deciding it are rather slow to realize what it means. It boils down to this; whether man shall live in constant apprehension of the brute oppression that governs him, or conduct himself as he pleases, work at his own behest, and in general endeavor to make this world, or his part of it, a bearable and sometimes even pleasant place in which to live.

I wish the people in the states, especially those who think they are "doing their part" and feel they have performed a valiant feat when they buy an $18.75 war bond, could see these men out here. Most of the people in the States are not fit to shake the hand of any of the men on Iwo, Leyte, or any of the rest of these Pacific deathtraps. And yet I heard somewhere that a certain lady asked a Marine who had lost an arm on Saipan if he was embarrased around girls. My God! The people in the States have little enough to do. They ought to be pushing this thing to the limit and past it. No price is too great. Not just words. Action.

Sorry I got started on this. I had intended to make it more personal. I'm glad Tom did so well at Birmingham.

Love,
Jim

TO: MAIBELLE SWIFT DICKEY

Postmarked 18 June 1945   *ALS, 2 pp; Emory*
                                               Philippines

Dear Mom,

We are having it pretty nice now. It is not raining much any more and not too hot either. I sure would like to be home now. It must really be nice.

When I get home I am through having a good time. Peg and all the rest of them can go to hell. I'm never going to run again or play football or anything else like that. I have been fooling myself long enough. I am going to school and just study for the rest of my life and work hard. I despise work and I hate to study, but after this I will go crazy if I don't do something. I never did have a very good time anyway. I don't get any enjoyment from drinking and I never got anything but despair from anything I ever really wanted to do.

I realize that I have made everybody at home very unhappy by my actions in the past, and this makes me feel pretty bad. I am truly sorry, but it is just the way I am. I wish I was some other way, but I am not. I am just different from other people, I guess.

I don't care much for fame now. I guess I wore it all out wishing for it before. It doesn't matter. All I want is for people to leave me alone. The important thing is for you all not to worry about me while I am over here and when I get home. I'll get by o.k. though it really doesn't matter.

Don't worry, Mom. You are much too wonderful. Tom is worth fifty of me.

Love,

Jim

TO: MAIBELLE SWIFT DICKEY

Postmarked 19 July? 1945   *ALS, 6 pp; Emory*
                                                             Okinawa

Dear Mom,

Please order from the

"Book Supply Company"

   0564-566 West Monroe St.

   Chicago #6, Ill.

the following books at prices quoted:

    1. Sigmund Freud's General Introduction to
       Psychoanalysis
    2. Standard Book of British and American Verse
    3. Story of Philosophy - Durant

                {all three for | $2.45

    4. This Above All - Knight   .85

    5. Invitation to Learning - Van Doren, Tate + Cairns
    6. Basic Teachings of the Great Philosophers - S. E. Frost
    7. What to Read in English Literature - Crawford

                { three for | 1.75

    8. American Harvest - Tate + Bishop   1.98

    9. Great Works of Music - Goepp   1.98

   10. Complete Rhyming Dictionary - Woods   1.98

   11. The Cambridge History of American
       Literature - Van Doren   2.95

13.[27]Bulfinch's Mythology   1.25
14. Contemporary American Authors -
      Millet   3.25
15. The Complete Greek Drama - Oates
      + O'Neill   4.95
16. A Treasury of Russian Literature -   3.85
      Guerney -
17. Fundamentals of Boxing -   0.69
      - Ross -

	total	$27.93
	postage	.94
		$28.87
	discount 3%	.87
	Send	$28.00
	Insurance	¢15
		$28.15

I realize this is quite an order; pay for it out of my account if you think its too much.

And, if that wasn't enough, see if you can buy from some Atlanta Bookstore, in the Modern Library Series,

Antic Hay   no. 209
Point Counterpoint 180   } Aldous Huxley

Origin of Species G-278
and Descent of Man   } Charles Darwin

Modern American Poetry 127 }   Conrad Aiken

If you can't get them in Atlanta, write Modern Library, Random House New York. 3 (You'd better get the Address of Random House from Davidson's or Someplace) and ask them to quote you the prices on the above books and also these

1. Poems -   W. H. Auden
2. On This Island -"   "   "
3. Another Time - W. H. Auden
4. Collected Poems - C. Day Lewis

After you receive the prices, order them.

Also, when you order the books from the "Book Supply Co." ask them if they have or can get the following books and to quote you the prices: The publishers are included whenever possible:

Poem - Trumbull Stickney -   Jonathan Cape
Blue Juniata - Malcolm Cowley   Harrison Smith Inc.
Cloth of the Tempest
First Will + Testament   Kenneth   New
Before the Brave   Patchen   Directions
Journal of Albion Moonlight
In Time Like Glass   W.   Sidgwick +
New Poems   J.   Jackson, Ltd.
The Dark Fire   Turner
Pursuit of Psyche
War and Love   Richard   Four Seas Co.
A Fool 'i the Forest   Aldington
Mood Without Measure   Richard
Twelve Noon   Church
Confessio Juvenis   Richard
                                   Hughes
The World I Breathe   Dylan Thomas   New Directions
The Destructive Element   Stephen
                                   Spender
A Hope For Poetry   C. Day Lewis   The Hogarth
A Time to Dance   Press
The Seven Sleeper   Mark van   Henry Holt + Co.
                                   Doren
Selected Poems   Robert Penn Warren   Harcourt
                                                              Brace + Co.
The Second World   R. P. Blackmur
Elegies   Alex Comfort   Routledge
                                                              of London
Always Adam   Sean   Faber +
                                   Jennett   Faber -
                                                              London
Blood for a Stranger   Randall
                                   Jarrell
anything by Selden Rodman
Also 20th Century Authors   {Kunitz and
                   Haycraft   {H. W. Wilson Co
British Authors of the 19th Century}
Well that's quite an order, when you get the prices, order them.
            All my love, sweetheart.

Be sure to write me when and what these Companies say.
>Everything is fine.
>Jim

TO: MAIBELLE SWIFT DICKEY

>*Postmarked 30 July 1945*   *ALS, 2 pp; Emory*
>*Okinawa*

Dear Mom,

We have been pretty busy the last few days (or nights) or I would have written. We are doing fine work. I am flying with two pilots now, Brad and "Little Joe" Vasa, a damned good kid who was in my class at pilot school. I am really getting in the missions now. After I make 1st Lt., which should be in another couple of months it won't be long 'till I come home. I think you can look for me from December to February.

The work we do here is exciting as hell. I have never had so much fun in my life. It is wonderful. Don't worry about me, though. I am perfectly all right.

Say Mom, will you do me a favor. Make a list of all the books I have received from the Fresno Bookshop and other places and <u>send</u> it to me. This is <u>very</u> important.

I sure <u>don't</u> want to get married. I have come to the conclusion that I never will. Boy, I have nearly been trapped on several occasions! I want to go my own god-damn way from now on out. No worries, no nothing.

There are so many beautiful things in the world, I can't see why anyone wants to obscure them with bills and babies. I despise babies. They are the horrible price you have to pay for a few good nights. As a whole I don't think much of the human race, especially after this, so why should I do anything to perpetuate it?

I am certainly glad I am not the "divine average" Whitman celebrates. I despise mediocrity. On the other hand I don't see why anyone should waste his whole life seeking the "bubble reputation" when he could be enjoying himself. The best way to live is to stand apart. With the crowd, but not of it.

If I was religious I could not stand this life here. Don't ever talk to me again about "God's justice." Maybe he is just, but certainly not according to his own Golden Rule. Eternal night is the greatest and most perfect heaven anyone could ever wish for. Why anyone should want anything else is certainly beyond me.

>I love you,
>Jim

TO: MAIBELLE SWIFT DICKEY

Postmarked 16 August 1945   ALS, 2 pp; Emory
                                               Okinawa

Dear Mom,

Sorry I haven't written for a few days (seems like I always start my letters this way) but we have been flying a hell of a lot lately. At present we are sweating out the Jap reply to our peace terms, but are still flying every night. I don't think they are going to quit, for they would have replied to Truman's note before this if they intended to. I think they are stalling. A few more atomic bombs should convince them.[28]

You should have seen the celebration here when the first Jap peace note was recieved. Everybody went absolutely wild. Several GI's got killed. It was a big disappointment to everybody when the Japs started stalling around this way.

I haven't gotten any packages from home since the wings Pop sent me. It takes an extra long time for packages to get over here.

Say, Mom, will you do me a favor and start buying a New York Times every Sunday and saving the book review section for me?

I sent $400 home the other day. It should be there in about a month, so be sure to let me know when it gets there. I should have around $3000 bucks by the time I get home. I <u>don't</u> think I will buy a car with it right off. I want to have some money in reserve for a while when I get out of the army, which should be next summer. I don't want to get married or anything, but I don't want to get rid of the money for a while yet. The red Ford is good enough for me, if Tom hasn't run it to pieces at college.

I was never so disgusted in my life as when that poll was taken at the Jap surrender offer and 75% of the <u>civilians</u> wanted to continue the war. It's not them that has to get over here and get their ass shot off. Most of the boys over here hate the civilians and war-workers more than they do the Japs. I wish some of those bastards could see what goes on over here. And they say fight to "the bitter end." Boy. That really takes nerve to say that, from the corner of Peachtree and Baker.

                                               All my love
                                               Jim

TO: MAIBELLE SWIFT DICKEY

1945   *ALS, 2pp; Emory*
                                                           Okinawa

Oct. 6

Dear Mom,

Say, pretty, if you can't send me anything better than Willis' letters, don't send nothin'. His is the only handwriting I ever saw harder to read than Tom's. He writes me occasionally himself, and even then I'm not interested much. I'd much rather read your letters. Are you really 58 now, Mom? Gosh, that's hard to believe. I'll send you something from Japan next week. Half our outfit is up there already. We are waiting to fly the planes up. New Guinea to Tokyo in 10 months. Not bad, eh? I sure am glad Delmore Schwartz's books came in. I wanted his books more than any, except those by Kenneth Patchen (Hint, hint!) I <u>sure</u> would like to find those books there at Christmas time, if I get there, or at least by my birthday, if I get there. Seriously, Mom, I can't understand why you're balking at the books, knowing how much I want them. You said yourself you were glad to pay for them. As long as I can get them now I want to order them now. As to the paper shortage, even when there is enough paper I'll have to buy these books the same way, for all the paper will be used in printing the 500<u>th</u> edition of "Gone With the Wind" or "Forever Amber" and such like crap, and not "Jewboy" Schwartz's "Coriolanus and his Mother" or Dylan Thomas's "Portrait of the Young Artist as a Dog."[29] So let's not balk any more. I haven't ordered any more books lately, but I <u>do</u> wish you'd get those I suggested.

So Tom is majoring in Phys. Ed., eh. Well, I guess he'll wind up coaching some high school track team. I want something a little better than that.

How is Peg? If you see her, tell her I'd like one more letter before I come home. I have had one from her in each of the places I've been: New Guinea, the Phillipines and Okinawa, and I shall expect my final one in Japan.

I sure am anxious for you to meet Gwen. She graduates from Bryn Mawr this June, or did I tell you? She is really nice.

Love you, love you, love you.
Jim

TO: EUGENE DICKEY

Early October? 1945   *ALS, 2 pp; Emory*
                                                        Okinawa

Dear Pop,

Sure was glad to hear from you once more. I'm mighty glad you like the ring.

There are no censorship regulations on now so I can answer any questions you want to ask. I think you already know where I was in New Guinea, so I'll just tell you where I was in the Phillipines. We were stationed at San Jose on the southern end of the island of Mindoro, as crummy a hole as ever I saw outside of New Guinea. We flew many intruder missions over Formosa, Indo China and China. When we did this we flew from a place in Northern Luzon called Loaog. When we were working over Borneo we flew from Sanga-sanga, which is southwest of Mindanao.

Right now we are on Okinawa at a place called Machinato. It is about 5 or 6 miles north of Naha, the capital. From here we were over Japan and China and Korea every night. In Japan many of the missions were over Kyushu, but there were also a lot over Shikoku and Honshu. One of the most interesting things I saw was over Nagasaki the night they dropped the atomic bomb there. It was such a terrific explosion you couldn't see down in the smoke. We got up there a couple or three hours after it was dropped and still couldn't see any thing. I had quite a few close calls. I really didn't think I had much chance of getting back. You can't imagine how this work tells on you, unless you've done it. Then, all of a sudden the war was over and now it looks like I'll be in the land of the living for awhile yet in spite of the Japs. To say I was stunned by the news of the peace is putting it mildly. It seems 15 or 20 years ago that I played my last game of football. You just forget about those things, that's all.

Now that I am actually going back to school I reckon I better start thinking of a good place. And before I forget it, Pop, how about giving me the particulars on this eligibility ruling? Do they still have the one-year rule or can't transfers play at all? I'd sure like to know. Now about Clemson. It's really a good school, for engineers and farmers, but I have less than no aptitude at all for either of those. Though I wouldn't be compelled to engage in military activities it would certainly be urged on me. I could remain in the army making $300 a month if I had any further inclination toward the military. Now that the need for being a soldier is past I have no wish to play at it. And as a place to have a good time, I had more fun in New Guinea than I did at Clemson. By the way, tell Mom that Jack Everson and I finally got together. I was sure glad to see him. He wants to go to Auburn, but I think he'll probably go back to Clemson.

As for being a writer I'm afraid my own efforts are pretty sad. However I'm very interested in reading other people's. You could say I was about as interested in writing as a career as Tom is in photography.

I don't know when I'll get home, but I imagine it'll be sometime before next June. At least I hope so. I don't think it will be quite as quickly as Mom thinks.

Love, Pop. Write soon,

Jim

TO: MAIBELLE SWIFT DICKEY

1945   *ALS, 2 pp; Emory*

Atsugi
Tokyo Nov. 8

Dear Mom,

We took these pictures in Okinawa just after the war ended. I sent Pop a bunch more of them which should arrive about the same time as these.

I am rooming with a Pennsylvania Jew named Leonard "Sugarlips" Frumer. He is quite a promoter and already has our room fixed up like the Waldorf. It is really a pleasure to live in barracks again after tents for almost a year. When I get home I'll tell you just how miserable the war was. I wouldn't go through anything like it again for anything, and we had it easy compared to the engineers, infantry, etc. Don't ever let Willis tell you how rough the war was. The navy lives better than most of the men in it would have in civilian life. I rode up on a Coast Guard L.S.T. right after coming from Sanga-sanga, where we covered the landings at Tarakan, Brunei, Balikpapan and other places on Borneo, and that Navy food was just like stateside chow. Much better than some I've seen in restuarants.

Well, Mom, you don't have to worry about Peg any more. She is married (as if you didn't know) What did you think I'd do when I found out about it, commit Hara-kiri? Not quite. Anyway here is the wedding invitation she was kind enough to send me. I understand there is a toilet-paper shortage at home.

I went into Yokahama to a geisha house the other night. During the course of the night's activities, one of the Jap pimps wrote "patronize Fuji geisha house, Yokahama, Japan" on the back of my flying jacket, which I was not wearing at the time, being otherwise engaged. Now I am greeted by gales of laughter whenever I walk down the streets. I tried to talk the proprietor of the house out of a 20% discount for pimping services, but haven't succeeded as yet.

Well, old gal, don't worry about me. All I do is lay around and read, and fool around Tokyo.

I'll be home in a couple of months.

Sugarlips sends his love.

So does
Jim

TO: TOM DICKEY

Postmarked 15 November 1945   *ALS, 2 pp; Emory*

Atsugi Field
Tokyo

Dear Tom,

Sorry I haven't written in so long, but I guess I am pretty lazy, as well as forgetful.

My orders are in to go home, also my name went in on points (I have 66, with three more battle stars [15 more points] pending) so either way I should be home in a month or two. Altogether I should have 6 ribbons and 7 battle stars. The ribbons are: Asiatic-Pacific, American Defence, Phillipine Liberation, Victory Medal, Air Medal, and one for the occupation of Japan. The campaign stars are: Southern Phillipines, Luzon, Western Pacific (Formosa), Borneo, China Coast, Air Offensive of the Japanese Homeland, Ryuhus. I might get the New Guinea campaign and the Bismark Archipelego (Raboul) but I don't think I had enough missions over Raboul. Only 2. I may leave the squadron before some of the campaign awards come through, but all they are good for are points, anyway.

I sure am glad the war's over. I can't get over not getting killed. This squadron was just like those in the movies where everybody sits around wondering who's going to get it next. We had the most impossible missions you ever saw. At briefing it would have been funny, had it not been so serious, when we were told our targets. My pilot wouldn't fly the real bad ones, so I flew with some other fellows. Once we went on an 1800 mile strike (round trip) way up on Honshu some place. When we got back and landed we didn't have enough gas to park the airplane. I took every mission I could get, to get all my time in so I could come back. I finished up on the night after the war ended (we got combat time until V-J day) and haven't gotten in an airplane since, except to fly up here. My orders have been in to come home on combat fatigue for two weeks now. If I come home that way I get 50 days leave (with pay) before discharge. If I come on points I get 30 days and then get discharged. Just so I get home.

We are living in the Jap Navy's "Kamikaze" pilots' barracks. It is really heaven after those islands. All I do is lay around and reflect on how lucky I am to be alive. Before the end of the war I was down to about 165 lb. from nerves and Spam every meal, but we are eating pretty well now and I guess I weigh around 175 or 180. I am too lazy to really find out.

> Write soon, Junior.
> Jim

TO: MAIBELLE SWIFT DICKEY

Postmarked 29 June 1946   *MS, 2 pp; Emory*
                                             Vanderbilt University[30]

Tacloban[31]

We were very crowded in the C-47. Armstrong and I were half-sitting, half-lying on barracks bags, parachutes and other equipment which members of our replacement shipment had brought with them from New Guinea. We had been riding in that fashion all the way from Peleliu, the last fueling stop between New Guinea and Leyte. We were all so fagged out it didn't create much of an impression on anyone when the co-pilot opened the compartment door and told us we had arrived.

By the time I reached the window we were already in the traffic pattern and the earth was tilting in that incredible way it does when seen from a turning airplane. I could see the metal landing strip for an instant and then the trees growing closer slowly and then more rapidly and all at once sweeping past in a smooth blending rush and I felt our wheels touch down.

After the airplane had been parked we broke out K-rations and ate the canned meat and canned chopped eggs which we had become so accustomed to during the last month.

At that time Tacloban was the largest of the two or three American airstrips on Leyte that were operational. There had been a terrific fight to capture and secure it, and since it had begun functioning the Japs had used every means available to them to destroy or render it impotent, even to the extent of attempted paratroop landings on the strip itself.

Armstrong and I climbed out of the transport and walked along the narrow beach paralleling the taxiway. Wrecked airplanes, most of them American, were everywhere. We examined a crumpled P-38 resting on the edge of the sand. The instruments had been removed and rust covered the battered instrument panel and seat. At least Armstrong said it was rust. I knew better, and I think he did, too.

It was beginning to get dark, and we had wandered a considerable distance from our C-47, so we started back, past a lone anti-aircraftman at his post, seriously reading a comic magazine, his skin a bright yellow from atabrine, his fatigues filthy, his face lean and placid.

Then we saw our four P-61's crouched in revetments looking ungainly and sinister, like tarantulas, black paint scaling from them in great patches. There was no one near them.

A squadron of B-25's was taking off. They came down the metal strip one after the other, bouncing a little over the uneven places and splashing water from the numerous puddles they had to run through. The sound of their engines was deafening; not the vicious whine of the fighter, but loud and thick and power-laden. On the nose of each was painted a huge blue bat with red open mouth, white sharp teeth and serrated wings extending evenly back along the fuselage. As soon as they began climbing we lost sight of them, for in addition to the gathering darkness the weather was rapidly becoming more threatening and the visibility poorer. Armstrong and I looked back at the '61's.

It was quiet after the '25's had taken off. Very still. The sea was smooth and there were no waves climbing onto the beach, but only a lapping sound, gentle and insistent. All the palms around the strip had been demolished by gunfire, or their tops blown off leaving only shattered stumps. There were many of these. It reminded me of cripples. We climbed back into our transport.

For a long time Armstrong and I sat in the open doorway looking out across the dirty invasion-littered beach and the calm sea where a few freighters were anchored. After awhile Armstrong lit a cigarette. The smoke curved up and back into the plane. He sat on an old barracks bag, his feet propped on the door, motionless, elbows on his knees, his long thin hand holding a cigarette. I had seen him like that, almost, many times, all the way through flying school and at bars in the States trying to pick up girls and be gay with them after his wife had left him, but this time there was a difference. He looked out toward the ships, and I watched him, thinking that he was the best friend I had, and while we were sitting there it started to rain, softly at first and then more fiercely until we could not see the ocean any longer. But we sat quietly and did not speak.

TO: MAIBELLE SWIFT DICKEY

Postmarked 14 April 1947   *ALS, 2 pp; Emory*
                                                    Vanderbilt University

Dear Mom,

I have finished studying this Sunday and am now listening to the Philadelphia Philharmonic playing Shostakovitch's <u>6th Symphony</u>, which seems to me to be pretty good.

I have a 100 average in Algebra this time, so I think I should make it through without any trouble. I am doing pretty well in all my other subjects, also. Here is a transcription of my last quarter's grades, in case you weren't sent one, or it hasn't arrived yet. I pulled that "E" I had at mid-term in Biology up to a B, which took a lot of work and which I think is pretty good. That means that, aside from that one quarter of math I failed, I haven't made below a B since I've been in school, or all during my Freshman year.

We had another track meet yesterday. I won the High Hurdles, as you can see from the enclosed clipping. The track was even slower than usual. I thought I ran pretty well. The boy from Southwestern had run a 15.5 the week before and I beat him without too much trouble. I can't understand why the time was so slow. I didn't Hi-Jump yesterday because I have a bad knee which I am saving for the Kentucky meet here next Saturday.

I have not written a whole lot of original things in some time except for the two sonnets on the back of this sheet. Pop will probably think his eldest son is insane if he reads them, so I don't think he should.

Be <u>sure</u> to get this hundred dollars up to me as soon as possible, for I owe everybody in town.

I have been going with some new girls who are very nice but very young. There is considerable social life here at this time of year and you can bet I am in on most of it. I am getting very tired of school, however. Just 3 more months and I will be able to "lay back" for awhile. I wonder if it would be possible for me to have the car here this summer? If it is not agreeable with Tom, though, I don't want it. I know how much I'd like to come home for a vacation and have to ride the bus everywhere.

They are building some swell new dormitories here. I am going to move into one of them this summer or next fall.

They are really nice.

Two Sonnets

I

Announced to me by trumpets and by tears,
by tempests in the silk, by paper wars,
how calendars of death in distant years
will well up in our eyes and wall our stars.
In ferns and forests, as the ghost appears
wrapped in his flags or swinging from his shores,
muffled with careful cloth, we stop our ears,
sing in our sleep to silence all his sores.

Pinned to our wrists, like butterflies to glass,
the alphabets of age, the wheels of grief.
A grain of salt, a nail, a lip, a leaf
reminds us that they melt and move through grass.

Announced to me by all they left to keep,
how soon they shall assassinate my sleep.

II

Sewn to my side, the shaken ships of love
move in their milky waste of pearls and blood,
let down their thorny nets to fire and flood,
splinter the roof of water, drown the dove.
First, in the breath of morning, all put out
in siren-light and glittering of grace,
savoured by weather; at the white look-out
sight simple islands moored in flowered space.

Then, on my banks of flesh as on a rock,
heave hills and heavens signalling the wreck.
Wild on the wave, they thunder in and shock
the red, remote cathedral where I work.

The bird-like boats, bringing their beaks toward home,
spin in my side, sail down and rest on bone.

                                                            Jim

TO: MAXINE DICKEY

Postmarked 19 March 1951   *TLS, 2 pp; Estate of James Dickey*
                                                    Maxwell Air Force Base, Ala.

My Darling;

I am writing this immediately on getting back from Atlanta. There, I had a really good time, but there is considerable (and mounting) tension over Tom's lack of a job. The family seems to think that he is trying to avoid going to work, but I think his efforts to find a place are more or less sincere. Patsy "wants her apartment," etc., and the poor boy is about off his rocker with worry. He'll have to learn to handle both himself and his wife, though, before there'll be any real satisfaction in that family.

I have been doing a good deal of thinking on the subject of you and flowers, and I have come to the conclusion that you are lovelier than any of them.

Most of the time here I don't do anything. I am sort of the squadron troubleshooter; I do what has to be done and nobody else wants to do. Not hard work.

I am glad you and your mother are having such a nice visit together, and I am also glad that you are seeing so many of the people we knew together. If you get a chance, see or call Spears, and tell him for me that I enjoyed very much his article on Auden[32] in the Sewanee. Ask him if he has had any repercussions from Jarrell.[33]

I am working on a long verse dialogue called The Red Garden.[34] It is likely to be very good. I want to get it finished by the time I leave here, which will be about in another month.

Tom says you are looking good, and that you are not sick at all, all of which relieves me considerably.[35]

I have decided one thing: that no matter what the air force offers me, no matter how little I can earn "on the outside," or no matter what, I will not (or could not) make a career out of this life. The life of an officer in the Air Force is essentially a surrender: a surrender to the "good deal", a surrender to an indolent, unthinking life, a surrender to expediency, a surrender to the officers' club, and a surrender of all I want most to do. Even now I can feel the insidious and delightful pull away from my work in the genial and innocent "Let's go up to the club and have a brew," and "Let's see what's going on up at the P X." Do what they tell you to do, and they'll let you have "a good time." Such is what the assorted mediocrities of the AAF want, believe in, and most fervently would live and die by. Not so for us, my love. A man is nothing if he doesn't sacrifice a good many things for the things he believes in. This last sounds a little adolescent, but it is a truth for all of that.

I love you a great tremendous amount. I want you to write to me and tell me all sorts of things. I want you to I want you

Love
Jim

TO: MAXINE DICKEY

Postmarked 25 April 1951   *TLS, 2 pp; Estate of James Dickey*

Dear Maxine;

Most wonderful of all wives: hail! I couldn't decide whether to make this THE IRONIC LETTER: ("Such hospitality in the Air Force!") the MOURNFUL LET-TER: ("I miss you so terribly, darling . . .") the FUNNY LETTER: ("Well, here I am in the Air Force again, Sugar-Lamb") or just the letter that tells you that you are the most loved woman in the world tonight and all the rest of the nights in which I participate.

News: I put in for instructor today, and there is a moderately good chance that I will get it. More of this in a week or so. If not, I go to Tyndall Field for another month, and then out to a tactical outfit. If the course at Tyndall Field is anywhere near as easy as this one is, I won't really know much about the workings of the All-weather fighters. The rumor is that the F-94 is a pretty hot aircraft.

I have found a fairly nice place to live. There are two other fellows in this deal with me. We live in a motel cabin, for which we pay eight dollars a week apiece. The place is about good enough to put George the yardman in. We get five dollars a day, however, and despite the holdup we will a good deal more than break even.

I have met a good many of the "old boys" here. They were all called involuntarily also, and are almost as bitter as I am, but I don't think quite as bitter; they didn't have you to leave. I love you. The field is fairly nice. The town, as you know, is a resort town, with the usual assortment of queers, ill-looking women, old men, grafters, gamblers and sun-burned housewives. The coast here is as wide open as you will ever find a coast: there are dice tables, card houses, whorehouses, damn near everything or anything you might or might not want to see. Ah, the lusts of the flesh! All the field personnel are pretty lustful, but all I want, ever, is to see and be near you once (preferably to last forever).

The instructors in the classes are very nice fellows, some of whom I knew before; they don't know much about what the hell they are doing, but then who in the Air Force does? After all, fellows, we're in this together. You know the attitude.

The car is wonderfully useful here. I don't know what I should do without it.

Tomorrow night I will write you a long, long letter full of meditations and love-passages and instructions for your reading and your education, and plans for our child and for us and for you, who I have decided is going to have the most considerate, non-nosepicking, clean, clean-shaven, deodorized, pants-pressed husband in the world as soon as he can resume his husbandly duties in the way in which he would like to be accustomed.

Take care of my two babies, and love me a little the way I love you both.

Thy

Jim

2nd Lt James L. Dickey
AO 2027173
3401 st Student Officer's Sqdn. (O)
Box 2401
Keesler AFB, Miss.

TO: MAXINE DICKEY

1 May 1951   *TLS, 3 pp; Estate of James Dickey*
                                             Keesler Air Force Base, Miss.

My Darling,

I wish very much that I could see you tonight, and that we could wander through the largest and most compelling zoo in the world, filled with raccoons and caoti mundi's. Biloxi is the very sink and cess-pool of the Western World; you can stand in the center of town, near the Earle Hotel, where the pimpled Pfc. snarls in a New Jersey accent at the miserable bar-maid and the rich retired grocery-man from Iowa shuffles to the Newstand (among the wretched soldiers aimlessly milling around the Crown Pool Hall) to get his evening paper, which he will sit on the sweltering front porch and try very hard but without much success to enjoy; you can do these things and see the star of the West decline. There is not much in or to us (the Western powers) anymore, except a tremendous power of production; the rest has been consumed by greed and the kind of desperate and fanatical dogmatism that Americans have.

But while there is the possibility, even the possibility, of the love that you and I have for each other, then, surely, all is redeemable, all is possible again, and the world is strangely and newly green, even in Biloxi.

To the boring Air Force business. I am to be paid Friday; on that illustrious date I shall send you the sum of two hundred dollars; one hundred-fifty of which you asked for, and the other fifty of which is a kind of present or call it what you will; it is a thing by which I say, inadequately, how much I adore you.

I have been getting in what the Air Force considers a reasonable amount of flying time. What it amounts to is that I get up in the nose of a B-25 and read for three or four hours, scarcely noticing where I am, occasionally looking out the bombardier's compartment at something relatively uninteresting sliding past on the flat and green ground, and then back to whatever it is that I am reading. I read through John Berryman's book of poems THE DISPOSSESSED[36] in that way, and I like it better than at any previous time. He is, in a limited range, extremely skillful, and his things are in rare instances moving. He has not a great deal of talent, but he is careful (as is Eliot, in another plane of accomplishment) with it; he has achieved something worth keeping in touch with.

I have finished Spender's book[37] and am reading it again. It is an extraordinary document of a sensitive but not clearminded man who is trying to understand himself throughout experiences for which his upbringing and temperament have not prepared him. These experiences are the great political and artistic upheavals of our time, and his moving among them is recorded faithfully and often painfully. I feel sure Stephen Spender is a real human being in the only way in which it matters at all to be one; in a way, therefore, that most of us are not (most of them, my darling; the others). I think you would like the book. If you have a chance check it out at some lending library. By the way, I want you to read Aldington's book; the one you took to Nashville with you. Tell me what you think. Read it carefully. I love you.

No one here has any aspirations, one way or the other. They care a little about what becomes of them, but not much; they are mostly interested in THE NEW BUICK, or something really important, like "Do you know what Arthur Godfrey said last Tuesday? How does he get away with that stuff on the radio? He practically came right out and said it. . . ." and so on and so on, as the line in the PX gets longer (or shorter) and the day gets hotter (or Hotter) and everything collapses in a huge mire of inconsequence and boredom.

My room-mates were curious about "why I lug all those books around with me" right away. I immediately got what has come to be almost standard procedure as a question: "You don't think everything in the world is in books, do you?" When I explained amusedly and a little tiredly why I lugged the books around there were only bemused and incredulous shakings of heads. It is best for them to think you a little odd. That satisfies them, and gives them their modicum of ridicule with which to nourish their fantastically protected ignorance. They are not bad fellows, really. That is the trouble. No one wishes harm; each wishes his own life happily mediocre. In that vacuum the engenderings of evil, corruption and death are, in those "fighting for freedom" as well as those "intent upon destroying it." The human animal, in the main, will never change in that respect; we must be saved, as Gide says, "by the few."

I love my darling child. Take care of my "growing" family, and write. I love you more than life.

Thy
Jim

TO: MAXINE DICKEY

Postmarked 4 May 1951   *TLS, 2 pp; Estate of James Dickey*
Keesler Air Force Base, Miss.

My darling,

This is a letter I hope you are glad to get because in it I say I love you, and not primarily because there is a hundred and fifty (no, two hundred and fifty dollars) in it. I love you.

In this letter I want to say how perfectly and unutterably marvellous I think it is that you are being such a good child about writing to your daddy, and how much I want to see you and how much you mean to me. All this I want to say. I also want to tell you what a wonderful loved childhood our little one is going to have both because it should have one and to make up for your childhood. I think the best expression of what I conceive your childhood to have been like is by Berryman . . . . this is you

> . . . whom sorry childhood had made sit quite still,
> an orphan silence, unregarded sheen,
> listening for any small soft note, not hopeful . . .[38]

This is mostly the same childish, semi-boy-scout life here. It is increasingly incredible to me how grown men can conduct themselves on the plane of imbecility these people here do. All of them I have met are simply idiots, that is to say children, and not bright or precocious ones. One of the boys I live with sold oil burners of some kind in civilian life. He is very proud of the fact, and at any rate I know, through his unceasing enthusiasm, something about oil burners. The triviality of the conversations we have would amaze you. It does me. And he is a nice enough fellow. So it goes on and on. Never any relief. This is the place for the books I have with me. You would never begrudge them to me now. (Not that you ever really did.)

Darling, don't think I am going to be "ashamed" of you if you don't read things, and do the things I am interested in. I don't want you to listen to music and read and look at pictures as a favor of any kind to me, but to open up the areas of response in yourself that are by all odds the best part of you. You are so wonderfully sensitive, and your natural taste is so good that it is nothing short of criminal not to develop these things. You are going to be a great mother for our child; so understanding and patient and kind; I adore you, Maxine.

My tubby little one, dont (as James Jones would punctuate) worry about getting fat as far as looks are concerned; do what the doctor tells you to keep in good shape, I don't want any slipups.

Take this money and get some nice things with it; if you don't I won't send you as much next time. Remember that.

Must tap off now. I have to get up at five in the morning to fly. After the B-25 takes off I get up in the plexiglass nose with the clouds and air flowing around and really sack out. The best place to sleep in the Air Force is in the nose of a B-25.

All love, little flower.

Thy

Jim

TO: MAXINE DICKEY

? May 1951   *TLS, 2 pp; Estate of James Dickey*
                                          Keesler Air Force Base, Miss.

Dearest Little Turtle Face,

You asked about pictures? Here is the latest. Fetching, what?

I was put in for instructor yesterday. As yet they haven't heard anything about its being approved yet, but it seems very much in the offing. As soon as I hear anything at all to confirm this delightful rumor, I will begin to look for a house (with no stairs), a beach and a puppy-dog for my children.

I haven't written for the last day or two because I have been getting my best poems out to various magazines. I thought at first that I would wait and see if I got any "offers" from any of them, but decided that while I had time I might as well get them in the hands of the people I most wish would publish them. Therefore I sent the two best to the Partisan, four (one much revised for the better) to Poetry and one to the Hudson.[39] The last one is the "Litter Bearers", the one in which I do my kind of playing around with Hopkins and sprung rhythm.[40] It seems to me to have some exciting things in it. I only hope that it gets read more or less sympathetically, or even just read, by the right people. These are good poems, the best I have written. If any of them get at all an adequate hearing I have no doubt that I will break into print again. So much for the life of literature. One note more. In revising one or two lines of another poem I wrote while at Rice, I ended up working on it for three days, hours at a time, and completely recovered (and added to) the enthusiasm for writing which I am convinced now constitutes (along with my great love for you and my hunger for experience) the only thing worth saving about me.

I have been rereading Dylan Thomas,[41] and am amazed how simple (not really <u>simple</u>, meaning "uncomplex", but "easy to understand once you ferret out the governing concepts of the poems") most of the poems are. There is wonderful round music in Thomas; he is very nearly a great lyric poet. Considered purely from a verbal standpoint he does or should not stand aside for anyone; Donne or Shakespeare or anyone.

For the first two and a half years of our marriage you have made wonderful progress in many directions. Best of all, you have been truly moved by at least one poem ("The River-Merchant's Wife")[42] and by many paintings, and for the right reasons, I think. The rest is simply learning, "feeling," analyzing, insisting upon getting things into some kind of significant relationship to yourself and love. I love you greatly. I love you.

This weekend I think I will go to New Orleans and wander fascinated among the stripteasers, the queers, the raised cemetaries, the "authentic jazz" and the expensive foods. I should, I really <u>should</u> go down there at least once during my stay here, and, as Saturday is "Armed Forces Day" (O joke of jokes!) and we don't have anything to do, I figured it might as well be then as any time.

I would like nothing better than to extend this letter infinitely and perhaps someday I shall, but <u>this</u> day I have a class to meet in approximately ten minutes. I have about ten miles to drive between here and there, and it is going to be plenty close.

Don't ever let any faintest shade of pain cross that little flower of a face. I love it and you.

Thy

Jim

TO: MAXINE DICKEY

Postmarked ? May 1951   *TLS, 3 pp; Estate of James Dickey*
                                           Keesler Air Force Base, Miss.

Dear One,

Not much news; the course is becoming more and more of a joke, the weather has turned unaccountably cold and rainy; I have been doing a good deal of flying; no drinking; not much sunning; much peeling; much thinking about you and the future.

I went in to see Captain Henderson about the instructor's job. He told me that he had blanket authorization to pull three men out of every class for instructors. He is not yet sure what he is going to do about our class; he told me to check back with him this time next week. He seems to like me very well; probably if he picks anyone out of our class of five it will be me. However, things are very uncertain, as always in the service, and we can only wait for whatever is coming to break.

I want to tell you how wonderful I think your adaptability is. You seem able to change with any wind, and not only "make the best of the situation" but make it downright desirable and even fun.

As far as the situation of getting out of the Air Force is concerned, it pretty well looks like I am in for 21 months. Given those terms, I am all for fixing it so I can stay alive for that length of time, do my "stretch" with as little fuss as possible, and then get the hell out of it.

I have been reading a good deal here and there; in fact, as I told you, I am getting more reading done here than I did at Rice, although certainly not more writing. I have read various articles in the critical anthologies I brought with me, a great deal of poetry from individual books (Tate, Warren, Wilbur, Lowell, Graham, Thomas, W. C. Williams, etc.) and a very interesting book (pocket edition) by the Spaniard Jose Ortega y Gasset called <u>The Revolt of the Masses</u>, a famous work which I should already have read but never have.[43] It bears directly on one or two of the problems which you and I discuss from time to time. Here is an excerpt which may interest you:

> As one advances in life, one realizes more and more that the majority of men—and women—are incapable of any other effort than that strictly imposed on them as a reaction to external compulsion. And for that reason, the few individuals we have come across who are capable of a spontaneous and joyous effort stand out isolated, monumentalized, so to speak, in our experience. These are the select men, the nobles, the only ones who are active and not merely reactive, for whom life is a perpetual striving, an incessant course of training.

I read <u>The Revolt of the Masses</u> in my private reading room, the nose of that most excellent and worthy aircraft, the B-25, under lovely conditions of cloud, sea and air. It is a recommended position to all interested persons.

I have a new haircut, This one is really <u>short</u>. It looks fairly presentable, however, and not nearly so <u>thin</u> as I had feared. There's hope yet for the old topknot (as a business man might say).

Darling, I hope you are caring for yourself; I know your lazy little ways when it comes to doing something you don't want to do (taking exercises, dieting, reading, painting, rubbing in the salve, etc.) I am going to demand a full accounting when you come down here, and everything had <u>better</u> be in order. See?

I finished Stephen Spender's autobiography and am now reading it again. I found parts of it extraordinarily moving; his self-analysis is frequently good and some of his descriptions of the many places in Europe he has been are lovely. He has spent his entire life not in making a living or sensually (in the common sense of the word) but in a sustained and exhaustive (and no doubt exhausting) effort to <u>understand</u> himself and the world he lives in, and I find that good. There are some revealing passages on his Oxford days with Auden, and others dealing with his "literary life" in London, Berlin (with Isherwood) and Spain (with Malraux).[44] Some of these I had read then printed separately in the <u>Partisan</u>, but enjoyed them no less for that reason when I encountered them in the book. You may read it for yourself (I hope you do) so I won't tell you any more about it.

Have you heard from Cal and Betty, or even "Captain" Hall?[45] I'd like very much to hear from Cal, so if you get a communiqué from them, or have got one, with their address on it, send it on to me and I will write him.

I have been patching up some of my poems, and may in a few days send one or two of them off to <u>Poetry</u>, the <u>Partisan</u> or the <u>Hudson</u>. Or maybe the <u>Kenyon</u>, although it doesn't seem quite as good as the others any more.

Well, time to desist. I love you more than I love anything on earth, or ever have. Or ever will. Be a sweet child and write your daddy soon and often. And take care of our "family" so that I can take care of it too in the near future. I love you.

Thy

Jim

TO: MAXINE DICKEY

Postmarked 7 August 1951   *TLS, 2 pp; Estate of James Dickey*
                                              Keesler Air Force Base, Miss.

Tuesday

Dear One,

Praise be! My orders came in today. The rest of the week will be taken up with clearing the field and getting everything ready for the actual move. I plan to leave Monday, so you can still write once or twice more, if you would like. You had better like! Joe Sokolowiscz is going to ride down with me. Here is the terrific joke of the matter: Holloway's orders, Joe's and mine came in, and Taylor's, Jackson and Rebert's didn't. On the bulletin board today was a note ordering those last three to report to <u>Supply</u> to be assigned duties! I'm sure glad I missed that detail.

I have a (crummy) room in the BOQ, but I am going to stay with the captain as long as I possibly can because of the piss-poor condition of things at the field. Well, I feel much better about everything now that I know what the devil is going on.

I have been working on a new forty-line poem called "The Son" which I have almost finished. It seems to me to be very good. I'll inclose it in the next letter, if you would like.

I am glad that you are reading a little in that Rodman anthology, but my poor child <u>will</u> pick those things <u>so</u> far over her curly little head. Perse, even in translation, is always worth reading, though not always understandable. No, the poem doesn't have much in common with Genesis, except in a general way. The Anabasis (from the Greek word meaning "journey," "migration") is a poem dealing with the conquests of vast distances and barbaric countries, packed full of esoteric lore about the customs of the Tartars ("the saddle of a coward was burned") and other great nomadic peoples. Even if you don't get all the exact references (and it will be some years when <u>I</u> get them all, if I ever do) you can sense the marvellous feeling for the tremendous distances traversed, the ritual customs employed by the people, and something of the voyage of the spirit of man through those same barbaric and dangerous lands of the mind. I'll explain some of it to you when we get together. You are right about Faulkner. That suicide scene in The Sound and the Fury was always terribly embarrassing to me. Anna Livia Plurabelle is beyond everyone. Someday I hope you and I both will understand and enjoy Finnegans Wake. That will be a measure of our progress. A partial explanation of the name may help you: Anna = "Annus": which in Latin means year . . . here it means yearly, that is, cyclic . . . "Livia" means "river", also "liv" is "life" or "living". So far we have "yearly, cyclic river of life." "Plurabelle" is

"Plura": "many", "Belle" is both "woman" and French for "Beauty," in other words, the river of life is seen to be flowing through all women, or through all women as they are exemplified or symbolized by Anna Livia Plurabelle, the character. You can see a little from this how Joyce works, and how suggestive and difficult (which you no doubt have <u>already</u> determined without my help) he is. No wonder Joyce said to a young disciple, "Young man, I expect the student of my works to devote his life to them."[46]

I love you

love you

Jim

The Son[47]

In the calyx of the apple-tree, cast
Around silk of warning summers,
At the fern's small irons lecherous,
You heard the distant drovers murmur;
The moon in the nostril of the fox burned red
Beyond your splendors, and a cool wind slid.
Slow builded blood thrown shadowd down
Rang then to the helmstone, lyrical exile;
By milk and hook, cloud and coil
From perjured membrane stepped the son.

From his gilled coign and animal smile
A god in marble among the yews
Dazzled, and a garden showered. You turned,
As the rills of the sacrificial pool
Glutted the doglike head, no more
To the long sailing motions shaken
From your tree, but to tide
Break at sorrow for the son
Passaged by blood and skill, the stone
Hurled at the women's hut, and the prepuce

Buried, at manrise, in the curious leaf.
No longer agonist, you paced
The vinewreathed bramble to the peal of horns,
As voyager ebbing, gross-stuck as boar,
And leant your ear to distance,
Its cored and breaking sound. Woodcloud
And aging tusk were lathered red
By changeling faint and rising lord;
In tapestried and dancelike radiance
Moved the parricidal vision from the loin.

A looseflamed soaring in the throat
Held temple post and ivy bread;
The waiting foliage gave upon
The golden hosted serpent, chaliced
Magnificent, the lichens of the gods,
The tabernacle which man seeks
Once only, to placate and destroy.
In strange munificence and love,
Calling upon your son, bloody at eye,
You crushed your effigies that he might live.

TO: MAXINE DICKEY

Postmarked 15 August 1951   *TLS, 2 pp; Estate of James Dickey*
                                               Keesler Air Force Base, Miss.

Monday Night

My Dear Wife,

This is (thank God!) the last time I will write to you from this delightful resort. Joe and I are planning to leave about eight in the morning, and to conduct a sort of leisurely trip out to Waco, with ourselves as participants. There is no need for us to rush, so we are not going to.

I have just come back from seeing "A Place in the Sun," which, as you know, is the movie version of Dreiser's "An American Tragedy", and it seemed to me a very good job of picture-making. Harry Brown scripted it, and the movie does as well as can be expected by that tremendous bulky elephant of a book. Montgomery Clift is quite good as George Eastman; he acts with almost desperate sincerity, with slow, tortured, deliberated statements that seem to be impelled from him against his will; just what is needed in certain of the scenes of the picture. Elizabeth Taylor is not allowed to clutter up much of the action, but what she _is_ in seems to me to be much better than it would have been, if, say, she had acted the part two or three years ago. She is becoming competent, which is all she is likely ever to be, besides an adornment. If you get a chance, see it. It will set you to thinking about a good many things.

The time for the birth of our first child is almost here, Maxine. I hope you look with a great joy on the prospect as I do. Let us teach it to try to <u>understand</u>, and not judge others selfishly, or judge them from its own selfish motives. ("But what about <u>me</u>? About <u>me</u>? About <u>me</u>?") There is too much of that kind of thing.

Let us teach it to see whatever it can see clearly, and to realize that action can proceed from a variety of motives, and is not limited to the most obvious of these,
and above all, not to condemn when it shall seem to best advantage to condemn.
That is the hard thing. And that a thing in one sense may be bad and in another
good, and teach it that because an act is advantageous to one (itself) it is not
therefore good of itself, but may harm another. And that "what people expect" of
one is hardly ever a way of being true to oneself. And to learn of people, and to
understand that people are lonely and mostly damned, and that they act to fore-
stall and conceal these things, and to hold on to what they have been led to think
rightly belongs to them, out of desperation that they may be again left alone, and
out of pride which is fear, and hatred.

Let us teach our child these things.

Again, I love you, darling, and I am thinking of you all the time, and of the
child, and of our great and quiet joy and anticipation and of the fearful responsibility we have taken on, and of the even more fearful and great responsibility the
child has to us, and to itself, in that it is a human being, half animal murderer,
part saint, sometime Anti-christ, pardoner and the fruit and consummation of
our love and the living knowledge of the guilt we all lie down in, that we may permit another to rise above us.

I love you. I will write to you as soon as I get to Waco.

Love, little Toodlum,

Jim

TO: MAXINE DICKEY

Postmarked 21 August 1951   *TLS, 2 pp; Estate of James Dickey*
                                              James Connally Air Force Base
                                              Waco, Texas

My Dear Wife,

I am sorry that I have not written since I have been here, but it is always likely
to be more or less like this when you change bases. I have been scrambling about
trying to do the more or less (I <u>said</u> "more or less" once, already) unnecessary
things the Air Force requires under these circumstances. I am squared away fairly
well now. I flew this afternoon, so I am all right as far as time this month goes. It is
rough here in the air and nobody likes the flying end of it, but everything else is a
great deal better than Keesler Field. You'll like it here a lot. We will be members of
this Baptist community in no time, and be bored and probably pretty well satisfied with it. The town is "friendly" and not large. There are no gambling joints

here. This is the kind of base, like Hammer Field, where you can go to supply and sign for watches, computers, dark glasses, flying suits, plotters, and damn near everything else, so I got some dark glasses and navigational equipment today, and a flying suit, all this after I flew. Our good friend Klein came through and lent me his flying suit to go up in. "Give you the shirt off his back, that guy!"

I have written on more short poem since The Son, and think it rather a good job. As to reading, I have decided to tackle the three toughest novelists in the twentieth century simultaneously, or successively, rather. Consequently I am now engaged in trying to decipher Finnegans Wake, (with key), Proust's Remembrance of Things Past, and Thomas Mann's Joseph tetralogy. I hope I have the fortitude. This time around (I have read these before, but with not nearly as much success as I would have liked, or would like) I should be able to come to terms with them with some measure of success and understanding, and profit.

Today before Joe and I went to the field we wandered around town and into a store that specializes in old pulp magazines. To our immense delight, the shelves were groaning with numbers of "War Birds", "Doc Savage", "Flying Aces", and "The Secret Six" which we remembered from our boyhoods. We bought a couple of them ("Flying Aces" and "War Birds") and have been roaring with laughter ever since. Excerpt:

Tucker was shaking his head.

"I'm no Jonah, Major, but death is standard equipment on these Nieuports. The wings are glued on."

McQuillen grunted. (wasn't that rather unexpected?) His keen eyes moved over the equipment on the line. It took no careful examination to confirm what Tucker said. The Nieuports were patched and sewed and mended and out of plumb. His lips thinned.

"C'est la guerre," he said. "Let's go."

Shades of Walter Mitty!! What a part for Danny Kaye!

O how I wish I could hear a little of that (almost) incessant bitching, from one who does it with such liquid sweetness! I love you, darling. Never cease to think of me, in my patched-up Nieuport, going to do battle with that scourge of the skies, von Richter, in his golden skull-marked Albatross. Up the Escadrille!

Love,

Jim

TO: MAXINE DICKEY

Postmarked 28 August 1951   *TLS, 2 pp; Estate of James Dickey*
                                               James Connally Air Force Base
                                               Waco, Texas

My Dear Wife,

Not much here to report. Joe and I have been taking it pretty easy. We are all
checked in here, with all passes and that tiresome stuff taken care of. We are working, as is usual with me, on "revising the course," an apparently endless task. We
work, actually, about 15 or 20 minutes a day. The rest of the time we sit around
and chew the fat, or go out for "coffee break," and at around three we take off for
home. Really a very easy time we have of it. I should have plenty of time to write,
but I can't seem to get much of it done without you. You are really all my talent,
and every accomplishment I have to my credit is entirely yours; yours more than
mine, as a matter of fact.

There is a show in town that shows old movies, is not air-conditioned, is generally crummy, and which costs 14 cents to enter. Today Joe and I went to see "The
Lost Patrol" with Victor McLaglen, Wallace Ford and Reginald Denny.[48] It was
one of the real landmarks and altarstones of my childhood (I memorized every
member of the cast, and could remember the names as Joe and I sat here in the
little inconsequential theatre in Waco, Texas). I enjoyed the show (which was
John Ford's, and one of the best of his) very much and enjoyed my sad bewildered
frustrated and normal boyhood also, and was quite nostalgic. The other night we
heard a radio adaptation of "The Informer", and have so really got a good dose of
McLaglen at his best, loudest and most brutally touching.

Child, child, where in what forest you lie alone tonight, hearing the horned
voice of the hunter break through the green pools and the unharmed birds cry
down the feathered wind, where your face is unseen, has never been seen, and
where you smile against the furred stone, and the blade moors its fires over the
raining font of birth . . . son, daughter, whose life and ruin I have wrought with
not one thought of forgiveness, where the great gentleness of all who have ever
been kind to me will find the soft lighted mouth of your mother, and the suns
gleam and make, and the great tribes of the silken and cruel sand throw down
their burdens and wander to the rich pastures laid on their unhooded skin, overture, Canaan and the great of earth, I shall come to you soon, fresh in your sacramental blood and the warmth of a great room, and watch your small lips curl and
try in that inarticulate music Beethoven heard when he saw the storm break over
his pure deafness, and we shall then meet, and what speech we shall have together
is already in whatever richness you have been allowed to proceed, cautiously and

cruelly, from, and has been in my heart from the time I was myself conceived, to lie wrecked and new and unsheltered save by love on what cast and lone shell of time the tremendous unceasing wind that blows us full of breath filled that night, and this night of all my loves, and my litten and hallowed wife.

Jim

TO: MAXINE DICKEY

Postmarked 21 September 1951   *TLS, 5 pp; Estate of James Dickey*
                                        James Connally Air Force Base
                                        Waco, Texas

LETTER TO ONE WIFE[49]

Dear Maxine,

I am more or less wound up to write to you a long time tonight, partly to make up for the poor correspondence I have been turning out and partly because I feel the need to talk about some things that I need to talk about.

First, some news. We will, I repeat WILL be able to go home for Christmas. The whole base closes down around the 22 of December and stays closed until Jan. 3. This period is called "Operation Sleighbell", and is designed for people like you and me, which is to say for everybody who wants to go home Christmas. Which is to say for everybody. Our poor lost friend Elliott is now in Anchorage, Alaska. A call came down from there for one RO, and naturally. . . . . . . Shall I elucidate?

It is settled that I am going to work in Group, at a nice desk job (editing 0520 training material), and things there will undoubtedly be fairly good.

They called the involuntary recalls in, got a little information from them, and now are rescinding our original recall orders to read 17 months instead of 21, so, if things don't get radically worse, we will be out around the 12 of next August. I am (or perhaps I will wait until you get here) going to talk to McKillop and lay it on the line. I am not going to grovel for any 210 dollar a month job. In fact I am sort of looking forward to expressin' my indignation.

It is still very lonely here without you, you children, and I wish I were with you or you with me in the little dream house I am going to build you when I make my first million (or hundred). I wrote three or four very good short poems while I was in Atlanta, and am getting them ready to send to Shapiro.[50] The best of them, I think (but I thought The Red Garden[51] good too, but now I don't), is one I wrote while I sat in the Airport at Atlanta waiting for them to repair a carburetor on

flight nine-oh-one. What I remember from the execution of St. Sebastian from
Fabiola, which has haunted me ever since, suddenly crystallized and I wrote the
following lines very rapidly, and revised only a little:

> There is
> One after one after one
> Drawn blind to the head:
> Teeth, leaves or hearts.
>
> Seven angels are pierced.
> Except the last, they turn
> And gather blood in wreathes,
> Sadly, as lingerers,
>
> And to such riven water,
>
> To the bolts of spring
> Snapt in the oak,
> Sing of endless freightage
> And scattered soil
>
> As one steps upward
> As into light filled and flying
> Over the stopped sun
> And the pied cuirass.

I am not sure about the meter of the third from last line, but the poem, I
think, is fairly successful. Does the scene come back to you?

I have been reading J. D. Salinger's The Catcher in the Rye.[52] It is really divert-
ing; quite the easiest book to read I have encountered since Uncle Wiggly.

How is the little button-nose?[53] I miss him and you like mad, and can't wait to
hear you both howl, as I undoubtedly will for the rest of my life.

Mother will be crazy about the little weasel, and wants you both to stay in
Atlanta for as long as you will. If you feel like it, take an extra week. I know how
good it is to eat once in a while stuff that you haven't had to buy and prepare
yourself. Or at least I think I know. You know.

Try, sweet, really to look at and feel things. Look at the paintings in the books
we bought. The world is not the dead lifeless mechanical wooden thing that the
others make out. Look at it, and feel it. Don't waste yourself on the artificial
restrictions, comments and observations, the million tiresome and commonplace and unimaginative opinions of others. See a little beyond the laundry bill,
and the new car, and the new house, and the "fifth of Old Forester," and the party
at the club and the things that most people think constitute the world, the real
world, the world that every night in your dreams rises and is new and terrifying

and various, the emotions in it new, and real, no boredom, only lust and terror and beauty. Don't let every emotion die except commonplace ideas about jealousy and "not letting so-and-so get away with such-and-such with <u>me</u>" and the other standardized substitutes for feeling that we seem obligated to entertain because someone once told us that we should. Rise, wake, like the Princess in the dust of thorns, the centuries fallen away like the brocaded robes and high collars of the Beast when La Belle wept for him, and take the world in your arms and hate it and love it and feel in it and try to <u>understand</u> it. Simple submission to it is no substitute. Certainly "but someone has to think of and take care of these things," but that is a poor excuse that the cowardly denial of life most people secretly wish for makes for you; your whole existence cannot be occupied with "these things," otherwise you have simply sold your life for a comfortable and busy mess of evasions. Wake, and your life will rise crying to you, and childhood will break marvellously over you like a wave, and you will know that we have created more than feedings and a "cute toy" and monetary problems.

But there is no sense in my ending on such a grave yew-like note. It should be obvious that I <u>must</u> love you or I wouldn't take such pains with you. All the women I have ever loved, or liked, existed so that I might meet you, return to you, love you and at last discover you.

Write soon, and give my regards to my image, and the mother, who, by now, surely, must be martyred.

Love,

Jim

TO: MAXINE DICKEY

Postmarked 5? October 1951   *TLS, 2 pp; Estate of James Dickey*
                                                James Connally Air Force Base
                                                Waco, Texas

Dear One;

I feel most like writing a long rambling letter about a good many things that are perfectly irrelevant and utterly bound up in the way we live and don't live and want to live. Letters about "what has happened since the last time I wrote you," are likely to be pretty boring, despite the best I or anyone else can do about it. So.

The first thing is this incongruous letter I received about our (for everything is always and now "our" which I have even the smallest interest in, knowledge of, and feeling for) "lot" or our "property" by some misinformed nitwit in Houston. See what you make of it. It seems incapable of explanation.

The next thing is this letter from sweet Betty Winton. No trouble in interpreting and loving that.

I miss and want to see you, and I won't miss you again until you go away Sunday, after we have wonderfully been together for three days. I have us a very excellent room in the Jefferson Davis ($6.50). We are likely to love each other in a very extraordinary way, this week-end. I don't want us to we bound in by the ordinary ways of loving and affection that you, frequently, and I, sometimes, are hamstrung by. The standards of loving of Gloria and Jack and Betty Woodard and your mother and my mother and father and Val and all the other petty and sometimes admirable people we know are not by a damn sight enough or good enough for us. If we could shake the million meaningless jealousies and envies out of the movies and radio programs and the other sources that we sneer and laugh at and are influenced and wrongly live by, we would then begin to know what each other is for, and what we are together for, and why that togetherness is such a marvelous and un-ordinary thing. My god, the good thing about us is that we are never alone, as I have sometimes been utterly alone in the inmost bowels and veins of the most "luscious blonde," and that we are together a refuge against the tremendous cold hate and indifferency of all human beings for their companions. But what we have and should and I hope shall always have is not achieved or helped by an insistence on it. I want you, and I love you dearly and always, and I want to be near you; I want to come back to you from other people and find you the same, always, but I don't want to wear you around my neck and feel you grow intolerable with heaviness. All this by way of attempting to define the kind of relationship we should have, and the kind I want. Love, if anything, is a freedom of choice; slavery is death to it. I have been very lonely here, and have been reading, mostly. I have not been out with anyone but Captians and first Lts. Don't take from your mother or anyone we know or don't know the kind of deadening middle-class morality that insists that one "act in this way," or says that "if he loves you, he wouldn't, ..." or ". . . if you have any self-respect, you won't, etc" all of which are perfectly meaningless when parroted by dissatisfied and ignorant and wretched people. Begin to think for yourself. Get out of the ridiculously small personal [way] that the inconsequential people you have known all your life have tried to build for you. The earth is opening like a tremendous flower. It is not a thing you can put in a window-seat. Be in it, and live in it, and take from it what you most love and want to live by. Don't let the petty merchants who have looked at the reflection of the flower in isinglass and never got any closer to it than that tell you what the flower consists of. The centre is love. That is where you and I lie, forever. What the merchants say can not change that. Only you or I could, forever. I love you.

Jim

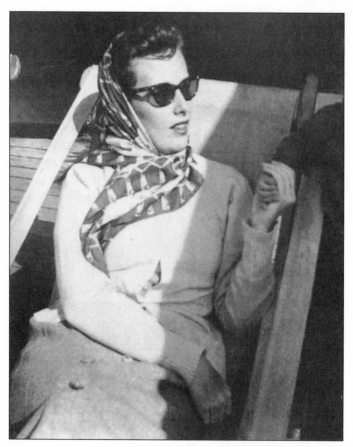

Maxine Syerson Dickey aboard the United States, *1955*

PART TWO

APPRENTICESHIP

August 1953–March 1956

Postmark obscured; 12 August? 1953   *TLS, 3 pp; Estate of James Dickey*
                                                166 West Wesley Rd. N.W.
                                                Atlanta, Ga.[1]

Wednesday

Dear Mac,

The book is finished, except for the closing three pages, which I will do tomorrow. I feel a kind of let-down, now that the thing is done, and want to get it off as soon as I can to Barker.[2] First, though, I'm going to write him and make sure <u>he's</u> looking for it, and reads it when it gets there. I'll write him tomorrow or Friday. We may have an answer by the time we get back to Atlanta, and then you and I'll send off the manuscript. Almost the end of the trail, huh?

Maibelle has a new car, and she's <u>so</u> thrilled with it! (!/?) and so on.

More good news: Mrs. Hamilton is due to show up in these parts this week-end. Pop thinks she'll move into the new house with Tom and Patsy and won't budge. They won't get in, though, before sometime in September.

Before I forget, I'd better tell you when I'll be there. The bus leaves Atlanta Monday (an express) and gets in to Nashville at 3:10/. You'all needn't meet me at the bus station, because it is only a couple of hundred feet to the hotel, which I can stagger very easily by myself. Then everything will be together again.

I have lived pretty much the life of a single man this summer, (with, of course, some notable exceptions), and I can report that I am very glad I'm not single. What I miss is the sense of continuity, of <u>belonging</u> somewhere, that I get from you and Chris. I sure will be glad to get back with my family.

I have had a very good summer, though. I have finished the book, and written ten or fifteen of the best poems I ever wrote, including the two or three best, and have relaxed hugely, got sunburned, for once in my life been swimming enough, and eaten and slept as well as anyone could want. In addition, we must have improved our financial standing greatly, and for these things we ought to be pretty thankful. Aside from being apart, the plan has worked out wonderfully for us, and now we can be together again with no loss anywhere, and really enjoy each other's company, more or less as new, or almost-new, people.

How is that boy? I dreamed about him last night. It's really very funny. I dreamed I was taking him to see <u>Trader Horn</u>,[3] the great jungle picture when I was a kid, and by God I look in the paper this morning and the picture is playing here in town. (So I'm going down to see it tonight.)

I am now finishing reading Isherwood's <u>Lions and Shadows</u>, Philip Toynbee's <u>The Barricades</u>, Wrey Gardiner's <u>The Dark Thorn</u>, D. S. Savage's <u>The Withered Branch</u>, and George Barker's <u>Janus</u>.[4] Quite a miscellany, eh? Isherwood's book is delightful: it is an autobiography, and Auden and Spender are in it, and very amusingly portrayed. I am very much looking forward to his forthcoming novel, which has one of the best titles I can remember: <u>The World in the Evening</u>. <u>The Barricades</u> is interesting and well-written, but really rather trivial: about a schoolmaster fired from his job, and his wrestlings with his social conscience over the Spanish War. Wrey Gardiner's book I have read before. It is also autobiographical, in the extreme "expressionistic" style of Henry Miller. It's a little pretentious, but the pictures of the 1943 fire-bombings of London are very good: in the midst of all this sits this poor bastard trying to write poetry, and edit a poetry magazine. His wife has left him, he spends most of his time drinking beer and worrying about his writing, and is in general frustrated as hell. But you do get a pretty fair notion of what the modern writer is like. Savage's book is critical essays: none of the modern figures are any good: Joyce is no good, Yeats is no good, Hemingway is no good, Virginia Woolf and Aldous Huxley are less than no good. The trouble with all these unsatisfactory people is that they have no consistent philosophy, or, as Savage puts it: "no center of opinion and belief from which to project their vision." In spite of this and similar absurdities, there are some good things in the book. <u>Janus</u>, by that fire-boy Barker, is completely formless, absurd, nit-witted, and really beautiful in places. God, what an imagination. You get the feeling that Barker, when he sits down to write, (Or maybe he's that way all the time: <u>I</u> can't tell) is drunker on words than the worst drunk is on whiskey: sometimes he sees visions, sometimes the words don't hold up. But even his misses are good, and it is very hard to find anything of his with nothing at all good in it.

Sorry to talk so much about books, but there's really nothing much else to talk about.

Oh, the tennis tournament. I got to the second round. If it weren't for the fact that the tournament was the only time I played during the summer, I could have beaten the boy that beat me, but I doubt that I could have gone any further than that, under any circumstances.

Love, darling, and I'll see you soon. Hold on.

Love again,
Jim

TO: DR. ROBERT M. HIGHFILL[5]

CC, 2 pp; Emory
Houston, Texas

January 5, 1954

Dear Dr. Highfill,

I have been advised by Dr. Cornell, through Mr. Jay Dennis, a student of mine here at the Rice Institute, to write to you concerning the possibility of an opening next year, or the year following, in your department. Dr. Cornell suggested that I inform you of my qualifications and interests.

I am thirty years old, and have a wife and a small son. I was educated in the public schools of Atlanta, and at Darlington Preparatory School in Rome, Georgia. I attended, very briefly, Clemson College, in Clemson, South Carolina, after which I volunteered for the United States Air Force. I served four years, as an officer, flying night fighters, in the states and in the Southwest Pacific and West Pacific combat areas, and was awarded three Air Medals and the Distinguished Flying Cross.[6] After I was released from service, I matriculated at Vanderbilt University in the summer of 1946, and graduated three years later Magna Cum Laude, Phi Beta Kappa, with the highest four-year average in my class. I was awarded a graduate scholarship, one of the two given each year, and with this took a Master of Arts degree in English Literature the following year. In the fall of 1950, I began my teaching career as an instructor in English at the Rice Institute, but was recalled five months later into the service, where I remained for seventeen months. Since my second release from service I have been teaching at the Rice Institute.

Because of my excessively long military service, together with family duties, I have been unable to pursue work toward the advanced degree which most schools seem to require. Aside from this, however, my commitments to my own writing tend to minimize the interest I might otherwise have in scholarly research. I have published widely in what I have been told are the more demanding literary periodicals, among them the Sewanee Review, the Quarterly Review of Literature, and Poetry: a magazine of verse, and have a novel, now about half completed, spoken for by Doubleday.[7] I feel that the knowledge of techniques, and the "live" relationship which a writer must necessarily have to his material, and by implication to the work of other writers, is of considerable value in teaching literature.

My desire to teach at Mercer is prompted to some extent by the fact that my father graduated there (he played on the first football team Mercer had, he tells me). We have always been "Georgia people," and I would like to resume my career as a Georgian before Texas naturalizes me.

Sincerely,

TO: ANDREW LYTLE[8]

TLS, 2 pp; Vanderbilt
Houston, Texas

March 23, 1954

Dear Mr. Lytle,

I have your kind letter, and am tempted to make all sorts of hopelessly grateful and inadequate responses, from which I feel I should restrain myself, for fear of seeming to dilute the clear core of extreme and sharp happiness your interest has set through me.[9] Just let me say that your comments are both the most intelligent and the most sympathetic criticism that my work has yet received, and that they have taken me a long way, in regard to poetry, toward that place I seem to have been trying to reach. Certainly you are right about the "chess-game" air of much poetry, all of which sounds alike. I don't think I will ever have written enough to make large, impressive statements about the role of the poet, or about poetry, but it seems to me that a poem has to try to rise toward form out of experience and conviction. The poet shouldn't look at something and say, "Why, I see how I can make a poem out of that," but rather, "This situation, or object, or person, has been lived with, lived in, thought about deeply and felt enough to justify what form I can give it."

In regard to my own work, I try to get a feeling of the subject's coming into being at the same time as the words, or of the words occurring at the same time that the situation takes place or the object is contemplated, a "live" feeling, one which will be both imaginative and true to the experience, and rhythms that will allow the words to say, through them, more than they would in other rhythmic arrangements. It is perfectly just that my only attempt at allusion, the one you point out, is unsuccessful, for I am not the Eliot or Pound type of writer. Robert Falcon Scott was an antarctic explorer who died, in 1912, on the return trip after having reached the South Pole. He left a journal, which records the wanderings of his party, and which tells of their coming again and again back to the same place. This has always been a powerful image to me, and the traditional association of the feeling of warmth and safety which men dying of cold are supposed to undergo, seemed to fit pretty well with the situation of the man in the poem, and there was the analogy between Scott's wanderings and his, and I thought that by reference to these things the central intent of the poem would be helped. Rereading it now, though, I can tell that this was a mistake. There is no certainty whatever that the reader has ever heard of Scott, and that part of the poem is lost if he hasn't.

As you say, I am probably writing novels too fast. I wrote and threw away one, which was only realized in one or two pages. After that, I had the feeling that I had better explore a bit, and not spend time "perfecting my mistakes." I think I have the makings of a fairly good book now, one which will justify all the attention I can give it. If you'd like, when I get it in some kind of shape, I'll send it on to you.

Thank you again for your letter. It is a kind of amulet against anything, from over-confidence to despair.

I should like very much to hear from you again.

Sincerely,

James Dickey

TO: MONROE K. SPEARS

CC, 1 p; Emory
Houston, Texas

1 April, 1954

Dear Monroe,

I wish that, by making the appropriate passes over this paper, I could cause to appear the most effective rhetoric summonable, the sincerest, the deepest- and widest-moving, to let you know how favored I consider myself, how proud and grateful I am.[10] I cannot, however; what small magics I have are stonily and bro-kenly my own, and pretty much left me, in awe, when I sat down to write this. Just let me say that I hope I shall not lose contact for one instant with the belief now falling away so deeply that I can't yet look fully into it, that during my year of tenure I am to be proxy to writers who haven't and never will have the chance that you and the Advisory Editors have given me, who can't know the sense of release I do now, who have no circumstances to lift them, even momentarily, wholly toward their work. If the poem I want to write can draw a little on this feeling, it will have its best chance.

Andrew Lytle has written to me, most encouragingly, and we are trying to arrange a meeting, probably to be in Atlanta this June.

I am very glad, indeed, to hear what Allen Tate has to say about my work, and feel rather as I imagine I would if D. H. Lawrence leaned down from his pedestal and said to me, very strictly, "Young man, you are not dead. You are one of the live ones." (But better! But better!)

I should like to write to Tate and to Dr. Fergusson and express my apprecia-tion to them, if you think it at all "good form," and could give me their addresses.

The method of payment of the stipend you suggest is entirely satisfactory to us. We shall go to Europe in August; I am negotiating with a bank in Atlanta to handle the money. We shall be passing through Sewanee in June (I am not yet sure just what date), and we want very much to see you and Betty. After about the fifth of June our address will be that of my parents: 166 W. Wesley Rd., N.W., Atlanta, Ga.

There is no worse time for a writer than when he discovers that he can't say, in an important situation, anything at all worthy of the occasion. But I want to thank you: you, personally, Monroe, for the whole perspective of time extending from the one freshman English period you taught my class (on <u>The Tempest</u>!) up to now, when I know a little more what I want in poetry (and not just exclusively what I don't): that is, the things I got: stole, transmuted, contaminated, and can't repay, from you, and for your great kindness and level-headed warmth.

Sincerely,
James L. Dickey

TO: ANDREW LYTLE

TLS, 2 pp; Vanderbilt

Mt. Vernon
Houston, Texas
April 3, 1954

Dear Mr. Lytle,

I am sorry I am a little late in answering your letter, which was one of the finest things I ever read, but since Tuesday my wife and I have been walking back and forth, passing each other with dazed looks, under the shadow of a great happiness trembling to be solid. We heard that day from Mr. Spears that we had been given the fellowship, which confuses and excites us progressively as the belief becomes more acceptably true to us. I think we both really <u>believe</u> it now, though it was very hard at the beginning. Allen Tate writes (Spears tells me): "Dickey seems to me to be one of the most original young poets I have read since the war." All this good fortune is a pretty terrible burden on the vanity of one who has not, until now, had much contact with people whose opinions on literary matters he respects. With luck I may, though, assimilate it in a valuable way toward a productive self-confidence, instead of, as now, feeling as though I have been given momentarily a marvellous kind of dream-strength with which to set the cloud-capp'd palaces and towers of the earth in a shrewder and more releasing light, but suspecting all the time that the strength will be rescinded, and I, waking, shall see that I have done or earned nothing. I am terribly happy, with only the fear that I shall not justify what seems to you and the other <u>Sewanee</u> editors to be worth encouraging.

Your remarks on "The Angel" poem are very much "on target": the two mazes do need to be dramatized; the poem needs something else: more strength, more clarity, at that point. But I have lost contact with the poem; it has set, like concrete or mud, and my efforts to tamper with it have not come out of a deep enough center: they miss in one way or another touching the other parts of the poem. So I shall have to wait a little,[11] always bearing your comments in mind. Someone (Elizabeth Bowen, I think) says that the essential problem of the novelist is "how to convey." This seems to me to be equally true of any art. There is always the problems of <u>means</u>, and of the employment of what one hopefully takes for possible means: the problem of selection.

I have always believed in the artist as much as in art, and in the freedom which to him is such a deep erecting of limits, through all of which he may once or twice burst, past all planning or preconception. It is not possible for anyone who has once had the feeling that a phrase, a set of two words in combination, even, is uniquely his, and is of possible value to other people, to be happy without trying to extend and complete what you call his subject, the one that is his rightly by birth, persuasion, and the slant of the blood as it runs. It is wonderful to know that you are working; I have not read anything new of yours since <u>A Name for Evil</u> (<u>The Long Night</u> has always seemed to me the best novel ever to come out of the South, Faulkner's not excluded). When I read "The Guide" in <u>A Southern Vanguard</u>,[12] I somehow got the idea that it might be part of a novel. Is that the case?

My own novel is pretty much complete in my mind, but there is the problem of performance, yet, of course. I am a very wasteful worker, and spend too much time trying to salvage or transmute what I have made unsalvagable, or what was no good in the first place. I don't want to work myopically on one phrase for hours without knowing at all what I want it to contribute to. To avoid doing this, I have blocked out the book fairly rapidly, and accomplished a kind of first draft, trying out a few alternative possibilities along the way. Because of this, I feel that the novel has a better chance to hold together; if the individual sections stand up, the whole thing ought to. But there is all that to do, yet.

We shall be leaving Texas right around the first of June, to avoid having to pay rent on the apartment. After that until we sail for England early in August, we'll be in Atlanta, where my parents live. I think, if you could manage it that way, that it would be easier for us to meet there, especially since Dallas is around 270 (instead of 30) miles from Houston. I shall hope very hard that you'll be able to stop off.

I'd like to try to stand up, here, and say without embarrassing either of us that I thank you from the strength of all the accumulated silences I have lived under and tried to articulate, for your part in giving me the opportunity that the fellowship allows: to pick up all this crippled shrillness of words and throw it with both hands toward the light, where the thing can truly be made.

Yours,
Jim Dickey

RTLS, 4 pp; Vanderbilt

April 17, 1954
Friday
Houston, Texas

Dear Mr. Lytle,

We are more or less shipwrecked here into preparations for leaving Houston; our rooms are beginning to have the look of a salvage operation like the hulk Crusoe kept taking things from, or the beach where he brought them. My son, at least, is unbothered by details; he sits on the old packing-barrels that my wife and I are trying to renovate, shooting at us with his cowboy pistol. There is the air of new things opening up for us, and the feeling that if we didn't hold the spirit in pretty severely, it would soar off forever on its own, and leave us just the details and exigencies.

Your letters have set me thinking along new lines, trying to define the artist for myself. I have never run much to generalization, as I expect you have already surmised; my mind is mostly images, and not propositions, and I can only hope that the images can have some of the value of propositions, but from their own angle. I heard once that Michelangelo, when asked how he cut stone, said that the form (of a woman, maybe) was already in the block of stone, and that all he had to do was liberate it. This is a real parable, I think, and not just of a certain theory of organic form, either. The artist (stone-cutter) is setting up something to stand against time, often quite literally (wind, rain, seasonal change, even animals). He is performing a kind of synthetic miracle, which is yet natural (the woman <u>is</u> originally in the stone). The result is both him and itself, and resides at that place where these two entities meet and enrich each other, and finally only the enrichment itself is left, for contemplation. If any human work ought to be able to stand up to time, and not only stand, either, but stand <u>significantly</u>, it is an endeavour of this order; and the later breed of artists is gratified and strengthened, always, to find that this is indeed the case. Of course, there are all those times when you stand off from what you have been doing, and the last of the dust floats down from the last mallet-stroke, and in front of you are only a few disrupted surfaces and places where the rock is starting to split. And when you dream of this, there is only broken glass there, and no image. But then, too, there are the times that are raised up, somehow, out of all the frustrations, when the form does start to show, and you know that it is <u>the</u> form, that it has arrived not out of adequacy but necessity, and everything starts to hold its breath with confidence. You know all this, though, having written <u>The Long Night</u>.

The library here does not have At the Moon's Inn. Someone told me that there is a story of yours, about the Spanish conquest of Peru, in an old issue of the Sewanee Review, but I've not been able to locate it.[13] I want to get all your work and sit down and read it from one end to the other, and write to you at length about it. Writers should be read entire; some of them have to be, but all of them should be. I am not widely read, but I remember what I read. Whatever taste I have seems to be native; there are not many critics I can profit from reading. I have come to dislike the kind of criticism that sets up in competition with the work. Tate's doesn't do this, but R. P. Blackmur's does, and most of the second generation of "New Critics" does also, insofar as I can judge. As you suggested, I got Percy Lubbock's book and went through it carefully.[14] It is very good indeed, but I don't think he's entirely right about War and Peace. To get back to the subject of your work, I reread "The Guide," and was struck by what is probably only a subjective parallel: Faulkner's "The Bear." I read "The Bear" again also, and the impression was not as strong. Nevertheless, part of what I felt remains. Your story is much less deliberately "mythical" than his: that is, you are not nearly so much after "universality" and "symbol" as he is. Faulkner so often seems deliberately to want to see his material so: the woods, fields, and so on, partake to such a heavy extent of this willed quality of his mind that they cease to be believable woods and fields in their own right, and become only examples. There is none of this in your story. I was much more "with" your boy than with Faulkner's, and his actions had a greater sharpness, particularity, and vigor simply as actions, for me, than did Faulkner's. And so there was real initiation, and real discovery.

From what I've read of your work, you seem to be much interested in the past, in history, and its meaning. In this you remind me of Robert Penn Warren.[15] Do you like his work? I very much do. "History is blind, but man is not," Warren writes in All the King's Men. Critics have not said much about this side of Warren, but it seems to me to be the central preoccupation of all his work to define and evaluate the past. That is, can we see in certain happenings behind us, on which we have a kind of perspective, symbolic patterns? If so, what are their value to us? How can this be assimilated to our lives?

We've kicked around my own book so much, and your advice has been so valuable, that I feel I should tell you a little about it. The problem is to show a middle-aged fellow, a mild, truculent, inconsequentially mistrustful man, for a few days at a Primary Training Base of the Air Force, during the early part of the last war. His son has been killed a couple of weeks earlier. Partly out of frustration and war-time boredom, partly on impulse, and partly out of curiosity he arrives in the small town near which the base is located, questions certain of the base personnel and townspeople who have known his son, and learns the dark side of himself, from what he thus finds out about his son.[16] I have tried out a good many possible routes through the story, and altered almost all of the original details, so you can see that when I talk of blue-prints and first drafts I don't in the slightest mean that I wouldn't abandon all such things if more fruitful paths made themselves felt. I simply wanted to wind up and sling the thread into the labyrinth as far as I could, and then follow it in, in hopes that it had gone around some of the right corners. I don't want to limit the material, but to try to open it up, to find a way into it. I would question the Minotaur himself, if I thought he could tell me anything. And stay in there with him, too.

Like you, I believe that a book should be an exploration, should grow out of what goes before; I don't believe in trying to write it before it is written, so to speak, which is obviously impossible. I believe that any successful work of art is like a result of evolution: a breaking through at an advantageous place, which means that something must, at some stage, have eliminated the eventual blind alley, or the wrong specialization. The problem is one of exploration, choice, and, to some extent at least, foresight based on what you already have.

I don't want to go on and on. But when you talk of responding to the quality of my mind and sensibility, I think I should tell you that your letters are the only <u>whole</u> wings I know. It is a very good thing for me that you didn't tell the gangster (in Fort Worth, incidentally) you were a writer, and even better you didn't tell the plain-clothesmen in St. Louis.[17] The latter, at any rate, would most certainly have shot you, out of that positive fury of misunderstanding which is probably the strongest emotional feature of our world. And I'd have lost the only Conscience I ever enjoyed listening to (and for!), much less profited by.

Yours,

Jim Dickey

TO: ANDREW LYTLE

TLS, 3 pp; Vanderbilt

April 26, 1954
Houston, Texas

Dear Andrew,

I am glad to know something of how your book is to shape up, and how your mind is fixed in the material. You speak of risks, and certainly the chance of failure increases (in some cases almost geometrically, rather than arithmetically) as you try more difficult and important things. With the scope of your subject, you must feel at times as if you are hunting the constellated animals of the zodiac, and, knowing that Orion himself cannot move, you must draw back a little, out of dismay, and the burden of looking such game in the eye. But you have so much:

so much skill, so much steadiness of talent. You have your knowledge of and feeling for history, of social process and change, and a principal of choice among the images and symbols of these, and you have both a deep base in the material and an eye outside it. If anyone does, I know the discouragement you speak of, when you feel the weight of all the published trash baffling the life in your own work, and the fear that this weight will somehow modify your work, by proximity, to something near its own undiscriminating image. But go back and read the part of "The Guide" where the boy and Goosetree enter the lake. The quality of good work is that it burns away the other as would acetylene; the artist's control of that wild sucking fire too fierce even to look at, narrows it and directs it, and makes out of all that heat and power a thing that will cut, and part of the cutting done is moral, eliminating falsity, irrelevance, the synthetic and the commercial, from the structure which the sensibility of an age is erecting, rod by rod, from its various angles and depths. The passage from your story has everything I have tried to mean by these metaphors, and a great deal more (I single the passage out for its quality of near-absolute <u>verbal</u> rendering), and the thing is that you made it, and nobody can unmake it, or could have made it to be as good, in another way. Now, you have the same blood, running in the same stream-beds among the same images, the same set to your eye, as you had when you wrote that, only the stream is deeper now, and a little longer, and so reflects better and carries farther. You have all the assimilative and modifying qualities that you had then, and in addition more knowledge of techniques, skills (of what Ford Madox Ford called "the game, as distinct from the players of the game"), and so you have every chance of producing even better work (though even holding that level seems to me to constitute an advance). You say, though, and I know you say this because I do, and so does everyone who writes: what if I fail? We all want to be assured that this won't happen, but whatever triumphs any of us ever attains comes from having given failure a chance at us; there are no meaningful victories when there has been no chance of defeat. As for me, I have my own thing to try to say, but it has nothing like the compass of yours, and never will have. I know no more about society's rituals (as seen as symptomatic, from an analytical perspective) than I do about astro-physics, much less how to go about separating out the valid and invalid things, symbolically, which appear through them. You are trying to create a realm wherein these manifestations will be caught and fixed in actions that will <u>determine</u>, in a sense, the past you are dealing with, much as we see Tolstoy's Russia as just that: <u>his</u> Russia; the Moscow retreat has hardly any being now, outside <u>War and Peace</u>. (By the way, I read your brilliant article,[18] and was delighted to see my own halting notions given so much basis and authority.)

The problem of unification of any work I do has always been the chief one. I am weak in what Coleridge called the "architechtonic" faculty; I fear that in his book I would be a poet of the fancy rather than of the imagination, and yet perhaps not wholly, either. But it is easy to impose form on words; that is, <u>some</u> form. What is hard is to arrive at that coincidence of individuality and necessity: to make the form absolutely a part of an utterance which is uniquely yours. I am working on some new stuff I want to show you. I can't of course tell when it'll be finished, but it looks good in the first stages, at any rate.

I don't feel myself capable of saying anything about the first part of your last letter, except that I feel like a man who has been sitting for some time, numbly, for no particular reason, in a quiet, open, cold place, with it coming on to snow, and looks up to see that someone has put a table in front of him, and a jug of milk on that, and bread, and then put a roof over his head, and has now begun to tell him in perfect and grave decorum what he has never had the courage to hope or believe about his own life, and still he can't say a thing to express himself, his grat-itude and awe, to this other, yet he feels the spirit rise up in him as if it had come unthawed, and powerful as a curve of structural concrete, and he wants to pull the whole thing out of his breast like a tangle of knitting thread and hand it to the man across from him.

It is hard to imagine what my life would now be like, had you not written.

Yours,
Jim Dickey

TO: ANDREW LYTLE

TLS, 3 pp; Vanderbilt

May 7, 1954
Houston, Texas
Thursday

Dear Andrew,

There is an intensity and drive in your letters that I have never encountered anywhere. You seem to lift them up out of yourself as God knows what force in the water raised up a white arm to grasp Excalibur when Bedivere flung it in. There is no blade I can throw that is worth that miracle; I feel very much like a young man in awkward armor looking out over a dark lake, commanding spirits he never knew of.

For a while I wondered why it is that I keep thinking of art as an edged instru-ment, a blade; I can look back through the few things I have written and see that this wasn't the case before we began writing to each other. And then when I got your last letter the whole thing came to me as I read. With your letters there is always the sensation of some hampered vital organ in me, just under my breast-bone, cut suddenly and softly and quite without hesitation free; I must have got my ideas on art filled up with the wonderful release of free breathing, alive beyond any state of being I have ever been granted.

You ask about my poems, and are so kind to them that they take from you some of what I couldn't have given them, and should have. I intended "The Anniversary"[19] as a kind of lament, and tried to give it the curious drive and exultation that comes to me when I associate longing and music (the guitar). The poem contrasts (in short lines, going fast) the same setting at two different times: on this day of the year five years ago, when the lovers had "lace(d) the river / An inch from sight," that is, when the river was running under their preoccupation with each other, and the time now, when the river holds only the sound of the guitar and the ear sliding out over its surface, now hearing nothing but the natural flow of the water under the changed music.

In the Angel poem[20] the man's wife has died. She is (has been, and is) his soul; she stands also for what you point out, which I felt I couldn't legitimately hope anyone would see. The poem tries to say something about the connection between the worlds of the living and the dead. The stone bust is an image out of the man's childhood which the soul, the angel, of the wife enters into, and in a sense helps him to create, to give him the kind of conventional mystery his mind and grief demand of the relationship. In a sense she is constrained, too, in being limited to that <u>kind</u> of image, and by the way he clings to it. She is born back daily into the head, and in the beginning of the second part of the poem she is presented as going through this change, waking from the darkness into the stone. The death of the wife is re-experienced by her each day as the light comes and the husband wakes, and is seen, according to her renewed relationship to her husband, as a kind of wedding, and a new childhood. The maze of the garden is both a place the man cannot leave, and one he takes comfort in not being able to leave, hence his reference to Scott, whom he envisions as having been in the same state. The maze is the changing and deepening mystery of that relationship which the living cannot understand, and the dead, despite their superior powers, cannot help. All this I intended, as I say. The quality of the performance I feel that I can't really judge, beyond saying that I feel the enveloping rhythm of the last part is nearly that which the poem needs.

There is no warrant for regret about your age. You have a hungriness of energy that makes me know that the spirit's fuel is everywhere. In addition, you have the staying power to feel the whole turning-force of the wheel determining itself between your hands, whereas I have to try to guess from occasional thrown-off sparks, the spinning shape.

It is very late, so I had better end this. Whatever you want to do about getting us together this summer, I want also to do.

Yours,
Jim Dickey

TO: MAXINE DICKEY[21]

Postmarked 17 June 1954   *TLS, 3 pp; Emory*
                                             166 W. Wesley Rd., N.W.
                                             Atlanta, Georgia

Tuesday

Dearest Mac,

Of course the big news here is Lytle's visit, from which I am slowly recovering in body, but only really beginning to assimilate in spirit. Of him I can say only what Lord Bolingbroke said of Bacon, "He is so great a man that I do not recollect whether he has any faults or not." He is so generous, so perceptive, so sympathetic, and so kind that I was left time and again absolutely unable to say what I wish I had been able to say, with gratitude, in immense assurance and eloquence. In appearance he is smallish and slim, graceful, with the face of a very kind duellist, and a kind of listening expression. He is a little fox-like-looking, and with the color to further this impression. He is always relaxed and friendly, and always alert and weighing things, so that you can talk in any manner and yet be understood by him. I showed him Chris' picture and yours, and, in connection with the (possible) Florida job, I remember his saying, "Then we can get the families together," which was just what I wanted, too, of course.

As to what he said about my work, there is just no way to begin to tell you what the effect of these things had on me. Once I quoted some lines from Shakespeare, and he leaned forward and tapped me on the knee and said, gravely, "But don't you see how much better your lines (that we had also been talking about) are? Can't you feel that?" The thing that gratified me so much about all the talk about my work was that the poems seem to have <u>meant</u> something to him, in his life as a man. And there is no need for me to tell you that is the best kind of compliment I could ever be given. There is more of this I could tell you about, but I'll save the rest to tell you when I see you. Suffice it to say that I "flattened" the opponents for the fellowship with what Lytle said was "ridiculous ease," and he insisted on talking about a renewal of the fellowship, though we haven't even begun this one yet.

And, My God, the people he knows, and has known! James Agee[22] ("a great big fellow, curly-headed, sort of lost-looking") and Phelps Putnam[23] ("he looked sort of like you. He'd have liked you"). He talked on and on, and then I talked, and we'd go from subject to subject, just as we wished, one thing leading to another. At one point he said, "I wish we could dig in here for a week, and really get started on something we could finish." We talked on until about three, and then fell into bed and got up again just as it was getting light and went to talking again. We went down and got some eggs and then came up and he broke out his manuscript. I sat and read it the rest of the morning, with him lying on the bed dropping off to sleep and waking again when I made some comment or other, and then being very interested and taking up the dialogue again, when we'd kick a point in the book around for a while, then I'd get back to reading again and he'd doze off. I finished about an hour before his plane left, and we got in the car and drove to the airport and had lunch (I bought him a steak, the only money he'd let me spend) and then they called his plane. We stood there a moment and said a few things to each other, quietly, and then he reached out and took my hand and put his other arm around my neck, the way fathers sometimes do with grown sons. Both of us were very strongly moved. Then I turned around and walked off, and went back home and slept for sixteen hours.

He wrote Pop a very nice note from Dallas, which I am keeping here for you to see.

As I said, I can't begin to tell you what his visit meant to me. There's a lot more I could say, but I think I can remember most of it until I see you, which is better, I think.

The Sewanee money (1,750 dollars) is sunk like a (gold!) plummet in the timid heart of the First National Bank (Buckhead), and I have the deposit slip (is that what they are called?) here in a safe place waiting for the financial genius of the family to take over. I am sending you Spears' note (I wrote him, and acknowledged receipt, so don't worry about that).

We also heard from David, and his letter is enclosed, if you can decipher that weird calligraphy (handwriting). I think I can catch the drift of one or two of the sentences, but the meaning I get is only an intuition at best.

I have been fairly lazy, but am enjoying myself, and rendering what service I can to the family crises (plural, darling, of crisis). The night of the Charles fight[24] I have to go over to Tom's and meet Tom Roper after, lo! these many years, in whom I have about as much interest as I have in Haile Sellassie (sp.)

Still no word from the travel bureau (sp).

I thought you might be delighted to hear that I haven't yet taken to wearing my new bathing suit, and consequently haven't succeeded in "Whowing" (where did you get this word?) any of the local debs. I just mention this to set your mind at ease.

I sure do miss you and the little fellow, and "old Mokey, all covered up with snow." I love you more than you, I, or anyone will ever be able to say, or even know, but only feel.

Take care of yourself. I got your card this morning, and thanks.

All the kinds of love,

Jim

TO: ANDREW LYTLE

TLS, 3 pp; Vanderbilt

166 W. Wesley Rd N.W.
Atlanta, Georgia
Sunday
June 20, 1954

Dear Andrew,

Your letter just came, and the week of thinking about you fell into place. I have calmed, now, about your image talking and drinking with people I do not know, but vivid, bright, and whole. The particular things I remember of you are so many, and each is so much fused with the others that it is hard for me to isolate even momentarily one from the others to cite, but your remarks on the Civil War (with which I associate somehow the quotation from Joinville you brought out at one point: "Sire, he is in Paradise"), the things you said about form, symbol, and the artist, and the session with your book are simply part of me forever.

I want to write something for you, but the writing will likely stretch out over a period of years, because I want the lines to test themselves against water, air, earth, and fire before I turn them loose against time: that is, I want anything I write for you to be as near as I can get it to enduring.

There is so much I want to say about your book that I hardly know where to begin. The scene at the pool where Beverly appears is irreducible; there has not been such power of imagination on paper since Portrait of the Artist. There is nothing in Faulkner, Warren or any of the other living ones than can hold more than a weak unsteady candle to it. And there are other passages almost as good: the "Nymph" scene, the first appearance of Eddie's cattle, Julia in her new dress, the fight between Duncan and Pete Legrand, the fatigue of Lucius on the water-witching expedition, and Jack's soliloquies: all these are going to stand up and hold on to time. When I got home (before I fell into bed and slept for sixteen hours like a man who has swallowed the thread to the labyrinth) I wrote down the story in as much detail as I could remember, so that I could add each episode as it develops. I feel a tremendous and valuable excitement over the progress of the book which must be akin to that of someone watching the construction of one of the Roman aqueducts: not the Pyramids: something not still in its bulk but moving, something with a structure that you can feel at the edge of your mouth (though perhaps this is too private a test), not a Miltonic edifice. I feel that the only way I can justify the trust you have placed in me in showing me the book is to tell you as strictly and as deeply as I can what I think of it, in detail and as a whole. If there is any way possible I'd like to keep up with the book as you write it, so that I can do this.

You sound tired, Andrew, and I know you must be. You are the greatest man I have ever known, and the only great one. But you give so much of yourself to others that I am worried for you. If I ever learned anything of value from athletics it is the absolute necessity of pacing yourself (this lack undid Ezzard Charles the other night, if you noticed), and of leaving yourself a reserve to draw on. As for myself, the fact that we were once together for a few hours would itself suffice to justify my life, but for the fact that I may do something to bear out the trust and confidence you have in me. This possibility takes me up like the hero his enchanted weapon, and I have begun to see in what ways I am held, and on what things the best strokes must fall.

There is nothing good that I have not learned from you, but most strongly these: the belief that the symbol must in some sense be lived to be valid (as opposed to those ready-made and applicable in any situation: applied from the outside), the dedication of the artist and the sacramental quality of his imagination. And courage, determination, and imaginative joy.

My father thanks you for the note. He says it is about things which are important in a way he had never thought about.

If you'd like, I'll write you a letter a week, whether you answer or not. How would that be?

Yours,

Jim

TO: MAXINE DICKEY

Postmarked 24 June 1954   *TLS, 3 pp; Emory*
                                                      166 W. Wesley Rd., N.W.
                                                      Atlanta, Georgia

Wednesday

Dearest,

I have not been very good about writing, but I thought it better to write longer letters, in which I would have more to say, than write oftener, and emptier.

Very little has been happening here. A couple of nights ago I went with Tom and Patsy to a cocktail party given by the Roumanian woman for her husband, the Colonel, whose birthday it was. Like a fool, I drank too much, but I did meet a nice family from Vienna, who, it turns out, live across the street from us here. I went over and talked to them for a few minutes last night, and they are certainly charming, very well read, and very much interested in our European endeavor. There are the old man, a doctor, his old-world-looking wife, and a daughter, about thirty (not very attractive), and a dachshund, who is rather attractive. There was some good conversation, and I ended by saying I would bring you and Chris by as soon as I brought you-all home.

I have tried to go swimming as often as I could get the car, which, as it turns out, has not been so often, after all. When it is too far (for the gas supply) to go to Venetian, I calmly drop in at the Driving Club.[25] No one says anything, and I have become quite friendly with all the functionaries there, including the manager (I forget his name) who treats me like a brother. I realize, of course, that this can't last, but certainly now it is very pleasant. Yesterday I played all afternoon with some children of a fellow named [ ],[26] whom I hated when I knew him in high school. He is married to a girl I went with at the same time as he did. She looks dreadful now, but the kids at any rate were very nice, and we exhausted each other with much pleasure.

Tom's business is picking up to some extent, I think. He is working hard, but seems reasonably happy with the results he's getting. Pat Huber (the partner) has now put his <u>brother</u> into the business, but even this seems not to be so bad, for it takes some of the work off Tom.

I have been reading a lot. The last thing I've finished is Forster's <u>The Longest Journey</u>,[27] which I had read years back and not liked much. Now I think it is wonderful. It is one of the best novels about wilfull misunderstanding I believe I know, and pretty well done, too. I read for hours, in a kind of half-drowse, but understanding without much effort what is going on the page. I lose track of time completely, and feel at the end, when I have to go eat, say, that I could go on for days without stopping. I read Forster's book in two sittings, which is contrary to my usual way of reading: just sitting down whenever I have time and picking up whatever I have started at some time earlier. I feel more and more that the books I have are a constant and immense pleasure: there is so <u>much</u> there: there are so many good minds, so much creation.

I want to write a little, probably before you come home. I have one or two ideas I want to try to work out, into poems.

It is wonderful to me, but a little sad, too, that Andrew Lytle seems so much to depend on me. I know what there is in himself that is probably producing this condition, and I want to do all I can to help him do and be what he wants to. I think I read you his last letter (Air Mail Special Delivery). I wrote to him promptly and told him that I would write to him regularly once a week whether he answered or not. I think that will relieve his mind a little, or at least I hope it does. He is easily the finest man I have ever known, but not at all a "professional" fine man: a speaker to Kiwanis Clubs, a Scout Master, or any of that. He is awareness, imagination, and sympathy themselves, and daily I feel myself growing more lucky to know him as I do.

I had a brief card from Mother, which I am enclosing, for it is driving me crazy (the picture is, that is).

I wonder how you are, and how Chris is, for without you and him I would not want to wonder about anything again.

I bought a bathing suit I like better than any that I have ever had, though someone said it makes me look like Rocky (Marciano). It is a ($2.25) pair of basketball trunks with elastic around the top. Maroon, with a gold stripe down the legs, and around the hem. Very comfortable, and I can swim and dive like mad (which is the usual way I seem to people to be swimming and diving). If my money holds out, which it seems very well to be doing, I'll get a couple more pair (different colors, naturally) since they are so cheap. Silky! Or at any rate rayon.

I love you very much, Suggie. Have you lost any weight? How much have you been able to get done on the sweater? How is the lightning-bug-catcher? Tell him that there are plenty of them here now, and when he gets here we'll catch a whole bunch of them and put them in a bottle. And won't that be fun?

I am holding all mail. We have a fair stack, including this one attempting to get the June rent for the Mt. Vernon apartment out of us. I send it on to let you deal with it with your customary vigor and (controlled!) outrage.

Be good, honey. I think I'll come after you about next Wednesday, if that suits you.

All loving,
Jim

TO: ANDREW LYTLE

TLS, 4 pp; Vanderbilt

21 Charles St
Berkeley Square
London W.1 England
Thursday
Aug 26, 1954

Dear Andrew,

There is no need for me to tell you how glad I was to get your letter. I delayed writing this one until I heard from you, not knowing whether you had gone back to Florida; I have a provincial distrust of mail-services, and won't risk the chance of a mixup due to forwarding, if I can help it.

I am quite recovered from my illness, though I was weak for a few days, and have been walking around a lot with my little boy while my wife does the shops (mostly visually). We are in London now, in Kensington, and have a direct shot on the bus in to Piccadilly Circus, in about ten minutes. This is such a vast place, and there is such a curious mixture of reserve and brashness (the latter not in the people, but in their works: American-type advertisements, TV quiz programs, nightclubs, and so on) that it is a bit hard to get a stable perspective on it. But it is marvellous to be here, where they have had no summer at all, but only a daily rain, and to fumble out the wrong change in pence, do all the wrong things, in fact, and be written off as Americans, and smiled at with a sort of wistful indulgence that, given a chance, turns into very real warmth. One thing I have noticed here, is that the customs, the ceremonies seem to be losing their efficacy, their vital power of suggesting a mystical and perhaps holy relationship between the body of the sovereign, the land, and the people. There is a terrible air of "going through the motions"; the people seem even a little rootless, which is the last thing you would ever be likely to say of the English; they seem to want comfort and convenience more than anything else. They don't realize what they're giving up, but maybe it is too late in the day for these things and the feelings appropriate to them to be preserved. I have come to believe that the old England is finished, or soon will be, but the last of its glory is magnificent, especially in the autumn, as it is beginning to be, here.

I passed a couple of afternoons with Stephen Spender, who edits a magazine called <u>Encounter</u>; Allen Tate suggested that I look him up. He is a very nice fellow, in a sort of misty, homosexual way (though I may well be mistaken about this inference). He asked me to bring around some of my poems, and I showed him the Maze and one or two others. I don't know whether or not he wants to publish them, he is so vague about everything, but at any rate he kept them in his office for (possible) action of some kind or another. You remember I told you that I would not bring out the Maze if you wish me not to, and I won't, for it is your poem, I believe now, as much as mine. I think it is a good poem, and if Spender wants to use it, I would like to see it published, if you would. But the final decision is yours.[28]

I can sense your excitement as you approach the place where you must battle it out with the Wake scene. The writing of the Wake will require, as the ore from which you refine the ultimate form of the scene, a release of your mind among the scene's possibilities: that is, when you begin you must not try yet to visualize or conceptualize the action as you would geometry (though I know you would not really do this any more than I would), but you must hold in one part of your mind the strands of the preceding and following action, so that there will be a kind of required direction, and then, between these two points, somehow slip the leash and let your imagination go in among these possibilities freely and watchfully, and <u>quickly</u>, like a dog into the brush. There will be a point where you will have to withdraw again and consider what you have done, with the colder part of your mind; there may be a good many misses, but for a scene like the wake should be, I believe this is the only way the right connection can be made.

You will have seen the Tates[29] by now. I hope they have helped you; I did not get to know her at all well, but he is so immensely intelligent, and withal human, that you could have no better critic. If, by any chance, though, the visit has thrown you off your stride temporarily, there is nothing to worry about. Your daimon sits in your own court, not Tate's, or Caroline's, or mine even. What that creature will say, if you listen to him long enough and keep asking him questions, will be right.

I was never able to ascertain what the Tates thought of me, and have wondered about it a good deal, though to no end. We talked mostly about writing and writers, and I think I was a pretty fair listener. Beyond that I can't say.

I hear sad things about James Agee, and they depress me very much. Arthur Mizener[30] tells me that he's had a heart attack, Tate that he's become an alcoholic, and Spender that "he's in bad shape," whatever that may mean. I wonder if there's anything we could do for Agee: write to him, or something. You never can tell; maybe we could help him in some way.

My own work is going well, but slowly, as always. About mid-winter I should have twenty or thirty poems to show you. There is a good war poem called "The Lemon Tree," and another about old people, both poems welling slowly up out of silence. And there is another, more exciting one, called "The Farm,"[31] dedicated to you, about your land inundated by TVA, where

> its noon work is to look
> For the sun wearing off
> Into new eyesight through a held dancing
> Wherethrough the trees are hanging skyward by their roots,
> Shining, vesting their candles with breath . . .

I have hold of only a corner of this one, but it is developing well.

There will be no powers to intrude and destroy what is between us, Andrew, for our courses have run far and deep enough together to be proof against anything.

A handful of sharp veins around the pen that puts down the Wake! We shall see that scene put beside "The Dead" and "The Open Boat"[32] (and beyond!), you and I.

Yours,
Jim Dickey

TO: ANDREW LYTLE

TLS, 2 pp; Vanderbilt

25 Sept. 1954
Cap d'Antibes

Dear Andrew,

Since I last wrote you, Europe has swallowed us like peas, and we are only just getting our bearings. Our money was running out in England, so we went to Paris to see a friend of ours there. There I got sick again, someone cut the top of our car open with a knife, we spent more money, and naturally were very depressed. When our friend left Paris, we stayed for a few days, and then started south, with no very clear idea of where we were going, except that prices were supposed to be less high in the provinces than in Paris. For a week we shuttled about, becoming more confused and less resilient, until we struck this vacation-coast down here, just as the tourists were leaving it. In one or two days the place had quieted so much that we began to look on it as a possible headquarters. Since then we have been searching for a place to live. Yesterday we found just what we need: a big house with a tremendous yard full of red flowers, cactus, lizards, and little birds, with a great yawning silence surrounding it, which I hope to fill with poems. We move in on October 1st; until that time we are staying in an apartment near the villa. Due to the off-season, the rent on the villa is about one-third that during the season, and so we have taken it until June. It would be wonderful if by some alchemical transformation in school administration, you and Edna and the children could be given time to come over, for we have all the room in the world, a little playground for children, and no neighbors or other disturbances at all.

Before I forget: Spender sent the poems back, with some faint talk about "skill" and "daring", though it was pretty clear they were not his dish. I sent them down to Marguerite Caetani at <u>Botteghe Oscure</u> in Rome, whom Tate had suggested. She edits a tremendous (physically) review in three languages, and is evidently receptive to new writers, from what I hear.[33]

Now that we have prospects of being settled, I can look back on the trip with some pretense of evaluation. Paris is a great city for writers; that is, for the kind of writers who need other writers around, who need the "literary life," who need to discuss and drink together, and the rest of it. I had a sample of that, but my writing felt too lonely there; I knew none of the latest writers, and had a good deal of trouble understanding what was going on. What money I had to myself, though, I spent on books. There are literally thousands of book-shops in Paris, as you know, and most of them carry good stuff. I've read nothing but French since we've been here, and am gradually getting to understand the written language, though as yet I can't speak it very well. Paris in some ways is as great a city as I have always heard it was, but I missed something there: perhaps it is the lack of personal discipline everywhere evident. I am not used to so much personal freedom: in dress, in language, in taste, sex, and so on. But I have an idea the city will grow in my mind, and then I will know and like it better.

Provence is the most beautiful place I have ever seen. Everything there: the olive-trees, the vineyards, the red and white mountains, is in a gentle and sustained state of crumbling, so that everything you see is soft-edged and half-luminous, and yet there is strictness of form: the grids of the vineyards laid subtly up the uneven hills, the poplars lining the roads, the Rhone leaning furiously on its banks, straight for miles.

The French writers have done me much good. The better I learn the language, the more sympathetic I feel toward the work of many of them. I begin to see, I think, what the imagination is capable of, at its full stretch. I see also that my own work has got to discover more surely its own laws and disciplines. I want to study a good deal here. And write. And write. I want to do some experiments in syntax and diction, toward developing the sense of immediacy in poetry, the controlled spontaneity that I am convinced my writing should have: a form like that of fountain water, wherein the shape is secured by the substance (poem) falling and arcing freely, and is maintained thereby. I am tremendously excited about having so much time to work, and I feel that the proof shall be delivered at the end of the year, so that you and the other editors may feel that you have not wasted the Sewanee's money.

By the way, there's a poem of mine in the current (Autumn) Sewanee.[34] At least there should be one, for I read proof, though I haven't yet seen it.

I have an idea that I will always be a searcher in these things, for nothing I do satisfies me. But I know now, though dimly, what I want from poetry: emotional depth: spontaneous, immediate: that the poem should strike the reader down through the more obvious levels of his being into the hidden and essential ones, and stay there, giving up its meanings as the reader's life does, not all at once. I want a poetry both human and imaginative: "forcer le plus réel à exister." But there is all that to do yet, of course.

We are all well. I promise to write oftener and oftener, swamping you with details of the projects, and with the projects themselves, as they develop. And may I be forgiven for this delay.

Write soon, and send me what you have done on the Wake, for I have been thinking much of it. My address now is % American Express, Cannes, France.

Yours,

Jim Dickey

TO: ANDREW LYTLE

TLS, 3 pp; Vanderbilt

14 Nov. 1954

Dear Andrew,

I got your letter the afternoon of the day I sent the note (and poem) to you. I was very glad to hear from you, needless to say. I knew that you would write, but I was afraid something might have happened to you: that you might be sick, or that your wife or one of the children might be.

It is good to know that you are all right, and are getting ready to tackle your book again. I wouldn't worry about the lay-off. There's more chance, I should think, that the book has been helped by it than otherwise: that the "deep well of unconscious cerebration," as Henry James called it,[35] has brought out the bones of the essential.

You ask about our quarters, and the weather. We have a huge house on the only hill of size on the <u>cap</u>. We are about three-quarters of the way up the hill, on the top of which is the <u>cap</u> lighthouse. It is very quiet here. Once or twice a week I take my little boy and we make our way up steeply behind the house, on a winding track (very roundabout because of the almost-sheerness of the hill-face), the Mediterranean broadening below us as we climb. At the top, beside the lighthouse, is a sailors' chapel. Sometimes we go in, but usually we stand beside the lighthouse in the wind that is always blowing there, and look down at the whole coast from Cannes to Menton, a huge half-opened wing preparing some hesitant and marvelling flight toward something never to be disclosed, blue with age and hope and inaction. There is nothing so calm, nothing so full of immediate and contemplative beauty.

The house itself, as I said, is big, and consequently rather hard to heat. Now that the weather is colder the sun does not shine every day. There are high thick clouds, overcasts, and often a fine thin rain. I tend the furnace a good deal, and have made some progress in technique (pine-cones are very good to start the fire with). We have coal and wood, and I use them in about equal proportions, and it keeps us warm.

You have only to turn inland to be among mountains, real ones, as wild as any. We go among them as much as we can, and they are fascinating. At one place there is what is left of a slender bridge that at one time spanned one of the gorges. The Germans demolished it before they left. All there is, now, of it, is a tall upright spine of masonry, very fragile, having that wistful and arrogant look of broken objects of use. And it is tall: it comes out of the bottom of a gorge you literally can't see all the way into, and ends at you level in the air, its two halves, where the road went, branching bewilderedly and serenely into the air, and you are left with it.

I have been working slowly, and studying, trying to clarify my intentions. The Spender episode hit, or left, a dead spot in me that is hard to make over. I have had rejections before, plenty of them, but somehow the memory of that professional shrinking violet condescending to me, talking about "compression" and "why don't you read Auden" wrung me about as disagreeably as anything can. I couldn't believe he read the poems well. I thought, then, in a rush, that if this was "literature," if this was the sort your work has to go through to reach publication, then he and the ones like him can have it. By the way, he told me that one of the poems (the first one) that appears next to mine in the <u>Sewanee</u> is the best one he has ever written.[36] And I sit down and look at it and am dazed. Can such things be? But the proof is there in print. There is his "best," and a fairly good one of mine, and I think that the comparison is beyond any doubt in my favor. And I feel somewhat better. Of course there should not be comparisons like this, but only the poet and his poem. But then I was raised, almost from the time I could stand, in the fiercest strain of competition: on basketball courts, in boxing rings, on fields, on tracks. Times like this bring all that back. But Spender is receding in my mind, and I hope will eventually be out of sight. To hell with him.

The more I read of the European writers, the prouder I am to be of the same calling. Since the war, which I entered at seventeen, I have never, until now, profoundly valued life.[37] Then, it seemed to me that I could see quite clearly that most of the things I had been told about human life were false: were constructions, rationalizations only, and would not stand up under any kind of forceful reality. But then I had not taken cognizance of the artist's way, the search for the hidden anatomy. Proust found a part of it, and James did, and you, certainly (and will, more, certainly, and perhaps more than any of these) and the Spaniard Lorca, and Valery. The better you understand life, the more you feel <u>clearly</u>, the more you begin to see the value of it (but perhaps it takes it value from this seeing and feeling more, and in a more pronounced order, even of spontaneity).

You ask about the people here. For a time we knew no one, but now we have a good many friends. We met Pablo Picasso a couple of times. He lives in the little mountain town of Vallauris, and makes pottery there. He is a small man, rather peasant-like, gentle and grave, with many children and relatives, most of the former, I am told, illegitimate. Then there is a retired admiral of the British navy who lives just down the street from us, also with a large family. I play tennis with his wife and daughter. Sometimes he and I sit out in his garden (everyone here gardens) and talk about naval strategy. He analyzes famous engagements and demonstrates at length what different admirals did in different situations, Nelson included. There is another man I know in Nice, an Englishman named Peter Bent, who has lived in France all his life and speaks with a French accent. Though he is married, the French government won't let him work, being an alien. He and his wife live with his father in a poor section of Nice. Bent is a strange, pale, weakly man who looks as if he is eaten up (but is not apparently, his only passion being book-binding) by some terrible ambition. A man named Nikos Katzanzakis, a Greek,[38] and twice runner-up for the Nobel Prize in literature, lives here. He is a poet and novelist (I have never read anything by him, though I think he has been published in America). Some people I know here insist that I meet him, and he seems to have been alerted for that purpose also, so we may go by his place some day. My friends tell me that he is receptive to company, and likes to talk poetry.

Before I forget, you mention in your letters someone named Berryman. I once appeared in a magazine next to someone named John Berryman. Is that the same one? Is he a good friend of yours?

Here is another poem I've just finished.[39] It rounds out a kind of design I began with the Maze: to write about the effects of death on people in different familial relationships: in the <u>Maze</u> an old man and his wife, in <u>Father and Sons</u>,[40] that, and in this one a boy and his mother: a hard subject. Here, the boy is an unthinking muscle-and-speed american type who has not the emotional equipment to assimilate his mother's death. He tries to go through the proper ritual (putting the flowers on her grave), but it is meaningless. In the desperate quiet of the situation his mind reverts to the most vivid of their relationships: his racing: (the 220 in point of fact: hence the "turn"), and in doing so grasps the fact that "it (the irreparable human situation) is all proved" by the spontaneous and necessary action of his mind to take in the death in its own way, in the only (and now pitiful) categories of his being that have been useful and vivid to him. And at the end, emphasizing the change, the new-life-giving rain comes, at last. I think that the two lines beginning "his legs are sleeping" do what poetry ought to do.[41] But you judge and tell me.

I am working on one now that ought to be far and away the best I have ever written. Its possibilities are so great that I feel like farming them out to Shakespeare or Dante. If I don't muff it, I ought to have it done by the end of next week. Whereupon I'll send it to you. It is all I expect ever to write about the war, and is called, tentatively, "The Confrontation of the Hero."[42]

I sit out on the upstairs porch and write going directly toward the sun, and a lot is coming. Since I have your letter, this is the plenitude.

Excuse the unseemly chaos of this format, but I wanted to send what I had to say as it came.

Write soon.

Yours,

Jim

Villa "Lou Galidou"
Chemin des Roches
Cap d'Antibes
France

TO: ANDREW LYTLE

Undated; late 1954   *TLS, 2 pp; Vanderbilt*
                                                         Cap d'Antibes

Dear Andrew,

By now I don't know which of us owes the other a letter, so let's call it square and start with this one.

I got your good criticism of the Father and Sons poem. You are just, as always, and more perceptive and kind than anyone could be. I feel like a dog (not one of those in the poem!) about the obscurities of the writing, but I, like you (as you indicate in your last letter) must work from chaos toward the light: at first there are only a few words, an image, a scene, things that have no logical but an emotive connection. There grows out of this a great mass of detail: tangential, irrelevant, confusing, through which the thread of the poem runs, if I can find it. The poem is thus a kind of long, slow discovery, more often than not only half discovered, touched, passed, missed. There is a shifting border across which the imagination, from its deep, hit-or-miss life, leans over into the actual world and touches something, then disappears. And you must wait. Sometimes it helps to fumble; sometimes that is destructive. In the poem, the knight is first, as you say, an image of the sun on the water, something not made, but suggested. The connection with the boys is intended to be this: the knight is their unfulfilled manhood, conceived as taking place according to a tradition. The knight's vigil is the most striking and clear-cut example of the Christian puberty rite I know. The idea is that the father's traditional upbringing (that of any Christian, say), being a product of the process which included this ritual as a way of seeing manhood achieved and confirmed, is seen momentarily as a vision by him, in the blinding sunlight; at the end, this leaves him, as it does most of us when we are struck with terrible knowledge of this kind, or the suspicion of it, and he is stripped naked, left in the face of the death of his sons with no mythical or traditional consolation or interpretation, but only the terrible realization of the grief. The poem takes place as the father comes to the edge of the lake in which his sons, whom he has been searching for with dogs, lie drowned.

By the way, before I forget, the <u>Shenandoah</u> people, who more or less commissioned the poem The Sprinter's Mother, have written a very flattering letter of acceptance. That is good for me; I have always worked in the dark, with no help, no readers, no encouragement, until your first letter. All that, or most of it, is over, now, and I am set toward writing as a life work, no matter what. The years in the dark were good for me, in a way, but not so good in another way. I have the hunger to see print, which is undignified and maybe even shameful, but very strong. I hope I shall pass through this stage, and have "the indifference of greatness",[43] but that is not yet.

You talk of the distinctive quality of my work. I hope you are right in what you say. The thing I wanted most, when I was given the fellowship, was that, this year, by throwing all resources and energies into the job, like the U.S. building the Atomic Bomb, I might fuse my style: establish and consolidate my scattered gains, solve most of the major problems of technique which hitherto I have only wormed around, hit or miss. And I think, with luck, that will be done. And yet I am not satisfied. My poems reread clumsily and blockily, with good flashes just missing being fused, and a great many thin, shadowy passages between.

In regard to the poem I enclose:[44] I intended it as a kind of personal farewell to the war, and to the use of myth. For a long time I wanted to work at the intersection of the classic myths and everyday life: to try to discover in what ways the ageless patterns contained in the myths are played out, most of the time unknown to the players, among the real things and situations of life. I tried to do that here, using the myth of Perseus and the Medusa as a glass through which to see the war. I wanted to lend the myth immediacy, and the situation of the wounded soldier timelessness. The first section gives the setting, wherein the central figure, a mechanic, is wounded while changing an engine on an aircraft, presumably, and actually, on Okinawa. The second section is a kind of mythological or universal projection (universal: hence the "you") of the wound, in which, in the pain and shock of the wound and ensuing amputation of his leg, he dreams of becoming a new constellation (there isn't one of the Medusa, though there is of Perseus). He returns by degrees to his actual situation, in the hospital amputee ward. In the third section he thinks disconnectedly of the Hero, of ceremonies of animal-killing: the familiar theme, reintroduced at the end, of the soldier as dead beef, or as of just a dead dog. The Hero, who ought also to be seen as Death, enters the ward, but the protagonist, in a kind of hallucinated fever in which he believes his leg restored to him so that he can flee (this often happened, by the way) leaps out, almost joyously, into the real things, the war materièl, of the island, with the Hero hovering over him, seeking the place and hour of confrontation. He wakes in the ward, remembering the time when he fought most conclusively for the airstrip on which he was later wounded, and the pride (which was also very real: you could not help it, and that is terrible, too) with which he enabled the aircraft to fly. This memory is coupled with a rendering of his death, both prefigured and seen as already having occurred, in which he becomes both the dead animal <u>and</u> the legendary figure with powers after death, in the actual confrontation. The snow of thistle blown by the enemy, which is as close as I could get to the old "all nature mourns" theme of the conventional elegy, and still keep an edge of irony, is also the Medusa's looking into the mirror of the shield (you remember the story). At the end he finds himself with the continuing and accusing power of his death confirmed, and unabatable.

There are maybe a good many things that need explaining: the Japanese fortified their ancestral tombs and machine-gunned from them, "line astern" is the standard ground-strafing formation, the "Ram" is Aries, the figure whose "house" the sun enters on March 21, in astrology. And so on. I struggled to hold clear the main line of action, but the tangential things swirled in, until the whole thing was a whipped snarl of lines and meanings through which the war, somehow, was held. And so it stays. It is maybe my best poem; not because of these meanings, but for the feeling of life, the terror and permanence of the wound, that is there. The second section, the wounding-constellation part, is the best writing I have done, I think.

Forgive this long gloss; I give it to save you time for your own work, which must always be as important for me as my own. I hope the Wake is going well, and that you will soon have something for me to read.

The weather here is cold, and it has rained for ten solid days. We are very close together here, now, and there is much happiness.

Yours,
Jim

P.S. In the poem, the change of sex of the protagonist is supposed to take place at the beginning of the fourth section.

TO: WILLIAM PRATT[45]

TLS, 1 p; William Pratt

28 January, 1955
c/o American Express
Florence, Italy

Dear Bill, (and, Ann, you are in on the greeting too, and the rest of the letter),

I am sorry I've waited so long to answer, but we have been in the process of removing to Florence (Firenze, here), and have been busy with the usual things that such undertakings require. We are settled, now, though, in a good <u>warm</u> pensione, and I promise to make a better correspondent, and to breathe the warm breath of <u>vino rosso</u>, <u>Etruscan</u> statuary, Michelangelo, Cellini, <u>heroic</u> statuary and brick paving-blocks (there is a lot of building going on) across to you as often as warrants (i.e. as often as I hear from you).

We hated to leave Provence; I had grown quite to love the place, the terraced hills, and the whole soft crumbling-and-held-together-with-vines look and air of it, but France, for our shekels, was <u>trop cher</u>, and too cold, too, despite the work I did on the <u>chauffage</u> every day, which, if translated into heroic action, would have slain a thousand Medusas, tracked and strangled the Minotaur, and lifted Prometheus' peak out from under him. Italy is better for us, though the majesty of it is hard to assimilate through the poverty of most of the people: you feel like you ought to be attending meetings and speaking out wildly against the conditions rather than standing mutely in the Uffizzi, looking up at the da Vinci's and Botticelli's. But these latter are unbelievably beautiful, nonetheless; I have not been to any meetings.

How did you make out at the MLA convention? Was there any excitement? I have never been to one of those, but I doubtless would not have been able to hold out much longer had I stayed at Rice.[46] And, for the Lord's sake, if you got a job, get me one. Allen Tate has promised me one, but I don't hear anything from him, and am beginning to wonder a little. We have written some letters to schools, but there has not been much encouragement.

The work has been going well. Spears is bringing out a long, confused "Confrontation of the Hero" of mine, which I expect is my <u>magnum opus</u> to date, and <u>Poetry</u> another,[47] even longer one. In two days I contracted for more poetry than I have published since I began to put it out, three or four years ago. I want to have a crack at something really big soon, and am holding off before diving into the mountain of notes I have for "The Vision of the Sprinter,"[48] which is superb in conception and, and I have no doubt I shall find, impossible in execution. But we must try.

You <u>must</u>, Bill, learn French, that damnable language. There is so much in it that the first look is breathtaking, and the subsequent ones slaying, except for the fact that you are being recreated all the time. Some names, all poets, which you will probably not be able to find, except in a foreign-language book-store: René Char,[49] Paul Eluard, Henri Pichette, Antonin Artaud, Pierre-Jean Jouve, Michel Leiris. The first writes (and I translate <u>very</u> roughly): "In the fabric of the poem should come together an equal number of secret tunnels, of harmonious rooms, at the same time as future elements, havens of the sun, specious tracks, and beings calling one another. The poet is the traveller through all that forms an order. And a rebellious order." <u>That</u> ought to give you something to chew on. The French are good at those fecundating, ambiguous definitions.

I must stop. Write to us, and we shall fire back with everything Europe has.

Yours, Jim

TO: WILLIAM PRATT

1955   *TLS, 2 pp; William Pratt*

15 May
Firenze

Dear Bill,

It is shameful, I know, to have waited so long to answer your letter, especially since in it you talk of things very important to you. I can plead only the extenuating circumstances of constant travel and a little work, and being very tired all the time from the rushing around, the packing and unpacking, and the rest of travelling, which you must know. We have been to Rome for a month (I got your letter Easter week-end in Rome), and to Naples and environs for about ten days. When in those places we were hardly ever in the rooms we rented to sleep in: we have been in literally hundreds of churches, museums, we have been to tennis tournaments (the big international winter circuit is just ending), horse shows, oh, everything you can imagine. Spring in Italy is, or ought to be, Italy. Festival after festival, much wine-drinking, music, ballet, the skirts and the prices higher, and the sun coming down on everything with all the heat in the world and no malice at all. Rome is crawling with American poets. Our best friends there were the Richard Wilburs.[50] A few days before we left, he had a mild heart attack, from overwork (he has four books coming out this fall), and from too much wine, pasta, late hours, and from four sets of tennis on top of all that. Then, one of his children and his wife got the mumps. They are all recovered now, though, and he is back to work on his "projects," which are multiplying all the time. We got to know Bill (William Jay) Smith and his wife pretty well (his wife is Barbara Howes, another poet, and it is her Guggenheim they are here on).[51] We all took care of two of the Wilbur children, and there was a good deal of zoo-going and picnicking, which lasted right up to the time we left to come back to Florence.

In Florence we know Peter Viereck very well,[52] and his Russian, inscrutable and charming wife, and their two dreadful children, who, you think every minute, are going to come out with "Neki Hokey," and push you off a cliff (this last reference will be lost on you if you don't read Dick Tracy).[53] We all went out to a monastery yesterday, Peter and I talking as wildly and churlishly as we could all the time (he must be, really, the most irreverent guy in the world), and the children milling and fighting (Chris, though outgunned and outnumbered, held his own, with a little help from Mac and me). We had a really good time, for they are the kind of people that you can have that kind of time with. And so on and so on. We do wish you were here, to share all this. I remember, as you do, the days at Vanderbilt, the "Thracian Athens" as Robert Lowell called it somewhere, and the feverish talk in little rooms, and the great world of the Other Poets, the published and prize-winning ones, like these I mention. Ah, but one day you will be here, or some equally good place, if there is such, on your own or a better fellowship, for you are waiting in that dark that we all have to wait in, the working dark, where now and then a little flitter of light comes to rest on the backs of your hands, and then is gone before you can turn it toward your palms: or, if you do catch it, seems, and probably is, common coin. But gradually, year after year, you come nearer, you catch more, and what you do catch is sometimes more inexhaustible than you ever could have thought, and then you begin to put the words down unchangeably. Ah, but you think: do I have talent? That is the word we all hate to hear, for it calls into the room with us the Unattainable, the gift of the gods to Dylan Thomases and Rimbauds, and not to us. But if my own case is worth anything as an example, the word does not have a crucial meaning. I had no more "talent" for writing poetry, in the beginning, than did Joe Louis, or Bobo Olson, or Mel Patton.[54] I was an obscure tryer in their world: that of language meant nothing to me; there was certainly nothing that such a world could depend on me to give it. What "success" I have had depends exclusively on my interest in the subject of poetry, and on the reading thus engendered, and on long meditations, mostly but not always sterile, on the subject of language, and on a great deal of trial and error, and on work. The farther in you go, the more underground dawns there are, the more you learn to experience, and/or re-experience in words, in rhythms, and the more you learn to fashion the "what goes with" what you already have, this last being one of the hardest of the controls you have to learn. Don't let your first efforts put you off, horrible as they may seem (and I suspect, from knowing you, that they are not nearly as bad as you say). There is always enough of a glimmer of promise to start again; there is always a little ground gained; though inevitably you always lose, at first, you never lose totally. And, in the beginning, don't worry too much about "form," though that must always be one of the basic and ultimate concerns. Try to get the words, in whichever way strikes you and keeps striking you through many efforts on the same subject or poem, to fall together in ways that seem natural to them, and try to see that the division of lines helps them to do this. For you don't want the adequate, but the inevitable movement: the words and their harmonics inseparable, and impossible without your experience and the slant of your own blood through them. And send me what you write. Before I forget, if you write fairly soon, you can catch us in Paris (c/o American Express, Rue Scribe), for we sail June 17.

My own work is going pretty well. I get overtures from publications now and then (it is hard for me to imagine a <u>solicited</u> manuscript!): from something called "The Beloit Poetry Journal", which Viereck tells me is pretty good despite the name, and from the "Quarterly Review of Literature" and the "Hudson Review." I managed to scrape something together for all of these, though I hadn't planned to work much the last month or so of our stay. The verdicts are still forthcoming, though they usually take things they ask for, I am told.[55]

We shall be in New York June 21, and will stay there until we can get squared away with the Rootes people about our car. Then, if you like, we can stop off in Washington and stay with you-all, or within whatever proximity you specify or can arrange, for a day or two. Or, if you will be at Vanderbilt then, we can of course see you when we are in Nashville, which is where we are heading from New York.

I am sorry all over again for waiting so long to write, as I end this. Please don't think the delay typical, though of course it is.

Do write to us in Paris. Maxine sends her love, and Chris would, if he knew you.

Excusez-moi du dérangement.

Bien à vous,

Jim

P.S. We have a job, at the Univerisity (sp.) of Florida. $4,000. Bourgeois, what?

J.

TO: WILLIAM PRATT

TLS, 2 pp; William Pratt

Paris

11 June, 1955

Dear Bill,

Paris is jumping, as it has always been except during the Resistance, and we are jumping with it, in our small way: into and out of huge panoramic shows of Picasso and Jacques Villon, night clubs, student dives, book shops, movies (some good new ones you'll be seeing, I hope), and sometimes just standing on the corner of Boul' Mich' and St. Germain and jumping up and down, to keep from stopping, even for a minute. My God, the <u>money</u> you can spend in this place really can haunt you. It must be more expensive here than in Hell (the American's hell must certainly involve a lot of <u>wasted</u> money, and the knowledge thereof.). We are hanging on, though, trying to wing the best punches our poor few dollars of the Sewanee's money will buy for us, where they will do the most good. But Paris is winning, and not so slowly any more either, and Thursday we shall be hanging on the ropes of the <u>United States</u>, headed out toward where the "great fields of the Republic roll on under the moon." (somewhere in the Great Gatsby this quote is).[56] I must say I'll be at least in some sense glad to quit this suit-case living, and settle a little, if not settle down. But we have given them a run! All the poems I have written (about ten) coming out in respectable places (and the money coming in, a few hundred dollars), and this not overly worked-for, either, and a lot of great new people, a new, good job (if the joker would ever write to confirm it), and Venice, Rome, Provence, Paris, Florence, all living and taking the color of the mind, and giving back their own. Ah! I won't go on. Some day we'll do all this. Again! Again!

Maxine tells me to tell you that the tourist court near you is fine with us. We arrive in New York the 21st, and will stay at least over the Olson-Moore fight the next night, and likely a day or two longer. As soon as you get this, write us at 155 East 72nd St., N.Y. c/o Miss Eliot Heiner, and tell us where and how we can reach you in Falls Church, or Washington, or wherever you say, coming in from the Philadelphia highway.

Sure I'd like to see Pound![57] I don't know, though, if we shall be staying there with you over the week-end. Can he get seen on week days?

Oh, really, we are tired! We have, all of us, lost weight, and the grim fascination of spending money all day and all night, every day and night, on <u>enjoyment</u> and <u>pleasure</u> is telling on us in many odd ways. Maxine wants more money, I want more time, several other lives even; Chris wants more toys, more animals in the zoos, more fireworks, more Walt Disneys. Life is earnest, here!

I have been in thousands of book-shops, and there are millions more here. The only cheap thing in Paris is books, and I have a friend in the publishing business here who gets <u>those</u> for me at a third off. So I am getting a good library. It is fine when you can read a little French (which, after all, is all I can do), and you can go in a book-store and pick up a surrealist poet (between covers, that is) who tells you that he would like to have a peninsula that dances like a fire, or an exiled tree that invents a kingdom. The other day I got a book full of the dreams of one of the best poets (an <u>ex</u>-surrealist) I have read over here, named Michel Leiris.[58] I translate <u>au courant</u>. You must be sure to try this one tonight:

> I am dead. I see the sky powder like the cone of air
> traversed, in a movie-house, by the ray of a projector.
> Many luminous globes, of a milky whiteness, are aligned
> far off in the sky. From each of them projects a long
> metallic stem, and one of these pierces my breast from

front to back, without my feeling anything other than a
great euphoria. I advance toward the globes of light,
gliding slowing along the stem and rising in a gentle
slope. By each of my hands, I hold the two nearest me
of a chain of other men who also rise toward the sky,
each following the rail which perforates him. No other
sound is heard than the light crackling of the steel in
the flesh of our breasts.

Sweet dreams! And do write us in New York, as specified. Maxine sends her
love.

Yours,

Jim

TO: WILLIAM PRATT

1955

TLS, 1 p; William Pratt
Atlanta, Georgia

20 Aug.

Dear Bill,

Well, here are your poems back, and a merry time they gave me, too. I might
as well plunge right in. I think it would be, or might be, wise for you to write in
the conventional forms for a little. Though this might contradict other things I've
said, I think it true nevertheless that your rhythmical faculty might be helped.
Unless one has that kind of ear, I should think increasingly rare in America, that
imparts to any words, even those of the newspaper, a strong come-and-go of
accent, he has to develop his rhythms over a long period, paying long, exhausting
attention to what he likes or doesn't like in other poets and in his own work, until
his attention passes into a kind of conditioned instinct, or reflex, and so on into
his poems. Also, I should like to see you cut loose with some genuine wildness,
risking incoherence (for which I should then call you down: you can't win, you
know, at these things), sentimentality, and all the rest of it in hopes that a higher
unity and order and precision might be made available. And fight down the
"literary", the cliché, as though they would send you to hell. One of the poems
is promising, and several have promising things (as I think I point out on the
manuscript), but you must not think yet, "I am writing with the best of them,"
as I used to do (and still, fatally, do, alas). All in good time. This is a long, hard,

unrewarding pull, until you say to yourself one day, after an unsuccessful fight
with a phrase

Bêtes! Devant vous mon corps
Est une grâce perdue

and there, by God, beasts are, and the poet, and the human being, and there is
that exchange, in the words. Dig after the ore, and dig rhythmically, even if it is
sing-song.

So much for the higher pleasures. Here, we have all been sick, I most of all. But
none of this happened until after we had gone down to Florida and got more or
less squared away down there. It is a huge high-schoolish University I am in, and a
little forbidding, with its kindly old gentlemen running the English department
and asking me if I have read Walter Pater, and if I thought Edna Millay and Emily
Dickinson were representative modern poets. But we have a nice little house
there, with a low rent (comparatively: $70) and several very good friends. The
salary is pretty good, and they tell me that "we don't insist on you writers working
summers," which naturally pleases me a good deal. All in all, it oughtn't to be a
bad place, at least for a while. You-all could come down if you could work out
some way for Ann to be comfortable. The location of Gainesville is very good:
about (70 mi.) equi-distant from Jacksonville, Daytona, and Orlando, with the
discreet fleshpots of St. Petersburg about 138 miles away and the indiscreet ones of
Tampa a mile or two nearer. Silver Springs is about 45 miles from here, and St.
Augustine about 60. So you see there will be plenty to do, if you can manage to get
away.

Before I forget, what is the Old Man of St. Elizabeth's[59] address? Since your last
letter I feel that I certainly should write to him. And Maxine, as I think I told you,
is going to knit him a sweater with the Gaudier-Bre. . . . . emblem on it.[60] Do you
think he'd like that? After all, he puts it on his stationary.

Keep working on the poems. I say so much about them on the manuscript
because I want you, eventually, to be able to do what you can do. Though of
course you will want to shoot me, I beg you to think better of it, for the good of us
all, and that of future Golden Treasuries.

Yr Ob't svt, Jim

TO: WILLIAM PRATT

TLS, 2 pp; William Pratt
Atlanta, Georgia

6 September, 1955

Dear Bill,

Day after tomorrow we leave to begin the "new life", and so for the past two weeks have been hustling hard to get things ready. I hope that will serve as some kind of excuse for my not having written, though I fear that at best it is a poor enough excuse. Anyhow, this is the last letter I can write before the movers come in, in the morning, and take this desk out from under me. Before I forget, I had better let you have our Florida address. It is: 1720 N.W. 7th Place, Gainesville.

I have heard from the Old Man. I quote (as best I can, for my typewriter don't know this langwige but a little): "the irresponsibility ethic and civic of most of my godamned "licherary" contemporaries, is food for thought on part of yr/generation." "The possibility of being irritated at Grampaw's prolonged incarceration alzo eggzists."

Indeed it does. I wish the possibility of springing the tough old bastard eggzisted, too, but I don't see much chance of it. If Hemingway can't get him out, I sure can't. But I keep thinking I ought to try. Anyway, I'm going to have Maxine get to work on the sweater as soon as we can get enough money to buy the wool. Maybe he and his wife can both get in it, and the ghost of Gaudier-Brzesca (sp) will lift them out over Washington and take them where Kung is setting down the rules for modern poetry and morals under some bo-tree or other, or the ideographic sign therefor. All this and Fellonosa too![61]

I hope that you are writing, at least some, and will soon have some more to show me. If you are bothered about about my reference to the "actual" world, I perhaps should have said "ordinary" instead, meaning what the French mean by quotidien. "Actual" or "real" (my fault, entirely) starts too many philosophical hares, and that's for damn sure! I think the hardest thing to get, in writing (especially in poetry is this true), is a feeling of inspired honesty, of an honesty beyond honesty, of a cracked kind of honesty that turns out to be more necessary that all our other kinds, and more whole. The truth, or a truth, is very hard to find, especially one that is bound up in the language peculiar to oneself. Yet that is the hunt we are committed to. For a very long time (I hope not so long in your case as in mine) every good, or half-good, or promising thing you can manage to say, amidst the universal slag and dead-wood of attempted writing, is owned lock, stock and the rest of it by someone else, until you feel, well, goddamn it, what else is there. But the something else is always there, hard as it is to come at: it is there because you have lived the life that you have, and not that that Auden has, or

Stevens or ____ (substitute any name.) So it is a question of time, and a long slow push, and much thinking, and a living with disappointment that turns it into your surest stake in the human emotions, and that leads out, finally, into the blessed state of "did I really say that? Myself? Why, I'm damned if it ain't my own child, come out from under that rock after all these years. Lord love him, look at the little bugger!"

Spears has put a long review in my hands, to appear in the winter issue.[62] It involves an evaluation of our friend Jarrell, and I am undecided whether to strike or spare. I don't think he is really a poet, for real. Do you? He makes all kinds of engaging noises, and he knows all about poets, their care and feeding, what they ought to be able to do, and all that, but I don't think any unprejudiced observer would say he has any real, ultimate business with language. Graham[63] is also in it (the review); there is no doubt about him. He has won: he has his own kind of thing on the page, and it is something. Something good, that is, and after so long, and so much Thomas,[64] too.

The only "original" work I have undertaken is a longish poem I have been kicking at for some months now.[65] The Partisan R. is bringing it out some time in the ambiguous future, for which I am very glad, since we are going to need all the cash we can get, until somebody endows me. Now I can get down to "The Cave Master,"[66] which seems to me to promise everything. I have several hundred pages of it, trying out one thing and another; working on this one is a pleasure, though I keep having that worst of feelings about it: that I may botch the handsomest woman that ever stepped out of Michelangelo's stone. More later, once the furnace's mouth is dared a few times in earnest. (bad rhyme here: you got to watch them things).

Maxine and Chris are fine. Tell Ann to take especial care of the Interior, Unknown, and Disclosing Image.[67] Hemingway says that beer is good for those.

Write soon (to new address)

Yours,

Jim

TO: EZRA POUND

TLS, 1 p; Yale

25 October, 1955
Gainesville, Fla.

Dear Uncle,

Thanks for the continued attention, which I fear I am repaying but illy and tardily. I thought of asking for measurements for the sweater, and all that, but I think the garment might have a better chance on its own, with only my wife's intuitions working and her attention nodding. We <u>will</u> put on the Gaudier head, which we have been at some pains to work out, on sheets of grocery paper, with rulers, pins, and a good many revisions. We have the thing started in gray, leaving you open down the front, as you say. If you want another color, speak up, and we'll try for a barber-pole effect with the (as yet) unknown color.

The poem is not ready yet, but I will send it when I find out, myself, what it wants to do.

Where dost get a hold of B. Bunting's poems? I saw a review one time of a Selected or Collected Poems published by something called the Cleaners' Press, but I can't locate either the press or the book.[68] He seems to me to be mighty good, in what I have read, and I'd gladly steal any volume or portion of one I could, or even buy it.

I have not heard from Bill Pratt for a good long time. If you are in epistolary or psychic range of him, tell him I resent his negligence.

Love to your wife. Winter Plans for Clothing and Shelter proceeding at all speed and dispatch, sir, I am

Yr O'bt Sv't
James Dickey

TO: EZRA POUND

TLS, 1 p; Yale

20 February, 1956
Gainesville, Fla.

Dear Uncle,

I render herewith the annual report of Florida sweater-growers, to say the one we (my wife, especially, but myself also, to some extent: you will recognize the holes) have been most concerned with. The winter is nearly gone now, and we are still "making progress"; that is, we aren't through with it yet. But it will be a warm one when finished, and you can use it forever. And it <u>is</u> almost finished.

There is not much else to say from here, except that a whole generation of Florida students is being brought up on the <u>ABC of Reading</u>, much to the astonishment of the Cerberi of the English Department.[69] Also, I lectured, I mean "lectured," to the American Pen Women's Society so furiously (and, I guess, controversially) that their National President wrote to the president of <u>this</u> place and demanded that I be kicked out.[70] I haven't been, yet, but the U. of Florida may martyr me still. I rather hope so, though it may just be possible that I am doing one or two people some good here.

There is a poem of mine to appear in the <u>Partisan Review</u> you may want to look at.[71] It is the only one that comes anywhere near doing what I want to do. Others have appeared, but on reading them over I can't for the life of me think they're what I want. But there are some new ones still baking that seem to have some of it. Also, there is a long omnibus review of poets in the Spring <u>Sewanee</u> that gets in some good licks against a man by the name of Jarrell, whose work has been to some extent influential, in a bad and sentimental way, here for the last few years. He should read Bunting, and either change or kill himself.

All my love to Mrs. Pound. We think of you often, up to our waists in sand, and burned by the winter (for it is a hot one here.) And we <u>will</u> finish the sweater, if I have to wear out a wife a day working on it.

By the way, is there any news of Pratt? He won't write to me, though I heard some way or other that he now has a child, a girl, specifically.

Yours,

James Dickey

1720 N.W. 7th Place
Gainesville, Florida.

TO: MR. AND MRS. WILLIAM JAY SMITH

TLS, 1 p; Washington University

11 March. 1956
Gainesville, Florida

Dear Barbara and Bill,

We are delighted to hear from you; we had about given up, and all that God-pouring of waters in the Villa D'Este was becoming a little remote and queer, since we had no word from you. Now all is well, and the fountains can go on working all right, in our memories, which would otherwise be in serious danger of dry-rot, here in this God Damned place. All Gainesville would have to do would be to think of Florence and Rome in order to cease to exist (incidentally, we are in Gainesville, FLORIDA, not Georgia, where your letter went. I don't know yet how we got it). And that might not be a bad thing, either, generally. What existence Gainesville has is not valuable to anyone, that I can see, and certainly not to us. There is nothing here for me but the genteel poverty of the University teacher, and the possibility, in twenty years, of its being a little more genteel. "Here lies one whose name was writ on fifty-seven thousand freshman papers." So we're thinking about chucking it, and trying to get into something where they'll give a man a salary he can ride, where the world is pushy, crass, and rich, and poets are eaten up with the disease of money and the "expense of action in a waste of shame." (misquoted, I think).[72] Over and against all this stand the Smiths, who are in Europe, struggling with the Real Things, and doing fine on all kinds of publications, and all. This is wonderful news to us, since otherwise we would simply sit around and burn our lips in silence, sinking slowly out of sight of Europe and What There Is there. Can you imagine what this life is like? I doubt it. The other day I was hailed into the <u>sanctum sanctorum</u> of the Head of the English Department.[73] At the door I raised my sword, and remembering the words of Victor Mature,[74] cried out, <u>Ave Caesar, morituri te salutant</u>. Caesar told me that I was spending too much time, on, well, on the structure, what you might call the <u>technical</u> part of <u>Huckleberry Finn</u>, when all the time I ought to be telling them about the <u>meaning</u>; i.e. what the thing was written to <u>tell</u> you. Mumbling a Spell from Baudelaire, I rose from Prisoner's Bar, blood and ink from my nose sprouting out all over my yellow and purple Artist's Cravat, and staggered home, not believing in anything I had heard. But it was true. I mean it was <u>true</u>. And <u>that</u> will shake you up, when you hear yourself admit it. No, there is not much for us here. If we stay another year I hope we're dead from it by the end.

You ask what have I done in Writing. Well, I had a couple of poems in the Summer <u>Sewanee</u> and the June <u>Poetry</u>. I have a tremenjus long review in the Spring <u>Sewanee</u> (not yet out, quite). I have some stuff coming out in the <u>P-rtis-n Review</u> (though when, I don't know; it was accepted last August). And there is some more in the <u>Hudson</u> if they ever get around to it, and in <u>Botteghe Oscure</u> (I think, only, on this one.[75] The stuff is good, though, and they <u>ought</u> to take it. If you can prevail on anyone you know over there in its behalf, why then prevail; although the pomes are good enough to make it on their own, you can't always tell if they will). I saw Bill's <u>jazz musician</u> in the PR, and your poem in New World Writing, both of which I liked very much.[76] You, Barbara, are showing a fine <u>particularity</u> which I don't remember to have seen before in your work.

We <u>told</u> you about living in France.

I should like to dedicate the poem (fairly long) in the Partisan to you, Barbara (it wouldn't work for you both), but it is a little compromising. So I'll wait until I get something that isn't.

Is there anything we can get or do for you here?

Love to David and the New(er) One.

Love to Italy. Love to Europe.

Love, Jim

1720 N.W. 7<u>th</u> Place
Gainesville, <u>Florida</u>

*Kevin, Maxine, and
Christopher Dickey, c. 1960*

*James, Kevin, and
Christopher Dickey, c. 1960*

PART THREE

ADVERTISING AND MOONLIGHTING

April 1956–May 1961

TLS, 2 pp; Emory

8 April, 1956
New York[1]

Dearest Ones,

The main thing is that I've moved. In case you didn't get the address "for sure" over the phone, it is Hotel Winslow, 55th and Madison. It is not a bad place, as I said; I have a little room on the 13th floor overlooking a wonderful industrial slum, and am now engaged (as I write) in watching it made over by snow, which certainly does something for it, though I haven't as yet decided what. At any rate, the room is fine for my needs, such as they are; it is warm and comfortable and small, and I can get my hands on anything in the room without raising them from my sides.

I just telegraphed in to 'Ol Jake[2] as follows: "I should like to resign my position at the University of Florida as of 5 April." I thought that had just the touch. I don't think it necessary to expand on it, do you?

I am sorry about Andrew,[3] though I suppose it couldn't be helped. He is so full of advice about "Integrity" for everybody else, that I don't suppose he could act any other way. I love and value him, though, and wouldn't want him to think badly of me. But if it must be, then it must be. My life and that of my family is at stake, as he certainly must know, and that is a good deal more important to me than fine words and sentiments. I should suggest that Andrew "learn to live in the world," rather than that of "artistic creation" (you remember his "advice" to me), and that he back up a little of that big talk about "dying" for people, fighting duels, and so on, with a little action, at least once in a while. If he won't face Wise about the Pen Women, how can he really face anybody? Much less "duel!" He wants to take credit for these attitudes without ever having to prove any of them in action, and that is too bad, for he deserves more from himself. Do what you can to get him back on our side; if all fails, why then tant pis, I say.

I am glad that the McHughstons came by, and that he is happy about what I did. If it will encourage others to stop their timid eating of the s... that Wise and others of that ilk think they can give teachers all their lives and get away with it, then I've done more than I set out to do, which is always nice.

The city is great big, of course, and all around me. I am not nearly so lonely as I would have supposed; I am lonely, all right, but it is a good loneliness, since I am working for something that we all want, something that will be some good, and not just working hopelessly to survive. And I'm going to spread-eagle the advertising field, don't worry about that. In three months (or less) we'll all be together, and I'll be "the Atlanta man," and we'll take it from there. If I don't make it, I still have my "talent" as a writer undiminished (how about that note from Rago!),[4] and the best family and all the love in the world. How can we lose?

Have all my friends write to me here: Bo, Andrew, and so on, and tell them to get all the ones they know to write, so that I'll have a little mail to look forward to, every now and then. And you just might mention to Bo to tell (as of his own accord) Andrew what a good 'un I was, what a genius, what a good teacher, and all that. Those things often help.

My new business associates are all good fellows; they are none of them dying of ulcers or drink, but only of enthusiasm and a kind of taut joy you sure don't find in teaching. I never felt completely right about teaching, anyway; it seems to me that there is something a man owes to his life more than sitting around talking about books all the time. And it makes literature itself boring, by divorcing it from life. This way is better, believe me, and is going to be better and better. I have a kind of feeling I was made for it. I think I can make Coca Cola into a Big Thing.[5]

I talked to Mom this morning, and she is going to send the fifty up to me here. She has my new address, and so everything is set that way.

The trip up was certainly tough; I never did get to sleep, and not the next morning after my arrival, either. I was all right during the morning of my "trial," but about the middle of the afternoon I developed one of those bright, clear headaches under which thinking goes on in a kind of intelligent desperation, hoping to hold out until everything collapses. I did hold out, though, and by damn I came through. Now I've got a clear track, and can really get down and run. I feel wonderful, and have the confidence of Achilles.

[   ][6]

It has stopped snowing now, just about; I watched the flakes for a long time this morning, lying in bed, reading a book (the only one, I swear) I bought up here from the Librairie Française (by Michel Leiris) and looking out the frozen window now and again, where the flakes were pouring like rain out farther, over The City, but close to the window were floating, even going upward a little; then, again, when I looked, the nearer ones were rushing past perfectly sideways, and the City ones were being held in somebody's breath. Ah! "The dazed archer's brain of snow has brought/ From itself the green of a beautiful prey/ Immobilized and flowering everywhere . . ."[7] How right I shall have been, when Spring comes!

> All my love.
> I love you,
> Jim

TO: WILLIAM PRATT

ALS, 2 pp; William Pratt

10 April, 1956
N.Y.C.

Dear Bill,

I have your fine letter, which Maxine forwarded to me here. There are a good many things in it I could go on about for pages, but a day's work in New York whips one down to creeping size, and the best I will be able to do tonight is to crawl over a couple of pages in a style that would help or dazzle no one, not even another creeper (this last wants only to go to sleep).

As you can see, I've gone for the big money, and they are giving (some of) it to me. There is considerable pressure here, for the account is a big one (Coca-Coca), and the writing done for it must be what underline{every}body wants. What everybody wants is a kind of calculated banality-trying-to-raise-itself-to-the-level-of-mediocre-pre-poetry-about-soft-drinks; once a man trained on language (poetry, say) gets on to what they want him to do, there's nothing to it at all: the only thing one must be careful about is giving them the impression that it is as easy as it is; then you would not seem to be earning the money! The life is fast, hard, full of organized pressures, but not heart-breaking, for your heart is not in it. How could it be to anyone who has read Pound's line "The sharp song with the sun's radiance under it"?[8] How could one possibly care when one of the "wheels" in this business is dissatisfied with you when you say "It's time for a Coke," and ecstatic over you when you say, "Enjoy your thirst, with Coke"? (that one slew 'em!) I am in advertising, in case that hasn't as yet filtered through. Boy, the sugar is heavy here! They're giving me a thousand a month to start, plus bonuses and the profit-sharing take, which ought to bring it up around 18-20 thousand a year. But what crap we write! Mercy me! There is a medicine we take here to get rid of scruples: it is called money. It is in a gentle, insistent raining state all around us all the time, turning everyone a little green and glassy. At a lull in the office clatter, you can pause and hear it shaking its heart out, gently, forever, in the air. Enough of this. I was not getting anything out of teaching (a grudging toleration and mistrust as a writer, a few good students, thousands of banal, listless papers, a poor life growing older. To hell with it! And the walls of New York, where cancer's three nymphs are dancing with knot-headed children and nurses of old millionaires, gave back the sound.—

The writing (<u>not</u> "Coke puts you at your sparkling best") is going pretty well. I am pending publication in the Partisan, and, under Viereck's insistence (he is "guest editor") in something called the Beloit Poetry Journal, and again in Poetry, whose editor even sent me a congratulatory note, saying the poem ("The Father's Body") is as far as he is concerned the best one the magazine has had since Dylan Thomas (get that comparison, will you! Mercy! Mercy! Archangel of Llarregub!)[9] The article on Jarrell and others is in the Current <u>Sewanee</u> (Spring). I softened up on him in the end, for, really, I believe as you do about him. I have got some new poems that I am very hopeful for: one called "The First Morning of Cancer" and another called "The Red Bow" (bow and arrow).[10] I have millions; the problem is time, though. This business world leaves me with a terrific head-ache every day, and it is hard to work well with that pronged brightness at you all the time to go to bed. I shall keep at it, though. If I quit, what would I have? Only money, and no life.—You know all about this, though, Bill, having listened a little to and worked a little to translate the endless song welling up out of silence.

I don't want to go on and on about <u>me</u>. Just let me say about <u>you</u> that I am glad you love your daughter, that I know how you can't help it, that your life has opened out in depth and terror through your commitment to innocence and helplessness. That is what happens to us, that is what should happen, and that is what we die of, in the only worthy death.—

But now we must live, as you say. Pray God you are having joy from it, and that I shall have, when I get to Atlanta in three months as "the Atlanta man." <u>That</u> will be the day. But now the struggle.—

Before I forget, the book-seller's name is Marcel Bealu. He is at 16. Rue St. Séverin, Paris (5ᵉ). Mention my name when you write; I just got a letter from him. You must write in French; he can't read English.

Do write <u>to</u> me here. It is so lonely. I shall read your letters falling downstairs, working the pulleys of Trade, and dancing all at once, like death, with cancer's three daughters, who know only blood. (There is something diseased about this town, and it <u>is</u> most evident in the <u>women</u>, and the "<u>gaiety</u>."—) Where is the love to give the children of cancer? (I write this half out of sleep, so if you want to know what I mean, crack your manual of Freudianism).

I give you a hot handshake, and a beat over the top of the back. I wish I could see you and your wife, and the child, whom I can feel in your letter.

Keep writing. You will write permanently valuable things some day, perhaps sooner than you think.

> O Europe! Still are you singing there with any sound!——
> O New York: Ave Caesar: morituri te salutant
> De profundis ex nihilo
> In extremis, "Bring home the Coke!"

Jim

1311 Winslow Hotel
55<u>th</u> + Madison
N.Y.C.

TO: MAXINE DICKEY

TLS, 1 p; Emory

11 April, 1956
N.Y.C.

Dear Mac,

Things are going very well here indeed. I wrote my first "copy" today. After you get the idea of what they want "consumer-wise" and "product-wise," the possible variations are infinite; a man with any degree of imagination can run circles around these fellows, without seeming to, holding plenty in reserve. My copy was shown to my biggest boss here, and he looked up gravely and said, "Dickey, this is highly promising. <u>Highly</u> promising. It looks like we're both lucky." I presume he meant the Company and I. At any rate, it looks good: there is no sweat here.

It is <u>that</u> end that worries me. I wrote Andrew today and told him how gratified I was that he was going to bat for me there, and all that; it ought to shake him, at least a little, out of the way he's been acting toward you. I ended by saying, "I should like you to go by and see Maxine as much as you can, for she is alone and must depend on friends." That, you see, puts it squarely up to him. Either he qualifies or he doesn't. I went to great pains to explain to him <u>why</u> my move was made as it was; if he doesn't understand it now, there is no possibility that he ever shall.

I have an awful headache tonight. After I talked to you last night about Wise, and all, I lay awake with my heart beating so fast for so long that it took a great deal out of me. I don't think it showed at "the office," but it sure has caught up with me now.

I got Pop's check for fifty.

I have not sent out any laundry yet.

<u>Do</u> get everybody down there to write to me, since I don't know anyone in N.Y.C. except account executives and other business men.

I send you, respectively, the pictures of Eliot and Chris at the Rome Zoo, a "pledge" from one of the best thrillers I have ever seen (the <u>only</u> entertainment I have indulged myself in as yet in the City), and a tape we cut on a commercial the other day (it says, in what connection I'm not quite sure), "You're <u>so</u> right," and all the love there is in my little cubular cubicle.

I went down to Miss Steloff's[11] for the <u>Sewanee</u> today, but it hasn't come yet. You say the Jarrell Review looks good? Read it and see if there are any mistakes. How long is it? How many pages?

There is not much else to report except tiredness and a very strong sense of accomplishment. We are making it here.

Keep Wise in check. Production-Wise? OK. Consumer-Wise? Well, you might get away with it. In <u>this ad</u>. In this one only. You get my point? But <u>Market</u>-Wise? You're dead. Send me in a report from Research and Development tomorrow. Yeah; I mean have it on my desk then. Check?

I love you, Husband-Wise.

I love you,
Jim

Wait'll you hear the new singing commercial we dreamed up: "Bring home the Coke, be-op-be-dop, bring home the Coke . . . ."
And so on.———[12]

TO: MAXINE DICKEY

TLS, 1 p; Emory

20 April, 1956
NYC

Dearest,

Everything is well here; everybody keeps coming in to tell me what nice things they hear about me, how well I'm doing, how much they're depending upon me, and so on. But, in this business, the better you do, the better they <u>expect</u> you to do, and every now and then I can't at first give them exactly what they want; but if they're explicit enough, I can sure give it to them the second time around, and do. And that is one of the things they like.

I am working on "trade ads" now: that is, ads directed toward the dealer rather than the public; we're trying to get the dealers to feature the <u>large</u> Coke at fountain sales, and so on. It'll take some doing, but it can be done, without a doubt.

I have the enclosed self-righteous note from Andrew (how does he always manage to sound so humorless and dour? There's no joy in the man). Get the reference to my making a show of the thing! Wouldn't that tie your tail in a knot? And the rest of his tiresome and pretentious posturing! My God, I'm glad I don't have to depend on having to get along with him, for my livelihood! He comes somewhere near being the biggest fake I've ever known. Yet he believes himself perfectly sincere and honest, brave and true, and all that. But it is all in talk. When the time comes to act, he shrivels up with fear and is worse than any filing-clerk worried about getting fired. It's too bad. For I sincerely and genuinely love Andrew. And yet he is such a fake, and so pretentious. All you can do is laugh hopelessly and helplessly, and not take him seriously.

I'll have to cut this a little short, since I'm writing in the morning, and time has about run out on me. I'll write again this week-end, and at greater length.

Be careful, and tell Chris that I love him, and love him, and love him.

And ask for the large Coke!

Love,

Jim

TO: MAXINE DICKEY

TLS, 1 p; Emory

14 May, 1956
NYC

Dear One,

Don't apologize for not writing; I haven't been so good about it either, this week. There has been a lot doing, what with Oscar Williams[13] rushing around inviting me to parties, and cooking dinner (hamburgers) for me with his own hands (he loved to do it!) and giving me sketches of and by "Dylan" and giving me also half his library, and all the literary conversation and wanting to use my poems in anthologies and wanting to quote my Sewanee article on Gene Derwood (his wife)[14] and all the other stuff that's been going on around here, I haven't had much time. But I have had a good time, though even in the midst of all this partying I "can't hardly wait" (as you and your mother say) to get home to my little room, so that I can really go to town with my screw-driver, with which I am building my own miniature Coca-Cola bottling plant! Won't Chris be proud!

The work continues about the same. I am working in something called "Radio and TV" and am doing about as well with this as with the other stuff, though it is kind of tiresome; they won't let me use anything but clichés. Impromptu example: "Your thirst will tell you that there's nothing like that real great taste of sparkling, ice-cold Coca-Cola to put you at your sparkling best in a hurry! And now that Coke comes in three sizes, you needn't worry about how much Coke to drink: there's the handy Standard Size you've known. . . . and loved . . . for years. There's the big new King Size, just right for that king-size summer thirst of yours. And there's the big, big Family size, perfect for meals, for picnics, beach parties, for fun in the sun and out-door get-togethers of all kinds. So get together with Coca-Cola today. And . . . bring home the Coke." (cut in singing commercial here). Et cetera.

How about that? Wouldn't that can your corn? "Corn" is right.

I have also been writing, well . . . really some quite wonderful poetry. No joke. By Heaven, now that I think of it, it is pretty good.

I didn't get the papers from the man in Atlanta until Monday night. I'll shoot them back to him tomorrow, as soon as I can find a Notary. He put twelve cents' worth of stamps on his envelope, so so shall I.

Things are not so bad up here any more, for I have met a good many people who have the poor bachelor around to dinner every now and then. And, now that I am "on expenses," I can get around and see a few shows. Here at the Winslow I am drawing 77 dollars and 51 cents a week (without laundry) and about 83 or 4 with laundry. (I just sent some out today.) I don't want to move from the Winslow until I hear from Sidney Phillips (Criterion Press)[15] and get my laundry back. Oscar says that Criterion is terrific.

I am finally going to get to see Waiting for Godot tomorrow night, after so long a time. It'll be the first show I've seen since Inherit the Wind, though I have been see-ing a good many films. (Martine Carol: Mamma Mia!) But she's just nuthin' com-pared to my little girl, who can really swing it. And does, all the time! Ah, I love you, little one. The "new Jim" loves you too, although maybe he ain't too lovable himself.

Love to Chris, the U-boat Commander. And all the future children, too.

And I love you.

More love, Jim

TO: MAXINE DICKEY

1956   *TLS, 2 pp; Emory*

15
June
NYC

Dear One,

I hope you got the money I sent. I thought I would probably send $175 instead of $150, but I thought that in the last week other things might come up, and there is no point in running myself short and creating a lot of confusion trying to get money. At any rate I will bring the rest home with me Friday, so you'll get your sticky little paws on it anyway. Or on <u>most</u> of it!

I am having the Gotham send some books home for me, so don't panic when you see the package. These are <u>paid</u> for.

The literary life has been going well. Sidney Phillips of Criterion Books is a wonderfully nice fellow. I don't think there is any doubt whatever that he will take the book, but I want to finish three or four other poems before I send him the completed manuscript. That should be around the end of the summer. He tells me that my work has attracted, as he said, "a tremendous amount of attention," and that there is even a "demand" for it! So it looks pretty good for a book some-time next year. I told him I wanted a red cover, and he thought that was a fine idea.

Oscar's party was nice. I met many good people there, and had a very pleasant time. Everybody was complimentary about my poems, and of the article in the Sewanee. One of the poets I reviewed, a fellow named Honig,[16] was there, too, and he was not so pleasant. He went around sniping at me verbally, following me around wherever I went, until I turned around and said, in a room full of sudden silence, "Look Honig, get off my back or I'll knock you off it." That seemed to do the trick, for he left soon after and everybody went back to having a good time. That kind of literary fellow doesn't want anything out in the open, but only a kind of half-hidden nastiness that nobody is going to call him out of. I changed all that for one son-of-a-bitch, at least. Doubtless he will be my enemy for life, but I would would much prefer him as an enemy than as a friend. To hell with him.

Last night I went to dinner with <u>another</u> editor, a Hindu named Tambimuttu,[17] who <u>also</u> wants some poems and articles from me. He had the best English poetry magazine there was during the war years, and now is editing one called Poetry London-New York which has attracted a good deal of attention, though they are sort of shaky on money. We had a nice time, me in my charcoal suit and he in his white night-shirt and long snake-charmer's hair.

Work at the agency is going well. I finished up my stint with the print produc-tion people, and now have only to return to my original office and work out a lit-tle copy for my friend Dave Boffey (half-rime not intentional.) Everybody here calls me Golden Boy, because, I reckon, they think I'm on some kind of inside track with the agency. My title, somebody said, in Atlanta is to be <u>Head</u> of the Copy Department, which surely will mean a raise as soon as possible. Of course they neglected to mention that I will also be <u>the</u> Copy Department <u>itself</u>. Boy, will I order myself around!

It has been terribly hot here. My room is like the inside of a blast furnace, and I can't sleep before twelve or one, or beyond around five-thirty or six in the morning. Oh well, I only have to sleep here for six more nights. I can "sweat it out," I suppose. And that is exactly what I'm doing.

I have not been having much in the way of "entertainment" besides going to a few movies. I just can't seem to get up any enthusiasm for the theatre here, and spend most of my off-time wandering distractedly around the city, or with these literary people, whose tastes are necessarily inexpensive, and who are fairly pleasant company. Allen Tate's ex-mistress is living in the hotel here, getting ready to go to England for the summer. She is absolutely the plainest woman I have ever seen: the old-maid school teacher come to unattractive life. I can't see how Allen could even get . . . oh well, I'd better not start talking dirty until I get home. Anyway she is fairly nice. She took Tambimuttu, the Hindu mystical snake-charmer and poetry editor, and me to dinner last night. I had <u>escargots</u> and all the good things we used to have in France. I thought it was very nice of Allen Tate's ex-mistress. Don't you think so? She is about forty, and looks like the side of a fence, sort of weathered and uninteresting.

There is not much else I can think of to say. This is probably the last letter I'll get to write from this burning room. I sure will be glad to pull out, you can well believe. But the point is that we've won the battle here, against every kind of odds. And we'll celebrate the new life in earnest when I get there. Make another pot of vichyssoise. I sure do like that stuff, as you may know. I buy it everywhere in New York, but it doesn't compare with yours, Miss Chubby of 1956.

Take care of you and Chris. I'll wire you the flight number when I find it out. And <u>that'll</u> be the day!

Love,
Jim

P.S. Tell Thad when I'm coming.

TO: BEN BELITT[18]

RTLS, 1 p; University of South Carolina

4 December, 1956
Atlanta, Ga.

Dear Ben Belitt,

I have your kind note, in answer to <u>my</u> note. Thank you very much for responding so promptly. I hope you will forgive, again, this imposition upon your time, but your letter aroused so many things I couldn't talk about to anyone but you, that I thought I should damn well go ahead and talk about them.

First of all, since you mention Randall Jarrell, whose review of WS[19] I read and agree with you on, was the subject of a long and "exhaustive" (and exhaus<u>ting</u>) article I wrote in last summer's <u>Sewanee</u>. Though I did not specifically intend it so, the review turned into an attack, and went on for pages and pages about the fellow's verse, which is essentially sentimental and bad. I tried to tack on a kind of being-fair-about-thing at the end, but my heart wasn't really in it, as you can see when you read it. In New York, where I worked for a time, disguised as a "business man," most of the literary people I ran into seemed to agree tacitly that it <u>was</u> an attack, and a few of them even congratulated me. One fellow even told me that in his opinion I had "out-Jarrelled Jarrell," which I don't yet know quite how to take, but may resolve some day. At any rate, <u>do</u> read it, if you haven't already, and tell me what you think.

As you know, I like your work very much. There is a tone of discouragement about your speaking of it, however. I shouldn't leap in with all kinds of remedies and advice and comments of all kinds, but your assuming that "all that was left of Wilderness Stair was the snicker of Randall Jarrell" disturbed me a great deal: made me want to draw the sword from the stone and go after the guy again. If I am any judge, the poems in Wilderness Stair will be read for a long time after those of Jarrell and his sycophants, as well as those of the genteel "garden-poets" like W. S. Merwin[20] and Richard Wilbur and the rest of the well-schooled young gentlemen and ladies, are all forgotten as they deserve to be. It seems to me that your poems have the virtue of taking chances, and certainly they come out of a very rich and very interesting unconsciousness. They have marked affinities with modern European poetry, of which I approve much more readily than I do English and American. If I can judge, your translations of Lorca have been wonderful for your own work, and I suspect that you have read a great many contemporary French poets, in addition to Rimbaud (your translations of whom I also looked up, and like). Let me urge you to keep your "impacted style" and let the critics worry about what "obscurity" they find in you. That style, and the judgment and placing of words, is the thing I find so good in your work.

Again, forgive. I work in a terribly deadening business, and hit whatever licks I can at my own writings, when exhausted, or drinking, or belligerent. It is wonderful for me to see someone like you turning out such a high level of poems I approve of.

If you want to see my work, there is a fairly long one[21] in the current (December) poetry.

Sincerely,
Jim Dickey

2930 Westminster Circle, N.W.
Atlanta, Ga.

TO: DONALD HALL[22]

TLS, 1 p; University of New Hampshire

2 April, 1957
Atlanta, Ga.

Dear Donald Hall,

I have your letter, for which much thanks. I have also heard from Geoffrey Hill,[23] and he has sent me some poems. I want to check with you and see what (of his) you have sent where, for there would not be much point in my submitting poems which have already been turned down, or (in the case of Poetry: Chicago) accepted. Hill has sent me these poems: "The Distant Fury of Battle," "Asmodeus," "Picture of a Nativity," "The White Ship," "The Scapegoat," and "Drake's Drum." You say you have tried some of his with the Partisan and Hudson. Were any of these among them? How about the ones you submitted to Poetry? Aside from those magazines, my chief contacts are with the Kenyon, the Sewanee, and the Yale reviews. I thought, if you have not already done so, I would try the <u>Sewanee Review</u> with "The Distant Fury of Battle," "Asmodeus," "The White Ship," and possibly "Picture of a Nativity," since these seem to me to be the best of the ones I have. I shall wait for your clearance before sending them, however, to avoid possible duplication.

I think Hill is a sure winner, and I am sorry to hear him sound so discouraged over his rejections (this from the letter of him I have). He is one of the few English-speaking poets I have read recently who have any imaginative daring. This is shown rather better in the "Genesis" poems than in those he sent me, but there is a good deal of it in these poems, too. I am glad you like Thom Gunn[24] personally, which undoubtedly I should too, if I knew him, and that you defend his work against the likes of me. I still don't think he's much good, being much too tenuous and propositional and generality-forming and stiffly proper, and totally without the <u>feel</u> of significant experience on any of his stuff. This is somewhat the case, too, with Richard Wilbur, whom you have made the best of all possible cases for (a better one, really, than he deserves), and James Merrill, that chocolate-frosting of a poet, and Anthony Hecht, with his tiresome and empty "elegance," and William Merwin, a prettified interior decorator with no subject and perfect manners and plenty of time to write. I'm sorry, here, to shovel so much earth (which, of course, you don't really think I've succeeded in doing) onto writers you have defended, expounded, praised, and promoted.[25] I don't include your own work among theirs, and like what of it I have seen.

In answer to your questions about English poets, I know Larkin's[26] work, and like it. I don't much like Tomlinson,[27] but feel he is genuine, though rather cold and finicking.

M^cCANN · ERICKSON, INC.	*50 Rockefeller Plaza* *New York 20, N. Y.*	*Radio-* *Television*

script title:	PARTYTIME	*client:* THE COCA-COLA COMPANY
code number:	TX 42 or 44, CUT 2	*product:* 10-OZ KING SIZE _ COMP
length:	1 MINUTE (CK-AM 7-92 K	*program:* AM - RECORDED & LIVE
typed:	1/12/57a COKE #183	*air date:*

RECORDING: 20-SECOND ET: "PARTYTIME" - TX 42 or 44, CUT 2

GROUP:　　Partytime's a good time for the good taste of Coke!
(SINGS)
　　　　　　Partytime's a good time for the good taste of Coke!

　　　　　　Coca-Cola starts the fun,

　　　　　　With a bright little lift for everyone!

　　　　　　Partytime's a good time for the good taste of Coke!

SOUND:　　MUSIC UNDER LIVE ANNCR

ANNCR:　　Parties are more fun when there's ice-cold Coca-Cola on hand.
(LIVE-
35-SEC.)　Because Coke is the best-loved sparkling drink in all the

　　　　　　world! So good in taste ... in such good taste. For extra

　　　　　　convenience, Coca-Cola now comes in the new, big King Size

　　　　　　bottle! It's perfect refreshment for a king-sized thirst!

　　　　　　Yes, there's lots of Coca-Cola in the big King Size bottle.

　　　　　　So for a great new buy in quality refreshment, bring home

　　　　　　cartons of Coca-Cola in big King Size, too! Always serve

　　　　　　ice-cold Coca-Cola - sign of good taste!

RECORDING: 5-SECOND ET ENDING:

GROUP:　　Partytime's a good time for the good taste of Coke!
(SINGS)

An example of Dickey's work on the Coca-Cola account

But that Geoffrey Hill!

It was good to hear from you at a little length, and you must forgive me for leaping into the breach and spouting my unstable opinions at you from all over the place. There is not much chance I get to do such, however, and I must take my chances when they come, at risk of abusing them, and the patience of those, who, like yourself, give me the opportunity.

I inclose an example of my latest "work."[28] Note the subtle play of plosives and double vowels in the opening "invocation."

Yours,
<u>Jim Dickey</u>

2930 Westminster Circle, N.W.
Atlanta, Ga.

TO: BEN BELITT

TLS, 1 p; University of South Carolina

22 April, 1957
Atlanta, Ga.

Dear Ben,

Pardon my not having written in so long, but the form of Usual Life has been so pressing and close-grained during that time I just have not had a chance. I have begun to write (poetry) in a real fever, and am kept at it night and day, and have been so for weeks. Some good things are coming of it, I think, and a book, too. The <u>Partisan Review</u> people (I may already have told you this) want the book for their house-organ, Criterion Books, and the editor, who is a brother of William Phillips,[29] has been and is being very kind to me. I have promised him the manuscript by Fall, and am breaking all canons and standards of Time to try to give it to him then. This necessitates writing five or six more poems, some of them of fairish length, and with my working-habits, and Advertising, the Abomination of Man, breathing down my neck from minute to minute, things get pretty interesting and frustrating.[30]

I finished the review for <u>Sewanee</u>,[31] but found I could not display you to your best advantage therein, and so have decided to write a separate piece on your work and get Rago to print it, if he will. Failing that, I shall write the next review around a comparison of your work and some (inferior) other, which I was not able to do in this one, there being around twenty other poets all demanding various kinds of attention. Sorry I promised and couldn't deliver, but I am like the tiger waiting my best chance to spring, and I don't want to waste it on a Rabbit or Turtle.

Your reports from the Freudian Underworld (I don't mean to joke about this) are fascinating. Don't worry about bringing your worries to me, for I understand (I think) most or at least something of what you must be going through, and sympathize with all the heart and body, as well as the brain. I am the twentieth century Laocoön, myself, and would drive any psychiatrist mad, as an uncle of mine was said to have got his assigned "friend" from Alcoholics Anonymous back on the bottle again. You sound more cheerful than I can imagine anyone ungoing your situation could, and I will read that as a good sign until I am told differently.

As things now stand, I am not, unfortunately, coming to New York any time soon, though I had been told I was. This is distressing, for I thought you and I could get together and talk about some of the things I encounter only through reading. There is a vast difference in the two approaches. To get one of your letters or to go back and read through your poems, in the midst of this mélée of junky writing and contemptible thinking, is. . . . is . . . well, as Cummings might say . . . just is. You are mighty good for me, Ben Belitt, and must certainly be a good man, as well as the poet you are.

A good many things are coming out, of mine. I have a little closer reading on when, though, and you might like to have the dates. There is a longish poem of mine in the current Partisan (Spring).[32] A very long one in the May Poetry.[33] A fairly long one in the summer Beloit Poetry Journal (Frost Chapbook)."[34] The long review in the summer Sewanee.[35] A long poem in the Fall Sewanee,[36] and another in the fall Hudson.[37] There is a short one (one is short) scheduled for next spring's Yale,[38] and several more for the Kenyon, god knows when.

Ah, but the best ones are in the typewriter. I am doing one for Howard Moss of the New Yorker,[39] and another for the Partisan[40] which should be the best of all. I hope so, anyway.

Well, enough boasting. (I don't mean it that way, really.)

Let me hear from you at some length whenever you have a chance, Ben. Do get better, and don't worry. You draw from the head of the Sphinx, every time you sit down with pencil and paper. Would that I did. There are no secrets, even Of the Ages, that are hidden from the talented man who writes.

Jim

TO: WILLIAM PRATT

TLS, 2 pp; William Pratt

7 May, 1957
Atlanta, Ga.

Dear Bill,

I was, as we say in advertising, "surprised and delighted" to get your letter. It raises so many interesting points, the kind I never get to talk to anybody about, that I had not better get, <u>really</u>, into any of them, else I should never get any advertising work done. No, nor poetry, either. Just let me say that I am supremely flattered (this word implies that there was ever "flattery," which is not what I intend) at all the nice things you say about me. I am far from worthy of any of them (<u>this</u> time, by Heavens, it is not <u>false</u> modesty!), though perhaps, in Heaven, we will be judged by Intention, too. And then I may have a chance. I am delighted also by the news of your job. It seems a good one, which is certainly lucky, though the deserving don't usually get much luck. That, however, is not why <u>I</u> was not able to get a good job teaching, and had to turn to the cruel world of Capital to make out. I was, I guess, a good teacher, but my main fault seemed to lie not in my relations with the students, which always seemed and I hope were good, but in my dealings with my colleagues. I imagine you have been around enough English departments to know more or less what to expect of the normal run of Ph.D's, but there is nothing like the full glory and horror of feeling yourself, as they say, "really a part of it," "it" in this case being as good a word as any to designate an ordinary Department of English. One always has the dwindling suspicion and hope that one can really "do something about it": get things (students and teachers) off their rear end, and heading in the direction of things that matter. And you <u>can</u> do enough of this to make teaching a vastly exciting and profitable venture. But there is no chance of moving the vast and sluggish mass of the academic mind, or rendering any permanent good except to individuals. I suppose, now that I think of it, that that is what the whole thing is about, anyway. You will make a splendid teacher, Bill. You have the two absolutely necessary requisites: you love the subjects you are talking about, and you remember how it was when <u>you</u> were trying to learn. This last is perhaps the more important, because it enables you to be the kind of teacher that you, and I, and all the others would have <u>liked</u> to have had, and never had. This is a definite ideal, and I am certain that you will fulfill it far better than I, who am naturally short-tempered and inclined <u>not</u> to suffer fools gladly, could ever have.

"Business as usual" is, well, business as usual. I find myself in a really key position with "The Coca-Cola Operation," and I can tell you right now it is a strange feeling. Big business is more like a war than anything else you can imagine. It is, for instance, a far-more seriously-fought war than athletics. The strategy covers years, and a company will plan damned near to bankrupt itself to put another one out of business, even if it takes thirty or forty years. Viz. "Gentlemen, our children will live to see the day when there won't be a Pepsi-Cola vending machine in the city of New York." And if you don't think that's a consummation devoutly to be wished, you have never worked in advertising! It is all done with the tacit assumption that this is O.K., rough on some people, maybe, but still and all the American way, and God-a-mighty, look what we've got! Rot-o-boils (or broils, I forget which), Waring Blenders, and the rest of the strange assortment of gadgets which have as an essential feature of themselves that they shall come to seem absolutely necessary, and thus, to the unhappy people who use them, the be-all and end-all of existence. There is no point in going on and on. You know all this as well as or better than I do. But you are not aiding and abetting it. I am. The pay-check is really not enough compensation; thus the Idealist in a quandary. What you are supposed to do, I reckon, is do their work for money and do your work for. . . . oh . . . what? Yourself? Yes, essentially. You have never worked in advertising, or you would know what immense proportions your own work (poetry) can assume when it is fastened-to as the symbol of your soul.

The single consolation I have, aside from my family, a great deal of tennis on the week-ends, and good letters like yours, is that my own work is going pretty well. Since you ask about publications, I might do well to give you the line-up, "so you won't miss anything." Last November there was a review of mine in Poetry which drew a barrage of senile fire from Rolfe Humphries, since I had said some uncomplimentary things about a protégé (read "disciple") of his, Charlie Bell. His "attack" is printed in the March Poetry, and my "counter-attack," which has maybe a little too much condescension in it, but answers his objections pretty well, I think.[41] There is another long poem in the December Poetry,[42] and another, very long one in the current (May) Poetry.[43] For these two I am supposed to get a "Prize,"[44] which I hope is indeed forthcoming in the fall. In the Spring Partisan is another longish one called "The Swimmer," which I wrote during my last days in Paris, and in the Café de Flore, too! Jean-Paul Sartre was there, a few tables away! There is a long review in the Summer Sewanee, in which I review one of Rolfe Humphries' books. Too bad it was a good book, but I was forced to say so, or feel like a criminal.[45] There is a Frost Chap-book the Beloit Poetry Journal is putting out this summer. I contributed another longish one they say they like.[46] There is the longest one I have yet written, in the summer or fall Sewanee Review,[47] and another good-size one in the Fall Hudson Review.[48] The New Yorker is printing one, though I don't know when. The Yale Review is bringing out a short one in the summer issue (I do write short ones, though I hate to!)[49] The Kenyon Review has just taken one, too, called "Standing With the Rope."[50] And so it goes. There are twenty or thirty in the works including three I think will be the best I have done (although one always feels this: one couldn't

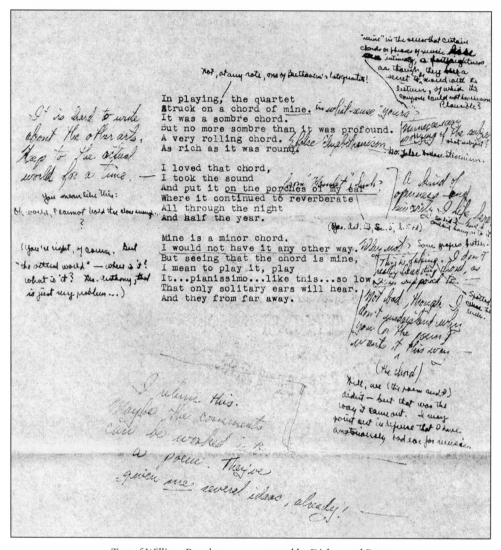

Text of William Pratt's poem annotated by Dickey and Pratt

work <u>without</u> feeling it): "To Be Dead On Earth," "The Exstasie," and "Patience: in the Mill."[51] I'll send them to you when they're done. I Have High Hopes, Great Plans, and the rest of it, for these, and I shall work like hell (although sometimes this is bad) to make them as good as they should be. When they are done, the <u>Partisan Review</u> people (Rahv and Phillips)[52] are going to bring out a book under the imprint of their house-organ, Criterion Books. I hope all goes well. I am to try to have the manuscript to them by November 15<u>th</u>. If by some chance they don't take it, Grove has asked for it,[53] so it looks like there will be a book, one way or another.

I am glad to hear our friend at St. Elizabeth's is doing well. It is hard to see what there is about Frankenberg's work he likes.[54] He was considered a promising poet ten or twelve years ago. He has one book dating from that time, "The Red Kite," which I remember as being fairly good. Since then he has been making anthologies. "Pleasure Dome" was one of his, and one other, more recent, with a title like "Invitation to Poetry," or something equally horrible. He is a very nice fellow. I knew him slightly in New York. He is married to Loren McIver, the painter, and lives the life of a typical youngish New York <u>literatus</u>.

We have a fine house here, and "ample accomodations," and we would love seeing you and the whole family whenever you can get down. Maxine is coming to Nashville in two weeks or so, but I shall be left behind. Do try to take a <u>little</u> time (you teachers have so <u>much</u>) to come see us.

I liked the little poem of yours. Keep writing! Keep sending me stuff. And cut loose on it! Nobody cares if you're wild! Try some free-association, à la André Breton. You'll be surprised what you'll dredge up!

Don't wait so <u>long</u> to write!

Yours, Jim

2930 Westminster Circle, N.W.
Atlanta, Ga.

TO: BEN BELITT

TLS, 2 pp; University of South Carolina

11 May, 1957
Atlanta, Ga.

Dear Ben,

I am sorry I let so much time slip by without writing you; there are many "excuses" I might use, but they are all beside the point. I am trying to make up for this by getting the letter off right <u>now</u>, in hopes it will reach you at your Bronx address before you set out for Yaddo.

A really terrible thing has happened here. The presiding spirits of the Coca-Cola company, and those of the Agency I work for (McCann-Erickson) have come in to talk to me "seriously" about my future. They tell me they consider me the best of the Coke "creative people" (the words "creative" and "art" are used with a certain latitude in the agency business, as you may know). What they want, actually, is a total commitment to them; that is, I must "eat, sleep, and breathe advertising," which is their striking originally way of saying I must give up my own work. They say, also, that "the rewards will be great." They want to bring me in to "the planning stage" of advertising for Coke, which means that in the not very distant future I must come to live in New York. None of this suits me, and I am at a loss to know what to do about it. I have no more intention of giving up my work than I have of flying to the moon on my own embryonic wings, and I told them so. Strangely, this did not displease them as much as you might expect. They said merely that it would "reduce my efficiency," which is certainly true. They were mildly amused by my counter, which they would not allow themselves to take other than as a pleasantry, that advertising seriously "reduces my efficiency" as a poet. So I must look for something else to do, privately and quietly, so that I can be prepared to get the hell out of this farcical business when a choice is forced on me. I have lived on my wits all my life, however, and I am sure I can make five or six hundred dollars a month, even if I have to go back to being a fisherman, which I once was.[55] I am strangely happy about "the crisis," though my wife is somewhat apprehensive. As long as my own work is going well, which it is, reasonably, I can fight the rest of the world off with the other hand.

It is wrong of me to unload all this on you, I realize, but there is really no one I know I can tell the <u>real</u> truth to.

I hope you know how much I appreciate your offer to put in a word for me with the Grove people, whom I esteem very highly. I don't anticipate being turned down by Rahv and the others, since the book was all their idea in the first place, but there is always a possibility that I will be, and in that case I shall certainly want to take you up on your very kind offer.

I believe, as though I were a child, a grown child with a family, in the relations between people. In the inhuman world of commerce, there is less than none of this that can be called "real." It is a wonderful relief to be able, even writing it on the typewriter, to be able to say to another human being, who is not trying to "use" you, "Yes, I love that poem. It means a great deal to me. I like so-and-so's last book. I believe in ____ as an artist."

Yes; it is something of a shock to me, too, to think I have never laid eyes on you in my life; no, not even a picture. You are known to me only by words on bits of paper. But it is as good a proof of the validity of poetry as I know, that I feel I have come to know a distinct personality, whom I call "Ben Belitt," through the marvelously imaginative poems of someone who actually has that name. (By the way, <u>could</u> you send me a picture?)

It is great to know you are getting better, and feeling better in yourself. Now you will be able to get on with your work, and touch off some more rockets like <u>Andaluz</u>.[56]

My own stuff is going well, but slowly, as always. Moss wants some stuff for the <u>New Yorker</u>, and I am trying to finish one for him. It has, tentatively, the refrain

> In a movement you cannot imagine
> Of air, the gulls fall, sailing.[57]

Yesterday I got "Standing With the Rope" off to Ransom,[58] since he asked me for something a good while ago.

"The First Morning of Cancer" is out, in the May <u>Poetry</u>.

Write soon, and take care of yourself.

How beautiful life is. Or, as Fargue says someplace, "Life is not good, but it is beautiful."

Yours,
Jim

2930 Westminster Circle, N.W.
Atlanta, Ga.

TO: WILLIAM PRATT

TLS, 1 p; William Pratt

27 May, 1957
Atlanta, Ga.

Dear Bill,

It is good to have your letter (and so shortly after <u>my</u> letter, too!), and I am making as much haste as I can to answer it, though certainly I can't match the Bobby Morrow-like speed with which <u>you</u> got off the mark last time.

Things are the same here. Slow plugging-away at poems. Correspondence with publisher. Correspondence with editors (If we may call this to your attention, Mr. Dickey, "cat" is generally spelled with a lower-case "c" as the first letter, followed in order by "a" and "t". If we may have your concurrence on the type change in your manuscript, we shall have the poem set up immediately. Sincerely yours). I have all but three or four of the poems for the book. Maxine is laboriously typing the manuscript, which we hope to have in to Sid Phillips by the fifteenth of November, God willing. Grove Press has also asked for it, so we have a backstop if Sid and his Partisan Reviewers don't come through for us.

The rest is work for the advertising profession, for a living, for Coca-Cola, and for the American Way of Life. This last is a perfect example of Good Coming from Evil, for Business is the death of the spirit, the death of every good impulse, the death of time, and the death of life. Yet, yet. . . . there is money in it! And that means I can support my family, raise Chris half-way decently, and take care of any and all succeeding off-spring, for before the time of arrival, on. And that is much. Only, I have to live like a schizophrenic, bowing and scraping before the Powers, and being the friendly young business man with good ideas, though with vague bohemian (that is to say, "literary") leanings, and, at night and early in the morning, the poet himself, in T-shirt and Bermuda shorts, payed-for in blood money and the slaughter of useful ideals, putting desperately down The Truth, and discovering in publication after publication that it is only groping, after all. But I am getting near something! And sometimes very near. I can hear it breathe at night, and it says words. And working them out is a terrific excitement. I have so many new poems I can't tell where one leaves off and another begins. There is much to do, and I can already feel the darkness begin to fall, maybe fifty years away. Wherein no man may work. And there is so much to do. So much. And to live, too. That is important. And to see Europe again, before they (or They) blow it up, this time for good. One way or another, I work as if my time is not long.

Maxine and Chris are coming to Nashville in a week, though, sadly, I am not. You still must manage your trip down here. I would certainly welcome seeing someone who is not paid-for, who is not for sale. Who is named Bill Pratt.

I'm sorry I don't have time to make a long letter, a really long letter, out of this, but I must get out a few more Commercials before closing time, and barely have time to do it.

Write and tell me all you are doing and thinking.

Love to your wife, and to Cullen.

Jim

2930 Westminster Circle, N.W.
Atlanta, Ga.

TO: EZRA POUND

TSL, 1 p; Yale

5 June, 1957
Atlanta, Ga.

Dear Uncle,

Good news to hear from you. I will write the Edge people[59] and see what they have.

I don't know whether I told you, but I am out of teaching. Had bad luck there and a passel of "Pen Women" got me booted. I am now making a living by half-successfully disguising myself as a "business man", coming down town to work in an office from nine to five each day, and banging away at lunch hour and evenings at poems and a few reviews. Partisan Review people say they will bring out a book for me if I can finish a manuscript by Nov. 15th, and I tell myself I am working toward that, though it goes very slowly.

Have a good letter from Bunting, though he sounds discouraged and says he cannot write because of the work he has to do. He says there is no more of his work besides the Galveston volume you sent and a long poem a few years ago in Poetry. It is hard to think that he thinks there will be no more. Can you prevail on him to get going on some new stuff? I would like to, but since I don't know him, can't, really.

Rock-drill good.[60] I think the image about the water-spider (or whatever) and the flower of shadow on rock is the best single image in Cantos.[61] Would not want to stand off Kenner[62] and others on this, but will hold to opinion anyway.

Nothing "cultural" here. Have a house where I can put books. Should like to read up on monetary reform.[63] Can you recommend? I know nothing about money except that it is hard to come by, but not so hard as when teaching gave it.

Heard from W. Pratt. He tells me you say good things about Lloyd Franken-berg's poems. Have F's "Red Kite." The stuff is good, but strikes me as more or less usual. Has Pratt got the name right?

Good, again, to hear from you. Let me know what you need, and wife and I will try to supply.

My best to Mrs. Pound. Thank her (belatedly) for sending me the Angold.[64] I had not known him. Some very good clumsyish poems.

Can't find anything of René Crevel.[65]

Yours,
Jim Dickey

2930 Westminster Circle, N.W.
Atlanta, Ga.

TO: JOHN BERRYMAN

TLS, 1 p; University of Minnesota

8 July, 1957
Atlanta, Ga.

Dear John Berryman,

Thank you very much for your letter of the 26<u>th</u>. I had no idea you would answer, much less provide me with so much information about Campbell[66] (and not <u>just</u> information, either). I am glad to know these things about him, and would like very much to look at the photographs you mention, if it would not be too much trouble to you to send them. I know you are pressed for time, however (indeed, you may already be on your way to Bombay by now, for all I know).[67] Just let me say that I appreciate your offer to supply me with the photographs, even if you don't get an opportunity to send them.

I would like very much to write several pages on Campbell's work, and try to determine which of his poems are the more valuable, but that would necessitate my spending more time writing, and your spending more time reading, than either of us has, at present. I am not sure whether you ever completely "got him out from under Auden" or not, but I am quite sure that the presence of Auden bothers me very little in Campbell's work. This is odd, since I don't much like Auden, and I like Campbell tremendously. Unless you are a professional critic, however, and have to hold yourself rigorously to account for your opinions (because the public will), you can dismiss the contradictions in your own judgments and simply resort to your feelings about the poems, regardless of influences, history, "tradition," and the rest. Where you first met Campbell "in New York, at the other end of the George Washington Bridge," I first met him on the remainder counter of a department store in Waco, Texas, where I was in the Air Force for the second time, and just back from Korea.[68] I picked up the book and read the introduction, and was struck by a statement Rosten quotes, wherein Campbell says he wants to "read all the books of criticism, rebore the block, and get ready to run steadily for five years" (I can't quote this exactly, since I am writing as hurriedly as possible on the office type-writer). The attitude struck me as very much like my own at the time, since I was happy that I was going to live for a while, had just had a son, and was beginning to believe I might write a kind of verse myself. I bought the book and took it home, and have since reread it so many times it is falling apart. I have a feeling I would have liked Campbell tremendously, as you so obviously did. It is not always true that the best of a man is in his poems, though perhaps the most enduring part is. Words can do a great deal that experience cannot do, and that is why we have poetry to try to do it with.

But they cannot give you the other human being, in the air from the river under a bridge, or dying, as, actually, he dies. It is very good of you to give to me out of your personal and essential memory of a man who has evidently meant a great deal to you (this is a necessary understatement). Again, let me repeat my thanks, and yet again, for your offer to send along the photographs.

Good luck, good sailing, and good reading (of "The People & Their Parks")[69] around India.

Let me know if there is any way I can help you, or anything I can send.

Sincerely,

James Dickey

2930 Westminster Circle, N.W.
Atlanta, Ga.

TO: DONALD HALL

TLS, 2 pp; University of New Hampshire

29 July, 1957
Atlanta, Ga.

Dear Don(ald) Hall,

I have your letter, for which much thanks. Since I am now "On vacation", as we say in the business world, I have a chance to leap wildly into the breach and answer like a shot, instead of waiting around till I could get a moment at the office.

You are right, I have forgotten what you are arguing with me about. I imagine I meant that the generalizing done in whatever poems I was talking about did not seem to me to be <u>earned</u>. This is of course a purely subjective interpretation, but of such is the kingdom of (individual) judgment. I don't care one way or the other about Merwin, who you say "Lives by his writing." This is of course is commend-able, if possible, but unlike you I have no wish at all to earn a living by poetry, or by reviewing, or whatever lies between. I don't wish to earn money by working in advertising, either. I would really like to be kept up by some rich woman, but since I have a wife and son, that might result in some embarrassment. Certainly it would present a problem in tactics I for one would not be able to solve. As you say of advertising, "I haven't the talent." The business of the American writer, the poor son of a bitch (excuse this uncouth language), has been rehearsed in so many thousands of articles (I remember reading one of yours that touched on it: How <u>can</u> you talk as if the blarsted university were a <u>good</u> place for him?) I have about given up on there being <u>any</u> solution, save that I suggested earlier for myself. No; we must leave this bookish, prettified poetry out, as history will leave it out, unless it preserves a few fragments to show that the "silent generation" was indeed silent, and should have been more so. I ought to go back to your article and dig up some more stuff to be ungenerous about, but I am afraid I would find there a thing which I hope I have only dreampt. It was something to the effect that we might eventually "have a great age" out of the likes of Wilbur, Merwin, Anthony Hecht, and perhaps some others of that ilk. No, man. There has to be something more than this well-meaning, mannered management of nothing. They ought to call this the "garden school," since it is almost devoid of anything but prettified description, impeccably presented, and absolutely empty of any human life at all. Surely you want more of poetry than this. If all poetry were like this, I would say to hell with it. I don't know what you mean by "storm and stress" poetry; I want a poetry that illuminates my experience. I want a poetry that gives me some of my life, over again; that restores something to me, or creates a need for more life, more feeling; something that gets me closer to the world: that gets me <u>inside</u> the world, in a new way, or in a way older than the world. Don't attribute these things to this cosmetic crap our academy boys turn out. Hold out for something good. Really good. Ted Roethke[70] has some of it. So does Richard Eberhart.[71] So does Geoffrey Hill. So do you, in what little of yours I have read.

What do you mean, you "like the new poetry better than the old"? Geoffrey Hill's new poetry? Inflation is <u>whose</u> enemy?

Yes, I have taught: at Vanderbilt, where I went to school, as a football "fellow," and then as a god-damned graduate student and teaching assistant. I taught at Rice, in Houston, and for a year I was Andrew Lytle's assistant at the University of Florida, in "The Creative Writing Program." I was booted from Florida for a controversial talk I made to a group of spiritual thieves called the "Pen Women's Society" or something to that effect. You can read the offending poem in last December's <u>Poetry</u>, if you like. I am more or less black-listed in teaching, and perhaps it's as well. I worked as a professional fisherman for a while, and coached track at a small college, and as groundskeeper worked in the mornings, before the boys got out of class.[72]

You are really very kind to want to see some of my "<u>Spare</u>-time writing." I am trying to finish the book for the Partisan people (Criterion Books), but my God it is going slowly. I have a great deal of luck to finish two or three poems a year. I haven't anything new at the moment, except a short poem out of the war. I have sent it to Botteghe Oscure, and to the Virginia Quarterly, who asked me for something (by the way, what <u>is</u> the rule about publishing things in two or three places?) If you still want to see the poem, or want to take it after (of if, perhaps I should say, as if knocking on wood) the others turn it down, I will send it along to you. I think it is a good poem, but my judgment is not posterity's, though yours, as an editor's, may be.[73]

I am still waiting to get together with Monroe Spears at the <u>Sewanee</u> to air Geoffrey's poems. I don't think it will be long.

In the meantime, if you want to look at things already published there are a good many floating around in the quarterlies currently. Let me know if you want them listed, and I will hunt around and try to find them all. (This should be in the second paragraph above. You must realize that I know this).

Yes, do write. And write soon, otherwise I shall think you are offended, which is the last thing I want. It is good to hear a voice off the paper, and I like yours. You must let me abuse you, and give you a hard time, for really I would not, except that you stand up to it so well. You always get the best of the arguments, in a few words (write <u>longer</u> letters!) It is good to know you are alive, and writing, and that you love writing. Who are you, anyway? What do you look like? Send me a picture. I am a tall blond tennis-looking man, still in pretty good shape. I still think I could fight three or four pretty fair rounds, though not ten. (My Lord, did you see Floyd Patterson slaughter Hurricane Jackson the other night?)

Glad you bought the Coke. At last, a letter from a "satisfied consumer!"

Yours,

Jim Dickey

2930 Westminster Circle, N.W.
Atlanta, Ga.

Ezra Pound has written about some of my poems in magazines,[74] but I can't tell whether he's for 'em or agin 'em.

TO: PHILIP BOOTH[75]

TLS, 2 pp; Dartmouth College

5 July, 1958
Atlanta, Ga.

Dear Philip Booth,

I have your letter, which was opened by mistake at the <u>Sewanee</u> and then sent on to me. Even so, I have had it for well over a month without answering, for which I hope you will forgive me.

Spurred on by your letter, I read <u>Letter From a Distant Land</u> again, and, though I found some things (like "The Lost Boy") I liked, I cannot for the life of me change my opinion of the book.[76] I paid special attention to "Barred Islands," keeping your patient and thorough gloss of the poem before me, but it is not really a good poem, despite everything. (By the way, is the term "barred islands" universally used to describe islands connected by sand-bars? Or is it used only by you?) The notion that the lovers, as you say, "discover what they hoped to find: that what is apparently separate is joined beneath the mere surface of their experience" simply because they see a sand-bar connecting two islands strikes me as one of those thought-out, approved-of, Brooks-and-Warren types of poetic conventions which has less than nothing at all to do with real human experience. Again, wouldn't the floor of the sea itself, as it "connects" the islands, and indeed all things, make your point better, if it is worth making? And look at the beginning: "Between their sandspit ends / we rowed, two spruce islands / moored in a blue Maine bay." Here the reader, before he corrects your syntax, is likely to take "we" as meaning "spruce islands," which is quite obviously not what you want (though I admit that, for me, it opens up some interesting possibilities). I don't mean to go on and on, primly and self-righteously, about a poem that is not as good as some others you have done. I wish merely to indicate that I could have been a good deal harder on the poem (though for other reasons, perhaps, than I stated in the review). If the reasons I gave in the Sewanee seem to you to take unfair advantage of your writing, I must ask you to forgive me, though certainly it is your privilege not to.

You ask me to explain how and where "good poems are good, and bad go wrong." It would take more time and effort than I now have at my disposal even to make a fairly adequate beginning. I think that the essential difference between your writing and someone like Graham's[77] is that he has felt the necessity (I hope from some inner compulsion) to construct, think up, think out, half-perfect, experiment with, fight for, fight with, overcome, come upon, or otherwise discover a kind of way of writing we would not have had unless he had done all this searching and fighting. The fruits of all this are apparent in a poem like "The Nightfishing,"[78] which I should like you to compare (for all the poetic reasons, including the undefinable one of poetic "reality") with your own poems about the sea and the sea-coast.

I should like to keep on writing this, for I don't get much chance to talk about poetry, but I must sign off here. If you like to argue poetry by mail, or even if you don't, write me again. I don't know any poets, since I am not in teaching or any of the approved professions for "poets and intellectuals," and have to spin all details about poetry and other important matters out of my own insides, sitting in a corner. Both the office and my home are now deep in webs.

Thank you again for your letter.
Yours,
Jim Dickey

2930 Westminster Circle, N.W.
Atlanta, Ga.

TO: PHILIP BOOTH

TLS, 2 pp; Dartmouth College

18 July, 1958
Atlanta, Ga.

Dear Philip Booth,

Many thanks for your letter of July 8th. I am very glad to have it; you sound a good deal more like a human being (although still somewhat angry at my "bad reading" of your poem), and I am happy to know something about you personally, for I like, if possible, to have some sense of the physical presence of the people to whom I write. Do you really look like the tall, mild, good-hearted fellow on the jacket of your book, absent-mindedly staying a shaggy dog with your hands, and looking across some Maine water at "barred islands" or whatever is out there? (Do not defend that poem any more. A defense of bad writing is the worst sign there is of artistic incompetence. I am now on your side, but I will have to be on it on my own terms, and can't be argued into it. I am looking for you to write some poems that please me, and that do so because they please yourself: really please you). I don't mean to be so pontifical (is this a word?) and god-like in my perfect knowledge of what your business as a poet ought to be, but (as I said somewhere else in the review) the thing our generation needs to be doing is moving somewhere or other, in some direction that is right for us as individual poets. If a poet gathers lovingly about him the things he's been taught in school and shows no inclination to use those lessons merely as stepping-stones toward his own kind of expression, why, then, gentlemen, I shoot him. And he ought to be shot. Nemerov[79] (to whom you refer me) seems to feel pretty much the same way about your work. The thing you must do (again I pontificate madly, and, certainly, maddeningly) is search, define, dare, experiment, do lots of different kinds of things. The trouble with this, is, of course, that your publications will be cut 'way down, and perhaps cut out altogether for a year or two. Being in the academic profession, this could act on your status as a teacher "without the calling-card degree" in a decidedly unfavorable way, and certainly must give you pause, in any event. (Please excuse the dangling participle, here). I was a teacher myself, and for a time was Andrew Lytle's assistant in the "Creative Writing Workshop" at the University of Florida. The guardians were always telling me to publish, publish, publish: either that, or go out and get a PH.D like an honest man. This attitude, coupled with some violent trouble I got in down there, ultimately prompted me to wrap my soul in gray flannel and sell it to the highest-paying flesh-merchant in Madison Avenue. Everybody threw up his hands, and said, there goes another poet (or something), selling out. He'll never write another line. But being in the business world has driven me back with a rather frightening fanaticism on poetry. I don't have to please anyone but myself with what I say in it or about it, and manage to do a few long poems and a couple of reviews a year, which is about all I ever did, anyway. Before I forget, there is a new long one of mine in the August <u>Poetry</u>.[80] Read it and tell me what you think. Before I get off the subject, I think I ought to say, in all truth, that I include myself in with you boys, as not yet being very satisfactory as a writer. But I would like to have a great generation of poets out of ours. I think we must try.

As to your questions about poets: I don't know who Snodgrass is, unless he is the W. D. Snodgrass of the anthology I reviewed.[81] Those selections are the only things of his I have read, and they are singularly unimpressive. I should think it difficult (or perhaps fatally easy) to get such doggerel printed. But when you say you are interested in Stanley Kunitz,[82] you interest <u>me</u>. Surely he is one of the two or three best American poets we have, profoundly neglected, and the victim of the queer kind of injustice that sometimes is visited on original writers. Yes, he <u>is</u> abstract often, but at times he is breathtakingly concrete; he is one of the few writers I know who seem to have had any philosophical training that has done them any good. There was a wonderful poem in <u>Botteghe Oscure</u> a few years ago, where he uses Plato to perfection (ever hear of anyone using Plato to perfection?), and talks of "hearing the sound / Of matter pouring through eternal forms."[83] Isn't that terrific? He has a cityish, Kafka-esque, nightmare quality I like, too, and there can be few poets who give you so much the sense of impending evil, and frail, possible good. Are you reviewing the book? If so, send it (the review) me when you finish, for I would like to read what you have to say about him.

Elizabeth Bishop[84] is a poet we have all been told (by Randall Jarrell and Marianne Moore) is good, but really she is not very. She has a carefully cultivated offhandness which charms academics like Jarrell, who are sure that this is the very voice of <u>reality</u>. She describes things in a half-cute, pert, half-serious way that seems to act on reviewers like the voice of the turtle, being heard throughout the land. All this I don't like, and can't say I care much for her.

Lowell[85] is good, but his world is so over-violent it often seems either comical or as though the violence were just being manufactured, and used here, there, and everywhere. He has done a few things well, but he is not nearly so satisfactory a poet as Kunitz. There seems to be nothing possible for Lowell to do, now, and the new poems add nothing to his stature. He seems doomed to be just another example of the brilliant, pampered American poet who spends the rest of his life, after the initial success, trying to progress and keeps falling down and down. This is sad, but it is perfectly true, I think.

I should like to go on and on, but must go, now, and wait with my wife at the hospital for our second child.[86]

If you like, send me some of the new work. I should like very much to see it. I promise to be as severe as ever.

Yours,
Jim Dickey

2930 Westminster Circle, N.W.
Atlanta, Ga.

TO: JAMES WRIGHT[87]

TLS, 1 p; University of Minnesota

19 July, 1958
Atlanta, Ga.

Dear James Wright,

I have your letter, which was forwarded to me here from the Sewanee.

Under the influence of God knows what powerful, self-protective compulsion, you have evidently invented a dreadful, irresponsible, arrogant fellow named James Dickey who thinks of you as a person congenitally unable to tell the truth ("I realize that you will consider this statement a lie." Why will I?), is capable of writing brilliant and important criticism except when he is overborne by something called "hatred" (and except when he is dealing with your work and that of Philip Booth, an almost equally uninteresting poet). Now it ought to be quite obvious that I have no cause to "hate" Philip Booth, or anyone else I write about. I have no reason to doubt your word, or even to care about it, one way or the other. It is true, however, that I dislike seeing a writer thrown into a state of convulsion over three words (including his name) about him in a review,[88] and then taking the first opportunity offered him to get what revenge he can by the perfectly transparent expedient of fastening on his "enemy's" reference to another poet, and seeking to discredit him by a good deal of routine cuteness about "bees and flowers" and the Handbook for Boys, the while never making any recognizable point. If you had submitted your review to me earlier, we might, together, have made something at least tolerably interesting out of it, instead of allowing it to appear as a pathetic exhibition of aggrieved, adolescent whimpering and "strucken" self-righteousness. It is too late, now, though, and I am afraid you will have to go it alone.

As for your letter to me, full of left-handed compliments, self-approval, false humility ("Sometimes students have cautiously and tentatively brought verses to me, . . . etc."), and absurd formulations like: "a good poet, is, I believe, by definition a good man," the less said the better. My God! By <u>what</u> definition? Not by that of literary history, I hope, or reference to real poets. Think, if you will, of Baudelaire, Villon, Dylan Thomas, even. But this is quite useless. If you deduce from this letter that I have no intention whatever of honoring your ridiculous "challenge" you are perfectly correct, and for exactly the reasons you advance.

One thing more: if you ever have occasion to address any further correspondence to me, do me the courtesy of leaving obscenity out. Childish as your references are, they nevertheless constitute a considered insult to me and to my family. As such, they effectively remove you and me from the plane of literary controversy. Such language addressed to the home of a total stranger must be taken either as the doing of a hopeless crank (which I do not believe you are, quite), or of someone who realizes the implications of his actions, and is prepared to be held responsible for them: i.e. to resolve the differences in personal action, rather than in print. If you persist, you have my word that this will be the case.

James Dickey

2930 Westminster Circle, N.W.
Atlanta, Ga.

TO: JAMES WRIGHT

TLS, 1 p; University of Minnesota

23 July, 1958
Atlanta, Ga.

Dear James Wright,

You could not more effectively have disarmed me had you held a gun to my head. <u>Of course</u> I accept your apology, and the tone of your letter strongly suggests to me that I had better do some apologizing myself, lest I be shamed out of existence. I am simply appalled at the dreadful condescending sound of my letter to you. Yet, if it has had the effect of allowing us to get together as human beings, it may eventually be seen to have done some good after all. The difficulty about reviewing books—especially books of poems—is that one may have some hand in destroying not so much poets, but the people who write poems. Nowadays one has to give up so terribly much to write poetry that one is driven back with a very real fanaticism on what one conceives as one's "talent." Let someone deny that it exists, and the poet feels that he is destroyed, since his talent is the thing that he has given up everything else to feed. I know this as bitterly as anyone could. I was a teacher myself (at the University of Florida, as Andrew Lytle's assistant in the

"Creative Writing" Program), and saw my poor family do without everything except the basic essentials. I worried and sweated over poems day and night, and many times felt that if someone should even hint that I had thrown away my life (as well as those of two other innocent people) I would simply not be able to face it. Before I go any further, do, please, let me say that you are entirely too hard on yourself. I have not read your work in its entirety (but intend to), but as far as I can tell, you have a very great deal more ability than you seem to want to allow yourself to think. Your beginning has been a good one. The only point I would make about it is that I think it should be beginning to show a direction. You seem to write very easily (which God knows I do not), and there is a very real danger in facility. You must watch out for the more sentimental and easy kinds of salable sincerity, and for a too-easy solution to poems. I expect you will do well as a poet, and as a teacher, also. Again, before I get off the subject, there is a long poem of mine in the August Poetry.[89] I would consider it a kindness if you would have a look at it and tell me what you think. I ought also to say that I am no more satisfied with my own work than I am with Booth's, Hecht's, Wilbur's, etc. The best I can say about my own efforts is that I am casting around, and that I have come close to what I want a few times. Close, but not really close.

I am sorry I don't have a chance to go on and on, for I very rarely get a chance to talk about poetry. As I look back on my life, it seems that I have been fighting with people to no decision forever. I am thankful (no; grateful) for your letter, your approach to the area we have in common, and for whatever courage (and I believe it to have been high) it took for you to write to me as you have done. If you like, send me some of the new poems. In the interest of literature, I promise to be as ruthless as ever, but not, any longer, in coldness. Please do write again, and let us sit down and talk away the miles between Minneapolis and Atlanta, not as two people who have to be right about poetry at all costs, but as those who simply love it and believe in it.

Yours,
Jim Dickey

2930 Westminster Circle, N.W.
Atlanta, Ga.

TO: JAMES WRIGHT

TLS, 2 pp; University of Minnesota

26 July, 1958
Atlanta, Ga.

Dear Jim Wright,

Please excuse my "leaping into the breach" and banging back at you with a letter so quickly, but I thought, in view of your own generosity in writing to me at such length, that I should try at least <u>once</u> to write a fairly <u>long</u> letter. The others have been banged out at the office, in between handling a thousand details concerning advertising for Coca-Cola, and I have, now, a whole empty Saturday night (at home, that blessed place), in which to talk across several thousand miles, about poetry, to someone I have never met, and, perhaps, will never meet, but whose letters are so intense that I can fairly feel him (or <u>someone</u>) breathing on the back of my neck as I write. Poets are lonely creatures, but they do get a few chances, now and then, to talk about the things that matter to them; because of this devouring need to be understood in their own way, we have many famous volumes of correspondence (among them, that between Jacques Rivière and Alain-Fournier, which I like almost as much as you do the works of Dickens). As for my part in writing long, immortal letters to poets, however, I am afraid that it must begin here. I have always been a little embarrassed by people (a few people) who wrote me about my work, saying that they had seen this poem and that poem in a magazine, and would I help to get them published, for they are sure (yes, <u>sure</u>!) that they could write as well as <u>that</u>, if only they knew a little more about form: "You know, meter, and . . . and . . . how to make it rhyme, and all that stuff." I have always written them decent, well-mannered notes. But this is different. If I have made you "face up to" yourself, you have certainly done no less to me. My situation is not really like yours, though. I have never been in the position of "having just about everything I write accepted for publication." I don't write much, but it is labored-at forever; I don't like to turn loose of anything that doesn't come as close to satisfying me as I can get it. And yet, of all the stuff that I've brought out, <u>none</u> is good. Since I have been publishing since 1951,[90] this is almost ten years of very hard labor for nothing. I have had the usual "honors" and fellowships, and been offered others I couldn't take, but I have never believed in that kind of thing, and go back patiently reading my poems after they are published, finding in their unfashionable sprawl only a kind of conventional groping after the allegorical, and a perfectly amazing clumsiness which is what passes with me for honesty. And yet . . . and yet . . . I can<u>not</u> say that I prefer to it the verse of Richard Wilbur, so perfectly self-assured and so perfectly empty of any ability to move me as a human being, or the stone-cold, pedantic, dry, patient, academic stuff of Yvor Winters[91] (who on earth but Winters would feel the need to write a poem "On the Opening of the William Dinsmore Briggs Room"?), or the poetry of any but a very few other living writers in English. No; we are all bad, except for a few flashes by Berryman, Roethke, Eberhart, Jock Graham[92] in England, and René Char, Alain Borne, Jules Supervielle,[93] St-John Perse[94] and one or two other continental writers. What we must have, Jim Wright, is a poetry that gives us life: some act of the imagination: the live imagination as it leaps instinctively toward its inevitable (and perhaps God-ordained) forms: something that restores our sense of continuity with tragic life, or joyous life, or dying life. Our teachers (mine were Brooks and Warren, in the regular students' edition)[95] have told us, as has Valéry, that in order to communicate (something, like, say, the sense of life), we need to be very particular about form. This is, of course, true, but it is not the whole truth. Once mastered, the formal technique is not only a vehicle for the sense of life, but for any damn thing you want to put in it. Our sense of values has got so twisted round that an intelligent man like RP Blackmur can write Lawrence off as a poet (because his "formal" sense is bad) and praise a minor, resourceful writer like John Brooks Wheelright,[96] as though this were the thing that makes, say, Wheelwright a good writer and Lawrence a bad one. The thing that gets left out of account, as if it were embarrassing, is the fact that Lawrence is 'way out of sight of Wheelwright as a poet: he is, because he is speaking (albeit clumsily) out of an urgent human need, out of human situations that are intense and real. It may be that had he been as preoccupied with the formal aspect of verse as Valéry was, he would have been say, almost as good as Edmund Blunden.[97] The important thing was, though, that he was obsessed with his response to life: everything he put down on paper is endowed with the passion of that response. Now, Lawrence irritates nobody more than he does me. But he gets me into the poem with him. And that is what we are going to have to do to whatever audience we have. We have got to get them into the poem, where the thing operates as a human gesture. Not let them stand off and admire our use of the short line, or the long line, or tot up our debts to Auden, Thomas, and so on. All that is death to the great, soaring, irrevocable motion that good poetry is. I am convinced that, even in the face of all that has been done, poetry is capable of as yet unheard-of flights, depths, and motions that, to contemplate, would put you in the presence of God. Or nearly. All our energy has got to be expended on getting the reader into our poem, where it can change him, or make him, or destroy him. Life and poetry at the best levels, are, so to speak, interchangeable. Or so we must believe. As I have said before, my own work does not have this quality. But I have it, and my work shall have it yet, even if I have to spend the rest of my life searching for ways to get it in. "The inexhaustible vitality and value of writing are there, and nowhere else," as a famous man once said.

I am sorry to expound at such length on my unhealthily chaotic ideas; so much so, in fact, that I haven't left time to thank you for your very welcome letter. Let me answer all the things that seem to need answering, allinarush: I am glad that Berryman thinks well of me. I think well of him. Yes, by all means write me about the poems of mine you have read. I shall be looking forward to reading your book at incredible leisure, and will write you all about it in due time. Your wife is the only woman I ever heard of (I almost said, "knew") with that name.[98] It is wonderful. Does it have a meaning? And, before I sign off (I am exhausted!) may I make a very modest request? If you have any photographs of you and of your family, would you send me a print? I like to have, if possible, some inkling of the physical presence of people.

Thank you again for your prompt and very gracious reply. Please write again soon. Send poems.

Yours,
Jim Dickey

2930 Westminster Circle, N.W.
Atlanta, Ga.

I enclose a sample of my latest "work." Read, and then throw away![99]

TO: JAMES WRIGHT

TLS, 3 pp; University of Minnesota

17 August, 1958
Atlanta, Ga.

Dear Jim,

Excuse my not writing sooner (I am now two letters behind!), but I have been very ill for the last few days. Luckily, my wife has not had our second child yet (she may go to the hospital today), else we might have had an uncomfortable situation here. As it is, I have been uncomfortable enough for everybody. I evidently ate something rotten or was poisoned, for I have not been able to retain food, and am losing weight by the tens of pounds. I have been lying here like a felled oak (or pine, rather, this being Georgia) thinking about my life, which I almost never get a chance to do, and reading some. I have gone through your poems in Poetry very carefully, and, like the recording angel I should like some day to be, want to give you a complete run-down on what I think. This will come later in the letter, but let me say first of all that the ode about the murderer Doty is by far the most exciting thing of yours I have seen (which damn well makes it the most exciting thing of <u>any</u> English-speaking poet's I have seen in a long, long time).[100] But before I get into an interminable discussion of poetry, I want first to say how much I appreciate your remarks about the Dover poem. I once heard a minor (and older) American poet say, "Son, you can write poetry all your life, and you're lucky if you find one reader." Well, I have found my one, and can only say now, rather helplessly, that I am very much moved by your concern with my work: by the trouble and time you have taken with it. Naturally I am delighted that you like it as well as you do, for it is a new kind of poem with me, and I thought for a long time that I was taking on something I couldn't finish. Some other people have written about it, though none so thoroughly or responsibly as you, so maybe the poem is good, <u>really</u> good, after all. I hope so. It may be that you would want to drop Rago a note telling him you liked the poem, as I intend to do about the Doty poem. Perhaps this is a shameless kind of log-rolling; I don't know. But he has been very kind about the poem, and I should like someone of your standing to give him the satisfaction of concurrence with his opinion. Please don't do this if you feel I am being forward (or even dishonest) in asking you.

Now, a few questions about the Doty poem. First of all, who <u>is</u> (or <u>was</u>) Doty? I notice another poem about him in your book, and conclude that you might even have known the man. These questions are, of course, irrelevant to the value of the poem; they are just questions I ask out of curiosity. Now for some comments. First of all, you have brought off a really amazing thing. Since the thirties, when people like Stephen Spender made kind of a literary parlor game out of the assumption of guilt for criminals, war-criminals, and other people who kill others, there has been an increasing difficulty in making themes like this believable. Here, at last, is a poem in which the guilt is <u>really</u> assumed. I believe the poem, absolutely. This in itself is a major technical accomplishment. When you talk about the Day of Judgment in lines like . . . "and we dead stand undefended everywhere," the word "undefended," in its absolute imaginative rightness and purity, makes me gasp and recognize, at the same time, and about with equal intensity. Talk about your visceral reaction!. There are one or two points I would (or perhaps could) quibble with, but I don't really want to. The whole poem is so effective that nit-picking comments have a way of turning quickly absurd, in its presence. Some reviewer has noted your capacity to identify with the "outsider," the criminal, the mad-man, and the child in his closed garden of a world, but this poem is by far the best fruit of what seems to be a natural tendency. I remember reading, somewhere in Henry Miller (who, despite everything, has some truly fine moments), of his preference for criminals and insane people; I too have this, though to nothing like the extent you seem to. I was out at the Atlanta Federal Pen the other day playing tennis with one of the inmates. After a set or two, we went over and sat down on a pathetic little green bench and leaned back on the Great Gray Wall, and another prisoner brought us some lemonade. I said to my opponent, "Dawkins, are you "going straight" after they let you out?" He thought a moment, and answered with surprising dignity, "No, I don't think so. I consider myself a criminal." Think of that!

In answer to your questions about sending me this book and that book: sure, send them all, and anything else you think I might like. You are so unfailingly kind I have just come to expect it; you are spoiling me to death sending me things, yet I feel somehow that I (or we, perhaps) have got past the place where I must embarrassedly fumble out repeated words of thanks. Let me say once and for all I appreciate everything you have sent, said, thought of, done, explained, not thought-of, believed, felt, and brought me since I have "known" you. There is no one in my entire experience like James Wright: no one so unfailingly honest, so talented, so human. You are always bothering about my thinking you are gushing "hysterically" about something or other: you just listen to me gush a little. I am so weak from lack of nourishment that I am liable to say anything: and yet all these things are true. I lie here the full length of the bed (for I am a huge man, almost six four) hardly able to move a finger (you should see me grapple with these damned type-writer keys), and for once in my life I don't have to fence with somebody, don't have to fight, don't have to crush somebody's arguments, don't have to lie, don't have to do anything but say exactly what I feel. To an advertising man (ex-teacher) this is truly a profound experience. I have great hopes now of writing good poems, imaginatively true poems. My guard is down forever (except against sons-of-bitches); that is the state of mind one has to have to respond truly to anything, and I hope to God it never leaves me again. I had almost lost the capacity to respond to anything deeply. This you have helped me regain; it is the gift beyond price. If I can just hang on and write a few more poems like Dover (or perhaps unlike Dover), and if the book comes out, I will for the first time in my life really believe I have some chance against the personal difficulties that have plagued me, perhaps forever: those, and the old spectre of suicide, which, along with drunkenness, seems the especial curse of my family.

Despite my air of assurance in literary matters, I am really a pathetically unsure, groping person. But, by God, I will not let a literary pimp and time-server like John Hollander[101] get away with being called a good-poet, when somebody like Kunitz has languished for twenty or thirty years. My God he is good! (Kunitz is good) Perhaps I should write him. Do you have his address? Who published his book?

I must fall back from the typewriter now, and try to get some rest. It is late at night, and I fancy I can feel the stars descend into the electric light bulbs, as they surely do into candles.

I enclose a sketch (O Ego!) of me done by my sister-in-law. It is not much, but it is a good likeness. I hope you like it.

Write soon.

Yours,

Jim

2930 Westminster Circle, N.W.
Atlanta, Ga.

TO: JAMES WRIGHT

TLS, 3 pp; University of Minnesota

6 September, 1958
Atlanta, Ga.

Dear Jim,

I have your last good letter, as well as the little book on Char,[102] both of which I thank you for very much. Put me down as "one of the foremost admirers" of your essay on Char, which goes a long way toward injecting the necessary human element into literary criticism. I liked especially your noting that Char's poem leads back into life, to the real woman the poem was written about. This I think no one has commented on; I believe this emphasis you make (and that Char certainly makes) is the needed antidote to the "well-wrought urn" idea that American critics fasten onto as the only way in which they can deal with poetry: as a "closed, self-contained system of language," etc.[103] Poetry interests me (despite Valéry, whom I admire) not at all, looked at simply as "a machine for evoking aesthetic emotions." When I examine my own reasons for writing, I am generally brought back to the assumption that a few incidents (usually concerning my family) have been of extreme importance to me, and in fact seem to contain and carry the meaning of a part of my life. I write verse in order to understand these times and states, and to perpetuate them. I write criticism almost by accident. Through writing poetry myself, I have sort of overflowed into making judgments on the work of others, which I am always somewhat reluctant to do. Once undertaken, however, such a task <u>must</u> not be faked. If it is, it is valueless. Whatever "influence" my critical writings may have will perhaps be traceable to the fact that I insist on poetry's meaning something to <u>me</u>: <u>really</u> meaning something. If a poem does not have whatever it takes to bring this feeling about, I have only a faint, cotton-candy sort of pleasure in it, at best, and no sustenance at all. I like to read, though; the American and English poets I had been reading up until a few years ago seemed to me so cautious and theory-ridden that I learned French as a relief, and for the past three years have read almost no other poets than the French. Some of them have been tremendously exciting to me. Char, of course, and René Ménard,[104] who is almost as good (I notice that the little book you send me has a couple of very astute things by him). Louis Emié[105] is good, too, and Marcel Béalu, whom I know slightly. The best young poet writing in French today, for my money, is Lucien Becker.[106] I shall write to Béalu, who runs a Librairie in the rue St. Séverin, and see if I can get some of Becker's stuff for you. He has a marvellous, glass-like clarity, and is capable (like Roethke) of saying the most amazingly profound things with the air of taking them out of the very fabric and air of the world itself: simply from "the way things are":

> Mais j'ai tant refait ton visage avec mes mains,
> j'ai tellement inscrit ton nom sur ma bouche
> que je n'ai qu'a fermer les paupières
> pour qu'en moi tu prennes la place de la mort.

How about that![107]

Meanwhile, we have struck a snag on the book. Faber says that they like it (with some of their publishers' half-exciting compliments), but that they have an iron-clad policy not to publish Americans until they have "established themselves in America, perhaps with two books, but better with three." So they will not do the book, and without them Phillips (at Criterion) can't move. So . . . what to do? Grove Press has written me, and wants the book, evidently. MacMillan say also that they would like to look at it. Also Scribners, with their abominable "Poets of the Year," out of which, still (in the fifth number), very little good has come.[108] I am debating now about what the hell to do with the book. I read it through again today, and it is a good book. What you tell me about your reaction to my work encourages me more than I can easily tell you, and there have been a few other letters which lead me to believe that the book would sell at least a few copies, which is I guess all one can expect of a book of poems. If you have any ideas as to what I should do, please give me the benefit of them.

You ask about Geoffrey Hill. He and I have been writing back and forth for a couple of years now. I think he has done extraordinary work. He has a mono-lithic, marmoreal kind of imagination (essentially static, unmoving, like Stefan George's) which has yet something human and tender about it. He sends me new poems from time to time, and very lengthy letters describing the things he is try-ing to do. He talks persuasively about "the rhetoric of didacticism" that he is attempting to achieve, but the later poems he sends are not nearly so good as his early ones. I told him so (you know me!), and he seemed to take it pretty hard. But he has a wonderful gift, I think, and he will come to (or back to) his best way of writing, eventually, I am sure. I have tried hawking his work about among the American Quarterlies, but, though some of them will take mine, they won't take Hill's, which is a damned pity, for there is no English poet who deserves more of a hearing. He would appreciate (I know) hearing from you. His address is 61 Grove Lane, Leeds #6. If you write, mention my name, and tell him (again) how I feel about his work. I don't want him to keep on thinking that I am (as we say in advertising) "not so high on him, any more."

You ask, also, about "Joel Cahill Dead."[109] It was a poem I conceived and wrote very quickly. It is actually a scene from a novel that I suppose I shall never finish, called The Table of the Sun.[110] The actual "Joel Cahill" was a boy named Pike, who was in Primary Training with me in Hemmet, California, in 1942. He went against his flight-plan and flew over a forest fire, crashed, and was killed. A farmer (or someone who lived in the country around Hemmet) rescued him from his plane, in a kind of clearing the fire had burned out within itself, and took Pike inside his house, where Pike died before anybody could get to him. This incident stuck with me for years, not so much because I was especially close to Pike, but because fatal accidents were comparatively rare in such an early phase of flight training, and because the circumstances were extraordinary. There was an investigation, some thought it was suicide, etc. I am glad you like the poem. It is a great deal less tortured and involuted and obscure than most of mine, and it has some narrative merit, I think. Beyond that I don't know about its value. But you are dead right about one thing. I want the poem, or any poem I write, to embody the experience: to come as near as it can to being the experience. I don't want to stand off and comment. I want to present. That is what I meant (I suppose) a couple of letters ago, when I talked about getting the reader into the poem. I want to write from the center of what's happening, and I want the reader to be there, too. At his own risk, of course!

In reply to your request for new poems, I must report being in approximately the same state you are: some are just about finished, but not quite. You may be sure that I shall send the new ones on to you as soon as they are ready. Meantime, I am very much looking forward to seeing the new one you are working on.

As to my health, I am much better, but still awfully weak. For a while I felt in real danger going down stairs, and never walked down any where there wasn't a hand-rail. But in a few days I should be ready for some tennis again, and that will be very encouraging. I love that game. I have been connected with sports all my life, as has my whole family (my brother just missed the 1948 Olympic team by about six inches, give or take a few, in the 880). It will be good to get out and move around a little. My son (my <u>new</u> son, that is), is making fine progress toward becoming recognizably human, and my wife is about back to normal. I have just got an immense raise at that legendary place (legendary in the same sense that Hell is), "The Office." I would be embarrassed to tell you what I make, it is so unfair. But I have been poor so long, I still have trouble believing that I am not so, still. As I say, I dream of teaching again, despite everything.

Believe that I think of you often, and hope very much that some day we may meet, and read poetry (our own, mostly, in very solemn voices), talk about Char, Becker, and Geoffrey Hill (that amazing boy), Berryman, Roethke, and the rest of the Heroes of this dread time. Believe me, Jim Wright, we shall not fail, in the end, and, when the stone angels of our tombs on Judgment Day drag us by our centuries-long hair into Heaven, "mile-high, through the rain,"[111] we shall go there singing. Keep writing, and keep living.

Yours,

Jim

TO: JAMES WRIGHT

TLS, 2 pp; University of Minnesota

3 October, 1958
Atlanta, Ga.

Dear Jim,

It is shameful of me to make you write two letters to my one (although I don't exactly <u>make</u> you, you do it because I don't write), but I know you will believe me when I say that things in the advertising world (what world is that, but Purgatory?) have been hectic, with all night hours being pressed into service to break the fascinating and humanly-important doctrine to panting customers ("consumers," <u>we</u> call 'em) that "King Size Coke has more for you." You can see that this requires some thought. "We want this," said our Creative Captain from New York, Mr. Roger Purdom, in an unctuous voice to make you hate the planet on which you were born, "to be an <u>assault</u> on the mind of the consumer. An <u>assault</u> we have carefully laid the ground-work for. An <u>assault</u> that <u>must</u> be successful, if Coca-Cola is to maintain it's (or its, rather) <u>rightful</u> place in the marketplace." Ten days of meetings of this kind, full of this jargoning, Kiwanis-type verbiage, and I am ready to turn slowly into a wild, really wild animal. Tell me, James Wright, what is life, real life, with real human beings in it, really like? I have forgotten.

As to important things. Your faith in the Dover poem, and my hopefulness for it, have received strong emphasis in the last couple of weeks. Mr. Rago writes me that it has received the Union Civic and Arts Foundation Prize of one hundred dollars, which I was very grateful to hear. Thanks again for your very kind comments on the poem, for which I was, and am, more grateful than I can say.

Thanks, also, for copying out the Neruda poem and sending it to me.[112] It is simply terrific! God! What _ease_ there is in the thing, as though these marvellously-arranged observations were just what a man _would_ say, if he were tired of being a man. I must try to get hold of some Neruda and puzzle it together with my high-school Spanish, a little of which (Buenas dias!) I remember, even if I don't remember how to spell it.

As to sports: I came up, as I may have told you, in a family in which there was simply no interest other than in sports. I was a scholarship boy (hired hand) at Clemson in 1942, and before that had played four years of high-school football, basketball, and track. All this proves, I guess, that there is no royal road to poetry, though I must say that the other American poets I have met have not had similar backgrounds. Anyway, I played on the freshman team at Clemson until after the varsity had played two or three games. After that, the Southern Conference passed the Freshman Rule, which allowed Freshmen to play with the varsity, this being at the beginning of the war and the draft. I finished the season with the varsity, and started the last five games, and was on the second All-Southern team. I played wing-back on Frank Howard's (the coach's) old straight-away power-type single wing, and did mostly blocking, though I got to run on a reverse every now and then, and catch an occasional pass. I was pretty fast for an 195-pounder, though, and tried my best to make them as good a back as I could, although I was too long-striding to be shifty, and too big to miss on a tackle. I could make a line-backer live hard, though, and I scored three touchdowns and was actually leading ground-gainer against Boston College, whom we played in Fenway Park, and who had an All-American back named Mike Holovak, whom we stopped cold that day, though we lost the game.

After I got out of the service in 1946 I enrolled in Vanderbilt, which made me permanently ineligible for football, since the Southeastern Conference militated stringently against having colleges swipe one another's players coming out of service. I finished college on a track scholarship, though, and in 1947 set a high hurdles record for the South in the Cotton Carnival Meet at Memphis. I think the record is still standing, though I am not sure.[113] I have always loved sports, though nowadays there is not much chance for me to do more than see an occasional football game or play a little tennis on the week-ends. I still weigh about the same (or a little less, actually) than I did when I was at Clemson, and spend a good deal of time trying (fruitlessly) to stay in good shape, since, after so many years of competition, I feel like hell if I don't.

This is the first time in a long time I have talked so much about myself, and certainly the first time in many years when I have done it without feeling embarassed. Now it is your turn. Do you come from Seattle? Or where? From some of your poems, I should judge that you are a farm boy. Is this correct? What about the service? I was in almost eight years, and they are threatening to get me again, God forbid.

Before I forget: I just remembered a curious thing that happened to me in New York, two years ago. A big blond gal picked me up in a book store (I don't mean this to sound like Jack Kerouac, but that's actually what happened). It turns out that she is (or was, rather: please disregard this syntactical tangle) or aspired to be a poet. She came from Seattle. Her name was Kizer,[114] I think (or maybe it was Kayser), and it was she who told me that you had won the Yale Younger Poets deal for the next year. We had a couple of drinks and hung around together for a day or two in fairly sordid circumstances. The other day I was reading Selden Rodman's[115] book on Artists (<u>Conversations with Artists</u>) in a book-store and ran across the woman's name, although I still can't remember how to spell it. It happens that this full-blown type (the woman) is a big patroness of the arts out there in Seattle, has pots of money, and knows all the artists (Graves, Tobey, et al) there are in that section of the world. Do you or did you know her? She's a very odd character, believe me. She used to talk about David Wagoner[116] (an entire mediocrity) as some marvellous, mystical type of genius, which is enough right there to make you suspicious that something odd is going on, either in the blond's mind, or between her and Wagoner. I just mention this as further fuel to your notion that there is some mystery in this correspondence between you and me, in which all kinds of unsuspected, marvellous, and hidden things come to light. Is this one more? I hope so.

Write soon, and tell me about yourself. Send some poems. My new son's name is Kevin, and he is getting as fat as an owl on Similac and attention. How about yours?

Did you ever hear from Geoff Hill?

Yours,
Lucky Jim[117]

2930 Westminster Circle, N.W.
Atlanta, Ga.

TO: PHILIP BOOTH

TLS, 2 pp; Dartmouth College

1 December, 1958
Atlanta, Ga.

Dear Phil,

Hey! You are beginning to prove my <u>Sewanee</u> opinion wrong. The poem about the big propellor is real poetry,[118] at least some of it is, and now I won't be satisfied until you prove me totally, incompetently, irrevocably wrong, at which point I will damn well say so, in print, or, even better, in private, to you. I will, as we former academics say, "confine my remarks" to the piece I mentioned, for I don't care much for the other one, which pretty badly pales out beside your "crated sun." First of all, the poem runs the danger of being exactly like ten thousand thousand others, which have, roughly, this kind of appearance: (1) Here is something interesting. I see a huge propellor stranded in its crate on a trailer on the side of highway #1 (or Route #1, rather). (2) A little description. (3) Some reflection on the thing, in its function, say. (4) Some "wider" reflections on the thing, including its relation to "civilization." (5) Its <u>real</u> meaning: that is, to the poet: as it is, or will be, in its "true" being, its "far interior impulse." The difficulty, as I say, is that the poem, or any poem of this kind will be, quite simply, only a poem written with the subject simply taken as an excuse for the exercise of the craft of verse: one really writes a poem, doesn't one? because one is or is supposed to be a poet, and poets must write poems. That is, by the way, exactly what is wrong with your friend Merwin. He writes poems, as Edmund Wilson once said of Stephen Benét, like the poems a man would write who has gone in for writing poetry as anyone else would go into the insurance business. But your poem escapes all this, and that is the thing I rejoice in. I mean <u>really</u> rejoice, for I have railed until hoarse trying to get "my generation" up off its complacent behind, and am glad to see one of our "leading young poets" doing just that. After all, Sir, it is <u>my</u> generation. And by God we will make something out of it, yet. Your poem, to get back to it, is good because, despite its conventional appearance and too-flatness, (I keep hearing the carping "chopped-up prose" objection come up in the back of my mind, but I put it down), the imagination has got hold of the propellor-thing and has made one or two really living phrases out of it, and has got these into a vital relation with one another. The cars' reflecting the blades "pure color" is one of them, and the beached propellor's being geared to a "far interior impulse" is another. The word "impulse" is far better than being just right: it is <u>inexplicably</u> right: that is, it is <u>poetically</u> right. Now: one or two objections. The last line is just conventional, beside the fact that "wheel will" diminishes the "sound effects" by the similarity of the words. I get the impression (though I may be wrong, it is still my impression) that the powerful statement of the propellor itself required, because it is in a poem, a completion, a "moral," a "clincher," and this seemed as good as any. It is, for any poem, but not for <u>this</u> poem. Consider, too, that when you're working toward a climax, such as it is, a phrase like "It's curious, here, to think . . ." is really not really strong enough to swing your reader into that orbit which leads to a true summation, or, if you like, consummation.[119] But, all in all, I am delighted: and how could <u>you</u> be more delighted: for he who delights Dickey, the Southern Antagonist, must himself be made forever happy, for that man is hard to please. Especially by Yankees.

I have taken on a couple of reviews for Rago, one of them on a number of "little" poets, none of whom I have ever heard of, and the other on Conrad Aiken, whom I don't have very strong feelings about, one way or the other.[120] Any ideas? I am also doing another chronicle for the <u>Sewanee</u>, but I don't know what books are going to be in it.[121]

I am glad you liked the "sprinter" poem in the <u>Yale</u>. I'm not sure, yet, what I think about it. It came out of a real dream I had, which in turn came out of seven or eight years of running on high-school, prep-school and college track teams. Beyond that, I can't say. The <u>Yale Review</u> is printing another, longer, one of mine soon, which is something like that one: it is about the obsessive effort boys have to "build themselves up" physically, along about their fifteenth year. It is called "The Other," and may just possibly be a good poem.[122]

Please let me hear from you further. I have a good deal of interesting gossip and talk from New York, where I spent a couple of recent weeks, but I don't have time to write any more right now, and thought you would rather hear my opinions of the poems.

I am keeping the poems. If you want them back, come get them.

Yours,

Jim

2930 Westminster Circle, N.W.
Atlanta, Ga.

TO: WILLIAM PRATT

TLS, 2 pp; William Pratt

8 January, 1959
Atlanta, Ga.

Dear Bill,

"Years dreams return . . ." said Mr. Earwicker,[123] and I return often to those curious dream-like years when we were at Vanderbilt together, with Jack Hall whispering of his strange sexual habits, Ann Locke living in that elevated rathole, Davidson softly intoning ballads, and Finney showing us about the circles (I think it was circles) of Proclus and holding forth on the Enneads of Plotinus (which, incidentally, are pretty good. I just read them for the first time). All that has changed now. The last time I went to Vanderbilt I drifted around the campus like a ghost, not even touching the ground. Our lives are set now, and we must think they are set as they should be. Of yours this is certain, but of mine there is still much uncertainty. I have advanced to a place in business where people trust me to get things done, and I do get them done. On the other hand, I have developed such an astonishing economy so far as time is concerned that I can write more, and work with what I do write more efficiently, than when I was a teacher. Though I loved that trade, I was, admittedly, pretty lazy in it, and mostly lolled around, telling my students all about how great D.H. Lawrence was, and hardly ever reading him myself. But now I do read him, and a great many others, too, whom previously I had only talked of, and nodded to, in the pages of the reviews. No less than seven (yes!) publishers have put in bids for the book. Right now, it looks like Malcolm Cowley and Viking have the inside track.[124] (Now, really, don't you think I <u>should</u> give Malcolm Cowley the inside track?) He wants to give me something called the Lamont Prize, which carries a thousand dollars or so, and I couldn't find it in my heart to object.[125] If something goes wrong with the deal, though, I can fall back on Scribners, MacMillan, Doubleday, Grove Press, and an exciting new outfit that is publishing out of Wesleyan University in Massachusetts,[126] to say nothing of some smaller places like Alan Swallow, etc. The quarterlies are full of me, I am reviewing books all over the place, people write in from all over, including South Africa and Australia, and I am pouring out new (and I think better) stuff all the time. All this is tremendously exciting, as you can imagine, and if I can hold together for a few more years I might succeed, finally, in writing one really <u>good</u> poem, god-like, unimaginable. I hope so.

Now, about Hilmer Saffell (I agree with you about the name). Yes, there is something here, all right, but I don't think this poem is adequate for the <u>Sewanee Review</u> or anywhere near it. I should like to see some more of this fellow's work. There are some good things here, especially the hawk's "wide swoon motion."

That is the real thing, but almost nothing else in the poem is. The point is that it is all "literatured" up, and full of poses (like the weeping at the end) that it is in the sincerest interest of good poetry (and good poets) to prune out ruthlessly, and be ashamed they ever thought of it in the first place. Your own comments on the poem are as good as any I would be capable of making. As general advice, tell him to read less of Hart Crane and Thomas, than whom I can't offhand, think of any worse poets for his own kind of subject matter. There is a new English poet named Jon Silkin[127] that seems to have a technical and sensible affinity with him. Hilmur might be interested in getting his one American-published book and reading it. It is called "The Two Freedoms," and is put out by Mac Millan.

Your course in poetry sounds simply terrific. It is set up like the very image of what a dream-course in poetry should be. I should not only like to teach it myself; I should like to take it. Aren't you going to have them read any criticism beside that of Eliot and Pound? As an "influence" on poetry, contemporary criticism has probably been the greatest of all, and if you can squeeze it in, it might be a good idea to have them read some of the stuff in Blackmur, Ransom, etc. Robert Penn Warren's critical essays (recently collected) would be helpful (as well as relatively easy to understand), and there is a new book on modern poetry that is about the best collection of essays on the subject that I have ever read. It is called Stewards of Excellence, by some unknown guy named Alverez.[128]

We have a new son, as you know. His name is Kevin, and he is getting as fat as an owl on Similac and over-attention. I think this is the extreme limit of the development of our family, though I would like to have at least one daughter before I die. Our family life is quiet. I go to work at nine, and come home at five. At that time I do something with Chris: either read to him, talk to him, or fight him (the matches are getting close!), and then we have dinner. I relax for a few minutes and try to read some French. Then I go into the room with the type-writer and get down to it. After three hours I am shot, and then I loll into the television room and collapse, half-reading something, and half-listening to television. On the week-ends I play tennis almost continuously, after using the mornings to write. Occasionally I go out to a bar and tie one on, and occasionally I give a lecture at one of the state universities, or one of the girls' schools around here, usually for a fee of from fifty to a hundred dollars (but I have, shamefully, done it for no more than ten). It is not an exciting life, outwardly. The excitement is channelled into the work, and comes out of the work, and I have a feeling that, for me, that is the way it should be.

I wish I could go on for pages, but I have to get back to work, since I am writing this at the office, during a (relatively!) slack time. Please do not be so damnably long about writing, for letters from good folk are the only contact I have with the world of Significant Things. Incidentally, before I forget, the old man of the Italian Mountains wrote me a post-card the other day. I wrote back to him, but it may well be that I misconstrued his address. Do you have it? Or perhaps I should just address it to E. Pound, Human Being, Somewhere in Italy. It <u>should</u> get to him that way, but I feel I should trouble you for his actual address, all the same.[129]

Our best to your wife, to Cullen, and to you. May the wind that blows over your grave fall dead, and you rise up.

Yours,
Jim

2930 Westminster Circle, N.W.
Atlanta, Ga.

TO: JAMES WRIGHT

TLS, 1 p; University of Minnesota

27 February, 1959
Atlanta, Ga.

Dear Jim,

Please forgive my not writing, but I have been unbelievably busy with business problems, with writing three reviews to deadlines, and with trying to complete the last two poems in the book, which has now been considerably revised. I got it off to Cowley on Monday. I read through it, and am proud that I was the one to write it. I hope it is as good as it then seemed to me, and as good as some of the pieces in it seem to you and Booth and Hall. But especially to you. You are forever thanking me for moral support, criticisms, comments, and so on, but now I need to do a little thanking of my own. Humility is not my forte: I much more easily run to arrogance and insolence, but I do want to come off that for a moment and tell you how grateful I am for your letters, but most of all, for being the kind of person you must be: striving continually for honesty in your writing, but most of all in your life. In the world I live in, there is no one else like that. I aspire to be the same way, but I really am not. But I know what that kind of honesty and that kind of life must be, and I admire it. I know, too, that there are plenty of frustrations in your life, and that among these is the continual one about money, which is one of the most strength-sapping and discouraging ones in the world. But at least you are dealing every day with important matters; you talk to students about them, and you think about them, and you perform them. I am not so fortunate, largely because I am fully as arrogant and unbending as I say I am, and would not, <u>would</u> not get a PH.D, because I am a writer and not a scholar, and don't pretend to be a scholar. That refusal was the only furiously honest sustained action I have performed since my army days. It cut me off from almost all teaching jobs, at least from those with any promise of permanency, and so I more or less had to go into business, or turn to crime. I now have, including money from publications, an income of right around $20,000 a year,[130] most of which goes to keep up an establishment none of us really wants or needs. I can buy the books I want (O holy joy!) but rarely have time to read them. I can buy the equipment I need for another passion of mine: hunting deer with a bow (I have killed one). I just paid $75 dollars for a new bow the other day. That is heart-lessly extravagant, but the bow is the most beautiful thing I possess. Maybe, some day, we can all get together and go shooting up there in Minnesota, where there's more game than we have in Georgia. Here, there're only deer and pigs (wild pigs, I mean). Anyway, for all this I spend seven hours a day writing and supervising the most pathetic kind of thing you can imagine, and chafing over the fact that the hours, the days, and the years are slipping by without my writing the things I know I could write. But we shall win yet! By God, we will! If I can't find the teach-ing job I want, I am resolved to get rich off this loathsome business, write great poems, live like a true human being, and pay it all off by going to heaven. Yes!

It was good talking to you the other night. I don't know quite why I called, but the Yale Review just paid me off, and I decided I might as well call you as not. And then, right then, I decided that I'd a whole lot rather call you than not, and I did. You sound so calm and easy-going it is hard for me to believe all the things you tell me of visits to psychiatrists, and so on. I am glad you are doing well. I am glad you are alive. Write soon and tell me everything.

Jim D.

P.S. The revised Doty poem is great! Even better than the magic letters of the dedication![131]

2930 Westminster Circle, N.W.
Atlanta, Ga.

TO: JAMES WRIGHT

TLS, 1 p; University of Minnesota

18 March, 1958 [1959]
Atlanta, Ga.

Dear Jim,

I did write to your friend Richard Hugo,[132] and received a reply almost at once. He sounds good to me; a "man after my own heart" (though I hope, somehow, that he doesn't get it). I have only read the one poem of his that you sent me; I don't think as much of it as you do, but it has many fine things in it, and I told him so. Exactly how much stuff has he published, and where can I find it?

The manuscript of Into the Stone, and other poems has been in to Cowley and his Vikings for a month now, and I am watching the mails as Death has been watching me for thirty-five years. If all goes well, maybe you would like to say something, a blurb, perhaps, on the cover, huh? At any rate, we should know something soon. The only thing that worries me is that I seem to be known in literary circles as a kind of maverick or strange one, and Viking may not want to go out on a limb with me. Then, too, I am bound to get a lot of bad reviews by people getting revenge on me for my reviews. I am all the time getting threatening letters from people like Edwin Honig, whom I ran down in a review three years ago, and also backed down at a party at Oscar Williams' in New York, when I was drunk and brave and he was drunk and cowardly. Ezra Pound, who wrote me once about some poems of mine he had seen, once told me that a man must be judged by the quality of his enemies. I don't think much of the quality of my enemies, but perhaps I can make up for that by the quantity. I sure have a lot of them, as well as a few loyal people. I know I need not enumerate those, though certainly I count you 'way up among them. But the book is good! It is! It is! And I hope we can get it out, with Cowley or without him.

In your last letter you took me to task, in your usual gentle way, for thinking of the teaching profession as I do. Yes, boy, I do know that there are places that don't demand that you have a Ph.D, and that there are some that are not as hidebound as I say they are. But I have never had the good fortune to be associated with them. Part of the source of my very real bitterness against the Universities is that people like Booth and Lou Coxe[133] and Wilbur and Tony Hecht all have good jobs teaching where they like, and what they like, and nobody ever asked me, who am a better poet and a better teacher and a better human being than any of them (Don't laugh; it's true. I know them all, and what I say is so). True enough, I was Andrew Lytle's assistant in the Creative Writing Program at the University of Florida, but I was only so in addition to carrying a full load of freshmen, and with the same salary as the freshman Instructors got. And that did not suit me, any more than it would have suited you, or Lytle himself, who taught two hours a week to my fourteen, and salted away seven thousand five hundred dollars a year for doing almost nothing. Well, I now have an income of almost twenty thousand a year, but I still feel I was had by the teaching profession, and did no good in it at all, except in the minds and hearts of a few people whom my honesty and extreme responsibility toward their talent (and it was extreme, and it was responsibility) may have helped toward seeing, feeling, writing, and living their own way. Now: you say you have some ideas about my getting back into teaching. Spill them, without further delay. Boy, you get me a good teaching job, and I'll take it. I mean immediately, and no questions asked, once I am satisfied it is a respectable job, commensurate with my abilities, such as they are, and with my wishes to build a future life for myself and my family. So tell me what you think.

I have to sign off, since I should by all rights be writing a new jingle for Coke. Perhaps you have heard my current one, which goes like this (and I quote) "King Size Coke has more for you. King Size Coke has more for you! / Get value . . . lift . . . refreshment, too"! Gad! That it should come to this! More important: tell me what you think of the two new poems, one in the current Yale Review[134] about the body-building craze young boys undergo, and the other in the current (both these "currents" mean the Spring issue) Sewanee Review, which is about Spring, rebirth, and the ancient sacrifices.[135] There is also a review of mine of Conrad Aiken in the April Poetry. Write soon.

Jim

TO: PHILIP BOOTH

TLS, 2 pp; Dartmouth College

19 April, 1959
Atlanta, Ga.

Dear Phil,

Sorry to be so long about writing, but we've been having a series of "meetings" with various agency clients, and I haven't had time to write anything but business letters. I am settled in here on a rainy Sunday now, when I am reasonably safe from the office force and the office forces of our various clients, and can take a little time to talk to you.

The first thing is James Wright. He wrote to me a day or two after you did, telling me much the same things you did, about his terrible depressions, his fits of angers, and so on, and I wrote back and asked him if he thought I ought to take a few days off and come up there and see him, which I would gladly do, since business and most other things, including poetry, are no good if you can't sacrifice them in favor of life, especially the life of somebody like Wright. I haven't heard anything from him, but I may very well leap forth from my garage all the way to Minneapolis in my new sports car (I traded in my Maserati racer for something more practical, since I never got to race very much, and it was no good for going to the corner liquor store. Even a bicycle would have worked better). I would like to meet Wright, for he has been and I guess still is the best correspondent I have ever had. When the Sewanee Review or somebody paid off a few weeks ago, I called him on the phone and we talked away about twenty dollars. I enjoyed it very much, and plan to spend the next money I get (which I suppose will be either from Poetry or the Partisan) to give you a call, if (as I suppose) you have a telephone on "RFD 1." What is your number, by the way? Back to Wright: just exactly how did you hear about his current troubles? You really don't tell me very much when you say you heard it "the way these things get heard." That implies, at least to me, that there is a kind of underground fund of busybodiness among teachers and poets, and that such private affairs as this are, aren't they, just sort of common knowledge. I hate to think of a boy who is suffering as Wright must be subject to having his troubles aired about by the usual crowd of literary harpies. Of course, if he told you, it is all right. I don't include you in the crew of fancy New York brain-pickers, of course, since you obviously love Wright and want to do something for him. Well, how about it? How about meeting me in Minneapolis, since you don't even have to get time off, being, you see, on a Fewwlowship?[136] As you say, this is a human being.

Yes; thanks for the letter where you talk about the poem in the Yale Review.[137] It is one of the best letters I ever got. I read over the poem in the light of your advice, and you are one hundred per cent right. (It must seem funny to you to hear me say something like this, rather than telling you that you are a hundred per cent wrong, as you sometimes are). I read the poem through at one of those rare times (lucky times) when it seemed like something somebody else had done. I thought it very interesting, a good try, but it should have taken another turn somewhere. I envy all your knowledge of prosody, which I don't have, since I work by listening in the dark, and not by what ought to be in the lines. I wish I knew more about that part of poetry, but my efforts in that direction are so painfully amateurish that they are not even in the same class with my son's work (a very fine poet, incidentally, who, the other day when we were out in the woods shooting arrows, asked me how the leaves of a tree could make stars out of the sun. I asked him what stars, and he said those we were walking on, on the ground). Anyway, I am glad that you find so much to like in "The Other." I think some of the images are good. Outside that, I can't say. It is not really what I want to do, but I don't really know what I want to do. I have a glimpse of the kind of poem I want to write, and can sometimes sustain this glimpse for a few lines at a time, but I can't keep it up. But I know that that kind of poem is somewhere, and that I am the appointed searcher for it. Whether or not I ever find it, I can't say, I don't know. I am working on a new one called "Drinking from a Helmet"[138] that may get closest yet, if I can bring it off. I'll send some of it to you, as soon as it's sendable. Yes; I will be delighted to have a look at your poem "The Owl" in the Hudson. Oddly enough, I have a poem coming out in the Hudson with an owl in it; the king of the owls, in fact.[139] Let your owl beware for his head. Or perhaps he is the crown prince of owls, in or out of disguise.

I thought you might be amused at the little newspaper squib on our favorite poet, which demonstrates better than anything could the paucity of literary news in this cultural cul-de-sac.[140]

My god, man, every reminiscence you have of Georgia concerns some girl you used to know down here. You know, there is <u>land</u> here, too, and <u>water</u>, and <u>stones</u>, and <u>leaves</u>, and "the laughter of children." Also males, old and young, and <u>old</u> women. I never had much truck with <u>girls</u>, even in the beginning. I was married at eighteen (in Australia: my first wife died).[141] From that time until I married my second wife, I knew a few hard-eyed, hard-bodied tennis court and arrow-shooting types, but the sweet pliable college-girl kind of female frightens me; I have a vision of myself as Humbert Humbert,[142] and I couldn't stand that. But you seem to remember <u>something</u> of Georgia, and that you are right about. It is tremendous this time of year. I go down on all fours and run through these dog-woody Georgia woods like a dog; I climb trees and suck eggs like a weasel. I sing and dance and fly, and the oaks follow me like they would Orpheus, as I strum on my bowstring like a harp. Ah! This is lovely! Wish you could come down. Come to think of it, why don't you?

I must sign off. Send some new poems, if you have any. And remember: we are all of us coming to nothing as poets, if we don't make a firm stand against the well-made poem. Let us not settle for the easy led-by-the-nose kind of inevitabil-ity. Read my long essay in the summer <u>Sewanee</u> called "The Human Power."[143] God told me to write it, and he was right to. Now, if he will just show me how to write some poems. . . .

Jim Dickey

P.S. Nothing from Viking, and this is two months now. Is this a good sign?

2930 Westminster Circle, N.W.
Atlanta, Ga.

TO: JOHN HALL WHEELOCK[144]

TLS, 1 p; Princeton

1 May, 1959
Atlanta, Ga.

Dear John Hall Wheelock,

Here is the book, and I hope you find in it some things to like. It is, of course, too long in its present form to be suitable for <u>Poets of Today</u>; if you think a number of the poems good enough, I would like you to select those for the book, and leave the others out. I ask this because my own judgment in these matters is rather wavering and doubtful, and I am not sure from one day to the next what I like or don't like in my work. The present collection is simply an assemblage of my poems which have appeared in major magazines, both here and in Europe. All these pieces have appeared in good publications; I must be, for example, one of the two or three poets alive who have published in all four major American quarterlies (Or perhaps this number should be increased to six, since I have appeared not only in the <u>Partisan Review</u>, the <u>Kenyon Review</u>, the <u>Hudson Review</u>, and the <u>Sewanee Review</u>, but in the <u>Yale Review</u> and the <u>Virginia Quarterly Review</u>, also).[145] Henry Rago of <u>Poetry</u> has just taken eight of these poems, including the title piece,[146] and writes me a most enthusiastic letter about them. He says, "We think the new poems are beautiful . . . congratulations on the work; everything about it suggests that you have felt your way into exactly the right direction." These are some of the shorter pieces ("The Landfall," "The Performance," etc.), and it may be, as some of my friends have suggested, that the shorter poems are uniformly the more successful. The Union League Prize poem, "Dover,"[147] is, I guess, the best of the longer ones, as well as being my best-known poem. It may be, though, that you will want to drop "The First Morning of Cancer" and/or "The Red Bow," though they appeared in <u>Poetry</u> and the <u>Sewanee Review</u>, respectively.[148] If this seems to you to be a good solution to the problem of length, I am entirely agreeable to it. After all, I want to show a good book to the public, and I want you to be convinced it is good, too, with no weak spots or dead wood.

Another thing: the divisions of the book, as I have them here, may seem somewhat arbitrary. If you don't think the way the poems are presently grouped contributes to their effect, either singly or collectively, then by all means let's take them out of their present sequence and arrange them another way: whichever way you think best.

Do, please, let me know as soon as you can, for I have had another offer or two, and I don't know how long these other people are willing to wait.

Before I forget: isn't Gene Baro one of the upcoming <u>Poets of Today</u>, 1959?[149] He and I taught together at the University of Florida for several months, three years ago, though I never knew him really well.

Again, thank you very much for your interest in my work, for which I am as grateful as it is possible to be. And perhaps a little more grateful than that, too.

Yours,

James Dickey

2930 Westminster Circle, N.W.
Atlanta, Ga.

TO: JOHN HALL WHEELOCK

TLS, 1 p; Princeton

27 May, 1959
Atlanta, Ga.

Dear John Hall Wheelock,

I am happy that you like the book; thank you very much for the handsome things you say about it. As to the omissions you suggest: yes, I will be glad to leave out the poems you enumerate, though it is difficult for me to relinquish <u>Dover</u>, which cost me a year and a half of work. If you don't think it fits, however, by all means let's omit it. Without these nine poems, will the book be long enough? If not, I have two or three more I have done recently. Most of the poems you suggest leaving out are early ones, and I have been moving steadily away from that style (or those several styles, I suppose I should say) for a number of years. I am glad to see that you wish to retain all those that I myself think most highly of. Eight of these will be presented in the July <u>Poetry</u>, and, if you like, I can have a copy sent to you. I am to be featured in that number; Henry Rago (the editor) seems to think that these are not only good poems but important ones, and I hope you do, too.

One thing more: you speak of the "eight finalists" among whose manuscripts mine is to be placed. In an earlier letter, you mentioned "only one poet" to whom you are "definitely committed" for <u>Poets of Today VII</u>. Shall I assume from this that there are in reality only two places to be filled, rather than three? As I mentioned before, I have had three offers which seem to indicate that these publishers would be willing to take my manuscript virtually sight-unseen. I hope it is apparent that I would most like to appear with you, especially in view of your own personal kindness to me. At the same time, I don't want to alienate the other people, and wind up by missing four opportunities instead of one, should Scribners decide against me. I realize I can't legitimately ask you for a definite commitment now, since there are other people involved, all of whom, I am sure, are equally deserving of attention. But if you could give me some indication of <u>possibilities</u>, I would rest more easily at night, and know better what to do and how to feel. Please forgive me if I seem to impose unduly on your prerogatives as an editor; I hope you will understand the temerity of one who has absolutely no knowledge of the publishing of books, and who at the same time feels an urgent, even desperate need of doing what he can for his own difficult and wayward talent, quite as though it were a separate and somehow better Being than himself, who at the same time trusts him implicitly.

Again, let me thank you for your confidence in my work, and for making this known to me in the gracious way you have chosen. I hope very much that <u>Into the Stone</u> may make a really good addition to <u>Poets of Today</u>.[150]

Yours,

Jim Dickey

2930 Westminster Circle, N W
Atlanta, Ga.

TO: PHILIP BOOTH

TLS, 2 pp; Dartmouth College

15 June, 1959
Atlanta, Ga.

Dear Phil,

It is unkind of me to repay your own extreme kindness with a note just every now and then. Believe me, I would like very much to be able to sit and write for hours on a <u>real</u> letter to you: one which would explain <u>everything</u>. But office hours do not permit such desirable situations, and the home hours are dedicated to the hectic, even desperate attempt to keep up with my own imagination, which outruns me at every turn, then comes back and hovers over me, to egg me on. The fruits of this are odd and wayward, but there are <u>some</u> fruits. My first book, <u>Into the Stone, and other poems</u>, will be published next year by one of the larger houses. I can't tell you which one just yet, for I have been requested not to. It is not Viking, because Cowley and I could not get together on which poems to leave in and which to leave out. I felt I had a number of legitimate objections to doing what he proposed, so simply gave the book to another publisher. I will let you know the full details as soon as the publisher wants to break the word to the great, breathless world. The arrangement which he proposes seems a nice one, and I am quite well satisfied. Before I forget: the June <u>Poetry</u> will carry a great number of my poems, and you might want to have a look at it. In case you can't get to a civi-lized library, isolated as you are on Concord: RFD.#1, I will send you a copy. But <u>do</u> let me know if you want one. Some of these poems are pretty good, I hope. Again, thank you for your post-card on "The Vegetable King."[151] I am glad it sings to you, if it does. There are some good images in it, I think, and I am glad to be able to do something to offset the monstruous use made of that myth (or fable) by Eliot in "The Waste Land." It is really a <u>human</u> parable, and not so much indicative of the growth, decay, and death of cultures as Eliot imagines. When I wrote it, I thought, "Now just imagine <u>yourself</u> in that situation," and I wrote my poem. But it is, quite likely, the only one of its kind I shall ever do. The myth of the Vegetable King (or Vegetable God) from Frazer is really the only thing that ever struck me with any actual force, of all the anthropological and ethnological stuff I have (dutifully) read. And I am glad you like it.

There is another long, hammer-and-tongs review in the Summer <u>Sewanee</u>. Read it, and disagree and agree with me violently. But violence is not your way, you "quiet man." I wish I was quieter, myself, but I am not: I am violent, unstable, and mostly incoherent. But I <u>do</u> feel, and live, and love, and write poems. I am about halfway through my second book, by now. It is called <u>Drowning With Others</u>, and if my present publisher doesn't want to bring it out, there are several others who do.[152] I think it is going to be a good book (a necessary illusion), and am working with feverish enthusiasm on the various pieces.

Now, something <u>really</u> important. I am to read at the Poetry Center (YM-YWCA) in New York on either December 17<u>th</u>, March 12, or April 8<u>th</u>.[153] Can you come down to New York and cheer me on? Or shall I make a quick excursion to the environs of Boston? Do write and tell me your thoughts on these important matters.

Listen: don't worry about what I said to you about gossip and Jim Wright. <u>Certainly</u> I don't think you carry tales (or tails) out of school. It's just that the notion that the thing, the news, and so on, might be in the air generally, that concerned me. That boy can take care of himself (else I would not be concerned with taking care of him). But I do hate to see private, delicate and desperate matters aired in public. You and I are not Public, but we hear when Public speaks. It is not us that bothers me, but Them. Jim also writes (Wrights) me that he and his wife have broken up, so the situation must be pretty acute. How can a man who So Loves the World (as he does) do such terrible things to himself? Half of his poems are about children (as more than half of mine are): that is, <u>his</u> children. How can he stand to lose his <u>heart</u>, that way? I could not. And yet, if he says it is necessary to him, then I must take it that it is. But how <u>could</u> it be?

Of your new poems, I like the Marin poem much the best.[154] I love his work, which naturally led me on into your poem about it with much enthusiasm and excitement. What I like most is "through a pane so / cracked by the lode- / star sun that he / swam back, blinded, / into himself . . ." That is <u>really</u> good, and is, to me, his famous picture of "Maine Islands," though it could have been many another. You are making good progress, and I look forward to (many) more poems as good as this. By the way, did you tell me the "Propellor" poem is due out in the <u>Virginia Quarterly</u>? Or where? Tell me, and I shall look for it.

There could be many other things to say, here, but I can only say good-bye for another time, plunging back into my typewriter the wrong way (the way that says TV commercials and not poems), and hoping you will continue to be so good a correspondent, where I am concerned, and so good a person where I am concerned (though I also hope you are a bad person where other people (or some of them) are concerned, because this brings balance). You can't be good to everybody. I know I'm not, but try to give what is good of myself to the ones that deserve it. Never give of your essential self to the dead, Lawrence says, and he is right. He means the living dead. There are so many, and we (or I) have only a few quick, living moments (there: I'm even beginning to <u>sound</u> like Lawrence, but I am really not like him. Would I were).

Please forgive all this chaos of print, and let me hear from you again soon. Your Marin poem is good. Send more. And live.

Yours,
Jim

2930 Westminster Circle, Atlanta, Ga.

TO: DONALD HALL

TLS, 2 pp; University of New Hampshire

15 June, 1959
Atlanta, Ga.

Dear Don,

Many thanks for your letter and the new poems. Let me answer a few questions first, and take care of other matters raised by your letter, and then I will get back to your own work. As to the book: yes, one of the large houses has taken it, and it will appear next year. I can't tell you who my publisher is just yet, for I have been requested not to. Believe me, as soon as I am allowed, I will give you full details. You and Wesleyan can certainly have a look at the manuscript of my second book, as soon as it is finished.[155] It is called <u>Drowning With Others</u>; there are only a few poems in it as yet, but I am writing them at a great rate, and feel very optimistic and good about the ones that will be in it. You might, if you like, take a look at the July issue of <u>Poetry</u>, in which the eight last poems of my first book, <u>Into the Stone</u>, appear as the featured ones. There are various others to appear in other magazines, but I don't have my "concise, annotated guide" to my own forthcoming work with me here at the office, though I can let you know later, if you're interested. I like very much what you say about the reviews. These are very hard for me to do, and I sweat and strain like a real Atlas of the intellect to try to say what I really think and feel about the books I review, and fight with all arms and legs to keep from saying just something that sounds good. There is another of my long, hammer-and-tongs treatments of bookloads of verse in the Summer <u>Sewanee</u>. I'd appreciate your having a look, and telling me what you think. I'd like to know, particularly, what you think of the section on James Merrill. His mother lives here, and he (I understand) called me when he was here visiting her, though I never got to talk to him or see him. There is also a section on Cummings, and another on Kazantzakis' tremendous <u>Odyssey</u>, in which I really went all-out. So have a look.

By the way, I remember that when you took <u>Poem from an Old War</u>[156] for the <u>Paris Review</u> you said it might take you "two years to print it." It has been just about that long now. Will we be coming out this year, or will there be a longer wait? Either way, it is all right with me, but I would like to know what your plans for the poem are, if it is possible for you to tell me. And thanks.

About your trip to England: this is tremendous news. <u>Do</u> look up Geoffrey Hill for me, if he has not already reached this country by the time you get to his. Also get with Jon Silkin, if possible, and tell him (I said this in a review once, too, but he may not have seen it) that he has one tremendous admirer here. And keep in touch with <u>me</u>, too.

"The Snow" is the best poem of yours I have ever seen. I rejoice in its strength. Let me tell you what I like about it. First of all, your sensibility has always seemed to me to be that of "the ordinary American" (a remarkable being, truly, at his purest) magnified a thousandfold and furnished with the technical equipment to write poetry. This is good, for it puts you in touch with your time as I, for example, a strange, half-magical, half primitive kind of poet, could never be. Coupled with this is a kind of nostalgic, childhood, innocent quality that gets into your writing, and produces, at its best, some remarkably <u>true</u> poetry. I find all this in "The Snow," and more, too. There are some things in it I don't like, and I resent these even more because I love the poem so much. The sun really shouldn't, for instance, "protrude," quite. And the great vague wandering of the snow, so good and right later in the poem, isn't helped by your saying that the sun "presses" the snow on your pane of glass. The second stanza is superb. Even <u>I</u> can't find anything wrong with it. In the third stanza, <u>please</u> take out the vampire. It is just theatre. Instead, say simply, in its place, "It is so." Just that sentence. Then begin again, in the next line, with "Whatever I touch, etc."

And that is <u>all</u>. It is a superb poem. It is a real poem. Though, by God, one more objection. Don't say, at the end, "The sun has gone back to bed." That is sentimental and untrustworthy and unimaginative.[157] And now, the end of my commentary. Read the first of this paragraph to find out what the poem is. It is, let me say once more: good, true, deep. It moves me. It is part of my life.

<u>Flodden Field</u> is good, too, though must, certainly, as anything would, suffer by comparison. "The wild horses are singing" is a great line of poetry.

I don't like the others as well, though there are some good things. The "Letter" poem is too much the kind of thing that too many other poets can do, and have done, just as well, or nearly. I don't like all the cultural pronouncements, comparisons, and so on. It is better to feel, and to know, that way. The "City of Grandfathers" I don't like greatly, either, though the way it is done is interesting. "To deepen floors in the house" is good. That is after all, I see, what Turkish carpets are for, and maybe all carpets.

Please forgive the obvious haste in which this letter is being written, but I wanted to get this posted before I go to Florida for a couple of weeks. I know I sound unbearably pontifical when talking about your poems, but these are the things I like and don't like about them. But, really, everything, all the "don't likes," cancel out before "The Snow." This is the kind of thing you can do, and should do. Send me all like this you do.

Thank you again for your good letter, Don. Believe me, I think of you often, and will the day to come when we shall meet, and "change the direction of modern poetry," and may the world, too.

I shall be reading at YM-YWHA (Poetry Center) next winter or next Spring. Any chance (but no; you will be in England) of getting together in New York?

Yours, and write again soon. Sooner than last time.

Jim

2930 Westminster Circle, N.W.
Atlanta, Ga.

TO: PHILIP BOOTH

TLS, 1 p; Dartmouth College

30 July, 1959
Atlanta, Ga.

Dear Phil,

Thank you for your very welcome letter. The mail about the eight poems is approaching flood proportions, and your letter came right in the middle of lots of others. Of these, not many were better or more helpful than yours, and very few as good. Most of what you say is undoubtedly true, though I don't remember writing anything about light breaking out of wombs (though I wish I had), and wondered momentarily as I read your comments if you had been looking at the right set of poems.[158] I like very much what you say about the poems, though, despite our disagreement about one or two aspects of poetry that look as though they are hardening into permanency. I wonder about my own "perverse wilfullness" toward bad lines. Now as you know (certainly you know) that nobody deliberately writes lines he thinks are bad; therefore it would seem that what you tend to think of as bad probably (at least in my own work) strikes me as good. It may be there are certain failures of ear in these poems. At times they fail my ear. But there are also some rather deliberate crudities (though I wish they were natural ones and not so deliberate as they are), and it is probably these that strike you wrongly. On the whole, I am satisfied with them, but the thought haunts me that these are really not yet what I want to do in poetry, and not so by a very long chalk. As yet I have only flashes . . . flashes . . . and then nothing: the nothing in this instance being a lapse back into "the way people write poems." Believe me, I hate this as much as you do. That is one of the things that galled me most about my correspondence with Malcolm Cowley. He went invariably, and with a truly awe-inspiring instinct, toward those poems which were just poesie; ordinary, predictable. And so I pulled out and went you know where.

Something far more important than any of these things: I thought, and think, I should tell you how much I enjoyed talking to you the other night. Since I have the money and you poor teachers don't (otherwise you'd call me, wouldn't you? or so I hope), I like to take the incidental payment I get for poems and reviews and whatnot, and plough it back into the literary life: either buying books, or buying something for some writer I like, or calling up "my most faithful correspondents." So far, with the Poetry check, three others from the New Yorker, one from the Atlantic and a gigantic one from the Sewanee Review, I have called Wright and Donald Hall and you. Of these three, your voice said by far more to me than theirs did. Believe me, Philip, I really felt something . . . something. You sound so much more like myself: I don't mean me, of course, but someone enough like myself and different from myself in the really essential ways of being alike and different that truly and profoundly valuable exchanges are possible. Without elaborating too much, for I enjoyed talking to Wright and Hall well enough, and am sure I would like them both, Wright struck me (by his voice alone, you understand: but understand, too, that I am never wrong on these things) as being pretty much the withdrawn, intellectual, ego-guarding, semi-precious type that one normally associates with the term "American poet." Hall is too withdrawn, talent-nursing, hesitant, and a somewhat calculating "don't quote me on this" kind of person. You are not: none of these things pertain to you. You sound to me warm, very human, very good, prodigal, interested, vital, and truly and selflessly responsible. If all this sounds like an advertisement for the ideal American poet, or the ideal human person, believe me it is, and I would run it in the Saturday Review tomorrow if I didn't think I'd already found my man. I felt this so much more talking to you than I ever have reading your letters, much as I have enjoyed some of those. It is this personal quality that I have never really sensed in your poems; believe me, it is worth getting into them. Go with the best side of yourself, instead of other people's opinions or your own opinions of words on a bit of paper. That is what I am trying to do, though as yet I don't know the way to do't. But the thing is there to be found, believe me.

All Yours,
Jim Dickey

2930 Westminster Circle, N.W.
Atlanta, Ga.

TO: JAMES WRIGHT

TLS, 1 p; University of Minnesota

27 November, 1959
Atlanta, Ga.

Dear Jim,

Thank you many times for the wonderful, life-giving letter. I have been struggling to write to you, too, and tell you how I felt about all of us, but I have been more afraid to begin such a letter than I ever have about anything else. There is still this dead-sure certainty: nothing I could ever write would do justice to the feeling of absolute <u>rightness</u> I had about everything we did in New York.[159] Hart Crane and Lorca were leaning from the windows saying "Yes! Yes! That's it! Go on and say it! Go on and do it! It's all right! It's all right! You're home, now!" And we were. I could hear the voices over my head in the middle of the night when I fell on my knees on some street in the Village when Bly was walking me home and prayed for everything. After he left me I tried to sleep, but it was no good and I got up and dressed and walked around all night, praying in the middles of some more streets and singing and weeping and wringing my hands for joy. In the morning I did come in and slept a little, and then packed and left the hotel and went to Bly's apartment. You were gone, of course, as you had to be, and I left a note and began to drift by easy stages, each more painful than the last, out to the airport. And the rest is another one of the Histories of Hell. I am back again: back in "real" life, and immediately had to begin travelling, seeing clients, and the rest of the time-consuming clap-trap of business life. One of the most terrible and frightening things about being in such a situation as we were in in New York is that you are permitted, just for a few hours, for a day or two at most, to see how things, how human life <u>could</u> be. Perhaps it is a foretaste of Heaven, or perhaps everyday reality is simply Hell itself; I don't know. But I share, I triumphantly share your conviction that we will get together again, and roar with laughter, tell jokes, drink and read poems together, look at each other and listen to each other again. But I don't think it will be in January, as much as I would like it to be. I am not due to read at the Poetry Center until March. See if you can get a reading around March 10th, if you can. Otherwise I will try to come up to see you and Bly this summer in Minnesota, if such a thing is possible. Charles Tomlinson, the English poet, is coming down for a week or so this spring, and it would be wonderful if you could come down during the same time. I can let you know more about this later.

I love Bly. He is one of the most marvellous men I have ever seen, and yet a human being like all of us, too. But <u>what</u> a human being!

I am still so full of all we did and said that I can't really take it in, even yet. God willing, there will be more such times, and we must set the machinery of coming together again, in motion, no matter what kind of machinery it takes. Time is running out on this letter, though. I must eat, I must sleep, I must die, I must rise again. But I do so thinking mostly of you and Bly, and the reasons that I must rise. Write soon, holy being that you are, and tell me how to live.

Jim

2930 Westminster Circle, N.W.
Atlanta, Ga.

TO: JAMES MERRILL

TLS, 1 p; Washington University

6 December, 1959
Atlanta, Ga.

Dear Jimmy Merrill,

I am appalled to find I have waited so long to answer your good letter of October 12th. I can plead only a vast, unnecessary involvement in the awful trivia of business and a desperate attempt to get the book into final shape. I have also written a couple of long articles for Doubleday Anchor Books.[160] All this is finished now, though, and I have a moment to breathe. And with the first breath I want to tell you how delighted I am by the things you say in your letter, including the objections you have to certain of the phrases. Almost everything you say I agree with. When you say, for example, that "Into the Stone" strikes you as having virtually "interchangeable parts" I know immediately what you mean. It strikes me that way, too, and perhaps it does have them. For a long time I have been trying to do two things in poetry, both of which I have been told one should <u>not</u> do. The first is to get away, by whatever means, from the idea of a poem as <u>objet d'art</u>, which is a notion I have always hated, however much it has been drilled into me. The other is to be able to make statements, one after the other: <u>this</u> happens, <u>this</u> happens, then <u>this</u> happens. To go with all this, I have also been trying to assert connections in nature where none exists: to make the world do what <u>I</u> say, rather than what it actually does. "Stars shine and (therefore) wings grow." And so on. All this I was consciously or unconsciously trying to get said in <u>Into the Stone</u> (which is also the name of the book), so the poem is bound to strike you as a little odd. It does me. But that is my direction, as I see it. Of course, I am delighted that you think so much of the end of "The Landfall." You are the only one who has ever felt about it like I want people to feel. It is the last poem in the book; I wanted the tone and feeling at the end of the poem to be what I had to say to people: the thing I would leave them with.

I am sorry you couldn't get down to the reading. It seems to have been a great success. I am sustained, however, by the fact that you will come down here again this winter, and that there will be some more talk and drinking such as we did for the few minutes we got together last fall. Also, I read at the Poetry Center in March, and perhaps you can get down to that. How have the reviews of "Thousand Years of Peace" been going?[161] Are you doing any new poems? If so, I would be happy if you'd send me some. And send Maxine some recipes. Especially the one for Shrimp and Oranges.

Write again soon, when the mood takes you.

All Yours,
Jim Dickey

2930 Westminster Circle, N.W.
Atlanta, Ga.

TO: JAMES WRIGHT

TLS, 2 pp; University of Minnesota

21 March, 1960
Atlanta, Ga.

Dear Jim,

Please forgive me for waiting so long to write. It is the usual dreary story of having no time to write letters, or anything else, but only time for pouring out the endless line of cynical, creeping-Jesus type of slop for the "markets," those mythical places where all good advertising men go when they die, as though to their appointed Hell. I am fed up with "business," its money and its strategems, its people and its methods, its aims and its rewards. Bob[162] says he thinks he can get me into the United States Information Service in some foreign country, and if he can I am going, regardless of where I may have to work. I can feel the best of myself leak away day by day, and nobody but me caring if and whether it goes. But I care. And I'll just be God-damned if I'm going to put the rest of my life into something as hopelessly corrupt and damned as this is. So if you can get me on up at the University of Minnesota, for God's sake do it. I'll come tomorrow.

.Last week I read at the Poetry Center, and the whole thing seems to have been a success. The other two writers were crappy, if I do say so myself (they were Paul Carroll from Chicago and a nice house-wifely lady named van Duyn).[163] So, see-ing I had nothing to lose, I cut loose with some new poems, and I think the place really rocked. I know I gave it everything I had, and I was satisfied at the end that I couldn't have done better under any conditions. Bob and I had some wonderful talks. But, as usual, I didn't have nearly long enough to stay, and had to leave after only two days. It was a wonderful week-end, the only trouble being that you weren't there with us. I told Bob that there is some chance I might get up to see all of you at Bob's farm this summer, but we shouldn't start counting on it yet, for the chance that I can come is rather a long one. But we can at least hope for it.

I read your review in the March Poetry. Very good.[164]

And I don't even have a copy at the office of the poems (all those poems!) you sent me, or I would comment on them at infinite length, enthusiastically and admiringly. Your "new direction" seems to me a good one, though I liked the old direction, too. The kind of Europeanized semi-free-associational stuff is good, it shows the imagination doing as it will, out from under the hutch of our university-oriented diction and "form," no longer being held for "Ransom," as it were (!), but the danger of the dolce stil nuovo is, quite literally, that anything goes, and this anything includes the wrong or the indifferent things as well as the right things. The poet has got to be able to make the good associations ("the images that hurt and connect," as Auden surprisingly says),[165] and not just any associations. To prove this, Bob and I and some other people sat around a bottle of wine in New York and wrote a "collective poem," each contributing one line, and so on and on. We called the result "Lobster," and when we read back through it, it was surprisingly like the verse of some of Bob's contributors in The Sixties.[166] So this alone is not enough. I don't know what measuring-rod you play your images back against (excuse mixed metaphor here), but I do know that it's a good one. But when this faculty of trying out lines, themes, and images against what for you is the truth, the imaginative truth, fails, it can be just as disastrous as the failure of imagination we're witnessing all around us in the quarterlies, the drying up of the stream, the general constipation of the inventive powers. But you are not in danger of any of this, as far as I can see. The human power, that I loved so in your early poems, is here, too. And that is all we really want, or need.

I have read the galleys on the book,[167] and we should be in print in about four and a half months. Meanwhile, Harcourt Brace has written and asked for the second one (they make no promises, but they were so flattering I'm sure they would be embarassed <u>not</u> to take it).[168] I'm not quite ready for them with a whole book, but I have a good many new poems and am having Maxine type these up and am going to send them in as the main body of the book, which is to be called <u>Drowning With Others</u>, also the title of one of the poems, which <u>Partisan</u> is bringing out fairly soon.[169] And there are some pretty good things in it. At least I hope they are good. I'll have Maxine make up some extra carbons of some of them, and send them to you, if you'd like. There is a hunting poem I particularly like, called "Fog Envelops the Animals,"[170] not quite finished yet, which I think is going to be the best I've ever done. At least it's on a subject dear to my heart!

I'd like to go on and on, now, talking about poetry: about Neruda, Char, Lorca, and the rest of the great ones, but my time is, as always, limited. If you knew how much I would give to be able to sit down and work—<u>uninterruptedly</u>—on a poem for at least an hour, you would know how much I have <u>got</u> to get out of the business world. Success is ruining me. And that's the truth. I had rather be poor. The only trouble is if I were poor I'd <u>still</u> have to do <u>something</u> for a living, and whatever I did would take as much as or more time than this does. So I will either go back to teaching some place, if I can get a job, or into the Foreign service. I have had my fling at "American business," and I have served that succubus for four years. That is all the time I have for it. And all I will ever have for it. Thank God.

Let me hear from you. All my best.

Jim

P.S. I almost forgot. Charles Tomlinson, the English poet, is coming down here to stay with us a week. Did you ever get together with Geoffrey Hill? I like to think that you did, or that you will. If you do, imagine me as there, and drunk.

TO: JAMES WRIGHT

TLS, 2 pp; University of Minnesota

18 August, 1960
Atlanta, Ga.

Dear Jim,

Ah Yes! The letters are flowing! It is like in the old days of two years back, when we were beginning to discover things that I hope we never cease to discover, from each other. There are some people who give life out of their eyes, and you are surely one who gives it in your letters. Believe me, they have that quality.

Miracles! I already had the White Pony,[171] though it was laid away, in its original trade edition, in a dusty corner. I have it with me at the office now, blowing the dust off and reading (naturally, since your letter) Li Po, Wang Wei, and the others. You are dead right: this is ungodly great stuff (or, rather, godly great stuff). I am very happy I remind you of Li Po. Please don't apologize about the "loud screeching voice" which Li Po had. I can screech with the best of 'em, brother. As the Zen Master says, "when the beasts hear me, their skulls crack open." Payne came to the reading at the Poetry Center, and then he and I and Norman Mailer[172] and some others went to a party. Payne and I had a long talk, mostly about China. I said I liked his own poetry (which I don't) and his two diaries on China, Forever China and China Awake (which I do like, very much). By the way, you ought to get these. They are far and away the best things he's ever done, among his thousands of books. He is a nice, gentle, intelligent man. Perhaps we both ought to write to him.

A couple of "business details": I am delighted that you want to do the book. I myself would review it (you know, like Whitman did him), but somehow or other nobody wants to give the book out for review on these terms! It's probably just as well . . . I don't think I'm as well qualified to review my book as you are, anyway. John Logan[173] and some others tell me they also want to do it, but I'd be quite happy if you get the assignment from Rago. That would be good.[174]

I am sorry about Anne Sexton, but she just can't write. Kinnell I ended up by being pretty kind to, largely, I think because of the long poem you mention, which was first published in the Hudson Review.[175] I don't know what you mean, or who you mean, when you talk about Mrs. Sexton's being "taken up" by all sorts of people "in the East," and so on. I am too far from literary centers to know anything about all that, and I wouldn't care anyway. I don't know when I've ever tried so desperately to like a book, I think mostly because of the appealing, beseeching, begging picture of the author on the cover and the appealing, begging tone of most of the poems, all about how she tried to kill herself, and all that. I am sure Mrs. Sexton has had a hard time, and all that. But I have a quick, bristling suspicion when people keep telling me that they've tried to kill themselves a number of times. In my opinion, there has never been a determined suicide attempt which didn't succeed, much less two or three. It is hard to say things like this, but this gal's book looks to me suspiciously like a parading of mental illness, which you, who have had a harder time than anyone since Hart Crane, have never done, for example. Besides that, her language is full of clever, supercilious crap. No; the only thing good about her is her picture, which I do like. She should keep her mouth shut and just look at people. Without the begging to be "understood."

This is cruel, I know, but there it is.

There are some new poems shaping up: "Don Yearwood's Death in a Flow of Wind," "Goodbye to the Serpents," "The Called Fox," and "The Movement of Fish."[176] I'll send them along as they are finished (If ever).

No word from Bly. Go out to the farm and stick him in the ass with one of his own pitchforks. Maybe that'll get some action out of him. Maybe.

Job still crap. Am much grateful for your proposed assistance as to a teaching job. Yes; it would be wonderful for all of us to be together, including Berryman, whom I am inclined to believe in as a great man.[177] He has written me some wonderful letters. We are both great admirers of a young dead poet, a friend of his, named Robert Bhain Campbell. I am writing a poem now about Campbell, "young poet dead within cancer,"[178] but I'll be almost afraid to send it to Berryman, who should have the final word to say on it. Anyway, I'll send it to you, too. If you should see Berryman, tell him to please write me, and tell me, in the words of one of his poems, "what satisfactions there are." Tell him also (But I should be telling him) that I think a stanza of his about men working in a flour-mill with "sparkling eyes" and "light hair" is one of the greatest things ever got down on paper.[179]

It seems that the final ritual slaying of Thom Gunn is really not in the Summer Sewanee, after all, which is full of Italian scholars writing about Emily Dickinson, but is to appear in the Fall issue. So look for it there.[180]

Fire back another seven-page letter. It is like a deep well where the sun still penetrates! God! That is the place for the sun to penetrate! Still! Deep! And floating forever!

All yours,
Jim

2930 Westminster Circle, N.W.
Atlanta, Ga.

TO: JOHN HALL WHEELOCK

TLS, 1 p; Princeton

19 October, 1960
Atlanta, Georgia

Dear John Wheelock,

I hope all is well with you. We are fine at this end. Occasionally I go around to the stores and see if the book is moving, and, although we didn't, finally, have the autographing party, the stores here must have sold forty or fifty copies, mainly on the strength of the review in the local paper. If you haven't yet seen it through your clipping service, I'll send you a copy of it. The young Creative Writing Teacher at Emory, a college here, did an exceptionally good job, I think.[181] I have seen a couple of other reviews in newspapers, but none other. Have you noticed any? It would be very kind if you were to inform me when and if the book is reviewed in various places, for I hardly ever see the quarterlies and the other poetry-publishing and reviewing magazines unless I have something in them and the editors thus send me copies. Incidentally, if you'd like to see some new poems (new, that is, since the ones in the book), there are some in the current (Autumn) issues of Partisan, Yale, and Kenyon, and another long blood-and-thunder review in the Autumn Sewanee.[182]

Would it be possible for me to beat Scribners out of a few more copies of the book, or to buy them at a cost below store price? This would help me a good deal, because almost every writer I know has written and asked for a copy, and the first ones nearly all went to relatives; a necessary thing, I suppose.

The Guggenheim Committee has just tapped me, and, though the announcements of grants won't be made until Spring, it looks as though I shall get one. If so, I plan to sell everything (except my books and archery stuff) and go back to Europe for as long as I can stay. After that, I may be able to get back into teaching on my own terms. Or at least I hope so. My main problem now is time, which I need desperately. I am full of new projects, and I will never, if I live to be a thousand, finish writing the poems that I carry around me in large, dog-eared folders, and work at, almost literally, twenty-four hours a day.

I think of you often, John Wheelock, and hope that we may meet again soon. I may come to New York this winter on business, and if so I shall certainly let you know in plenty of time to make plans.

My best to you, and to your work, which, to judge from the examples you send me from time to time, is taking on a power and authority that must be a source of steady delight to you, as it is to me.

All Yours,
Jim Dickey

2930 Westminster Circle, N.W.
Atlanta #5, Ga.

TO: RADCLIFFE SQUIRES[183]

TLS, 1 p; Washington University

21 October, 1960
Atlanta, Georgia

Dear Radcliffe Squires,

I have your generous letter, and am very glad to have it. I am happy that you like what poems of mine you have seen. Scribners has just brought out my first book, called <u>Into the Stone</u>, and as soon as my editor sends me some more copies (the first ones, inevitably, had to go to relatives), I would be pleased were you to accept one. It is kind of a mixed book, but if the "responsibility to life and experience" you see in the poems <u>is</u>, in fact, in them, it is justified. The second book, <u>Drowning With Others</u>, is finished, and I have sent it along to the publisher who has been writing to me the longest, Doubleday. I have no way of knowing whether or not they'll print it, for I know nothing of the publishing of books.[184] Anyway, all that is behind me, and I am moving toward something. . . . something else: something I can only glimpse very dimly. From what you tell me of the poems you wrote in Greece (which I would dearly love to see), the impulse, if not the execution and subject matter, is very similar to yours. After your letter came, I went back and read "Compass" again, and I want to tell you, Radcliffe Squires, that the end of the poem on Mark Twain, in fact the whole last twenty or thirty lines, are among the two or three best damned things I have ever read in my life.[185] That <u>you</u> should have trouble getting published, as you intimate you do, is one of the most amusing and disheartening things I can think of, when the quarterlies and the rest of the places that print poetry are filled, month after month, with the most appalling kind of crap. You are exactly right in what you say about most poetry's "suffering from an abstract concept of things called creativity and art." I hate any kind of officialdom, and the kind of university-ized officialdom that now has a death-grip on American poetry is one of the most truly horrifying things that could happen to a great art form. There is a long review of mine in the current <u>Sewanee Review</u> (Autumn) in which I tilt with some of these windmills, and I'd like it very much were you to have a look at it and tell me what you think.

Before I forget to ask: <u>which</u> publisher is bringing out your book? I'll be sure to get it when it appears. Are the poems from Greece going to be in it? By the way, did you meet Seferis when you were over there? I would like to know him, though I can't read Greek, or speak it, or anything. A man named Kimon Friar wrote me a nice letter, as a consequence of my review someplace of Katzanzakis' <u>Odyssey</u>, which he translated, and he told me that he was bringing out an anthology of modern Greek poets, Seferis, Elytis et al, which I am very much looking forward to, since, in translation, they all seem very good to me, and maybe great.[186]

Is Don Hall still around there? He used to write to me a good bit, but he went to England some time ago, and I haven't heard from him in a long time. If you see him, tell him he owes me a letter, and I mean to collect. Also, the last time I heard, a curious little fellow named Jack Thygersen, with whom I taught for a while at the University of Florida, was there. Did you get to meet Geoffrey Hill, the English poet? He and I wrote back and forth for a long time, but have since quit. I think he is very good; the best of the over-formal formalists: "the new men" in England.

Again, I don't mean to run on and on. Really, I just wanted to thank you for your letter. It has life in it, and I am always happy to have more of that! And more!

Good luck, and write, but only if you feel the need. Don't do it as a "duty". Duty letters are no good. No life. The letter killeth, but . . . . . etc.

Jim Dickey

2930 Westminster Circle, N.W.
Atlanta, Ga.

TO: JAMES WRIGHT

TLS, 2 pp; University of Minnesota

20 November, 1960
Atlanta #5, Georgia

Dear Jim,

It is good to hear your voice again, which I would recognize, either in my ear or on paper, among a hundred million others.

I am happy that you are reviewing the book for Poetry. Certainly you don't need to hear me say that I had rather have you review me than any other man, living or dead, but nevertheless I will say it once more; it is so. In answer to your question about Lee Anderson: I don't know his Nag's Head, but I did review his only previous book, The Floating World (a good title!), a year or so ago.[187] It came out as (I think) one of the three books in Poets of Today III, and I roasted not only Anderson's book for its culture-conscious pretentiousness and (as you say) incoherence, but the whole idea of the three-decker book of poems. I have had a good many letters from people who think similarly, asking me how on earth I ever let myself get sandwiched this way. I can only say that Wheelock has been so unfailingly kind to me and so persistent that I finally went ahead and gave him the book. I don't really regret it, because the second book is about set now, and this one will be mine! Back to Anderson: you may want to look up my remarks in an issue of the <u>Sewanee</u> two or three years ago, which contain about all that I will ever have to say about Mr. Anderson. I am glad he writes: he appears really to put his back into it. I think he hits an astonishingly good lick every now and then, but then assiduously buries it under "learning." That is not what we want. If there is anything good about my own work, it is the banishment of this kind of thing in favor of a kind of <u>mindlessness</u>, as though the world itself spoke in its sleep. That is what I am trying to get at. Your own work, especially the new work, has this quality, and nowhere more than in the three new poems you send. I think the one about lying in the hammock is especially terrific![188] By the way, I saw Hoffman's review of <u>Saint Judas</u> in a recent issue of the <u>Sewanee</u>, and he seemed rather to slight your "conversion" from 19<u>th</u> century poetry (as you say) to your new phase.[189] In my opinion, this change of yours is quite likely to rank, in the end, with Yeats' change from the Celtic twilight stuff to the poems in <u>Reponsibilities</u>. Again: back to Anderson. <u>I</u> think he goes at the thing the wrong way, and doesn't produce anything that means anything to <u>me</u>; but he is a serious man who has given his whole life to poetry (he goes around recording poets at his own expense), and so must be listened to seriously. If the final verdict must be no (as I think it must) we should know (and say) exactly why.

Last week-end I read with Randall Jarrell at Hollins, in Virginia. I mean, it was like crazy, man! After the readings, which were received with an enthusiasm which actually frightened me, Jarrell and I sat for two and a half hours arguing in front of the several hundred students and guests, and let me tell you it is exhausting! We agreed on almost nothing (and I <u>mean</u> nothing!) and we cut and slashed and parried with deliberate and desperate urgency. The audience was violently partisan, and seemed to me more or less equally divided; there was wild applause after each bit of repartee (by Jarrell) and each bit of raving (by me), and at one point I thought I actually detected the wonderful sound of "Go! Go! Go!" as we went at it hotly: the sound of a crowd cheering for the home team to score in the last quarter, or the sound of a good, knowledgeable and enthusiastic crowd at a jazz festival, when one of the musicians (for some reason I think of tenor sax players) goes from technical virtuosity into inspiration, or art. It was a great experience for me. God knows what I said, but I certainly said it, I am sure. After it was over we fell into each other's arms (literally!) and there was more applause and we then went out and got drunk and promised each other we wouldn't be influenced by the other's work, swore undying fealty to poetry, and so back home! By the way, he thinks highly of your work: says it is the best of the younger fellows'.

As soon as I got home to Atlanta, my son and I strung up the bows, touched up the edges of the arrows, picked up Don Yearwood, the mighty hunter, Bud Adair, a Delta pilot who is a friend of mine, and ascended into the Blue Ridge to hunt. My God, it was great! We stayed a week, and almost froze to death. I took my guitar along, and we sat around the fire a hundred miles away from the nearest house and balladized the day's hunting. Yearwood and Adair were both very good, and contributed much better stanzas to the ballad (for it turned out to be all <u>one</u> ballad) than I did. Adair and Yearwood both got deer; Bud killed a 135-pound doe and Yearwood killed a <u>300-pound</u> ten-point buck, and so became the hero, not only of our camp, but of the whole Blue Ridge. I didn't fare as well, mostly (I suppose!) because I had Chris along, who is a good young hunter and good shot, but can't make the long, 15-mile stalks like a man can (he is only 9). Anyway, it was wonderful, and I wish you and Bob could have been with us! We had all kinds of weather, from fog in which you literally couldn't see your hand in front of your face, to sunny days like the end of summer. I shot another fox and three big grouse. But no deer. Here is the refrain of our song, "The Ballad of the Blue Ridge," though I won't give any of the rest of the hundreds of stanzas because I don't remember them.

> The sunlight is cold in the Blue Ridge
> And the deer is as smart as a man,
> And it's seldom the arrow flies truly
> From the archer's frozen hand.

And so it goes.
    Write soon, and tell me how your life goes. And give my best to your family.

All yours,
Jim

I think I could not take a teaching job now, though thanks anyway. The Guggenheim people have written to me, and if I get a fellowship I will sell everything (except books and bows!) and go back to Europe for a while.

TO: JOHN LOGAN

TLS, 1 p; SUNY Buffalo

12 May, 1961
Atlanta, Georgia

Dear John Logan,
    Please forgive my not answering your good letter (or letters, now, I reckon; I forget how many), but I have been terribly busy trying to get out of the advertising business and be poor again. I think I have found a way. I have just been given a

Guggenheim Fellowship, and when I pay off a few more family debts (I belong to one of the old crumbling Southern families, going to pieces, though not so spectacularly as those in Faulkner)[190] I am going to hoist my wife and two boys on my back and head for Europe for as long as the money holds out. And then I guess I'll be on the mercy of the teaching profession, or I'll go to working for the government, for I won't write another hack line as long as I live. Six years of that is enough for anybody north of the eleventh circle of Dante's hell. I have had it, as the boys used to say in the army. Really had it. Another six years in this business and I'd be dead. Or worse, I'd be a businessman.

I have the issue of Choice you were kind enough to send, and I thank you very much. I knew only a few of the poets therein, but met some good new ones. I think the venture is a very worthy one, and I'm very happy to be part of it.[191] Continued good luck!

Thanks, too, John, for the things you say about my Scribners book. The reviews have been pretty flattering, but I have an idea they're all praising me for the wrong things. I guess it's fatal when, after reading the reviewers, you say, "Oh, well, maybe these are the right things and I just didn't know it." Anyway, I'm pleased enough with the reception. The second book, Drowning With Others, will most likely come out with Wesleyan next year. I am about through with the third one, too. I thought of calling it The Secret Law or The Dream Flood, or A Helmet of Water, or The Conquest of Heaven or The Enemy's Peace.[192] Do any of these strike you as good?

I continue to enjoy your own poems with awe and admiration; I think that the sacramental quality they have is one of the most precious characteristics our poetry possesses. It is much the same thing as I am after, though I come at it without orthodoxy. Let us hope we both arrive at the same point, at the same time. There, surely, we shall meet at last.

All Yours,
Jim Dickey

2930 Westminster Circle, N.W.
Atlanta #5, Ga.

James Dickey, c. 1959

PART FOUR

POET AND TEACHER

July 1961–August 1964

TLS, 1 p; University of Minnesota

10 July, 1961
Atlanta, Ga.

Dear Old Jim,

I've done it at last. Five minutes ago I quit my job as "Atlanta's fastest-rising young businessman" (a term used by my present agency to its own purposes). I will probably be around Atlanta until the end of next winter, doing odd jobs and trying my best to live on my wits, until we leave on the Fellowship next March. But the main thing is that I am <u>out</u>. I am OUT, thank God! I simply could not do it any longer, and now that the break has come, "everything I look upon is blest."[1] I feel like overhauling the poetic engine, grinding the valves, re-boring the block, and getting set to run like hell on the poetic Road to Glory (or elsewhere) for the rest of my life, God willing. No longer do I have to give lip-service to a thing I despise, nor spend the best part of every day buttering up the great gray public. I don't care what my life involves from now on: I will never write another hack line as long as I live, and that's a solemn promise.

You are the first one I tell all this to, before even my wife, for as I sat at many desks for many years I have always had your kind of intellectual honesty before me, both as a reprimand and as the promise of the kind of integrity that I might attain to myself, if I ever had the guts. Well, now I have the chance, and I intend to make the most of it. From now on out I am a writer: not an <u>advertising</u> writer, not a scholar, not a free-lance hack, but a writer: one who believes constantly in the possibility of his standing on his own feet, on his own terms, on his own ideals and ideas. And that, so help me, is what I intend to do.

Nothing else new here. I shot another fox in North Georgia, and I spend a lot of time up in my ancestral haunts (around Nimblewill and Noontootley Creeks in the Blue Ridge Mountains) canoeing and camping and Wordsworthing around. I hope eventually to live there. I have a little property near Blue Ridge, Georgia, and if I can get together some money, enough to build a house on, I can go up there and live full time. And then all your friends and you and all my friends and me can get together up there, where the foxes bark all night "clear and cold"[2] and the geese are always flying over, and live in the sheer <u>beauty</u> of the world, which is great and God-like and never-ending. Let me hear from you soon, and tell me what satisfactions there are.

And I will <u>need</u> a job in the fall of 1962, so do what you can for me. I'd appreciate it.

Love,

Jim

2930 Westminster Circle, N.W.
Atlanta #5, Ga.

TO: DONALD HALL

TLS, 2 pp; University of New Hampshire

15 July, 1961
Atlanta, Georgia

Dear Don,

Big news! After five and a half years of working in these dark Satanic mills of American business I am out at last. After consulting my finances, savings, and so on, I found that my family and I could pretty well get along until March—when we take the Guggenheim—without my having to work. So, after considerable preparation, which included just sitting in my effusively decorated office and looking at the walls in pure joy, I walked in and told my elegant, fatherly employer Mr. Burke Dowling Adams (better known in the trade as "B.D.A.") that I was leaving. There followed such a scene as was never before enacted, comparable only to Priam's weeping over the body of Hector. I was ungrateful, the agency had spent a lot of money on me, and so on. Well, I have spent a lot of time on them: time I won't get back. Anyway, I am out now, and feel in possession of myself for the first time in a long, long while. What happens now I don't know, but I am awfully tired, and I just want to lie around, get the book in shape, write a few short, undemanding poems (this is the way one always thinks of new poems, and it never turns out that way) and "loaf and invite my soul,"[3] if I still have one. Believe me, it is a joyous time, and I want you to rejoice with me. And, if you hear of any good jobs in teaching which will be open by September, 1962, I'd appreciate your doing what you can for me; we'll need something when we get back from Europe.

I'm glad you were able to use two of my poems for the Penguin Anthology, and I'm rather happy, too, that you picked the ones you did.[4] As to why I write such long poems: well, on some of them I can't get myself or the reader into the situation without a good deal of detail and build-up, or so I feel. There are some marvellous short, short poems, as we all know: those little crystals. I have done some myself, not marvellous, maybe, but workable. On many things I start, though, I feel myself being pulled into trying to make a larger, in-the-round kind of experience; one that envelops the reader slowly and totally. There are a lot of these coming out in the New Yorker, and some shorter ones, too. I am all for concentration and compression when it is right for the poem, but I am also for dilation and expansion when that approach seems right, or righter. Needless to say, I am not invariably right when I choose one or the other. Some of mine are too long, just too long; these are the ones where I get fascinated by the detail for its own sake, a not unheard of thing in many other poems too, but sometimes approaching a vice in mine. I think I do less and less of this, though. At least I hope so.

As to the book; yes, I am recasting it, though I am not fooling with the individual poems much, having lost the impulse on many of them. Since I last wrote you I have written three new ones, all to be published by the New Yorker. This makes eight new poems, plus the long, long Dover poem, which should make a fat, new-looking manuscript. Again, I shall write at least four or five more before August, since I don't have to do office work any more. I'll just put all the poems in the book which I should like to see come out, and let the editors fight over which ones finally do. I can only include the poems I like; one never has any assurance that editors will agree with one; on the contrary. What time in August shall I send the manuscript back? Shall I send it to you, or what?

How is your own work going? Send me some new poems written like you wrote the one about the old aircraft.[5] That is great; I've read it over and over again, and like it almost as much as the snow poem. In the others, tighten down some; don't go laconic and self-satisfied and half funny like in the one about eating, or over-eating.[6] That kind of thing is too slight for you to fool with. Try some things with the elements, with rain or wind, or with more snow. There, judging from past performance, you can't go wrong. The snow is your father and brother!

As to Wilbur and his remarks about my criticism: he is quite persuasive and totally wrong. One could say—I wouldn't want to say it because I like his work very much and I like him more than his work; but of course I am saying it—that he simply wants an excuse to rest on his laurels, which are certainly considerable, and not do the pushing out and trying new things and risking failure that poets ought to do. Believe me, the fifties were a bad time for poetry; if our generation can't do better than let some other folks, barbarians, even (other than beatniks), who can give the Word a little life blood instead of using it as a beribboned exercise bar, take the ball and run with it for a while. In my last review in Sewanee (which will, incidentally, probably be my last review there, since one of my ene-

mies is now editor)[7] I have, maybe, a little more charity toward my own generation of poets; many of them, like Wilbur, <u>are</u> good poets. But it is a limited and
sort of self-aggrandizing and rather predictable (certainly, by <u>now</u>, predictable!)
kind of good, and we must look to something else. Something like Lawrence,
maybe; I don't know. Perhaps something totally different from Lawrence and all
others. Somehow or other, the time is right for poetry now; people, all kinds of
people, would read it if poetry itself were not like it is. That is our fault. But I get
letters from strangers all over the place, even as far away as South Africa. We all
do, I'm sure. And now more than ever. I think we can do something great for
poetry, and for humanity, too (I risk sounding undegraduate, but then I essentially am, and probably always will be) if we can just break through.

My love to you and to your wife. I hope some day we may meet.

All yours,
Jim

2930 Westminster Circle, N.W.
Atlanta #5, Ga.

TO: DONALD HALL

TLS, 2 pp; University of New Hampshire

18 October, 1961
Atlanta, Ga.

Dear Don,

Good letter, great letter, and thanks. When letters like yours come in I really
ought not to wait so long to answer. My excuse this time is that I have been out of
town most of the time since your letter came. I took a long, two-week swing up
through Virginia and North Carolina reading from my own works in a solemn
voice at Washington and Lee, University of Virginia (where R.W.B. Lewis[8] and I
are giving something called the Rushton Lectures in February, just before I take
off for Europe) and some other smaller schools. I made enough to keep us alive
for a couple of months, but will need to read some more before we leave. I am
supposed to be pretty good, or so everybody tells me, though I like to think that
it's the poems that are good and not just the reading. My closest reading date to
you is at Miami of Ohio, which doesn't yet have a date set for it. I don't know how
far that is from you, but it's closer than Atlanta is, anyway. Yes, I guess I could
come up there to read, if you could "make it worth my while." I don't know
exactly what my "while" is, but if Michigan wants me to read, have them make
me an offer. I have gotten everywhere from $250 (plus expenses) to $500 (plus

expenses), but don't believe I could come for less than $250. The main thing would be to get together with you, in what should be a meeting for which they (or we) should roll out the cloth of gold. I'll bring half if you'll bring the other. Anyway, let me know what the prospects are.

I have the galleys of the book,[9] and am living with them in that slow process that all writers know. The proofs certainly look good, and the poems seem to hold up well, too. My God, Don, thank you so much for the things you say about the book. I hope it is just half as good as you say it is.

About teaching there:[10] yes, I too would like that, and the climate wouldn't bother me, I don't think. The business of mimeographing things and going around to schools with my hat in my hand I won't do. If I go back into teaching, it will be because someone makes me a good enough offer of his own free will. I have no desire whatever to "sell myself," as we ex-ad-men say. Whoever I end up teaching with will have to want me and make active efforts to get me. I had rather teach in a small school, even a high-school, where I was genuinely wanted than in a Yale or Harvard where I was just tolerated and made to feel suspect and "grateful" all the time. You know what I mean, I'm sure. My process of getting a teaching job is simply to put out, among my friends in teaching, the word that I'm more or less available to the right offer, and then let the schools do what they want to about it. Already seven or eight have written me, and it's likely I will go to Washington and Lee or possibly the University of Virginia next fall. Or I might work with the Louisiana State Press as senior editor, another job that's been offered me. Right now I'm just waiting until all the bids are in. If Michigan wants to negotiate on that basis, I'm ready. If not, thanks anyway, as always, for your efforts on my behalf, which have been the best efforts that have ever been spent thereon.

The people I know at Michigan are you (I wish I did), a fellow that used to teach with me at that unspeakable University of Florida named Jack Thygersen, and Radcliffe Squires, with whom I have some correspondence, and possibly Allen Seager,[11] whose work I greatly admire (Amos Berry, particularly), and whom I wrote a couple of fan letters a few years back. So it must have been one of those you talked to about me.

The fellow you talked to at the Yale Book Shop was Royce Smith,[12] a very likeable homosexual boy who used to be in charge of the book shop in a large department store here. He is the great and good friend of another man of the same persuasion named George Marion O'Donnell, who is also living at Yale, I think. He used to teach here at a tiny school called Oglethorpe, and he and Royce lived in a little cabin out near the campus. They used to give some good parties, but I always felt a little out of place, needless to say.

On my trip up through Tennessee and Virginia I stopped off at Tellico Plains, Tennessee and went hunting for three days with an old country guy up there I know who has some good dogs. I had a chance at a bear, but missed him. I didn't get a shot, but followed him for six hours. He treed, finally, a mile away, and another fellow killed him with a gun. I did get a big hog, which seems to be becoming my specialty. I am going hunting next week down in the Piedmont Game Management Area, and if I get any venison I'll freeze some of it and airmail it to you. Have you ever eaten air-mailed venison? Neither have I.

Yes, I am still under contract to the <u>New Yorker</u>. I am more or less living on them now, and will be until I take up the fellowship. Moss has been a very good editor for me, though I understand that Simpson[13] and some of the others (you?) don't like him, or at least don't like the way he does business. I have eighteen or nineteen more poems coming out with them, and they are asking for more all the time. I am busy with poems! Luckily I have a big backlog. I counted poems the other day, and I have about half enough for another book, which I am calling <u>Springer Mountain</u>,[14] after a place in North Georgia where I hunt. The Appalachian trail starts there. This book has some experimental things in it which are strange and exciting, at least to me.

Robert Bly is coming here to see me this November. His wife is going to have a baby, and won't <u>that</u> be something! He'll be raised on the mother's milk of Neruda and Trakl![15]

My best to you, Don, and write soon. You once told me that I didn't say much to you when I talked about poetry having to have a "life-giving" quality. Well, I was right again, as usual. Just read your own letter to me to understand what I mean. They give <u>me</u> life! Look!

All yours,
Jim

Who wrote the jacket blurb for the book? Wilbur? Thank him, or whoever.[16]

2930 Westminster Circle, N.W.
Atlanta #5, Georgia

TO: BROTHER ANTONINUS[17]

TLS, 1 p; Bancroft Library

20 May, 1962
Positano, Italy

Dear Brother Antoninus,
    Your letter finally caught up with me here in Positano, after being forwarded from my home in Atlanta to my mother's home and then to Rome, Naples and

Salerno. I am very glad indeed to have it, needless to say. I have regretted the whole controversy[18]—if such it may be called—perhaps more than you have; I have been in a good many, some of which I welcome and some not, but I had a feeling from the beginning that this one was not based on the real issues; what issues there were I tried to make plain as best I could, but I couldn't really lay my hands on the right ones, and so I was always having to defend a point of view that I only partially believed in. I am heartily glad the whole thing is over, and even gladder than that that you have seen fit to write. Your writing (instead of my writing first) proves, I guess, that you are a better person than I am, which I am not only willing but eager to admit. Please accept whatever portion of my total apology you can, and let us look forward to having that drink you mention, even if it never happens that we are able to do so. I have been approached to do some readings out that way, but I have to have five or six more colleges before I can make expenses. Since I quit my business job to take the Guggenheim Fellowship I am now in Italy on, I have prospects in the States only of living on my wits and on writing. Since I write only poetry and critical prose, that is going to be a pretty tough row to hoe, and I take as many readings as I can to supplement my meager winnings from the literary pool. Can you get me a reading or two out that way? I'll be home in September, and available any time after that. The best thing about such a trip would be, at least from my point of view, that it would give me a face-to-face chance to tender you the apology I certainly owe you. So, if possible, see what you can do; I'd appreciate it.

Understand, too, that I fully sympathize with your dismay over the way you've been reviewed; first you were unlucky enough to get a glib-talking moron like Fiedler,[19] and then me, whatever I am. The most distressing thing about one of your letters to the editor of the Sewanee was that you seemed to think that I simply used your first book as a stick to beat your second one to death with. Believe me, that was far from my intention: The Residual Years is a wonderful book, I think. When the dust jacket says that it is time for poetry to take its foot out of its mouth and talk language that can be understood, it isn't just selling books: for once a blurb really tells you something you can use. And the poems do so wonderfully speak, about places where "the peace is enormous," and there are "bent-winged birds." I guess the full fury of my carping fell on your later book because I had liked the earlier one so much; I am terribly suspicious of orthodoxies for poets, though I realize that they have been good for some writers. Tune in to the Summer Sewanee and watch me take Yvor Winters apart on this score, by the way.[20]

Do you see what I mean in the article on Logan?[21] Or am I wrong completely?

My own second book has been out a couple of months, and someone has called me, I am told, a (if not the) leader of something named "the new mysticism."[22] I don't know if I am or want to be, but I think the book, which is called

Drowning With Others, is a fairly good one. If you get a chance, have a look at it. I'd send you one, but I had to sell all my author's copies to buy gasoline to get to the boat in February.

My best to you, and write again, if the spirit should happen to be on you at any time in future. I'll be in Positano another month.

All yours,
James Dickey

Via Boscariello, #13
Positano (Salerno), Italy[23]

TO: ROBERT BLY

TLS, 4 pp; Robert Bly

30 June, 1962
Venice, Italy

Dear Bob,

Delighted to have your letter and the new copy of The Sixties, which I'll talk about later. First, before I forget, I want to give you the Italian of the poems you ask for. I haven't a copy of "Tappetto," for I sent home the book it was in; if I come on a copy in a book-store I'll write it down and send it to you; otherwise I'll have to wait until I get home. Here are the others:

Invitation

Come into my bed to hatch the cold ashes.
Just as death dawns, we'll fall apart:
When the potency of the sexes is beaten down
Into petrified birds
And the glorious being that has destroyed us
Is nothing more than our two hostile cadavers.

André Frénaud

Poem

Each stands alone at the heart of the world
Pierced by a single ray of sun.
Almost at once it is evening.

Salvatore Quasimodo

Here are three more of Ungaretti's I have done, which you may want to put with the first three to make a larger group. I won't give you the Italian yet until you decide whether or not they are successful English poems, which is the whole point. Actually, I see, there are four rather than three:

Nostalgia

When
The night is about to vanish
A little before spring
And only rarely
Someone goes by,

Over Paris densens
An unclear color
Of weeping:

At a corner
Of a bridge
I watch and think about
The limitless silence
Of a slender
Girl:

Our
Sicknesses
Melt into each other,
And, as if carried away,
We remain.
* * * * * *

This is one of early war poems I think is real good:

Vigil

All night long,
Thrown down beside
A massacred
Friend,
With his wide mouth full
Of the full moon,
With the congestion
Of his hands
Reaching

Into my silence,
I have written
Letters filled with love.

I have never been so close
To my life.
*   *   *   *   *   *

Evening

At the foot of evening's steps
Clear water runs by,
The color of olives,
And reaches the brief, memoryless fire.

Now in the smoke I hear crickets and frogs

Where grass trembles tenderly.

*   *   *   *   *   *

This next one is probably Ungaretti's masterpiece. If I do it any kind of justice at all you can see how good it is.

Rivers

I lean on this lopped tree,
Abandoned to a despair
That has the lethargy
Of a circus
Before or after the performance,
And look up into
The quiet passage
Of clouds across the moon.

This morning I stretched out
In an urn of water
And like a relic
Lay still there.

The Isonzo streaming over
Rounded and polished me cleanly
Like one of its stones.

I gathered upon me
The four great bones of my limbs
And went away

Like an acrobat
Over the water.

I hunkered down
Beside my clothes,
Filthy with war,
And like an Arab
Bent down
To receive the sun
Into my head.

This is the Isonzo,
And here, best of all,
I know myself
A peaceful thread
Through the universe
Woven.

My worst torture
Is when
I do not believe myself
In harmony.
But those secret
Working
Hands
Grant me
Rare
Happiness.

I have gone through
All the stages
Of my life.

These are
My rivers:

This is the Serchio
From which have been drawn
For two thousand years, perhaps,
My country's people,
And my father and mother.

This is the Nile
That saw me
Be born and grow
And burn with unknowingness
In the stretching of plains.

This is the Seine,
And in that turbidity
I have been stirred
And have known myself.

These are my rivers
Said over again in the Isonzo.

This is my nostalgia
Which in each of them
Glows to me through water
Now that night comes
And my life appears
A flower's crown
Of shadows.

*   *   *   *   *   *

Let me know what you think of these while I am in Zurich, which will be from the 9th through the 13th of July. If your letter misses me there it will be a long time catching me, for we are doing some hard travelling from then on out. And could you pay for the other poems now (and any of these you want to print?)?[24] I'd appreciate it, for things are expensive over here and we can use everything we can get. If payment before publication is "outside the policy of the magazine," I understand, of course; far be it from me to interfere with editorial policy.

About the New Yorker: I know well your feelings about it, and the people who write for it. Now know mine: The New Yorker has sustained life in my family for well over a year now; they have lent or given me money when I needed it most, and they have printed the best things I have written. I don't share your contempt for money (that is, for other people's earning money); I am not that pure. Don't talk to me about "kissing their rump": that kind of talk you can get away with with other people; not with me. You're not all that good a friend of mine; nobody is. I'm not interested in "justifying" writing for this that or the other place; that I do as I see fit. I am interested in letting you know just what bounds there are in my regard for you; they are wide, necessarily; I like them that way. But they are not infinite, and we'd get along a lot better if you understand that they do not include remarks of the kind you see fit to make on occasion. I'm sorry, truly, if I seem like an ill-tempered son-of-a-bitch, which I may well be and definitely am a good deal of the time. If you think all this tirade is excessive, you're probably right. If it is, forgive me, for you are one of the few people that I genuinely care for; that is precisely why I am saying these things.

Well, with that out of the way, I can close by saying how much I do hope we can see you again in the winter, when my family and I drive up to Reed to stay for a couple of years. I wish we could all be together here in Venice, where the weather is beautiful and even the tourists are happy. We are buying Mary[25] a few little things we hope she'll like.

Yours,

Jim

C/o American Express
Zurich, Switzerland

TO: DONALD HALL

TLS, 2 pp; University of New Hampshire

27 August, 1962
London

Dear Don,

It is surely very good to hear from you again, and at such length, too! It makes me feel like sitting down and writing one of those long, youthful letters (maybe letters of that kind are the only way back into youth for such as us, even more so than our "official" or hopefully immortal writing in poems and stories) about the future of poetry and <u>our</u> future as poets, and what is wrong and right about all the poems we know and the ones we hope to do. One of these days I hope to write such a letter again, and by all rights it should be to you. I used to write them back from the Pacific twenty years ago, accompanied by long, excruciatingly poetic descriptions of night missions over burning Manila and the Pacific sea-phosphorus; those were the great days of poetry for me, when it was all to be discovered, and being discovered, along with sex and death. It is not often I can catch more than a faint notion of that time any more, as I get more bogged down in the technicalities of poetic statement, and in the <u>ways</u> of saying things, and I still harbor a kind of delighted notion of poetry as a <u>saying</u>, a divine communication, "where only necessary things are done / With that expert and grave dexterity that ignores technique."[26] I am very glad indeed that you like my stuff so well, and even gladder than that that you should write and tell me so. But what I have done now is only the beginning. I remember reading in William James[27] (who speaks as everybody's father should or would, if he could) about what he calls "fatigue points": sorts of physical barriers to energy something like the sound and heat barriers in the paths of high-speed aircraft, and how, if you push yourself determinedly past them, then whole new areas of energy open up. I am feeling, these days, about poetry like that. With the third book, <u>Springer Mountain</u>, I want to pass out of the first phase and on to something totally different, as yet only hinted at. And then . . . God knows what. But I have a great, bursting sense of the untried <u>possibilities</u> of language, and think continually of people unleashing tremendous reservoirs of human energy, faith, love, and human accomplishment for good out of places in themselves which have been waiting, and are waiting, for something like the truth of poetry—of <u>their</u> poetry—to turn loose. There are truck drivers and waitresses who could write better poetry than I ever can, if they just <u>would</u>, if they just wanted to (<u>I</u> want to, and they <u>should</u> want to); I feel, as Neitzche said, like one "who prepares the way for one greater than myself". John the Baptist also said something like this, but even in my present soaringness I know better than to evoke such an image. Well; we'll see. My grandiose ideas had better be kept for the poetry, where the iron will of lines and ideas will provide the tests they require, along with time . . . or Time.

I spent some fine time . . . three or four days . . . with Geoffrey Hill, and I am so <u>damned</u> glad I went. I didn't get your letter until I got back to London today, so was not able to avail myself of your advice, which was all, as they say, right on the money. Geoffrey kept telling me, and almost from the first, about how we "sat there, hating each others' guts," and then in the next breath saying, or mumbling inaudibly, "But . . . now . . . for God's sake . . . can't you stay another day." Well, we did stay another day, and disagreed violently, and agreed even <u>more</u> violently (and when Geoffrey agrees with anyone, the sun comes out all over England, a thing which, as you know, it rarely does). He showed me some new stuff he has done which is <u>wonderful</u> (by which I mean incredible, stupendous, Ezekiel-saw-the-wheel-in-the-air stuff, and I mean, as the Bible says, in the <u>middle</u> of the air. But it's like his <u>early</u> stuff, as I was exstatically careful to point out to him (as I am to you, and triumphantly).) His worst tendency is to go cold and dead and academic, making poems which are just excercises and complicated explanations of what he's talking about, and which have no <u>reality</u> to them, no urgency, no nothing, but the trimmed bones of discourse. Wait'll you see these <u>new</u> ones! My God! I hope to write something on him when I get home.[28] And I may call on you for help, for his own grumbling notions of what he's doing are next to no help.

About my own book: in keeping with your advice I'll wait and send it in to you in time for your winter or spring session[29] (you'll let me know, I hope, the best dates for this). That'll give me time to finish two long new poems I've begun, and which I want in the book. But most of it is finished, and slated for publication, mostly in the <u>New Yorker</u>. Bob Bly disapproves of this, but I don't. Moss seems to me a very straight guy, and never hesitates to tell me what's wrong (usually plenty) with what I write. Anyway, you can gauge something of the tenor of the book from what is appearing in <u>New Yorker</u>, if you usually see it.

Again, I would like to do a reading there, and could probably arrange the date you mention (from the 6th to the 10th of January), and would take any fee you could muster, if you could get me a couple of other readings in that area to make good the extra travel. I would very much like to get together with you, for I owe you a very great deal, and would like to say so, looking you in the eyes.

My best to you, Don. And write again as quickly as you can; by return air if possible. I shall be here until September 5th.

All yours,
Jim

p.s. I haven't gotten any fee from Meredith.[30] The only address they have for me is at home, in which case my mother would forward. Is there anyone there I could write to? I could sure use the money. Do let me know about this.

TO: JOHN LOGAN

TLS, 1 p; SUNY Buffalo

18 November, 1962
Atlanta, Georgia

Dear John,

I have just crawled back down out of the North Georgia woods, covered with dead beggar-lice and live tics, and contracted with John Hardy to come up to Notre Dame around the 8th of December, which isn't far off. I am not sure of the exact date, and Hardy didn't at the time seem to be sure either, but it will most likely be the 8th or a day or so after. I haven't heard from Hardy on this exact date, which is pretty important, so if you see him tell him to get in touch with me right away and let's wrap it up. I'll be coming to you from Washington University in St. Louis, and I'll be flying in, but I don't know the schedules as yet; I'll let you know later. A day or two before the Washington reading I have to give a joint prose-poetry reading with Peter Taylor[31] at Miami of Ohio, which makes it, all in all, a pretty hectic three or four days. I'm glad I'm ending at Notre Dame, which I look forward to as a very relaxing time.

Things go well with us, though we are in process of a general upheaval occasioned by our pulling up roots here and going out to Portland to live. We must sell the house, arrange with the movers, and all that sort of thing. My wife and I counted up, the other day—in a kind of awed and queasy fascination—twenty-seven places we've set up "permanent" housekeeping in, everywhere from Buffalo Speedway, Texas, to Naples. I hope we can stay in the Northwest a while, but right now it looks as though we'll probably be there no more than three years, or even just two. I like the world, though, and am interested in seeing as much of it as possible. One of my permanent nightmares and redemptive hopes is that right now, as I sit here writing to you, there may be—there <u>is</u>—someone in Aswan, Burma, in Smolensk, Russia, in Paris, London, Berlin, in Shrewsbury, Dubuque or Fresno, California, that would make all the difference and justify everything. That person—those persons—are living now, and I'll never know them. If I meet one or two during the rest of my life, I'll be lucky. But the One—man, woman, or child—I shall never meet, and that is the most tragic thing in experience, for me as for everybody else.

Well, I won't go on and on. Try to give me a final confirmation on the reading date as soon as you can, or get Hardy to. And please say hello to Ernest Sandeen[32] for me, if he's around. Tell him I look forward very eagerly to meeting him.

One thing: I'll be very much interested to see what you say about the book in Critic.[33] Send along a copy whenever it happens to come out.

My best to you, and write soon.

All yours,
Jim Dickey

2930 Westminster Circle, N.W.
Atlanta #5, Ga.

TO: DONALD HALL

TLS, 1 p; University of New Hampshire

10 January, 1963
Portland, Oregon

Dear Don,

This is just a note to tell you where I am, and to tell you how very, totally much I appreciate all the things you say about the new book, and also to discuss whatever possibilities there are of my coming there to read sometime next spring. As to the latter: yes, I'd be glad to come, but I guess I shouldn't definitely commit to anything until I see which way the wind is blowing in these parts, among the Department Heads, and so on. Needless to say, I'd surely like to do the reading, for it would give us a long-deserved chance to get together and solve the State of Things, in Poetry and Life. Meanwhile, since I am in charge of a kind of reading program here, I'd like to offer <u>you</u> a chance to come out here and read. I suppose that your coming here would be contingent upon (as we used to say in Advertising Plans Boards Meetings) your being able to get enough other readings in this area to make your coming out financially worth while. I'm not sure yet what we could give you, but we would put you up with us, in a great draughty barn of a place we've rented from a Political Science professor on sabbatical, and so you could tack part of the expense money onto your reading check as profit. Well, think about it. If we can't get together at Michigan, we shall here. But both, of course, would be infinitely desirable (as we also used to say in Advertising).

I won't go on and on, but will close so as to get this in the mail, and the epistolatory monkey on <u>your</u> back. Can we expect to hear about the book pretty soon? Or when? I've written a couple more poems to go in it, all to come out in <u>N Yer</u>.[34] Yes, the big spread there—a bold experiment from Moss's point of view—seemed very nice, and there has been a mountain of mail on it.[35] People <u>do</u> read the verse in the <u>N Yorker</u>, evidently, and a lot of them can tell you the exact place you stood when you saw or wrote something (down on my old grandfather Samuels' place, right off Highway 116, just after you turn off at . . .) and so on, all places that I have never seen, but now, for some reason unconnected with poetry, I would like to see. I am writing away on a lot of new things, and trying to get my prose book into shape, and filling some old boxes with notes for a new novel, a strange kind of thriller called <u>The Deliverer</u>, some of which is to come out in various magazines,[36] and the movie rights to which are beginning to be dickered for, even though I haven't actually written a word of the book as it will finally be! I have a high-powered agent in New York (for prose fiction, though I've never written any!) who evidently can sell stuff by prose synopses. Talk about monkeys on backs! What a burden on the poor writer! Especially since I am clumsy in prose; writing it is like trying to put on a wooden coat. Well, we'll see what happens. But it is all fun, and I am pushing ahead on some new poems I hope you'll like. I'm trying some new tacks and departures, and there are more opening up all the time. It is exciting, and the critical reception given to <u>Drowning With Others</u> is heartening indeed; in fact it is astounding: I keep thinking, on reading something like Simon's or Thom Gunn's review, "I wish to hell someone would say those things about <u>me</u>," and it is strange to realize that that's just what they're doing.[37] But what you say, in private, in letters, is worth them all, and more than all.

Write soon, when you can.

All yours,
Jim Dickey

NOTE NEW ADDRESS:
3807 S.E. Harold
Portland #2, Oregon

TO: DONALD HALL

TLS, 1 p; University of New Hampshire

13 February, 1963
Portland, Oregon

Dear Don,

Yes to two things: yes, you have sent me the Pale Blue Poems, or the Tinged-With-Purple Poems, hot from the mimeograph machine. "The Stump" is still the best, and for the same reasons. The ending is good, though it does remind me a little of Roethke's poem about the greenhouse riding out the storm, "Still bearing her full cargoe of roses."[38] Maybe just getting the word "cargo" out would kill the resemblance, if you feel it needs to be killed. I like "Birds," too, though Bob Bly's hand is beginning to be felt, as it needn't, so much. His way of writing is as constricting as it is releasing: no narrative (and so no real interest in "what comes next," in the sense of a story, no associations but rather fortuitous ones, no real rhythmic structure). Jim Wright was written his whole third book this way, largely at Bob's prompting;[39] he (Jim) seems to me diminished thereby; I love some of his early stuff; I can't love any of this; it is too arbitrary and drifting. I like a strong sense of <u>necessity</u>, as in "The Stump." That is better; that is good, or at least to one reader.

The other yes: yes I can do two (or more) readings in one day. And very easily. Set 'em up in the other alley!

I am going to have to do some negotiating to get you the money you want. Donald Justice, my beloved predecessor,[40] used up the year's fund of the school's money for bringing poets here—including <u>my</u> part of the year—on bringing a couple of his mediocre friends here and entertaining them like royalty. The student part of the fund is still intact, so I have a hundred dollars guaranteed. I am going to see the President (of the University of course; not Kennedy) today to see if he will give me the other hundred. But come out you shall, even if I have to pay you myself, with the last of my ill-gotten gains from the Ad game.

I cut this short to get it in the mail, looking forward, on the way to the mailbox, to seeing you in a month.

All yours,
Jim

P.S. Tell Squires I will bring his manuscript when I come.[41]

3807 S.E. Harold
Portland #2, Oregon

TO: HENRY RAGO

TLS, 1 p; Lilly Library

3 March, 1963
Portland, Oregon

Dear Henry,

Thanks so much for the note. Sure, I'll take on the Aiken for you, plus the chronicle you see shaping up in future.[42] I have plenty of time here, and can give all these the attention they should have. I have a couple of other reviews and articles that are in the mill, but they should be out of the way by the time the Aiken book reaches me; I can meet your middle-of-April deadline easily, and also any deadline you want to set for the chronicle.

My own new book, <u>Springer Mountain</u>, is set for next February, and I am already at work on a fourth one.

Could you help me with a problem? I want to write some poems under another name—a couple of other names, in fact—to see if I can take on different "writing personalities" in case I get tired of the one I have. I'd like to send some of these to you and see what you think of them, but, in case of publication, I wouldn't want my real identity known. Is this a legitimate kind of pursuit, in letters? A Portuguese poet named Pessoa did this some time ago—he had <u>four</u> alter egos!—and I wanted to try it, just to see what would happen. On the other hand, I don't want to submit poems to my editors—such as yourself—without letting them in on what I am doing; that would somehow seem wrong to me. Could you advise me on this? If you don't think it's a good idea, I'll publish the poems under my own name, though they're quite unlike anything I've ever done before.[43]

I'm glad Juliet[44] likes the guitar pick; it seemed a good one to me when I used it. I'm making some progress on the great instrument myself; there are some good pickers out here at Reed, a strange place where barefooted eighteen year old philosophers with beards walk under the campus trees debating the finer points (only the <u>finer</u> points!) of the <u>Critique of Pure Reason</u>. They are a good bunch of kids, though, and I am enjoying myself hugely. I'll be here all next year, then down in California for a year, and then maybe back to Italy, though I'm not clear, yet, as to what's going to happen that far ahead.

Caroline Kizer came down here yesterday for a reading I'm doing tomorrow. She seems in good spirits, and asked to be remembered to you.

Could you tell me the name of MacCaig's book?[45] I'd like to get (buy!) it and read it.

My best to you. And I look for your own book soon; it will be good to have it.[46]

All yours,
Jim Dickey

3807 S.E. Harold
Portland #2,
Oregon

P.S. I enclose a couple of new poems, which you may want to put with the "Folk Singer" piece if they're any good. I think "The Being" is not bad.[47]

TO: ALLAN SEAGER

TLS, 1 p; Bancroft Library

24 March, 1963
Portland, Oregon

Dear Allan,

Well, that is a good letter, and I'm glad to have it. I, too, have trouble finding people I take to—I almost never respond to anybody right off—and most of the time am pretty much off to myself, slowly trying to put the world together. It was doubly good to meet you the other night, not, as you say, too, entirely because I like your work so much, but because you are somebody I can talk to, and have the feeling that relevant things are being said. That doesn't happen to me very much, as much talking as I do with these eager students around here. Your comments on the novel I was stumbling around trying to explain were very helpful; I already think I can see a way to take out the implausibilities you noted. I haven't written much prose fiction—hardly any since I got out of college—and so consequently the conventions are strange to me: trying to write prose is like trying to put on a wooden coat. Verse I can move around in easily, or fairly easily, but the whole other apparatus of fiction is something I am going to have to get used to. I wouldn't have tried this book, except, like an idea for a poem, the story kept coming back to me, tightening and tightening down and into an orderly sequence, and I felt it was too good—too neat, maybe, to lose. Like the Joyce of Ulysses— but only like him in this respect, unfortunately—I thought for a while of turning the idea over to somebody else to do, or making a TV play out of it, or something of the sort, but in the end decided that, since the idea was mine and the experiences it is based on were mine, I more or less had an obligation to try to write it, if anyone did. And you have helped a whole lot, already. When I get it a little more together, I'll send you parts, if you like.

I am reading slowly through the issue of <u>Critique</u>, and finding a lot to like, though I was amused at the selection of cuttings from the reviews concerning <u>Amos Berry</u>.[48] Some of them are right, though, in noting that the novel turns on the believability of Amos's action in shooting Walter Rickert: the assumption that a man would or could believe that the essentially <u>symbolic</u> act of killing "the big organizer around here" would have any real or <u>actual</u> significance, or bring about any change in the things that the man has come to abhor. It's not the crime and its reasons that I like so much about the book, though. It's the outlining of Amos's predicament as a man who subtly but strongly feels that his real life has been taken from him by perhaps unfathomable means: that reality is retreating more and more, so that all he is being left with is a kind of soft, insulating fuzz of mean-ingless sensations. That is a thing we have all felt, and the seeking of a solution for it—if indeed there is one—is something we must all try for. This the novel superbly shows; it is one of those books in which one is inclined—no, <u>forced</u>—to leave out of account all strictly aesthetic concerns: those matters of literary device—and turn directly to oneself saying: this has got something—or every-thing—to do with <u>me</u>, as I actually live in the world. That is a better thing than art, I believe; it is better to reach someone where he lives than have an airtight plot: I am sure that this is the real <u>raison d'être</u> of all art, artful or artless. It is this that makes D.H. Lawrence a better novelist, a more lasting influence, and more meaningful to people, than Ford Madox Ford, and James Agee better than Philip Roth.[49] Well, I won't go on and on; I must take on faith that you'll get something from this drift, and write again soon, whenever the spirit is on you.

All yours,
Jim

3807 S.E. Harold
Portland #2, Oregon

TO: DONALD HALL

TLS, 1 p; University of New Hampshire

28 March, 1963
Portland, Oregon

Dear Don,

Good that you are coming on April 8<u>th</u>! I scheduled the reading at Reed for that night, at 8:30, so that Portland State could have you the next day—it'll proba-bly be in the afternoon there, Warren Carrier tells me. I also got on the phone and started pushing the Bard of Lake Oswego (Stafford),[50] and he now thinks that Lewis and Clark can come up with something: at least fifty bucks, and maybe more. They'll most likely want you to read on Wednesday the 10th, from what Stafford tells me, though that time's not firm yet—as we used to say in the ad game. Anyway, we should do all right. Stafford has also written some other, smaller, places that may come through also. I wrote to Heilman in Seattle, and should hear from him today, if the mail can get through a big windstorm we're having. Has Carolyn[51] done anything yet? I mean about getting you booked into some of her schools (no need to ask about her other activities: her private ones that she talks about ceaselessly in public; they go on all the time).

Don't worry about causing trouble between Bly and me; we argue all the time anyway, and I didn't say anything to you that I haven't said to him personally many times before. He might've been bothered that I would tell you the same things, but anybody as free with his tongue—or his mouth, as we Southerners say—as he is, should develop a tough skin, because he is going to get plenty of it back. I have seen a couple of small notices of Wright's new book, and they bear out what I was afraid of: that the poems, instead of being James Wright's, are just sort of anonymous bucolic surrealist-Oriental poems that hundreds of other poets, English, Spanish, French, Chinese, and American, could have written. In his first two books he had a tone and a voice you could recognize, and listen to quietly, with instruction, a sense of purpose, and delight, but now that is gone; there is just the drift of fortuitous association. If poetry were that easy to write, all things would become miraculously simple, and we could all quit sweating over what we put down. But it isn't, and none of Bob's endless pseudo-reasoning and wild generalizing, and none of his picturesque and not-very-enlightening characterizations of poetry and poets (John Logan is "like a great white heron standing on one leg in a stream with his eyes closed" for example) is going to change that. Well, I won't go on and on. I am fond of Bob; very fond. But this is not to say that I agree with him when I don't, or encourage him to meddle with other—and better—men's poems. He must learn to go his own way, and not ask for disciples. Let him write, and not politic.

Naturally I'm delighted about the things you tell me concerning the (continuing!) aftermath of my reading there. And please tell all those who have written to me that I will answer them, just as soon as I can.

Maxine will be at the plane to meet you, and I will, too, if I can get out of class at that time (a peculiar time, but the only one there is, for that class). We should have a good time here; I believe in it.

Love,

Jim

3807 S. E. Harold   p.s. And you will get the
Portland #2, Oregon   Guggenheim: I have spoken!![52]

TO: DONALD HALL

TLS, 2 pp; University of New Hampshire

25 May, 1963
Portland, Oregon

Dear Don,

Very good to hear from you. I figured you were down among them North Carolina sandhills having a wild time, and couldn't write. I'm glad you made it there and back safely (a feeling I always have when I come back: happy to be in one piece, happy to have a few extra dollars, happy to have had such a good, dissipated, <u>un</u>domestic time with other unstable folks). Rago tells me that he is booking me into the Midwest circuit for next February, but of course you'll be gone by then.[53]

Well, to business. I figured Wesleyan would kick over the length of the book, but there are some things we can do to alleviate the situation. First of all, we can drop out all the section numbers, which are half-arbitrary, anyway (these, I guess, are what Lockwood[54] calls "Part titles"). There's no use publishing empty pages when we could be publishing poems, so let's cut all these little roman numbers out; if the book has any sequence, it'll come through anyway, without the divisions. We can also cut out the dedication, since I have already dedicated one book to Maxine; that'll get rid of another page (or two, if Lockwood is counting front-and-back). That leaves us 11 pages of poems to cut. Your selection of poems to be cut is good, though there are a couple that I don't quite agree with. We can agree, right now, though, to drop out "Chenille" and "In the Child's Night." That leaves us seven pages to cut. I had as soon drop out "Horses and Prisoners," which, if you agree, gets us down to four pages. I would prefer to keep, if possible, the other three poems you mention as possible cuts: "Breath," "Goodbye to Serpents" and "The Beholders," which, if kept, would gave us a book of 84 pages. If Lockwood is adamant, we can drop out one more of these or possibly two, and that would enable us to meet his strictures. But if you can persuade him to keep the book at 84 pages, I would be most appreciative. After all, he did not—as he says he must do here—"keep to our 80-page format" in <u>Drowning With Others</u>; why should he suddenly feel bound to keep to it now? After all, I've gone along with all Wesleyan's policies without kicking (too much); it seems to me that an extra four pages is not asking awfully much. So see what you can do, when you have the chance.[55]

As to the title: I have no objection to going back to <u>Springer Mountain</u> as a title, if Lockwood feels all that strongly about it. As a matter of fact, I think I would prefer to do so. I like the local reference (to N. Georgia), and the fact that many people remember the poem as winning the Balch award, which may help to sell it,[56] and I have also such a good design idea if that title is used that I cringe at the thought of not making use of it on the cover, considering the kind of thing that Boultinghouse does best. Helmets are mentioned in just a couple of poems, plus, of course, the "Drinking From a Helmet" poem which ends the book. If there were a title piece called "Helmets" it might be all right for the book title, but I would have to write one (which I am not sure I could do, to order), and that would mess up our page count again. So we can, if everybody is satisfied about doing so (including yourself, of course) go back to <u>Springer Mountain</u> as the title.

Let me know how all this strikes you—and of course, how it strikes Lockwood. Then we can go on from there.

You are right to fight hard over the 500 copy moratorium.[57] The Wesleyan poetry program has only one thing to recommend it—for any house can put out well-packaged and attractive books—and that is the quality of the poetry it publishes. In order to keep that standard, Wesleyan is going to have to have something about it that makes new writers—and old writers—want to publish with Wesleyan. And people are going to shy away if all these strictures hedge publication around, plus the fact that the only market the poet can <u>really</u> count on—that which buys his book partly for novelty when it first comes out—is automatically taken away from him. It is humiliating to get bi-annual royalty checks of $3.75 and such figures. I have been luckier than that, but some haven't. My sales must be up around 1500 or better by now, but I have made only $110 from <u>Drowning With Others</u>. I did a good deal better with Scribners, although I had to split the pot three ways, and the sale of the book was never much more than a thousand copies, if that.

But as to your resigning over the 500-copy moratorium—well, I'd think about it a long time before I did it. Of course <u>I</u> don't want you to resign. But the main thing is that I don't believe it would serve any useful purpose. People get wind of a thing like that, and it would be a hard blow to Wesleyan prestige if you did it. It would also be a hard blow if the Wesleyan authors started pulling out and going to bigger publishers, which I am afraid they—or some of them—will do if Wesleyan doesn't dream up a better arrangement than they have now: a couple more of the "cutbacks for the sake of economy" and there will be little difference between publishing with Wesleyan and publishing with a vanity press.

After <u>Springer Mountain</u> comes out, Scribners wants me to come back with them. They say they plan—or could plan, if I were willing—to bring out a big sort of collected poems, or new and selected poems, or something like that. They guy who wrote to me, name of Hutter,[58] is full of great merchandising plans "using the full Scribners resources," and so on, but I have not definitely committed myself either way as yet. Don't for God's sake let this get out; I am still undecided about it. I don't really want to leave Wesleyan, largely because you are my editor there, but if you pull out, so will I. Let me know what you think of this, for I am in a deep quandry about it.

Yes, I like your new book title,[59] but I'd also like to hear some other possibles. I am pushing away on two new poetry manuscripts, <u>Reincarnations</u>[60] and an odd book called <u>The Morning of One-Legged Men</u>.[61]

I don't hear anything from Bob Bly. Could you induce him to write? Or does he consider me outside the fold; a wolf or coyote (sp?), maybe?

All yours, and write soon
Jim

3807 S.E. Harold
Portland #2, Oregon

"Kudzu"[62] is in the current <u>N Y 'er</u>. We got the package, and <u>thanks</u> from all of us. Kevin wants a lion.[63] I told him you'd grow him one back in Michigan! Send C.O.D.[64]

TO: AL BRASELTON[65]

TLS, 2 pp; Al Braselton

16 June, 1963
Portland, Oregon

Dear Al,

Please forgive the long silence, but I have been very busy with the bearded Jewish geniuses out here, herding them through finals, arguing with them about their term papers, and so on. They are good kids, very smart and intense, but exhausting. They are all gone now, and I have simply been living with the type-writer all day every day, using up ream after ream of paper. I am going so good that it seems a shame to stop, and so I don't. I just go on and on, for some kind of dam has burst in me and everything is flowing. The new book, <u>Helmets</u>, will be out in about six months. In addition, I am about halfway through two others, <u>Reincarnations</u> and <u>Them, Crying</u>, and have made at least a reasonable start on three others, tentatively titled—or four, rather—<u>Living in Logs</u>, <u>Sterilities</u>, <u>The Stepson</u>, and <u>The Morning of One-Legged Men</u>.[66] These last four will probably mix with each other, but as of now I have separate folders, and as far as I can tell they are separate books. I have been trying out some stylistic changes that are very exciting—at least to me. Some of these new poems the <u>New Yorker</u> will do, partic-ularly some of the <u>Reincarnations</u>, where I try to create a kind of new universe of animals, fish and birds with human characteristics, or the remnants of these from former lives lived as human beings. The first one <u>New Yorker</u> will do is the one about the rattlesnake.[67] I also have, to date, a turtle, something living in a shell (a little sea-creature whose fossils make up the Dover cliffs), a crow and an elephant. There ought to be—as I see it now—about twenty five of these creatures when I've finished; I hope to have them all by the time I leave Reed for California.[68]

First, though, I'm coming home for next summer. I will be in Atlanta all summer, and we should have a lot of time together. That is something to look forward to, believe me. I should be home—for we will be driving—about this time next year.

I have a whole first draft of the novel, and Scribners wants it—God knows how they get wind of these things. I am not satisfied with it at this stage, of course, and will redraft at least twice more. What is emerging from the book as a kind of theme—unbeknownst to me until I got on into the material—is that there is a lot of violence in people that doesn't get a chance to come out in the pleasant circumstances of suburban living, and that this violence takes the form of a kind of unspoken yearning, an unfulfillment in people—men, mostly—and then turns into a kind of poison that they have no way to get rid of. The narrator of the story must be made a kind of vehicle to show this, and then is freed by the secret crime of killing this stranger that is threatening the life of him and his companions. In other words, murder allows him to enjoy being average, and be content with it, and happy even. I have used almost everything you, I, and Lewis did, saw, talked about or ate on our river-trips; I had no idea I remembered so much; but the great thing about writing is that it does bring such things back. Here is part of a paragraph which you can try on for size; it is actually based on that big turn on the Toccoa river: the one you and I almost made twice, and didn't quite get all the way around:

> . . . he did not look back, and I had no way of knowing whether or not he had heard me, for now we were going hard. We were in the main roar, and I dug in on the right to keep us straight. "Get your paddle out of the water," I yelled as loud as I could, and Bobby pulled it up just as we hit the little jolting ripples before the first drop-off. We went over; the nose tipped, Bobby fell back from his seat the moment after, the canoe grated under my tailbone, and we went down another, smaller one, a rough shove upward through the spine that nearly unseated me and drove the canoe partly over on its side. Our speed righted us, and we swung and ran over two step-downs, hard shocks at the base of the brain, and between them I heard a faint, then a quick loud shout or singing or call from somewhere, and thought it might be Lewis screaming, and then we were down, having lost speed but picking it up almost at once, and were going for the spray. Bobby looked ahead, and then, as if by pure recoil, dropped back on his rear on the floor of the canoe, with his legs still over the

bow seat and his hands on the gunwales. I dug in hard, backwatering on the left to turn the bow, and we swung, swung and jumped shooting into the spray.

For a second I couldn't see anything at all, and rode like I was standing still, my mouth filled with aerated water and little fluttering bumps coming up through the canoe-shell. With nothing to see go past, the sense of motion died out altogether and it was like being in an odd, open room or a shaking cave filled with cold steam; I was wet clear through in an instant from the water flying back off the walls of the gorge. I lanced out and down and in backwards with the paddle on my left, to turn, turn, keep turning left, and not let the bow swing into a rock on the right, spin us, and the river catch up with us in a second from behind, the whole river, and come into the broadside canoe in ton after ton, never-ending. I dug again, but still couldn't tell whether we were straight in the current, or curving with it as we should be doing, or what. Something snatched with great suddenness and authority at the paddle-blade. I pulled it back and dug again, and the river showed in front, blinded like an eye, showed again in a leaping rush, and we came out shooting forward as though launched to take off into the air, with the bow high and bumping and flying and everything but the river just ahead of us a flickering blur, half drowned and drunk to the bone. We were going faster than I had ever been in a canoe; the force of the water around the paddle-blade was tremendous; the paddle felt as though I had dipped it into some supernatural source of primal energy, and from this there flowed up through my hands a feeling that I was taking the energy on, each time I moved. The river had turned blue. . . .

and so on. This is still an uncorrected passage from the first draft, but it should give some inkling of what the final style will be like. It's a book which is a lot of fun to write; it writes itself, as they say.

The guitar is going well. I got a good trade-in on my old Framus—more than I paid for it—and acquired a Gibson "Country Western" model for two hundred dollars, though with the trade I only paid a hundred and twenty. It's real good; "lots of clang," as Kipnis[69] says. Another year with that fellow and I'll really have it made with the guitar. I tried to figure out a way to show you what Kipnis has showed me, and by mail, but really I will have to show you in person, or you won't really be able to see how this kind of style is played. Suffice it to say that three-finger picking is the thing that the guitar was made for.

All yours, and write soon
Jim

3807 S.E. Harold
Portland #2, Oregon

TO: RADCLIFFE SQUIRES

TLS, 1 p; Washington University

30 June, 1963
portland, oregon

Dear Jim,

Thanks so much for your June 6 letter; it was very surprising and touching, and I am so sorry I am so long in answering it. One reason was that I was not sure what address you had at the Utah shindig, and didn't want my letter to miss you. The other reason is that I'm wildly busy with dozens and dozens of projects that all have deadlines. I can see a little light at the end of the tunnel now, though, and so I have a chance to write at least a few letters, of which this one is the first.

Your Frost book is great: it is not only the best thing ever written on the subject, but is so good—and so <u>different</u>—that it really constitutes a radically new <u>kind</u> of criticism, I believe. I will mention it in a long review I'm doing for <u>Poetry</u> in which I deal with Jeffers' last book, <u>The Beginning and the End</u>.[70]

Tell me about your Prokosch book.[71] John Dimoff tells me that Twayne is going to do it. Is it on his novels, his poetry, or both? I think he's a terrific subject—I have always been crazy about his stuff, even though I, as well as most others of my generation, could tell you why the New Critics don't like it—but have never seen much written <u>on</u> him. Do tell me what you're doing; and, of course, send me a copy when the book comes out. When is it due, by the way? And what is the title? Evidently you know Prokosch himself, for you say you plan to spend some time in Europe with him. What is he like? From his work I would think he'd be rather Byronic, and one or two pictures I've seen of him are very handsome, though I expect he's up in his fifties now, isn't he?

You're right about the "Lifeguard" poem, and maybe when Wesleyan reprints I will cut out the last "water."[72] And thanks for the suggestion. Yes, I think it is a good poem; it always moves me, and that is more than I can say for a lot of my stuff. Please forgive my immodesty here, but you'll understand, I'm sure.

Is Don Hall still around there? And if he isn't, do you have an address for him? I need some editorial consultation with him.

Thanks so much, Jim, for the personal things you say in your letter. Yes, I am very happy to know you, too, as I always am happy to know the good ones, the intelligent and honest ones: the ones with <u>more</u>: more joy, more pain, more life.

Let me hear from you when you can. The future is going to be <u>great</u>; every-thing is beginning.

All yours,
Jim

3807 S.E. Harold
Portland, Oregon

TO: DONALD HALL

TLS, 2pp; University of New Hampshire

August 20<u>th</u>, 1963
Portland, Oregon

Dear Don,

Thanks so much for your long, <u>long</u> letter, with so much so patiently explained. It is strange news about Wesleyan—how on earth can they afford to keep shifting board-personnel around the way they do? I'm sorry Nemerov is out, for I think he stands for some very good things, but I am most concerned about your position with Wesleyan—are you in fact in or out? If you are out, I will leave Wesleyan after this book, but if you are in I will stay on. So do tell me what your final status is; it makes a big difference, believe me.[73] By the way, your fulmina-tions against the 500-copy moratorium must have borne fruit, for Lockwood just wrote and asked me if I would prefer some kind of complicated percentage based on <u>all</u> copies sold, which I would; it's a little better, anyway. <u>Drowning With Others</u> is now well up over the 1500 mark and Wesleyan is going to reprint and raise the price. With the reading tour next winter we should go 'way over 2000 and I very much hope up around 2500, which would make me the leading money-winner amongst Wesleyan poets, which I very nearly am now. Well, here's hoping, anyway. Also, the new book will be out just in time for the tour, and we can push that, too.

As to the business between us concerning the <u>Paris Review</u> editorship: even after your letter I am still undecided.[74] My indecision, which you will (I hope) understand, is based largely on the fact that after this year at Reed and next year in California I will have no official job, and so will need all the time I can get to take on writing and editing assignments that do bring in money. I am just afraid of a position as exacting and time-consuming as this one is, particularly in view of the facts facing me as the provider and head of a family. Let me put it this way: I don't believe, Don, that I can really justify taking a job without <u>any</u> pay: I just couldn't swing it. If there were pay of some kind connected with it, even token pay, $500 a year, say, I might: that is, if I could count on buying groceries for one month of every year with money from the editing job, I think I might take it on, though God knows $500 a year is little enough for that amount of time and work put in. But no salary . . . no; there is something in my Scotch ancestry that won't let me; I can't work for nothing. I wouldn't expect anyone else to, either. That is too much to ask, either from you, from me, or from Joe Kennedy[75] (or Jack Kennedy, either, for that matter). The prospect of participating for an evening every year or two in Plimpton's[76] dolce vita is not quite enough, though it sounds interesting, and the imponderables and intangibles you point out as having been true in your case—I think they would be likely to be less consoling in mine—would not, I am very much afraid, compensate for the time required. I am in a good period now, writing a lot, and into a great many projects that I have always wanted to try. Everything is moving well, and I would resent very much having to "tear myself away" periodically and sit down for hours, weeks and months of the year plodding through others' poems when I wanted time to write my own. I sweated out every minute of the day for years, fighting tooth and nail to get time to write, and I don't want to go through that again, now that I have just come out of that tunnel. I have an idea that that's why Joe Kennedy is quitting and probably was a factor in your quitting, too. I would be disgruntled at having all this happen, all the sacrifice it would certainly entail, and no revenue coming in from it. Surely the Aga, or Plimpton, or the Kahns, or somebody connected with that rich, losing-proposition of a magazine could ante up a little something for a poetry editor? If I'm not worth any more than petty cash, I doubt I'd have much enthusiasm for the job. So . . . still, I won't close the door entirely, but wait to hear from you once more. Perhaps in the meantime you could contact Plimpton or whoever and tell him my views, and maybe work something or other out. I'll wait to hear from you.[77]

Yes, surely I will send you some new things, just as soon as school starts and I can get to the thermofax room, or whatever room it is that they reproduce things (things on paper, I mean) in, here at Reed. I have a lot of new poems that the New Yorker is going to do, plus three or four long, ambitious pieces I have been working on for years, now poised at the edge of the nest and thinking, God, it's a long way down: they're eagles, you see, and live way up there.

We have moved (our address now is 1200 S.E. Lava Drive, Portland, Oregon 97222) and have a spectacular house on the Willammette River (I am looking right at it now; it practically comes into the room with me). Gulls sail up and down the river and pheasants walk through the yard, and there is a friendly garter snake with .0000003 at the bone instead of zero.[78] Chris's arm is better, and he is beginning to do some boy-things again instead of having to be so careful all the time. I have made some progress on the guitar, and have been playing with a little folknik group around town this summer; a lot of fun, but little money. School is about to start again, as you undoubtedly remember and rejoice at being away from, and I am oddly looking forward to it; I work better on a schedule at least of some sort, and the kids here are eager and sharp, as you will remember.

Maxine sends love, and so do the boys. We have our lion now (you know, the one you sent Kevin) I know you have to say lollipops in children's books, but I know you must've meant gin, for he is drinking us out of house and home! Our best to all in your house. And let us hear from you soon, for we worry doubly about friends when water is between.

All yours,
Jim

1200 S.E. Lava Drive
Portland, Oregon 97222

TO: JAMES BOATWRIGHT[79]

TLS, 1 p; Washington and Lee

3 November, 1963
Portland, Oregon

Dear Jim,

Thanks for the note. I'm glad you like "Mary Sheffield" and are going to print it.[80] Yes, the line you mention should be "all things spread sail." Sorry about the typo at this end. The poem is, as you say, kind of unusual for me. It is the basis for a long, long poem the <u>New Yorker</u> is going to do: the basis, I mean, in that sort of "burst writing," the grouping of words with space between them and no punctuation.[81] At any rate, you have the first of these poems: if they make "literary history" (?) I'll see that you get credit.

Now I <u>think</u> I remember you, from those old Fred Bornhauser[82] days. It clicked in my mind who you were when Carolyn Kizer told me about the impression your Southern manners made on her at the small-magazine conference recently in New York. The <u>good</u> impression, I mean, in case you don't already know.

Glad to be on your masthead.[83] Shall I dig up some new writers for you? I'm having a few students send you things. I'd appreciate a word or two of handwriting on the rejection slips you'll almost surely be using. And thanks.

All yours,
Jim Dickey

1200 S.E. Lava Drive
Portland, Oregon 97222 ZIP!

TO: JONATHAN WILLIAMS[84]

TLS, 1 p; SUNY Buffalo

25 November, 1963
Portland, Oregon

Dear Jon,

I take time out from watching the President's funeral cortege[85] to write you, whom I have so long and shamefully neglected, first failing to answer your letters from England and now also neglecting to answer several good ones from the States, too. Well, I mean all that to end, and will promise to answer, and promptly, any letter or other communication you may wish to send my way, and I hope they are many. I am temporarily out of my first Wesleyan book, but will send you a copy of that and the new one, Helmets, due out in a couple of months from Wesleyan, and in addition a copy of my critical book, The Suspect in Poetry[86] (the Patchen essay is in it) due out at about the same time. That ought to keep you in reading for a while. I am finishing up my fourth book of verse, The Common Grave,[87] this winter, and this spring I am bringing out a limited edition of two of the poems in it, called "Two Poems of the Air." A student here is doing the edition in calligraphy for her thesis,[88] and as a maker of fine books (some of the finest) I thought you'd be interested in seeing what she's done. So I'll send you that, too, when it comes out, if you like.

My term as poet-in-residence (how we renegade literary types love titles!) at Reed ends in June, and I have taken a job (also as poet in residence—and full professor, no less) at a new school in California for a year—San Fernando Valley State University. After that—who knows? Probably back to Europe for two or three years—and then—well, God Almighty! Maybe I'll settle back up in those hills that you and I love so. I have some property on the Toccoa River (I have just bought my grave plot in Gilmer County) and could build a little kind of house up there and write and play the guitar (I could show those hillbillies a thing or two I've picked up from Jewish boys out here) and live out the rest of my fourscore and ten in the place I came from; I'd like that. Well; we'll see.

The friend of mine who owns Sautee Manor is not named Lewis Allen but Lewis King.[89] He is a very good man; a real outdoorsman and a rich man who's not afraid of the devil himself. A smart guy, too, and could be a good writer if he wasn't interested in so many other things, and if he could sit still for long enough to get something down on paper. Look him up in Atlanta; he'd be glad to see you.

I won't go on and on, but will just get this in the mail to let you know where and how I am, and know also that I believe implicitly in what you are so courageously doing with your life. Know also, that I saw a poem of yours somewhere about cabbages in a field (or lettuces, maybe) that was just terrific.[90] More like that would sure be welcome at this end.

I leave in February for a tour beginning at the Poetry Center. Is there any chance of your being in town, or environs?

Say hello to Ron Johnson[91] for me.

All yours,
Jim

NOTE NEW ADDRESS
1200 S.E. Lava Drive
Portland, Oregon 97222 ZIP!

TO: RICHARD HOWARD[92]

TLS, 1 p; Richard Howard

15 December, 1963
Portland, Oregon

Dear Richard Howard,

In the course of making up the jacket-copy for a new book, Wesleyan sent out to me your review of <u>Drowning With Others</u> which appeared in <u>Poetry</u>.[93] I had not previously seen what you had to say, and I'd like now to tell you how much I appreciate it. I was once introduced at the Poetry Center as "the American poet with the largest collection of poison pen letters," and that's probably the case. Reviewing has made me ten enemies to every one (doubtful) friend, and it is good indeed to find someone like yourself who likes one's work quite outside the conventional and disheartening orbit of professional and private log-rolling. Though I am teaching poetry temporarily for a living, I deplore the increasing tendency to treat poetry as "a subject": that is, for "discussion and analysis." My optimum picture of the poet-reader relationship is that of someone sitting down, perhaps under a tree but in any case certainly <u>alone</u>, and reading a poem. Your review gave the impression that this was the case with you: that you were a human being in live touch with language: not a semanticist but someone inhabiting the earth for his little time, reading what someone in the same situation had to say about his view of their common lot. Your review moved very deeply indeed someone who has never really been sure whether or not he was a writer at all, and confirmed him in his determination to go on with it. Surely that is a good service, and I must say so. Again, thanks.

It's odd that when I heard from Wesleyan I had just been reading your translation of Gracq's <u>Balcony in the Forest</u>, which I think is just terrific.[94] Has <u>Le Rivage</u> <u>des Syrtes</u> ever been translated? That is Gracq's best, I think. Would Braziller be interested in your doing it? I'd sure like to see that happen. How about translating poetry? Why couldn't you do a big collection of Supervielle? He is to my way of thinking the best poet of the twentieth century, and he is totally unknown over here. Who would be interested in doing such a book? My God, when you think of the things that could be! And also of the things that aren't.

I won't go on and on, but thank you once more for your remarks. It sure makes me happy to think of myself in the same boat (perhaps on fire, but that's all right) with Heraclitus.[95]

Yours sincerely,
James Dickey

P.S. I'll be in New York to read at the Poetry Center the 2nd and 3rd of February, and I hope we can meet at least for a few minutes. Let me know how your schedule looks, and we'll make some plans, if you like.

1200 S.E. Lava Drive
Portland, Oregon 97222

TO: DONALD HALL

TLS, 2 pp; University of New Hampshire

20 December, 1963
Portland, Oregon

Dear Don,

Good to hear from you, and I hasten to respond, on the hope that this may just reach you by Christmas, or at any rate some time during the holiday season, and let you know how much and with what affection we think of you out here, and rejoice in the good life you seem to be living, and at all the writing you are getting done. You seem to have the problems with your new book about ironed out, and it would be funny indeed if Deutsch did the book and then sold the sheets back to Viking.[96] But in any case you won't have any trouble getting a publisher; not with your reputation. The main thing is to push on with some new poems, to do new things, to take on things you really don't think you're capable of. The longer I write the more I am left with just one criterion of worth in regard to any poem I happen to be working on: if the poem is saying something I didn't think I knew, then I know it is going to be good, or at least that it has a chance to be good. If only the old ordinary poetry-writing voice is speaking, then it is just going to be an old ordinary Dickey poem, and I try to change it into something else. Well: I have a new, <u>new</u> book finished (at least I think it is finished), and am hung up between titles. These are <u>The Common Grave</u> (though I shudder to think what the Opposition could do to me in a review, using my title against me), <u>Slave Quarters</u>, and an odd idea I had, taken from a guitar piece I play: <u>Buck-dancer's Choice</u>. Tell me what you think of these whenever you can.

I also have a little limited edition, done in this fancy calligraphy which is a kind of Reed trademark. This will be out in May, and will be called <u>Two Poems of the Air</u>. I will then incorporate them into the new book, which should be really good, for these new long things have really turned out well, I think; I'm anxious for you to see them.

The book of criticism of mine that Bob Bly is doing hasn't come out yet, but should be out soon.[97] A man at MacMillan, Arthur Gregor, wrote to me and wanted me to write a book on poetry "bolstering the defense of tradition that underlies all your criticism," I thing I had no idea was the case. I doubt I'll do it, but I may, if he can put ideas enough in my head, for I sure don't have them by myself.[98] And <u>another</u> funny thing happened, too: a mysterious man, a senior editor for Houghton Mifflin, turned up out here and absconded, over my weak protests, with the pre- pre- <u>pre</u>-first draft of my novel, shoving various monies into my hands.[99] He thinks it's wonderful—though this may be because he can't read it in its present state; nobody could—and so I may have to go to work trying to make something of it, after all, though I know nothing whatever about writing novels. I'll probably call on Allan Seager, who has turned out to be one of the best correspondents I've ever had, for help, and perhaps Andrew Lytle, too, and anybody else I can think of. Since I've just been made an advisory editor of <u>Sewanee</u>, perhaps Andrew and Tate can't turn me down.

One more important thing, before I forget about it: I must take the midwest tour in February—Stafford says it is mighty tough getting around to all those places—and I'd like you to tell me what to do to get that reduction in airplane fare that you told me about. This is very important, for it involves money, so do write me about it whenever you can, before I leave the last of January.

When will you be back, boy? We sure miss you, and look forward to seeing you again. Though I will be living in California next year, I may also come up on a Minnesota reading tour, and then may be able to get by your place. I'll sure try, and will do it if it's at all possible.

Have you seen Michael Hamburger?[100] If you should, or should communicate with him in any way, please give him my best, and tell him that I will surely write. Tomlinson I'd also like to be remembered to, though you may not see him, for he lives near Bristol. And of course Geoffrey Hill, whom I am promoting like mad over here. Tell him I got his new address, and will write, though it is my impression that he owes me a letter, going 'way back. And when you're in London, do go by and see my friend John Hall at <u>Encounter</u>. Tell him that I will write, and will try to send him something new, after such a damned long time. By the way, they never did send me a copy of that anthology of theirs, <u>Encounters</u>, that I was in.[101] Kristol or somebody wrote and said they were sending it, but I never did get it. Anyway, give the <u>Encounter</u> people my best. And while I'm scrounging free copies of things, could you nudge your publisher to send me a copy of that massive thing that you and Spender did recently?[102] I'd like to see it.

Things are well with us here. We have an old house, a magnificent estate on the river: the damndest place you ever saw. Seagulls bash into the window of my study, convinced that a man is sitting in the middle of air they could be flying in, and ringnecked pheasants walk through the yard at all times of day and night. It really is a wonderful house, and it grieves us to think that we must leave it in another six months.

That's about all the news, I guess. I am working away on the guitar to pretty good effect, and have gotten to the point of playing an occasional job at a local coffee house—luckily this does not entail singing. The novelty of three-finger picking is interesting to folk buffs, for there are lots of better traditional pickers. Anyway, guitaring is a good alternative to writing, for my trouble has always been in keeping away from the typewriter, and this keeps me away as much as I need to be kept away, so that when I sit down to write it is when I literally <u>have</u> to, not just when I can, with nothing better to do. Anyway, life seems pretty good now; it is not so hard to push on.

Take care of yourself and your family. Write when you can, and send me what you've been doing.

No, I don't have any idea who will take the <u>Paris Review</u> job. It really wouldn't have been right for me, nor I for it. Perhaps Seidel[103] will do it; he seems to aspire to hang around with that crowd.

All yours,
Jim

1200 S.E. Lava Drive
Portland, Oregon 97222

TO: ROBERT DUNCAN[104]

TLS, 1 p; SUNY Buffalo

7 March, 1964
Portland, Oregon

Dear Robert Duncan:

Thanks so much for your note, and for the things you say about my work. I am very happy that you like "The Being"[105] and "Drinking From a Helmet,"[106] and I hope, as you do, that my true and final direction will be that indicated by those poems. They are both in my new book, just out, called Helmets. The folk-singer poem,[107] which I guess I like better than you do, is also in it, but you are certainly 100% right about "Why in London the Blind Are Saviors,"[108] which is a good idea bothered and botched by my inability to make it come off; I left it out of the book. Well, there's no telling who's going to like what: my editor at Wesleyan, Dick Wilbur, tells me that my best poem is the Civil War Relic one[109] (I don't think it is, or anything like the best) and the other one you mention, "The Performance"[110] has been anthologized just about everywhere, if that means anything (it probably doesn't.) But about the inwardness and the personal, intuitive conviction about things that should get into poems you are dead right. The question is how to do it. I have never found just exactly how yet, myself, but I am sure it can be done, if not by me then maybe by you. My most outspoken critics have griped endlessly about my poems being too inward and private, too subjective and something they are pleased to call "mystical," but that is the part of poetry that appeals to me the most, and if I am damned by those qualities I consider myself well damned. I have a new manuscript now that is farther-out than any of the other three, and has, I think, the best stuff of all in it, particularly a series of poems called Reincarnations,[111] all about people coming back to life as animals and birds. A couple of these are going to be printed in an elegant private edition in May as Two Poems of the Air, and I'll send you a copy if you like.

Please forgive the brevity of this, for I usually write—and like to write—long letters. However, I am momentarily leaving for Canada, and wanted to get your note answered before I left, so you wouldn't just think I didn't care enough about it to write. I do care, and am very heartened by what you say. I have a lot of enemies—mostly culled from ten years of reviewing—and it is good to know that I have some people (good people, good poets) favorably inclined, too. (By the way, did you see the review I did of The Opening of the Field last summer in the Sewanee?)[112]

Perhaps we shall get a chance to meet, and not in the hazy, indefinite future, either. Someone named James Schevill asked me to come down to your town and do a workshop from the 15th to the 19th of June, and I told him I'd come. If you're in town, we'll get together. I look forward to that, and hope for the possibility.

Yours sincerely,

James Dickey

1200 S.E. Lava Drive
Portland, Oregon 97222

TO: JOHN HOLLANDER[113]

TLS, 1 p; John Hollander

7 March, 1964
Portland, Oregon

Dear John Hollander,

Please forgive me for waiting so damned long to answer your letter of February 24th, but I am only just now getting back out here to the coast after a five-weeks reading tour. I'm sorry, too, that I couldn't get to Yale, but even with optimum conditions it would have been a terrific scramble, considering the places I had to be and the scanty time I had to get to them. No, I haven't any plans for coming east next year, but I can't tell what will develop between now and then, and I may come after all. If I do you may be assured that I'll come to Yale. The most frustrating of my regrets is that I didn't get a chance to meet you; it would have been good to talk awhile.

Yes, the so-called symposium was really ghastly (level of discussion: "Nemerov, why are you rich?"—G. Corso) It was the low point of the trip; things seemed to take an upturn after that—after all, they could hardly have gone down. I did get to meet Richard Howard, whom I liked tremendously. He told me of a project you and he once had to translate some of Jules Supervielle—I think you should go on with it, if only for the reason that he is my all-time favorite poet in any language, and I've never seen any translations that did him any kind of justice at all. People who really care for poetry would appreciate having Supervielle available.

As for poems for PR—I haven't anything right now, but am cautiously edging back into writing, and will doubtless soon be buried in two or three very ambitious things I've been carrying around with me, in my head and other places, for the past few years. When I get anything I think is any good I'll send it on to you.

Meanwhile, thanks again for your letter. It is good to hear from you. I hope very much that you are writing some new poems. I think history is going to have it your way, rather than the way of the nit-pickers who balk at your poems and carry on stupidly and wittily in the reviews, extolling the likes of Anne Sexton and (my God!) W.D. Snodgrass as writing about "reality." Well, Time is the best (and perhaps only) critic, and he is riding favorably on your shoulders. You are tapped in in some strange and wonderful way with the real concerns of my generation, as I said in a review somewhere.[114] That is a big responsibility, but writing such poems must be enormously exciting, as it is to read them. I look for more—I am always looking.

My best, believe me.

Jim Dickey

1200 S.E. Lava Drive
Portland, Oregon 97222

TO: JAMES WRIGHT

TLS, 1 p; University of Minnesota

5 April, 1964
Portland, Oregon

Dear Jim,

Thanks so much for your long, good letter of March 8th, and please forgive me for waiting almost a month to answer it, but I have been enormously busy catching up with all the work that had piled up in the five weeks I was gone—I still am 'way behind—and have had no opportunity to write letters. I am making a little headway now, though, and so can get this off to you today, telling you how glad—no; overjoyed—I was to see you in Minneapolis, and say a little of what a good occasion the whole weekend was. I was happy to see Bob, also; in fact, the occasion was one of those that come along so rarely that you feel sometimes that times of that kind are impossible, really, or just happen in the best of dreams or reveries. Well, I won't go on and on, but will just close by saying that it was a grand, eye-opening, life-renewing time for me, tired as I was at the end of five weeks of steady, sleepless travelling, and finished the tour off for me in so much better style than I ever could have dreamed of.

It is good, too, to know that you have a good girl, and that you can now see "the light at the end of the tunnel," for it is going to be a good light indeed. During most of life I have the sense of strangulation, of a kind of strangulation and compression of a ghost which is myself, where everything is seen through a thickening pane of glass that is really the deadening of the senses that comes with aging. I also have, rarely, the sense of breathing deeply, suddenly becoming a full-blooded human body, and being able to reach out and take up things and hold them, touch them, with exquisite and meaningful intimacy. That is the kind of thing, the kind of time that I live for. It is because poetry helps or even perhaps causes such states that I care for it; it can, as Lawrence says somewhere, help you "not be a dead man in life." It is the sense of that deadness that is most frightening to me, and it is also the sense that such deadness can't really be got around or done away with by liquor, sex, or other stimuli that both scares me and stimulates me. Whatever does militate against the deadness has got to come from deep within; one has to be able to sit still and receive, so that the flow of a river becomes something so inexplicable, haunting and uplifting that it is past all telling, the air-spines in an ice cube of a rare and delicate essence, fragile and there. This is where I am going—or want to go—in poetry. That is, as far as I am concerned, where poetry is. It is in lines like yours about the horse dung blazing up like golden stones.[115] Yes, Lord, it is.

I am slowly getting back to myself, and a little writing. I banked the proceeds of the trip, with an eye on an eventual Europe, my only extravagance at this time being to buy myself a big twelve-string guitar. Boy, when that thing booms out the trees try to shuffle out of the woods, and the rocks, as Valéry says, "know the full horror of dancing." I also took Maxine and the boys up to Vancouver Island in Canada. We had a good time, a time full of cold sunlight and seagulls. By God, life is good: just hold your hand up and look at it; that is enough.

Write again soon; whenever you can. And would you do one favor for me? Find out from the Tates if I have done anything to alienate them? I have been in agony, since I stayed drunk at their house and left too early the next morning to say goodbye, though I did, I think, leave a note. Please give them my good wishes and thanks.

All yours,
Jim

1200 S.E. Lava Drive
Portland, Oregon 97222

TO: A. L. BADER[116]

TLS, 5 pp; University of Michigan

22 April, 1964
Portland, Oregon

Dear Mr. Bader:

Here are the results, at least the results according to Dickey. I spent a good deal of time with the manuscripts and found a lot to like in all of them; the choices—or some of them, at any rate—did not come easy. Some of the poets, notably Brian Craig, Skarell and perhaps Mr. Tetunic, were obviously not of the calibre of the others. Mr. Craig, in particular, is so obviously at the very beginning of things that he showed at somewhat of a disadvantage in the company of accomplished writers like Mr. Nickel and Miss (Mrs. ?) Bodin. The poem of his called "Aftermath" is the only one which seemed to bear comparison to even the most ordinary pieces of most of the others. Skarell had some slightly better moments, particularly in "Speak Soft in a Monotone," "Alas For Grass," "For Lao Tze," "Legends," and "Ballad," but in large is not much in advance over Mr. Craig. Mr. Pedotti is altogether better than these two writers, though his poems are marred, most of the time, by a certain youthful-conventional diction. I liked "800-1400 A.D.," "Poem in Yellow," "Independent Pleasure" (a good one, that!) "In Praise," and "Chaucer's Spring." Choosing between the three remaining contestants in the Minor Contest was very much harder. In my opinion, Miss Bodin, Miss Keith and Mr. Nickel are all superior to anyone in the Major Contest, though I am not sure I would say (as you specify I might suggest) that they are "<u>noticeably</u> superior": not all <u>that</u> noticeably, anyway. At any rate, they are all very good. I think Miss Bodin is very slightly better than the other two, due mainly to a certain unconventionality of outlook and the ability to think (or feel) her way more deeply into her subjects than the other two. "Rapture," "Week-end," "Unfolding," "Old Knives" (<u>very</u> good!) "Cynthia's Wish," "His Mistake," and "On the Sound" are very good poems indeed; I am delighted to have encountered them. Rebecca Keith is also very good, though her near-prose rhythms are a little monotonous and she seems to have comparatively little technical resiliency. She is perceptive, though, and often her breathless meters are in exact accord with her matter. "February, 1964" is a very interesting poem, but the best of her pieces are those about people, such as "Aunt Bess," "Love Poem," and "You, Who." I also liked "Let's Go Away." Miss Keith is a little mannered and often verges on the cute, but she should surely have a good future. So should Mr. Nickel, though he is often slightly precious and literary in the bad sense, as Miss Bodin and Miss Keith are not. He has a very sharp eye, however, and a good ear, and can write movingly, as in "Visiting Aunts in

Boston," "Poem," "Student," "Poplars With River," "A Metaphor," "The Abstract Painter," and particularly in "Old," which in my opinion is one of the two or three best poems in all these twelve manuscripts. To sum up the "Minor" poets, then: I think that they are all very promising, and if you were to give all of them encouragement and also give the top three special awards of some kind, that would be all right with me. I do think that Miss Bodin, Miss Keith and Mr. Nickel are the three best and most interesting poets in the lot; I'll leave you to take whatever action this may seem to indicate.

Now, as to the "Major" Poets: Nathan Tetunic is rather good; so good, in fact, that I am a little dismayed to see him at the bottom of my own list, for he has a fine satiric wit and some interesting ideas, and is able to do something fresh and new with mythology, which is no mean feat. His best poems are "Tantalus," "Phoenix," "Eden," "Theseus" (a wonderful, very powerful ending!) and, best of all, "Paros." Mr. Tetunic flounders a good deal, though, and engages in a lot of poetic wheel-spinning. When he has traction—or a myth—under him, though, he is fine, and should develop very fast from this good beginning. Anne Saverude (I am not sure of the spelling of this, since you spell her last name one way and the manuscript another) is very accomplished also, though her preference for knotty language and choked rhythms is a little hard to take over a long stretch of poems. I liked her book very much, though. Her feminine sensibility is beautifully projected in such poems as "For the Sculptor Milonadis," "Veils," "Late Autumn Pond," "Matins Read Thrice," "The Assurance of His Coming," "The Preacher," and "Poverty in the House of the Dead," which is another of those two or three best-of-all poems that I mentioned in connection with Mr. Nickel. R. F. McGurk is very interesting, though very nearly completely amateurish. He is violent and unpredictable, and doesn't yet know when he has really hit on something and when he hasn't. He has a wild, unconventional imagination, however, and when he learns to let the language itself help him a little he will surely be worth watching. "Lily Pond," "Automobile Accident at Brush Creek and Paseo," "Genesis Regenerate" (but please prevail on him to change some of these titles!) "Nordica," "Half-Gainer for Icarus," (his best effort, despite the flipness of the title) and "The Ice Rider" are all extremely vivid and striking. The writer who struck me as having, in a tantalizingly elusive way, the most poetential (the typewriter actually invented this word, but I'm letting it stand as a beautiful Freudian slip) is that one who goes by the name of St. B. His (her, I would bet) is the smallest of the books, but it contains poetry of a consistently high order. "I Never Said" is a fascinatingly worked-out sustained metaphor about queen bees and people (My Lord, who but a poet would ever have thought of a thing like that, I kept mumbling to myself as I read it), and the Rilke adaptation (it isn't that really, but just takes off from the famous Rilke "Archaic Torso" poem) is curious and successful. The ballad "The Demon" has some of the authentic scary-ness and incantation of the old anonymous ballads, and "Archaic Poem" (the first of these in the manuscript) is beautifully conceived and executed. Leslie Dickerson is a powerful and in the main a successful writer, though alternating with his (sometimes profound) individual perceptions and judgments is a disconcerting conventionality and a certain show-offiness (is that a word?). But his book is sustained in a way that many of these others are not; his level of performance is generally higher than the others. His best pieces are "To an Old Plum Tree, Newly Pruned," "Remembering Hart Crane," "Sunday Morning," "Landscape With Three Verticals," "Hillscape With a Listening Girl," "The Phoenix," "Anniversary," "Second Encounter" (<u>extremely</u> fine, particularly the end!) "The Hero," and "Elegy for John Kelley," which I would pick as the best single poem in all these manuscripts. Miss Kline has an even more sustained level of good poems than Mr. Dickerson. She has obviously been writing for a long time, for she is aware of the ways and means of poetry to an extent that none of these others, even Mr. Dickerson, is. It is true, however, that just this fact causes her to write period poetry, the period being the present, and I am a little worried that Miss Kline will not see fit to break back into the primitive part of herself for the new images that make good poems: a place already inhabited (in <u>them</u>selves) by St. B and Mr. McGurk, to mention only two. Compared to these writers Miss Kline is a little dull and predictable, but her poems are finished performances rather than brilliant fragments, and there are a lot of them. Some of them are very good poems indeed. None of them really shook me up, like Mr. Dickerson's "Elegy," but I admired nearly all of them, but most particularly "In the Park," "The Nun," and "The Pool." Judges of contests would, I should think, secretly like to give prizes to those poets who have given them the most pleasure. If that were true I would give it to St. B, Mr. Dickerson or Mr. McGurk. But prizes should be given not to promise but to performance, and that is where Miss Kline has it over these others, though she may not always have. At any rate, to quote Judge Roy Bean ("the Law West of the Pecos,"), "That's my ruling."

After all this, I'd very much like to say how much I enjoyed reading these books, and how interested I am in the futures of these people. I don't send their manuscripts back willingly, I can tell you. I look forward to seeing them in print in various places, which they all will be, I believe, if they keep at it.

A few matters of business: You ask for my Social Security Number, which is [ ]. I'd like to have your check as soon as you can conveniently send it, for I will be leaving Portland soon, and it makes me nervous to have checks following me around; they might get lost somewhere.

One more thing: I'd like very much to know the results of these prize-givings, and will hope to hear the final decisions as soon as you have them.[117]

I enjoyed talking to you on the phone the other day. Perhaps we may meet some day. I'd like that, believe me.

Meanwhile, my best to you, and the work you're carrying on.

Sincerely yours,
James Dickey

1200 S.E. Lava Drive
Portland, Oregon 97222

THE AVERY HOPWOOD AND JULIE HOPWOOD CONTESTS
1964
MAJOR CONTEST IN POETRY

Please list the names of the six contestants in the order of your preference:

1. Ruth Kline — The Reeves Pheasant
2. Leslie Dickerson — Blood From the Winepress
3. St. B — Constellations
4. R.F. McGurk — Inside the Grape
5. Anne Savenrude — Between Winter and Spring
6. Nathan Tetunic — Calibration

_____James Dickey_____
signed

THE AVERY HOPWOOD AND JULIE HOPWOOD CONTESTS
1964
MINOR CONTEST IN POETRY

Please list the names of the six contestants in the order of your preference:

1. Jean Bodin — The Civilized Cistern
2. Rebecca Keith — The Small Voices
3. Peter Nickel — Poems
4. Oren Pedotti — Statics
5. Skarell — Assorted Meants
6. Brian Craig — Morning is When the Moon Dies

_____James Dickey_____
signed

TO: DENISE LEVERTOV[118]

                                    TLS, 1 p; Stanford University

11 May, 1964
Portland, Oregon

Dear Denise:

New Directions have kindly sent along your new book. I don't know whether or not they did so at your instigation or of their own free will (if publishers may be said to have such), but I have been lost in wonderment and gratitude ever since I received it. I shall surely review it for <u>Sewanee</u>[119] and perhaps a couple of other places, and thought perhaps you might enjoy looking for these notices to appear (though you know how God-Almighty slow the quarterlies are about these things). But the main point about the poems is that they exist, and that you have somehow got the inner feeling of events, as though there were no <u>real</u> difference between things as they exist in the world and the way they exist in us. That is the quality in poetry that I care most for, and which none of the hacks of sensibility or the poetic careerists can fake: the irreducible element: the thing itself. There is so much of that quality in your book that I go from one set of marvellings to another, and then start the whole thing over again by turning back to the first page, as back to the beginnings of all things. Again, thanks so much for your book, and the sensibility that made the poems possible. Thanks also for sending it along, if indeed you did. But I <u>have</u> the book, and that is the main thing: it exists.

                                    Yours sincerely,
                                    James Dickey

1200 S.E. Lava Drive
Portland, Oregon 97222

TO: DONALD HALL

                                    TLS, 1 p; University of New Hampshire

21 May, 1964
Portland, Oregon

Dear Don:

Thanks so much for your letter. Yes, I did indeed notice that you had some poems in the May issue of <u>Poetry</u>,[120] and remembered very warmly discussing them with you a year ago in Portland, at the time we went through my own manuscript and you decided we should call it <u>Helmets</u>, which was a real stroke of inspiration and has helped the book tremendously, I am sure (it has <u>already</u> sold nearly a thousand copies. <u>Drowning With Others</u> is well over 2000, by the way, which tops the Wesleyan list; though Simpson may now outdo me, with the Pulitzer prestige.[121] However, I'd bet against that, since I'm lined up for a couple more long reading tours next year, and that's what sells books, at least according to my experience). Anyway, you have been a wonderful editor for me, the best I have ever had (you are still my official literary executor, if you'll remember, though you can back down any time you want to; I wouldn't hold you to it against either your better judgment or your will). Believe me, I am not in any sense asking you to "go to bat" for me on this new manuscript, or to do anything but approve it or disapprove it. Lockwood will give me the money I ask for if the book is approved. If not, it will officially cut my tie with Wesleyan. So it will be all right either way. I can go or stay; there are advantages both ways. As to publishing another book a year after <u>Helmets</u>: Wesleyan tells me they have no book planned for that period, and the editors there seem excited by the prospect of bringing out another one of mine. I <u>have</u> a book, the best yet (the mail on the separate pieces has been very large), and people will therefore buy it. Why not strike while the iron is hot? Wesleyan might well be jammed up with books later on, and I'd have to wait around, something no one likes doing, and also something which is always par for the course with a small press which can bring out only four titles a year. The business you cite about Frost's sitting on his poems in order to "surprise people" with them is not something I am equipped to understand. I have a number of poems I want to get before the public; if they are good they will make their own way. Nothing could matter to me less than the deliberate hoarding and juggling with poems, the strategic employment of them in the interest of my "career." That has no fascination for me. And it shouldn't have for you, either: not for a man of your gifts. That kind of thing should not even occur to you. We are not in the gold market, after all, but are trying to get something said. And if it's said it should be heard.

About the manuscript. If you want to see it, I'll send it. But if you are predisposed to be <u>against</u> the idea of my publishing a book <u>at all</u>, then there is not much sense to it. I had sooner simply ask Lockwood to let me out of my contract and go ahead with plans to connect with another outfit. Naturally I would leave Wesleyan with misgivings (though I also have some misgivings about staying); the misgivings are mainly connected with a reluctance to disassociate myself from your editorial direction. But I seem to be much in demand these days, the poems are getting read, people want to pay me money for "gracing their imprint" (as one of them said). There is no reason Wesleyan can't pay me <u>something</u> (far less, in fact, than I have been offered). I will stay for what amounts to no more than a token sum, but something I must have. I hope you will understand all this, and write back an airmail letter as soon as you can. I must wrap up all these matters in just a few weeks.

Love to Kirby and the children. And ask Bob Bly where the hell that prose book is.[122]

Jim

TO: ROBERT DUNCAN

TLS, 1 p; SUNY Buffalo

28 May, 1964
Portland, Oregon

Dear Robert Duncan:

Thanks so much for your letter. I got it at school an hour or so ago and walked over to the bookstore, the only place they have any copies of <u>Two Poems of the Air</u>, and had them mail out a copy to you. I'd have sent you a copy myself, free, if I had any, or bought a copy and sent it if I were not already broke, with the prospect of moving my family all the way back to the Southeast next month. But since you say "herewith my order for the book" I hope that my action was all right. Anyway, it's a beautiful book, at least the format and calligraphy are, and I hope very much that you will like it. I am happy indeed that you are to review it for <u>Poetry</u>,[123] and will look forward very much to seeing there what you have to say of it. Your comments on my work are very heartening. I am very glad that you like the poetry so much better than the criticism; so do I. I am not really very much interested in writing criticism, though more and more people these days seem to be wanting me to do it, and a collected (or selected, rather) volume of it has just come out. I had not thought, however, that I dealt just with shop talk and what is "in" and "out" this year or will be next year. I would have thought that my stuff was not really open to that kind of attack, but rather that of being too subjective and personal. But, as I say, if there is to be a ground on which you and I can meet—and I am persuaded by your remarks that there may well be—I am glad that it is poetry rather than discourse, criticism. That is the proper place for it.

You ask about my religious beliefs in the poems. Is there a God in the poems? Are there angels? My position is this, as nearly as I can tell. There is a kind of state of mind—a state utltimately religious and perhaps akin to the Zen teachings, though really I know little of these—in which the mind seems to cancel itself out and the barriers that intelligence or ratiocination set up are quietly dissolved away, leaving nothing between the thing one contemplates and itself. One does not become the other thing, but there is a kind of intimacy between the beholder and the thing beheld that could not obtain in any other way. This is perhaps being close to God; feeling that there is no <u>necessary</u> wall between entities, essences. It is to some extent a kind of visionary state. I myself have never had any visions while in it, but all the same the state seems to me to call for such, to be only one step this side of them. That step I try to take in the poems; that is what the poems are for.

Again, thank you so much for what you say about my work. I am enormously heartened by your good opinion. In just a few remarks you have got so close to what I have been trying to do that my jaw dropped when I read them (<u>actually</u> dropped, and a long ways). There may be some way to get the poetic intelligence, as you call it, into criticism. I obviously have not been able to do it, but perhaps you can. I hope so, and shall be looking for what you say.

See you in about two weeks.

All yours,
James Dickey

1200 S.E. Lava Drive
Portland, Oregon 97222

TO: JOHN HOLLANDER

TLS, 1 p; John Hollander

2 June, 1964
Atlanta, Georgia

Dear John Hollander:

At last I have something I think is worth showing you, even if it is about a sex maniac and murderer.[124] It is a new kind of thing for me, and I'm much interested in hearing what you think of it. I don't believe that the poem is vulgar in any way, though if you're trying to depict what happens to a man who climbs trees and looks in women's windows you have to report what he sees. The thing that intrigued me initially was that a person of this sort would have a look—a look from a secret, unsuspected place—at American life that no one in another position would have, and a poem about such happenings might have therefore a chance to say something about the hidden or usually unobserved side of this life. Whether the poem does all these fine things is of course another question. But do let me know what you think of it as soon as you conveniently can; I only hope that it is not too much of a betrayal of your more-than-generous asking for poems for PR.

Present plans call for me to be in your vicinity around the second week in

October. Let me know if you'd like me to read for you at that time, and I'll do my best to work it out.

Best regards. And I look forward to meeting you in not too many more months.

Sincerely yours,
James Dickey

c/o Mrs. Eugene Dickey
166 West Wesley Road, N.W.
Atlanta 5, Georgia

TO: JAMES KORGES[125]

TLS, 1 p; Rice University

10 June, 1964
Portland, Oregon

Dear Jim:

Well, that is a wonderful letter. There is the kind of understanding in it that writers hope for and secretly think they don't deserve, and when they get it there's nothing for them to do but feel humble and exalted. I'm happy that you chose to defend me at the Tates against Robert Kent,[126] and am even happier that you should choose to write and tell me what you said. Should you see Mr. Kent again, tell him that he has paid me the greatest compliment of my life when he says he thinks I just "pour it out." If I were able to do that, I would be much more talented than I am, and would probably live longer as well. Incidentally, I have not seen your <u>Minnesota Review</u> article,[127] and would welcome having a look at it, if you could take the trouble to send it along to me in Atlanta. I'll be there all summer, c/o Mrs. Eugene Dickey, 166 West Wesley Road, N.W., Atlanta #5, Georgia. I'll look forward to reading what you have to say.

Yes, it's odd to remember those days at Rice, when, as you say, you "didn't really like my poems." Well, I don't blame you. I didn't like them much, either, but was looking, I guess, for "the way." Pater says somewhere that "the way to perfection lies through a long series of disgusts,"[128] and I suppose I may as well admit that my time at Rice was just that. I cared for a few people there, but the English Department was so intolerable, with McKillop (a really bad man: small-minded and vindictive), Will Dowden, Carroll Camden, and the rest. What profit is there in such a crew. I'm glad even after ten years, to be out of it. Incidentally, Monroe Spears has just gone down to Rice to teach. I wonder how he's going to like being in Will Dowden's department! Someone told me (perhaps it was you) that Dowden was the head of the English department down there. I hate to believe it, but I am not surprised, even so.

I won't go on and on. Thanks so much for your letter, Jim. It comes like a drink of Jack Daniels on an empty stomach, and that is good whiskey and a good feeling. Let me hear from you again when you have time. Incidentally since you say you "haven't been asked" to do any more reviews for the <u>Minnesota Review</u>, how about doing an omnibus poetry or fiction review for us for <u>Sewanee</u>? Let me know how this strikes you, and send along your <u>Minnesota Review</u> article so that I can sample your wares. Then we'll swing.

All yours,
Jim

c/o Mrs. Eugene Dickey
166 West Wesley Road, N.W.
Atlanta #5, Georgia

TO: DENISE LEVERTOV

TLS, 1 p; Stanford University

26 July, 1964
Atlanta, Georgia

Dear Denise:

Well, that is a wonderful letter. I'm very happy indeed that you like the new book. I heard from Lockwood on it, and everything seems to be in order, though Wesleyan seems to want to go along with Don Hall's advice, which I'm agreeing to mainly because it will give me time to finish a couple of things I've been working on for years, one of them a long one about a love-hungry poor boy working in a candy factory[129] and the other an even longer and very curious poem about Appalachia, a kind of ghost story, called "A Mayday Courtship Legend of Gilmer County."[130] I'd like if possible to get these into the book, and so will wait until next August to bring it out. I agree, at first secretly but now more and more openly, with your opinion of Don Hall, whom I like very much personally but whom I have been putting entirely too much trust in. Half the stuff I threw out of <u>Helmets</u> on his advice ought to have been kept. There will be, though, a kind of collected or new and selected poems in a few years, and then I can put all those pieces back in. And your remarks on Bob Bly are exactly on the mark as well: the kind of thing he does is so fatally easy to do, and often good fun into the bargain. But it has no real significance. He is trying to start a revolution with a pop-gun, and things just can't be done that way, or that easily.

Don't worry about my thinking your letter a result of a kind of literary recip-
rocal trade agreement. When I got your book in Portland I had no idea you were
connected with Wesleyan University Press[131]—the fact still startles me a little—
and wrote purely out of admiration for the poems, which are the best I have seen
in years.

An idea I just had: I remember seeing some wonderful translations of Supervielle in your next-to-last book, and this set me to thinking of the desirability of
someone's translating Supervielle, who is my all-time favorite poet in any and all
langauges. Who don't you and I take on the job? I did some stuff of his for the
Bollingen Foundation,[132] I have his books available to me, and so on. John Hollander once started such a project, aided and abetted by Richard Howard, but
gave it up, and as far as I know the field is clear. I am sure Gallimard would
approve, and I have seven or eight publishers in this country and a couple in
England, as you also must have, who would be at least mildly interested. My
French is adequate and yours much better than that, and we both love the guy.
So . . . what do you think?[133]

I'll be in New York around the first week of October, and we can talk some of
these matters over. And drink them over too, a prospect that I look forward to
with the utmost eagerness.

I am sending you, under separate cover, a kind of gift edition of the first two
poems in the manuscript you read: "The Firebombing" and the one about the
man being reincarnated as an albatross.[134] The whole thing is called Two Poems of
the Air, and was very handsomely calligraphed by a student at Reed, Monica
Moseley. I hope you like it.

All yours,
Jim Dickey

166 West Wesley Road, N.W.
Atlanta #5, Georgia

TO: ROBERT BLY

TLS, 1 p; Robert Bly

2 August, 1964
Atlanta, Georgia

Dear Bob:

Good to hear from you again! That should be some talk you're getting ready
to make, and I hope you'll send me a tape or a transcript of it when or after you do
it. In answer to your questions: yes, I played football for Clemson in 1941 or 1942. I
was a freshman and played two regular freshman games, but after that the South-

ern Conference passed the Freshman rule (everybody was beginning to get drafted) and I moved up to the varsity and started the last six of their eight games. I was honorable mention for all-Southern, which was supposed to be pretty fair for a freshman. I played wingback under the old singlewing formation, not much used any more except by the University of Tennessee, though the pro "shotgun" formation is a variation of it. When I got back from the war I went to Vanderbilt, but was declared ineligible for football and so couldn't play there. I had played in three basketball games also at Clemson, and so was also ineligible for that. But I did run track all three years I was an undergraduate at Vanderbilt. I ran the sprints and hurdles and broadjumped. My best race was the 120-yard high hurdles, and my best time was 14.3. The biggest race I won was the high hurdles at the Cotton Carnival invitational meet at Memphis in 1947, but I won pretty regularly in Southeastern Conference meets for three years. My best time in the hundred was 9.7 (done only once, but I was fairly consistent under 10) and for the 220, 20.9 (on a straightaway). My best broad jump was around 24′ 5″. Yes, I was field archery champion of Georgia one year, but there are a lot better shots around now than I was then. My best field round was about 450. (Field archery is the kind we were doing when I took you out with me that good day).[135]

I hope all this immodesty on my part will be helpful to you in your talk. Good luck with it. And say hello for me to both Anubis and Hilary Corke,[136] should you see him again.

All yours,
Jim

166 West Wesley Road, N.W.
Atlanta #5, Georgia

TO: MAXINE DICKEY[137]

TLS, 1 p; Emory

8 August, 1964
Atlanta, Georgia

My Dearest Heart:

I'm so happy to have your long wonderful letter, which sounds exactly like you, misspellings and all. I'm glad—and relieved—to know that all the people I care most for in the world are well and having a good time, which is the only kind of time to have. As for me, I am working pretty well. Every day is pretty much the same, and sometimes monotony sets in. But mainly I am content, and the work is going well. I'll have quite a lot to show Bob Lescher when he comes down.[138]

Here is some news: I went down to Tucker Wayne yesterday, and to my surprise Matt Connor, the large Cheese down there, had not heard more than very vaguely what the situation in regard to "Young Blood" was. He listened very attentively, kept nodding, and then asked the all-important question: "How much do you want?" I was shook, I can tell you, but finally mumbled something about five hundred dollars. He asked me to submit a bill, which I have just done. I still don't know whether he's going to pay me, but he very well may. He told me I was "a cool one," whatever that means. Connor is a very decent fellow, not at all like Schaefer, that Doug Smith-like character that writes such charming letters.[139]

Wesleyan is sending along the two hundred and fifty dollars this week, and the sales manager tells me that Helmets has already sold a thousand copies! Now that's going it some! Drowning With Others sold less than five hundred during the first six months, so I'm pointing for 2500 or 3000 with Helmets.

The Times wrote that they are reviewing Two Poems of the Air. So Helmets should also be reviewed pretty soon, if it hasn't been already.[140]

San Fernando wrote and tells me that the first faculty meeting—which I take to be the first time I'll be required to be on hand—is on September 14th, which to me is good news, for it'll give us a little more time in the Southeast, and means that we won't have to rush quite so much when you get back to Atlanta.

Nothing much else has happened. I thought I might get a physical check-up while I'm here and have the leisure time for it. (Don't worry, I'll pay for it out of the Heaven Fund, which is what I've taken to call my savings account). There's nothing wrong with me, but I keep hearing such dire warnings about having check-ups (all, I'm sure, propaganda from the AMA) that I've gone more than halfway back to my old hypochondria, which is a place I don't like. I haven't done anything about all this as yet, but I may soon, particularly since your physical seemed to please you so much. I guess it really is a good idea to have one every so often.

Lewis[141] is proposing another of his wild canoing trips, this time down "a real tough one," the Chatooga,[142] but I'm putting him off. My novel has scared me off all such projects! Lewis and I are going out to shoot Sequoiah today, if we can find a way to get in.

Everything is pleasant, but very lonely without your griping and kissing. I love you very much, and don't care whether you "get skinny" or not. Just come back to me.

I enclose some bills and letters.

Love to all I love,
Jim

On Thursday,
April 20th, 1967
at 8:15 p.m.

Dyckman Hall

Friends OF THE Scarsdale Library

present

"The Unlikeliest Poet"

JAMES DICKEY ...

*athlete, pilot, ad man and a
fresh, emerging literary voice.*

Barnstorming for poetry

PART FIVE

MIDSTREAM

September 1964–June 1968

Dickey moderating a 4 March 1968 Library of Congress reading and discussion by Reynolds Price and John Cheever

Winners of National Book Awards for works published in 1965: Arthur M. Schlesinger Jr., Janet Flanner, Katherine Anne Porter, and Dickey. Mayor John Lindsay of New York City is in the center.

TLS, 1 p; Bancroft Library

19 September, 1964
Northridge, California

Dear Allan:

I am happy (no, it is better than that) to hear from you. Sure, I'll recommend you for the Guggenheim, and with the drive—and overdrive—that comes from utter conviction. What happens is this: you are supposed to fill out all those forms and give a list of people you'd like to have recommend you. The Guggenheim people then take all the material and get in touch with the recommenders. The recommenders then furnish the Guggenheim folks with a very confidential (supposedly) report on what they think the abilities and capacities of the applicants are. When that stuff comes to me, I'll swing into action. For some reason, Gordon Ray, the high priest in matters of money with the Guggenheim people, keeps asking my advice on things that don't seem to have much to do with the dispensing of all those foundation millions, and so I feel I have a kind of in with him that maybe some of the others don't have (I may be all wet about this). Anyway, when it comes to opinions on writers, he'll listen to me; he sure as hell did in the case of Don Hall and Robert Bly, and he will this time, too. So leave it to me; I'll get the dough for you if I can. And I think I can.[1]

It is interesting to know that Bea asked you to do the life of Ted.[2] I know but little about his life, but it ought to be interesting. He was such an odd guy. With me, he always wanted to fight (for some reason or other), taking wild swings and falling down on the sofa, where somebody always brought him another drink. We had some hilarious badminton games in his yard in Seattle, both of us drunk and very disorderly; they were among the few badminton games I've ever played when, out of the five or six shuttlecocks you see, the middle one isn't the real thing to hit; in my case, most of the time it turned out to be the second one from the end.

I am happy to know your wife is well enough to go out. My God, your daughter playing all that Shakespeare! And I welcome hearing any news you have about Mary,[3] whom I remember well; I took her to the poetry-panel fiasco at the Poetry

Center in New York, and to the very posh party afterward. I hope she is doing well, and that you will remember me to her when you write.

I am working some, though I did little this summer but play the guitar in some dark joint in Atlanta. I hope to get going on some new stuff now that I'm out in the California sun. Houghton Mifflin will do the novel you and I talked about at Don Hall's. It seems to be developing pretty well, though I know nothing of the writing of novels.

Thanks for the tip on the agent. Some other guy snagged me though.

Write when you can.

Jim

8950 Balboa Boulevard
Northridge, California

TO: RICHARD HOWARD

TLS, 1 p; Richard Howard

6 December, 1964
Northridge, California

Dear Dick:

God! Thanks so much for your enormous letter from Kentucky (or, Letter From Kentucky, as future historians of our genius will have it). I haven't enjoyed anything so much for months, swamped with work as I have been (in fact, the only movie I've seen since I've been in California has been "The Three Stooges in Orbit"). It is wonderful to know that you have worked yourself into a situation where you can write your own work your own way; you must get all kinds of royalties and residuals and what not from all those hundred-odd books you've translated. I hope very much that <u>Making Scenes</u>[4] is moving forward, and I will surely get it for review (possibly in three or four places, for that seems to be the way I've been reviewing lately: I hit Fred Seidel[5] from so many sides he must have felt like he was <u>between</u> Sonny Liston and Cassius Clay—that is, if they'd fought). Anyhow, let me know what progress you're making on it. And tell me, young fellow, are you in the market for a grant? I've been called in as advisor to the Rockefeller Foundation and they seem to be <u>begging</u> to give away money. Tell me what your situation is, and we'll go into the Rockefeller vaults like Goldfinger, though I hope more successfully than the famous Ian Fleming heist at Fort Knox.[6]

Your book for Horizon Press sounds great.[7] Let me know if you need any kind of help. In answer to your question about new work: the new, <u>new</u> book, <u>Buckdancer's Choice</u>, will be out in September. Then, as far as I can tell at this early date, I'll most probably move to Scribners, Knopf or Harpers for a New and

Selected poems, a big book, in 1968 or thereabouts, though perhaps even a year earlier than that. And sure, send along your list of poets about whom you're planning to write the essays of your book, and I'll advise accordingly.[8]

I got the Barthes book, which is <u>great</u>! Thanks so much. Good to hear, too, all the stuff about the New York scene. I read Snodgrass' piece about the Lowell plays in <u>Review of Books</u>,[9] and was sickened by it, as I have been by everything else that snivelling, self-serving little bastard does. His patronizing piece on Roethke was one of the most disgraceful things I've ever seen in print.[10] How Roethke would have holwed (I mean howled; but maybe I mean holwed after all) with laughter, though he hated Lowell and everything that pertained to him.

And I know what you mean about Jarrell. I read with him at some school in Virginia a few years back (Katherine Anne Porter was also aboard the stage in that strange place, which we called the Ship of Schools). Jarrell glosses everything for hours before reading it, and one has the distinct impression of the mountain laboring wittily to bring forth a m(o)use (perhaps from Jarrell's beard, though it looks a more likely place for birds).

Well, it is late, and I must close and get this in the mail. Write again soon and let me know if you are in a position to take some money from Mr. Rockefeller. I'll defer my list of the select (or the Angelic, as Mr. Rockefeller and I delight in calling them) until I hear from you.

My best to Sandy.

Yours,

Jim

TO: DONALD HALL

TLS, 1 p; University of New Hampshire

16 January, 1965
Northridge, California

Dear Don:

I expect we ought to be pulling the book into final shape pretty soon, don't you? I have a couple more thing I want to have go in, and one of them is a long poem on the Negro-white agony—my only statement on the matter—which the <u>New Yorker</u> will be doing. It is called "Slave Quarters," and I want your advice as to whether to publish the version the <u>N Yer</u> will do or a slightly longer version.[11] These and other questions are things we'll have to be conferring about during the next few weeks. This is going to be a smash of a book, I believe. <u>Partisan</u> is doing the poem about the sex fiend in the spring issue, and the editors tell me the poem already has a considerable underground reputation. So we want to get out the very best book we can, for it will in all probability be my last with Wesleyan, for I intend to follow your suggestion—and you—to Harpers, if the price is right. After all, I can't do without my executor. My God, what if I died?

You are naturally looking for poets for Harpers, and want to get the best you can get. I reckon you'll be bringing in Bob Bly, as I believe you indicated.[12] I also have another suggestion for you: something I would do if I were the great Power in Publishing (at least in poetry publishing) that you bid fair to be. This would be to get hold of Brewster Ghiselin and bring out a collected poems.[13] His first two books are out of print with Dutton, who did not handle him well, but they are mighty good books, in my opinion, and he also has a third book which is just now being completed. The whole thing would be most impressive, in my opinion; he showed me some of the new stuff this past summer in Salt Lake City, and it floored me. Of course, you may not care for his work as much as I do, but if you do like it as much—or almost—you should get hold of him; he's definitely cut loose from Dutton.

MGM wants to make a movie around the January 3rd article in the New York Times,[14] and I've given a tentative consent. I am working up a step outline of the material now, and my director, Jeffrey Hayden (who, incidentally, is married to the actress Eva Marie Saint), is most enthusiastic. There's a lot of quick money in the project, though every mirror I look in I expect to see Scott Fitzgerald's weary ghost looking back. But so far I haven't seen him.

Love to Kirby. And let me hear something from you as soon as you can get a moment from all your projects and duties.

Maybe we can get together this summer, for I'll be in Milwaukee for a month.

All yours,
Jim

8950 Balboa Boulevard
Northridge, California

TO: DONALD HALL

TLS, 1 p; University of New Hampshire

26 January, 1965
Northridge, California

Dear Don:

Thanks for the card, and the information about the book. I am enclosing "Slave Quarters" and two or three others I've written since I sent the book to you; I'd like these to be considered for the final selection; New Yorker is doing all of them.

A couple of things: first of all, this is the first I have known about Denise[15] helping edit the manuscript. As it turns out, this is all right with me, for I respect Denise and like her. But suppose it had <u>not</u> been all right? In other words, I expect to be consulted about such things; this is a definite change from the way you and I have worked before, and when such changes occur they should be subject at least to my review, if not my consent. Secondly, I expect you as editor to give me your opinion, as you have done so effectively before, as to what should and shouldn't be in. When this book was first accepted you wrote to me that we wanted to have as strong a book as we could get—"ninety pages of pure gold", as I believe you put it. You went on to say that it would be best if we had a larger selection of poems from which to choose all this precious metal. It seems to me that this is the situation we are now in. If we have too much stuff, let's cut some of it out; the pomes in this letter are, I believe, a good deal better than a lot of the ones in the manuscript as you now have it.[16] We're in the position of making up the book simply by exclusion, and that shouldn't be awfully hard to do. If we are left with nothing but very good stuff—or at least the best I can do—why, that is what we have been aiming for all the time. We don't have to ask Lockwood for a lot of extra pages— though I would like, maybe, a few more: it is not a question of cramming in everything I've written since <u>Helmets</u>—you have taught me this, and I have learned it well—but of making the best selection we can. And there are a lot of ways in which we can do this. For example, we can leave out the whole first section of "The Shark's Parlor." The <u>New Yorker</u> is only printing the second section, which <u>is</u> a good deal better, though if you think the first section sort of "sets up" the second, as it was intended to do, of course we can keep it.[17] But do let me have, as soon as you can, some sort of idea as to how you think the final form of the book should be: what it should contain, what the order of poems should be, and so on. Then we can go on from there.

As to your other questions: you can reach Ghiselin c/o American Express, 11 Promenade des Anglais, Nice, France. He's living for a few weeks at Villefranche.

Before I forget—now that I look back through these poems in the letter—: "Dust" is the only one of these not to be in the <u>New Yorker</u>, though I think it is one of the best I've done for some time. If Denise wants it for the <u>Nation</u>, she's welcome to it. If you could convey this information—and a copy of the poem, which she'll have to see anyway—to her, that would be good.[18]

My best, and get back to me on these matters as soon as you can.

Yours,

Jim

8950 Balboa Boulevard
Northridge, California

TO: DENISE LEVERTOV

TLS, 1 p; Stanford University

14 February, 1965
Northridge, California

Dear Denise:

Don Hall has sent along your letter, and I wanted to thank you for taking the trouble with my manuscript that you did take, and also for holding out for the poems that I myself prefer to the ones Don prefers. I had no idea that you were to be involved with the selection until Don told me that you wished to be; therefore it is a little hard for me to understand some of the things you say, such as "I simply can't see why he can't figure this out for himself instead of our having to put up with all this headache." Believe me, it was none of my intention to be troublesome to you; as I say, I had no idea you were involved in the project at all until Don made the fact known to me. I did not solicit your advice or approval, though of course I am glad to have both; neither do I particularly care, as you do not, for "this business of two people messing around with a third one's manuscript." I can understand your reluctance to do that, and I can only reiterate that I had or have nothing whatever to do with your being involved with my mss., as you surely must know.

As for the difficulties that would necessarily be involved with your printing "Dust" in the <u>Nation</u>, I can understand them perfectly. I sent it on to some Australian outfit that is putting out an issue on something called "The New American Poetry," and so the poem has found a home, more or less. And I will, if I turn up anything good in the near future, send it along to you; I'm working on a couple of things that seem pretty promising, and I'll get them to you if they don't collapse before the final lines.

Something in your letter to Don—the tone of it, maybe—bothered me a good deal. It's not so much that you're thinking about quitting the editorship of the <u>Nation</u>, but that you seemed pushed and frazzled and at bay, as it were. I don't like to think of that, for I remember you as having a number of remarkable resources of your own that I do not believe the world could easily get the better of. Of course the letter to Don may have been written only out of a temporary period of depression, which is what I hope for. But I won't know until I hear from you, which I hope will be soon.

Wesleyan tells me that <u>Helmets</u> is up for the National Book Award, as I suppose your book is too, though I don't really know anything about who the other contestants are. I guess Lowell and Berryman are in, which probably should wrap it up in favor of the elder statesmen or Original Witnesses. Oh well, you and

I can't finish any worse than seventh and eighth, which ain't as bad as it might be, I guess.[19]

Please do write and tell me what your life is like. I may be in New York briefly this summer, and perhaps we could get together for a bit. I am off alcohol, and all manner of strange, delicate traits are surfacing through the old mannerisms and the ancient obvious tiresomeness that I had grown accustomed to thinking of as myself.

Best to Mitchell.[20]

Yours sincerely,
Jim Dickey

8950 Balboa Boulevard
Northridge, California

TO: DENISE LEVERTOV

TLS, 1 p; Stanford University

27 February, 1965
Northridge, California

Dear Denise:

Well, that is a good letter. After reading it, I would no more doubt anything you say than I would question the order of words in a good poem; one of your own poems, say. Don Hall's letters have never had that feeling for me; there has always been something slippery and time-serving about them. It is true that he has worked with me on the two previous Wesleyan books—and now on this new one—and that I have taken some of his advice. Some of the advice has been bad, but I have not by any means taken all of it, as I am not doing now; the new book will be much closer to what I (and you) want than what Don wants, and I think that is all to the good. It galls my very soul to have Don going around saying that he is a kind of Maxwell Perkins to my Thomas Wolfe; that I can't exist without him. There is no truth at all in that; I hear from him hardly more than once or twice a year. As for his rather pathetic slavery to Bly (my God, have you seen Don's new book?[21] It has nothing at all), the less said the better. I like them both person-ally, but neither has any talent, or certainly neither has any talent worthy of the claims being made (mostly by them, Bob especially) for it. It is all so politicky; I am sick of the whole affair. No; don't worry; I won't be patronized by Don or by anybody else. And I think I shall probably leave Wesleyan for the next book any-way. Every large publisher in the country is trying to shove money into my hands—I suppose partly because I am doing a novel—and there's no use going to Harper's with Don and being a stablemate of Bob's, and still under Don's supervision. No; that won't happen.

And I do thank you so much for the remarks about the poems. There is something important in me somewhere, if I can find the way to get it out.

I know what you mean about correspondence. I am about six months behind in my own; it is all over the desk like a huge paper dragon; one that I shall never slay in this earthly life.

Yes, I know I was troubled at Colgate—and probably troublesome, too. But that is not me, really: it is a kind of condition I subconsciously felt I owed myself. I am really such a healthy square that I had come to be a little ashamed of it. But I am squarer than ever now, running five miles a day in the warm California dawn, hunting and walking a lot. It is good; it is my way, and I shall never set foot on any other. Liquor was trying to finish me, so I finished it. Now the world is very clear and steady, and very deep in every direction.

I'm sorry I don't have any "lovely short poems," but only this one, which I fear is too long. It is about the dream of intensity that middle age aspires to in its mild judiciousness. Anyway, it's all I have, and you're welcome to it if you have room.[22]

Please don't let this letter add to the woes (but only, hopefully, to the joys) of your correspondence. Answer it only when you feel like it, or just throw it away. But do remember from it the feeling I would like to think is in it; gratitude for your courage and tenacity on my behalf, and a continued admiration.

Sincerely,
Jim Dickey

8950 Balboa Boulevard
Northridge, California

TO: FRANCES STELOFF

TLS, 1 p; Berg Collection, NYPL

20 March, 1965
Northridge, California

Dear Miss Steloff:

First of all, congratulations on the book about you,[23] and on the recognition you so very much deserve. The Gotham Book Mart has been my book supplier for twenty years, and it is not too much to say that the Mart has been more responsible for my literary education (and whatever writings have come from it) than any college or any library. And my example could be multiplied by dozens—hundreds, even. Anyway, congratulations again.

Second, I have taken the liberty of having a good many of my students order books from you. Many of these must come from England, and I hope these orders have not inconvenienced you. Believe me, the students appreciate knowing of a bookstore that can get these things for them, and many of them will be lifelong customers, I am quite sure.

Third, I'd like to order a couple of books myself. I'm not sure of the name of the first one, but it is by G. S. Fraser. The title is something like <u>Vision and Reality</u>, or <u>Vision and Design</u>, or <u>Vision and Form</u> (as you can see, I'm pretty sure that the word "vision" is present somewhere!)[24] The other books are by F. T. Prince[25] and Norman MacCaig (or maybe it is spelled McCaig). I don't know the name of either of them, but I know that they exist. I already have Prince's <u>Poems</u> and <u>Soldiers Bathing</u>, and the title I want would be anything of his except those I just listed. Similarly, I have MacCaig's <u>Riding Lights</u> and <u>The Sinai Sort</u>, and the title I'd like to get my hands on is anything other than these two. Anything, that is, which has been published recently, for I also have an old book of MacCaig's called <u>The Inward Eye</u>. Also I'd appreciate it if you'd see if you could get me a copy of John Peale Bishop's short stories, called, I think, <u>Many Thousands Gone</u>,[26] and J. N. P. Barbellion's <u>Last Diary</u>. This last one may be hard to run down, but it is the companion to Barbellion's <u>Journal of a Disappointed Man</u>, one of my favorite books of all time, and I'd like to get it if I can.[27]

Again, thank you so much for everything, these last twenty years. I realize this letter is long overdue, but I am very happy to be able to write it at last.

I'll be in New York at least twice next year, and I'll make sure to drop in on you, as I always so much enjoy doing. The same thrill of poetry, of creativity and those devoted to it, comes over me every time I come in the door, as it did when I came in for the first time. As long as the Gotham Book Mart exists, all is not lost.

Regards to Mr. Lyman![28]

Yours sincerely,
James Dickey

8950 Balboa Boulevard
Northridge, California

TO: ROBERT BLY

TLS, 1 p; Robert Bly

On the last letter you got my address wrong. The right one is 8950 Balboa Blvd. Northridge, California (NOT 9850, as you had it)[29]

23 March, 1965
Northridge, California

Dear Old Bob:

Good to hear from you! I hadn't written because I wasn't sure whether you were still in Paris or not. How long will you be there, and when will you be back in the States? I haven't seen you and Jim Wright since we walked on the frozen Mississippi a little over a year ago, and you took us over to the Tates'. By the way, in connection with the National Book Awards (always with capital letters, I am told), in which Helmets was one of the finalists, I hear—I suppose by much the same kind of grapevine by which you heard what you tell me of the board meetings of Wesleyan in connection with the last book you submitted—that Tate, who was one of the judges, was "loud in denunciation of Dickey's character and his influence." I'm not sure exactly how he arrived at that estimate, but it surely had something to do with that afternoon, for I had only seen him one time before in my life. I got pretty well gassed on his liquor, and I remember making an eloquent speech, with gestures, in defense of you and some of your ideas—mainly, I believe, in connection with foreign-language poets, none of whom Tate knows anything about—and his attitude may well stem from that, though I can't and probably never will be entirely sure of <u>what</u> it stems from. This is all just between you and me, Bob; I sure don't want any of this to get around—that would be unseemly, I reckon. But what a lot of crap it all is!

That is <u>great</u> news about <u>Suspect</u>! I had no idea it would do anything like as well as that! And all in hardbound, too, which seems a kind of bonus! How many volumes does our first edition run? If we sell out, as we may well do before long, are there any plans to reprint? Also, how many copies do we have to sell before you get back your $150 advance? Do tell me about this, particularly, for I have worried about it.[30] And could you <u>please</u> send along my twelve author's copies? I'd sure appreciate it, for if I lose the one copy I have, that's it.

Yes, I did have my attention called to the piece in <u>Saturday Review</u>.[31] I thought it was very funny, particularly in his praise of Ciardi, the poetry editor (you and I and Spector and everybody else knows) of the magazine. I've seen a few other reviews, and am very happy at the reception of the book. Where to, now?

I did get a good many letters on the "Barnstorming" piece, some of them from good people. Also, a guy at MGM here wants to make a movie of it. I had to acquire an agent to deal with him on this, and they're still sitting down with each other and working out clauses in the contract. I'll probably be the last to hear what they've decided.

How are your own projects going? Are you going over to Harpers with Don Hall? I've been thinking about doing the same, but haven't absolutely decided yet. Tell me what you think of this possibility.

Glad you like Marcel Béalu. Remember me to him affectionately when you see him again.

Love to Carol and the children. And write again soon; it is always good to hear from you. <u>Very</u> good![32]

Jim

TO: DENISE LEVERTOV

TLS, 1 p; Stanford University

19 April, 1965
Northridge, California

Dear Denise:

I wonder if I might ask a favor of you? This would be no trouble to you unless I were to die, but if that should happen I'd like to think you'd be my literary executor (or executrix, I guess it would be). Don Hall has had this dubious distinction up to now, but he seems to know less and less of what I'm doing, and the experience with the last book, in which he gave me the worst conceivable advice, prompts me to change this situation. I got the book straightened out, finally, and I think it is really going to be good, but if it hadn't been for your stand in the matter I might have gone along with Don's judgements, and that would have been disastrous. Anyway, let me know if you'll take on this gloomy duty. Believe me, I've thought a lot about whom I'd like to have do it, and the choice has circled back to you via all kinds of alternatives and possibilities. I hope you won't be pressed into service to <u>do</u> anything for a while yet, but I'd like to know you're there just in case. It would be a tremendous load off my mind.

My best to you and Mitchell; I'll hope to see you both this summer, or, failing that, next fall or next spring.

All yours,
Jim Dickey

8950 Balboa Boulevard
Northridge, California

TO: RANDALL JARRELL

TLS, 1 p; Berg Collection, NYPL

2 May, 1965
Northridge, California

Dear Mr. Jarrell:

Thank you so much for that letter; it is sure good to have it. Lord, if Randall Jarrell likes my work it is better than the wild acclaim of multitudes (though I have scarcely had that). Anyway, I appreciate very much what you say. As to the poem you ask about, it must be one called "Fence Wire"[33] and it's collected in a book of mine called <u>Helmets</u>. The one about the junkyard is called "Cherrylog Road,"[34] and is in the same book. I've got a new book coming out in the fall with some very different kinds of things in it, and I hope you'll like these too. I have learned more about poetry from you than from anyone, and your example has been more life-giving for me than I could ever possibly tell you. I am not one to gush about these things, but I thought I should at last give you some indication of how I feel. Anyway, you are sure welcome to any poems of mine you'd like to print in the anthology you mention; I'd be very pleased to see them, no matter which ones they turned out to be.[35]

As for "Gleaning,"[36] it is probably the best poem I've ever read. The beginning is so good I actually cringed, as I dropped from line to line, afraid that the whole thing was going to collapse and drop me into the void, but it kept getting better and better and stronger. It was hard to believe, but there it was, and so I sat down and wrote a letter.

The fall of '66 I'll be going back to Hollins for a year, and I hope very much that we can get together during my stay. I'd like that.

My regards to your wife.

All yours,
James Dickey

8950 Balboa Boulevard
Northridge, California

TO: DENISE LEVERTOV

TLS, 1 p; Stanford University

9 May, 1965
Northridge, California

Dear Denise:

Thanks so much for your letter; it makes me feel a whole lot better. But please don't be alarmed by the things I say. I am not planning to die for a while yet, if I can help it. I am so full of projects now that I'd have to live several hundred lives to complete even a small part of them. But ever since the war (the two wars, really, for I was in Korea too) I have lived very close to the thought that I might wake up dead one morning, or be killed on one of these dreadful American freeways, or develop cancer (my family is full of it), and have lately taken to wondering about the fate of my work. The appalling lack of comprehension of what I am trying to do on the part of Don Hall in relation to this last book worried me a whole lot, because I suddenly realized that if anything happened to me all the stuff I've been working for for so many years would be in the hands of somebody who not only was not awfully sympathetic toward it, but had very little idea of what was going on in it. That is a bad prospect, and I decided to do something about it. So I sat down and wrote you a letter. Believe me, I'm not anxious for you to exercise your new "duties" any time soon, either. I plan for you and I to take a trip to Sweden when we are magnificent, witty old people, too old for people to say we're running off together, but are just going over there to get up on a platform and receive a certain prize jointly, and then expire together, pelted to death with roses.

Anyway, don't worry, and don't fret about any of the points you bring up in your letter. My wife is well acquainted with my wishes in the matter, and she'll see to it that you get the papers and the correspondence, and the rest of it. It'll never happen, but if it surprisingly should, I'll feel better, up there on the crown of Parnassus, knowing that you are the one shuffling my papers.

I'll be in New York for a week this summer to be on Camera #3, and some other things. Will you be in town? I do hope so. Meanwhile, love to Mitchell.

And thanks again, Denise, ever so much. You don't know how much this relieves me.

All yours,
Jim

8950 Balboa Boulevard
Northridge, California

TO: MAXINE DICKEY[37]

TLS, 1 p; Emory

16 June, 1965
Atlanta, Georgia

My Dearest One:

I love you, and I can't sleep without you close to me. The only solution has been to stay up late, out with Inman or Worley or Al and Lewis, but that isn't really a very good solution; it would be much better—infinitely better—to have you, my one true earthly lifelong woman, with me and near me, bitching and loving. The only consolation is the rapid mounting-up of the bank balance that this way of operating helps. According to my latest count, we are somewhat upwards of $11,700, which is a pretty good place to be. Don't forget to get the bank interest added onto the Great Little Book at the end of this month. That'll bring us up to around $11,800+, and the $250 for the last two essays—on Smart and Hopkins[38]— will set us on the grand peak of $12,000. Then Bill Hale's $500[39] plus the $1500 I hope to net from the Milwaukee venture will put us up to $14,000! We are really going good, and it is a vastly comforting throught to me that Chris's college education is already in the bank, and most of Kevin's, too. The terror about money is the worst, most destructive psychological force in our society, and we have got it licked, and with a few more thousand can bury it forever. That leaves only death to worry about, and I worry about that less and less. Life is good to us, right now, and we have only to concentrate on becoming magnificent, witty old people together.

Really, there is not much to do here. I learned a couple of new things from Worley and taught him a couple I've picked up in various places.[40] Al and Lewis are as fine as ever, though Al is unhappy with his work, as we predicted. The Braseltons have moved to a larger house in Ansley Park. And so on. Not much has changed. I listen more or less patiently to the grievances of the family, to the talk of Patsy and Mrs. Hamilton and the cottage at St. Simons—the cottage that I am tempted to lable the Cottage of Miseries—but I am anxious to get on with it. This is a pleasant enough interlude, but after a few days I begin to rattle around. It is better for me to get into a regular orbit, and I look forward to whatever I'll end up doing at Milwaukee. I wrote Dunleavy when to meet me, and I am sort of slowly phasing-out things in Atlanta in preparation for Milwaukee.

Bill Hale called from Washington, as I told you just now on the phone, and is floating around on cloud #17. He said the people had the highest praise for the script; in fact, Bill said that he had the distinct impression that they thought the narration was too good for the film. But they liked the film too, and Bill has a go-ahead to finish it. If he calls, you might like to have him take you and the boys to the session where he and Mel "mix" the sounds, music, commentary, and the rest of it. I'd like to see that part of it myself, only I won't be able to. At any rate, ask him about it.

My greatest love to the boys. And be sure to tell Kevin that I will bring him a <u>big</u> present. Say hello, too, to Michael,[41] and thank him for all he's done. I am deeply moved by it, and by him.

All my love, my darling wife,
Jim

TO: BEATRICE ROETHKE[42]

TLS, 1 p; University of Washington

16 June, 1965
Atlanta, Georgia

Dear Mrs. Roethke:

Thank you very much for your note of June 8<u>th</u>, and for the things you say about the <u>Poetry</u> article on Ted.[43] I had had no previous notion as to whether you liked it or even saw it, and I am very happy that you did see the piece, and that it meant something to you. This was one occasion when I did not want to write "literary criticism," but only wished to say what I felt. Such an attitude has its dangers, for it opens one to the charge, not only of sentimentality—that, writers must always risk, and the best ones do—but stupidity as well. But if I had the article to write over again—and I shall surely write again on Ted, and again and again—I would do it the same way, only more so.

I have looked through my correspondence, and don't find anything from Ted. I remember getting a letter or two, but these were mostly in connection with the possibility of his coming down to Reed for a few days, or with my going up to read at U. of Washington. If there had been anything in the letters which was more than just routine, I surely would have kept them. As I remember, Ted and I did more talking over the phone than we did letter-writing, and of course that record of him is lost, though <u>I</u> certainly remember it with deep affection.

On Sunday I go up to be writer-in-residence at the University of Wisconsin at Milwaukee, and then later, around July 17<u>th</u>, will be coming to New York, where I must be on Camera #3 and some other things. Should you change your plans and stay on in New York, it might be possible for us to get together for a little while and talk; I'd like that. Or if you could stop by Milwaukee or Chicago on your way out to the Coast, we might also be able to meet. I like to think of the prospect of that, for I remember Ted with the greatest personal affection, though I never had any idea whatever of what he thought of me, beyond his telling me that he liked some poems of mine. Anyway he is a very great poet, the greatest we have ever had in this country for my money: small change, maybe, but all I have—Hopkins and Ted are the greatest poets in the English language.

Please give my love—<u>really</u> love—to Carolyn[44] when you see her. And also to Allan Seager, that good, impressive, intelligent man.

Yours sincerely,
Jim Dickey

English Department
University of Wisconsin at Milwaukee
Milwaukee,
Wisconsin

TO: CHRISTOPHER DICKEY

TLS, 1 p; Emory

10 July, 1965
Milwaukee, Wisconsin

Dear Chris:

I write you on sudden impulse, which is the best way to write letters, knowing that the sound of my voice on the printed page will be much different than the sound of it that you're accustomed to. But it occurred to me that, though I've talked to your mother and Kevin a good many times on the phone, I have rarely heard your voice, and I hunger for it in the way that human beings hunger for those things that are most precious to them. I have nothing particular to say, but in a way I have almost everything to say, too. I want most to tell you, just simply to tell you, how much I love you, my dear, irreplaceable oldest boy, and how proud I am of you. I want to say, too, what I think you and I ought to do about insuring your future as one of the great ones: one of the great human beings, which you have a chance to be, and one of the great futures. You already have, I think, an inkling of what I mean.

You have seen the world. You know, as I do, that it is <u>there</u>, from the bikini-covered (almost) bottoms of the Riviera to the high snows of Everest. The world is the greatest place for the human consciousness to flourish, for the mind and body to grow wings in, that could ever be conceived of. And there are, basically, two approaches to it. One approach says that simply to live in it is enough. The other approach says that, in order fully to live in it, one must <u>do</u> something in it, contribute something to it. Myself, I think the answer lies somewhere in between.

The beatniks think that just to live in it is best, though they make a kind of show of contributing something, with their unread copies of Sartre in their ratty lofts and basement apartments. But they are not Frank Lloyd Wright, nor are they Sartre. The best of living, Chris, is in the abandonment to the fact, the reality of living wherever you are, after having earned your place, your right to live, for that moment, as you wish. Some earn it by ways that you and I wouldn't consider adequate. You and I earn it by creation, by making something that couldn't have existed without us, by something strange in us that will not let us rest until it gets put down, gets built, gets written, gets said. And that, I think, is the best thing. After that, secure in the knowledge of what we are, which is what we have done and what we are going to do, we can for a time swim in the sea, love women, drink whiskey, or loaf and invite our souls, as Whitman did, "observing a spear of summer grass."

Well, enough. But remember, too, this rather practical but very much <u>meant</u> advice from a father: in fact, <u>your</u> father. (My God, what a strange role being a father is. A <u>father</u>!) Love, really, is all we as a family have. When your petty side wants to gripe, wants to be lazy, wants to talk back to your mother, that great, troubled, lovely woman, think about it a little. And then maybe you won't want quite so much to nag at Kevin, to be insolent to your mother, to shut yourself away from us like the Wounded Fawn of romantic eighteenth century novels. We are all in this together, son. That is the way it should be and that is the way it is. We all irritate each other somewhat from time to time. But under the great stars of night, and against the Enemy, which is Time, Death, Separation, we cannot afford to spend too much time in irritation with those we are in the human condision most closely and essentially with. The essential, the great, the best Team is you, me, Kevin and your mother. Let us spend more time living as though our every day with each other were the last. Then we will have a more adequate idea of what a human family means, and the basis on which it rests.

Always, —Dad—

TO: LOUIS D. RUBIN JR.[45]

TLS, 1 p; University of North Carolina, Chapel Hill

16 July, 1965
Milwaukee, Wisconsin

Dear Lou:
Thanks so much for the letter, and for the things you say and the information you send along.

Now, to your questions: If you like, I can teach a kind of year course of modern British and American poetry, taking both these together. Or I could teach modern British poetry the first term and American the second. If it were left to me, I believe I would choose the former, but could easily do the latter if it is preferable to you. And, surely, I will be glad to give a reading, a public lecture, or anything and everything else you think would be interesting and/or instructive to the students and faculty (and townspeople, too, if they want to come). There is no problem about any of this at all, though I would welcome your thoughts on the kind of course you'd most like me to teach: that is, what kind of course you think would serve the greatest benefit.

I'd prefer the classes to be scheduled in the early afternoon, if possible. I like to work in the mornings, and things seem generally to work out better that way for me.

As to housing: I have the requisite wife, and two boys who by then will be (just) fifteen and eight. And, yes, we'd like three bedrooms if at all possible, for the boys are not all that compatible. I think we should plan to be there for only the actual term, for by that time we will have been living away from our home folks for quite a number of years, and will probably want to spend the summer previous to our stay at Hollins with them.

As for this other mysterious, delicate subject you broach, for God's sake don't worry about any such where I am concerned (though I am not quite sure what you're alluding to, insofar as any exactitude of conjecture is concerned). In other words, I can only surmise that someone—or several someones, since you say there were "several" incidents last year—has or have been either actually intimate with students or proposed such intimacy. I do wish, if you possibly could, you'd tell me a little more about the actual circumstances which prompted all this dire forewarning, for I'd really like to know what the story is. In other words, if this is so serious that you must bring the subject up, as you say, with all new faculty members, I'd like to know what the violations have been, and exactly what a violation, strictly speaking, is. Communications like yours scare me to death, because I don't know, really know, what the exact bounds of propriety are. In case of rape or pregnancy, of course, it is clear enough, and such as that is what I think of immediately. An affair with a student is also clearly a violation of what you call "the proper student-teacher relationship." But how about something like serving someone a beer in your house, or something like that: something that some schools, Baptist schools, like Baylor, call "immoral conduct"? I will be glad to bear with any rules you have, and it will be no trouble to me, but I really would like to know what the rules are, and know this as exactly as it is possible for you to tell me. Believe me, I'd appreciate it if you'd enlighten me on this.

Meanwhile, everything looks great. Let me hear from you on these matters as soon as you conveniently can.

I'll also try to get a poem or two to you, soon.[46]

Yours, Jim

8950 Balboa Boulevard
Northridge, California

TO: ALLAN SEAGER

TLS, 1 p; Bancroft Library

7 August, 1965
Northridge, California

Dear Allan:

Thanks so much for the letter, which I only just now got, for I have been in the east for the last couple of months, and spent a month in Milwaukee teaching at some kind of arts festival. Anyway I am mighty glad to hear from you. I see also that you got the Guggenheim, so it may have been that my nagging of Gordon Ray did some good, or at any rate didn't do any harm. It's good that you have the money—you deserve it more than any of those curious Entemologists and Geologers and Specialists in Hypertrophy that fill out the list of Awardees which Ray sent along to me. And you don't have to tell me that your book on Ted is going to be good (though I like to listen to you say that it is; the tone is full of authentic grandeur and self-knowledge, and I like that, just as I hate false modesty and phony humility); I know it will be good, and I am looking forward to it eagerly.

You ask me about Ted (by the way, do you remember when he and I, drunk as owls, called you from Seattle?). I never really knew him well enough to make any definitive pronouncements about him, for to do that you should know a person over a long period of time, and have seen him with many people and in many situations. That was not my situation with Ted. I saw him maybe half a dozen times. I liked him very much most of the time, and he seemed to like me, partly because I had referred to him in print as the greatest poet in English—alive poet, that is— and partly because I played the guitar, which for some reason he seemed to enjoy a great deal, and also, I suppose, because he considered my work at least somewhat in his "tradition." Anyway, we got along very well, which I was told was unusual. As for my impressions of him, he seemed to me pathetically unsure of himself, and fanatically self-protective, not so much of his work but of his reputation. He talked incessantly of this, and kept showing me things in letters and in journals in which people—famous people or at any rate famous literary people—had spoken well of him. He was extremely jealous of other writers, but most particularly of Robert Lowell, whom he disliked to the point of mania. He felt that there was an "eastern conspiracy" to boost Lowell and to knock—or, worse, ignore—his, Roethke's, work, and he would hold forth on this topic for hour after hour. He had very little good to say about any of the younger poets' work, and considered them all rivals; I remember his calling Donald Hall, for example, an arriviste. The picture that emerges in my head of Ted Roethke is of a curious, big, bumbling man who was eminently unlikeable except at rare intervals when you could get him off by himself, but who was also somehow loveable, someone you felt you wanted to protect from the things he most feared: poetic rivals.

Well, if you'd like me to go on in this vein, I can probably summon the muses of memory some more in the next letter. But do write and tell me what you're doing. Chances are I can get up that way next school year, or the school year coming up, rather, and may even manage to come twice, once in the fall and once in the spring. Anyway, I'll look forward to it.

Please give my warmest regards to Miss Mary when you write her.

                                                                            Jim

8950 Balboa Boulevard
Northridge, California

TO: HOWARD NEMEROV

                                        TLS, 1 p; Washington University

6 September, 1965
Northridge, California

Dear Howard:

Rutgers has kindly sent along your new Journal of the Fictive Life, and I read through it in a single afternoon, leaving my children, whom I was supposed to pick up, scattered about as widely as two people can get scattered. Anyway, I think it is a wonderful book and very like what I remember of you personally, this being intended as a very high compliment. There isn't much like the book in English, though the French tradition has some precedents, for those folks are always keeping journals and records, particularly journals of what they're writing, how they're going about it, what it all means or doesn't mean, and so on. But I think your book is a lot better, more useful, truer, than any of those others I've read, including Gide's, Montherlant's, Jouhandeau's, Julien Green's, and some writers' whose names I don't feel like stopping to recall. It is the kind of book I could never do—or certainly not do well—but is also the kind that every writer feels he'd like to do, or owes it to himself to do. But anybody who <u>does</u> try it will have to measure his book against yours, and that is pretty intimidating. Meanwhile it is very fine to have the book, and I wanted to write and congratulate you on it. I'm proud to know you.

Maxine sends her love, and I send mine.

I'll be east again in October and again in April, and maybe we can get together, either in New York or Bennington. I'd like that.

Yours,

Jim

8950 Balboa Boulevard
Northridge, California

TO: JACQUES DE SPOELBERCH[47]

TLS, 1 p; Jacques de Spoelberch

2 October, 1965
Northridge, California

Dear Jacques de Spoelberch:

Thanks so much for the note, and for the things you say about <u>Deliverance</u>. It's going to be a wonderful book, the only question being whether or not I'm the one to write it. I know very little of the writing of novels, and I'm going to have to lean so heavily on you that you're in danger of being driven right down into the ground, like the cat in the Tom and Jerry cartoons when the mouse hits him over the head with a sledge-hammer. Anyway, I'm delighted to be working with you, and look forward to getting the manuscript back and heading back up into the woods, inexperienced as I am at canoing, murder, or novel-writing. I haven't as yet received either the ms. or the letter from Brooks,[48] but will let you know what I think when I get them.

There's going to be some difficulty in getting time to finish the next draft, so you may have to be a little patient. The trouble is that my poetical career is sort of running off with all my time and energies. I'm not only writing a lot—and better, too, than I ever have—but I am constantly being asked to lecture and read at places all over the map, and some of these offers are hard to turn down. No; impossible to turn down. Anyway, as a result I'll be travelling pretty constantly all this year. There is one stretch, though, when I'll be writer in residence for two months at the University of Wisconsin at dead of winter[49] when I may be able to do a good deal of work, and if it's possible for me to get anything at all done before that time, I should be able to finish another draft by the end of March. I'll try, but I can't promise.

Again, thanks so much for the letter. With luck we'll bring off something that'll shake 'em up.

                                                        Yours,
                                                        James Dickey

How do you pronounce your last name, by the way? I feel I should know, and I don't.[50]

8950 Balboa Boulevard
Northridge, California

TO: L. QUINCY MUMFORD[51]

                                              TLS, 1 p; Library of Congress

27 December, 1965
Northridge, California

Dear Mr. Mumford:

I accept with pride and humility the position of Consultant in Poetry of the Library of Congress for the period 1966–1967. I understand and will comply to the best of my ability with the stipulations set forth in your letter, as well as with any and all other requirements which you or the Library may see fit to impose upon me in the capacity that I assume with this acceptance. I hope it will be permissible at this time for me to say that I accept the position in the name and spirit of the American poets of my generation.

Since I am no longer to be connected with San Fernando Valley State College after the termination of the semester ending this January, there is no problem as to my commitments to that institution. In reference to Hollins, where I had originally intended to be in residence during the school year 1966–1967, there is likewise no difficulty, for I have talked with the Chairman of the English Department, Louis Rubin, and he has assured me that Hollins gladly withdraws its claim to my services in favor of the Library appointment.

I plan now to take up residence in Washington at whatever date next September is most consistent with the duties of the position that you have so graciously tendered me. I shall be in touch with Dr. Basler[52] as to details of housing, schooling for my two children, and so on, as the time of my residency approaches.

Again, let me thank you profoundly for your letter, and assure you of my happiness in accepting the position of Consultant in Poetry to the Library of Congress for the term 1966–1967.

Sincerely yours,
James Dickey

8950 Balboa Boulevard
Northridge, California

TO: ANNE SEXTON[53]

TLS, 1 p; HRHRC

27 December, 1965
Northridge, California

Dear Anne:

Thanks so much for the lovely, <u>felt</u> note. I had no idea you would write, but I felt myself obligated to do so, and I am very happy you've answered. I realize how busy you are, and I am also very busy myself, but there are the letters you write out of and around and because of the busyness—and business—and there are those you write because you want to write them, and the ones that go between me and you belong, so far as I am concerned, to the latter category. I would very much like to see, for example, the letter you wrote and, as you say "tore up." Ah, those torn-up, forever-lost letters are always the ones we'd like most to get—isn't that so? Anyway, the letter that you <u>did</u> send is plenty good enough, and I am most glad to have it.

What is the future for you and me? Lord, I don't know. It would suit me fine just to write back and forth and see each other, as decent married, <u>responsible</u> literary folk and earthlings subject to social limitations, but I don't know if this is what is going to happen. I do know that you have touched a new tenderness in me, and that the feeling is very strong when I think of you. I'm not much of a believer in mad, passionate affairs. What I do hope is that there will always be a good strong man-woman response between us that has nothing whatever to do with the fact that we are writers, but only with the possibility that we may become fuller men and women—or man and woman—because of knowing each other. I would like that, for I have reached the time of life when I can no longer give of myself—or my essential self, at any rate, whatever that is—to people who are not put together right or geared right to receive it. I'm sure you know what I mean: if you don't, just consult that pile of unanswered letters on your desk: all those notes from people who say, in effect, "Please Anne Sexton, tell me I'm great. I wrote also to James Dickey and he never answered, and I know from your poems that you are more gracious than he, as well as much better looking." The best-meaning people in the world will cut you and your time up a million ways, if you let them, and think nothing of it except how they can get more of your time and attention. But that way lies madness, or something fully as horrible, and one must resist.

Again, my love to your children, and my regards to your husband, who must be an awfully good man for you to have married him. Anyway, remember that the human creature was made for joy, and that the things that give it are always close enough to touch, if we knew how to reach. I don't mean to sermonize, for that is not my sort of thing, my "rhythm," but I do want to affirm certain things, and that is one of them.

Again, with affection,
Jim D.

English Department
San Fernando Valley State College
Northridge, California

TO: RICHARD HOWARD

TLS, 1 p; Richard Howard

10 January, 1966
Northridge, California

Dear Richard:

Well, I am overwhelmed, that's all. I have read your essay over several times, and I will just say that if I had written it myself—that is, written a review or essay on my own work, as Whitman is said to have done—I could not have been either as eloquent or as accurate.[54] I felt, really, the uncanniness of a Presence in your lines: something that has a view into my intentions and my methods which no decent critic should have, for critics should, like the rest of us, be subject to mortal limitations. Surely, I said, the things this man says are the things I have been trying to do. And now he says that they are what I have <u>done</u>, and if he, this man, <u>gets</u> these things, these themes and rapports and extensions from what I have put down, well, it is possible that I have been successful in a very long and painful endeavour. That is a good thought to go to sleep on, believe me; the best I have had in a long time. What the writer wants, always, as you know, is that moment when he feels himself <u>understood</u>, and understood technically as well as understood in the matter of his work and its intentions. That I do feel, and I thought I would write and tell you so. Again, thanks. To say that this essay is the best thing that has been written on my work would be an understatement so blatant as to seem comical. I had as soon bring the essay over into the canon of my work itself: let it join the poems in that united front that I, like every writer, wish to present against Time and all its array of destructive powers.

Why not send this essay along to <u>Sewanee</u>, <u>Shenandoah</u>, <u>Hudson Review</u>, or one of those places? It would surely be good to see it in print, for if my poems don't make it a piece that any magazine would be proud to print, your prose surely does.

A couple of things. One, I shall be in New York for a couple of days—January 18<u>th</u> through the 20<u>th</u>—to pick up a lit'ry prize of some sort given by the Poetry Society of America, an outfit I had always vaguely associated with maiden lady geniuses in country newspapers.[55] Anyway, I'll be at the Hotel Winslow, and I'll hope to see you and Sandy when I'm in town.

Second, I have just been appointed Poetry Consultant at the Library of Congress for the year beginning next September, which means that we'll be able to have you down for various readings, and so on. Maybe between us we can straighten out the war in Viet Nam! But I must ask you not to let the information about the appointment get around, for the government is touchy about these matters, and likes to release such news itself, grandly, as befits the Great Society.

Well, thanks again for the magnificent essay. May I be worth it.

O yes, I just sent your Guggenheim forms in with my strongest recommendation to date. And I also put you in again—Number One choice—for one of the new Rockefeller grants, that run all the way up to $14,000.[56] All this may sound a little like <u>noblesse oblige</u> or something, or spoils system or nepotism, or something . . . or something. But it isn't; I'd have recommended the same recommends anyway.

All yours,
Jim

TO: ANNE SEXTON

TLS, 1 p; HRHRC

1<u>st</u> February, 1966
Madison, Wisconsin

Dear Anne:

Thanks so much for the sweet letter. I'm sorry we won't be able to get together in Boston, for I had hoped to meet your husband, but it may well be that we can meet in Baltimore, Washington, or some such other place. Believe me, I'd like that a lot. I don't have a full itinerary of all the spots I'm supposed to hit this spring, but Bill Thompson[57] tells me that I'll be in and around Baltimore for a few days, and if you are there at the same time, why fine: that would be great. I have neglected to bring with me any kind of prospective schedule, but Bill will be very happy to tell you where I am going to be, and if he doesn't I'll be sure to have a Master Plan—<u>supplied</u> by him—before I take off in April, and I can then tell you myself. Meanwhile, let's hope for a meeting; it is something to look forward to.

A good deal has been happening, the main thing of which is that I am told that I have just been made Poetry Consultant (how these beaurocracies love capital letters!) to the Library of Congress for two years. I don't know all the things that this will mean, other than the fact that my family and I will be living in Washington for a couple of unexpected years, but as far as I am concerned—who after all ought to be allowed an opinion in these matters—it should mean that we may be able to have you down for a reading and/or some of the other things which poets are occasionally able to tap the government for. Let me get set behind the great oak desk with the chaste light of the Capitol dome shining full into my bewildered face, and we'll see what can be done.

No; believe me, I am not trying for any relationship with you other than the tenderness you describe. We should go no deeper, even if we were so inclined, which I doubt either of us is, really. That is where the Demons are likely to get stirred up. I don't know about <u>your</u> Demons, but I had rather have mine stirred up by a situation in which there is more repose and stillness, more handholding and long soulful looks into eyes—as well as the sexual part, which I can't quite visualize, or conceptualize, with you, no matter how much I would like to—than there is likely to be in your case and mine, in this mortal life. So let us have a long, intellectual dinner together somewhere in the east, and I will give up trying to think of you either in a see-through negligee—<u>à la Playboy</u>—or in one of those long flannel New England granny-type gowns (in which, I admit, I come nearer to you in thought than the other). It is better to have what we already have than to risk it in what is at best an unlikely venture. But men will be men, and women will—well, be what they are, too. Let me know where you are—in other words keep in close touch (ah! close <u>intellectual</u> touch!), and we will see what the Cruellest Month brings.

Meanwhile, my best to The Starfish, as always, to the new dalmations, and to the nervous Midwife.

Yours,
Jim

I'll be here two months.[58]
Room 410, Claridge Apartment Hotel
333 West Washington Street
Madison, Wisconsin

TO: ANNE SEXTON

TLS, 1 p; HRHRC

17 February, 1966
Madison, Wisconsin

Dear Anne:

Sorry about the phone call. It was one of those things that those I like the best are privileged to have visited upon them when I get lonely and drunk enough. I dread it, myself, but there is a strange excitement in it as well. When the Mau Mau were slaughtering whole villages of Kikuyus in Kenya, the times came to be called "The Night of the Long Knives." Well, episodes like the other night are called, in the privacy of my mind, "Nights of the Drunken Phone Calls." Some interesting things have happened as a result of them, but mostly bad things. Still, it is good to hear the voices of people you care for, even if they are perplexed and finally, outraged. I am sorry if all this got you in trouble with your husband. It must be shocking and saddening and bewildering to hear your wife tell another man over the phone that she loves him not one but fifteen times; after all, good solid men don't expect their wives, the mothers of their children, to receive drunken phone calls from fiends and idiots who carry on in such a fashion. It's just one of the sadnesses of husbands that things like this sometimes happen to them. I hope I haven't done any permanent damage to your marriage; I can't believe I have, really. But I <u>am</u> sorry, and I hope that, if you won't forgive me, you'll at least not fret any more over it.

I liked (a lot) the talk about love in the letter, even though you were mostly mad at me. This mental love is something new to me, for I am essentially a peasant, and such things have little meaning to one so physically-oriented (may God forgive me such phrases!) as I am. But I am willing to go along with it if it means as much as it seems to mean to you; I'll do as you say. And, no, the sex part is no good—and I mean <u>no</u> good—if the woman doesn't desire it desperately, so that she will do just about anything to bring it about. These situations when one of the partners is full of doubts, so that there is a general air of embarrassment and hanging-back about the whole affair (!) are worse than useless; they are humiliating. So we will do as you say. Just tell me what I should do to meet you specifications of tenderness-without-touch.

As to my schedule: it looks as though I shall be arriving in Baltimore on the morning of the 19<u>th</u> of April, and will be staying there for that day and the next, to leave on the 21<u>st</u> for Boston, so that should accord with your plans.

I hope it does; I'd like to see you. But if the other night aroused misgivings of any destructive sort, you might like to let the whole thing go, and agree to become strangers again. I would rather that were the case than cause you any further embarrassment or trouble. We might enjoy seeing each other very much. Again, we might not. But that shall be as you wish.

Love,

Jim

Room #410, Claridge Apartment Hotel
333 West Washington Street
Madison, Wisconsin

TO: ANNE SEXTON

TLS, 1 p; HRHRC

22 March, 1966
Madison, Wisconsin

Dear Anne:

Thanks for your note, which still seems to be harping on things I thought we had settled. Your concern and anxiety seem excessive to me. I am not some dark—or light—demon lying in wait for you, trying to demoralize you. Believe me, I am not interested in physical love under such circumstances. You seem to associate it with pain and guilt, and nothing could be farther from my own feelings about it, which have to do with joy and warmth. Anyway, you say you would flee out of town to avoid any such relationship. Believe me, before you got out of town I would be out of the state, heading in the opposite direction. There is really nothing for you to worry about, believe me.

Now, where does that leave us? I confess I don't know. Other than apologizing for my one drunken phone call—which, you're right, I _did_ enjoy, though of course you didn't—yet again (shall I do it again? and again?) I don't very well see what I can do to rectify things, though I must say I don't really feel awful enough about any of this to go through all _that_ much apologizing, though I will if it will make you feel better. Anyway, live or die, but don't poison everything. I myself don't feel like having any of that particular brand, and if we're going to sit down and brew it up together—the poison that only men and women can concoct— and hand it 'round as a kind of cordial—well, as Louis B. Mayer once famously said, include me out.[59] I suppose it's that I don't really know you well enough to know what you are really like, or why you do things, but I still would like to. As to various social conventions, I don't care a fig for all that. I would like to loosen the universe up, make it capable of more contact and more meaning, and that includes the relationships between men and women, which have gotten into an awful state through too much timidity. To hell with all that. I remember what little I know of you with affection and interest. You are in some ways a fascinating woman. Oddly enough, I had rather hear you talk about your children than anything else. That really touched something in me. Despite my avowals of "freedom" from social conventions, I have a great love for family life. These two viewpoints are supposed to be opposed, but they aren't at all. A wide enough viewpoint will include them both, and affirm it with a great all-brothering shout.

I'll be here for another ten days, so you can write again, if you like. Yes, do write again, even if it's only to tell me that you don't want to write any more. We can go on with more, or we can become strangers again (though never <u>entirely</u> strangers, for I have the furry touch of your coat in my fingers, and we have stood under a tree together. Let it live or die. It's up to you.

Yours,
Jim

TO: ROBERT BLY

TLS, 2 pp;[60] Robert Bly

16 July, 1966
Milwaukee, Wis.[61]

Dear Bob:

Thanks so much for the check, and the royalty report. How come we are selling so many more hardbounds than paperbacks? Is it because the price is comparatively low for a cloth-bound, or what? And since we're getting low on copies, are there plans to reprint? If we've sold out—or almost sold out—of an edition, doesn't this indicate another printing? Surely we could sell a lot more copies if we had 'em.[62] Let me know about all this, if you can, without my having to nudge you. I let you have my book as a publisher, and was glad to, but this also puts a certain monkey on your back as regards doing the things that publishers normally do. But as I say, your distribution system, whatever it may be, is fantastically good, and I have nothing, but thanks that it is working in my favor—or perhaps I should say our favor, for I like to think you're making money, at least a little, on <u>Suspect</u>. Could you give me our total sales figures, cloth and paper, if you have them? It would help to know these.

Sorry you had a bad experience at Knox College, which I found rather a nice place. As to the quotation you charge me with, I'll stand by it. I did say it, and I hold out for my right to be forthright and honest in just exactly the same way you do. However, the complete text of that part of the talk I gave is . . . "Robert Bly, an energetic and vital, though often stupid farmer from Minnesota. He is what someone called Ezra Pound, a "village explainer," and he has a good many of the characteristics of the young Pound: enthusiasm and drive, and the excitement about poetry that only those have who come upon it as the great discovery of their lives. In the current scene he is one of the most interesting figures . . ." and so on. As a matter of fact, I put you and Jim W. as one of the four major prongs in the shoving-forward of the new poetry, and, though I did not mince words about what I considered wrong in your program, I also did not hold back when I came to what I thought was right. What's wrong with that? It's what I think, and exactly what I think, and that's the way it is. In future it might help you to quote the whole of a thing and understand what you hear in the light of its context, as you so seldom bother to do.

As to the Viet Nam thing: you are mistaken in what you say, and mistaken in the wilful and irresponsible and self-seeking way that seems entirely characteristic of you. I have been on no "platform" "in favor of the Viet Nam war." Platforms and propaganda poetry seem rather more in your line: have you in all truth not been doing some such lately? Come on now, confess it. No, I have been on no platforms. If someone comes to me and asks my provate opinion as a citizen (emphatically not as "a poet"!) I try to point out the dangers of appeasement, as exactly as I can make them out. This is as honest as I can be about the thing, for it is what I really do think, though I don't like killing people any more than you do, and possibly less. You seem to think that it is somehow dishonest to be honest if such honesty is not in agreement with yours, and, again, I can't buy it. If you want to run with the rest of the herd on this matter, that is all right with me. But you can also, as Sam Goldwyn once said, include me out. I am no politician nor statesman, and would not presume to tell the government what to do, nor would I make propaganda or public capital out of any such.

                                                                          Jim

TO: MARY ANN BLATT[63]

                                        CC, 1 p; Library of Congress

October 7, 1966

Dear Mrs. Blatt:

Your invitation does me much honor, but at the same time puts me in difficulties. You do not mention any honorarium, and I incline to assume you mean none is available.

The poet is so placed in our country that he can earn only negligible sums by the direct practice of his art; nothing like a living wage is even contemplated. But the by-products of his art, the lecturing, the teaching, writing, which devolve from the fact of his doing poems, can enable him to live, and on the monies brought by these activities he is compelled to rely.

I regret that this is so, and have made exceptions, where poverty, enthusiasm, and prior personal acquaintance have been involved. But the rule is that public performances are done for money, even if it is generally not very much money. This is partly for the economic reasons just outlined, and partly because such performances cost me, in addition to time, the labor of preparation and considerable apprehension.

Should you find it possible to comply with the above conditions, I would be very happy indeed to fulfill your most kind request. I shall hope to hear from you in due course.

With best wishes,
James Dickey
Consultant in Poetry

TO: ALLAN SEAGER

TLS, 1 p; Bancroft Library

6 January, 1967
Leesburg, Virginia

Dear Allan:

Please forgive me for not answering your other letter about Barbara's[64] death, but I have been in the hospital with a bad back injury and then with the flu, and have had to let everything go but my body. I don't want to offer the usual condolences on Barbara's death, for you have already told me how the situation was, and I could see that well enough the one time I ever met her. You speak of a weight being lifted, and surely it must be so. There is nothing so terrible as the tyranny of the body when something is wrong with it, especially the tyranny of somebody else's body—somebody's you love—when something is wrong with it. All my life I have been aware of this—maybe overaware—but I have always looked on my body as a thing that would betray me at the slightest or no opportunity. Mostly there is nothing, no good the doctors can do; they are hardly more than hopeful alchemists, really. But your own life will have a chance to move now, in the directions it needs to take. You are a good man, Allan, the best I know, and the next years will be your best. I feel it; I know it.

What word on the Roethke book? Is it actually finished now, or what? If so, what is the publication date? I want to get it and review it—maybe for the Times—as soon as it comes out.[65]

By now you will have your grant—or at least have word that you got it. The government never spent money so well, or so productively, I think. I was in on the consultation concerning the grant (though it would be best not to noise this around), and I am glad things turned out so well. What will you do with the dough? Maybe you should go off somewhere, maybe to Ireland. What do you think?

My own Poems 1957–67 will be out in April. I think it will be a good book, with the newest stuff the best of all. I have a long one coming out in the April issue of the Atlantic that I want you to see;[66] I think it is awfully good, and I've been living with it for a long time, so I am not dazzled by some momentary production of my own.

A thought strikes me: since you have entered the poetry business with the Roethke book, why not review my Poems for somebody this spring? If you think you might like to do this, let me know, and I'll suggest some possibilities. Believe me, I'd like it![67]

My love to your daughters—one met, the other unmet—and to Joan.[68]

All yours,

Jim

47 North King Street
Leesburg, Virginia

TO: ROY P. BASLER

CC, 1 p; Library of Congress

January 16, 1967

Roy P. Basler
Director, Reference Department

James Dickey

Consultant in Poetry

Here is a list of five possible Honorary Consultants,[69] in the order in which I would recommend them:

(1) John Hall Wheelock
(2) Norman Holmes Pearson

(3) Marianne Moore
(4) John Berryman
(5) Allen Tate

TO: FAMILY OF JOHN MASEFIELD[70]

c. 12 May 1967   *CC text for telegram, 1 p;*
                                                       Library of Congress

IT WAS WITH GREAT REGRET AND A SENSE OF PERSONAL LOSS THAT I HEARD OF
THE RECENT DEATH OF JOHN MASEFIELD. INDEED, HIS GOING IS A GRIEVOUS
DIMINISHMENT OF ALL MEN AND WOMEN WHO LOVE THE ENGLISH LANGUAGE,
AND RESPOND TO THE MOVING SEA AND THE STILL EARTH. PLEASE ACCEPT MY
SINCERE CONDOLENCES.

                          JAMES DICKEY
                          CONSULTANT IN POETRY IN ENGLISH

TO: HENRY RAGO

                                                       TLS, 1 p; Lilly Library
2 June, 1967
Leesburg, Virginia

Dear Henry:

I have been meaning to write you for some time, simply to let you know I
haven't forgotten about Poetry, and that I regret very much the fact that I haven't
published anything with you since "The Firebombing," three or four years ago.
Now that I have the big Poems 1957–1967 finished, finally, I can turn to some new
things, and I'll be able to let you look 'em over in maybe two or three months, if
all goes well. But do know that I have Poetry in mind, and will give you whatever I
think is good enough.[71]

May I make one small request about the new book's reviewing-situation in
Poetry? I ask only that you not turn it over to anyone of the Bly faction (though
Jim Wright would be OK, though he's already reviewed one book of mine for
you). Bly insists that there is bad blood between us, principally because I told him
I would have nothing whatever to do with his clique, claque, movement, or whatever it is, and he now tells me he is "after me." I thought you would probably want
to know about this, for you can't get impartial reviewing done under such cir-

cumstances. The last fellow that reviewed me in Poetry—at least insofar as I
know—was Wendell Berry, who had just prior to that published an open letter in
the <u>Sewanee</u> denouncing me for my views in an article I did that included some
harsh words on his friend Robert Hazel.[72] Yet, though he had some reservations
(this was <u>Helmets</u>, as I remember), he still was very fair indeed, and as a consequence he and I have become good friends. But Bly and those that follow him
(John Haines, Louis Simpson, et al) are not that large-souled. They are vindictive
and revenge-minded, and these things have nothing to do with evaluation of
poems, being <u>personal </u>reasons for finding fault with literary works. Well, I won't
go on and on; all this shall be as you wish.[73]

By the way, as to reviewing, I've been awfully much impressed with what I've
seen of Michael Benedikt and Laurence Lieberman.[74] They have a good grasp of
what they're doing, and they can write. Please find your own way of conveying
these sentiments to these critics, for I don't know where to find either of them.
Also, do you have Lisel Mueller's address?[75] I'd like to get in touch with her about
a personal matter. Also, I admire what of hers I've read.

Let me hear from you on these matters whenever you can. I'd appreciate it.

All yours,
Jim Dickey

47 North King Street
Leesburg, Virginia

TO: CHRISTOPHER DICKEY[76]

TLS, 2 pp; Christopher Dickey

28 October, 1967
Leesburg, Virginia

My Good Boy:

Well, you almost didn't have a father, but—luckily, I hope you think—you still
do. Montherlant[77] says that if life gets boring, then risk it. Life was not exactly
boring to me before I went to Terry's Paradise Acres,[78] but, whatever it was before,
it is something else now. On opening day, Terry and I went out at dawn, but didn't
see anything where we expected the deer—"<u>them</u>", as Terry calls them—to be. We
came back and had some of Terry's famous eggs, and he said he wanted to go back
down across some fields, over on the other side of the ridge. That didn't sound
like much to me, so I told him I'd work back up the creek by the road, and then

strike off through the woods to the west of the creek, and meet him back at the house around noon. I set up my compass and took off.

It was a good day, and the foliage was beautiful, burning with all those fall colors that just last a couple of days at that level of intensity. I had Bud Adair's old bow with me. I had shot it in for the various ranges the day before. It's not the fastest bow in the world, but up to about forty yards it throws the arrow, the broadhead arrow, just exactly right, and very straight, though the arrow tends to fall out pretty rapidly after forty-five yards. Anyway, I was ready to kill something, the hunting fever was on me, and I went on up a little branch absolutely shook-up with the kill-fever, like being drunk on the air and the leaves: the whole works. I found a good deer trail, and then the place that it crossed another, and made myself a blind out of some dead limbs and other stuff. I sat down, and knew that something would come. Something.

About a half hour later I heard a great crashing in the bushes behind me. I thought, well, old Terry has thought better of it and come around to my side of the creek. I thought this, but I wasn't sure, although I knew no deer would make any such racket. I craned up out of my blind with an arrow on the string. There was a little ridge in front of me, and I saw a huge—I mean huge—black shape sliding along it, just on the other side. My marrow froze. I took another look, and there he was, about fifteen yards away, a good 500 pounds of him, upwind of me, luckily: the biggest black bear you ever saw. The mast is heavy this year, and he had evidently been eating like a hog, for he was tremendously heavy and waddle-footed. He stood for a minute sniffing around, and then went down to the creek to drink. I said to myself, All right, let's go: you've got a bear tag. He was about three quarters turned to me, quartering away, with his head down, drinking and also messing around with the big rocks of the creek, trying to turn one of the biggest ones over, maybe to get at a crawfish or something. I pulled the bow to half draw and stepped out of the blind, keeping out of his eyesight. I was not particularly afraid, for I knew that if I could get into him good, through both lungs, he couldn't last long, and if I could manage to work it so that he didn't know where I was, he would just go off and die in a couple of minutes. I walked over to about twenty feet from him, still behind some brush, and drew.

But something had happened to the light behind me. There was something—a change, a flicker—that told me I had better look around before I committed myself. I did, and that was when I knew it was all over, because there was another bear standing on his (her?) hind legs, behind me, looking straight at me, making a low sound, with the teeth just beginning to show white. I said to myself, well, what to do. If I hit the one that is drinking, even he won't die immediately, and if he bawls, the other one will be on top of me like a half-ton of pure mayhem. On the other hand, if I turn around and hit the one behind me, the one drinking, the biggest one, would be unwounded, and then <u>he'll</u> be all over me. On the other hand, if I wounded one—either one—and he ran, maybe they both would run. But I've got to do something, for the balance of the moment wouldn't last forever. I thought, well, there's maybe one more thing I can try. I took a step back, and slid back into my blind, down behind the ridge, because I honestly didn't think the odds were at all favorable. One I would take my chances with, but not two. Anyway, the moment I was out of the sight, the second bear's head dropped below the level of the top of the ridge, and while he was out of sight, I pulled back, jumped the creek, cut back over another rise and came out on top. I could still see them both at the creek, but they didn't seem interested in me, so I stayed low in the bushes and watched them drink, cuff each other around a little, and then move off the way they came. And that was it. Maybe we could have had a bearskin, but I am very thankful to have mine, you can bet. But it was great, just the same. My God, the pure <u>energy</u> of the world, and the wildness of it!

I just got back from Andover, and some of the Exeter people were there. Everyone spoke well of you, and I was glad of that. I am happy to have you going to school with such boys. And they are lucky, too.

About graduating this year. Well, I hope very much you will reconsider that. I shouldn't think it would be desirable to go to school in France in order to graduate from Loudoun County High School. No, that decidedly is not the plan. Let us carry it through the way we originally planned it. There are no difficulties that can't be overcome—social ones or otherwise—and the difficulties of your going to college at such an early age would be infinitely greater. I know you are anxious to get going into the world—every young man is, particularly every talented young man—but we can do this better by giving you as much time and preparation as we can: as much ammunition, as many guns, as we can get for you. We must gear up for the long haul. And the Viet Nam situation is very much in my mind, also, as it is in everybody's. Since you are already ahead a year, you have a legitimate reason to get back with your age-group, and that fact is pure gold as far as your intellectual development is concerned. The thing to do is <u>use</u> it, as I know you will. I was also at Harvard a day or so ago, and that is where I want you, if you still want to go; it is a remarkable place. But I want you to be <u>ready</u>: I mean <u>really</u> ready, and you are not yet, quite. So don't rush, and don't overmatch yourself when you don't have to. That is bad, all the way round, whereas, if you don't, you'll take the place by storm, and get from it what there is to be got. Trust me on this, my son, and the whole project (your life, that is) will swing.

All my love, always,

Big Spider Beek

TO: CHRISTOPHER DICKEY

TLS, 3 pp; Emory

7 November, 1967
Leesburg, Virginia

My Dear Good Boy:

Lord God it was good to hear your voice again; I am still rejoicing. The troubles that you speak about are very real ones for you now, but they are not so serious as you think. I can very nearly categorically guarantee that your hair will not fall out until you are my age, if then. The same thing is happening to you that happened to me at your age. You have exactly the same kind of coarse, horse-tail-textured hair that I have, and what happens is that a couple of years into puberty (? !) some of the hair at the front of your head and at the temples comes out, your hairline goes back a little ways and then, as it were, settles down and stays where it is. The attrition rate is very very slow after the first traumatic hairfall, the one you're now in. As for Val,[79] you don't resemble him at all, though your mother does, particularly as to the nose. The business of brooding over such things is in part brought on by your loneliness, when such matters get exaggerated beyond all mortal control. I can't help feeling that my own preoccupation with the same thing as you are worrying about, has made you overly conscious of it. If so, please forgive me; it was a condition—that you might be made to worry, too—I didn't give enough thought to.

The loneliness bit is bad, I know. But, though you like social life well enough, you have never been a particularly gregarious person, requiring mostly to be let alone, and so I was a little surprised to find this bothering you. But it is always going to be tough going, at least for a while, for a sixteen-year-old boy on his own in a strange country. The thing to do about it is to have a lot of projects going, a lot of things to look forward to, a lot of things to learn. Your new-found enthusiasm is the greatest thing that ever happened to you, and that ought to be played for all it's worth, for that combined with your intelligence is simply an unbeatable combination. It is also a healthy sign that you are afraid of death. This symptom is what I would call "talented young-manism." The same thing still bothers me, when I think that, as Thomas Wolfe says somewhere, "Something has spoken to me in the night and told me I must go."[80] But things are always speaking to me in the night and telling me I must go, and I haven't gone yet. I feel, like you, that there is so much to do, see, and above all, so much to <u>be</u>. But when you are my age, you will be the original world's wonder, if you can turn the things that bother you into assets: turn aloneness, for example, into that essential creative state of being which the artist, above all men, knows. When loneliness becomes creative rather than destructive, the artist is alive, and in his element. Out of that, anything can come. Real creative work is not done by committees; it is done in the dark night of the soul, in the labyrinth of being, in fear and trembling and the solitary exaltation beside which Heaven itself is pale and commonplace. "Great things are done when men and mountains meet. / They are not done by jostling in the street." Blake said it.[81]

I am sitting here working away at the proofs of my critical book,[82] and writing the introduction. Bly is still making trouble, but I think we are going to scuttle Captain Bly's ship, though legally.[83] Anyway, the book is due out in February, and I think will be pretty good, though I tire out quickly, reading so much of my own prose, which, really, I don't write as well as I might. Anyway, a little snow is coming down, and I am listening to Kipnis play "The Cuckoo." The tape-recorder is turned up so high (on both outlets) that I'm surprised you can't hear it in Rennes. Everything Kipnis does on the song, which used to be so mysterious and wonderful to me, is very simple now. It is still wonderful, that is, but not so mysterious. One thing pleases me very much: though I am not and never will be a Doc Watson[84] (his stuff ain't so awfully hard, either!) I can play pretty well. I gave a kind of concert at Harvard and used a mike, and I must say I was amazed at how it sounded. It was almost exactly like the first time I heard Kipnis play at Reed. I like very much the sensation of getting better at things I like: that pleases me more than just about anything. "We are not here to be Gods," Sartre says, "but only just to improve a little."

I'm delighted you like Fitzgerald, for I do, so much. You must now read <u>Tender is the Night</u>, which, though <u>Gatsby</u> is a lot better structurally, is really his big book. Boy, it will tear you apart; I know it did (and does) me. <u>The Last Tycoon</u> is very promising. The scene with Boxley (Huxley, surely) is one of the most imaginative things I know in fiction: when he explains to Boxley how movies are made, and what they <u>are</u>. But there are a lot of things about the book that a scrupulous craftsman like Fitzgerald would certainly have cleared up. For one thing, the point of view doesn't always work. Celia (or is it Cecilia?) tells most of the story, which is all right in some places, such as in the opening scenes. But this doesn't allow you to see or be with Stahr enough to know what his work (on which so much depends) is like. So Fitzgerald has to find some way to get around this, and this forces him, after the passages featuring Stahr-without-Celia, to begin chapters with such clumsy devices as "This is Celia, taking up the story again." And surely Brimmer is the most unconvincing Communist in American literature. But I agree with you: it would sure make a great, <u>great</u> movie. Would you shoot it scene by scene, or take some liberties with the chronology?

We'll abide by your wishes on the college thing. It seems to me that you are anxious to get into an atmosphere which permits more freedom that the Exeter environment does, and this is understandable. But remember that the whole reason for the Exeter thing was that we were going for the Big One (Harvard, the whole bit), and you are now in position to do exactly that. If you deliberately want to settle for less, you certainly may. But I don't want you to be disappointed in later years that you did less for yourself than you could have done: were, in fact, doing. The course you are set on now—that is, going to Exeter with expectations of Harvard year after next—will definitely do a great deal more for you than Chapel Hill next year will. As for the Army, you seem to discount and dismiss it, saying that you can still carry on your work. That you may do—I did, to a certain small extent—but believe me it will not be easy. If you think you dislike Exeter, wait until you get in the service, which is really a form of going to prison. It really is, you know. So think a little more about that part of it. But, as I say, you can surely do the thing your way, and we'll help, as we can.

I want to try to do some translations from the French, and I want you to help me, for my formal grammatical knowledge is shaky indeed. How about trying a couple of the Supervielle things, and sending them to me. We could surely work out something. And he is such a wonderful poet, too! Also, do send your journals and themes. I'd love to see them.

I enclose a copy of the new poem about you and the crows; the New Yorker will do it, apparently.[85]

Here are the opening lines of "The Eye-Beaters," which describe the visit of a man who can see to the Indiana Home for the Retarded and Blind.

> Come something   come blood sunlight   come and children break
> Through the white hall-wall, taking heart from the two left feet
> Of your sound   are groping for the new one, the Visitor in the Home
> Of homes   in the white-halled corn-green air-blue and vast
> Of Indiana brooding on its children   mid-August-brooding over
> The Retarded and Blind: those in: those in out of and beyond
> The earth, and those who have seen it, once: seen the red County
> Home fade from around them   bricks fade therapists and corn-green
> Fade   heard sight passing, eye to ear   heard that in counting
> Its stalks, the field grinds and presses with insects and goes round
> Right and left to the back of the head   coming in at three
> In the afternoon, green like you, all the way   all the way to the dead
> Stop of the walls.   You man with the magic eyes, you strange feet coming
> Through the corn . . . . . .[86]

I'll probably not use all of this, but you might be able to get the idea of the beginning, as it is now. I'll close now, and get this in the mail. Also enclosed is a copy of Larry Lieberman's essay on me in the current Hudson Review.[87] It is very good, though I can't always cotton to his verbiage, his talking about "the shifting sands of the personality," and suchlike. But it says some rather perceptive things, I think.

Keep going, my dearest son. The world is going to be a great place for you. Remember what John Davidson, an otherwise undistinguished poet, says:

Men to know and women to love are waiting everywhere.[88] Amen![89]

Love,

Dad

TO: C. DAY-LEWIS[90]

CC text for telegram, 1 p; Library of Congress

JANUARY 3, 1968

WARMEST CONGRATULATIONS UPON THE LAUREATESHIP. WILL BE LOOKING FORWARD TO NEW POEMS, BOTH OFFICIAL AND UNOFFICIAL.

JAMES DICKEY

CONSULTANT IN POETRY IN ENGLISH

TO: RICHARD JAWORSKI[91]

CC, 2 pp; Emory

47 North King Street
Leesburg, Virginia 22075
February 28, 1968

Dear Mr. Jaworski:

Thank you very much for your letter. I am very happy that South Florida Review would like to feature my poetry this year, but I am afraid it will be impossible for me to send you a poem of mine due to my contractual tie-ups with the New Yorker, Atlantic, and other magazines. I guess the best thing to do is to let me answer a few of your questions in this letter, for your use as you see fit. I deal with the questions by the numerals you give them. (1) I am a Southern poet by birth, and by the incidental but vital details of upbringing. However, I have no wish to be progromatic about being Southern. I leave that to others more capable of endowing such an approach with value, and to those more interested. (2) As in the case of any poet, my early influences touch my present poetry through a system of recall altogether too complex and mysterious to pronounce upon definitively. I will say that, the longer one lives, the deeper, more haunted and value-ridden it becomes. As writers and poets, we try to make it truly ours, for thereby we make it ours as human beings. (3) I have no notion as to what you mean by "philosophical position", or "philosophical poet". But if you mean that I am more interested in physical experience than in the abstract world of ideas, then you could say that I am not philosophical. (4) In reference to Mr. Jack Moore's comment, I can tell you very little about how excitement gets into poetry. It is partly a question of the poet's <u>use</u> of language, but it is mainly a matter of "personal vision". You can't write in such and such a way unless you are such and such a way, or at least unless a part of you is. But excitement is a quiet deep thing as well as a noisy surfacy one. (5) I don't reflect "any trend" at all as far as I can tell. I hope to help American poetry go toward a kind of clairvoyant simplicity, toward a singleness of vision and being, and to help it find a way to be simple without being thin. (6) I think American poetry compares very favorably with the current European poetry but about the South American I am not qualified to say, though I do think that Borges is fascinating, and Jorg de Lima is extremely fine. In my opinion the greatest living poet is Eugenio Montale of Italy. (7) Largely disastrous. Too many writers are writing out of a sense of public duty, and not out of something that moves them as individuals. Other poets without the slightest talent—Robert Bly is a perfect example—are mounting the platform ostensibly to "protest" but actually to call attention to their writings by this means: attention that the writings themselves do not and would not under any other circumstances merit. A great poet is a man with the gift to produce a remarkable sensibility and vision in linguistic forms which actualize the vision as well—theoretically, anyway—as words can do. As to my own position or influence, I must leave that to the jurisdiction of time.

I hope you can use some of this. It is the best I can do on such short notice, for I must leave for Australia in a few days.

I look forward very much to meeting you and Miss Stewart-Moore in April.

Sincerely yours,
James Dickey

TO: MRS. MARTIN LUTHER KING JR.[92]

5 April 1968   *CC text for telegram, 1 p;*
Library of Congress

I PRAY, WITH YOU AND YOUR HUSBAND, WHO IS STILL PRAYING, THAT THE GREAT WORK MAY NOT FALTER, BUT GO ON.

JAMES DICKEY
CONSULTANT IN POETRY TO THE
LIBRARY OF CONGRESS

TLS, 1 p; SUNY Buffalo

6 April, 1968
Leesburg, Virginia

Dear John:

Please forgive me if I said or did anything that offended you the other night; I wouldn't for the world, ordinarily. It is only that I think so extraordinarily much of your talent. You are the best of us, as I've said in print more than once, and I know from sad experience how Captain Bly tries to use, subvert and suck dry the men of talent who hold him a friend of theirs. As I also know, he is not much of an enemy, but he is sure death to his friends. You may accept or reject this opinion as you see—or feel—fit, of course, but I did want to register it, having then done all I could in the matter. But as you said as I left you, you are your own man, and will write as you will write. That is all I wanted to be assured about, really; everything is in that.

I also want to thank you for coming along with the others, the other night; it was kind of you, and kind also to bring along the new <u>Choice</u>, which looks fine indeed. And, yes, I would like very much to see those papers of your students that you mentioned. If you don't have time to gather together a bundle of them, speak to the students themselves and have <u>them</u> send them. Either way, I'll be most happy to see what they've been doing.

As to a reviewer for the book, anyone would be fine, except Bly or someone Bly is using. I would trust Jim Wright in the matter, even so. Or Michael Benedikt would be all right, in New York. Or John Simon, or Saul Maloff of <u>Newsweek</u>, or Michael Goldman or Denise Levertov or R.W. Flint (whom I admire more than almost any other critic writing), or Paul Carroll, or RWB Lewis or Robert Penn Warren. I'll wait to see who finally does end up doing it.[93]

It was good to see you, as it always is. Let's try to do it again, whenever and wherever possible. The end is not yet, God willing.

All yours,
Jim

TO: MRS. ROBERT F. KENNEDY[94]

7 June 1968   *CC text for telegram, 1 p;*
                                                  Library of Congress

SINCEREST CONDOLENCES. I AM AS SPEECHLESS AS THE REST. I HOPE YOU WILL
UNDERSTAND THE DEPTH OF FEELING THAT UNDERLIES THE DUMBNESS OF
THE MAN OF WORDS.

JAMES DICKEY

CONSULTANT IN POETRY TO THE

LIBRARY OF CONGRESS

Teaching a class at the University of South Carolina, 1969

PART SIX

UNIVERSITY OF SOUTH CAROLINA AND *DELIVERANCE*

September 1968–June 1970

Early 1970s: Dickey was an enthusiastic archer and guitar player.

TO: LOUISE BOGAN[1]

TLS, 1 p; Amherst College

2 September, 1968
Columbia, S.C.[2]

Dear Miss Bogan:

The Pulitzer Committee has just sent on to me your book, <u>The Blue Estuaries</u>, and I simply wanted to tell you how absolutely splendid I think it is.[3] Perhaps this is a breach of form, though I hope not. Even if it were, however, I would still write to tell you how much I think you have done for the formalist spirit in American poetry, so that when one speaks in public or thinks in private about the utmost concentration of which our language is capable, one speaks or thinks of you. Please let me record my gratitude, and my admiration.

Sincerely yours,
James Dickey

4620 Lelia's Court
Lake Katherine,
Columbia,
South Carolina 29206

TO: RICHARD WILBUR[4]

TLS, 1 p; Amherst College

16 September, 1968
Columbia, South Carolina

Dear Dick:

Please forgive me for delaying so long in writing the letter I said I'd write, but we have been engaged in moving from Washington down here, with all the attendant misfortunes and frustrations, and there just hasn't been time to write letters. We've settled in now, though, and I wanted to write you about a number of matters.

First, there is the <u>thing</u> of changing publishers, which has come up for the last couple of times I've had a new book, or one in progress. I have about half of a new one, and it is surely the best yet, <u>I</u> think.[5] Meanwhile, I have the critical book just out with Farrar Straus, another publishing connection with Doubleday, and a novel to come out with Houghton Mifflin. All these people are constantly telling me that I would be better off by far with them (or one of them, rather) as my publishers, and I must say they offer some awfully convincing arguments. I have nothing to complain of with regard to the attitude Wesleyan has toward me and my poems. In truth, I could hardly have done better, all things considered. But I am at a stage now where I can reach a really <u>mass</u> audience, and I am fearful that Wesleyan simply does not have the money to throw into advertising and promotion. Some of these other publishers are talking of advertising the book as they would a best-selling (hopefully bestselling <u>to be</u>, I mean) novel, and that has a strong appeal, I must say. There is no question but that they can do it, and if I change to one of them I will demand an advance that will make them <u>have</u> to do it, in order to get their money back. Maybe these are crass commercial considerations, but if there's one thing I've learned both from business life and writing, it is that it's not a question of whether your book is going to compete in the marketplace or not: it <u>is</u> going to compete. The point is whether it is going to compete successfully or not. This can be an awfully paid-attention-to book, or it can just be another poetry book, though by a more or less "established" writer. And there is no doubt at all in my mind that publicity, and the money spent on it, will inevitably have something to do with this. Of the poems themselves I am confident. But as to methods of getting them before the public, I am not so confident, where Wesleyan is concerned. They would spend the money if they could, but they simply don't have the money the larger outfits do. Lockwood would be the first to tell me that; in fact, he <u>was</u> the first to tell me. So—where does that leave us? The book is about a year from being finished, so I have a chance to consider all the possibilities, which I want very much to do. Let me know your thoughts on this, particularly as to what you would <u>do</u>, if you were me.

But oddly, despite that last long paragraph, that isn't the reason for the letter; not publication at all. But I wished to speak of the really extraordinary closeness I have come to feel for you personally, though I have only seen you twice. I don't know exactly how to account for this, but it is there. I won't go on and on about it, but just register it. I hope we can get together soon. I feel closer to you, <u>personally</u>, than to any other poet alive. And that means a lot to me, believe me.

Yours,

Jim Dickey

4620 Lelia's Court
Lake Katherine
Columbia, S.C. 29206

TO: ROBERT PENN WARREN[6]

TLS, 1 p; Yale University

17 September, 1968
Columbia, South Carolina

Dear Mr. Warren:

I simply had an impulse to write, for I am just finishing a poem I think is really good, called "Under Buzzards",[7] and I thought to dedicate it to you. But surely I wouldn't think to do it without permission. As a rule I don't dedicate poems, but I wanted to do it in this case, mainly because I feel some root-deep kind of affinity with your poetic effort—that kind of yearning-toward in your poems is what I mean—that simply stood up and told me to do it. If this embarrasses you, please don't let it; such emotions are not intended to be shaken. Please understand that I think of you as the best of all of us.

Sincerely,
James Dickey

4620 Lelia's Court
Lake Katherine
Columbia, S.C. 29206

TO: WILLARD LOCKWOOD

CC, 1 p; Emory

15 November, 1968
Columbia, S.C.

Dear Will:

I have done my best, from the standpoint of examining everything—including my conscience—to find what might throw any light on the particular ground of this decision-making: have consulted my agent, have consulted you and my wife and a good many other people and things and frames of mind. I had a good letter from Wilbur on the subject, and this was very helpful. But Doubleday has offered me a contract the like of which no serious American poet has ever been tendered, and the conviction among most of those that are closest to me is that I should take it.[8] My agent strongly advises it, and he gives convincing reasons. As you should know by now, this decision is not in any way based on any dissatisfaction, real or imagined, with Wesleyan. I have nothing but gratitude and admiration for you and the other people there. But it is really time for me to move, I believe. The Wesleyan program is really for young writers, and I personally think it can best serve the cause of poetry by being just such an operation: an operation for discovery and chance-giving. I have had my chance with you, thank God, and now it is somebody else's. I am increasingly chary of taking your time and efforts which might be given to discovering new people, as I was discovered.

But this is really not the main reason for the decision. The real reasons are financial, as so many—if not all—others in America are. The money from this contract will take care of my family in case anything happens to me, and, since I can get no insurance, being diabetic, this is even more of a factor than it might otherwise be.[9] Again, since I am to be into Doubleday for such a huge chunk of dough, they will <u>have</u> to throw their muscle into advertising and promotion, and, since they are used to doing it and have the means to do it, it probably will signify a rise in sales which, if we are lucky, will mean something new in the relationship of the American public to the poets they produce. At this stage, I <u>need</u> something like this: something enormous and organized, and not—though I wish it were the case—the small and valiant Wesleyan operation. Surely you see this, Will, deplore it as you may—as I do myself.

But you have done four of my books; you have in your charge, in fact, my entire life-work up to this date. This work will continue to sell, and I will cooperate in any way I can to help sell it, as I have done in the past. Until I produce another book—and even, in a way, after I have produced it and any others I produce—I am still a Wesleyan author, and am so identified in the public mind. This is good, and I am glad to have it so. But now, for reasons pertaining mostly to the future of my family, I must turn elsewhere, though I do so reluctantly and with a heavy-blooded heart indeed.

All yours,
Jim

4620 Lelia's Court
Lake Katherine
Columbia, S.C. 29206

TO: JONATHAN WILLIAMS

CC, 1 p; Emory

4620 Lelia's Court
Columbia, S.C. 29206
January 23, 1968 [1969]

Dear Jon:

Thank you for your last letter, and for all those other letters and newsletters and perspectives and other materials which you are so unfailingly kind to send to me, who deserve none of it. But do know that I think of you often, and in a way very special to me. I have always believed, though I have never said anything about it to you, that some of the beatniks and hippies that you seem to know and to have approved of—and that you now apparently disapprove of like Mr. Olsom, Mr. Creely, Mr. Patchen, and so on—were none of them worth a minute of your devoted earthly time. It seems to me that you have undertaken a solitary work so demanding and so difficult and so unrewarding from the standpoint of recompense as to be inconceivable to someone who did not know you. I have believed, and I still believe, that your work for old and all but forgotten poets like Alfred Young Fisher, Basil Bunting, and R. E. F. Larsson is, in more ways than simply the literary, saintly.

I would also like to say—and you can look on this as pompous if you wish, though I hope you don't—that as a man, a poet, and a joyous laborer in the literary world, my generation has not the equal of you, or anything like it.

And as Samuel Johnson said in his reply to James MacPherson, you may print this if you wish.

Let me hear, and I'm sorry I missed you in Columbia.

All best wishes,
James Dickey

JD:rhu

TO: MELVIN B. YOKEN[10]

CC, 2 pp; Emory

4620 Lelia's Court
Columbia, S. C. 29206
February 11, 1969

Dear Dr. Yoken:

Thank you very much indeed for your lovely letter of January 27. It would be unduly modest of me to say that it is the only letter of its kind that I have received, but it would be quite truthful to say that it pleases me more than any other. It is particularly gratifying to hear from someone unknown to me, like yourself—someone that is, "out there in humanity somewhere"—, and I have received not many of <u>that</u> kind of letter, I can assure you! And I surely had very little idea that anyone at all remembered my first book, <u>Into the Stone</u>, which came out as long ago as 1960, which is practically prehistory! That book, I imagine, had only a very few readers outside my immediate family, and it is surprising indeed to know that you remember it at all. You asked me about my particular activities, literary and otherwise, and I'll say a little bit about them if you like, and if you really <u>are</u> that interested, which I am delighted to believe you are.

Like most poets I have read a good deal of poetry in addition to my own, and I am no exception. My favorite American poet, as you may see from my essay in the October or November <u>Atlantic</u> is Theodore Roethke. He is a very great writer to me, and seems to have more insight into the earth that <u>I</u> care about than any other American poet known to me. I like Whitman very much also. I like Emily Dickinson very much although I don't know of any writer who is better in single poems and less good over long structures of poems. She tends to tire me out. As to English poetry I'm a great admirer of Wordsworth and some of the lessor Elizabethan playwrits like John Webster for example or Cyril Turner, for the rashness and daring and what I like to think of as the essential craziness of their language. As to French I don't know their literature very well before the time of Boutlare, but I have read a good deal of the more contemporary French poetry. Of the ones now writing, I like Andre Frenaud, who seems to have—and let no one tell you this is not important—a personality somewhat like I conceive my own to be. In German I like Trakl and of course Rilke, and also less well known ones like Richard Dehmel, and a contemporary named Gotfried Benn and an even more recent writer, Gunter Eich.[11]

Leisure time activities and so on, I can sum up rather easily. I play the guitar both six and twelve string and I spend as much time doing <u>that</u> as I can. I also am an ardent bow hunter and archer and what money I can get for my own uses, I spend on arrows. For, as I say, I am a regular fanatic about archery and bow hunting and the woods and outdoors generally. I go canoeing whenever I can, though naturally this is not as much as I would like, and those activities, coupled with an excessive rage to write, plus a good deal of travelling, plus lecturing and giving readings, plus judging contests, serving on panels, serving on juries of various literary kinds, plus teaching, plus writing a good deal of critism, plus attempting to write a novel and a play, plus caring for my wife and two boys, pretty much takes up all the time there is; yes, and more than that, too.

I must break this off in the interests of a great many of these and other projects. But do know that I deem important indeed the letter that you have been kind enough to write to me. I would welcome hearing from you on any other occasion which you choose to write. Let me thank you once more, and sign off.

Sincerely yours,
James Dickey

JD:rhu

TO: JAMES AND BARBARA REISS[12]

CC, 2 pp; Emory

4620 Lelia's Court
Lake Katherine
Columbia, S.C. 29206
February 27, 1969

Dear Barbara and Jim,

Thank you very much for the chapters you've sent along. I shall be returning to you the edited manuscripts in a few days.

But let me get right to the questions you asked. I don't know exactly how we could have missed talking about the May Day Sermon, but it looks as though we did. So now let me say a few things about it.

The poem came in some manner from a statement by Edwin Arlington Robinson, which I read years ago in a collection of his letters. The quotation, as I remember it, says that "I have been reading the Old Testament as though it were a novel, and I am convinced that God is the villain."[13] It hit me that God, whether by nature a villain or a hero, can be <u>made</u> a villain by villainous people. I am not sure whether or not the Old Testament shows this, as Robinson thinks it does, but I have seen a good deal of evidence for this supposition in events of my own life. "May Day Sermon" is about that, and about the malevolent power God has under certain circumstances: that is, when He is controlled and "interpreted" by people of malevolent tendencies. In this case God is neither more nor less than a combination of the Old Testament and a half mad Georgia hill farmer. The natural inclinations of his daughter, particularly in the spring of the year, are interpreted by him as "sin," and he drags her into the barn, strips her, and beats her very nearly to death. What I wanted to do most in this poem was to make a kind of mythological framework for the action by casting the poem in the form of one of the legends that are prevalent in such communities. The ghost story, the house which everyone avoids because of what happened there years ago, the land that surrounded such a place, and the absorption of these details into the minds of a community, are what the poem is about. It has, I like to think, something to do with the ingrained attitude of mythologizing that rural communities have. What originated as a story of rural blood lust and religion and sex and escape has now become something of a legend, and the woman preacher who speaks the poem has taken that legend as her text, and also as her valedictory to the Baptist church, which is in some manner connected with the events of the legend. I have always liked local stories and reminiscences and legends, and it seemed to me that in the telling of this one there were a good many elements which are present in, and a good many elements which are absent from most of the legends that we hear. I wanted to make the Bible, or a certain interpretation of the Bible which permits cruelty, the central focas of the poem. I also wanted to connect what happens to the people in the poem with the animals—in this case those in the barn—of the world. I wanted to do what I have for many years attempted to do: that is make a long, long poem which has a kind of unbridled frenzy about it, something like that frenzy found when a preacher—particularly of the rural, Baptist variety—works himself up into a state of fanatical, Biblical, unbridled frenzy, "as though he were pure spirit, beyond good and evil." I like to think that readers will notice the parallel between the frenzy on the part of the father—a kind of frenzy of cruelty and self-righteousness—and the frenzy of the woman preacher, who is convinced she is right in telling the women of Gilmer County to throw off the shackles of the Baptist religion and enter into an older world of springtime, pleasure, love and delight. Various readers and critics have made various things of the poem, but it really is a very simple one. It is just a retelling of a local folk myth.

You asked me to say something about the book Helmets, the book Buck Dancer's Choice or the book Falling,[14] and I will do so if you like. I liked them all, naturally, and don't want to make a choice among them. But Helmets was a book in which I was working half with the anapaest and half not.

I will conclude this in another letter.

Sincerely yours,
Jim

JD/fw

TO: JAMES AND BARBARA REISS

CC, 1 p; Emory

4620 Lelia's Court
Lake Katherine
Columbia, S.C. 29206
February 28, 1969

Dear Barbara and Jim,

Buck Dancer's Choice was a continuing exploration of some of the themes I had started to explore in Helmets. Falling represents a further extention, and a kind of exploration of the long, long broken line that I had begun to experiment with a little bit earlier.

You asked me also for something on "The Step-Son."[15] "The Step-Son" has not been finished yet, so I can't send you a copy of it. But it is a poem, I like to believe, that has something to say about the nature of love and work. It is about a high school drop-out who works in a candy factory, and sees the working women and girls all as potential wives. It is, hopefully, a poem about courtship, where the protagonist does not know exactly whom he is to court. She may be working in the packaging room, or she may be playing third base on the girl's softball team. The poem is about the step-son's search on this basis, also about his drinking beer with juke boxes playing Ernest Tubb and Merle Travis records around him on Saturday night while he watches the rich girls water ski on one of the local lakes. It is in the form of a dialogue between the step-son and another person who is either his working buddy or his alter-ego or God or his own consciousness or anything, any other enmity that the reader wishes to supply.

And that's about all for now. Let me know how else I can implement the book. And do let me know what the market prospects are. I may have told you this, but I may as well tell you again. When I saw Theron[16] in New York he was most enthusiastic about the whole project: as for myself I have no doubt at all that it will appear in many, many places, and be enthusiastically reviewed and attacked when it comes out as a book.

I have been giving some thought to the title, and I think your suggestion a good one. It would please me, though, to drop out the idea of this being an auto-biography, because I am strongly opposed to any notion of auto-biographies. About the best I can do, I don't think it a bad best, is to take your suggestion for a title and shorten it a bit. I think we should call it Listening to James Dickey: the Poet in Mid Career.

Love to all in your house, from all of us. Let us hear.

All yours,
James Dickey

JD/fw

TO: ROBERT FITZGERALD[17]

CC, 1 p; Emory

4620 Lelia's Court
Lake Katherine
Columbia, S.C. 29206
March 16, 1969

Dear Mr. Fitzgerald:

I hope you will permit the intrusion of a stranger on your time, but I have just finished your introduction to Jim Agee's shorter prose things,[18] and I would very much like to tell you how moving to me it was, and is. I never knew Agee, though I know a good many people who did, but none of the others—Dwight McDonald,[19] or any of the older crew on Time magazine—seems to have known him so well or so splendidly as you have. That is a valuable thing, and one senses just how valuable it is in the way you write about Agee and yourself and Time magazine and the days at Harvard and those in New York during the depression. As for my own opinions of Agee's work I can say nothing more nor less than that if it had not been for his example, I would not myself today be a writer. If that is pompous, so be it; but I can think of no other way to express the debt I owe to the man's writing, and to the kind of man he was. I won't go on and on about this, but I did want to give you some sense of what Agee means to me, and what your editing of him and your writing on his behalf also means to me.

I am slated to come and give a reading at Harvard sometime in the latter part of the summer, and I hope very much that we can get together. Of all of the writers of your generation that I admire I have met most of the ones I want to meet, except you. I know a great many of your close friends: Robert Lowell, Allan Tate, Red Warren, and some of the others you have been associated with. I knew Dudley Fitz[20] very well, and read for him at Andover about a year and a half ago. So— at least from my point of view—we should get together at some place—at some time. But do know that I admire you and your work enormously, only I wish that you could have more time for your own creative work in poetry than you seem to be giving yourself these days. I remember talking to Flannery O'Connor about you,[21] and she said that you worked so hard teaching and translating that you had very little energy left for poetry. With your style, as urbane and incisive as it is, with the enormous amount of learning and labor it must have taken you to develope it, we have a right to be disappointed that we do not see more of the results of it. Please do not take this wrongly, but only as a sign of the greatest admiration and affection. Again, this from a stranger.

Sincerely yours,
James Dickey

JD/fw

TO: FRANK KERMODE[22]

CC, 2 pp; Emory

4620 Lelia's Court
Lake Katherine
Columbia, S.C. 29206
March 20, 1969

Dear Mr. Kermode:

Please forgive my intrusion, but I should like to record my gratitude for a number of things. First, the <u>Atlantic Monthly</u> over here has kindly sent along your letter of response to the article that I wrote on Theodore Roethke in a recent number of the magazine. No one agreed with me about Roethke's stature, but that does not greatly matter to me. If the <u>Atlantic</u> sent you a copy of the number in which the replies to the article appeared, you will see that there were a good many, and varying responses. But I simply wanted to tell you that if you found anything to be favorable about in the article, I care nothing whatever for the opinions of the others who wrote in. I quite agree with you about the kind of critical jargon that is rife in the magazines and literary journals. It is very difficult for me to read through one of these periodicals, and I have just about given up doing so.[23]

Another thing that has been deviling me for several months is that I came on a quotation from William Blake which is printed under the title of your book <u>Romantic Image</u>, and used part of it in connection with a poem I wrote.[24] It occurs to me that I should have credited you in some way, for, though the quotation is from Blake, I wouldn't have found it if I had not been reading your book. I don't know what protocol is in matters of this sort, but simply wish to write you and tell you that if I would have credited you with discovering the quotation to me, I will try to make ammends in the future by including some kind of acknowledgement to you with the poem when it is published in book form next winter. Please do advise me about this, for I know little or nothing of such matters.

The other things are more personal. Some one sent me your last book <u>Continuities</u>, and I read it, and then went out and got the little book on Wallie Stevens and <u>Puzzles and Epiphanies</u> and <u>The Sense of an Ending</u>, and have been reading through them.[25] I am no good at flattery, so I won't try to tell you in detail how much I enjoyed these books. As Santa Anna[26] once said of himself, "I am an ignorant man almost a poet." But I would enjoy criticism almost as much as the best poetry if it were more like yours. You write exactly as I myself would wish to do if I had a better education and a more organized mind. But it is not necessary that <u>I</u> do this, but that somebody does it. I am very greatly indebted to you for making the reading of Ernest Dowson[27] at least a <u>little</u> respectable, for I read Dowson during the worst part of the Pacific war, and I cannot look at certain poems of his even today without feeling the tremor of the guns in the ground around me and the tremor of the possibility of poetry inside of me. I, too, think his translations from the French are extraordinarily good, and his story, "The Dying of Frances Donne,"[28] is, I think, about as good as the Nineties did in short fiction. I also am much in your debt for what you say about Nabokov.[29] I have seldom read a writer who appears to me more tiresome and disgusting as he does. He is exactly the kind of writer that I most detest, with a built-in intellectual smirk and a kind of feeling that everything, and especially every<u>body</u>, is in some way contemptible. That is an eminence from which I think there is little profit in viewing humanity: <u>that</u> kind of intellectual superiority and snobbishness. I am rather a heavy breather, myself, and I am sure Nabokov would find me more contemptible than just about any body else, except perhaps those young American novelists who type out, as he says, "heavy autobiographical novels with their thumbs."[30]

I won't go on and on, but simply record my gratitude for a multiplicity of things. I hope that some day we may meet, and I can tell you the same things, and some others I am bound to discover in the near future in your work, looking you right in the eyes, as such things should, ideally, be done.

With every best wish, I remain,

James Dickey

JD/fw

TO: JACK KESSIE[31]

TLS, 1 p; HRHRC

4620 Lelia's Court
Lake Katherine
Columbia, S.C. 29206
April 15, 1969

Dear Mr. Kessie:

Thank you for the copy of <u>Playboy</u> and your note about Mr. Carroll's interview of Allen Ginsberg, which I read through.[32] I have no interest, myself, in Mr. Ginsberg either as a writer or as a public personality. He is one of these actor-type writers who are cluttering up the scene at present, and his work is going to blow away like the thistle-down of many other literary fads have done in the past. I don't know Mr. Ginsberg personally, but I have read his so-called verse, and it is pathetic beyond all the patheticness that I have previously known. I don't intend this as a put-down of a fellow American writer; only as a put-down of the kind of public personality that the poet, in some cases, feels constrained to become in our time, poetry itself not being enough.

You asked me to contribute something to your Letters column, but I don't really want to do this at all. So please don't print this. This is only a private communication to you, and if private communications, as in other areas of American life, have no validity at all, then simply throw this in the wastepaper basket, or fold it into a model airplane and sail it out toward Lake Shore Drive.

But I would like to think that you would tell Robie MacAuley that I have some fiction about ready to go somewhere, and if he will get in touch with my agent Theron Raines, at 244 Madison Avenue in New York, we might be able to get together, in some fashion.[33]

Please tell Mr. Carroll that I greatly admire his interviewing skill, and I hope that next time around it will be exercised on a real American poet, instead of a self-serving actor with no talent as a writer, and none but the most obvious kind—and the worst kind—as an actor.

Sincereley yours,
James Dickey

JD/fw

TO: STANLEY BURNSHAW[34]

TLS, 1 p; HRHRC

4620 Lelia's Court
Lake Katherine
Columbia, S.C. 29206
May 4, 1969

Dear Stanley:

Thank you so much for your last letter. It is wonderful to hear from you. I will make only a few comments on The Seamless Web, which I have now completed reading.[35] If I had never heard of you and I read the book it surely would have changed my life, as well as the kind of poetry I write. I think it is the most original book on the subject that has ever been written, and probably more important than Aristotle's Poetics. As far as criticism is concerned, people around the country tell me that I make excessive statements, which I do. Sometimes I mind making these, and am unsure of them myself. But in this case I am not. I don't want to offer any kind of nitpicking "comments" on the book, for if it has any blemishes they are very minor ones. It is a stunning amazing book, Stanley. The whole section about the connection of imagery with bodily functions and things of that nature seems to me to be the only valid writing about the subject that exists. I would like to know what on earth induced you to take this approach which is so much deeper than the kind of textual criticism that I was reared on at Vanderbilt. Surely what you say poetry does is what it does: <u>does</u>. I hope very much that you will send me a bound copy of the book—or a couple of them—when it is published. Did you say that you want to dedicate this book to <u>me</u>? Please forgive me if you didn't say this, or if you have other plans for the dedication, but it seems to me that you did at one time say something of this sort. Of course, if I do remember rightly, and you do dedicate it to me, I would be most pleased, for it is very likely that having my name on your book will be the thing in me that outlasts everything I have written.[36] But the real matter at hand is not the dedication, but the book itself. The only other book that is as daring, or anywhere near as original, is Robert Ardrey's <u>The Territorial Imperative</u>,[37] and that is just a kind of shot in the dark thing. Yours isn't; you've got the documentation, and you can prove what you have been bold enough to hypothesize. I won't go on and on, for we can talk about all this when we finally get together once more. Maxine and I have to come to New York in a couple of weeks so that I can close out my business with the Rockefeller Foundation for this year, as well as see a couple of agents and publishers. I hope that we can all get together at that time, for there is very much to talk about.

I can't write longer, Stanley, but I did want to let you know that I had read your book, and that it is wonderful, as it should be.

All yours,
Jim

JD/fw

TO: MARK SCHORER[38]

CC, 1 p; Emory

4620 Lelia's Court
Lake Katherine
Columbia, S.C. 29206
May 13, 1969

Dear Mark:

Please forgive yet another fan letter about your <u>The World We Imagine</u>,[39] but it is, as far as I can tell, inevitable. I have just read the whole thing again, and partly as a result of this I went and read through <u>Sinclair Lewis</u>.[40] There is something major working here, I have no doubt at all, as well as the best prose style since the age of Burke and Johnson. I have never in my life had so much the sense of a _man_ writing about something that concerns him deeply, as I have in your essays and the rest of your prose. My own, which you are kind enough to praise, seems a pale business indeed beside yours. I won't go on and on in this vein, but will simply tell you again how much of an inspiration the example of your commitment to literature and your intelligence and talent have meant to me. And _do_ mean to me, with every breath I draw. You are the best of all of us, I think.

All yours,

James Dickey

JD/fw

TO: STUART FRIEBERT[41]

CC, 1 p; Emory

4620 Lelia's Court
Lake Katherine
Columbia, S.C. 29206
May 15, 1969

Dear Mr. Friebert:

Thank you very much indeed for your letter. Surely, I remember my visit there a few years ago with very great pleasure. But I am sorry to have to say that I cannot contribute to your new magazine, though I am much interested in your effort. I am so cut up between various periodicals and publishers that, if I were to give you a poem, even if I had one, I would end up in Leavenworth next week. It is very nice of you to say the things you say about my work; I hope the new things that I am now doing will at least in some measure justify your extremely kind commentaries. I look down your list of contributors and, if I may make bold to comment, I have a good deal of regard for.[42] Synder is adequate, Stafford is very good, but Bly is nothing at all, and Merwin is not much better. Rich is all right, though of a period style which will fade away quickly, Eich is good indeed, Krolow is also good, Salinas is interesting and one of the old Spanish guard, Hall would be a disgrace to your magazine, Simpson is a little better than average, Jim Wright is just a slight bit better than that. But, as you say, at any rate we hope you feel the company is responsible enough. I must make it plain, that I don't think the company is really as good as the company might be, and I don't think that any kind of fad poet like Finlay is going to matter at all.[43]

I am delighted that the faculty wife whose knee I put my graceful hand on, as you say, still gives off gamma rays from the event. I cannot even summon up beta rays, myself, and I could only become radioactive if I were to renew the physical contact, which is unlikely to happen. However, please give my regard to the lady.

No, I would not much relish being photographed in a bathtub, even if I were in one of a field full of bathtubs. But please <u>do</u> let me see the first number. I would like that very much. And do remember me to David Young, your big boss editor. Please understand that I send my very best regards, and hope for a success for your magazine, and for your personal life and writing.

Sincerely yours,
James Dickey

JD/fw

TO: E. LEWIS KING

CC, 1 p; Emory

4620 Lelia's Court
Lake Katherine
Columbia, S.C. 29206
May 15, 1969

Dear Lew:

Thank you very much indeed for your letter of May 9th. It is always great to hear from you. I hope very much that Maxine and myself will be able to get up to Sautee at the time you designate for the Great Canoe Run. But in one sense your letter chills my blood indeed. You sound so much like the character in a novel I once read.

Oh I'm trying to write. Right now the book looks awfully good, and huge feelers are coming out of Hollywood and other places about it. I talked to both my agent and my editor, and we are surely on to something, on the Coosawattee. I don't believe you'd recognize the novel, from the amount of talking we did about it, which was <u>sort</u> of what I am doing but not exactly like, when you read it, I hope very much that you will be pleased by what I have done. The book is dedicated to E. Lewis King and Al Brazzelton, companions. But none of us is really recognizable as the characters we were on the Coosawattee: that has all been rendered strange by the Alchemy of the Word. But it is an awfully good book, Lewis; I believe you will be proud of it. At least, I hope so.

I am happy that Susan is feeling better, but I am so awed by the crossies[44] of the <u>higher surgery</u>, that I don't feel qualified to express any opinion at all. I hope she will be all right, and grow up into being what she can surely be: one of the world's great beauties.

As to the writing, I hope you will do it, and I hope that Al will do it too. There is not much really good prose writing—or poetry, either—around. And it is good to know that there might be some good things coming up, out of the creeks, and out of whatever else there is for it to come from.

I'll be in Atlanta again in a couple of weeks, and will let you know when I'm coming. Meanwhile, my old friend, hold on. Good things will be coming up the river soon.

All yours,

James Dickey

JD/fw

TO: GLENWAY WESCOTT[45]

CC, 2 pp; Emory

    4620 Lelia's Court
    Lake Katherine
    Columbia, S.C. 29206
    May 21, 1969

Dear Mr. Wescott:

Last week I picked up your <u>Images of Truth</u>[46] in an airport news-stand somewhere, and read through it in the next few hours. I simply felt that I must write to you and tell you how much I liked what you say about Catherine Ann Porter and the others. I am quite sure that Somerset Maugham will never again have such an eloquent defense, and I believe what you say is more important than what Edmond Wilson says.[47] I have always thought of Wilson as a tiresome kind of old literary hack, and to see people like Robert Lowell and Lowell's wife Elizabeth Hardwick, refer to him as "a great writer," is as appalling as it is amusing. Anyway I think your essays are wonderful indeed, and I thought you should know that I think this. Also, a couple of years ago, I remember seeing you on television—it might even have been the Today Show—talking about E. E. Cummings. I thought what you said was the best thing I had ever heard said about Cummings. I introduced him at what I am told was his last public reading, and I remembered on that occasion what you had said about his work, and used it, in some way or another, in the introduction.[48]

I remember meeting you very briefly at the National Book Awards the year I won the award for poetry, but I don't remember anything of what we said. Be that as it may, I'd like you to know how much I liked your essays. There is a new thing coming into criticism, I think. This will be a more emotional, a more involving, and a more <u>committed</u> participation of the critic in the work that he reads, and will also be a kind of criticism that is more partial, more prejudice, and altogether more interesting. I think your <u>Images of Truth</u> points the way toward this, and I like that; I like it quite a lot.

Whether or not any of this registers with you, I still wished to tell you that I think <u>Images of Truth</u> is a fine book indeed. There has never been anybody more absolutely <u>right</u> about Thomas Mann than you are. And that is a very great deal.

Know that I think of your work with admiration and honor, in criticism, in fiction, and in the other things you do, like some of the personal reminiscences in <u>Goodby, Wisconsin</u>.[49] Has that book ever been reissued? I bought it for 29¢, and would not take $29,000 for it.

My best to you, and to your work, both past and future.

Sincerely yours,
James Dickey

JD/fw

TO: F. W. DUPEE[50]

CC, 1 p; Emory

4620 Lelia's Court
Lake Katherine
Columbia, S.C. 29206
June 4, 1969

Dear Mr. Dupee:

I hope you will forgive the intrusion of a stranger, but I have just read through your edition of the letters of E. E. Cummings, and I think it is simply wonderful. Not only are the letters wonderful, but the selection and arrangement is also wonderful, and it is wonderful that you and the other fellow should have taken the time to do the thing. Surely the world ought to <u>have</u> the letters, and I am very happy to be one of that world. I introduced Cummings at what I have been told was his last public reading, at the Poetry Center there in New York, and it was the only time I ever saw him. Afterwards, we went out to a party and sat around and talked for a while, and I enjoyed him very much. I have always enjoyed him very much, since the first Cummings poem I read. The bright thing about him is his absolutely unique personality, and his refusal to compromise it under any conditions, or for any political system, or for any thing at all.

I am also an enormous admirer of your own critical writings. I bought <u>King of the Cats</u> in Madison, Wisconsin, three years ago when I was writer-in-residence up there in the dead of winter, and read through the whole thing in one evening. I can't think of any critical writings that I more admire. Beside yours, mine seem puny indeed, and aggressively puny.

I wanted you to know these things, because I have been thinking them for some time, and because it seems to me that writers owe such letters to each other; after all, one is not usually moved to admire. Or at least I am not.

One more thing: I have read a good deal of reminiscences of James Agee, but yours—in just a couple of pages—gave me more a sense of the man than any of the others, or indeed, of all of them put together.[51] I never knew Agee, though I wish I had, but I have a very vivid image in my mind of what he must have been like, personally. Your account of him jibes almost exactly with this, and therefor I am doubly grateful for it. It is what you might call a literary unearned increment.

Thank you very much, and from the deepest place, for the work you are doing for all of us.

Sincerely yours,
James Dickey

JD/fw

TO: CHARD POWERS SMITH[52]

TLS, 1 p; Yale

4620 Lelia's Court
Lake Katherine
Columbia, S.C. 29206
June 5, 1969

Dear Mr. Smith:

Thank you very much for your letter about the Robinson essay; I'm very happy you liked it. As for myself, I am a great admirer of <u>Where the Light Falls</u>, which I don't think will ever be replaced by another book on Robinson. Coxe's book is good, but it is nothing like as thorough as yours. I don't think Coxe likes your book quite as well as I do, but he has surely used it very widely. If I have offended you by not, as you say, crediting you with the description of Robinson's family, I hope you will forgive me.

Thank you very much as well for taking the trouble to point out the qualities of Robinson's life which you do point out. Certainly you understand Robinson better than any one else does, and I'm very happy to be part of a public which can admit this and enjoy it.

As to the other part of your letter, I don't know, or have any idea at all, of what you mean by "greatness." Roethke has surely written some things that I would call great, and maybe Jarrell in one or two things, but Louis Simpson—well, no. He is just one of the boys; just one of the slightly above average American versifiers, and is getting more and more that way. I hesitate to be in such company, for, as I say, I don't know what you mean by greatness, and if Simpson has this, in your opinion, then I don't wish to have it at all, but rather something else. I don't know, either, exactly what your situation is with your anthology. If you want my opinion of something that I think is good, though only Time will decide the issue of greatness, why don't you use my poem "The Sheep Child"? It appears in the latter section of my last book of poems, Poems 1957–1967.[53]

But again, thank you indeed for your handsome letter. It is good to have it. And the best of luck with your literary projects.

Sincerely,

James Dickey

JD/fw

TO: MRS. ELIOT JANEWAY[54]

CC, 1 p; Emory

4620 Lelia's Court
Lake Katherine
Columbia, S.C. 29206
June 12, 1969

Dear Mrs. Janeway:

It is a monumental relief to me to get your letter, and I am very happy to have it. I talked to Gene McCarthy last week out at Reston, in Virginia, and he is as maddening as ever, or maybe he is even more maddening. History casts the man in a role in which he could have been at least influential, and probably crucial, and he did nothing with it, or about it, at all. Just to sit down and talk to him is to have the whole unspeakably frustrating thing of his candidacy and the rest of it happen all over again. I am very glad indeed that I do not have to go through that but one time in a life time. McCarthy has got a way of sliding off an issue with a remark that he thinks of as enigmatic, a remark that may have a great deal of wisdom in it, and may not, and even as he says it you think, privately, that it doesn't. This is such a stock in trade of his that it is almost impossible to talk to him directly, and if American politicians cannot talk directly, they cannot talk to the people, and if they cannot talk to the people they cannot do anything at all in politics. People want simple answers, even if the answers turn out to be, in action, more complicated than they are, at least in a campaign they must <u>seem</u> simple. For example, Gene's great appeal to the young and to the liberals was that he was against the prolongation of the Vietnam war. If you talked to him during those days, you could see that he had no really well conceived plan of <u>doing</u> anything about it; it was just the fact that he was registered in the public-mind as a man who had stood up and spoken out against the continuation of the war. He was fairly direct about <u>that</u>, and that is what got all the kids and the liberals and the others kind of like myself, who believed in him, to working for him and helping him. But the final thing that defeated Gene was his personality: he wants to say and not to say, and above all not to be held accountable <u>really</u>.

I won't go on and on in this vein, but will just thank you once more for your letter. I hope you will remember me to Eliot, and even to Senator Hartke,[55] should you have occasion to see him or write to him.

Keep in touch, in whatever manner you would like, and we shall surely get together with you again, I hope in the not too distant future.

Sincerely yours,
James Dickey

JD/fw

TO: SELDEN RODMAN[56]

CC, 2 pp; Washington University

21 July, 1969
Columbia, S.C.

Dear Selden:

It is a great pleasure to hear from you; yes indeed. Thank you very much for the remarks on <u>Babel</u>. It got some hard knocks from the New York beatnik boys, but that's fine with me; I would be disturbed if, say, John Ashbery was crazy about it, instead of just crazy.[57] You might drop my editor at Farrar Straus a letter about the book, if you're of a mind. I'm trying to get him to do another critical book called <u>The Self as Agent</u>[58] with the long Roethke piece in it that kicked up such fuss in the <u>Atlantic</u> last fall. But that shall be as you wish.

On your project: sure, I'll help you all I can. And I agree with New American Library that you should revise your anthologies, which came out, as nearly as I can remember, when I was in college, back in the forties. There are dozens and dozens of new and important poets working in lots of different languages now, and these should have some space in your books. You ask me about specific poets, Neruda and Borges,[59] and some others. I think Neruda is wonderfully good, but only in individual images and lines. I love some of those, but his whole poems seem terribly diffuse and arbitrary to me. Borges is good in a different way, but he relies too much on one <u>kind</u> of presentation: the person dreaming something into existence, for example, when the point is that someone else or something is dreaming him. But they are both very good, and you should have them in. Paz I like pretty well; he has a kind of interesting tropicalizing of surrealism that I like but am not crazy about.[60] Yevtushenko is good but too political-minded for me. He has enthusiasm and youthful "accessibility to experience," though, and is important and worth reading. Since he is my Russian translator and a very good drinking companion (You should have seen the show he and I put on at the Library of Congress) I can hardly recommend that you leave him out.[61] But he is really not as good a poet as Voznesensky, who is very powerful and direct and chance-taking.[62] And that's what I think of <u>those</u> fellows: the ones you mention.

As to who <u>else</u> should be in, there's no way to start telling who I think is good. In French, Francis Ponge should be in. Yves Bonnefoy should be in, and (in my opinion one of the best poets I have ever read) a man named Lucien Becker. Supervielle should be in, Rene Char should be in, and O, lots more. In German, Gottfried Benn should be in with one of his more gruesome efforts, and Gunter Eich. But <u>not</u> a phony like Hans Magnus Enzensberger, a real no-talent, and a shit personally, as well. In Italian, surely Montale. And Ungaretti. Maybe Quasimodo, and maybe Saba. In Spanish, Luis Cernuda. And also Vicente Aleixandre.[63]

But maybe these people are too specialized or little-known for your anthologies. Or anthology, rather. But that should be part of the point, I'd think: to get them less little-known.

Anyway, this'll do for a starter, I hope. Let me know what you think, and we'll go on from here.[64]

Do know though, that I remember what little I know of you fondly, and think of you with affection and honor. And I like your poetry very much, too. The wreck scene in the <u>Death of the Hero</u> thing is awfully powerful; it could not be better. And, since I have diabetes myself, I could not be more interested in a hero than in <u>that</u> hero. I wouldn't be around if it weren't for him.[65]

My best, as always.

All yours,
James Dickey

4620 Lelia's Court
Lake Katherine
Columbia, S.C. 29206

TO: R. V. CASSILL[66]

CC, 1 p; Washington University

4620 Lelia's Court
Lake Katherine
Columbia, S.C. 29206
July 29, 1969

Dear Verlin:

Many thanks for your note; I will be overjoyed to see you when I come to Harvard. I don't know whether I will be able to get out to Truro with you, but I will if I can possibly do so. My situation is this: I shall be bringing my family—or part of it anyway: my wife and youngest son—with me and that may present a logistical problem. Anyway, after the reading at Harvard we plan to go up to Martha's Vineyard for a few days relaxation. I don't know the relationship, geographically, of Martha's Vineyard to Truro, but it is not entirely impossible that there may be some interplay. I surely hope there is, or, if there isn't, that we can invent one. I would love to see you for as many hours as our mutual schedules will permit. I want very much for you to meet my wife and my little boy, who is the goal of God Himself to me, and for us to get together once more. But that will be as it will be, and as it is possible for us to arrange it.

After I supplied the enconium for "Buckthorne"[67] I was not able to find out how the book did. It was my impression that it did well, but I have no real figures to back up my assumption. But we can talk about this when we get together in August.

We had a kind of a little literary festival—or mini-festival—here at South Carolina and Peter Taylor came down for it. He was full of reminiscences of Salt Lake City, where we lived in that strange limbo of cinderblock motel rooms, disguised as girls dormitories, with a tack board in each room with a single note on it that says, "M.S. please pick up your laundry." Peter, overcome with sentiment about our lost youth in the hills of Utah, said that it was the best time he ever had. I doubt any of us would want to go back, but I remember it, myself, with great affection indeed. And probably you do too. Anyway, Peter said to tell you hello, and that we would all be reunited in the Lost Writers' Colony which we glimpsed briefly going over on the cable cars out of Garden City, Utah. He said he would feel sure he was in Heaven if Verlin Cassill refrained from giving the Cry in Tiny Alice.[68] As for myself, I remember the Cry with affection and honor.[69]

We'll hope to see something of you, Verlin. The end is not yet; no by God, and not by a very long chalk.

Meanwhile, much love.

All yours,
James Dickey

TO: RICHARD WILBUR

TLS, 1 p; Amherst College

4620 Lelia's Court
Lake Katherine
Columbia, S.C. 29206
July 31, 1969

Dear Dick:

I have just received your new book[70] as part of the material for judging the next Pulitzer Prizes (I expect this part of it should be kept quiet).[71] But I just wanted to tell you how good it is; it is the kind of writing that I have always wanted for you. There is a lot of new nerve and muscle and iron here; the breaking through to intense personal concerns is becoming more and more apparent. I won't go on and on about this, but simply let you know how delighted I am with the book. It is by far the best you have written. As for reviewers—especially awful ones like Chad Walsh in the (I think) Washington <u>Post</u>[72]—there is very little to say of them at all. I read Mr. Walsh's omnibus review of you and Anne Sexton and some others last week, and I am absolutely dumbfounded at the inadequacy of the man's mental equipment and his sensibility. It is very obvious that none of the other books in the review are in the same category with yours at all, and yet he contrives to hedge this bet, and at the end, though he compares Mr. Clark— surely the no-talent of all and every generation—to Rod McKuen,[73] he nevertheless concludes that his is the most promising of all the "voices" in the review. Well, this kind of thing is just enough to make one laugh. No wonder I never read reviews! There are only things that throw you off your stride. And your stride, like in your poem on jogging,[74] is very good indeed. There is really no point in my drawing this letter out any longer; I hope you get the general notion of my delight and happiness over what you have done here and are doing. My best to you, as always.

Jim D.——

JD/fw

TO: ERIC FIEDLER[75]

CC, 1 p; Washington University

4620 Lelia's Court
Lake Katherine
Columbia, S.C. 29206
August 1, 1969

Dear Eric Fiedler:

Thank you for your green letter. I admit, however, that I am a little nonplused at your appeal for help from me in the case of Wally Burckhard. The fact that he is a poet—and from the samples you send I think he is one, or sort of one—is not really a contributing factor to his altercation with the Law, however. I realize that he surely must be a very close and particular friend of yours, but from your summary of his career, he is something over and above just being a good old fun-loving buddy who writes (pretty good) poetry. He is a criminal, period. I am sure there are a lot of good people in prison, and I am equally sure, from what you are kind enough to tell me, that Mr. Burckhard is one of these. Far be it from me to hold out for the Law as against the creative intellect, but I am at a loss to understand on what grounds you think Mr. Burckhard should be released from prison. He is obviously guilty as charged, and not only of the selling of marijuana, but of car theft, burglary, and God knows what else. How, then, am I to intervene? What could be the possible grounds for my writing to the Adult Authority on behalf of Mr. Burckhard? The case is clear, legally speaking. And I don't even <u>know</u> the man, other than what you tell me of him. Furthermore, I am, God save the mark, rather a clean-liver, and take a very dim view indeed of drugs, drug users, and drug peddlers. This stamps me, I guess, very much as a square; that, I am happy to be. I am answering this letter because you have interested me in the case of Mr. Burckhard. However, I am not at all sure that I can do anything for him, or, if I could, would do anything. If this particular letter moves you to write me a more personal communication—that is, something other than what is possible by means of a mimeograph machine—we can go on and maybe try to work something out. But I can promise you nothing.

Meanwhile, please remember me to your father and mother, whom I last saw in London a little over a year ago. Tell your father that I would like to have some news of his poetry book with Paul Carroll,[76] and that I will give him a jacket statement, should he desire one. Be happy to.

Sincerely yours,
James Dickey

JD/fw

TO: BARBARA AND JAMES REISS

CC, 2 pp; Emory

4620 Lelia's Court
Lake Katherine
Columbia, S.C. 29206
August 3, 1969

Dear Barbara and Jim:

Glad to have an address for you, for we are moving into an important time on the book, and so it is necessary that we communicate. It is not only necessary that we communicate but that there also be some communication between all of us and Ken McCormick at Doubleday, and with Theron Raines also. Theron called me a couple of days ago and said that for some reason or other the contracts had been lost, or had gone wrong in the mails. This is serious. Let us get those contracts in, for there is some money which will result from it, and will not result until the contracts are signed and returned. Please look after this, for Theron says he sent the contracts to you in Ohio and they have not been received back in New York. I was in New York about a month ago, and I can assure you that the Doubleday people are very enthusiastic about the book. But they have the regular big-publishers' situation with schedules, and they cannot allow a thing like this to hold up the production of the book. So please do get this straightened out, and very quickly. At the suggestion of Norman Mailer I am now calling the book Self-Interviews. I hope that will meet with your approval; the people at Doubleday seemed to like the idea and title very much. If you have any objection, please let me know.

Next item: let me see the draft of your introduction, Barbara. We have a choice of doing one of two things, or of doing something inbetween these two things. We can really make a statement about this kind of book, considered as a relatively new kind of genre, or we can have a sort of throw away introduction: the kind of introduction that almost always is the introduction of a book of this sort, if there is any such sort, or at least of books that have a distant kinship with this kind of book. So let us step out and make some very bold statements. It would not be a bad thing at all if the book were controversial; I intend some of my remarks to incite this kind of reaction. Let us make some bold claims for me. I will leave these claims to you, but if we can stir up the Lowells and The New York Review of Books people to a violent attack, we can then rally our forces and as the result of the interplay the book will sell rapidly. Controversy is the very name of the game in the case of writers and their opinions; I would be very disappointed indeed if the book were not violently attacked from many quarters some of which

I can predict, and some of which I could never imagine in a million years. But we will have our defenders too, this is a foregone conclusion; the main thing is for the book not to be simply a throw away item much as the Williams'[77] book turned out to be. We have a chance to do some rather startling things here, and I think we should play those things up, and make statements that we both believe in and that we know in advance will constitute controversial items.

Enough of that. But I do very much believe that we have a chance to do something important for the human sensibility here: to do something about shaking it out of its "dogmatic slumbers." And I think that if we are not bold enough and not forthright enough and not controversial enough, all three of us will regret it bitterly for a very long time. It is very exciting: how this work, instigated by you, has mushroomed from a relatively timid graduate product into a situation in which we can make major statements. I believe a good many people will be shaken up by this book, and shaken up in far deeper ways than people are shaken up by the deliberate shaking-efforts of people like Norman Mailer. I believe that the tremors from this particular shock will be deep indeed, and will cause a certain revaluation of poetry, and, yes, of existence in this time and place.

I won't go on and on, but will hope to hear from you soon. In the meantime, please keep in touch with Theron, please do get the contracts back to him signed, and please keep in touch with Ken McCormick as well. Publication is set for August next year, and a good deal of publicity, parties, and other things are being planned. This can all be terrifically good for all of us.

Meanwhile, my love to you both, and to your lovely little girl. I was in Colorado this time last year, and remember it with affection and honor. Please let me hear something from you soon, and we will go on from here. Onward and inward, as the poet says.

All yours,
James Dickey

JD/fw

TO: HAROLD T. P. HAYES[78]

CC, 1 p; Washington University

6 August, 1969
Columbia, S.C.

Dear Mr. Hayes:

Thank you for your communication concerning Cassius Clay.[79] I will sign the statement: I do believe that Cassius Clay should be allowed to defend his title, particularly against Joe Frazier or Sonny Liston (who may be honest now), or even Jimmy Ellis or Jerry Quarry. And I also think Clay (none of that ridiculous Muslim stuff) is the champion, for there is only one way of dethroning a man who can still (physically) fight, and that is in the ring, not in the courts. The part of us that goes back to the flickering of cave-fires knows this, and no amount of legal hocus-pocus is going to change the fact that physical champions remain so as long as they <u>are</u> so.

Enough. And a couple of other things: please tell Jill Goldstein[80] that I have decided not to pose nude; that, really, is not for me. And Mr. Gingrich[81] solicited an eloquent (!?) statement from me as to the most pressing "challenge of the seventies." When will that run?[82] Lastly, I have a first novel coming out in April that will knock you on your ass, as it does everybody else including me. If you want to print part of it, get in touch with my agent, there in New York; Theron Raines, 244 Madison Avenue.[83]

Otherwise, best wishes. I'm slipping into town for a couple of days beginning Friday, and if you can also slip (away) we might get together for a drink, or something; I'd like that. Anyway, I'll be at the St. Moritz. I'll be in around noon Friday.

Again, thanks for communicating.

Sincerely,
James Dickey

4620 Lelia's Court
Lake Katherine
Columbia, S.C. 29206

TO: VICTORIA J. WHITE[84]

CC, 1 p; Emory

6 August, 1969
Columbia, S.C.

Dear Miss White:

I have your letter and your poems. I do not usually answer such letters—my waste basket is heavy with them every week, and I am damned glad to get rid of the stuff people send me—, for I consider them a god-damned imposition on one who has, if he is serious about his writing and living, no time for the work of strangers. The supposition on the part of people who write to poets is something like this: "I realize you're busy <u>and all that</u>. But I don't really mind taking up your time. I don't know exactly <u>why</u> you should sacrifice your work to the work of a stranger, but I <u>do</u> think you should, especially in my case." It is very tiresome, I can tell you. As there is a kind of saying in American life for would-be advantage-taking of this sort, I'll quote it: What's in it for me? The answer is, usually, nothing: nothing but a gratitude quickly forgotten on both sides, and the loss of time which, like any other time, one can't get back.

But your letter is a little different. First of all, you can write. I won't say any more about this until later, though. Second, there <u>is</u>, in this case, something you can do for me. And if you will, maybe we can get together on some detailed commentary on your poems, though I can't promise anything as yet. This latter is:

There is a good paperback bookstore on your campus, and it has a very good department of folk guitar books. I'd like you to go up there and make a list of all the books that have to do with either blues or finger-picking or flat-picking, and send it to me. What I want are books with <u>pieces</u> in them, and not instruction manuals. Make a list of all these they have, and send it to me. I want to get several of these books apiece and give them to my friends and guitar students. Also see if the record department (anywhere in town) has an instruction record by Stefan Grossman called "How to Play the Blues": the only useful folk instruction record I've come across.

When you've done all this, maybe we can talk about your poems. <u>Maybe</u>. Otherwise, no. If all this doesn't strike you as a good idea, let me know, and I'll return your poems.

With every good wish, I am

James Dickey

4620 Lelia's Court
Lake Katherine
Columbia, S.C. 29206

TO: LOUISE NOBLE[85]

CC, 1 p; Emory

22 August, 1969
Columbia, S.C.

Dear Louise:

Thanks for sending along the (proposed) design. I'm afraid I'm in entire agreement with you in rejecting it, and also with your reasons for rejecting it. This was why I talked to you last week about the way we're going about this, which was (I was afraid) going to lead to something like this. In most cases it is a mistake to leave this much autonomy to the artist, and to let him go this far along with what may not have been an accurate conception of the problem on his part, in the first place. The only good thing about what he has done is his rendering of the actual peep-sight part of the string, which is very good indeed. But that dreadful, too-detailed, rotogravure eye is plainly not going to do at all. What I had in mind was nothing like this. I conceived the design as being strictly in line drawing, with just so much of the sight as in this case appears in orange, and no more. I wanted behind this—or in combination with it—a line-drawn eye of the same color as the sight, and stylized, reduced to the barest suggestion of an eye, so that the whole thing would make one design, eye and peep-sight—and with luck, and with the right kind of stylization, would be, as to the book and the theme, a kind of industrially-designed logo or trademark. Can we still not do something with this? It is a much better idea than I have yet been able to think of, or that I have had presented to me. I had also conceived of the jacket in black and the design and title and author's name in the same orange as the peep-sight and the eye, and the whole thing on paper of relatively rough stock (not slick paper): something simple and mysterious. I would like the reader to look at our "logo" and wonder what the hell it is, and what it has to do with "deliverance."

And that is the trouble with showing an actual bow, an actual arrow, a stylized bow, and so on. That gives too much of the game away. It gives too much of the book away, for I want the reader not to know that the bow and arrow plays that much of a part in the action until he sees, gradually, and by reading, that it does. We don't want to telegraph this by the cover, if we can help it. Let us let the reader discover what there is for him to discover.

Meanwhile I enclose a number of shots of archers, archery gear, and so on, so that you can get some idea of what's going on in the book. There are a couple of pictures of different types of broadhead (or hunting) arrows in case they spark something—though again, I'd rather not be too specific, here—a picture of Jim Dougherty shooting with a bow-quiver equipped bow, though left-handed Jim is using a covered-head type of quiver, not like ours, and an ad for an open-headed bow-quiver that ours is something like.

Next time around, do some sketches of your own and let's agree on what we want, before we go on to the next step of having the idea rendered. That would save everybody a lot of trouble, and have the best chance of satisfying us all.[86]

Again, thanks.

TO: DIANE WAKOSKI[87]

CC, 2 pp; Emory

4620 Lelia's Court
Lake Katherine
Columbia, S.C. 29206
September 9, 1969

Dear Miss Wakoski:

Thank you indeed for your letter of September 1st, and for the things about my work that you are kind enough to say. Also, I am very happy that you are persistent in your pursuit of Guggenheim fellowships and other things of that nature. If I had not got fellowships at crucial times, I doubt very much that I would still be a writer today, or, in fact, would even be alive. So I hope you get what you desire from these foundations, and that it will do for you what you hope it does, once the fellowship is forthcoming.

It is not up to me to give a stranger advice, but the second paragraph of your letter is as strange to me as if it had come from the planet Uranus. The number of <u>assumptions</u> about writers and poets and poetry and social protest are nothing more or less than a kind of compendium of current attitudes, especially those to be found in every alleyway of Greenwich Village. You talk of "the 60's image of the poet as . . ." surely this is group-think of the most blatant, obvious, and ephemeral. I am very happy that, as you say, you have "defended" my work against people "both academic and otherwise" who are ready to write me off as a terrible poet simply because, as you say, I "make a good living from it." These are all people, I would be quite willing to wager, who do themselves give readings, publish poetry, and other things that I do, so it can't be a generic thing that I do that they object to, for most of them are doing the same thing, or trying to do it. No; it is not a question of my doing something wrong, according to their likes. It is simply that I do it better than they do, and that I get paid more for it. This is not arrogance on my part; it is simply a fact that I as well as they must take cognizance of. All this red-herring business about being a war lover and so on is simply the product of envious people who cannot and will never do what I have done, are conscience of this, and wish to find some other weapons rather than poetry with which to attack me. It is all so benal, uncreative, and stale. For, as you say, the real thing is the poem itself, and not the aura that surrounds the poet or his political opinions. Mr. Bly—surely the most laughably untalented poet of them all—has called "The Firebombing" a war poem in the sense that it is a war <u>mongering</u> poem.[88] It is nothing of the sort. Your particular relationship to it seems to stem not from the poem itself, but from Bly's opinions: another example of the herd instinct that you seem to partake of rather liberally. But all one has to do is to <u>read</u> "The Firebombing" to see that it has nothing to do with being a war mongering poem. This propensity to parrot accepted opinions is the saddest thing in the whole poetic corpus just now. New York is full of it, and so are a lot of other places. But New York seems to be more full of it. From what I have seen of the situation there, the New York poets are like crabs in a bucket: scrambling over each other, pulling each other down, backbiting, calling each other names, faulting each other's politics, and so on. It is all such bullshit. It has nothing whatever to do with poetry. The unspoken notion here is that one can knock a man's <u>work</u> if his politics, his ideology, his married life, his life situation, are not what the current Greenwich Village status quo is. Nonsense. A man does the work that he must do, and the world can just damn well reckon with it. That's all. The poetic scene now is one very much like advertising: that is, one deliberately writes poems in view of a predictable audience reaction. I would not do this for one million dollars. The poetry I write is exactly what I would write if nobody ever saw it; after all, I did write it for years, and no one <u>did</u> see it. I will go my way despite the opposition of any othodoxy at all; whoever reads my work or discusses it is just going to have to reckon with that, because that is the way it is going to be.

Again, thank you very much indeed for your letter and for your—rather curious—vote of confidence. If you read the poems and like them, close your ears to the Village gossip and to the people, "academic and otherwise", with whom you've been arguing about it. Poetry is poetry, and it is rare enough at any time. If I have written any that is genuine it has not been written to a formula. That is the main thing to remember. Let the Devil take the hindmost, but a man must say, not what people want him to say, but what he wishes to say, and, in the end, <u>must</u> say. I don't mean to turn this into a lecture or seminar on Integrity, but simply to respond in kind to your very honest and sincere communication. It was very kind of you to write as you have done, and, as I say, I hope the fellowship will be forthcoming.

Again, thanks.

Sincerely yours,
James Dickey

JD/fw

TO: JOHN UNTERECKER[89]

CC, 2 pp; Emory

4620 Lelia's Court
Lake Katherine
Columbia, S.C. 29206
September 16, 1969

Dear Mr. Unterecker:

I hope you will pardon the intrusion of a stranger; I understand how time consuming not only writing letters but reading letters is. But I am pleased to trust that you will permit me to make a few comments on your recent biography of Hart Crane, which I have just completed after literally weeks of reading. If the reading takes this long, how long must the writing have taken? You say ten years, but surely more than that, even, is involved. I will just say that I was absolutely enraptured by the book, and hope to read it many times during the next years. I have not been so caught up in a poet's—or a human being's—life since my initial fascination with John Keates. Crane was a marvelous, that is to say miraculous, human being. I had never had such a sense of this until I read your book, where it is documented and completed. I doubt very much if there will ever be any need for there to be another biography of Crane, no matter what new evidence comes to light. Surely such a work as yours is the ultimate kind of devotion in literary matters, as in human matters generally, and I wanted to tell you that I for one am enormously grateful for it. My own life, in some ways so much like Crane's and in some others utterly unlike it, is uncommonly enriched and broadened by the enormous and intelligent work that you have done. Again thanks.

I happened to glance through a number of reviews of the book, and settled finally with an almost absolute anger on Louis Simpson's review in, I believe, one of the Chicago papers.[90] Surely this is a spectacular low in the reviewing of biographies. Simpson, himself a very mediocre poet, displays the almost inevitability present characteristic of condescension to his betters, and does it in an infuriatingly smug way, talking about the "confusion" of Crane's ideas, and so on. Surely all one has to do is to read through the letters and statements about poetry of that enormously gifted and original-minded man to see how thin and how altogether ordinary Simpson's mind is. If I were given to literary controversy, I would surely call Simpson's hand on this; it would be very easy to make a public fool of him. But I thought that you, personally, would rather have this letter, and so I am writing it. Again, I know your time is valuable, and I know that you have other projects in the works. I surely do hope you do, anyway. But I thought I should record these sentiments and send them along to you, for whatever they may be worth.

Please accept my heartiest congratulations on your great book, surely along with Allan Seager's recent book on Roethke—the most significant rehearsals of a poet's life and time that we have ever had in this country.

I hope you will remember me to Fred Dupee, in my opinion a very great critic. I hope to meet you both the next time I'm in New York.

I remain,

Sincerely yours,
James Dickey

JD/fw

TO: PAUL MASON[91]

CC, 1 p; Emory

4620 Lelia's Court
Lake Katherine
Columbia, S.C. 29206
October 15, 1969

Dear Paul Mason:

Well, that is a wonderful letter. I'm glad that one of the <u>original</u> Buckhead boys saw the poem,[92] and am doubly glad that he took the trouble to write. Yes, it's true, my brother in Atlanta tells me that, that Wender and Roberts are finally closing up at Buckhead and moving out into one of those new chromium edifices somewhere around but not in Buckhead.[93] But that is all right, I guess, because it has to be. As the poem says, one can go back only in memory.

The Tom Dickey you went to Peacock School with is my brother, that I mentioned in the previous paragraph. Ed Dickey I have heard of but don't know; it seems to me he spells his name a different way, and consequently isn't any kin to me.

As to the other things, Tyree's Pool Hall was really Red Dorough's. Red, I hear, has since made a million dollars in real estate in and around Buckhead, which is al right, I guess, but there's no reason to close up the pool room, is there? As a matter of fact, where Red's old pool room was, there <u>is</u> a shoe store, though I forget the name of it. But the main thing, as I see it, is the <u>feeling</u> of the thing, and you have certainly persuaded me that I have got through to at least one nostalgic hometowner. And I thank you very much for taking the trouble to communicate. If you want to do us all a favor—and I include poetry in this "us"—take the time to dash off a note to the editor of the <u>Atlantic</u>, Robert Manning, telling him what you told me. They are great believers in letters to the editor at the <u>Atlantic</u>, and they will probably print what you write, as well as considering, as I would very much like them to do, featuring more poems in prominent position in their magazine.[94] The editor is hoping for a big response to this particular one, and it would please him very much if the poem were to get one, as well as pleasing me personally very much, and making more such ventures possible in the future. But all this shall be as you wish.

Meanwhile, thank you again for your very kind letter. I hope to meet you again face to face one day, and tell you this, looking you right in the eyes, as all such things should be done.

Sincerely yours,
James Dickey

JD/fw

TO: ROBERT LOWELL

TLS, 1 p; Harvard

4620 Lelia's Court
Lake Katherine
Columbia, S.C. 29206
October 29, 1969

Dear Cal:

Thank you very much for the card; it is very gracious of you to submit to such as this, but who knows what posterity may make of it?.[95] Since <u>Encyclopedia Britannica</u> is sending a whole crew of technicians, producers, and so on with me, I can assure you that we won't have to stand or sit around any studio while the really <u>important</u> things like commercials and quiz shows are going on. Believe me, I know what you mean when you tell me how death-promoting such occasions are. This won't be anything like that at all; probably won't take over an hour, while you and I just sit around and get everything straightened out: everything, that is, like Love, Fate, Poetry, Time, Art, and the rest of those things. The main point, though, is to get together again. We see each other about every three or four or five years, and if enough of such time periods add up, then it is all gone, and where did it go?. At least we can have a little time sitting around talking under the lights for whatever posterity may make of it, and then maybe have dinner, or a drink, or something which we agree would be nice. But believe me, I <u>do</u> look forward to seeing you once more under these or indeed any other circumstances. I'll let you know more of exact times and schedules when <u>Encyclopedia</u> lets <u>me</u> know more. Meanwhile, my best to you and Elizabeth, and to your little girl.

All best,
Jim D.

JD/fw

TO: E. LEWIS KING

TLS, 3 pp; E. Lewis King

4620 Lelia's Court
Lake Katherine
Columbia, S.C. 29206
November 1, 1969

Dear Lou:

Please forgive me for waiting so long to write, and to thank you for the maps that you have been kind enough to send along; they are an enormous help in some writing that I am doing. Meanwhile, the book, Deliverance, is done, and it is really good. Your help on it has been absolutely beyond praise, and it is quite safe for me to say that the book never would have been written at all if it were not for you. Not only did you take me up into that country canoeing, but I have used a good many things you have told me, as well, and it seems to me that such incidents and conversations as I have selected were made exclusively for this book. Anyway, the novel will appear, officially, the 23rd of March; I am reading proof on it now. Part of it will run in Atlantic Monthly in a couple of months, so you can get a preliminary look at it then, if you like. It is dedicated to you and Al, and I hope this pleases you as much as it does me.

There is an enormous pre-publication excitement about the thing, my agent tells me, the editor at Atlantic tells me, and all my editors at Houghton Mifflin tell me, too. The publisher is blowing just about his whole spring advertising budget on the book, and he hopes that it will make all of us rich. The initial printing is 25,000 copies, and they expect those to be gone within just a few days after the book appears. Frankly, this is a very strange situation for me, who have been scratching around for the nickels and dimes that poetry affords for so long. The novel-publishing business is nothing like that, I can assure you very quickly. All the hullabaloo, all the promotional stuff, all the cocktail parties and celebrations and so on that are coming up are likely to do me in, but I'm looking forward to the whole shebang, never having, as Huck Finn says, been anywhere like that before. I hope very much that you and Al can get in on some of this. Anyway, I'll keep you posted.

More news. Steve McQueen wants to do it as a movie, but so does Warner Brothers, and they are now battling it out over who is going to pay me the most for it.[96] Burt Lancaster also wants it, particularly since my agent was wily or crazy enough to tell him that the part of the fictional Lewis was written with him in mind, which we know has not a grain of truth in it. Anyway, Lancaster may wind up playing the part, so you can take your family to the movies and tell them that

that guy thinks he's Burt Lancaster, but he's really me. The character is a very strong one, the center of the motivating action of the book, and though you will recognize some things that you and I have talked about, you will see that the character is not really based on you at all, but on somebody who is, oddly enough, much more like Lancaster than he is like you. Al, so far as one of the other characters representing him, has all but disappeared, and in his place is a figure who is kind of like Dave Sanders,[97] or a combination of Dave Sanders and Robert Goulet. The fourth man I just made up out of various Driving Club types that I have known in the past, as well as a few folks in the Coca-cola Company and the ad business there in Atlanta.

What I propose to do about your suggestions in your last letter is this: when the contract for the movie, either with Lancaster or with Steve McQueen or with Warner Brothers, is made up, I propose to have you hired as a consultant.[98] The movie people will be very happy to do this, since they are not likely to get a better one, nor one who knows the country around here any better. Of course, production is yet a good ways off, but it is well to plan for these things, so do let me know whether or not you would be interested in doing this, or whether you would have time for it or not. I think it would be an awful lot of fun. Though I wrote a couple of documentaries while I was on the west coast,[99] I have never worked on a real movie: that is, one with characters who speak dialogue, with a plot, with "action, suspense, drama," and all that business. This story has got all those things, and you'll allow, and it would be interesting to try to translate these things to the screen in that particular country. So, let me know what you think.

I'll be in and around Atlanta—actually, Clarkston—on the 19th of November, and, though I am going to be in rather a hurry, I hope we can at least have a drink or something together. Speaking of movies, Encyclopedia Britannica is doing a movie on me, for some reason, and the whole crew—producers, cameramen, technicians, and whatever else it takes—will be with me in Clarkston, so you see the whole business is going to be rather hectic.

Where all this is going to lead, or end, I have no idea whatever, but he who rides a tiger fears to dismount, and I guess I'm in some such situation. Anyway, though wearing, life is an awful lot of fun right now, and the more fun it is, the more ways I see to make it fun. I hope you and Al will be able to get in on these good times.

I went hunting up in the Virginia-West Virginia mountains last week, and had a great, great hunt, though I came back, as usual, without any head or hides. I almost got a shot, though. It was at dawn, and I was going through a little field of pine trees toward the highest mountain in the area, and there was a deer across the clearing from me about 55 or 60 yards away. I managed to get up around 50 yards from him, and was going to take a shot from there rather than not get a shot at all, but when I got back to about half way to full draw, he took off. But, hopefully, there'll be next year, and some other years, too, I hope. Anyway, I couldn't have had any better time if I had killed a whole battalion of deer. I have a good friend who lives in Alexandria, and he owns a little shack in the mountains, which is our base of operations. He is crazy about bow hunting, and scouts out the area for weeks before deer season opens. Maybe next year you could go up there with me, if you would like. My friend, whose name is Terry Miller, would be delighted to have you, I have no doubt at all. It really is beautiful country, and there are always deer around there. We always see ten or fifteen, and one of these days we're going to bring something down.

Well, I won't go on and on, but will just close now and get this in the mail. As soon as I have bound proofs of the novel, I'll send a copy along to you, and one to Al.

All yours,
James Dickey

JD/fw

TO: PETER DAVISON[100]

CC, 2 pp; Emory

4620 Lelia's Court
Lake Katherine
Columbia, S.C. 29206
November 4, 1969

Dear Peter:

Of <u>course</u> I will give you a statement for your book. I want it to be a good one, and so will work on it for a couple of days, just as I would on a poem. After all, anything that one writes, and that is important, should be done properly. I have made a few public statements for poets before, some of which I have regretted; I see these, especially the latter, all the time. But this must be something over and beyond what I have done for other people, for they are not as good as you are. I won't go on and on, but will simply tell you that I agree with you entirely that <u>Pretending to be Asleep</u>[101] is the best thing that you have done. It is not only that, but <u>promises</u> a great deal beyond what even you have yet conceived of doing. The event of such a book must be tremendously exciting for you. There is no better feeling for a writer, or for a human being, than to be good at what he has chosen to do as his life's work, and to know, from looking at what he has done to date, that he is going to be a whole lot better. And, yes, better than that too, even.

As to what you say of my novel, I will only record that I'm very happy that you like the book. I have never written prose fiction before, and may not write any after this, though I might, even so. Anyway, I'm delighted that you think the book goes well. I have worked on it a long time, and the hardest work of all was to bring down the stylistic fireworks to what I would like to think of as a kind of steady and believable glow. At the beginning, the style was kind of like Updike or Agee or somebody. It took me a long time to realize that stylistic hijinks were the last thing in the world that the book needed. It had to be, first of all, believable, and in a way that would seem plausible for my protagonist to have come up with: a kind of personal account by an intelligent—fairly intelligent, anyway—guy who is a little different from what he thinks he is. I do think the book is exciting, and I am delighted that <u>Atlantic</u> is going to print a section from it. My agent tells me that there will have to be some rearranging of your format in order to be able to include this part of <u>Deliverance</u> in one of your issues before the book is published in March. I hope very much that such rearrangement will work no hardship on you and Bob,[102] and the magazine.

But do know, Peter, that your letter is a marvelous shot in the arm to one working in a medium strange to him. Strange, but exciting. And, since you wrote, even more exciting.

I will be in Boston around the 19th and 20th of November. I hope very much that you and Bob will be available for at least a drink. And could you get Ed Sissman[103] on this little get together, too? I'd like that.

All yours,
James Dickey

JD/fw

TO: JOY C. BEAUDRY[104]

CC, 1 p; Emory

4620 Lelia's Court
Lake Katherine
Columbia, S.C. 29206
November 5, 1969

Dear Miss Beaudry:

Well, that is quite a letter. The most amazing one that has ever descended to me from out of the blue. It is very kind indeed of you to share your interest and some of your work with me, and it is also very kind of you to say the things about my own work that you do say. Yes, I believe that there are certain sensibilities that are like each other, and these should become known to one another, either personally, through poetry, or through some other means that is the best kind of communication between those particular people.

You mention Ezra Pound and St. Elizabeth's, and I remember both very well. I had lunch in New York with Pound about three or four months ago, and we talked a little about the old days at St. Elizabeth's when I used to go out to see him on Sunday afternoon, during visitor's hours. He has sadly deteriorated; I have never spent such a depressing lunch hour with anyone in my life. There is not much to the old man any more, though he is struggling to finish the cantos and has only two or three more to go. I hope he makes it; he has been working on them for such a long time and there are so many good things in them.

I am not at all sure I know what you mean by advice. I think, from your letter, that you love poetry very much, and I think probably that you will be able to write it well when you have worked at it longer. The first little four-line thing you sent me about the grasshopper is rather good, but the other one is awful. The thing to do is to encourage the first vein and discourage the other. The main thing about writing poetry, at your stage of things, is to write a very great deal, throw a wide net, experiment in all kinds of ways, and gradually out of all this work consolidate a style that is like no other, and which, after a great deal of labor and disappointment, can legitimately be called your own. You are a long way from this yet, but the search for one's own style is the most exciting thing that a creative artist can undergo. I hope you make it; I believe you will. Let me hear from you further whenever you have the inclination.

Sincerely yours,
James Dickey

JD/fw

TO: ROBERT LOWELL

TLS, 1 p; Harvard

4620 Lelia's Court
Lake Katherine
Columbia, S.C. 29206
December 10, 1969

Dear Cal:

I cannot even begin to tell you what a great day it was for me. I don't much care about the movie, nor the movie folks, one way or the other; the main thing was that we had a chance to sit down and talk, and drink, and the rest. I wouldn't have missed it for anything, believe me. Though I haven't time for a long letter now, I just wanted to send this and let you know how I felt. I have seldom in my life had such a damn good time, such a day full of fun—yes, really—nor one about which I felt and feel so good. Frank O'Conner[105] once told me that, though he really didn't like Yeats very much, he always left the old man "feeling like a million dollars." It surely must be obvious to you that I like you very much indeed: like you, like your wife, like your little girl—what I've seen of her—like your apartment[106] and your writing and the way you go about the business of living. The camera crew sensed all this, for they commented on your hospitality and graciousness at a good deal of length. Even so, they had nothing like as close an apprehension of these things as I did. Again, thanks. I won't go on and on, but will conclude simply by saying it was good lived time—good human time, and how much of that do we get?

Maxine sends love, and so do I. I hope you won't have to edit my papers, and all that melancholy job, but it is a source of great consolation to me that you will do it if you have to.[107] Believe me, I'm grateful.

All yours,
James Dickey

JD/fw

TO: MRS. ELLIE SCOTT[108]

TLS, 1 p; Brown University

Lelia's Court
Lake Katherine
Columbia, S.C. 29206
December 15, 1969

Dear Mrs. Scott:

Through Scott Donaldson,[109] I have received Win's Exiles and Fabrications,[110] and I wish to thank you for your kindness in sending the book to me. As I did not make, I am afraid, sufficiently clear to him during his life, I was a great admirer of Win's, and my only consolation in this regard is that I reviewed The Dark Sister very favorably,[111] and received a very handsome letter from Win in response. We corresponded a little after that, but, as such things almost inevitably do, the correspondence dwindled away and then became silent. So—I thank you very much for sending me Win's only prose book. I have been reading it, and finding a very great deal to admire. Win was the kind of poet and man who does not fool himself about his own work, and this shows in every line that he wrote whether in verse or in prose. Webster Schott,[112] who evidently knew you and Win very well, tells me that Win was discouraged at the end of his life. I am sorry to hear that, for he need not have been. I knew the late Theodore Roethke during the last couple of years, and he was very much the same way. I don't know exactly what I could do or say now, though, except to thank you very much for being so kind as to send along Win's book to me. I shall prize it highly, and for the rest of my life.

I am helping Scott Donaldson—or at least I hope I am helping a little bit—on his book.[113] If there is anything that you want to know from me, in the way of opinions, allegiances, and so on, please let me know. I will do what I can to honor the work and the <u>being</u> of a fine human creature, a man of sensitivity, dedication, and talent.

And could you tell me if there will be any further publication of Win's notebooks? Those reproduced in <u>A Dirty Hand</u>[114] not only have whetted my appetite for more—a great deal more—of the same, but have prompted me to embark on a similar enterprise.[115] And writers who are as jealous of their time as I am do not take on new writing tasks either willingly or easily. So you see what the man has done to me! And <u>for</u> me!

My best wishes to you. Yes, indeed.

All yours,
James Dickey

JD/fw

TO: HIRAM HAYDN[116]

CC, 1 p; Emory

4620 Lelia's Court
Lake Katherine
Columbia, S.C. 29206
December 19, 1969

Dear Hiram:

You asked me my opinion as to the most neglected book published in the last quarter of a century, and I would nominate Crawford Power's <u>The Encounter</u>,[117] a novel about a priest, his dreams—that is literal <u>dreams</u>—and his human commitments, and seems to me to be the best and most mysterious and compelling statement of the strange ways in which the Lord works—or doesn't work—that I know. It is a moving and original book.

It was good to see you up at the Vineyard last summer. Let me know if there's anything else you'd like me to do for <u>The American Scholar</u>, and I will attempt to comply, though this is going to be a very busy spring, what with four books due to appear.

By the way, with your connections with Phi Beta Kappa, could you tell me where to get another key? I seem to have mislaid mine, and need one to impress my students down here. Any information you could give would be much appreciated.

Meanwhile,

Sincerely yours,
James Dickey

JD/fw

TO: PETER F. NEUMEYER[118]

CC, 2 pp; Emory

4620 Lelia's Court
Lake Katherine
Columbia, S.C. 29206
March 16, 1970

Dear Peter:

Thank you very, very much for your letter of March 1st. It has been a long time since I have had a letter from another writer which seemed to me to be so life-giving. Your remarks about Rilke are very interesting, and help me to understand that strange poet better than I had previously been able to do. He seems to have such a strong identification with other forms of life—even with inanimate matter—that it is often difficult for a person like myself, who is always so conscious of his <u>own</u> identity to understand exactly what is going on. I guess the difference between his attitude and mine is that we <u>merge</u> with things differently. He seems to be able to <u>become</u> the other thing, while I am very conscious of the fact that <u>I am also involved in the merging</u>, and that I am giving something to the thing I am merging with as well as getting something back from it. Please excuse all this mysterious and cloudy talk; I can only hope that you have at least some idea of what I am talking about.

Your reference to Edwin Muir[119] is nothing less than uncanny. Yes indeed, I <u>do</u> know his work, and if there has been any one person I would acknowledge as being an influence on my own work, it would be him. I don't have anything like his diction, or his mythic concerns, but there is something about the way the man <u>takes</u> the world that I am very sympathetic toward. It is too bad that Muir did not have a great gift of phrase, for his <u>situations</u> are fascinating, even if his style is not. He is a very great man to me; I wish I could have known him. But, in a way, I guess I do, through his poems. That is the only real way of knowing, anyway.

I can't make this the long letter I would like to, for I must get on yet another airplane. The real purpose of <u>this</u> communication, though, is to invite you to a party in New York on the 23rd of this month, when my novel, <u>Deliverance</u>, is coming out. If you can make it into the city, the party will be from five to seven at the St. Regis Hotel. I hope very much you can come in, for I would love to see you. Anyway, let me know if you can come, and I will be guided by what you tell me.

About Louis Simpson, I just don't know. I think he is a man of talent—that is, of <u>some</u> talent—but these wild pronouncements he makes simply seem to me to indicate that he is incapable of reviewing judiciously or fairly. I saw a review of his about John Unterecker's <u>Biography of Hart Crane</u> which was simply appalling. It was not so much that it was appallingly bad, which it certainly was, but that it was appallingly <u>arrogant</u> in its badness. When a man of Simpson's ordinariness of mind talks about Crane and his supposed inability to get his ideas straight, and so on, one simply wants to kick Simpson's ass. Crane, though uneducated by university standards or other ordinary standards, had one of the most vivid, incisive, volatile and above all <u>original</u> minds that have ever been concerned with poetry. I cannot see how anyone, even Simpson, could fail to see this. But a kind of planned obtuseness seems to be becoming more and more part of his critical "equipment" and it will simply result in his being laughed at by anyone who takes the time and trouble to <u>read</u> the things that Louis purports to review. I won't go on and on, for I consider Simpson a friend of mine. It is simply disheartening to see him do these things to other writers, but more importantly to himself. I expect he knows pretty much how I feel about all this, so I don't think it will be necessary for you to tell him. I expect also, that you are as dismayed as I am.

But, to come back to happier things, please <u>do</u> come into the city, and to the party, if you possibly can. And if you can make it, make your presence known to me. I would love to see you, I can tell you.

Thanks so much for your long, detailed letter. It is moving, and, to me, permanent.

Sincerely,
James Dickey

JD/fw

TO: EDGAR K. SHELDON[120]

CC, 2 pp; Emory

4620 Lelia's Court
Lake Katherine
Columbia, S.C. 29206
March 19, 1970

Dear Mr. Sheldon:

Here, after a good deal of deliberation, is my final judging. In the main I found the poems not very good, and was easily able to eliminate about half of them. Then the judging became more difficult, because there was a great deal of difference in quality between the first ten and the other, eliminated ones. I had a difficult time deciding between my favorites, for all these ten poems are good in different ways; yes, and <u>very</u> good. I finally came out with the rating sheet as you see it. In case you need a kind of check on my choices, I list them herewith:

1. Pilot
2. Birds
3. By Ourselves
4. A Second Coming
5. Always in a Soft Voice
6. The Aviator
7. untitled (Blind tired I sat down to rest)
8. Raymond's Letter
9. The Politics of Water in Arizona
10. Gorgo Speaks

I enjoyed doing this very much, though I hate to be associated on <u>any</u> project with Kenneth Rexroth, who is as detestable person as I have ever known or seen in my life. I was at the National Book Awards a couple of weeks ago when he rose up and called Robert Lowell a fascist. Shortly thereafter, when the ceremonies were over and everyone was standing around talking, he made a point of coming up to me and calling me a Nazi. Why he does this kind of thing I have no notion whatever, but he did, and I damn near threw him down the stairs. Wish I had.

Anyway, let me know if there is anything else I need to do in connection with my function on your committee. And please <u>do</u> let me know how the contest comes out, and who, finally, wins.

Thank you very much indeed for the comments that you are kind enough to make about my work. The new collection of poetry[121] is, I think, about the most interesting collection I have done, though a good deal different from other books of mine. Let me know what you think of it when you have a chance to read it. Also, I have a novel out, called <u>Deliverance</u>, that you also might like to read. I think it is pretty good, though I suppose it shows the regular defects of the first-novelist's work. But Balzac says somewhere that the main thing in the novel is not the psychological nuance, but that the work should possess a force that carries all before it. I persuade myself that <u>Deliverance</u> has that, and that, I believe, is enough. Or at least it is as much as I can hope for.

My best to you, sir, to Webster Schott, and to the others out there I hope to meet.

All yours,
James Dickey

JD/fw
enclosure

TO: PETER F. NEUMEYER

CC, 2 pp; Emory

4620 Lelia's Court
Lake Katherine
Columbia, S.C. 29206
April 10, 1970

Dear Peter:

Thank you very much indeed for your two good letters, and please forgive me for waiting so long to answer, but I have been traveling, and only just now got back to Columbia, and found your letters here. The long one would take so long to answer that I despair of ever doing so. I can answer a couple of your questions very briefly, if you like.

Yes, I like Christopher Smart very much, and a few years ago wrote an essay on him for <u>Oscar Williams Last Anthology, Master Poems of the English Language</u>.[122] You might like to see what I have to say there, though I understand a couple of the factual points are mistaken.

I don't know what to think about Louis Simpson. His work is not getting any better, and he seems to be putting most of himself into those ill-conceived critical essays. But he is not going to be an important writer, I am quite sure.

No, I have never written anything of Basil Bunting, though I have read about everything of his. He is an interesting writer, in rather a minor way, obviously an off-shoot of Pound: a little more coherent, but very Poundian withall. I think those long things of his are probably the best, though a few shorter ones are very good as well. He has a kind of steely hardness I like, and is surely not at all sentimental. I'm very happy you liked Allan Seager's book on Roethke. The reason for my article[123] was that I knew Allan very well toward the end of his life, and I saw what Beatrice Roethke put him through on the biography that she herself had commissioned. She wanted to slant the biography <u>her</u> way, and Allan, with his fine integrity and thoroughness and honesty would not have it so. He spent the last years of his life, bedridden with cancer of the lungs, trying to work out a way to write the book he wanted to write and still get it by Beatrice Roethke, who had control of the material, and of the issuance of the book. It was a terribly sad story, but Allan came out of it looking good. Only he was dead.

I'm sorry I can't make this the long letter I'd like to: one to match yours in length and enthusiasm, though not in quality, but I can't. I am very hard pressed with travel these days, mainly in connection with the promotion of my novel, <u>Deliverance</u>, now on the best seller lists and moving up, I am told, very rapidly.[124] This noveleering is a strange business, particularly to one who has been publishing in the literary quarterlies for twenty years at fifty cents a line. It's a whole new ball game, as they say, but I must play in it as hard and as well as I can, for it promises to make my family well off—even rich—for the rest of our lives; yes, and for my children's lives, too. At least, no one will want, if we do the thing right.

So I must travel, appear on TV and radio shows, sign books, and so on. I hope you'll understand this, for, though in a way it is none of my doing, in another way it is, and I must go where it bids me go. All this will be over in a couple of months, and I will have more time to read, and above all, to write. I have just been asked to deliver the Phi Beta Kappa poem at Harvard on June 9th,[125] and this is one thing I plan to do which has nothing whatever to do with novel writing, autograph parties, and so on. As you know, it is the same occasion on which Emerson delivered his <u>American Scholar Address</u>, and, though I may not be in quite that league, I hope to do my best, and something entirely different from what Emerson or any of the others has done.

I hope you will, though, continue to write, for yours are by far the best letters I get. Only, they are so thorough and long, that I worry a little about your taking off too much time from your own work, your criticism and scholarship, and so on. But, if you want to write such letters, I am only too happy to have them. However this turns out to be, it shall be as you wish.

My very best to you, as always. Hang in there!

All yours,
James Dickey

JD/fw

TO: JONATHAN WILLIAMS

TLS, 2 pp; SUNY Buffalo

4620 Lelia's Court
Lake Katherine
Columbia, S.C. 29206
April 13, 1970

Dear Jon:

Thank you very much for your letter; it is always, and I <u>mean</u> always, good to hear from you, and to find out what part of the world you are currently in.

I don't, in all honesty, <u>want</u> to say anything about Dahlberg,[126] because the more I read him the more he palls on me, and if I said something nice about him, it would not be something I really felt, but would be a thing I did because of my regard for you. That is not, I think, quite what one wants to do. If it were someone I thought more of, both as a writer and as a man, I would be only too happy to comply. The trouble is, though, that I once intervened to get Dahlberg's <u>Aphorisms</u> published after the University of Minnesota Press turned it down. Horizon finally brought the <u>Aphorisms</u> out in a very handsome book, and I was very glad that things turned out this way, for he seemed to me to be a desperate and relatively deserving old fellow.[127] The aftermath of this was that I was inundated with letters from Dahlberg, then at the University of Missouri at Kansas City, or some place like that, giving me the moral imperative that I <u>must</u> review the book, promote it, proselytize for it, and in general do all the things as a reviewer and a literary man that he sees as only venality in others. This seemed to me to be the worst kind of hypocrisy, and I told him so, flatly. I have since heard nothing else from him, and all his talk about friendship, the meeting of the minds, and so on, disappeared into very thin air indeed.

This did not really piss me off as much as some other things that have happened, but it surely did not predispose me in favor of Dahlberg or his writings. I don't refuse to comply with your request because of this, but because his conduct with me simply set me free of attempting to see things in the work, because of good will, that I did not actually see. I don't like the man's stuff; it seems to me to be phony-Old Testament in a particularly irritating way. He says something good every now and then, as any writer of a modicum of intelligence must if he keeps at it, but the content of his work is not, as far as I'm concerned, of sufficient value to bother with more than once every couple of years. I liked a few of the things he had to say in the exchange of letters with Herbert Read, but that's about all I can honestly say I ever enjoyed or learned from in his work.[128]

Basil Bunting means a good deal to me; another neglected writer. He and I had an exchange of a few letters about fourteen or fifteen years ago when I first began working in advertising, and I remember some of the things he had to say with a very great deal of affection and honor.[129]

You asked about the novel. It is called <u>Deliverance</u>, and this week it is seventh on the best seller list. Next week it will be fourth and then, the computers tell us, will be first for something the computers coyly refer to as "an indefinite period." All this is very strange to someone who is use to counting his literary earnings at the rate of fifty cents a line, doled out on that basis from <u>The Kenyon Review</u>. But it is very nice, even so. Warner Brothers are going to do it as a movie. I am writing the screenplay, and Roman Polanski is directing. We will most likely film it around the north Georgia country you and I love so well, so, if you're in the area, come over. We'll probably start shooting next fall, on the Chatooga River, the Toccoa River, maybe the Coosawattee, a little further west. I told the Hollywood people that it would be fine with me if Polanski directed, but don't ask me to go to any parties at <u>that</u> guy's house![130]

I much enjoyed your <u>Collected Poems</u>.[131] How has the press been? I have just sent your name in to <u>Esquire Magazine</u> as one of my favorite writers. They asked me; I told them.[132]

My very best to you, and my best to Bunting and the others I either know or admire.

All yours,
Jim

JD/fw

P.S. At the National Book Awards your friend—or at least acquaintance—Kenneth Rexroth called Robert Lowell a fascist and me a Nazi within about fifteen minutes of each allegation. How's that for getting two birds with one very sharp stone! I damn near threw the old paranoiac down stairs, and wish now that I had done just that. What a total ass!

Again, please do keep in touch. And I'll see you when you get back here.[133]

TO: FREDERICK EXLEY[134]

CC, 1 p; Emory

4620 Lelia's Court
Lake Katherine
Columbia, S.C. 29206
April 13, 1970

Dear Exley:

Thank you very much for your very welcome letter. It is good to have word of you. The last time I heard from you, you were somewhere in Florida, and I have no means whatever of knowing where you are disporting yourself these days. Where on Earth is Antwerp, N.Y., anyway? Thanks also for your condolences on the death of my uncle, Ervin Dickey, but he was an awfully old man, very senile, his mind gone, his eyesight almost gone, and all the other grim, factual things that happen when you get past a certain human limit of time. Still, it is death, and we must pay attention.

I'm very happy you like the quote I gave you for your paperback.[135] I hope it sells a million copies. I also hear that Warner Brothers is going to do it as a movie. They are the same people who are doing Deliverance, and that fact gives me an odd pleasure. They both should be awfully good movies. Are you writing the screenplay?[136]

As to Deliverance, what is happening to it dazes and benumbs me. As of this Sunday, the 12th, it is seventh on the best seller list, and next Sunday will be fourth. It is substantially ahead of Portnoy's Complaint[137] at the same period, and this is frightening indeed. The computers tell us that it will be first on the list in about three weeks, and this is queer, though naturally I am very happy about it. The critics have been very kind, and most of them even seem to know something of what I think I am talking about, so that is good, too, I guess.

As to your feeling that I display a distaste or contempt for humanity, I am not quite sure that this is so, though indeed it may be. The point is that the whole novel deals with both the worst and the best in men, or very nearly, and I may have emphasized the worst more than the other; I don't know. I intended to show a man who, in defending his own life and the lives of people who depend on him, becomes both a hero and a criminal: intended to show, in fact, that there is no real line of demarcation between these two types, some or even most of the time.

I must close now, and get this in the mail. Please keep in contact, and maybe we will have a chance to get together later on, in New York, Columbia, or, God willing, maybe even in Antwerp.

All yours,
James Dickey

JD/fw

TO: HAYDEN CARRUTH[138]

TLS, 1 p; University of Vermont

4620 Lelia's Court
Lake Katherine
Columbia, S.C. 29206
May 4, 1970

Dear Hayden:

Very good to hear from you again, and to have the anthology that you have edited.[139] No, I don't have any plans to come up to Crow's Mark at Johnson, Vermont, although I must admit that the locale sounds fascinating, judging from the names. I hope you are well up there, and are doing your thing, which is one of the best things going on in the literary scene. I always look for your poems, and I know of no better literary criticism being written anywhere. I thought <u>Appendix A</u> was an awfully good book, and the book on Camus is one of my favorite books of its kind, but, since there aren't any other books of its kind, it has to be an <u>especial</u> favorite.[140]

Now let me come to the point about your anthology. I think it surely should be a commercial success, despite the enormous number of anthologies being published these days. You must understand, however, that I deplore the inclusion of so many rotten poets, most of them of the Ginsberg-Ferlinghetti ilk. I cannot for the life of me see why a man of your discrimination feels called upon to include these people who, no matter what their final place is in history, will find it in the history of sociology rather than poetry. Therefore, I must say that I cannot in all good conscience give you a quotation which embodies my feelings about your anthology, and have these feelings be entirely favorable. This is painful to me, as it must be to you. And I will add one further thing. I think so highly of you that I will give you a quotation if you ask for it under these circumstances. That is, if you ask me for a quotation knowing that I have serious and grave misgivings about your anthology, I will make up something favorable. Doubtless this is not the first time such has gone on. But it is certainly the first time that <u>I</u> have offered to do it. Almost all plugs for books come from friends or acquaintances of the authors or the anthologists. There is nothing new in this, and doubtless almost all of the opinions expressed on book jackets and in publicity quotes are to some extent falsifications of the writer's true feelings. Myself, I place my regard for a man and his work above any quoted opinion of mine. As I say, then, if you still want a quotation from me, knowing how I feel about your book, I will give you one. If you <u>want</u> it, ask me, and don't draw back under some kind of false feelings—or true feelings—of integrity. My own integrity is quite well satisfied by my unburdening myself to you in this manner. But I did think I should let you know how I feel before giving you the quote. So let me hear from you on this. Perhaps I am making too much of the whole thing, but for some reason I thought I should tell you all this.[141]

As for quotations on your own work—either in poetry or in criticism—I have no qualifications at all, of any kind.

The acquaintance of mine that you mention is, I think, not a man named Philip Horton, but a young politically-minded guy from Atlanta named Jerry Horton. If his name indeed was Philip Horton, I don't know him; but if it was Jerry Horton I quite agree that he is an extraordinary young fellow. Jerry Horton is very bright, and is crazy about politics and poetry. The last time I saw him he was taking on a good deal of weight, and already looked like the politician he so desperately wants to become.

Do keep in touch with me, if you like. And let me know what I must do about your anthology.

My very best to you, and to your writings.

All yours,
James Dickey

JD/fw

TO: JAMES WRIGHT

TLS, 2 pp; University of Minnesota

4620 Lelia's Court
Lake Katherine
Columbia, S.C. 29206
May 11, 1970

Dear Jim:

Please forgive my not answering your letter immediately, but I have been doing so much traveling in connection with the promotion of <u>Deliverance</u> that I just haven't been home either to receive mail or to answer it. I'm back, now, for the month of May, and hasten to answer.

First thank you so very much for your letter, and for the things you say about the new poems. If I can run down a copy of the <u>New Yorker</u> where "Root-light" appeared,[142] I will have it Xeroxed for you and send it on. I have about half a new manuscript, and the poem will be in that, whenever it chances to appear. I haven't written any poetry, now, for about eight months or a year, and it feels very strange indeed to do nothing but travel and not write. I have taken the month of May off, for I must somehow contrive to write the Phi Beta Kappa poem for Commencement at Harvard next month. I am told that this is the same occasion on which Emerson delivered the American Scholar Address, which, you may imagine, filled me with a sense of total inadequacy! Nevertheless, I am pushing ahead with what I think is a rather interesting idea, whether or not I can bring it off. This is to take a man's entire lifework—in this case, Trumbull Stickney, an old Harvard man, minor poet and a corpse at the age of twenty nine—and go through it laboriously time after time, picking out some lines that have meant a great deal to me personally. Then we take these lines and phrases and write a poem out of them illustrative of what the phrases evoke in <u>me</u>, personally. The whole question of poetic imagery is so fascinating that I hope to get some of this fascination into the poem. For example, when I say "tree" there will flash up in the mind's eye of anyone within earshot a different tree for each person. When Stickney says "the burning season shone" you and I are going to see different burning seasons, and different shinings. So the poem is actually going to be about Stickney's imagery's effect on me, and therefore will be about poetry, and therefore will be about my life more than about Stickney's life. All this may sound rather vague at this stage, but it is yielding some rather interesting stuff, I think. I hope I can get it done by June 9th, which is the target date for Harvard graduation, and probably for a huge riot in which poets will be stoned to death like St. Stephen—or not like St. Stephen.

Also, the Apollo Eleven boys want me to come up to New York and read at a program for them on the 1st of June, which I plan to do.[143] I will try to contrive to spend a couple of days in New York, and maybe you and Annie[144] can go out to dinner together with me. I would sure like that, you can believe.

By the way, I taught your entire lifework yesterday in an hour and a half class, and I got a finer and deeper response to your work than to that of any other poet—English or American, great or small—than I have taught this year. These kids are really crazy about the stuff, I can tell you.

Love to Annie, and to everything surrounding you. Even to Old Bob,[145] who has tried his God-damnedest to make an enemy out of me, but will never succeed. He is a good man with no talent, and he ought to be content with that. He is killing himself trying to be a "great writer and great literary influence." Terribly sad. But I have good memories of Bob, and when can one ever have too many of those?

Love,
Jim D.

JD/fw

TO: CHRISTOPHER T. BUCKLEY[146]

CC, 3 pp; Emory

4620 Lelia's Court
Lake Katherine
Columbia, S.C. 29206
May 13, 1970

Dear Christopher:

Please forgive me for delaying to answer your very welcomed note, but I have been traveling and have only just returned to Columbia, and consequently have just got your letter. I am dismayed to see that the date for your paper is the 14th, but will answer your questions anyway in hope that you may be able to take them up with your instructor, or perhaps use them in some later paper, at another place and another time.

But first let me say I certainly <u>do</u> remember you from Cape Kennedy,[147] and am only sorry that we didn't have more of a chance to talk down there. But there will be lots of other times. I surely do hope so, anyway.

Now let me get to your questions right away.

1. You asked me whether any poems of mine have been written under the influence of mescaline, and I can assure you that none has. My only experience with drugs occurred a few years ago in California, when I was spending a few days with a colony of fanatical folk-guitar players. They were all turning on on various things, and I thought I would give it a try. I tried, I think it was three buttons of peyote, and they affected me for around three or four hours. I didn't much like the experience, and have never repeated it, or anything like it. The trouble with depending on outside agencies, such as stimulants, depressants, and so on, for inspiration, "insight", and so on, is that they destroy the critical faculty of the writer which is his best ally. In other words you think, under the influence of some drug or chemical, that your writing is a great deal better than it is. It requires the cold, analytical, unfoolable inner critic that every writer ought to have, in order to bring the writing up to the level that is sometimes potentially in it. Without this critical faculty, the writing is likely to degenerate into something less than good. Besides, I have found that I like the uncorrected world better than I do the corrected or drug-amended world. As the French writer Gide once said, "Lucidity is my disease." There is nothing so crazy or hallucinatory in drugs as the actual world itself, and there is an added increment, at least to me, in knowing that what I see is <u>real</u>, and not an illusion. It is this reality that I try to write about.

2. As far as I am concerned the modern American poet's task is a good deal like the poet's task at any time and in any culture: to preserve the integrity of the true individual response to experience, against the standardization of the mass-response, the conditioned reflex, as it were. As Auden said somewhere, "Poetry makes nothing happen."[148] That is true, and people who try to use it as propaganda for various causes are doing the cause of the imagination and the integrity of the individual sensibility no good. The poet's job is simply to cultivate his own garden, and to try to discover some real toads among the imaginary leaves.

3. There are several biographies of me around in books like <u>Who's Who</u> and other such places. However, if you have a little more time, you could write to Ken McCormick at Doubleday and Company, my new publisher, located at 277 Park Avenue, and he will be glad to send you any number of fact sheets, photographs, and any and all imaginable kinds of biographical references. If you don't have time to do this, most of the book jackets on my books—or if they're paperback, just on the back of the book—contain thumbnail biographical sketches of a kind.

4. Yes, I suppose <u>Deliverance</u> is the work of a poet, since I <u>am</u> more or less by definition a poet. But I did not want the book to be written in convention-ally "poetic" prose, for the first-person narrator that I chose to tell the story would not think in terms befitting, say, Robert Lowell or any other poet known principally or exclusively <u>as</u> a poet. So what poetry there is in the book must come in in a very subtle way, in small observations and not in long perorations of the more obviously literary kind, the sort of thing that John Updike indulges himself in at great length. If the poetic quality you noticed is part of the novel—and I hope it is—it is not of an <u>obviously</u> poetic sort. This is intentional.

5. As to my favorite poetic theme, I should say that it would have something to do with process: natural process, evolutionary process, process of all sorts. The world was made for me, as it was made for most poets: that is, the world as it existed before man got to messing around with it too much. If you look at any part of the Creation, you will see that the ingenu-ity of it is boundless and matchless. We make intricate machines, and we can go to the moon, but we could not make a grass blade. And if we do manage to make a grass blade, eventually, in a test-tube, it will only be because we're imitating the grass blades that were made without us, made before we came.

I don't intend to get philosophical here, but only to answer your questions as well as may be.

Again, I am terribly sorry that I was not able to get this information to you in time for the deadline of your paper. I hope very much that you will be able to use it in some way, or that it will be valuable or at least useful to you if you can't actually employ it in the composition of a thesis.

Meanwhile, you may be sure that I am very deeply moved by the things you say about <u>Deliverance</u>, and about the poems. I don't know whether or not what your family and I, or, better still, your family and my family, will be able to get together in the near future, but I for one would like that very much. Maybe at some later time this summer, we can all meet for a few days, either in Stamford, or down here in Columbia, or in the Big City where your great father works. Please, when you communicate with him, tell him that I look forward to seeing him any time he can manage it, that I was very sorry I was not able to get in on his public performances down here in Columbia,[149] and that I was very happy indeed to see him for an evening in Camden.[150]

With every good wish, I remain,

James Dickey

JD/fw

P.S. Yes indeed, I do indeed give a shit about seventeen year olds. I have a boy a year older than you at the University of Virginia. He is married and will be making a grandfather of me in about three weeks.[151] By the way, his name is Christopher.

TO: IRVING HOWE[152]

CC, 2 pp; Emory

4620 Lelia's Court
Lake Katherine
Columbia, S.C. 29206
May 20, 1970

Dear Mr. Howe:

I hope you will countenance the intrusion of an (almost) stranger, but I have just read your Robinson piece in the current <u>Harper's</u>, and wanted to thank you for it.[153] I am not given to writing letters of this sort, but since, a few years ago, I struggled for around a year to put together an anthology of Robinson's work from the effort that the late Morton Dauwen Zabel had made previously, and then wrote a long introduction to the book,[154] I feel I have a special stake in the Robinson game, and read whatever new has been done on him. Yours is by far the best of the criticism that is attempting to re-evaluate Robinson for us and succeeding generations. I wish, now, that you had done the introduction for the Robinson book that I ended up doing for McMillian, for your piece on him is far better than mine, and I say this without any degree of false modesty. You come to the point a great deal quicker, say more cogent things, and make the case for Robinson as a major writer much better than I was able to do. Anyway, I think your piece is great, and I wanted you to know that I do think so. Although I have only met you once, I think it was at Colgate several years back, I have followed your work in Harper's and elsewhere, and have never been disappointed in anything you have done. I think the work you have done on Hardy is very good indeed,[155] and your essay on Hemingway a few issues ago is the best one I know.[156] You are quite right in believing that "A Clean Well-Lighted Place" is the best of the best of Hemingway. I have always thought so myself, and it is good to have such confirmation. Also, years and years before that, you put me onto Crawford Power's novel The Encounter, and I have never read a more powerful book about the religious experience. Afterwards, when I was at the Library of Congress, I lived in Leesburg, Virginia, where Power also lives. His real name is Francis Power, but he uses Crawford for some mysterious reason of his own. I don't know whether you know him or not, but he is kind of a rich idler, and professes no further interest in writing novels. I used to go out to his place—he evidently has some money—and sit around talking and drinking with him. I came to like him enormously, though he is a mysterious and elusive northern Virginia type. His main interest now, he tells me, is in collecting stones, and he says that the only writing he is now going to attempt is a book on megaliths. Curious, eh?

I won't go on and on in this vein, but will simply close as I began, by thanking you for your fine article on Robinson. Surely any poet, dead or alive, ought to be very happy in one world or the other to come upon such a reader.

I'll be in New York in a couple of weeks, and if you're in town, maybe we could have lunch or at least a drink together. I'd like that, believe me.

Sincerely yours,
James Dickey

JD/fw

TO: HAYDEN CARRUTH

TLS, 2 pp; University of Vermont

4620 Lelia's Court
Lake Katherine
Columbia, S.C. 29206
May 20, 1970

Dear Hayden:

Thanks enormously for your long, full and friendly letter from Crow's Mark. I felt like a dog, as they say, about my rather aloof reply to your asking me for a quotation in connection with your anthology. Thank you for being so understanding. Would it be possible for you to have me say something like "There is an astonishing amount of good poetry here?" Or something like that? I wouldn't mind giving you a quotation at all if I could find something to say which would stress the qualities of the book I do like without intimating that I like everything. Couldn't we do something on the order of suggesting that I have gotten a good deal of enjoyment out of the book, have found some new poems and poets I didn't know about previously, and so on? That would get everybody out, with honor satisfied on all sides.

I know something about your personal situation from Henry Rago and others, and my conscience has been bugging me a great deal over the matter of your anthology, because I respect and like your work so much, and because I know that you are usually fairly strapped financially. So, if you can figure out something for me to say that meets the conditions I've just been talking about, you can use a quotation from me if you like. It really is a good anthology, with an awful lot of good poetry in it, as well as some bad.

Have you ever thought to collect your reviews and other criticism? My two critical books—and now a third that is coming out in the fall[157]—are almost all composed of reviews and pieces I did on commission for one magazine or another. If I can collect my reviews, why can't you collect yours, which are so much better? Also, it seems to me that you have done even more reviewing than I have, so you would have a lot more material to work with.[158] I remember especially your estimate of Ted Hughes a few years ago in Poetry, and if that isn't telling it like it is, I have never heard it told like it is. That was an intelligent murder, and absolutely and completely deserved. The English critics are always whooping it up over Hughes, who to me is a very predictable kind of pseudo-energetic D.H. Lawrence-type British phony. The reason the British like him so much is that he has at least a semblance of energy amongst so much great intellectuality. Anyway, your review of him was first rate, and it is not the only good hatchet job you've done, or by any means, I hope, the last.[159] You also praise very well, and that is the surest mark of a good critic.

And how about collecting your poems, too? It seems to me that now would be a very good time for a large edition. Tell me what you think of all this; I'm eager to know.[160]

Thank you very much for the things you say about my own work, and particularly about the last poem of mine in the <u>Virginia Quarterly</u>.[161] All those things were such a long time ago, but I believe I could get in a Stearman[162] right now and take it off, and go anywhere I wanted to in it, and set it down again more or less safely. As you may know, I have a novel that is now topping the best seller lists, and my editors are already after me to write another. I don't think I will, but if I decide to do so, I believe I might write something about those old Stearman days, when flying <u>meant</u> something, and one actually did have the sensation of one's body being carried through the air, rather than being blasted through it.

When you have a chance, write again and tell me what your life is like. Someone said to me once that you had some kind of place-phobia, and I would like to know about this, if it is possible for you to tell me. But that shall be as you wish.

All yours,

Jim D.

JD/fw

TO: PAUL BOWLES[163]

CC, 2 pp; Emory

4620 Lelia's Court
Lake Katherine
Columbia, S.C. 29206
May 20, 1970

Dear Paul Bowles:

Thank you very much for taking the trouble to write, for I hadn't really expected that you would do so. Yes, I inquired about you from Dan Halpern,[164] for you are one of my favorite writers, and are probably my favorite composer of all the new fellows. By the way, Ned Rorem[165] was down here in Columbia a couple of weeks ago in connection with a festival of the arts that I put on here at the University, and he spoke of your work as though you were a kind of new messiah of music. He is really very knowledgeable about music and musicians, and I was delighted to hear his high opinion of your work. I have only the one record that was put out about fifteen or twenty years ago, but it surely has some beautiful stuff on it. Are you writing some new music? You may be sure I will try my best to get hold of your A Picnic Cantata[166] and will ransack the record magazines to see if I can find anything else.

Meanwhile, are you writing some new things? I have read almost everything you have written, beginning with The Sheltering Sky,[167] which as I remember came out when I was going to Vanderbilt. You have a very great gift, and it must be a terrific pleasure for you to sit down at the writing desk whenever you do so.

If you'll let me know, I'll send you a copy of my book Deliverance; I'd like very much to do so.

Do you know my old friends Alec Waugh and his wife?[168] They have been going to Tangier for years and years and years, and must be pretty well known among the English-speaking folks down there. Alec has recently married the lady he has been keeping company with for a good many years, and he tells me that he now lives in Tangier. I don't have his address, but you could probably find out from other people, as Alec gets around a good deal socially, and probably any of the people in the British Consulate could tell you where he lives, if you don't know already. He is a very sweet old party, and it is absolutely impossible not to be crazy about him.

How do the prospects look for Dan's magazine? If you see him, please tell him to send me a copy of the opening issue, for he has got me interested in the damn thing.[169] Surely an international kind of journal like that is sorely needed. To my knowledge there hasn't been any such since the demise of Botteghe Oscure, which I—probably among many others—miss sorely. You used to publish a good deal with them, as I remember. My former poetry publisher, Wesleyan, recently sent me a complete file of the magazine, and I have been reading through it slowly, issue by issue. If Dan's magazine is half way as good as Botteghe Oscure, he is doing everybody a real service.

I can't make this a long letter, for I must get on yet another airplane. But I did want to let you know how much I appreciate your taking the trouble to write. Let me hear from you again, from that far, exotic place, whenever you have a moment, or have the inclination.

Meanwhile, my very best to you.

Sincerely yours,
James Dickey

JD/fw

TO: PHILIP RAHV

CC, 1 p; Emory University

4620 Lelia's Court
Lake Katherine
Columbia, S.C. 29206
June 17, 1970

Dear Philip:

My apologies for not meeting the generous deadline that you had given me, but I have hardly been home for two days in a row. The whole trouble is that I had no idea that Deliverance would be accorded the reception that it has; apparently these occasions of best-sellerdom occasion enormous outlays of travel, time, expense of spirit, and so on, and may not be denied. I have certainly put my time and spirit in at the request of the Houghton Mifflin people, and now that Deliverance is on top of the best seller lists, I must apparently make some efforts to help it stay there. All this is disconcerting and very exhausting, but I have been attempting to do what Houghton Mifflin wishes me to do about it. Anyway, I think I can meet your July 1st deadline, and if I can't I will shoot myself, or something.[170]

I don't know whether or not I am supposed to tell you this, but on one of my visits to New York in connection with some TV appearances that Houghton Mifflin set up for me, I sat in as a member of the nominating committee for the Gold Metal for American Literature given by the National Book Committee. It was one of these meetings where nobody can agree on anything or anyone, but as a result of it you are one of the five final nominees on which, apparently, about 80 or 90 judges will be voting. But you are definitely on the final selection list of five, and Elizabeth Hardwick, who was also on the committee, and I are keeping our fingers crossed for you. I have of course no idea what all these many judges will render as a final decision, but the consensus of the nominating board is that you have an awfully good chance. Don't be disappointed if you don't get it, but at this date, everything looks pretty good for you. As I say, I don't know whether you are suppose to know this or not, but I can't really see any harm in your knowing it, and I hope it pleases you.[171]

Thanks very much for the things you say about Deliverance. It is the best novel that I can write, and I am very happy it has been so well received. All very bewildering. But gratifying, as you may guess. But none of the hullabaloo is nearly so gratifying to me as the things you are kind enough to say.

My very best to you, as always.

All yours,

TO: RICHARD HOWARD

TLS, 2 pp; Richard Howard

4620 Lelia's Court
Lake Katherine
Columbia, S.C. 29206
June 17, 1970

Dear Richard:

Thank you so much for your June 11th letter, which I am awfully happy to have. No, I most emphatically did <u>not</u> find your <u>Nation</u> piece disappointing.[172] The contrary was true: it seems to me one of the most favorable and penetrating things yet written on anything I have done. I might have expected this of you, for you have written so much about my work elsewhere, but you surely seemed to understand the wave length that the new book[173] is tuned on, and, though there have been a good many reviews, none has been so close to the mark as yours. I can only thank you once more for this, and move on to wherever I am going from here.

Most interesting news about your editorship of the <u>New American Review</u>, and the new poetry series that Braziller is going to do under your editorship. I don't know very much about Chester Kallman's work, though I haven't read much that I've liked by him, but I <u>do</u> like Charles Simic very much, and once wrote him one of the few fan letters that I have ever sent to anyone. And of course Eleanor Taylor is one of the really good women poets in the country; quite possibly the best now writing.[174]

Meanwhile, I, too, have become an editor, and in rather a curious place. <u>Esquire</u> is starting a poetry program, and I am, God save the mark, their editor.[175] Why I took this on I can't quite say, though it is most likely for some such reason as that which prompts me to serve on committees, nominating boards, and so on: if I don't do it, some bad guy will do it. After all, I was the chairman of the board that voted <u>you</u> the Pulitzer Prize, and God knows who would have got it if_____had been on it! So many things like this are the luck of the draw, (fill in the blank)
and I would rather have my hand on the deck than somebody else's I could think of. Anyway I would like to ask you for a short poem or two, if you think you will have anything ready in a couple of months. I think I should have something from you, something maybe from Jim Wright, maybe something from Archie Ammons,[176] something from Wendell Berry, and so on. Do you have any suggestions as to the really good writers now? I am not up on the very latest fellows, and so, were it left to me alone, I would probably go with people like Bill Stafford,

whose work I know best. But I would surely welcome suggestions from you, since you are, as they say, on the scene.

Good to know that Sandy is writing again. I had no notion of his monumental depressions, as you call them, but then I see so very little of him that it would be impossible for me to know. But it is good to know that he is feeling better, and getting back to work. As to your own hyperventilation attacks, I am concerned, naturally. But since you tell me that you can control them and that there is no real danger in them or surrounding them, I am not so worried as I might be. My God, how mortal and fragile we all are! My own diabetes seems to be all right, or at least it hasn't found a way to bother me yet other than mentally. But that is a plenty bad way, as you may know. Christ, the damn curious disease has made such a hypochondriac of me that I can hardly walk to the door without feeling some new pain, probably having something to do with sugar and a regulatory system I had no notion, four years ago, that I even had—well, I won't go into all that. You, like everybody else, has his own troubles. But I did want to let you know that I am all right, only very rushed, what with doing the screenplay of <u>Deliverance</u>, bringing out two more books in the fall, writing some new things, traveling around a bit, the considerations of a new grandchild—a boy—and a good many other things—that I simply have not had time to write anybody. But now, home for a few days, I can get off some mail to those who really matter, foremost of which is yourself, as always.

My very best to you, and to Sandy. I will be looking for what you both write. Take care of yourself, Dick. I will try to do the same, down here in my own hot, sandy, South Carolina way.

All yours,
Jim

JD/fw

Dickey as the sheriff confronting Jon Voight as Ed Gentry in the movie version of Deliverance *(1972)*

William Styron and Dickey meeting with a class at the University of South Carolina in 1974

PART SEVEN

CELEBRITY

July 1970–November 1980

TLS, 2 pp; Lilly Library

4620 Lelia's Court
Lake Katherine
Columbia, S.C. 29206
July 15, 1970

Dear Gordon:

I haven't time to look up my last letter to you, but if I haven't already, I want to tell you now that I will be in New York—for the Today Show on the 20th and the Cavett Show the evening of the 22nd—from Sunday afternoon until the following Saturday: from the 19th to the 25th, I guess it is. I will be, as usual, at the St. Moritz, and will hope to hear from you there. I have a good many ideas about our first issue, and want to talk them over with you. Mainly, though, I have got hold of a remarkable young—or I guess he's young, anyway—poet from California by the name of Jesse Shields,[2] and I want to know what you think of him. He is apparently a very curious kind of a recluse, for he doesn't seem to want to talk about himself, but the stuff he has sent me is absolutely dazzling.

The other thing is that I am absolutely bowled over by your sending along the poem of Helen Sorrells.[3] If there is any one writer that I think I can personally take complete responsibility for it is Helen Sorrells. She was a member of my writing class when I taught in California, at San Fernando Valley State College. She is now between 60 and 65, I should judge. You should have seen the first stuff that she turned in! But, all during that year, she began to see the light, little by little, and to write some interesting and original things. I haven't seen any of her recent work except what you send me. I like this a lot, and, if you can come up with an address for her, would like to get in touch. I may have her address around somewhere, but I am not sure that I do, after all this moving around. Anyway, Helen Sorrells has got the seeds of grace, I believe. But what an extraordinary coincidence that it should be <u>her</u> whose work you were struck by, and have sent along! Well, good things can happen, every once in a while: to you, to Helen Sorrells, to me, to <u>Esquire</u>.

Please <u>do</u> let me hear from you in New York, and we'll have lunch again, or something. And I do indeed want you to come down here and stay with us for a few days. It is very pleasant, though hot. We have a lake, a speed boat, and some other things you might enjoy fooling around with. Anyway, I'll see you in a few days in New York, and we'll talk it all out.

Meanwhile, my best as always.

All yours,
Jim

JD/fw

p.s. By the way, would you be kind enough to do me a favor? The last time I was there I promised a lady named Mary Cantwell—or at least I think the first name is Mary,[4] and am sure the last name is Cantwell—at <u>Mademoiselle</u> Magazine that I would come by and pose for a couple of pictures, as she suggested, since <u>Mademoiselle</u> is running part of <u>Self-Interviews</u>.[5] Would you call her and tell her the dates that I'm to be in New York, and where I'm staying? I feel as though I owe the people there the courtesy of doing what they suggested and I agreed to, though, as I say, this must be done belatedly.

All yours,
Jim

Meanwhile, I have your last note. See you in a few days. Hang in there! J.—[6]

TO: JOHN CALLEY[7]

CC, 2 pp; Emory

August 6, 1970

Dear John:

Here is the first draft of the screenplay,[8] as promised. Get back to me on it as soon as you have read it through. I think it turned out very well, myself. It was great fun to do, and, since the novel is conceived scenically anyway, it was comparatively easy to translate it over into visual terms. It may be that I have gone into too much detail in places; I can't of course know what you will think of this. I read through the scripts that Barry Beckerman[9] sent along, and it seemed to me that they were pretty thin. I had much rather try to do a James Agee-type script, and perhaps put in too much rather than too little. Anyway, you will tell me what you think. This is, as the agreement has it, a first draft. Doubtless there will be some changes suggested, perhaps by you and almost certainly by whatever director we select. Nevertheless, this screenplay is essentially what I want to do, and when I thought I had come up with a good shot or camera angle, I said so. This is for the director to accept or reject, as he sees fit. As you will notice, I have changed the ending and several other of the parts to include material that is not in the novel. But I have stuck pretty closely with the story, for I think that any changes we make should be in the interests of making a better film of our material, and not simply to change for the sake of changing. I pondered this story, its characters and scenes and implications for eight years, and I have everything fitted into place exactly as I want it. So, if the dialogue in the book seemed right, I included it in the screenplay. As you will see, I have shortened down the narrative after the men come off the river, and have taken care of everything that it took me two or three scenes to resolve in the book, in one scene on the riverbank, as I have it in the script. The end is changed completely, though the implications are the same.

The next step, then, I guess, is up to you. Let me know what you wish me to do after you've read this carefully. I say carefully, knowing you will do so without my saying it, because I have worked the script out very carefully, and anyone reading through it too quickly will chance missing a good deal that I have tried to do.

I am now planning to stay in Columbia for most of the rest of the summer. Playboy is doing what they call a profile on me,[10] and the interviewer is coming down here to stay with us for about a week, and I am planning to take him over into north Georgia and show him some of these rivers. Other than that, and a trip to England for a week around the tenth of September for the British publication of Deliverance, I will be here, and could even come out to the coast, should you deem it necessary or advisable. Again, I will wait to hear from you on this.

One more thing: several magazines—Esquire, McCall's, Atlantic, and a couple of others—wish to publish parts of the screenplay. I told them I would consult with you on this, and see what you said about it. We can publish with any or all of them, or not, as you say. I have no wish to infringe on our original contract, but since my agent, Theron Raines, takes care of all this for me, and since he is out of the country right now, I am not quite sure what the contract does say about matters of this sort. It might be good publicity for us; on the other hand, it might not. Let me know, and I will swing with what you want to do.[11]

My best to Barry Beckerman, and to yourself. But if you think it would be a good idea for me to come out there at some time before the beginning of school here—September 16th—please let me know, so that I can make plans accordingly, and save the time required from whatever else might impend.

Sincerely yours,
James Dickey

JD/fw

TO: GORDON LISH

TLS, 2 pp; Lilly Library
Columbia, S.C.

September 24, 1970

Dear Gordon:

I enclose the two poems by Sheinkopf,[12] in which I don't find very much. I assume we are firm on the two first issues: first, with the poem by Helen Sorrells, "Amputation," and second, with the Berryman poem.[13] I will soon follow up with the long-promised poem called "Women at the Well,"[14] which I just read today, and which I think you will like.

Another thing: I really liked getting together with you the other day in New York. It is <u>impossible</u> for friends to get together in New York without getting smashed. I apologize for my part in this, and would apologize twice as much if the damned occasion hadn't been so much fun. I am sure you will understand what I mean by this and be guided accordingly, whenever I come back to town. One must exercise some kind of Aristotelian mean in these matters, otherwise one simply blows up like a bomb, as I very nearly do every time I come up to that crazy place where you work. Anyway, I remember the time spent with you as very good human time. The main thing now is to go forward and do something quite remarkable with this poetry business in <u>Esquire</u>. Keep sending me the stuff, and I will tell you what I think of it, and will keep trying to get new material from my particular and peculiar sources. The main thing is to keep up the contact, and swing, under these conditions we find ourselves in.

Please remember me to the people I met when I was up there, and understand that I'll be back from time to time. But next time, let's just sit down across a table with a glass of Orange Crush and work out what we want to do. I am crazy about being drunk, as should be obvious, but we have other considerations which might be better if we did not indulge this particular madness every time we got together. Believe me, I <u>like</u> it; that is the damn trouble. I like it like Patton liked war; more than my damn life. But we can do a better job if there were not so much of this damn liking present on the scene. I don't speak for you, but for myself. You will know what I mean.

With all good wishes, as you know,

All yours,
Jim

JD/pch

TO: LAURENCE LIEBERMAN[15]

CC, 3 pp; Emory
Columbia, S.C.

October 12, 1970

Dear Larry:

Thank you for the good letter. I was allowed two recommendations for Guggenheims this year, and had I known that you were going to apply, you would certainly have been one of them. However, they have already gone in, so I can't work with you from the standpoint of <u>my</u> initiating your nomination. However, that is not so important anyway. You can surely be absolutely certain that I will back your play for the fellowship in any way that I can. If you have any forms, or things like that, that you want me to fill out, please send them to me and I will do so right away. Meanwhile, I will write to Dean Alpert[16] and make that recommendation also.

I like the new poems a lot. They are awfully good, Larry, as you certainly know. I also like your "Description of Project," for it sounds like something very much worth doing, and, knowing you, I'm quite positive that they will get done, whether you get these fellowships or not.

I'd like to know a little more about the book on modern poets that you're writing.[17] I have read a good many such books lately, and most of them are rather disappointing. It is not that they are not thorough, or not very kind to my own work, but that they seem academic and going-through-the-motions criticism that I have read so much of—and doubtless written a good deal of—in the years that I have been on the poetry scene. What it needed is a truly and brilliantly <u>biased</u> book: one with the stamp of a strong personality on it. I am convinced that you can supply this, and so I'd like to know exactly what your situation is in regard to your plans for the particular book.

It is also good to know that you are going to work with John Palmer.[18] This business of being a <u>regular</u> poetry reviewer can be good and it can be bad, according to who the reviewer is. You have a serious and good and very exciting chance of being a real <u>power</u> on the scene, a real taste-maker and mover and shaker of the poetic firmament. This is a position of a good deal of authority, and I am very happy that you have taken it. It will be hard work, but when did Larry Lieberman ever draw back from <u>that</u>?

Yes, indeed, I'll be there Monday, November 2, and stay with you through the fourth. As soon as I have my reservations, I'll let you know when to meet me. I don't have a very good idea about distances between Chicago and Urbana, but I had a lot rather ride down with you, and talk along the way, than sweat out one of those little local air lines, especially in cold weather. I have sat for so many hours around so many airports waiting for the aircraft of such air lines that I would surely welcome <u>not</u> having to do it on this occasion.

Things continue well here, though very hectic. I finally have the director for the film version of <u>Deliverance</u> that I want. His name is John Borman, and he's a Dubliner.[19] I talked to him for about a half hour on the phone yesterday, and he canceled out a contract with MGM in order to be able to do <u>Deliverance</u>. I met with Sam Peckinpah, who directed <u>The Wild Bunch</u>, in London, but I'm not at all sorry that I turned him down, though I liked him very much. I also requested that Roman Polanski be taken off the picture, for he is essentially a mood director, and does not handle an action line at all well. Borman does. The pictures of his that I have seen—<u>Point Blank</u>, with Lee Marvin and <u>Hell in the Pacific</u>, with Marvin and the Japanese actor Mifune—have exactly the ingredients I want, mainly action with a philosophical dimension. Peckinpah tries for this, but achieves it only intermittently. Borman's score is very high, I think. Anyway, he's going to do it.

Meanwhile, <u>Self-Interviews</u>, is due out the seventh of November; I'll see that you get a copy when I get the box of copies that Doubleday is supposed to send me. I think you'll like the book, though it is rather naive in places. The naivete, though, is really the best thing about it. It is not one of these carefully considered, over written books, but sounds exactly like talk, which in fact it is. It was taken off tapes, and I did very little editing on it. Since you have written about so many of the same things in connection with my work, I think it will be interesting to you to have a look at it. Anyway, as I say, I'll get the book to you in a week or so. I have another critical book building up in which I'm going to mix essays with entries from a kind of undated journal that I've been keeping for the last couple of years. I think I'll probably call the whole thing <u>Assertions</u>,[20] with maybe a subtitle reading "Essays and Journals," or something like that. I'm getting the book together now, and it seems pretty good. I <u>want it to be good</u>, for it is probably the last critical book I'll do, at least for a long time. I'm starting on another novel which I like a lot so far, though I don't understand it completely. The working title is <u>The Field of Dogs</u> and its about a blind man and also about the early days of training in the Air Force for World War II.[21] Strange book, but very exciting, at least to me. I haven't got very far with it yet, but am beginning to see what can be done with the material, if I can do it. Am also translating twelve poems of Yevtushenko for a volume Doubleday is doing. My Russian is not much, but I have the help of a very knowledgeable young fellow in Russian studies at Harvard, and he is helping me very much indeed.[22] I like some of the translations pretty good. Yevtushenko's knock-about enthusiastic style is just what I need to be working with right now, for my poetry, such of it as I have written in the last few weeks has gotten awfully solemn, and I want to open it up some to joy and recklessness. I don't know whether I'll publish any of these solemn ones or not, though one or two of them are, I think, pretty good. I have about half of a new manuscript, and should bring out another volume of poetry about fall of '71, though I am not absolutely sure that this will be the case. It will depend on how much of my time is committed to the film, and how much time I can get to work on poems. I am trying out a couple of new directions, mainly in connection with metrical innovations, and some of these are promising, although some of them are dead, flat failures. But the exploratory sense of language is strong in my make-up, and is what I like most about writing poetry to begin with.

My love to all in your house. See you soon.

All yours,
James Dickey

JD:lah

TO: GORDON LISH

TLS, 2 pp; Lilly Library

14 October, 1970
Columbia. S.C.

Dear Gordon:/

Well, here is the mini-manifesto, right in there with Plato, Shelley and Sir Philip Sidney, ah! Anyway, let me know if it's what you want, for this kind of thing is easy for me, and I have a little time, before we start filming Deliverance.

With this issue Esquire opens a poetry section, and one may well ask why. It surprises the editor more than anyone that the section is being put in because of what used to be called popular demand. Again, why? And why now? I can't say, though naturally I am moved to speculate. It may be that Americans, lied-to in an increasingly intensified, desperate and professional form by politicians, government agencies, advertisers, continually deluged with propaganda of one sort or the other in the mass media, have turned, are turning—or at least some of them are—to poetry as the last place where one human being can communicate in depth with another, with others, poetry being a use of words that, as Auden says, "makes nothing happen." It is not part of my intention to come up with an immortal or eminently forgettable "defence of poetry" here. I can't change things; that much at least should be obvious. But they seem, even if only on a comparatively small scale, to be changing themselves, and part of this change of heart—of mind, of desperation, and maybe of a kind of hope—has brought poetry to Esquire.

I will publish what interests me: the best work of my friends (always a prime editorial function, whether admitted or not) and what the other editors at Esquire will pass. Practically, the poems that appear in these pages will be what I like, what I can get (which depends on what I know about, which in turn depends on what I dig up myself and what the Screening Force at Esquire sends me), and what Esquire has room for at the time. I have no interest in publishing the work of "schools," in "being fair to all factions," or any of that. I have no wish to indicate "trends in modern verse" or to make life easier for future literary historians by giving, over the months, a kind of capsule version of current fashions in poetry. If this venture has anything to do with literary history and its making it will be because we discover a new writer or a new and better side of an old one. The editor's preferences are strong and constantly fluctuating, so this should make for a wide and eccentric variety. I hope so. Anyway, there's only one way to find out.[23]

How does that grab you? Does it have the requisite bratty, intelligent-arrogant Esquire tone.? I do hope so, because it is the kind of thing I'd do anyway, for Esquire or any other organ I was editing for. Anyway, let me know if you want anything changed, and I'll get on it. And excuse the typing.

More business. Dick Howard sent me four poems, and I think we should do the "Snake-swallower" one. I'm enclosing it with this letter for your approval, and keeping the others, as he instructed me to do. He tells me that he's talked with you, and told you that these four poems will appear in something called Findings, to be published in early March. I'm not sure about protocol on these matters, but Dick said that he explained to you that we could use any of these poems in issues up to and including the March number, since (to use his words) "the March number is published on February 12th." I'll let you settle this, but I'd like to use the poem if there's a way we can do it.[24]

So . . . with the manifesto in and a backlog building up (and some very good poems in it, too: I'm sure satisfied that that's the case!) we should be in pretty good shape. I'm glad you like the format of our first issue: I'm eager to see it.

Let me know if there's anything further you need, and I'll supply, for, as I say, I have a little time right now, and can put it into this particular area. My God, I might be able to sit down and try to work out a poem or two of my own! Wouldn't that be something!

Let me know if you want, meanwhile, to look at some of this Yevtushenko stuff I've been doing. It's real hell-for-leather, and funny, too, a lot of it.

All yours,

Jim

Is the stationary ready yet? If so, send some of it along to me, when you get a chance.

TO: RICHARD HOWARD

TLS, 2 pp;²⁵ *Richard Howard*

October 19, 1970

Dear Dick:

Thank you very much for your last two letters, but I am worried about Sandy and you, as maybe you are not, or needn't be. Both of you are such precious people to me that these dim, subterranean rumblings of—what shall I say?—disaffiliation, or something, are deeply disturbing to me. They are disturbing in the ways in which things are disturbing which one can, at one's particular remove, do nothing at all about. I know that your life with Sandy is intensely private, and a person like myself, married for twenty-two years, with two children and a grandchild, cannot really presume to know anything, <u>really</u>, of the circumstances that are disturbing you. Please <u>do</u> know that I understand as fully as it is possible for a person like myself to understand, but more importantly, I sympathize, whatever may befall.

I am much indebted to you for the quotation from Jimmy Merrill to the effect that after forty, the lid comes off. How damn true that is! People do not understand, actually, the desperation that begins to settle on one at this time of life. Erotic experience comes to seem not only the best of answers to the Void, but the <u>only</u> one. If people—wives, lovers—would grant us this very obvious fact and let us go our way and do our thing when the body and the mind most demand that it be done, things would be very much easier all around, and we would no longer live in the world of phoniness that we now inhabit. I won't get on the soapbox about this, but believe me, I understand what you mean when you talk about getting <u>around</u> more.

<u>Self-Interviews</u> is out, at least in the twelve-volume version of the complimentary copy box I've been sent, and I'll get one of them to you in the next few days. Meanwhile, you might <u>ask</u> the <u>Times</u> if you can review it for them,²⁶ but even if they send you a copy, I'll send you one too. Get one free, get <u>another</u> one free!

Meanwhile, I've sent on your snake swallower poem to the people at <u>Esquire</u>. <u>I've</u> accepted it, but since I'm new to this business of editing for <u>Esquire</u>, I don't know whether Harold Hays will accept my acceptance or not. Anyway, I'll let you know. There shouldn't be any trouble about printing the poem—and very handsomely too—but I don't <u>know</u> yet, so I'll have to inform you when the Powers up there let me know. But it's a damn good poem, in a crazy kind of Yeatsian mode which is kind of beyond Yeats, both fore and aft, by which I mean it's in the nineteenth century and also in the present and future. I like it a lot, and also the other stuff. I am so <u>damned</u> glad that we got the Pulitzer for you!²⁷ As I may have said earlier, Auden was for it, and all I had to do as chairman was to say, OK! Phyllis McGinley²⁸ was in the hospital with some kind of bathtub accident at the time, so

I don't really know if she was ever consulted or not. But it wouldn't have made any difference, for we were for you, and we <u>got</u> it! Thank God.

Your project having to do with printing, say, a poem of mine and an earlier poem is very interesting. My God, what <u>will</u> editors think up! I pondered this for awhile, and I think that I have come up with something that <u>might</u> be pretty good. Why don't you print my poem "The Sheep Child" with the lines from Christopher Smart's "Jubilate Agno" beginning, "For I will consider my cat, Jeffrey"? That might provide a pretty lively kind of essay for <u>somebody</u>! The lines I allude to are printed in Auden and Norman Holmes Pearson's anthology, <u>Poets of the English Language</u>, put out by Viking. They are on page 564 and run through 567. A great deal could be said about the relationship of men and animals, and many other lighter and darker things by an astute commentator. Anyway, since you ask me, that's my choice. Let me know what you think.[29] As to all these lectureships you are either now fulfilling or planning to fulfill, I think they are all great. I would like to get into your Princeton class myself! The business in Kyoto is fascinating, and it might be a great thing for you to do. I was there about two and a half years ago, and liked Kyoto very much, and the university as well. What's the name of it? Do-Shisha? Something like that? Anyway, it's a very good school, and Kyoto is still one of the greatly beautiful cities of the earth. As to how much you might like <u>living</u> there for a period of time, is maybe another thing. It could be great. A couple of American poets live there. One of them is Cid Corman, and another one teaches at the university: a very good woman poet named Edith Shiffert.[30] There is a kind of colony of American poets there.

I must close now. Please remember me to Sandy, and buoy him up any way you can. I know what these hard times are like, believe me.

All yours,
Jim

JD:lah

TO: JERRY QUARRY[31]

CC, 1 p; Matthew J. Bruccoli
Columbia, S.C.

November 2, 1970

Dear Mr. Quarry:

Untill the last minute, before your fight with Clay, I was to come to Atlanta and interview you and cover the fight for <u>Harper's Magazine</u>. I got sick, though, and couldn't make it, though I very much wished I had been able to.

I don't know how much good communications of this sort do, but strangers must assume that they can occasionally do <u>something</u>. Anyway, I wanted you to know that I sympathize as much as can be done with your bad luck in the Clay fight. I read your comments after the fight, and I believe everything you say is absolutely true. I have not seen the fight films, or anything like that, but I have seen you on television on several other occasions, and I know that you do not indulge in a lot of idle talk about your own capabilities, your opponent's or the fights you are in. I will make a prediction right now, though you yourself may not believe it. You will be heavyweight champion, if you keep on. I very much believe that you could knock Cassius Clay's brains out, given a proper chance. Yes, and Joe Frazier's too. You are twice the fighter now that you were when you fought Frazier. Hang in there!

Sincerely yours,
James Dickey

JD:lah

TO: FREDERIC PROKOSCH

CC, 1 p; Emory
Columbia, S.C.

November 9, 1970

Dear Mr. Prokosch:

I have your kind note in regard to <u>Deliverance</u>, and I wish to thank you with whatever powers for doing such things I possess. I would rather have heard from you on <u>Deliverance</u> than have all the money, the notoriety, and all the rest of that sort of thing that has inundated me since the book came out last March. It is nice to have the money, the recognition, and all that, but I would swap all of those things in one blink of the eye for the note that you have been so kind as to write. I doubt very much if I would be a writer at all if it had not been for you and your work. I read <u>The Asiatics</u>[32] when I was in the service in New Guinea, and I can very truthfully tell you that it changed my life. I like all your things, and the poetry I like enormously. I teach your work here, and the University of South Carolina students respond to it probably more than they respond to the work of anybody else, including Yeats, Elliot, and all <u>those</u> people.

I hope you are writing some new poems, and, since I have just become poetry editor of <u>Esquire</u>, I would love to see anything that you may be doing in poetry. I have not seen any poems of yours since a kind of memorial issue—or something—of <u>Poetry</u> came out about fifteen years ago, as nearly as I can recollect. But you <u>should</u> write poems, and if you do, I hope you will let me see them for inclusion in a future number of <u>Esquire</u>. But that shall be as you wish.[33]

Sincerely yours,
James Dickey

JD:lah

P.S. I talked to Jim Squires a couple of years ago, and he sent me his book on you for the Twayne series. I thought it was a very creditable job, didn't you? The book put me on to a couple of novels of yours that I hadn't known about, and for that I am very grateful to Jim. But more especially to you for writing them. Hang in there! I'll be in Europe next summer, and maybe we could have a drink together. That itself would be sufficient reason for my coming, for you are a very great hero to me.

TO: GORDON LISH

TLS, 2 pp; Lilly Library
Columbia, S.C.

November 19, 1970

Dear Gordorn:

Thank you for your unfailing attention to the area that lies between us. I have been soliciting like mad, and enclose three poems that I think we should consider very carefully. Two are from the Cambridge don, John Holloway. The one about the poet and his black girl is good, I think, but may be a little too long; there's no way that I can know about <u>that</u> part of it. The other, Breakfast Poem, is OK, and I don't think should raise any objections. The strange thing by Brotherson really took me, though, if you don't like it, let's throw it out. Of all the responses to my solicitations, these three seem to me to make the best case for the poetic imagination.[34]

About Graves, throw the God damn thing out if you don't like it. As an editor—ahem!—I thought it might be prudent to publish Graves for the <u>name</u>, though, like you, I don't think it's any great shakes as a poem. I want something with a lot more guts than that. If you haven't already paid the crusty old son of a bitch, send the God damn thing back to him, with my blessings.[35]

Now about the other business in connection with the "Attack" by someone with the strange name of Midwood, I haven't seen it.[36] I'm glad you told me, because I will surely avoid it. There is no good at all in going around filled up with the poison of resentment against some guy, if you don't have to. I am getting a little tired of adulation, anyway. What I need to do is to pick up a really strong enemy. Maybe this guy is it; I don't know. I have been hoping for Dwight McDonald or Mary McCarthy, because they are both supporters of Lowell, and I am shaking the great man's throne. Anyway, don't worry about my feelings of chagrin at Esquire's printing somebody's work that doesn't like my work. That is quite all right. My acquaintance with Esquire is limited to two things. First, picking it up occasionally in airport newsstands, and editing the new poetic venture. There is something nervous-making about reading through, in detail, every issue of any magazine that one is working for. I read, just by chance, an excellent thing in one of your recent issues by a guy who went to interview the hard-hats. I also read the Hemingway thing, every word, and loved it, just as I love anything by the old man.[37] Other than that, I have very little notion of Esquire's policies, writers, or whatever. Don't think that I am shook at all by any adverse comment that comes out on my work, whether in Esquire or anywhere else. Short of the guy's taking a forty-five and blowing my brains out to prevent me from writing, there's nobody that can do anything to me at all. My work is what it is, and the world can make its peace with it, kick it out, shit on it, or do whatever the world figures it should do. But as for my feelings, don't worry. I have gone through a lot tougher times than anybody alive can ever give me on the printed page, so, to use your favorite phrase, feel good.

Meanwhile, let's do have that party! I must go to Washington for the presentation of the Gold Medal for Literature to Robert Penn Warren on December 2nd. I then have to go up to Brockport—out of Rochester—to read on the 3rd and 4th. That would bring me back down to New York around the 5th, or maybe the evening of the 4th. Don't we come out on a Monday, doing such-wise? I'm not sure, since I don't have access to a calendar, but if we do come out around a Monday, could we not have the party then? I will be in the city for several days, and so we could have it on Monday, Tuesday, Wednesday, Thursday, or whatever. I really ought to be getting back here to Columbia around the weekend, so set it up as you wish. Let me know right away what you plan, and I will go right along. I look forward to getting together with you again, as I always do.

Hang in there, and don't let these guys bug you. My Self-Interviews has just come out and it's going to give every person in Christendom a chance at me with the ax. Let 'em have at it!

All yours,
Jim

JD: lah

I enclose the revision of the Linda Pastan thing, which I think is okay.[38] Also the "Women at the Well" thing, which is amateurish and crazy, but maybe too long. And too amateurish. Anyway, tell me what you think——[39]

TO: DAVID BUZZARD⁴⁰

CC, 2 pp; Emory
Columbia, S.C.

December 4, 1970

Dear David Buzzard:

Well, I'll just be damned if I believe there <u>is</u> anybody named David Buzzard! But, if there is, I am quite prepared to entertain the notion that it might as well be you! Anyway, thank you indeed for your comments on the poems, and about my novel, <u>Deliverance</u>.

Let me get right to your questions:

1. I think of the cliff which Ed Gentry scales as being between 175 and 200 feet high. As the passage dealing with this event makes more or less clear through Ed's feelings, his physical situation, and so on, the cliff begins as a rather steep slant and then becomes more vertical toward the top, where Ed nearly falls off, and then breaks into a kind of little canyon that he uses to ascend the rest of the way. Neither Ed Gentry, Lewis, nor I know whether it would be possible to reach its top by another route. You'll remember that at one point Ed considers trying to do this, but can find no way to get back down from the position he is currently on. The point is that one would not be able to get up another way from anywhere along the river where the men find themselves. Ed is satisfied about this in his mind, and that is why he tries it at the place he does. Also, this is a gauge to enable him to tell his particular spacial relationships to the men in his party below him.

2. I am not crazy about the eye on the novel's cover, myself. It is supposed to be Ed's eye looking out through the pine needles as he lies in wait for the man with the rifle. It may, as you say, also represent Ed's fear of his deed being discovered, but the other meaning is the primary one. Or at least that was the intention, anyway.

3. You are very perceptive to note the same name being used for Lucas Gentry in "On the Coosawattee" and Ed Gentry in <u>Deliverance</u>. I did run up on a country family on a canoe trip up in north Georgia named Gentry. The boy's name was really, if I remember correctly, Ira Gentry, but I just changed it to Lucas for the poem, and took the name for my protagonist in the novel just because I thought it would, well, be a good name for him to have.

4. My brother, as I wrote about him in the poem "The String" was named Eugene Dickey. He died when he was six years old of what was then called "brain fever," but which was almost certainly meningitis. Yes, I have an older sister, Maibelle, who is about 59 or 60, and a brother, Tom, two years younger than I am which would make him about 46. Yes, I was raised up north of Atlanta, not in the

city proper, but in what was then called the "County": that is, Fulton County. I went to North Fulton County High School.

5. I admire Theodore Roethke very much indeed. But there is no stylistic affinity between my work and his at all. I think he is the best <u>kind</u> of poet for American poetry to have, especially right now. He deals with eternal objects and eternal feeling, and does not throw the sop of temporality or headline-mongering at the audience. For that reason, he will be around a long time. But his work has no relationship at all to mine. He is essentially a meditative poet, and I am rather, I guess, more of a dramatic poet. That is, I deal in <u>incidents</u>, and feelings about them, where Roethke deals mainly about feelings and thoughts occasioned by, say, landscape, seascape, and so on. But he surely is a wonderful poet. As for other writers, you seem to assume that there is some kind of influence of Roethke working on my poetry, but I assure you that there is none at all. The main injunction that I have to myself, when I admire a writer as much as I do him, is to say to myself, "go thou and do otherwise." I don't want to do Roethke's thing; I want to do my thing. The more I like a writer, the less likely he is to be influential on what I write. I think that I belong more to the European tradition than to the English. The best poets I know are little-known modern French poets like Louis Emié, Lucien Becker, and André Frénaud. I read French, as well as other foreign languages, indifferently, but with the greatest excitement, and I read them all the time.

6. I don't know <u>what</u> you should know about me that has not appeared in print. My God, how could I answer <u>that</u>? I don't even know what you have seen in print! But I just have had a new book come out last week from Doubleday called <u>Self-Interviews</u>, and that would answer a great many of your questions, in one way or the other, I am sure. Why not get hold of that, read it, send it down here for me to autograph, and ask questions pertaining to the answers I give in the book? That might be more helpful to you than anything else that either you or I could think of. But that shall be as you wish.

Again, thank you very much for the things you say about my poetry, and about <u>Deliverance</u>. We will film the novel this spring, and I hope you will like that, too.

Sincerely yours,
James Dickey

JD/lah

TO: MARK STRAND[41]

TLS, 2 pp;[42] *Lilly Library*

January 1, 1971

Dear Mark:

Thank you very much for sending along the poem. I am kind of new in the job, and I am told that I must try my selections out on the other editors at Esquire, which makes for quite a mare's nest of complications. So—I'll try this one out, and see what they say. They have rejected some of my choices, mainly two or three by Berryman which were so dirty that they couldn't even consider printing them in Esquire, which is some kind of switch, is it not? Anyway, I'll try with this one.[43]

Meanwhile, who are we going to give this dm'd (Bollingen!)[44] thing to? I looked over the list of other winners, and they don't seem to want to give it to any young fellows. Again, are we giving the prize to a book, or to the life-work of somebody? I thought, with the other winners considered, that the prize sort of went to somebody who had operated with distinction in the field over a long period of time. But the Gallup[45] fellow seems to indicate that we are giving the prize for a specific book. If that is so, all sorts of people would be eligible that I didn't think would be. Anyway, what is your opinion in this matter? Barbara Howes seems to think that either Elizabeth Bishop or Wilbur or her ex-husband, Bill Smith, should win. I would be quite willing to give the prize to Wilbur, but I don't think Bill Smith should even be considered, no matter whose husband he used to be. He is just not of the caliber for a prize of this caliber, doesn't it seem to you? Anyway, if you have time before we meet in New Haven, let me hear some of your opinions, your candidates, and so on. It might facilitate things when we get up there. I hate these long meeting where people sit around deliberating for hours, putting their friends up for prizes, trying to put down their enemies, and all of that stuff. I know Barbara Howes fairly well, though I haven't seen her in a long time. She is a nice lady, and I think we can work with her OK. But I do think it would help to get some kind of preliminary reading from you by mail on your candidates, opinions, and the rest. So—if you have a moment or two, write to me down here in Columbia, and maybe we can make things easier for ourselves, the candidates, and everybody else next week. I've been on a lot of these committees, as I'm sure you have, and things can get awfully sticky if the judges don't know where each other stand, and sometimes they can get sticky even if they do. I hope we can make this relatively painless, because I have an awful lot of work to do and very little time in which to do it.[46]

But I did want to close by saying that I very much look forward to seeing you, even if only for a couple of days, a couple of drinks, a couple of dinners, and the rest of the things that go on in occasions of this sort. Maybe we might even have a good time, too!

Sincerely yours,
Jim D.

JD: lah

TO: JAMES WRIGHT

TLS, 2 pp;⁴⁷ University of Minnesota

January 15, 1971

Dear Jim:

Please forgive me for waiting so long to answer your wonderful letter of December 21st, which came as the finest Christmas present I have ever received in all my 48 years. I am very happy that you like the comment that I made for publicity for the jacket of your <u>Collected Poems</u>, and you can know that I meant every word of it. It was just a question of saying something that was right <u>enough</u>, out of all of the good things I might have said.[48]

The things that you say of my own work are very sustaining to me, I can tell you. I am very happy that you like it as well as you do, that it has meant as much as it has to you, for the things you say make me very happy that I spent the time, time that I might have spent living and doing other supposedly necessary things, in trying to compose these poems. It costs me blood to write, as you above anybody else knows. I am very happy that someone of your eminence thinks as highly of my work as you do. I won't go on and on in this effusive way, but will simply thank you once more, as warmly as I know how.

I get all kinds of disturbing reports about Robert Bly, and if he continues to do some of the things he has done in regard to me, I am going to have to confront him in some manner, either through lawyers or through a personal encounter of some sort. One simply cannot allow someone to go about in public meeting after public meeting, at reading after reading on college after college calling one a racist, a fascist, a nazi, a nigger-hater, a toady of the government, and so on. This is quite clearly slanderous, and if you have any contact with Bob, you may tell him that I am not going to put up with it any longer. I will either come after him myself, or I will have lawyers deal with it. I have consulted a couple, and they say that if I can prove that he is saying in public the things about me that he definitely <u>is</u> saying, I can take him for all he's worth. I doubt if he has much to be taken for, but if he continues as he is doing now, I will surely ruin him. You can tell him this and let him be guided by whatever conscience he may have. Or perhaps I shouldn't depend on <u>that</u>! It is not that all this is disturbing to <u>me</u>, but that the laws of this country are set against the kind of character assassination that he is bent on doing. I am sorry for Bob; a life spent in envy of another person, in spite and frustration, is not an enviable life. But neither is a life of being consistently slandered and lied-about in public. He even goes around telling people that he has <u>heard</u> me read and say these things: things like "tell that nigger down in the front row to get me a mint julep or I won't read." Now can you imagine my possibly saying that, or anything remotely resembling it? I think Bob should be in a straight-jacket, and I am either going to put him there, or in jail, or in the poor house, or in the hospital. As I say, I won't put up with this any more, and if you see him, you can tell him exactly that.[49]

I don't mean to take up this letter with talk about such unpleasant matters, but you can surely see how I might be concerned about them. I wanted this letter, though, to be simply a letter of thanks for <u>your</u> letter and for the things you say in it. You are a very precious friend to me, Jim, and I don't think these things can ever be said too often. I am very happy I said what I did about your book; I mean it all, you can well believe.

Love to Annie, and to all those who visit that good house of yours. With <u>one</u> exception!

All yours,
Jim

JD:lah

P.S. I thought your poem looked awfully good in <u>Esquire</u>.[50] Give us a little more time—a couple of months, maybe—and we'll do some more of yours. The response to that one has been extraordinarily good.

TO: JONATHAN WILLIAMS

TLS, 1 p;[51] SUNY Buffalo

February 8, 1971

Dear Jonathan:

I have asked <u>Esquire</u> to forward your letter to Bart Midwood, and they have done so.[52] I remember your telling me once, in regard to your publication of Robert Duncan, that, "if you ever want to make an enemy of a man, become his publisher." I have always considered you a friend of mine, and so am completely at a loss to explain the untoward and underhanded viciousness of what you say. It may be that you didn't like <u>Deliverance</u>; you wrote me about it and indicated otherwise, or so I interpreted what you said. At any rate, it was nothing like <u>this</u> paranoic outburst. You evidently felt some need to do this, though I would not want to pry too deeply into the reason my old friend did feel such a need. At any rate, I don't want you to write to me any more. I would accept one letter of explanation, though of course there isn't any. Whatever explanation for your action in this case is within you, and is really not guided by any reasonable or objective principles. I was profoundly shocked and dismayed to see what you had done, and I still am. Particularly since you had told me so many times how people have stabbed you in the back, your friends betrayed you, people spoken behind your back, and the rest. How do you square your behavior with those lamentations about others who have wronged you?

Again, Jon, I am very sorry. Let us become strangers again.

Sincerely yours,
James Dickey

JD:lah

TO: PETER BIRD MARTIN[53]

CC, 3 pp; Emory
Columbia, S.C.

March 4, 1971

Dear Peter:

Thank you very much for your note of February 25th, which I have just come in from California to receive. We have a kind of embarrassment of riches on casting for Deliverance. Apparently everybody in the world wants to be in it, and we have to narrow the field down within the next few weeks. By the time I left out there, day before yesterday, it looks as though Jack Nicholson will play Ed Gentry, if the studio can get his price down a little bit, and Marlon Brando will play Lewis. However, there is nothing in this that is by any means final, and I expect, judging from my experience up to this point, that there will be still some more shifting around. But that is the last I have heard, and, until I hear different, I will assume that that is what the studio is going to go along with.

As to my getting together with Vonnegut[54] on March 9th, that is fine with me. As to inviting Willie,[55] I'll leave that up to you. I need to see him about some things, but I could easily see him at some other time. You very well may be right about Willie and me; we carry on in kind of crazy ways, and maybe this wouldn't be suited to Vonnegut's taste. Again, I don't know. Handle it however you like, and I will be guided by your wishes. But I can tell you one thing: I am sick to death of alcohol, and hope sincerely to never see another shot-glass. It is amazing how much one can get done without the continual back-drag of drink.[56]

As to the actual filming of the movie, it looks like this is going to be more or less the way we'll do it. We'll spend most of the month of March and probably about ten days of April setting up in Clayton preparatory to shooting the film starting the second or third week in April. With a ten-week estimate, this will bring us well into the summer before the movie can be actually completed. Boorman will then take the thing back to Ireland and brood over it in the cutting-room, in that strange monk-like atmosphere of those kinds of priesthood. If we finish the film by, say, the second week in July, we can release it about this time next year, which would be very much to our purpose.

But there's all that to do yet. I have to come up there to talk to Brando in a few days. I am sitting here waiting for the non-existent phone call that tells me that I got the National Book Award. When I got it the last time, I think I was notified only a day or two before, so, as I write this, I still may get it, and still may come up within the next couple of days. But I rather doubt that this will be so. I expect that Eudora Welty has already got it and been notified by now, which is a good thing too, since she is a very fine lady.[57]

But this movie is another thing. Hollywood studios operate on such a great, lavish schedule that I have little notion of what to tell you about accommodations, and the rest. Clayton is a small place, though they have two very nice, large motels there. I am told that Warners will commandeer one of them, and me, I'm taking a new light-weight tent up there in case they won't even let <u>me</u> in! Anyhow, I'll let you know more about the actual physical details of the filming as soon as Boorman and Calley and the others let me know.

Very good about your novel.[58] It is an awful experience, but one that one would not take anything for; I wish very much that I could write <u>Deliverance</u> again, and I'm so glad that I don't have to. I am getting together a lot of notes for another novel, called <u>Death's Baby Machine</u>,[59] about blind men and airplanes. This should take a couple or three years, depending on how much time I can get to work on it. I want to write some more poetry, too, for I have written only two poems in the last two years. I just finished one, though, on the death-scene of Vince Lombardi,[60] and it seems a promising kind of direction to me. Anyway, we'll see what happens as a result.

I simply can't get through Norman Mailer's work, as much as I like him personally. The stuff is so rhetoric-blown and high-falutin' that I feel that I must <u>run</u> for the nearest copy of some simple-stark writer like Hemingway, or like William Humphrey.[61] I may come to Norman in time, but I think it is best for me to stay away from him now, when I am so damn bugged by the rhetoric that I simply could not do the man justice.

As to the fight. As luck, or something, would have it, I must read at the Poetry Center at the same time that the fight takes place on March 8th. I <u>sincerely</u> hope that I don't take <u>too</u> much of the fight's mob away from Madison Square Garden. I am a born gambling man, taking after my father, and I will bet you that breakfast of country ham, grits and red-eye gravy that Joe Frazier wins. Further than that, I will bet you that he knocks Ali out before the tenth round. So—what say you?[62]

Depending on whether the book award comes in, I'll be in New York either the 3rd or 4th or, say around the 6th. I expect the latter is by far the more likely, and I will let you know where I am going to be staying. It almost certainly will be the St. Moritz—but, as I say, I'll let you know when the arrangements have been made.

Again, much thanks for the good, chatty letter. It will be very [good human] time to see you again. And tell Vonnegut that I will be very [glad] to get together with him, too.

All yours,
James Dickey

JD:lah

TO: JOYCE CAROL OATES[63]

TLS, 1 p;[64] Syracuse University

March 22, 1971

Dear Mrs. Oates:

I cannot tell you how very much gratified and much moved I am to receive your new book and the dedication you were so gracious as to inscribe in it.[65] I have received a good deal of mail lately, as you may imagine, but nothing I have gotten has given me nearly the gratification—nor the occasion for gratitude—that your book has done. Sending it to me was a kind human act, and when can there ever be enough of them?

I read through the poems too, and found much to admire. It seems to me that, despite all the Anne Sextons and the Adrienne Riches, that there has been very little real womanly sensibility in American poetry. Many are called but few—well, very few women can or do write like women. Your poems of love-making are very beautiful indeed, and I hope there will be a lot more of them. A man cannot really understand how a woman feels about these things, as a woman cannot understand how a man feels, but with poetry like yours the man can come a lot closer to understanding them than he otherwise would have been able to do, in his blundering, mortal way.

Again, thank you for your poems, your book, and your inscription. It was wonderful of you to send them all to me.

Sincerely yours,
James Dickey

JD: lah

TO: EDMUND WILSON

CC, 1 p; Emory
Columbia, S.C.

May 25, 1971

Dear Mr. Wilson:

Please forgive the intrusion of a stranger, but I was uncommonly shook up by reading somewhere, for some reason or other, your comment on your own work concerning Memoirs of Hecate County[66] which, as I recall, you thought the best of your books. I think so too, and it seemed to me more or less fitting that I should write and tell you this. I first read Hecate County when I came out of the Air Force in 1946, and was very powerfully taken with it. I also remember reading a commentary on the book, I forget who it was by, that said that the reviewer "believed every word of it to be true." So do I, but it is the truth of art, and probably not that of fact, at all. Anyway, if the remarks of a stranger, coming in to you in your venerable position, make any difference, I thought I might as well send these words along to you.

My very best to you, and I hope to read more work of yours in the future.

Sincerely yours,
James Dickey

JD:lah

TO: JONATHAN WILLIAMS

TLS, 2 pp;[67] SUNY Buffalo

August 2, 1971

Dear Jon:

It is fine to have your letter and to know that you are not mad at me for being mad at you for your Esquire letter. It was just that the thing was sprung on me by the Esquire people as such a complete surprise. I think that we can get back on the same level of warmth and respect as we used to have. Believe me, I am surely for that!

Ron Johnson writes to me from San Francisco, and sends poems, some of which I think we will probably use in Esquire.[68]

The filming on the movie is done; now my director, John Boorman, and I will go to London to cut it and edit it, then bring it back to New York, edit it some more, and show the work-print to a selected audience of distributors, critics, and so on. I have no idea how all this will turn out, but the footage I have seen would make your hair stand up and then tie itself in knots. If we can edit this thing right, I don't believe anybody who ever goes into a theater to see the film will come out the same person as when he went in. But that's all to do yet. The last shot we did, Burt Reynolds, who plays Lewis, is catapulted out of a canoe about twenty-five or thirty feet in the air. I was talking to Burt before his stunt—or "gag", as he calls it—and he said that he was not fooling himself about why they were taking this as the last of the footage. Burt said, "Boorman wants all his footage to be in the can in case I get killed."

But he didn't, and we have the stuff, and it is mighty, mighty powerful stuff, too. Well, you'll see when the thing premiers in March. We plan to premier simultaneously in London, New York, and Los Angeles, and there is a chance that we will also include Atanta, which promises us the biggest premier since Gone With The Wind, a hell of a long time ago, as you may remember (I was in high school, myself). Anyway, if you are in the States, anywhere around any of these locations, I'd like to invite you to come to the premier as my guest. But that shall be as you wish.

I like your collected volume very much indeed.[69] Are you printing some new things? Do you have John Wain's address, since I need to write to him about something? When I got your last letter, I went back and read that little volume of post cards that you were so kind as to give me with an introduction by Wain.[70] I think the whole damn thing is absolutely wonderful. You are quite a learned guy, you know? Where do you and Ron Johnson get all these strange, Blakean references, and the rest? I never saw any of the things that you guys use before, in my life, and I'm not such a bad 18th Century man, myself! But I sure didn't know any of that stuff!

Take care of yourself, Jon. And when you want to write a letter to some asshole that reviews your buddy's book unfavorably in the pages of a big slick, don't do it with me, the next time. I've already had mine, and didn't really like the feeling, as you may imagine. I wouldn't mind you telling me what you thought, for many others have, a lot of it adverse. But I don't want them—the Esquire people—to say they have got this savage vituperative, condemnatory letter from some fellow, and the fellow turns out to be my old friend. That is very shocking and very discouraging, as you may know.

Anyway, I don't want to end this on a doleful note, but only to reaffirm the friendship that I had—and have, and do—feel to be so solid and fruitful.

Again, my best, as ever.

All yours,
Jim

JD: lah

TO: STANLEY BURNSHAW

TLS, 2 pp;[71] *HRHRC*

27 August, 1971

Dear Stanley:

Well, as they say in South Carolina, that is some kind of good letter. Let me get right to your points about your book. The Terrified Radiance is good. However, you might consider dropping off the article, or changing the phrasing in some kind of way, such as In the Terrified Radiance, or something like that, maybe, or something like Facing the Terrified Radiance.[72] These are just possibilities to fool around with, as I would do if the poems were mine, and the book mine—that is, really, the only way in which I can approach your book, as another poet would be the first to know and recognize. But the idea and the concept—and above all the possibility of the Terrified Radiance is very powerfully taking, as they also say in South Carolina. Question is, how to get a phrase as good as this one to give out with its maximum power. Well, it can be done, and I'll depend on you to tell me what you finally decide. I look at it this way: you've already got very much of a winner as a title.

Now, as to your dilemma about chronology, I can say this: I think you are entirely too worried about such things as "showing progression," and so on. I don't think that the poetry-reading audience cares nearly so much about when poems were published, what collections they first appeared in, or any of that. You are, after all, not presenting something for graduate students to date and write about, but are putting forth a book of living, vital poems. In other words, you are getting in front of the reader a number of good poems, and that matters more than the notion of showing the reader how and by what means the later poems evolved from the earlier—if they did; and that is always questionable. My point is to throw the emphasis on the artistic and imaginative quality of the poems, and not on their historical dating, or anything of that kind. If it were me—and again, that's the only actual and honest criterion I've got—I would mix the whole business up. I would have only one standard, and that would be this: in what sequence do I want to hit the reader with these poems? How do I want him to go through my work? And I think that historical periods should, ultimately, have very little or nothing to do with it. You think your later poems are your best work. Very well; so do I. Print those first, and then scale the book on down, for a while at least, through poems that you think are good and should be printed, but are not as great as the ones you print first, and then finish the book with another bunch of pieces that you do think are great. There is no substitute for starting strong and finishing strong. Pace the thing, and your readers will go right with you. I not only believe it: I know it.

To get onto something else, I heard from the Warners people yesterday, and it looks as though we'll have some kind of private screening in December, and I'll sure try, by guess and by God—as we used to say of our navigation in the old days of the Air Force—to get you in. Some of the film is so utterly horrifying that the author himself can't even face the screen. But my God, what <u>excitement</u> we've got here! And what dealing with gut issues! I don't think that any of us connected with the film have any real idea of what we're sitting on top of, here. But that's all to see, in the future. I am scared to death that we've got an unbearable masterpiece on our hands. To tell you the truth, I don't know exactly what to feel or how to respond. But the thing is in motion now, and, as the Chinese are supposed to say, he who rides a tiger fears to dismount. Anyway, by God, we'll see what happens.

About the National Book Award jury thing, I am also about as confused as it is possible to be. I wrote to Roger Stevens[73] about the fact that I didn't want to screw up the chances for <u>Sorties</u> by serving as a judge in another category. He wrote back immediately that my serving on the poetry panel would do no such thing: that it would, in fact, have nothing whatever to do with my candidacy in the Arts and Letters category.[74]

But I would rather take your advice than his. But the thing is, that they are leaning on me awfully hard for a decision. So—I'll wait to hear from you on this, and make the decision on the basis of what you tell me. What you said in your other letter about getting good judges, competent judges, for these things, is very important to me. Otherwise we are going to end up with things like the Bly fiasco, or the unspeakable travesty and horror of the Ginsberg performance last year.[75] None of this is good for American letters, or for American poetry, or for poets or the imaginative life. But if you think I shouldn't serve this time, I'll tell Stevens and his boys just that. Again, let me know what you think I should do.

As for your own judgeship—or whatever one might call it—are you the only one doing it, or what?[76] Stevens tells me, for example, that there are now <u>five</u> judges for poetry. And what the hell do you do with <u>that</u> kind of a thing? If there are other judges in Arts and Letters, who are the other ones? I've been up against some bad juries, as we all have, and I think it's just as well to know what the situation is, in these cases. If you're the guy—the only guy or the main guy—it will sure make a difference. If there are other fellows involved who might, say, swing the thing to Leslie Fiedler, or if there were any of my numerous enemies on the panel, I had just as soon take Stevens' offer and get on the poetry panel and make a stand against the assholes who clutter up and often dominate these things.

Again, I'll wait to hear, and will move when you tell me how.

Love from us,
Jim

And Kevin says you needn't warm up the water at the Vineyard. He likes it like it is, like it was, like he remembers it.

TO: STANLEY BURNSHAW

TLS, 2 pp;[77] *HRHRC*

September 8, 1971

Dear Stanley:

I have acted on your advice, and declined to participate in the poetry jury for the upcoming National Book Awards. Believe me, I realize that the chance of <u>Sorties</u> is an outside one at best. But, as I said in another letter, it is almost certain to be my last critical book, and I would like to give it the best chance I can to win the award. I know Fred Morgan[78] from being a long-time contributor to <u>Hudson Review</u>. Mr. Lahr I know only from seeing him on the Today Show when his book came out.[79] I was not so moved by his appearance as to go out and buy the book, though I <u>did</u> see his father on opening night in <u>Waiting for Godot</u>. I also ran into the elder Lahr in a bar after the performance, where there were a lot of people milling around and clapping him on the back, and I asked him what the hell the play was about? His answer, as I remember, was, "Believe me, son, I don't know. But I do know that my appearance in it is the best thing that my career has to show, after all these years. But don't ask me what it's about! I don't know what the hell I mean when I say 'It looks like my shoes are green.' " Anyway, at least I don't feel like I'm up against a stacked deck, as though Robert Bly, Robert Creeley, and other of my numerous enemies were on the jury. No; I will just put <u>Sorties</u> up there, and see what happens. Edmund Wilson will surely be the sentimental favorite, but there is a heartening trend in literary awards these days <u>not</u> to give the award, as though one were giving John Wayne the award for <u>True Grit</u>,[80] on the basis of his having been around a long time. I myself think Edmund Wilson is the most over-rated literary critic I have ever read. Though he is relatively astute, he is, as a critic, exactly as he characterized Stephen Vincent Benét as a poet: "He writes the kind of criticism that anyone would write if he had gone into the writing of criticism instead of the insurance business." His work is one long tissue of selfindulgent clichés and self-aggrandizement. And when I read the Lowells in the <u>New York Review of Books</u> talk about what a "great writer" he is, I feel the sudden cold touch which indicates the prevalence of literary log-rolling in this country. Edmund Wilson is a great writer to the Lowells and to the <u>New York Review of Books</u> simply because he endorses Lowell as a poet. That's the kind of thing that must be broken down, if we are ever to have a true and free literature in this country. End of sermon.

I am very happy that you have decided to follow my advice and begin with all the new poems. I also think it is a good idea to follow with selections from your three earlier books. And your idea of going in reverse order, after that, is also extremely interesting. I would have to see the manuscript—and I hope you <u>do</u> send it down—to see how this works out. But it surely sounds good. I am looking forward very eagerly to the manuscript, and to the book, too. I have asked Roger Stevens to hold off on my being a member of the jury this year in favor of my being a member of it next year. I have never sat on a five-man jury before, but the fiasco last time, with Ginsberg using the judgeship simply as another platform, and the business a couple of years ago with political-minded friends giving Bly the award for the express purpose of his being able to get up and make a political speech, does not entrance me, to say the least, with the notion of serving as a National Book Award juror in poetry again. But the good thing is that your book will be one of the nominees, and though one man can't do everything there is to be done in a five-man jury, he can sure as hell do <u>something</u>. Carolyn Kaizer— almost a man—swung the jury in favor of Mona Van Duyn last time, which, regrettably, set Ginsberg up for his public pronouncement, but also, on the good side, gave Richard Howard a chance to come back at him, publically in the <u>New York Times</u>, with a very witty put-down of Ginsberg and his ilk.[81] Anyway, I will begin to arrange things with Stevens and these other people about this time next year, if they still want me on the jury. And from their letters to me urging me to serve on this one, I am sure they will. But—we'll see how all that comes out.

Meanwhile, <u>do</u> send me a Xerox of the whole manuscript, and I'll go over it carefully and come back to you with my comments.

I am very happy that <u>some</u> good people are getting into positions of authority. American poetry and American letters generally, are at stake. And nothing can be more important than that.

I'll be here for about three more weeks, so if you need to communicate, just write to me here in Columbia.

My love to all. Maxine and Kevin send love too.

All yours,
Jim

JD:lah

TO: GORDON LISH

TLS, 1 p;[82] Lilly Library

November 3, 1971

Dear Gordon:

We might profitably consider these few poems for a future number. Dacey is pretty good, don't you think? And old John Betjaman probably ought to have a modest place in the magazine too. Well—let me know what you think.[83] Meanwhile, I have a lot of other stuff that I am gradually working through, and will send most of it back to you in the next few days, perhaps with a few suggestions for other publications.

As to your astonishing note of October 28, I hardly know what to say.[84] You <u>surely</u> must know that I could not consider for a moment doing something like this. I have no intention whatever of getting into the Hemingway-Mailer camp, and talk all <u>around</u> the game rather than playing it. There would be nothing at all for me in putting down all of these people in favor of myself, particularly since most of them are friends—or at least acquaintances—of mine. So—there is no possibility whatever of my going through with a kind of universal put-down of other poets of my generation in favor of myself. The work is going to have to do that, and not publicity. I'm sorry to nix your idea, particularly if, as you say, Harold[85] is crazy about the idea. But it would have to be somebody other than myself—your editor—who took this particular kind of advantage, with photographs, yet. I'm sure you understand my feelings about this and will be guided accordingly. Incidentally, aside from Lowell, none of these other people you list would be even in the first <u>fifty</u> American poets, as far as I, personally, am concerned. Ginsberg, Snyder, Creeley, and Duncan indeed! Lord, Lord!

Anyway, we'll move along to some other things. But, really, I don't conceive of a kind of junior olympics. I think Mailer has done himself and literature great harm by the kind of posturing that he has seen fit to indulge himself in. I won't do that. Again, I'm sure that you must understand that my work is too valuable, at least to me, for that. If these things are said, they will have to be said for me, and not <u>by</u> me. End of sermon.

I hope everything is well with you, and that we can get together when I come up to New York in about three weeks. I'd like that a lot, believe me.

Meanwhile, all love to your wife, and to the new little creature, whom I hold in a particular favor, for what reasons you know.[86]

All yours,
Jim

I'll be at St. Moritz on Nov. 21–24—[87]
JD:lah

The ten best poets, I think are—(in no particular order)
  1. Pound (I <u>guess</u> he is still an American)
  2. Auden
  3. Dickey

4. Lowell
5. Wilbur
6. A. R. Ammons
7. Wm. Stafford
8. Elizabeth Bishop
9. John Berryman
10. James Wright[88]

TO: STANLEY BURNSHAW

CC, 2 pp; Emory
Columbia, S.C.

27 November, 1971

Dear Stanley:

Some strange things have happened, just in the last couple of days. The main thing is that the French edition of Deliverance has won the Prix Medici, given— or so I was told—for the best foreign language book published in France during the year. This is all quite confusing to me, but I felt that I am more or less obligated to go to Paris today to receive the prize. It is supposed to be a great honor, and all that, but I had so much rather stay here and work on the new poems I have finally been able to start; some kind of new direction, and maybe, with luck, several of them. But, as it is, I'm getting on yet another airplane in a few minutes and going to Paris. At least I'll have Maxine and Kevin with me, and it will be fun to show Kevin what little of Paris I know. I haven't been over there in nine years, and perhaps it is time I went back. Anyway, here we go. I thought it would please you to know that your judgment on my work is vindicated—yes, and in several languages! It is good for me, too, to know that the man who has written the best book ever written on poetry might be pleased at this latest thing.

I'm also very happy that you like Sorties, and will be indulging in that hope you speak of. I had a copy of the book sent along to Fred Morgan as you suggested. I don't know where in the world Lahr is—that is, is in London, which is a mighty big place. But if you and Fred like it—particularly you—I will be plenty satisfied. And thanks, also, for the backstopping on the typos. I am wretched as a proof-reader. The only only of my books that doesn't have any is Helmets, and that was only because Dick Wilbur was my editor then.

Your questions: Jefferies' Story of My Heart[89] is an old, old book published sometime in the late nineteenth century. His publisher was Longmans, and, when they published Helmets in England I asked the present editor if I could get any of

Jefferies' works. He said they were all out of print, that he no longer had any requests for them. But the Gotham Book Mart might be able to get it for you; that's where I got my copy.

Yes, Lucien Becker is very good; by far the best of the more recent fellows that I, personally, have read. I feel that he has something special for <u>me</u>, which is the way one wants to feel about poets.

My nomination of you was indeed for the National Gold Medal. But not a single one of my candidates was on the final list, which shows you about how much clout <u>I</u> carry around there! Anyway, when one has the chance, one should try. Andy White[90] finally won it, which is a complete mystery to me. He's a nice fellow, but clearly not of that calibre. Well, there'll be other times, and the right man will win it yet.

The business about Epstein[91] I just picked out of a local newspaper column. The gist of it was that Epstein was kept by the FBI for a period of time—a couple of weeks at least—and then emerged from their dungeons to make a statement about the self-aggrandizement that New York intellectuals—he says—indulge themselves in concerning politics. He issued a complete recantation of his own position. I'm not sure where you could look this up, but the <u>New York Review of Books</u> (an organ I simply cannot get through an issue of, myself) is bound to have had a lot about it. Question is: when? I should say about eight months ago.[92]

Maxine and Kevin and I all send the best and deepest love we have. And please <u>do</u> stop by and stay with us when you come through Columbia. I would look forward to such a visit with a lot greater eagerness than I would going to Paris, I can tell you.

All yours,

TO: STANLEY BURNSHAW

TLS, 2 pp;[93] HRHRC

January 5, 1972

Dear Stanley:

Thank you very much for your lovely Christmas letter. The <u>New York Times</u> book review of <u>Sorties</u> was so inanely silly that it could scarcely bother a ninny, which I ain't—at least most of the time, anyway.[94] I don't know what gets into these Greenwich Village people when they start talking about Southerners. The irony of it is that Broyard is furious with the hayseed Southerner for being taken in by the big city slickers of the East Village, because I wrote an introduction for an anthology—rather a bad one, too—which featured some of their work.[95] The truth of the matter is that I dislike the work of these people very much indeed, and, if I had it to do over again, I would not have done the introduction. The editor sent me the book, and I told him I didn't like the poetry in it, or at least most of it. He then asked me to write a short piece describing the kind of poetry I would like to see come along. This I did, and the result is that ever since the book appeared, I have been bracketed with the very writers I dislike the most. But Broyard would not have it that way, until he says what he says. It is all very stupid and foolish, and I have already forgotten most of the gist of what he's talking about. The other reviews, though, have been awfully good, and the book is selling surprisingly well. It has been out less than a month and has already sold 5,000 copies, and had extremely good notices in the Saturday Review Syndicate, in Cosmopolitan, by Elizabeth Janeway, and best of all, in the Boston Globe by a lady named Manning.[96] My God, if you read that notice and then read the one in the Times you wouldn't know that the reviewers were talking about the same writer! Well, so it goes.

Yes, I remember Tom Goethals,[97] though I didn't get to talk to him very much when I was at Skidmore, since I was only there overnight. I liked him very much, and would be very pleased to renew the acquaintanceship. That's the damn trouble with this traveling: you meet people that you would be absolutely crazy about knowing and then you have to go somewhere else where there's maybe some other good people, or no other good people. Thank God I am able to justify passing up most of those readings because of the fact that I would simply be giving the money to the government. Just in the last few days I have got down to try working out some new poems, and make a tentative start at getting the notes together for what will surely prove to be the only other novel I an ever going to write. I have been running around so much in connection with the film and other matters that I have not really written any poetry to speak of for the last year or so. I have got something strange and new moving now, though, and will send it to you as soon as I get some texts worked out. I got the idea from The Seamless Web, which surely did open up the world of poetry to me, but more especially the world itself. I don't know how you are going to feel about what flowers your seeds have planted in this particular head, but I will show you some of them when they grow a little more.

Keep in touch, from down there in the sunshine country, and we will make plans to get together. I'm sorry you're not going to be in New York or thereabouts in about three weeks, for Yevtushenko and Eugene McCarthy and myself are going to give a reading up there, and there might be some good times connected with it. It's something my publisher wants me to do, and, since I know Yevtushenko from his reading during my stay at the Library of Congress, I thought it no more than courteous to reply in kind with a reading for him—or at least with him. I don't know about McCarthy as a <u>reader</u> of poetry, but he is certainly no poet. However, he is an old friend, and I linked up with him in his bid to get Lyndon Johnson out. I was there in Washington, and, though I knew little of politics, I am very glad I was in on that particular venture. Gene is going to make another try, but I believe the crest of the wave has already passed over him. Anyway, I need to talk to him, whatever that enigmatic soul plans to do next.

You should have your book back from Seaver[98] by now; I assume that he <u>did</u> receive it, since you say he is trying to place some of the newer poems in magazines. Believe me, I'll sure look for <u>those</u>!

Our love to Leda, and to you. Let us know when you arrive down there, and if you get this letter. I have had a lot of important mail lost, and most of this has been because I sent it to a new address for someone who was going there from some place else. I'm sure you've had this experience in Europe. My God, all those American Expresses that have never heard of you! Especially when you expect a check to be awaiting you!

All yours,
Jim

JD:lah

TO: GEOFFREY HILL

CC, 1 p; Emory
Columbia, S.C.

January 18, 1972

Dear Geoffrey:

Thanks for sending along your book, <u>Mercian Hymns</u>,[99] which I like very much. You seem to be as mysterious and as gifted as ever, and as obscure a poet as I have ever read. But you seem to me to be on the right track, and have developed in a way that I think is absolutely unique and amazing. Of course, the question of obscurity is sure to come up with reviewers, as it has with me, and fortunately, or unfortunately—but I think fortunately—I like poetry which I despair of ever getting to the bottom of. And yours is surely that kind. I won't go on and on in this immoderate vein, but do want you to know that I think you are one of the best poets in England today, and that your work is timeless, while the work of others, like Ted Hughes, is already reeling with time.

Meanwhile, whenever you have the time or the inclination, write and let me know how things are with you these days. And if you have anything you'd like for <u>Esquire</u> to have a look at, send that along too. I can't promise anything, of course, since our space is limited to what they can squeeze in between the men's deodor-ant and underwear ads, but we will have a try at it, all the same.[100] But <u>do</u> commu-nicate, with or without poems.

We hope to get to England either this spring or summer, if all the hullabaloo over <u>Deliverance</u> dies down enough to permit it, and perhaps we can get together at that time. It would be good to see you—and to hear you play the piano.

All yours,

James Dickey

JD:lah

TO: STANLEY BURNSHAW

TLS, 2 pp;[101] HRHRC

March 15, 1972

Dear Stanley:

Thank you for your long letter, and for all the tiresome business you have had to put up with on my account at what surely must have been a hellish kind of ses-sion. From what you tell me, none of the three judges can agree with another on a single choice. I am indeed surprised at Morgan's actions. Though I don't know him well, I have been a contributor to the <u>Hudson Review</u> for many years, and have recently been on closer terms with him than at any previous time. If he doesn't care for <u>Sorties</u>, that is, of course, his privilege, but it is very odd to learn of his advocacy of his own regular contributors, Haggin and Simon.[102] All these judgings and ring-giving ceremonies are so shot through with personal conflicts, self-aggrandizements, and other such unpleasant things that participating in them is one of those "never again" affairs that one, usually because of other rea-sons, participates in the next time, even so. I have been trapped into seven or eight of them, including three National Book Awards and three Pulitzer Prize's, and, though I thought each of them a hideous experience—all in different ways— when I thought of what might have happened if I hadn't been on the jury, I approve in retrospect of my participation. I was able to help get some good choices, and was able to prevent some disasters, though most of both types of outcome were effected by compromise. And I expect that if <u>Sorties</u> should hap-pen to win, it will be by some such compromise route. But that kind of win is just as much of a win as a unanimous decision, and that gives us continuing hope. But in any case, <u>do</u> know how very much I appreciate your championship of what will almost certainly be my last critical book.

I am not quite clear on the "announcement" business. I understand that this year there won't be any pre-award announcement of finalists,[103] but I also wonder if there will be an announcement of finalists <u>after</u> the prize is given. There ought to be some way of guaranteeing what is certainly a great plus—in advertizing and publicity—to around fifty books which don't get the prize, many of which are very deserving. In other words, if we don't win, I'd still like to take advantage in some way of being in the finals, particularly since Doubleday very nearly gutted itself trying to get the book out at the time it did. All this has really very little to do with anything but my own situation, of course. Anyway, let me know, when you can, how this is to be handled, and I will be guided accordingly. Meanwhile, I enclose a smashing review from the March 11th <u>Saturday Review</u>, which may even convince Fred Morgan, the small-magazine tycoon, himself.

It was great to have you and Leda with us, even though for just such a very short time. It may very well be that my family and I will be able to come up to the Vineyard, as we all very much wish to do. The house your friend has sounds fine, but Maxine has just rushed in to tell me that if possible we want to try to have my oldest boy and his family come up while we are there, and that this would make three bedrooms almost mandatory. We'll certainly understand, even down through the grandchild, if you can't come up with a house of this sort. But we will tentatively arrange our time so as to be able to come up as you suggest. That would be great, believe me.

And even if we aren't able to make it, I would like very much to work out with you this anthology of "creature poetry." That is surely a great idea. We can talk about it as the format develops in your thinking. You know so much more poetry than I do that I would suggest that you carry most of the load and prestige, though it is my hope that I will be able to suggest some things to you that you may have missed.[104]

Meanwhile, I'll sound out the editors at <u>Esquire</u> to see how much space and backlog we have, for they schedule things a good long time in advance. If we are able to use the one dedicated to me, I think we ought to take off the dedication for reasons that are probably obvious, since I'm the editor, and it would seem almost like self-praise if we retained it. Could you send me a couple of carbons of this one? I'll see what can be done.[105]

Any chance of your coming through here when you go back to New York for the final Gunfight at the OK Corral? I'll have to be in New York on the 5th of April for the dinner to be given to the inductees of the National Institute,[106] and maybe if you can't come through Columbia, we could arrange it so that our times in New York overlap. That would make that hideous city bearable.

All yours,
Jim

TO: GORDON LISH

TLS, 1 p;[107] Lilly Library

March 22, 1973

Dear Gordon:

I will get some poems to you in just a few days. The trouble is, however, that I have been blind for the last week, and my eyesight is only just now slowly returning, and consequently, I haven't been able to read manuscripts. I had a freak accident in the mountains of North Carolina, where a cast of my face was being made. The thing broke, and filled my eyes with calcium dust, and, since calcium reacts with water, I had a pretty bad time. Don't worry about all this, for things seem to be working out at least fairly well. Look at it this way: I can now not only write you a piece on withdrawing from alcohol, but on blindness and alcohol combined! The experience will also help us on "Dark Riding," the excerpt from the novel that I'm planning to publish with Esquire. I might call it "Dark Riding," or call it "The Wheedling of Knives," which is what the wind sounds like over the guy wires of a primitive aircraft, a bi-plane trainer.[108]

Let me recover from this ghastly business with my eyes, and I'll move right into some stuff; I'm fired up to write.

I have a tremendously exciting new long poem, which I may have told you about.[109] I sincerely think it is a major work. But the question is whether or not Esquire will have the room to publish the thing entire. If it does, I will bring it out with you; if the magazine doesn't have the room to do the whole thing—and do it right—it may be possible for me to publish a section or two with you, though naturally I would prefer to see it all come out in one place. Anyway, this can be worked out.

Love to all in both your houses, publishing and private. And love to my great god-son. Jesus, would I love to put him in my guitar case and run off with him! Why, that little super-man and I could go anywhere, and make the place jump and glow.

All yours,
Jim

JD:lah

TO: GORDON LISH

TLS, 1 p; Lilly Library
Columbia, S.C.

11 July, 1973

Dear Gordon:

Please forgive the long silence, but I have been run absolutely crazy for the past couple of months—I not only have bats in my belfry: I have <u>wombats</u>—and in view of the fact that all this involves not only my trying to write things inbetween terrible family crises in Atlanta in which my <u>soi-disant</u> business interests are under the sword of Damocles and various other troubles, I just haven't had a chance to communicate with anyone at all except lawyers and other shysters. Bill Buckley, an old friend, and I have decided just to pull out of family and writing woes for a couple of weeks and hole up at a weird place in California called Bohemian Grove,[110] and try to shake off my family traumas and his ulcers. But you can always reach me through Maxine at the Columbia address we all know.

I enclose a couple of poems. I expect you won't want to print the Phrydas boy's thing,[111] but if and when you send it back, I hope you'll want to put the touch of a human hand on the rejection. The strait machine can crush a writer in more ways than one. But that shall be as you wish.

The Warren piece is a more serious matter. It is long, I realize; longer than most poems we print. But might we not possibly run this alone in one issue? That is, devote our entire poetry space to this particular poem, rather than having, as we usually do, a number of short ones? It's a good poem.[112] Old man Red has a lot of raw, troubling power, and old age is giving him more of it. We might, of course, exerpt sections from it; I'm sure that would be all right with him. But if we printed the whole thing, and in addition gave it some prominent space, it would call more attention to our poetic effort in the magazine than several short poems in inconspicuous places, down there among the male deodorants and other accoutrements of swingers and would-be such.

Anyway, I'll let you communicate with Warren, whose current address is West Wardsboro, Vermont, and with Andy Phrydas, living, apparently, at 212 N.W. 32nd Street, Gainesville, Florida, 32601.

Write and tell me what you need, and I'll try to keep in touch. Meanwhile, <u>The Zodiac</u> goes well, and so does the airborne piece, <u>The Wheedling of Knives</u>.

Love to all in your house.

The Godfather,

Jim

TO: ROBERT PENN WARREN

CC, 1 p; Emory

11 July, 1973
Columbia, S.C.

Dear Red:

Sure; I'll make it a good strong point to be here whenever you decide to come. I've made an heroic attempt to keep the travel down, this fall, in favor of some work I've projected. About the only definite commitment I have is the University of Pittsburgh on October 3rd, and, if you'll tell me when the best time for you to come down here should happen to be, I'll make certain that whatever schedule I may develop between now and the time you come will give us some time together. I long to see you.

Meanwhile, the poem is one of the best of all of yours, and I have sent it along to Esquire with as powerful a recommendation as I can command that we put the thing up front and shove out all the little, with-it poems that're all I'm getting these days, in favor of devoting all of our space for an issue to "Rattlesnake Country." Whether the smart-asses in New York will want to do this, I don't know. But they'll hear from me if they don't.

And so will you, one way or the other. Your work is the most powerful voice in American poetry at this time, and you're getting better and better. I had Allen[113] come over to read—it was a great success, which pleased him—and he said as much, himself. Cal Lowell sent me three books which I simply cannot read, full of self-justification and irrelevant description. No; you are the big man now; there's no doubt in my mind, at all. Keep giving us whatever you can give us.

Love to Eleanor,[114] and to all in your house. And let me hear, whenever you should the wish to communicate. I'm here for you.

All yours,

TO: ROBERT PENN WARREN

TLS, 1 p;[115] Yale

January 7, 1974

Dear Red:

I have sent the sections of the new poem on to Gordon Lish in New York, with the strongest recommendations. We still don't have much room, and I don't believe we could possibly do the whole thing as you have it here. I have made some suggestions as to how we might print a part or a couple of parts of the poem, and I have asked Gordon to give me his thoughts on this idea and to come up with suggestions of his own as he wishes. But anyway, the poem is now in the hands of the New York editorial staff, and you will hear either from them or from me on the matter. It is particularly good, Red, and the end is nothing less than smashing, especially the very end.[116]

Well, we'll see.

The pictures we took down at Litchfield came out very well, and we will have reproductions made and send them along to you as a reminder of how human life should be lived and almost never is.

Maxine has been deathly ill. At one time there were indications that she might have as many as four potentially fatal diseases at the same time. It was a dark night not of the soul but of the guts. But one by one the tests came back: the danger of the high blood pressure and coronary problem seem to be over-rated, the diabetes suspected apparently either receded or did not exist in the first place, the test for cervical cancer came back blessedly negative (though Maxine had to have a kind of exploratory operation), and now remains only the gravid liver, which she is combatting with a fine mixture of fury and temperance. So we are not as bad off as we thought we might be. But we have been pretty much out of circulation, what with all this medical runaround, and I am only just now getting back to editing and to my own work. I have only been working a few days, but lots of pieces are falling into place, and the new book of poems, Slowly Toward Hercules, is going to be on all counts the best I have done to date.[117]

My warmest love to Eleanor, and keep some for yourself. I hope your flu is better, or, hopefully, now "vanished quite away."[118]

All yours,
Jim

JD:lah

TO: GORDON LISH

TLS, 1 p;[119] Lilly Library

April 2, 1975

Dear Gordon,

I have just received the news from Theron that Esquire will not use the Zodiac, and I am truly amazed. Theron is furious, but I myself am not furious. The decision against the poem simply strikes me as an example of supreme foolishness. For Esquire to turn this poem down is the equivalent of the Dial's refusal to print The Waste Land.[120]

I don't know exactly what my reaction to <u>Esquire</u>, in general, is. I know that you are there and that augers well. But I do not like the magazine, I must say. The fiction is not much good, despite the efforts of a valiant editor, and the attempts to build up readership through a crude kind of cutsieness and one put-on after another is extremely depressing. Despite our personal friendship, the <u>Zodiac</u> should never have appeared in <u>Esquire</u>. Yet, the expectations that one was led to believe, plus personal loyalty, seem to indicate a major <u>coup</u> having to do with the magazine. Too bad. I will now publish the <u>Zodiac</u> in either <u>The Atlantic</u>, <u>Harper's</u> or <u>Playboy</u>.[121] This fiasco in no way damages the relationship between me and you, nor between my family and your family, all of which relationships take transcendent precedent over anything that <u>Esquire</u> has ever or will ever do. Don't worry; the big poem will knock 'em dead anywhere it appears.

Love to Atticus, and all in your house.

Ever,

Jim

TO: MARY CANTWELL

TLS, 1 p; Mary Cantwell
Columbia, S.C.

April 30, 1975

My Mary,

Thank you for your marvelous letters, from which the spirit of a woman alone—with children and animals to care for—shines with what Marianne Moore once called a "grass-lamp glow." It is wonderful to have these; and I draw on them continually for sustenance, in my hectic life.

I have just completed what people tell me is the most important long poem since <u>The Wasteland</u>. Editors keep wanting to break it up and publish various sections; and something like this, of course, could be done. But I will have none of that. If the poem appears at all, it is going to have to appear intact. I realize what space limitations are in magazine work, since I have fought so desperately for space in <u>Esquire</u> for six years. But any editor who lets this one, called <u>The Zodiac</u>, get away from him or her deserves to lose it. Let me know if you would like to see it, and if you would, contact my agent, Theron Raines, at 244 Madison Avenue. The agency is Raines & Raines, and the telephone number is 683-7012. Whether or not you publish it, I'd sure like to hear what you think of it. I can't believe that I wrote it, to tell you the truth.[122]

I will be up for the Spring meeting of the National Institute (I don't have the date with me as I write—but it's a week or ten days away). My wife will be with me, and I'd like you to meet her, and her you. That is not the usual basis between myself and yourself, but it might be a good occasion even so. Check the Institute date, and give us a call at the St. Moritz the day before the occasion.

There will be other occasions.

Love to all in your house, and keep writing to me from the 18th Century, as New York should recognize such in your letters, had it but the wit. As for me, I have half the wit.

All yours,
Jim

P.S. Keep writing me, even about the poem, here at school and not at home.

TO: STANLEY BURNSHAW

TLS, 1 p;[123] HRHRC

April 13, 1976

Dear Stanley,

Sorry to be so remiss in answering your good letters, but I have been pushed beyond all resonable human boundaries these latter days, with the build-up for The Zodiac, the new novel, the Call of the Wild television spectacular—which, incidentally, you will be able to see on the 19th of May at 8:00 on NBC—and various projects concerning a new television series to come from the May 19th show.[124]

I am much honored to have Mirages dedicated to me.[125] I remember a remark in a poem by Robert Lowell wherein he talks about a visit to Gettysburg with Allan Tate, where Tate says to Lowell, "I don't know whether to call you my father or my brother."[126] I would say of us, Stanley, that I would prefer, and feel, the latter.

I am delighted that Doubleday is doing Mirages, and that Sandy Richardson is your editor. He came through Columbia and visited us only yesterday, and it seems there is an awfully good relationship, for once, between top writers and top publishers. I am delighted to have been in a position to help bring about the publication of a major work by a major American poet who just happens to be a close personal friend.

My love to Leda; Maxine and the children send theirs also.

Ever,
Jim

P.S. Kevin is going to Washington & Lee, where Sandy Richardson went, and we are happy about his going to a Virginia school as well as to Sandy's alma mater.

I got so carried away with the actual writing of this letter that I forgot the most important part; <u>Mirages</u> is a work of such major importance that it will endure for all time.

Jim—— thank you for sending me <u>the Lugano Review</u>![127]

TO: THOMAS C. WALLACE[128]

August 1976

CC, 1 p; Emory
Columbia, S.C.

Dear Mr. Wallace,

Please forgive my belatedness concerning the third and last volume of the Robert Frost biography.[129] I can plead only a very heavy work schedule, illness and travel. I have long been a great admirer of Frost, in his poems, prose writings, aphorisms and letters, and am herewith very happy to give you a publicity quote, if you still want it. I did a lead piece for the <u>Atlantic Monthly</u> on volume one of the Thompson biography. There was something repellent about the man, and perhaps I overemphasized this. Nevertheless, from personal acquaintance, plus a long familiarity with his writings, I have since come to admire him very much. I admire also the heroic effort that Lawrance Thompson made to finish his monumental work, and I admire also R. H. Winnick's aid in finishing the third volume. You can take any portion of this letter and reproduce it with a couple of provisos. First, that you let me know exactly how you use what I have said and where you say it. The second proviso is that you send me a hard-bound copy of the third volume.

And yet there is a third, also. Please give my personal regards to Mr. Winnick, and tell him that I am very proud of him. It can have been no easy task, his.

Sincerely,

James Dickey

JD:sea

TO: LOUIS SIMPSON

CC, 2 pp; Emory
Columbia, S.C.

August 10, 1977

Dear Louis,

I have just finished <u>Three on the Tower</u>[130] and wanted quickly to write to you and tell you how fine I think it is. It must have been a tremendously difficult job but I don't think such difficulties have ever been dealt with before in such an urbane and readable way. At first I thought your approach—part scholarly, part critical, part biographical, and part personal opinion on the part of the biographer—a little curious but I soon got to like the effect of what I was reading and now I would not wish to go back to perusing more standardized or compartmentalized biographies, especially those of writers.

The section on Eliot, that secretive man, is most enlightening. Like you, I doubt very seriously as to whether any official biography will ever be written on him. As I remember he took some pains to specify that no such <u>Life</u> should be authorized. The only other example of this attitude I can think of is, curiously enough, Matthew Arnold. It seems odd that a man of Eliot's influence should have so little biographical interest. I imagine this fact would have pleased him, but there was something terrible, perhaps unthinkable, underlying all of that scholarly reasonableness. You have certainly fixed my conviction in this matter and it will most probably not waver.

Again, this is only a very brief note to let you know how highly I esteem the book and my acquaintance with you which though reasonably long, has been lamentably infrequent. But I am in and out of New York city a good deal and perhaps it will be possible for us to meet for a drink or even dinner at some time during the upcoming school year. I like to think of that; it would be good human time.

My best to all in your house. Please accept my continuing good wishes for yourself and all your projects.

Yours ever,
James Dickey

JD:sea

TO: ELIZABETH HARDWICK

13 September 1977   *Telegram, 1 p; HRHRC*
                                                      Columbia, S.C.

THIS MAN OF WORDS HAS NO WORDS. I LIKE TO THINK THAT CAL WENT IN A
GREAT RUSH OF PRIDE IN THE WONDERFUL ACCOMPLISHMENT OF HIS LIFE
AND WORK.[131] I CAN GUARANTEE THAT I WILL HAVE SUCH A FEELING FOR HIM
WHEN THE SAME THING HAPPENS TO ME AND AS I DO NOW. PLEASE KNOW
THAT I AM WITH YOU AND HARRIET ALWAYS, NOW THAT ALL WE CAN DO IS TO
LOVE HIM FOREVER.

                                                      JAMES DICKEY

TO: A. J. VOGL[132]

                                                      CC, 1 p; Emory
                                                      Columbia, S.C.

February 14, 1979

Dear A. J. Vogl:

My choices of musical selections for a record to be sent to other worlds are the
following:

1. George Frideric Handel, Water Music Suite
2. Bix Beiderbecke, "Royal Garden Blues"
3. Richard Wagner, "Overture" from Rienzi
4. Bela Bartok, Concerto for Orchestra
5. "Duellin' Banjoes," recorded by Eric Weissberg and Steve Mandel
6. Wolfgang Amadeus Mozart, Horn Concerto in D Major
7. "Ragtime Annie," recorded by Doc and Merle Watson

I am looking forward to receiving Carl Sagan's book[133] as well as a copy of your
magazine.

                                                      Sincerely yours,
                                                      James Dickey

jaw

TO: JAMES APPLEWHITE[134]

TLS (Xerox), 1 p; Emory

25 February, 1980
Columbia, S.C.

Dear Jim:

It is good to have your last letter; please forgive me for not answering it sooner. Life here has been very busy, continuously being interrupted by the interminable and confusing medical tests. But something has <u>got</u> to be done, for my esophagus is twisted and has set up a curious situation where my guts are strangling each other, and as a result I am not able to assimilate food properly, and am slowly starving to death. I have narrowed the choice of surgeons down to a fellow in Charleston and another (the better, but so <u>remote</u>!) in Seattle, and I am awaiting their comparison of X-ray reports, suggestions, and the rest. This really needn't bother you, for what will be <u>will</u> certainly be, and all will be resolved in a couple of months, one way or the other. I'll keep you posted, you can bet.

How is your manuscript coming? You mentioned revising some of the pieces, and of giving some thought to another title. I still like <u>Shadow Brother</u>,[135] and am most eager to see what you have come up with in the way of revisions. If North Carolina puts forth a poet, it should certainly be you, rather than someone like Archie Ammons (who must certainly be the dullest writer of all time, bar almost none) or Fred Chappell.[136] Bob Watson[137] is a little better than these, but not much. We need to get a book of yours in front of people, so that they can see these things. What thought have you given to publishers? Though I like Doubleday fine, the big presses are on the whole not so hot, though if you'd like to come out with one of them, let me know. The trouble with them is that most are not really interested in or knowledgeable about poetry for its own sake, but will publish poetry as a sop, in order to get the author to write a novel or a travel book (or even a cook book!) for them: something they believe will <u>sell</u>! It is all a dreadful pain, and I think a really good poet, such as yourself, would do better with one of the good university presses, like Wesleyan, or Texas. If you'd like me to explore some of these possibilities for you, let me know, and I'll get right on it.

I must go along now, and get back to what I am supposed to be doing. But I am delighted with the things you say about <u>The Strength of Fields</u>. Your words make a lot of difference, and your presence in the world even more.

My best to Jan, and to all in your house.

Yours, Jim

TO: ROBERT PENN WARREN

TLS, 1 p;[138] Yale

May 12, 1980

Dear Red,

I am leaving for Seattle in a couple of days for an occasion which involves some "major" surgery, and I wanted to get this off to you before I left on a trip whose outcome may be uncertain. Really, though, this is just to let you know how much your work and your existence mean to me. Rob Cowley[139] has just sent along your Talking book,[140] and I have been going through it, noting points of similarity (so many!) between your background and convictions and mine, and also being rendered absurdly grateful, time after time, for your insights into the creation of poetry, the structure and technique of fiction, and your whole manner of taking life and responding to existence. I seldom write letters to writers; most of my correspondence is of inferior quality in a literary sense, as doubtless this one is, but I wanted to tell you, once more, that whichever writer has been valuable to me is going to have to be identified as you.

One of the fellows who edited your interviews, Floyd Watkins, has approached me as to the possibility of my giving-over my papers, drafts, letters and so on to Emory University in Atlanta, and at the same time spoke of his wish to acquire yours as well. I don't know what I am going to do about this suggestion, but being coupled with you in such a way I take as a good sign, no matter how actuality may eventually resolve things.[141]

Later, when I have more time to dig into comparisons, I will write you at length about the new version of Brother to Dragons.[142] I haven't time to do the poem justice under the present circumstances, but do know that though I believed the original version to be a classic, I now think that you have made of it a super-classic, and I plan to tell you in detail later on why I think so.

I am happy, also, that you believe Audubon[143] to be one of your best poems. So do I, and from it I chose the end, Section VII, to be read at my wife's funeral.[144] I could think of nothing of my own so fitting, or so likely to last, or to hang longer in the bearded oaks of Waccamaw Cemetery, at Litchfield, where we were all together.

My best to you, always, to Eleanor, and to your children.

Yours,

Jim

TO: RICHARD HUGO[145]

CC, 1 p; Emory
Columbia, S.C.

June 13, 1980

Dear Dick,

I am back now, lying like a stepped-on lizard in the flowery sun down here, with your many phone calls still in the realest of all inner ears, which are those of the spirit. It may be that you won't believe me—though I hope you do—when I tell you that your messages from Montana were more effective medicine than all the knives, drugs, and radioactive magics of the doctors. You are someone I could always talk to, and your calls to Seattle rank with the letter I got from you after the poetry-doings at the American Embassy in London, so long ago.[146]

I am busy working on a situation whereby you might come down here for a few days, talk to our kids, and be pretty well paid for it. By the time you get here, you may be sure that they will know your poems as well as the magnificent Triggering Town;[147] the best ones already know these things, but when you come, the worst ones will know them too. It is those "worst ones" that the teacher really exists for, whether he knows it or not. As for me, I had rather be surprised by a student's performance than gratified by one, though both are surely desirable.

The trip back was only a minor nightmare, though when I protested that the film shown en route not be the scheduled Little Miss Marker but a buried classic called Ride a Crooked Road (starring John Agar), I had to be restrained and placed in the seat next to another handcuffed transportee, a fellow named Ted Bundy, who was being returned to Florida.[148]

Again, without jokes, I want to thank you for your calls. I wish it had been possible for you to drive through the stone snows of Mount St. Helen[149] to spend a day or two with us in Seattle, but I surely understand the circumstances and can hope very strongly that we will make up for all these lost years when you come to South Carolina.

My best to Ripley, whom I must meet. You and I must get the new wives together (yours not so new, mine fairly new).[150] It's just as the general said to the admiral in King Kong versus Godzilla after they had outlined the paths of the monsters on a military map and saw that the inevitable was inevitable: "There's no doubt that when they meet, they'll destroydestroy each other." I hope this won't be true of Ripley and Deborah after all, I never did believe in the prophetic powers of Japanese horror movies.

Please write soon; I need you still, and always.

Always,

TO: PETER VIERECK

TLS, 2 pp;[151] Peter Viereck

June 26, 1980

Dear Peter:

Thank you for the letter about <u>The Strength of Fields</u>. Of all the poets of my time, you have the most integrity and courage; when you say something, you mean it. I am not given to gush, but I do indeed thank you with whatever heart I have. Your letter was especially welcome, since when I got it I was facing major surgery. This was done in Seattle during the very heighth—if that is the word—of the Mount St. Helen's eruption, and I credit your letter and your opinion as being foremost among those agencies that enabled me to arise more or less in one (renewed) piece from under the surgical snows of Seattle and the stone snows of Mount St. Helen's.

Also, your material on the death and "wake" of Georg Heym[152] was most welcome, and vividly interesting. Heym is such a violent writer that he is almost dangerous, and despite my indifferent German, I am very much moved by him, and solidly in his corner. He has not been done any kind of justice in translation. Michael Hamburger[153] has the end of "Judas" as "his feet were small as flies / in the shrill gleam of golden skies." I thought "the golden hysteria of heaven" much better, though it is not really what Heym said.[154] The phrase is neither Heym nor myself, but something in between, and perhaps better than either. The phrase has become a favorite of Red Warren's, incidentally, so he tells me.

Come to think of it, your admiration for Heym and for Roy Campbell indicates very definitely—and has indicated for these many years—that you and I are just as surely mavericks as those two are. I myself count it very good to be a wolf among the sheep that mill complacently around in poetry, these days. There are so many mild-mannered half-talented forgettable people: sheep in sheep's clothing, I call them.

Something you could do for me, if you like. In fact, a couple of things. My literary executor down here, Matthew Bruccoli, has a daughter who is beginning at Mt. Holyoke in the fall, and any help or little kindnesses you might be able to extend to her would be much appreciated. She is a fine little girl, and I'm sure you won't find any association with her onerous.

The other thing is that I have a new poem, in a completely different style from any of the others, in the July <u>Atlantic</u>.[155] It is a kind of elegy for Jim Wright, who died a couple of months ago of cancer of the tongue. If you like it, let the editors at the <u>Atlantic</u> know it, for I have a number of other poems written in the same idiom, and I would like as receptive an audience as I can get.

Let me hear from you again soon, and send along as many of those wild off-beat Xeroxes as you care to: they are always welcome here.

My very best to you as always, Peter. As I remember, the last time we saw each other was on that strange television show with Muriel Rukeyser. Though I never saw her on more than one occasion other than that one, it is still strange that she is gone.[156] Those left, the best ones, must close ranks; the rest I don't care about. So keep in touch, as you will.

Yours,

Jim

TO: ELIZABETH LASENSKY[157]

CC, 1 p; Emory
Columbia, S.C.

30 July 1980

Dear Ms. Lasensky:

Here are the answers to your three questions:

1. Some books that I read as a teenager:
   <u>Baseball Joe and the Silver Stars</u>
   <u>Gary Grayson's Hill Street Eleven</u>
   <u>Poppy Ott and the Stuttering Parrot</u>
   <u>Poppy Ott and the Whispering Mummy</u>
   <u>The Land of No Shadow</u> by Carl H. Claudy
   <u>Tarzan the Terrible</u> by Edgar Rice Burroughs
   <u>Bomba the Jungle Boy in the Temple of Vines</u>
   <u>Tom Swift in the Caves of Ice</u>
   <u>Of Human Bondage</u> by W. Somerset Maugham
2. A book I like very much:
   <u>Collected Letters</u> by Rainer Maria Rilke
   My favorite writer: James Agee
3. What I would say to encourage teenagers to use the library:
   "Every book is a separate new life. I would stress potential, intellectual, and physical excitement, adventure."

I hope these notes will be helpful to you in your display.

Sincerely,

James Dickey

JLD:lb

TO: SEYMOUR KRIM[158]

CC, 1 p; Emory
Columbia, S.C.

30 July 1980

Dear Seymour,

Thank you for your last letter and for sending along the piece on Henry Miller which I thought was excellent and enjoyed very much. I never met him, but I got a weird letter from him one time about something I had written. I don't even remember whether or not I answered him, or even what the letter was about, but I did read a couple of books of his that he got Jim Laughlin[159] to send me. One of them was called Books In My Life and after I read it, I read a notice about it in Partisan Review. The guy didn't like the book, and said it was like listening to some amiable, mildly intelligent old fellow in a bar.[160] When I thought it over, I saw that is what Miller's work is like, but maybe too many people put down such conversation. Personally, I like mildly intelligent old guys; I'm one myself, more or less.

The New York plans are still on. My wife Debba and I will be there a week during the middle of October, and we and you and your girl(s?) can have some fun. You'll like Debba; she's a demon from the pit, and very beautiful. Some pit, she comes from!

I am much better after the operation, though this is one of those kinds of recovery that take a lot of time and idleness. But don't worry; I'll make it.

I'm sure looking forward to getting together with you. If all Jews were like you and all Southern rednecks like me, we could straighten this World thing out for the rest of humanity, right quick.

Yours,

JLD/lb

TO: TRUMAN CAPOTE[161]

CC, 1 p; Emory
Columbia, S.C.

11 August 1980

Dear Mr. Capote:

Would you like to come down here to South Carolina and speak to us sometime next spring? If your schedule might permit such an occasion, and you were inclined to it, I can get back to you on the details—including the financial—once I hear from you.

When you can, do let me hear from you on this. Needless to say, I hope very much you can come. When I first moved here from the Library of Congress twelve years ago, I asked the President of the college what might be the advantages of living in South Carolina, which I as a Georgian had always thought of as a depressed area, full of pellagra and prejudice, and he answered, simply, "Flowers and birds." They were here—are here—and so am I. You come too. (Though I hate to quote that super-jerk Robert Frost to end a letter intended as friendly, and as at least a mild enticement.)[162]

With best wishes,
James Dickey

JLD/lb

TO: ROBERT PENN WARREN

TLS, 1 p;[163] Yale

11 August 1980

Dear Red,

Thank you so very much for the book[164] and for the inscription, which Debba and I will prize for as long as we can stand up and see lightning and hear thunder; yes, and longer than that, too. As it happens, I have just reviewed the book for the Saturday Review,[165] and I believe on my honor it is the best piece I have ever done, in all my reviewing: surely the closest to my intent, and to what I really do feel about a writer. The kind of criticism I do is closer to Ruskin or Walter Pater than it is to Eliot or somebody like William Empson; I am a very emotional critic, and am as likely to be talking about myself as about the poet I'm supposed to be dealing with. But I believe that in this piece, I subordinate my own reaction to your work (which is intense) to the work itself, and I believe I have got pretty close to the heart of it. I haven't seen the printed article yet, but am told it is in the August issue, so have a look and let me know what you think.

Debba sends her love, and I do mine. Please remember us with great fondness to Eleanor.

Ever,
Jim

TO: SEYMOUR KRIM

CC, 2 pp; Emory
Columbia, S.C.

August 22, 1980

Dear Seymour:

I haven't heard from you in some time, and I've been gone a lot and wanted to check in with you and see how you are getting along. Since you have an unlisted number, I tried to get the number from the <u>Village Voice</u>, and called, but the phone company told me that the number had been disconnected, and so I thought you might have moved, or something. This letter is just to keep the contact established. The October dates are now firm: I'll be coming up there October 17th, and will stay until the 23rd, which should certainly give us at least a little time to ramble around the Village, listen to some blues, or do whatever you think might be right for us all. Do let me know about your situation, and I'll swing right with you.

The enclosed piece is an introduction I did for the new edition of the <u>Diction-ary of Literary Biography</u> for the volume on American poetry since the second war. Since you broke open the whole idea for me with some of your remarks on Thomas Wolfe, I wanted you to see this, and to check the part you play in my assumptions and assertions. Right or wrong, this is something else I owe you for. It will bring me plenty of flak, but I've got my own shortsighted cannoneer in the top turret, and he uses twenty-millimeter cannons rather than the usual twin fifties.[166]

There is another guy who has—or had—the same free-swinging, powerful, individual approach to literature and culture that you have. No; not the same, for he is not as good as you are. But he is plenty good, and he has just died. His name is George P. Elliott,[167] and you may have read him in some of the journals, for he wrote a lot for them. He is not a bad fiction writer and he is <u>sort</u> of a poet, though not really distinctive. But he is a first-rate cultural and literary essayist, and all his books are out of print. I have no stake in his (posthumous) gain, except that I think his example and his work should go on, and I thought that I could, maybe, get his widow to collect his things and publish them all in a big book, if I could get a good enough editor, someone of like mind and like daring, to arrange the pieces and write an introduction. If I can get this going, and find the right publisher, would you be interested in handling that part of it? Again, it's a long shot, but I am a born gambler; as Whitman says, it tastes right to me. So—what say you? If you like, maybe you would want to read some of Elliott's stuff. The best of it col-lected between covers is in two books, called <u>A Piece of Lettuce</u> and <u>Conver-</u>

sions.[168] Those are out of print, naturally, but you could get them. You could also look up Stanley Edgar Hyman's review of <u>Lettuce</u> in Hyman's book <u>Standards</u>,[169] if you would care to get a preliminary overview of all this.

Do let me know how you're doing, for you and your city-psyche are much with me these days; these are things I need to know more about than I do, and I am much looking forward to getting together with you, you can believe; you've got that open head and heart, and there are damn few of those.

Ever,
James Dickey

TO: LANCE MORROW AND/OR MARIA LUISA CISNEROS[170]

CC, 1 p; Emory
Columbia, S.C.

September 15, 1980

Dear Mr./Ms. Morrow/Cisneros:

Thank you for your letter, and for attempting to clear up some confusion for me. Certainly it is nice to know that you intended a link-up of myself with Lyndon Johnson as a compliment,[171] though I suspect that this intention was lost— since it appeared without your ingenious and quite private rationale—on all of your readers save yourself; certainly it was on me. Johnson is irrevocably and forever the Viet Nam President, and that is the association your readers will inevitably make. I supported McCarthy because I felt he was right in his stand. What I may or may not have risked in taking such a stand while serving under Johnson is known to me, and not to you. How, exactly, do you know that I "realistically risked absolutely nothing" by doing what I did? And what do you mean by "posturing," and "a few fairly easy moral points with the antiwar movement"? If I had wanted to score points of this nature, either hard or easy, I would have been engaged in the various public demonstrations against the war that so many of my generation saw fit to participate in. I did none of this. I was approached by phone by your people—a Mrs. Leviton of the Atlanta office—as to my views on laureateship, and I told her what I thought of it, which is not much. Instead of using what you asked me for, I find myself in your article bracketed with the most detested president of our time. You may appreciate my confusion here, I should expect.

Anyway, it was good of you to write, for I am sure you are busy, as I am. And please forgive me for quite honestly not knowing who you are. If you are offended by this, as you seem to be, I hope to be forgiven. I'll be in New York in about a month, so maybe we might talk some of this out, if you are of a mind. I had just as soon not go on thinking of you as an irresponsible jerk, nor myself as one, either.

Sincerely,

James Dickey

JLD:lb

TO: JOHN BUDAN[172]

CC, 1 p; Emory

Columbia, S.C.

November 3, 1980

Dear John Budan:

Thank you for your very moving letter about the death of your swimming teacher at the Y, and your kindness in telling me of the poem of mine that he used to keep, and now you keep.[173] In answer to your question: yes, the poem is about a lifeguard at a summer camp for boys who tries to save one of the boys—maybe one about your age, or a couple of years younger—from drowning, but can't do it. This makes him feel very guilty, and he can't face the other little boys who thought he could do just about anything. At night, hiding out in the boathouse, he has a fit of grief and guilt like going out of his mind, and in this fit of craziness he believes that he can walk out on the water on nothing but the moonlight and bring back the boy who has drowned to life. For a moment he believes he can do this, and that he actually is doing it: that he sees the form of the boy rising to him from the depths of the lake, breaking the surface of the lake with his forehead, but then—but no, he sees that it is only a dream, and that the dead boy, who seemed to be rising back into life from the water, is water forever.

But you have most of the poem figured out just fine, for yourself, and I hope you will keep it with you, for you and me, for the lifeguard and boy in the poem, and for your swimming teacher at the Y: for all of us, the living and the dead.

Your friend,

James Dickey

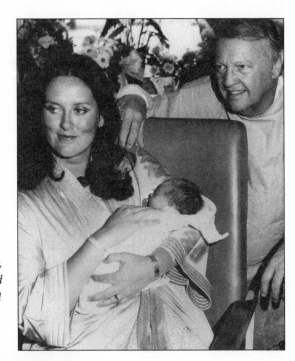

Deborah Dodson Dickey,
Bronwen Elaine Dickey, and
James Dickey, May 1981

Dickey and Bronwen, winter 1981–82

PART EIGHT

MAN OF LETTERS

January 1981–August 1988

Robert Penn Warren with Dickey in a still photo from the CBS Cable video Two Poets, Two Friends *(1982)*

TLS, 1 p;[2] Emory

January 15, 1981

Dear Mr. Bottoms:

Thank you very much for your book, which I am reading with great pleasure, and for the things you say about my work. It is curious that you should mention the passage in <u>Self-Interviews</u> where I talk about Malcolm Lowry and Nordahl Grieg, for I do indeed feel about certain writers as Lowry did about Grieg;[3] in fact, I felt and do feel that way about Lowry, and last September when I was in England making some telecasts with Malcolm Muggeridge, I went by Lowry's grave in a little village in Sussex called Ripe, took some pictures and did what I could in the way of keeping company with the dead. The fact that you have some of the same feeling about me is strange and heartening, and I assure you that I would be very happy to meet with you, anytime you could get up this way. Let me know how your spring schedule is shaping up, and maybe we can get together. I'd like that a lot, believe me. I am on sabbatical this semester, and though I must travel some, I am still relatively flexible, so we could probably work something out, according to your own allotment of time. We could talk, maybe read some poems and swap out on some guitar stuff. What make of instrument do you play, anyway? Since "Dueling Banjos" I have had so many endorsement requests that the house is full of an almost unimaginable number of guitars of all makes, though oddly enough nobody ever sent me a banjo. But guitars I have got, canoes I have got, bows and arrows and knives I have got by the gross, by the carload, by the tens of racks. If you like music, and if you like the outdoors and primitive weapons, you would like it here, and I hope you come here. But that shall be as you wish. Meanwhile I have your strong, individual, real, uncompromising and enlivening book, and it is welcome in my house and so are you.

Sincerely,

James Dickey

TO: PAUL HEMPHILL[4]

TLS (Xerox), 2 pp;[5] Emory

January 16, 1981

Dear Paul:

Your book just came, and I read the whole thing straight through last night.[6] Some of it is quite marvelous, especially the war pieces and the piece on Wallenda. A compilation of journal and magazine pieces depends for its effectiveness largely on variety, and you have plenty of that. I am interested in this not only because you wrote it and because it is good, but because two other things are also true. The first of these is that some of my friends—close friends like Mailer and George Plimpton and Willie Morris, and acquaintance-friends like Marshall Frady and Harry Crews[7]—are always hammering at me and at everybody else who will listen on their main philosophical thought regarding what they do, which is the "higher journalism," the journalism of sensibility. Another of these, Tom Wolfe,[8] was here last year and stayed with us a few days, and he is quite convinced that the real literature of our time is in this form. He may be right, for he is an exciting writer, as are all these others, and as you are, who belong right up there with the best of them. The second consideration I mentioned is that my own oldest son is a journalist, doing exactly the same thing; he is in El Salvador, right in the middle of all that high-speed random lead, and he feels the same way as Mailer and the others do. The form has developed its own set of standards and techniques. The danger of the "journalism of high sensibility" is that it is already tending to run to a formula in which the main ingredients are over-heavy and obvious irony and self-consciously colloquial diction. Too much of either one of these, or both of them at the same time, wear out very quickly, and the formulaic quality tends to submerge the individual sensitivity that brings this genre, at its best, close to the art that Plimpton and Wolfe and the others want to make of it. Among these writers, you are certainly among the top-flight, if not indeed the best of all of them already, or surely potentially so. But the dangers of any literary approach, any literary form, are real dangers and are peculiar to that form. The avoidance of them or the turning of them into virtues are[9] the main tasks that must be faced. And that's the end of <u>that</u> catechism.

I also return the poem you sent over a few weeks ago, with some tentative edits and suggestions. Keep me informed as to the progress of the thing; I feel I have a stake now.

My best to everyone in your house: or houses, maybe I should say: your publishing house and your real house.

Yours,

Jim

JLD:lb

TO: SAUL BELLOW[10]

CC, 1 p; Emory
Columbia, S.C.

March 6, 1981

Dear Mr. Bellow:

Though all I remember of you personally—doubtless more than you remember of me—occurred a good many years back when we were both on some sort of Rockefeller committee to give money to other writers, I like many others have followed your work with great interest, fascination, and joy, and on the basis of these general credentials would like to ask some running advice from you, if you have time.

I have entered into an arrangement with United Artists, and with the director and producer Jerome Hellman,[11] to write what the trade papers call an "epic" film, this one dealing with the Yukon and the Klondike gold rush. United Artists has given Hellman and me the money to go ahead with this, and it will be done, one way or the other.

Where you come into this is that I am quite intentionally basing one of the characters on Delmore Schwartz,[12] and if you want to see how Delmore would influence and perhaps dominate the Klondike in 1898–99, you will have to see my movie, which is scheduled for 1983. As the author of Humboldt's Gift, which is surely the best book ever written by a writer about another writer, and quite possibly your best book as well (if I may judge), I wonder if I might ask you from time to time for some information about Schwartz's personality, his kind of imagination, characteristic attitudes, and sayings of his? This is only a preliminary sort of venture, here, a preliminary sort of letter, but I thought I might as well lay it on you early, for I am drawing heavily, even in the first stages, on your version of Delmore. I hope this is all right, for if it works out as I intend, the film will be the second-best tribute to Schwartz that anybody has yet conceived, and with luck may even be in the same class with the first-best.

Let me know what you think of all this, and I will be guided accordingly. Meanwhile, thank you for your work, and your existence.

Sincerely,
James Dickey

TLS, 2 pp;[13] Jerome Hellman

March 19, 1981

Dear Jerry:

A short note to get these letters from Bellow's agent and Delmore's biographer to you.[14] Both of these sources seem interested in the project, and apparently they see no difficulty about libel actions of any sort, or indeed any displeasure or interference on the part of Delmore's executors, relatives or friends. Just how we might want to use the cooperation of these people—or of others like Dwight MacDonald—I am not sure, but that is something we can work out later.

In our phone conversation of the other night—much enjoyed, I can tell you!—I mentioned, in connection with our interest in Delmore's background, a book by Irving Howe that might prove useful to us. I have since looked it up and read it, and I think we should definitely assimilate this into the material of the story. The book is called World of Our Fathers, and is a social portrait of the East European Jewish immigrants in America. It won the National Book Award for History in 1976, and is, like almost all of Howe's work, extremely imaginative as well as informative. I can see all kinds of possibilities here, particularly in relation to Delmore's—the original Delmore's—family recollections of his grandfather's hiding in a "wine-stinking barrel, / For three days in Bucharest" before he "left for America / To become a king himself."[15] I also think you should read through Delmore's Genesis, which is a quite undisguisedly autobiographical account of Delmore's early life, particularly since you are reading the Atlas biography, which deals with the same material. The libraries out there may not have Genesis, but if they don't I'm sure that either the Gotham Book Mart in New York or James Laughlin's New Directions can get you a copy. My own book is so heavily annotated that it would be more confusing than enlightening, I am quite sure, though if need be I can send it.

Keep digging for the title, and I will do the same. A possible field of interpretation, or a couple of them. I have already suggested working with the word claim as part of the title. If we took maps of the location up there and scanned them for local place-names, and used the most evocative of them in conjunction with the word claim, we might come up with something in line with what we want. As an example, but only as an example, and not recommended at all, would be something like The Dead Horse Claim, or The Featherfoot Claim. Look over some of those maps in the Berton book, Jack Hope's book, or Keith Tryck's, or the others, and see what might spark.[16]

Another possibility is the world field. In the Klondike, there were not only claims, but fields; in fact, the whole thing was a gold field. Field opens up a whole new set of referential possibilities, quite different from those given rise to by claim. I think immediately of the Field of the Cloth of Gold, somewhere in English history, though I forget where. Of course we can't use that, nor would we want to, but field itself might be much to our purpose.

I'll close now, to get this in the mail. But work is going forward here, I can tell you, and I'll be ready whenever you are to carry things forward in any way you like.[17]

Our best to you, and to Nancy. We hope to see you soon.

Ever,

Jim

JLD:lb

TO: STANLEY BURNSHAW

TLS, 2 pp;[18] HRHRC

May 13, 1981

Dear Stanley,

It is wonderful to hear from you, and especially to hear the details about The Refusers.[19] I am studying out, now, what I might do to be helpful, and I guess the first thing I need to do is to read it. At this point the difficulty that presents itself is not whether I will furnish you with a jacket quote, for I will certainly do that, but whether I have the background and the knowledge of your subject matter to make it the supremely effective quote that I would like it to be, that it must be. As soon as I get the galleys I will read straight through them and take notes, and maybe I will be able to come up with something worthy of being used in connection with the "capstone" of the writing career of one such as you. Well, we'll see what can be done. But know that you can count on me. I'll do my best.

The subject of The Refusers is of great interest to me right now for other reasons, even, than that you wrote it. I am writing a new film—one with a huge budget and almost infinite resources—and as I have conceived the story, one of the two main characters, the one on whom the main events turn, is a young Jewish fellow from the Bronx: a wild-eyed, enthusiastic, likable, exasperating and very Jewish tummler very much like what I remember—but mostly what I have heard—of Delmore Schwartz. My producer is Jerome Hellman, who did the much-awarded-to Coming Home, Midnight Cowboy, and other films of note, and he is much taken with this character, and wants to build the film almost exclusively around him. I don't know how the final balance will come out, but I do know that in developing this character I must delve more deeply than I have ever had occasion to do into the Jewish experience in this country, particularly that of the Jewish immigrants of the late nineteenth and early twentieth centuries. To this end I am not only reading all of Delmore, some of which is extremely good and some not so good, but historical work like Irving Howe's World of Our Fathers, which has certainly been a revelation to me, especially about the first-generation of Eastern European Jews transplanted to New York City. I don't want to bore you with all this, but would only like to indicate that I may well draw on your knowledge of Judaism, particularly the conditions and attitudes of the Jewish intellectual inclining to poetry, whether he is a tummler like Delmore—or like my character—or not. I'll let you know how the project goes forward as it develops. I went out to Hollywood in February and Hellman and I spent two weeks, 9–5 every day—and sometimes longer—working out a story that suited us both. We have 1000 pages of transcribed notes, and still the story is at least to some degree nebulous, though the possibilities are exciting, or at least I think so. I'll tell you more about this later on, but right now there is a big Writers' Strike on and not much further can be done until all that is settled. But we have begun the thing and eventually you'll see it.

Debba and I are now within two weeks of changing the human race by adding to it the element it has lacked from the beginning: namely, a child consisting of us. The target date is the 27th of this month, and everything is ready. Biology itself is in the final stages of readiness, and the Little Hero will come forth, as they say, "on or around" that date. Believe me, we'll let you know.[20]

My love to Leda, and keep plenty for yourself. Keep in touch, and we'll bring all projects to great climaxes. Keep well, my old friend.

Ever,
Jim

P.S. I enclose a recent publicity photograph showing how I appear when I read my animal and military poems.

TO: RADCLIFFE SQUIRES

TLS, 1 p;[21] Washington University

June 9, 1981

Dear Jim,

How good the stuff is! I am so very sorry that I have waited even this long to write you about Gardens of the World.[22] I don't know of any poetry anywhere—

Lord how these generations struggle with the Word! Many are called . . . —that is any better than "Men and horses: Wyoming" or that is as good as "The first day out from Troy." It seems to me that you are totally remarkable, and Anne Stevenson is fairly right, but has missed the essential gist, in what she says on the jacket. I think that the conjunction of the American western wilderness and the great classical themes of Europe that gets into your poems is the most totally remarkable thing I know, not only in the poetry that is being written now, but in that which has already been written, or could be written, even. The poet who could say <u>When you are cold and wet enough that / The weight of clothes proves naked-ness</u> . . . could say anything, and also <u>would</u> say anything. I won't go on and on, because I am not given to gush, but I did want you to know how your poems, your new poems, come over to, get down into and stay with one who defers to no man—or woman or child or animal—in his admiration, and in his gratitude for the states of spirit you have made available.

My best to you, my old friend.

Ever,

Jim

P.S. I wonder if you have news of Frederic Prokosch? I lose these things, these people. If he is still alive, and if you are in communication with him, please say hello for me.

TO: RICHARD HOWARD

TLS, 2 pp;[23] *Richard Howard*

June 23, 1981

Dear Richard,

Thank you so much for the letter about Bronwen. She is now going forward into her sixth week, and is small and healthy, with a very good sense of humor and a good-time nature. It is wonderful to have her around, since my other two boys are gone, Chris in El Salvador in his flak-vest[24] and Kevin in medical school at Emory, in Atlanta. My grandson Tucky the Hunter is just 11 years old, but it may be that his destiny is in the air, and I plan to take him out to the Air Force Academy next spring, to see how he likes it. I'd like it myself; I wish there had been a place like that around when I was going to school; it certainly beats Clemson. Anyway, we'll see how all this turns out.

I had no idea you were in Austin, Texas, but it is a place I have always liked, and there are some people there that I like. One of these is David Wevill, who as you may remember was involved in the whole business of Sylvia Plath and Ted Hughes and the rest of that wretched business. David's first wife, Assia, was the one Hughes ran off with that precipitated Plath's suicide. Hughes then deserted Assia in the same way with the result that she killed herself and her two children, one or both of them David's. But David has recovered and married a splendid big tall friendly girl, nothing like Sylvia or Assia, thank God, and they have three children of their own. Their family is very close to Debba's and mine, and if you don't get to know them down there I will be most disappointed. But perhaps you already do know them; I think that's probably the case, since David is very keen on knowing other poets and talking poetry, though he may seem shy at first.

That is very good news about Baudelaire and you.[25] When I got your letter I immediately began rereading the great man, and also got together all the translations I had around here. After doing this I was more than ever sure that you should take on the project. There are few people who are as misrepresented in translation as Baudelaire is. The most famous renderings are the most ludicrously inept, such as those of Roy Campbell and the even worse Millay-George Dillon ones,[26] which Valéry said he liked, though that is hard to believe. Lowell did fairly well by a few of the more famous pieces,[27] but his Baudelaire sounds altogether too much like Lowell, as one would suspect beforehand to be the case. Oddly enough, the best translations I know are by Aldous Huxley, though there are not many of them. His version of "Femmes Damnées" is at least in part as good as the original, at least insofar as I am able to judge. But enough of this, for this is your new project and mine only insofar as it is yours. Please put down these unsolicited opinions to mere enthusiasm in this quarter, which is great.

Please let us keep in closer touch, for we have lost the time we have been out of communication, and that is time that I would prefer to have.

Could you not come down, along with David Alexander, and spend a few days with us this summer? We have a second house in a condominium closed-circuit kind of place on Pawley's Island, which I'm sure you would like. It is a three-story house, and you and David could have a whole floor!

My best to you, your talent and your soul. And remember me to Sandy, when you communicate.

Ever,

Jim

TO: PETER BALAKIAN[28]

CC, 1 p; Emory
Columbia, S.C.

June 29, 1981

Dear Peter,

Thank you for your deeply-felt letter. I am very happy that I could have done something for your state of mind at a time, really, when nothing can be done.[29] I am dictating this from a plantation down here on the coast, and my wife of thirty years lies buried only a few hundred yards away. But the dead have their place in us, do they not? That is maybe little consolation, but maybe, also, it is more than we think.

Here are the last two poems I have left from Puella; I have been saving them for something I considered special, which this is.[30] One of them is simply an evocation of the craziness of adolescence, and is just a depiction of two girls too full of sap and energy to go to sleep, blasting out of the house and running down a dirt road all out, in long gowns. The other one is a kind of spell which builds up image by image, and is meant to be spoken by a young girl to her first lover, somewhere out there in humanity with God knows what characteristics or what background; it is all right with the girl casting the spell: whoever comes will be all right, whatever he may be like: it will be him. The accumulative structure, where a line is added to each stanza, is also supposed to bear a parallel to imaginative process, generally, and to the mental associations that go to making up the composition of poetry. One thing calls forth another, and the process is endless, and should be.

Anyway, I hope you like these. Let me know what you think of them when you can, conveniently. And tell any ladies that you know, whether maidens, whether virgins or not, that the spell works! Don't ask me how I know!

My best to you.

Ever,

James Dickey

P.S. I did find a carbon of the previous letter, and am enclosing it. I would like to think that you will be able to share it with your aunt,[31] and will remember me most kindly to her.

JLD/lb

TO: L. M. ROSENBERG[32]

CC, 2 pp; Emory
Columbia, S.C.

July 22, 1981

Dear Liz,

Debba is asleep now, with Bronwen, and I thought I would take a minute and answer the long, delicious letter you wrote her a month or so ago. Bronwen is a remarkably trouble-free baby, but she is a baby—now two and a half months old, and growing fast and fat—, and has to be looked-after and cared for 24 hours a day. That is, one is always in some kind of relation (no pun) to her, and she is the first consideration, no matter what else you may have to do, or want to do. This induces a rather odd frame of mind, but at the center of the frame is a very warm area which radiates out into the rest of one's activities, informs them with humanistic and mystical feelings, and is altogether to the good. We like Bronnie, and we can't imagine existence without her. Why don't you and John come down here, and see all this for yourselves? You know the place here, and if you could stand to be put up in Kevin's room while he is over in Atlanta in medical school, we'd sure love to see you. As to the room, it is still full of huge posters of Jimi Hendrix and King Kong, which are said to induce nightmares, particularly due to the influence of the former. But such as it is, it's here for you. So are we.

I'll surely be looking forward to seeing the poems when they come out in MSS.[33] Who else will be in the same issue, by the way? When will it appear?

About your novel.[34] I have been giving it some thought, but I haven't been able to come up with much. Though I am of course a Southerner, the social amenities that are peculiar to Southerners create a climate that I have assimilated only by osmosis; that is, I have seldom paid any deliberate attention to any of them. But it is my impression that the caste system is strong here, and particularly so in regions that have a certain amount of social longevity among their families. All big Southern cities like Atlanta and Birmingham—those which are expanding rapidly—as well as those smaller, tradition-bound places like Charleston and New Orleans and Savannah, have "Old families," and these have a very definite way of doing things, particularly those things which have to do with events involving the intermingling of the sexes, particularly the young sexes, such as dances, debutante initiation rites, coming-out parties of other sorts, and so on. Southern women have a great deal more interest in genealogy than Northern women. I never cared much for this part of things down here, but I remember that when I was in the Air Force I was shocked when a California girl told me she didn't know who her first cousins were. I expect that the famous Southern version of anti-Semitism is due more to snobbery than to any actual feelings about race. The snobbery would be as much exerted against, say, a poor white or a redneck as an old-family girl's escort as it would against a Jew. But of course the character in your book is a Jew, and the scene would have to be written on that basis. If you like, I can cogitate a bit more on this. Meanwhile, there are a couple of things you might want to read. As to anti-Semitism in general, though only tangentially related to the South, I can think of nothing better than Delmore Schwartz's story, "A Bitter Farce," in his collection The World is a Wedding.[35] For Southern social traditionalism, the chapters on Charleston and New Orleans in John Gunther's Inside U.S.A.[36] Though these are quite frankly journalism, they are full of quite accurate observations on social attitudes, and the supposed "facts" behind them. I also recommend John Peale Bishop's essay "The South and Tradition," in his collected essays published about thirty years ago by Scribner's.[37]

I must close now, but in doing so I'd like to end with expressing the hope that you do get the position you want at the Kenyon Arts Festival. Debba and I were there last winter, and liked it a lot. The Kenyon Review has two ambitious and intelligent young editors; they are bringing out a whole slew of poems from Puella, so naturally they are intelligent![38] Anyway, if you go, you'll like them. The head of the English department, Perry Lentz, is also a friend of mine. As I say, we had a good time there, at the old school of Robert Lowell, Paul Newman and Johnathan Winters. In fact, we've decided that if we ever have two sons—the first will still be Tal—we'll call one Kenyon.

Our love to John, and to you and all your works.

Ever,

TO: ROBERT PENN WARREN

TLS, 1 p;[39] Yale

July 24, 1981

Dear Red,

Thank you for your letter. I am glad you like Ghiselin, for he is a deserving fellow, from what I know of him, and an altogether better poet than William Jay Smith, who is amiable and rather skillful and charming, but strikes me as disastrously thin and almost totally unmemorable. Ghiselin does really have hold of something, or makes significant grabs at it, I think. He is good with the ocean, especially, and with deserts and bare hills. He is less good in writing erotically, though even here, not at his best, he is better than Bill Smith at his best. So I think we should go ahead and give the prize[40] to him, for despite what Stern may come up with as a judgement, there has never been a time in the history of the race, or of mathematics, that two could not out-vote one. If you are firm on Ghiselin, so am I, and if you like—as you seem to suggest you would—I can assume the pose of "chairman" and convey these determinations to the committee, so that they can go ahead and announce Ghiselin as the winner and pay us the pittance they owe us for reading all these unrewarding and well-meaning books.

We are well here, and Bronnie, in her third month, is thriving. Life when it is this new is certainly a wonder. I don't know how I could have gone so long without a child in the house.

Please convey my love to Eleanor. Debba sends hers too. We'll hope you can make the fall Institute meeting, for we will almost definitely be there, and would sure like to see you.

Ever,
Jim

TO: BEVERLY JARRETT[41]

TLS, 2 pp;[42] LSU Press

July 27, 1981

Dear Beverly:

Thank you indeed for your letter and for the Stuart and Cotterill manuscripts, which I am returning. Here is my report on them.

Dabney Stuart's book I am not in any doubt about. His faults—a certain monotony of subject matter and a lack of rhythmical interest—are not so great as his virtues, by a long way. He seems to care genuinely and deeply about the events of his own life. He is honest, clear and clean, and though he lacks several of the characteristics I most esteem in verse—open excitement and an on-going, surging feel—his own actual virtues may be more important than those I like and which I miss in his work. Though he is not proliferatingly imaginative (an evidence of this is his constant recourse to images of things—or himself—spinning or turning), he is most convincing; his speech and tone of voice are honest, listenable-to and leave the impression of an actual human being rather than the group-think of a writing seminar. Some of the pieces, like "Doing Time" and the elegies for Walker Dabney Stuart, Jr., are genuinely moving, and I think that the most sensitive part of the public would welcome Mr. Stuart's poems and his book. I think you should definitely publish it.[43]

Sarah Cotterill I also like. Whether you should publish this book of hers, though, I am not sure about. I think you might take a chance with her, if someone like Herbert Scott, who really is good, doesn't come along. If there is any kind of crunch, I would prefer either Scott's book or Applewhite's to this one, though if there is room and sufficient money within your purview it might be a fairly good idea to bring this out. And yet, there is so very much writing like this, especially by women. Ms. Cotterill has little real vitality, and writes as though she had made a composite voice out of all the laconic-imaginative, wry, shoulder-shrugging, dowdy, neurotic women poets of our time:

> In that dream everything is clear:
>
> I am a wall
> on which sparrows light.
> A man sleeps at my feet
> Who has just buried his dead.

And so on, and on. On the Xerox, I thought briefly that the poet referred to a man who sleeps at her feet who has just buried his head, and my attention flared briefly, but unfortunately this was a misreading, and the commonplace quickly reappeared. If I could, I would discourage the kind of writing that Ms. Cotterill does, the beseeching, cringing attitude out of which it is written, the imitation of other not-very-good poets, and the whole genre of such poetry, which had little interest even when better poets, poets like Elizabeth Bishop—not so good, either—made it familiar and critics like Randall Jarrell—very good, usually— praised it. And yet there are good things here. The suggested title, itself, is one of them. Some of the nature images are faintly interesting, faintly genuine, and if she had a good enough editor who could cut out a lot of the dreck and kapok, Ms. Cotterill might have an interesting book; at least it will be more interesting than it is in this form. But, as I say, this is worth taking a chance on if you can't get any-thing better; not a whole lot better, maybe, but any better.[44]

So—that's what I think. Let me know what transpires in regard to these books, and also what you decide in the case of Herbert Scott—if he has any-thing—and that of James Applewhite.[45] I'll wait to hear about it all with the great-est interest, needless to say.

For the record (and payment!) my social security number is:

[   ]

Cordially,
Jim

jld:LB

TO: DAVID BOTTOMS

TLS, 2 pp;[46] *Emory*

August 18, 1981

Dear David,

Thanks so much for the letter and the picture of your dog. There is very little mail I get that is in the class with yours for vividness and interest: I mean that they deal in things that have a great depth of interest for <u>me</u>. So much of my correspondence is so very dull—business matters and such: dull on the part of the people writing to me, and dull on my part, writing back to them. It is ironic that all this, or most of it, has to do with poetry, for the poets should be trying to make a stand against all this computerized impersonality. But impersonal your letters are not, and that <u>not</u> is what I value. Keep 'em coming.

Yes, I know Harry Crews, and like him. He is a good writer, a kind of folk-poet, and especially good with the dirt-poor Southerners. A couple of years ago he and I were in North Dakota, of all places, at a writers' conference in Grand Forks, and for two or three days he and I and Debba were together continually. He has given himself a hell of a bad time, particularly with alcohol, and after we both came back south, I tried to get in touch with him in Gainesville to recommend him for a job in Virginia that I had been asked to administer. But I was not able to find Harry, and I still can't locate him, and therefore I have some doubts, knowing him from those few icebound days, as to whether he is still alive, though I damn well hope he is, for he is some kind of good man, good companion, a tough son of a bitch, tough and mystical, and that is what I like. If you have word of him, do let me know.

You ask about some of the contemporary British poets, and I'm not sure how much help I can give you, for I don't like any of them much. Heaney[47] is all right; fairish, I'd say. We have had him here twice, and aside from his front-row view of the turmoil in Northern Ireland and his opinions on it, had no real interest for the students, the people here; they did not respond to the poetry at all, except where it evidenced some social stance or another. I like his work well enough—he and Ted Hughes are much alike, with Heaney being maybe a little better, at least in my judgement. But they both have that sort of <u>ersatz</u> violence that is so very easy to use, and rely on; it is all agitation of a predictable surface; nothing coming from the depths. Philip Larkin is only mildly interesting. The British seem to see much point in him, but I don't. He seems to me only one of those wearily laconic Englishmen of the welfare state, superciliously self-effacing, writing poems on how much he hates his record collection, and judging historical time by the appearance of the Beatles' first LP. There is not enough there. Geoffrey Hill, though I know him personally better than I do any of these others, and like him, remains a complete mystery to me; I cannot understand more than a third of what he is saying. His subject matter seems rather private and more or less arbitrary; he seems to want to write religious poetry without any truly religious feeling. He sends me his books, and I read them dutifully, but take little away, except an occasional line which is sort of hermetically good, as such lines in Mallarmé are good. But there ain't much worth reading, from over there in the Isles. Maybe something later will come through.

I'll have to close now, to get this in the mail. Let me know when you want me to write to Ed Shannon for you.[48] If there's a real opening at UVA, we'll try to get you a real job.

Ever,

Jim

TO: GORDON LISH

TLS, 2 pp;[49] Lilly Library

August 28, 1981

Dear Gordon,

I have your couple of letters, for which many thanks. I don't know whether Lugar[50] and I will ever be able to do anything, but like you I think he's all right. He seems to have some sort of drive, almost a mania, to make movies, and I respect that sort of enthusiasm, even if it comes to nothing, which it usually does. I set him on the trail of a novel that I would like to make a film of. Elliott Kastner, the producer, who wanted me to write something for him, acquired the book about ten years ago, but he's never done anything with it, and if Lugar can buy the material from Kastner, and afford my price (pretentious comment!) I might see about doing the story with him. Well, we'll see.[51]

Though I haven't read any of your fiction, I know, as they say, the author, and I would bet on <u>him</u>, in anything he did. I am quite sure that East of the South will surely take your book of stories,[52] and I look forward to <u>that</u>, I can tell you, as well as to "Dear Mr. Capote," which, you tell me, William Abrahams has intelligently taken.[53] Where is this to appear? In other words, what does Abrahams edit? If you see him, tell him that his biographical work has a great admirer in South Carolina; I mean the books that he and Peter Stansky have done together; and not only the two Orwell books but the wonderful <u>Journey to the Frontier</u>, which you should certainly read.[54] It is about those two idealistic upper class poet-Communists, Julian Bell (nephew of Virginia Woolf) and John Cornford (great-grandson of Darwin) who fought in Spain in the thirties and were killed. Lord, what a double-action film there is in that material! I can see the Australian director, Peter Weir, going to town with it. But that, like a lot of other "potentially" good things, shall never be, I guess; malheureusement.

Sure, I'll do what I can for Jack Gilbert's[55] work, if you'll send me a Xerox of the book. I really don't know his work very well, or him either. His one book, Views of Jeopardy, came out at the same time as my first book, which is to say around 1960. I reread it the other day, in keeping with your publication of his poems, and was struck by the relative mildness and dreaminess, the rather gentle and mystical quality of the work. It does not strike me as being very distinctive, to tell the truth, though maybe the latest stuff is better. Certainly what I have read does not accord at all with the small, wiry, savage little guy that I remember. Two of the occasions that I recall were public, one at San Francisco State on a panel with the other Dickey, William, and the Irish poet John Montague. Jack spent most of his part of the time inveighing, in multi-obscenities, against academies and academic poets. The other public time was also on a panel, this time in New York, at the Poetry Center. As I remember, John Simon moderated, and in addition to Jack and myself, there were Ted Weiss, Allen Ginsberg, Terry Southern (of all people), Howard Nemerov, and some woman poet whose name I can't remember. True to form, Jack leapt into open opposition with everybody, but most especially with Nemerov, who represented academia, and most, most especially with Ginsberg, with whom, in the sleazy, self-justifying night-world of the dope culture, one would think he had some very obvious affinities. But these public encounters tend to sink without a trace, and mainly I remember Jack from the few days in San Francisco—after the conference, or Conference—when I pulled out of the west coast en route to Washington and the Library of Congress. Here Jack would come, balancing his twin teenage dope-glazed inamorati on the precarious—and I mean precarious—back stairs of Kay's house.[56] The stairs sounded, at 3:30 in the morning, like the prelude to the falling-away of the scaffolding of the tower of Babel. And then Jack and his girls would come in, which was into the bedroom, and we would all sit and talk until morning. Sometimes Kay would join us, for she had trouble sleeping, and those disastrous stairs would waken anyone, and she would spin long tales of herself and Hart Crane carrying on together, in one way or another that did not involve sex, in the moulin of Harry Crosby outside Paris. Well, I like Jack, and remember him with all the affection that one can summon on such slight—but intense—acquaintance. I will do what I can for his book, because he is involved, and because you're involved. Maybe we can get it some real attention.[57]

I am sorry to go on and on, but I am tired of pushing so hard on the novel[58] every day, and wanted to speak to somebody, if you know what I mean. That helps, you know, particularly when you know that the other person is as receptive to your communication as you are to his.

My best to Atticus and to Barbara. Let me know your developments, as you can and wish.

Ever,

Jim

TO: STANLEY BURNSHAW

TLS, 2 pp;[59] *HRHRC*

September 24, 1981

Dear Stanley,

Thank you so much for your letter, and your advice. The writer's strike has now ended, and I can go back to work on the Yukon project, the material for which is sitting around the house in bales, whose assimilation into a coherent story is very slow. My situation is this. The producer with whom I am doing this, Jerome Hellman, is very prestigious and rich; at least he is rich <u>now,</u> and although wealth and affluence come and go very quickly in Hollywood, at this time he has or can get as much money as he wants to spend on any project he comes up with. It is the kind of situation that used to be called a "dream of a lifetime." The dream of a producer's lifetime is to produce and direct a movie about a subject which has had a lifetime fascination for him. In this case, the fascination is the Yukon and the Klondike gold rush. Jerry is a Jewish fellow from the lower East Side of New York, very conscious of his ancestry on the one hand and drawn to wildernesses and mountains and forests as only a city person can be. He came to me with this project a year or so ago not because of <u>Deliverance,</u> but because I had done Jack London's <u>Call of the Wild</u> for NBC a few years ago. He wished me to invent a story which would be interesting and unusual in itself as to the delineation of characters, and would also "tell the real truth" about the "Klondike experience." Also, without knowing very much about the story—even <u>I</u> don't know much, at this stage, about the story—Dustin Hoffman expressed, as they say, a desire to play in the movie. I don't know Hoffman at all well, but he is a Delmore Schwartz fanatic, and his obsession with Delmore, his identification with him, and so on, gradually got to be part of the story we were concocting. It now appears that Jerry doesn't <u>want</u> Dustin Hoffman to be in the picture, can't pay his price, doesn't like him any more, or some damn thing. At any rate, by this time Jerry <u>himself</u> has fallen in love with the Delmore—or Delmore-like—character and wants the whole picture to be built around him. I have to go out to Hollywood next week and thrash some of this out with Jerry and his people, for every-body is bound up contractually with everybody else, and now there is no getting out of it, for I have taken the dollar from the drumhead, or at least part of the dol-lar.[60] But I still don't know exactly where things stand. But if I have any kind of orientation at all, it is the one you have given me, for I know almost nothing, except that, about either Delmore's background or Jerry's, or about the Jewish immigrations into New York, the customs, mores, language, or anything of that sort. But I do have the flicker of a feeling that this might just turn out to be an extraordinary film, for Jerry Hellman is no fool, and what I have seen of his directing abilities convinces me that he is not bad at that, either. Well, we'll see.

But I did want to write and thank you for your help. In connection with all this, I too have reread Humboldt's Gift and I don't like it as much as I did, either. Bellow is rather too much addicted to trivia—details of dress, women's make-up, and so on—for my taste. But you needn't worry that I am taking more than should be taken for my character from either the actual Delmore Schwartz or "Humboldt von Fleisher." As the character has evolved, he is really not much like either one of them.

Keep me informed about The Refusers because it is a book that is going to matter very greatly to a very great number of people. Let me know what more I can do to help out.

Meanwhile, you are almost a kind of folk hero down here with The Seamless Web. Among others the head of the department, who sits in on my classes, is presently deep in the thrall of it (and even, as is the wont of professors, in the bib-liography as well!).

All three of us send love, and Chris and Kevin too.

Ever,
Jim

TO: SEYMOUR KRIM

CC, 2 pp; Emory
Columbia, S.C.

January 11, 1982

Dear Si:

Sorry I'm late getting back to you. I am terribly sorry about Klonsky,[61] whom I greatly admired. I remember especially his long and good essay "Along the Mid-way of Mass Culture," which, though most of the comic-strip figures he writes about have long since passed out of the comics, was the first and best exploration of the real meaning of such things. I also remember a long poem of his in the Partisan Review written in terza rima or some difficult form, that I liked and never saw collected anywhere. I return his book to you, and can certainly understand why you would want it back, especially now.

Yes, I did get a lot of manuscript from Michael Seide, and though I haven't had time to read it all, I think it is most extraordinarily good. I'd like to help in any way I can, and I also want to get your own feelings on the material. Could you give me a couple of statements that both you and Seide would like to have made about The Common Wilderness?[62] If you could do that, we could get this thing going in plenty of time for the spring publication. Let me know what you think, and I'll swing with you.

I much enjoyed the piece from the Columbia magazine about teaching;[63] things are just like that, sure enough, though I expect your students as a whole are better than mine. The problems and the personality relationships are the same, though. Randall Jarrell once told me that he liked teaching so much that, were he rich, he would pay to be able to teach. I don't feel quite that strongly, but I do like teaching well enough, and will go on with it for a bit, I think.

Here is something I'd like you to consider, though I will only suggest, and not outline in detail. As you know, I am doing a movie, an expensive movie, with Jerome Hellman, of Midnight Cowboy and Coming Home fame, as well as The World of Henry Orient and The Day of the Locust unfame. The movie is about the Yukon of 1898, and the gold rush, in a kind of oddball and dreamlike overview. One of the two principal characters—and much beloved by Hellman, who identifies with him, as does Dustin Hoffman, who wants to play him—is quite frankly based on Delmore Schwartz, whom you knew and I expect have cause to dislike. Anyhow, the character is even named Delmore, and as it is turning out, is not a bad character, either. At any rate, I have been able to understand the character as he functions in the story pretty well, I think. But what I lack is his idiom: the manic flavor of his rapid-fire New York Jewish intellectual patter. I can't fake this, and I can't really approximate it, because I don't own it, was not raised with it, and am to a certain extent alienated from it by birth, geography, milieu, and just about everything else. That is where you come in. You do own it, are at home in it, use it naturally, and could be of enormous help to me, for my character does little but talk—except to get killed in the end—and he must talk like that. Would you make bold to come in with me on this? Hellman has come up with a couple of "advisors," but they are not in your class, I can tell you. I don't know what kind of financial arrangement might be made, here, but some kind not only might but could, if I insist on the arrangement, and with your consent I would. Let me know how you feel about all this, and I will be guided accordingly. The thing might actually be some fun, into the bargain, for we can have (the fictional) Delmore say anything we want, so long as it is far-out, infectious, rapid-fire, New Yorkish, intellectual and Jewish. Since you are a better writer than Delmore, and know the scene, you are my choice, if we can work it out.

Debba sends love, and so do I.

Ever,

TO: BETTY ADCOCK[64]

CC, 1 p; Emory
Columbia, S.C.

April 2, 1982

Dear Betty,

Thank you indeed for your nice note. I meant what I said about your work, but it is surely among the best I have read in years, and I read a lot. I can't remember that we have ever met, and if we have and I don't recall it, I certainly apologize. If I have had the influence on your work that you say I have had, I certainly must have been doing something right. I have a private stable of four women poets that I think are the finest ones writing. The others, besides yourself, are the Canadian girl, Margaret Atwood, a new woman named Mary Oliver, who lives in Provincetown and is apparently a lesbian—though she is certainly more interesting about it than Adrienne Rich, whom I can no longer read—and a very gutsy California woman named Adrien Stoutenburg, whose Short History of the Fur Trade is one of the bitterest and best and most imaginative poems to come out in the last twenty years.[65] Your work is right up there with theirs, and since you are the only Southerner among them, I have a special interest in it, apart from but also connected to the fact that it is so sheerly good. I won't go on and on in this immoderate vein, but just reiterate what I have said, and my vote of confidence, which will not waver.

Thank you indeed for the things you say about the poems in Kenyon. All of them are Deborah poems, and are part of a book about her which Doubleday is bringing out next month.[66] I'm sure the editors at Kenyon would be much pleased if you were to write to them and tell them what you tell me. They are young and ambitious, and would be most appreciative and grateful. But that shall be as you wish.

I am much moved by Tom Walters,[67] his personality and his predicament, and I hope you will look after him, so that we can all meet some time later on, in some good place.

Cordially,
James Dickey

JLD:lb

TO: DAVID BOTTOMS

TLS, 2 pp;[68] *Emory*

June 28, 1982

Dear David,

Well, the tape is just great. I had never heard any of these before, but all the pieces are good, and the flat-picking is simply astonishing; makes me want to get back on all the stuff I've been trying to steal from Dan Crary, who up until now has been my favorite flat-picker next to Doc.[69] Anyway, thanks so much for sending the tape, which is just mighty fine. By the way, do you have anything by the Bullsboro Bluegrass Band? I can't get a piece of theirs that I want to use in a movie; it is called "Pleasures of Quebec." I heard it on an airplane once, took down the name of the group and the record company, but haven't been able to find it. If you have a copy, please tape it off for me, for I must route it to my producer. And thanks, in advance (if you have it).

As for my own playing, I have not been able to work on flat-picking enough to get the speed I want. My attack is all right—good enough to play without accompaniment, being very loud—but I can't get the speed and the cleanness, what some guitar players call the "sparkle," that I'd like to have. What work I have been able to do consistently is in the area of finger-picking, where I am trying to branch out from straight bass-alternations or monotonic, rag-style bass into something more complex, more pianistic, such as the sort of stuff Charlie Byrd plays. He is a classically trained musician, and the difficulty about following him is that the chord changes all have to be made very quickly, and nearly all of them extend across the board, requiring all kinds of left-hand positions that folk musicians don't even know exist. In addition, the right hand must use the thumb and <u>three</u> fingers, whereas I have always done finger-picking with the thumb, the index, and the middle only, and a good many pieces with only the thumb and the index. This voicing of chords, including a good deal of counterpoint, is, I tend to think when discouraged, for the Julian Breams and John Williams of the world, and not for sixty-year-old folk players trying to get onto such very sophisticated and difficult techniques. But what I have been able to do in this line is so exciting and so beautiful—at least to me—that I just can't get enough of it. When I get sufficiently good at some of this, I'll make a tape and send it down to you. But that may be a while; I improve very slowly, and sometimes not at all. But I keep at it, and that's the main thing. That and the love of the sound.[70]

Incidentally, thanks also for sending along the copy of <u>Poetry Pilot</u> you edited,[71] and for the things you say—surely excessively kind—about my playing. I won't say any more about <u>that</u> except to offer equally excessive gratitude. In the issue I noticed a couple of things that I hadn't known. One was the death of

Adrien Stoutenburg, whom I considered the best woman poet around, and the death also of Isabella Gardner, who was one of the worst.[72] Also, I was surprised to see a poem by Joe ("Edgar") Simmons, for whose posthumous work I have just written an introduction.[73] He was an old friend, a real snake-bit worthy fellow, and I was happy to write about him. The book will be out in November, and I'll send you a copy, if you like.

Meanwhile, Nona Balakian, of the New York Times Book Review section, has asked me for the names of some possible reviewers, and I mentioned you. She is very high on Puella, and if you'd like to have a shot at a review of the book for the Times, you might care to write to her in care of the Times Book Review with some possibility that you will be able to do the review. Anyway, if you write to Ms. Balakian, she'll be expecting you.

And if you review the book somewhere else, I had just as soon be dealt with alone, for it is late in the day for me to turn up in omnibus formats. I'm sure you can understand this, and will act accordingly.[74]

Your ideas about "the poetry of situation" are very good, I think, and I will proceed with the idea, and see what I can come up with.

The new book of essays and miscellaneous writings, Night Hurdling, is finished, and will be out in October.[75] I'll send you one of those, too.

Thanks a lot for all the stuff you do for me. It is very gratifying to me that you do what you do, especially since you are, it surely seems to me, the best of the younger horses.

Ever,
Jim

TO: MICHAEL ALLIN

CC, 3 pp; Emory
Columbia, S.C.

July 9, 1982

Dear Michael,

Thanks so much for the letter, and for the poem, which I think is quite remarkable, particularly in some of the individual lines. The idea of the voyage— either real or imaginary or hallucinatory—has always fascinated poets, particularly the best ones, like Baudelaire and Rimbaud. The connection between real sailors, here, and those who find temporary release in dreaming of being sailors, the while drinking, is an awfully strong theme, with which almost anything could be done, and you do plenty. Why not try this one out on Jim Boatwright at

Shenandoah, Box 722, Lexington, Virginia? I don't know whether he would take it—it may be too long for his space—but he will certainly read it, which is a better condition than one will find at many magazines. Anyway, try him out on this one, if you like. I am supposed to be an advisory editor, and he keeps asking me to scout stuff for him, and certainly I have seen nothing in the class with this for a good long time.[76]

My business with Jerome Hellman is, I think, dragging to a close. He is always asking me to come out there on the slightest pretext, and the only result is that we sit around trying to make cinematic sense out of his thoroughly predictable and mediocre ideas, and show old movies, by means of which he hopes to get some ideas, which he then childishly disguises, hoping that I will disguise them even more slightly and feed them back to him so that he can claim that they were his ideas. After two years of this, I've had enough of it, and I'm telling Theron that I will forfeit the final $20,000 Hellman owes me for the treatment-phase, in order to get out of the whole business, get clear of the entire film connection, forever. It is not my real work, and I detest group-think of any kind, and out there there is nothing else. I'll keep you posted on what happens, but as of now I consider myself severed from the cinema, and on another shore, for good.

Your own situation in movies, as you outline it, sounds interesting, and I think you should get into the directing end of things, for there one has some power, some sway. Keep me posted about this, too, and I'll offer whatever I might be able to do—from my farther shore—for your projects.

The novel is going very well. I have been living with the story so long, now, that the writing of it is automatic, almost like taking dictation, and yet, during the writing, and the intense concentration on parts, all kinds of new fields of inter-pretation open up, and frequently I have to go back and recast previous sections in accordance with what has opened. I suppose every writer experiences these things, but this novel is booby-trapped with such situations to an uncommon degree, and so goes forward slowly. But it is very exciting, and if it is not a master-piece, it is certainly unique; I have read a lot, and I have never read anything like this. It is a good feeling, though possibly based at least somewhat on illusion. But the illusion is strong, and that's why we do it; all of us.

Meanwhile, there is a lot of new stuff forthcoming. Harcourt Brace will bring out a new collection of essays, poems, translations, criticism, debates, interviews, afterwords, graduation addresses, and god knows what all, the whole thing to be called Night Hurdling.[77] It's due in October, and I'll send you a copy. The False Youth poems, plus "The Birthday Dream," will be published in February by a good new small press in Texas called Pressworks, out of Dallas. The title is False Youth: Four Seasons and, again, I'll send you a copy. The longest of the poems, "The Olympian," has just come out in an ecology magazine, of all places, and I enclose a copy.[78] Oddly enough, they set the poem up better than anyone else has ever done one of these "balanced" poems of mine, for which I am grateful, needless to say. I think you'll recognize the locale, and perhaps you'll murmur to yourself, as Rimbaud did in quite another connection, j'ai seule la clef a cette parade sauvage.

All are well here. Bronnie has taken her first few steps, and the family has just had the perhaps dubious honor of being interviewed for a feature in People magazine,[79] which you will probably be seeing in the grocery stores in about three weeks, with the girls beautiful and myself looking like an especially unfortunate version of the Leviathan, doubling as the mighty behemoth. What the interviewer will want to say about us, I have no idea, but those people always have at least a small needle concealed on their person somewhere, so don't be put off by whatever happens to be said. If it's bad, it ain't so, or it can be made not to be bad, whatever that mysterious pseudo-statement might be taken to mean.

Robert Penn Warren and I have just finished a film for CBS-Cable[80] which I think may turn out to be pretty good, because he is a good talker—very intent and intelligent—and because we kept to the good subjects, about which both of us had a lot to say. We did half of the shooting up at his place at Yale, where we gave a joint reading, and the other half down at Litchfield, walking or rowing around the landscape. He is certainly an impressive old guy, and I am very happy that the public—or a little of it, anyway—will be able to see and hear him, and understand that this country, despite everything, can produce such.

I can't go on and on as I'd like to, for I must close and get this in the mail. I very seldom do get a chance to write a real letter, to anyone who is real, and so I would welcome the chance to run on and on in this one, if I had the time. But it is best to get it off, this Friday afternoon, while Leslie[81] and the mails are outgoing, before the weekend.

Our best love to you, and to everything about you.

Ever,

TO: ROBERT PENN WARREN

CC, 1 p; Emory
Columbia, S.C.

September 10, 1982

Dear Red,

I have been out of the country, and have just now got hold of your poem in The Georgia Review, and read it last night. It is absolutely remarkable, as you surely must know, and the only thing I can say about the poem itself is that it reconfirms my notion that narrative is—and has to be—the basis of all really big poems. The lack of it is the main trouble with pieces like The Waste Land and The Cantos, and the presence of it is what makes The Iliad as great as it is. Narrative answers to something very deep and fundamental on the human psyche, and of all the poets who have practiced it in my time, there is none that can approach you. Indeed I don't mean to offer some kind of estimate of your qualities, except to say once again that a combination of narrative strength and energy and thrust, plus a deep sensitivity to words and their placement, seems to me the secret of the thing, or at least of the big thing. This is very remarkable stuff, Red. And I think you have also rendered the world of the Indian—not only the hunting and fighting Indian, but the dreaming, the mystical Indian—better than it has ever been got before. You certainly have my congratulations. This new poem is the latest part of your on-go, and that's got to matter to all of us, but to none more than to me.

As to the dedication—well, what can I say?[82] I am most humbly pleased and honored. I will say that, and hope that the depth and reach of what lies under the words will be felt. I have never before been part of such an astonishing thing.

Meanwhile, the producer of our film, Stephanie Sills, called yesterday when I was at school, and talked to Debba. She is most pleased with what she has seen, though editing is still going on. She tells us that you and I own all the rights, which may in future be of some value to us. I haven't seen any of the film, myself, but it would be hard for me to forget the making of it, and some of the things we said. I am glad we have those things down, and so will the public be, and from now on.

When you have a minute or two, let me hear from you, and tell me how your life goes.

Meanwhile, my best to Eleanor, and to all those you love.

                                                        Warmly,

TO: STANLEY BURNSHAW

                                                        TLS, 2 pp;[83] HRHRC
        September 10, 1982

Dear Stanley,

Debba and I managed a trip to Paris for a couple of weeks, and so I have sort of been out of things, and am just now getting back to teaching, and being able to answer your letter of July 13th, which was long, good and most welcome.

I am back working on the long novel, and some other things. The Hollywood business is being phased out, for I don't really like Hellman personally, and he has such a conventional mind that it is impossible to get anything over to him that is even in the least unusual. All he wants to do is to screen old movies and try to pick up suggestions from them that he might be able to use. He wants everything to be like every other movie that everyone has ever seen. I don't have time for that kind of thing, so I am taking the last payment on the preliminary part of the film-making and getting out, for I have a good many projects I had rather put my time on.[84]

Puella is doing well, and has sold out the first printing of five thousand, which is rather heartening. However, the fellow in North Carolina who originally commissioned the poems for use in another book he was never able to publish, now wants his money back, or at least some of it. I consider the fifteen thousand dollars he paid me as payment for a year and a half he took out of my life, when I suspended work on the novel, turned down a good many readings, and went through multiple other vicissitudes to complete the project, only to find out that he could not find any way to bring the book out. The poems were written independently of his photographs, however, because under no circumstances would I ever have any poem of mine depend on an illustration, and I brought them out in magazines, and, eventually, as Puella. The lawyers are going round and round about all this, and I may eventually have to give the guy a little money. This is only a minor irritation, but it will resolve itself fairly soon, or so my lawyer tells me. Anyway, we'll see.[85]

Red Warren and I finished the film we were doing for CBS-Cable; even the editing has been done, I am told. I don't know when the thing will screen, but the producer called yesterday and said that it was being put through the final stages, and is just about ready to go for an October date. Again, I'll let you know.

And, yes, Warren does like and esteem your work very much. I'll sound him out as to the possibility of his seconding my nomination for you at the Institute.[86]

About the matter of honorary degrees: my God, you should have a whole wall of them. I have been asked to be on some committees in connection with these things, and I will certainly militate strongly for you, in any case in which I am a participant. I'll also see what I can do with the Boston outfit.[87]

Odd you should mention Helen Vendler, who was at Kenyon last May with Wiesel and myself.[88] For some reason or other, the college had mixed up my hood and hers, and she came into my room at the college guest house with what turned out to be my garment in her hands. "Is this your academic hood?" she asked.

"Madam," I answered gravely, sweaty and unshaven as I was from traveling, "I am the academic hood." And that's about the extent of my association with her, though she is certainly a very poor writer, who writes a kind of jargonish substitute-poetry—and very unimaginative, too—which she passes off as "criticism." And I don't like her main subject, Wallace Stevens,[89] either. If all poetry were like his, I would have no interest in the subject, or certainly not enough to write it.

I have just finished the second week of teaching, and most of the time spent in the composition class has been concerned with <u>The Seamless Web</u>. In preparation, I read through the whole thing again, plus my notes, and came to the same conclusion, all over again, that my class came to for the first time: that it <u>states</u> and <u>documents</u> what the whole sentient human race has been waiting to hear, but didn't know it: that we are bodily linked with natural process, with <u>rerum natura</u>. Incidentally, my class liked especially the section illustrating the connection of the body with the rotation of the earth, with day and night, sun and moon. Man, <u>that's</u> the stuff to give the troops! I became an instant hero in about ten minutes! Thanks so much for this, Stanley, as for all the other things I have to thank you for.

I must close now, but will be in closer and better touch from now on.

My love to Leda. To her, first, and then to Stan Hart, Tom Maley, and all my other friends on the Vineyard.

Ever,

Jim

TO: WILLIAM F. BUCKLEY JR.

CC, 1 p; Emory
Columbia, S.C.

September 10, 1982

Dear Bill,

Thank you indeed for the book and the dedication.[90] Your account is certainly fascinating, and I was particularly interested in the navigational stuff. The back-up sextant that was apparently stolen is a Davis, probably a Mark Twenty, for that is a Davis case on—it looks like—page 57, on the dresser. It is probably the best of the plastic sextants, though the EBBCO from England is also very good, of its kind. The Vernier of the EBBCO reads backwards from ours, and Plath's, and takes some getting used to, but I would recommend it as a good back-up sextant, if you don't get your Davis back.

As very much a landlocked sailor—with papers, though!—[91]I would recommend your leaning up against something solid when you take a sight, as you don't seem to be doing in any of the photographs. You can cut down a whole lot on error if you're firmly based and stanchioned. If this is true sighting from land, it must be doubly true on shipboard, where everything is moving and swaying around. Incidentally, have you ever tried a bubble? I have the Plath bubble attachment, and it is useful at times when you don't have a sea horizon, or the body is too high to use an artificial horizon. But a bubble, though fascinating to play with, is very hard to calibrate, and even when calibrated correctly, is not as accurate as a natural-horizon sextant, even with the dip.

I offer all this unsolicited advice because your own remarks on navigation have contributed so much to my enjoyment of the activity. If I were instructing in the subject, I would send the students to your two books as a preliminary assessment of the whole celestial navigation problem, or, if the case arose, as a crash course.

Debba and I will be in New York on and around October 13th, and maybe we could get together with you. Let me know your plans, and we'll be guided accordingly.

My best to Pat and Chris.

Ever,

P.S. Is that Time machine I gave you working okay?

TO: PETER BALAKIAN

CC, 1 p; Emory

Columbia, S.C.
October 6, 1982

Dear Peter:

I enclose a carbon of the letter of recommendation I have sent to the Career Planning people at Brown, for your file. I hope it will do the job, for it says exactly what I mean, and what I feel. Let me know if there is anything further I can do.

Don't worry about Bookie Binkley, the Winston-Salem haberdasher and soi-disant photographer. You don't even need to write him, for my lawyer, Kirkman Finlay, who is not soi-disant, will handle everything. Not to worry.

I look forward to your review in ABR;[92] they seem to give people and books plenty of space, and I am glad it is you who will be taking it up. Puella is controversial, and will be attacked plenty; I expect Helen Vendler will come down on it, for she wishes to put one of her chicks, Dave Smith[93]—who is a kind of follower of mine, and did his doctoral dissertation on my work—up at my expense, and of course there are always people like Robert Bly and Donald Hall, who would do anything on earth to get at me. So I am glad I have strong champions, like yourself, and now, I am told, Denis Donoghue.[94] It would be lovely if you could tell the readers that almost any line in any poem of Puella would make the reputation of a new poet, and perhaps, if you took this tack, you could quote some of them, like "The Near Hills," "Thinning With Overreach," or "The Sea's Holy No-win Roar."[95] Anyway, I'll be most pleased to see what you have to say, whether this or something.

Remember me to your aunt with great warmth, and keep plenty for yourself.

Ever,

TO: JACOB CHERNOFSKY[96]

CC, 2 pp; Emory
Columbia, S.C.

December 9, 1982

Dear Mr. Chernofsky and Readers of <u>Antiquarian Bookman</u>:

Please let this letter serve as notice to you and to your readers that any books, broadside editions, or manuscripts bearing the stamp "Library of James L. Dickey III," or the white, blue-bordered bookplate reading, "Ex Libris: James Dickey," have been taken <u>without my knowledge or consent</u> from my personal library, and are <u>stolen property</u>. I appeal to readers and collectors of rare books worldwide to help me recover my books. These include, but are not limited to, first edition copies by Robert Penn Warren, Allen Tate, Randall Jarrell, John Berryman, and W. D. Snodgrass. Any help in this matter will be rewarded.

Sincerely yours,
James Dickey

List of Missing Books

by Robert Lowell

Land of Unlikeness
Lord Weary's Castle
For Lizzie and Harriet

by John Berryman

Poems
The Dispossessed
His Thought Made Pockets & the Plane Buckt
Delusions, Etc.
Henry's Fate and Other Poems
Recovery

by Allen Tate

Reactionary Essays

by Robert Penn Warren

You, Emperors
All the King's Men
World Enough and Time

by Randall Jarrell

Poetry and the Age

by Richard Wilbur

The Beautiful Changes

by W. D. Snodgrass

Heart's Needle

by Theodore Roethke

The Lost Son[97]

TO: ROY H. WINNICK

TL (Xerox), 1 p;[98] Emory

December 21, 1982

Dear Dr. Winnick:

I have been reading through your edition of the letters of MacLeish,[99] and I feel I owe you a very great deal for the work you did in making the book possible. Surely they are remarkable letters, like none others I know. It strikes me, now that I think of it, that everything of Archie's should be in print, including the miscellaneous prose pieces. I remember, for example, an extraordinary prose thing he did on the Dry Tortugas some years ago; it was I think in one of the women's magazines.[100] I would think that, considering Macleish's energy, there would be a goodly number of such things around, waiting only to be collected. And how about his political writings? I remember a long television piece on democracy he did for one of the TV networks, and surely there are others in the Domain.

Really, however, this is not intended as a letter full of unsolicited advice, but a note of congratulation on your edition of the Letters. This is a fine service, and I appreciate it as much as such faculties have been given to me can register such things.

I knew Archie only slightly. I had him come to South Carolina to read, and we spent a day or two together, mainly talking, as I remember about Mark Van Doren, whose dialogues with MacLeish I had been using in class.[101]

I doubt that there's anyone who has a more genuine liking for MacLeish's verse than I do; he is one of the few American poets to have a <u>sound</u> of his own, as one would say of a musician that he had a sound. His poetry is like the poetry that Hemingway might have written, if he had been able to write it. MacLeish is sinewy and masculine, and the work has true resonance, which is a lot, and not given to many.

I won't go on and on, but will thank you again for what you have done. I look forward to the biography with the greatest interest.[102]

TO: DANIEL DAHLQUIST[103]

                                                        TLS (Xerox), 1 p;[104] Emory

January 14, 1983

Dear Dan:

Please forgive my belatedness in answering your Christmas letter, which I greatly enjoyed, together with the new poems. "Copper Man Creek" is really good, one of your very best so far. Some of it is not entirely clear to me, but the middle of the first stanza, about the extracted teeth, is better than just merely good. I haven't time to go into detail about the poems, because I have to get on yet another airplane, and rustle up some more dough for my youngest son's medical school tuition, which is plenty. But the poems are coming along fine, and I am sure that Stanley Plumly and Marvin Bell are being helpful to you;[105] they are reputable and good people, and should be considered very lucky to have a young writer of your caliber. By the way, have you met John Leggett yet? Surely you must have. Tell him I admire his <u>Ross and Tom</u> very much; a true horror-story of American literary success.[106]

Since the aircraft is waiting, I must close, with just this little bit. But you have misread the "message" of the Zen archery master to his pupil![107] The Master told Herrigel to send him photographs of his drawing the bow, and enjoined him to "perform the ceremony every day." He didn't direct his student to send him news of himself only when he had made progress in the "artless art," but just to give him evidence that he was still engaged in it, no matter where he might be. That's all. These new poems are your drawing of the bow, and your aim and form are right on the pinwheel. Plumly's advice to "let the poem happen to you" is in itself very "Zen"; it is like the release of the bowstring without releasing it; it is like what happens when "It" shoots, and "the bowstring has cut right through you." It will all happen; as I say, just keep doing what you're doing.

Warmly,

Jim

My best to Lucky Jacobs, too!![108]

TO: THEODORE WEISS[109]

RTL (Xerox), 1 p;[110] Emory

February 1, 1983

Dear Ted:

I have prevailed on the Princeton Press to send me a copy of The Man From Porlock[111] for review, and have not only read through the whole thing twice, but have used it extensively in class, with the result that my kids are so enamored of Lucretius that I cannot get them to jump the fence between the ancient world and the medieval; Dante must wait in the wings for another week because of Lucretius' grim beauties, and because the case you make out for him is the best that the centuries have yet made. But, then, the whole book is remarkable, Ted. The part on Pound is better than the whole corpus of Hugh Kenner's exhaustive—and exhausting—would-be-ness about Pound, and your statement about Pound's attempt to weld a whole lot of imagistic fragments into an epic is what somebody should have made a long time ago, and didn't; it is the definitive statement about that sometimes amazing but frequently stupefying would-be epic, The Cantos.

You are also right about Larkin, and his foolishness. John Betjeman, indeed! Larkin himself, as a poet, is fairish, but only just so. He lacks open excitement, and most of the other qualities that I esteem.

But you have said all this better than I could possibly do. I mean only to congratulate you, here. I always feel wonderful when one of my close and old friends proves out, as they say in the South: is as good as you want him to be. I want to help you feel as entirely good as this book—and your recent poetry—should make you do; I would be glad if I had a hand in that. But really you don't need me for such. The sturdiness and deep flash of your talent, together with your incorruptibility, should give you all the self-esteem you need. Please accept my congratulations, though, for your extraordinary work, and for your extraordinary life.

Let me know on what basis we might meet again, the sooner the better. Meanwhile, I enclose an invitation that comes out of my current—regrettable, but not as yet fatal—sixtieth birthday.[112] Though the invitation arrives maybe a little too late for you to come down, I will hope for you in spirit. That is <u>some</u> spirit.

Ever,

TO: DANA GIOIA[113]

TLS (Xerox), 2 pp;[114] Emory

May 19, 1983

Dear Mr. Gioia:

Thank you for sending your article, and for some of the things you say in it.[115] Did I talk with you over the phone about this, or what? Forgive me if I don't remember, but there is always a lot going on around here, and I can't keep track of it all. But I do thank you for sending it; that was considerate.

As to the article itself, I thought it fairish, but hardly worth four years of time. You purport to give facts, but you have them entirely backwards in my own case, so most of your "illustrations" using my example cannot therefore hold up, and places your credibility regarding the other instances you use in some doubt as well. I went with McCann-Erickson <u>first</u> in New York, where I worked primarily on radio-TV commitments, mainly the Eddie Fisher show, "Coke Time," and <u>then</u>, when the network show was phased out, I came to Atlanta in charge of all local bottler radio-T.V. advertising, and worked there on that and other McCann accounts, including the First National Bank of Atlanta, until I went with Liller-Neal as copy chief. The rest of it you have more or less accurately, though my "rise" was not all that "meteoric" (and you really should get away from such clichés as these, which are worse than any of those in advertising.) I won't go on and on, but simply tell you that I found your article of some interest and some use. What more can I say?

As for your feelings about <u>Puella</u>, I am sorry you have them, though there's nothing I can do about that, either. I don't know whether the poems are better or worse than the earlier ones, but they are different, and that is what I wanted, and still want, and will have. I got rather tired of versifying anecdotes; it had become rather too easy. I could have gone on doing it, of course, and written the same poem over and over, doubtless satisfying the expectations of those, like yourself, who wanted to read more of these. If you want to do that, write them yourself, as many, both male and female, are doing these days—I won't give names; open any magazine, and look for the approach to subject matter; look for the split line. As I say, why not get in on it yourself? As for me, I'll be somewhere else. Repetition, self-imitation, no. Change, and more change, yes. I intend more phases than Picasso, and some of them will be good. And some of <u>Puella</u> will be around when the rest is gone, despite your protestations, or anybody else's.

Your interest + concern, I like, though, so keep in touch.

With best wishes,

James Dickey

/rl

TO: JOHN BENEDICT[116]

CC, 1 p; Emory

Columbia, S.C.

December 19, 1983

Dear John:

Thanks so much for sending along Dick Hugo's book, which in design and format—as well as in content—is certainly a proud memorial to my old friend.[117]

It's interesting; three and a half years ago I had an operation—it was the day after Mt. St. Helens erupted—which had to be done in Seattle, because the main specialist who did the surgery was there. I had the operation, and the first person who called me was Dick Hugo, and we discussed—very reasonably, as I remember—whether I would make it through. He wanted to drive out from Montana, through all the drift of volcanic ash, but the government disallowed traffic on those roads, otherwise I am sure he would have come. After I got on my feet I invited him to give a reading down here, which he did, and after that I never saw him again. But I did get a phone call from him, and it was from the same room in the hospital I had occupied. He had had a lung removed for cancer, and we had the same kind of conversation. After that, when <u>he</u> got out, we talked a couple of times more, and the next thing I knew he was dead not from cancer but from Leukemia.

Well, I don't know about these things. As John Berryman said in a poem, "be dust myself, someday. Not yet."[118]

Let me know whatever I may be able to do to promote the book. I hope, for the sake of all of us, that it will be in print forever.

Cordially,

James Dickey

/rl

TO: WILLIAM PHILLIPS

TLS (Xerox), 2 pp;[119] Emory

December 28, 1983

Dear William Phillips:

I have your letter, and am glad to have it.

Let me say this. If it would not be presumptuous of me, I would like to tell you that I most probably would never have been a writer at all, had it not been for the <u>Partisan Review</u>. When I came back from the war in early 1946, I had never heard of a literary magazine, and chanced on an issue of the <u>Partisan Review</u> in a book-store in Nashville, Tennessee, where I had just enrolled as a freshman at Vanderbilt. I bought it, and read in that particular issue, as I remember, your essay on Dostoyesvky's underground man, and I remember saying to myself in the dorm, this kind of thing is for me. Later, when I had written some things and published some of them in <u>Partisan Review</u>, I came to know Phillip Rahv and Dwight Mac-Donald, and I met a good number of the regular contributors, like Randall Jarrell. It was always with an enormous uprush of enthusiasm, a sense of a renewal of intellectual possibilities, that I opened each new issue, and read most of them through on the day they came out. Later, evidently because of the interest of someone at the <u>Review</u>—perhaps it was yourself, or Rahv, or Delmore Schwartz maybe—it was suggested that I might like to publish a book of poems with your brother Sidney's firm, Criterion Books. Though nothing came of the venture, I remember with extreme gratitude and pleasure an afternoon spent with your brother on this subject, and, though I have not seen him since, I hope you will pass along to him my remembrance.

As to my giving you something for your fiftieth anniversary issue, I will be more than glad to do so, if anything I have at hand is suitable. I don't have any new poems, except in fragments, and I don't believe I could do any kind of article, even a short one, in that length of time. But, since you say that such a selection could even be an excerpt from something currently being worked on, I might, if you like, send along a brief section of a novel I am finishing. It is simply a description of a blind man in a hot bathtub drinking whiskey, still inhabited by the snow-storm he has just left. It is, I guess, about how the blind experience snow, and as such I suppose could be construed as a kind of prose poem, though actually it is part of another thing.[120]

Let me know how you feel about this, and if this sort of selection will do, and I will be guided accordingly. I'll wait until I hear from you before sending the pages.

My best to you, from a past almost forty years deep.

Sincerely,

James Dickey

/rl

TO: SHAYE AREHEART[121]

CC, 3 pp; Emory
Columbia, S.C.

July 18, 1984

Dear Shaye:

Just checking in, because it is now a good while since we communicated. The family is well, Kevin was married to a fine girl, a classmate in medical school at Emory, and in general life is moving forward fairly well, as nearly as I can make out, on several fronts. The novel is about done through the Friday section. This is the hardest to write, and takes the most experimentation. After I finish this there will be only the Saturday portion, during which not much happens except for Saturday night—this in keeping with sequences of other action on that particular evening both in fiction and out—and the final debacle on Sunday, plus a short aftermath section, a kind of reprise in which I want to do some explaining but not too much.

A couple of things about the novel. Partisan Review has a fiftieth anniversary number coming up, and wanted some of the book, so I gave them a short section. Now George Plimpton wants one for his twenty-fifth anniversary number of The Paris Review, and I told him I might be able to send him twenty-five pages or so, if my publisher would agree to that much. Matt thinks it a good idea, and Theron has no objection, but I thought I would ask Doubleday first before I sent in the pages, called "The Tattering of Algol" to George.[122] It seems to me that these magazine publications along the line are helpful; I still get a good deal of mail on the part that was published in Esquire in '76, and it seems to me a good idea to keep the public attention on what we are doing. So . . . do let me know about this as soon as you can, and I'll be guided accordingly.

As to the Appalachia book, I have only one letter from Kate Medina[123] in which she says she likes what I've done but wished for there to be "more Dickey" in it. There is no possible way I can evaluate remarks of this sort, much less comply with them, or at least not until I get something more specific. At any rate I go with what I have sent in, as overseen by Hugh[124] and agreed-upon between us. I plan no extensive revisions, in other words. I was asked to do the book as I did Jericho, in which there was not one editorial change—except in one of the recipes, which called for one half cup of peas instead of one fourth!—and I proceeded the same way here on the plan that Randy Green[125] and I laid out. So there the matter rests, as far as I'm concerned. Tell Kate that we can change some things, maybe, but that the general format should stay as it is—I'm not prepared to work with any other, or to recast the whole thing—and that certain sections, such as the ghost stories, <u>must</u> stay as they are. I've read them at a good many places, and the audience wants them and is expecting them in that form. Again, inform me on these things, or get Kate to communicate.[126]

One more item. I gave the graduation address at the University of Arkansas in May, and Miller Williams, head of the new poetry-oriented Press there, asked me about some strange off-the-wall poems I have been experimenting with. These take off from Spanish translations, after which I rewrite them in Spanish for the sound-resonance and then translate them back into English. I showed Williams, at his request, about fifteen of these, thinking that, if he and his editors liked them, the Press might want to do a little gift edition, something like Palaemon Press did with <u>Head-Deep in Strange Sounds</u>, before the poems were incorporated in <u>The Strength of Fields</u>. Williams sent the manuscript out and received several readers' reports that verge, I blush to say, on the ecstatic, and now he wants a whole book of these odd hybrid tentatively called, as the original manuscript was, <u>Immortals, and Others</u>.[127] Before I went ahead with the project, though, I felt I should check with Doubleday for you-all have a lien on all my original poetry, and these are original poems, despite the take-off from Vicente Aleixandre's originals, which they do not in the final version resemble in the least. Clue me in as to what to do, and I'll be guided, as I said above, accordingly.

The Binkley thing drags on, though we have now got a situation where he can only sue me for what he thinks he would have made out of the book if it had appeared. Since we can prove that the book would not have appeared—that he couldn't get it off the ground; that it wouldn't fly—my new lawyer thinks we have quite a good case. But I don't worry about it; there are other things to do.

The children's book will be done by Harcourt Brace Jovanovich, and the editors there tell me they intend to put some real muscle behind it. Rather than rush production, we plan to publish in the Fall of 1985.[128]

A favor, as I depart this letter. I have been working a good deal on the Brother EP-20 typewriter, the tiny little flat one that you can practically carry in your pocket. I gave Chris my original one so that he can take notes on it down there in the Central American jungle—or Bungle, as I call it—and I got another one, but have used it so enthusiastically that I have run out of the cassettes it uses. I'd appreciate it very much if you'd go to one of the typewriter stores in the big city and buy me a package of five cassettes for the Brother EP-20, and send them and the bill to me right away. Please do this <u>today</u>, and send them UPS, so that I can use the typewriter on aircraft, in the bathroom—and in the bathroom on aircraft—on the world famous backyard literary dock, on my Sunfish sailboat, where we're having a cocktail party on the afterdeck late next month; you and the entire Doubleday staff are invited.[129] Anyway, please <u>do</u> send the box of cassettes today, so that I can get back to work in my various locations.

And one more thing, if you will. At the Museum of Natural History, please buy me two more dinosaur T-shirts, with as many teeth showing—on the dinosaur(s)—as possible. I take an extra large, but a large will do if they don't have them. And get Bronnie a little one, too, please, with equal or only slightly smaller teeth.

I'll wait to hear on these matters, and to know whether you got this letter, and my love. Debba sends hers too, and so does Bronnie.

Ever,
James Dickey

/rl

TO: KATE MEDINA

RTL (Xerox), 2 pp;¹³⁰ Emory

April 8, 1985

Dear Kate,

Here is a bundle for you,[131] sure enough! As you requested, I have made a copy of the whole thing up through page 872, so that we both have identical manuscripts, and consequently can refer to any passage, line, or word, on any page, without confusion. The enclosed copies of the two sections are a kind of amalgam of various typewriters, papers, (and typists!), but they should be legible, I think. If there is any spotting or other illegibility, please let me know and I will correct from my text.

At the beginning, I include all the epigraphs that I have set aside to choose from among, so that you may have a look and do your own choosing. As for myself, I think that the two from David Hume are virtually musts, and possibly the words from Lucretius should also appear, since the novel is really about the air, in the sense that Moby Dick is about water.[132] Again, let me know what you think.

The end is written, and if you want me to send it to you out of sequence I will do so. The part I am laboring now to revise is the flight material into which we are getting with page 872. This sequence, originally called "A Wheedling of Knives," is the real heart of the book, and, though I think the first pass at it was pretty good, I feel that the revisions strengthen it greatly, and with luck will make it unforgettable, even if I do say so myself. All but a few pages are at the typist's now, and I will have the whole thing in your hands very shortly.

Meanwhile, go back over the story and make some notes on whatever aspects of it strike you as needing attention. I am constantly making my own notes, and find that they help a good deal. There are some actual research points we will need to check out before we set the book up in type. For example, in the long navigational sequence about the Rabaul raid out of New Guinea that Captain Whitehall tells Cahill and the others about, I don't know whether the stars I refer to are the actual stars that could have been seen on that night forty-odd years ago, and I suppose I will have to check with the United States Naval Observatory or someone to find out. But in cases like that I thought it better to go ahead and guess, and keep on with the story rather than waiting until I heard from someone who had gone to the trouble of looking up declinations in old Air Almanacs for me. All that can be done later, but some of it <u>should</u> be done, for, though historical accuracy is not really my aim, I don't want to vitiate the story, either, by introducing material that could not possibly be as I say it is.

But read through all this again just as soon as you can, and get back to me on it. Meanwhile I will get McCaig and Cahill into and out of the air by means of the revisions I am doing, get the other pages back from the typist, and we'll have the whole thing.

My best, as always,

JAMES DICKEY

TO: KATE MEDINA

CC, 2 pp; Emory
Columbia, S.C.

June 14, 1985

Dear Kate,

Here is the rest of the Friday section, through to the end. This section, the only flight in a novel that centers on aircraft, is the most crucial scene in the book, as well as the only extended action sequence. For these reasons I have re-written this whole portion, and so you can now fit it into place with the rest of the pages which go before it; these are numbered in accordance with the pages I sent in April, so that when we talk about details we can refer to the same page on the two copies.

The Saturday and Sunday sections are being typed. These are not nearly so long and difficult as the Friday part, and I will send them along soon. The very last part, which is a kind of coda or aftermath, I am trying a couple of different ways. I am not sure of how much to explain; what explaining I do is done by dialogue, and the speculations of several of the characters, mainly Cadet Shears, the Flight Surgeon, Major Ianonne, and the Navigation Instructor, Captain Whitehall (Captain Faulstick is killed in the climactic event of Sunday, the destruction of the aircraft by the Alnilam plotters, in which Cahill's dog Zack is also killed), and it is a question of how much speculation or summation I want them to do. I'd like to leave certain things, important ones, up to the reader, but there are also some hints I would like to give as to the <u>possibilities</u> of the events that have taken place. I could, I should think, have a long scene dealing with the probe into the destruction of the aircraft, the Alnilam plot, the disappearance of Joel, and so on, and could have an investigation-scene, something like the <u>Caine Mutiny</u> court-martial proceedings, but I feel that such would be anti-climactic, and would violate my notion of leaving certain things up to the reader. Such an investigation, by the way, would lend itself to another short work, perhaps, or even a play, for it seems to me that the situation and the characters are far more interesting than anything in Herman Wouk's perennial and predictable set-up.[133]

Let me know how all this strikes you, and meanwhile I'll be finishing up.

My best to everyone up there.

Ever,

JAMES DICKEY

JD/pg

TO: JAMES B. T. DICKEY[134]

TLS (Xerox), 1 p;[135] Emory

July 12, 1985

Dear Tuck,

Well, a lot has happened; things keep on happening, no matter how you might want them to stay the same. But a lot of that is good, I think. I want to start writing you more or less regularly, so that so <u>much</u> won't have happened without either of us hearing about it. For example, I know almost nothing about your school, about the subjects you are taking, about your athletic doings, your sailing, or indeed your life in general. So catch me up on as much of that as you can, for I want to know; I want to know a whole lot; as much as you would like to tell me.

I am trying to study out some ways in which I might be of some use to you, and am doing this by going through the kind of stuff I know something about, maybe not from having any native talent for the things, but because of the interest I have in them, and a long acquaintance with them. Almost anything in the school (sp.) curiculum I could help you with, I think, even chemistry and physics (up to a point: <u>only</u> up to a point!), but especially anything dealing with philosophy or the world of ideas, generally. I have played almost all sports except polo and lacrosse, and could, I believe, call on memory for those I don't participate in any more; memory is strong when it has to do with anything physical that you learned at one time. Music I could help you with; the guitar, if you wanted to get started, or to some extent the piano. I think music would be a good thing for you, if you like it already; like to listen to it, like having it around. Photography I know something about, though not a great deal about the ultra-tech of some of the equipment.

And so . . . let me know what you need, and whatever I can do, I will do. Meantime, tell me what your greatest interests are right now, and I'll see how much I can swing with you. I'll sure do what I can, because it is for the best cause in the world, which is your development and your life. As I say, I'll go with <u>that</u>.

Ever,
Fun Man[136]

TO: BEN BELITT

TLS, 2 pp;[137] University of South Carolina

January 19, 1987

Dear Ben:

Thank you so very much for sending your book to me,[138] and for the inscription, which I value more than any. It is a terrible thing to have to admit that I have not been in touch with you for such a terribly long time, but what I hold in my mind from the association is the best that memory gives, and I draw on it frequently for lessons of uncompromising dedication as well as poetic excellence of a kind perfectly unique in the English language.

I also go back and back to your translations, for it seems to me that the whole question of translation and the cross-pollinization of cultures by means of translation, is very large and important, and will be more so. People are not only coming forth with more translations, but with <u>theories</u> of translation, which is to say defenses of the kind they themselves practice. Since Pound at least, a new kind of curious form, which I try to experiment with myself, has come into existence. This is neither a translation or a completely original poem, but a kind of hybrid which for want of a better name I am tempted to call "the rewrite." Such an approach may seem on the surface of it contemptible, but it is not, and I think more and more people, either those who don't know the foreign language very well or those who <u>do</u> know it well but want to do something <u>different</u> in English, will be the ones to watch. Your own verse seems to me to come into this situation in the best possible way, for you understand instinctively what good effects Neruda, Alberti—to say nothing of Rimbaud—can have on poetry in English. I think the well of this resource is very deep—indeed, bottomless—but a lot of the water is impure in the wrong way, because it is being drawn up by untalented hands. I thank God for you, whose hands are very talented indeed, and for the part you will inevitably play—no; are already playing—in what I quite sincerely believe will be the most profound change our poetry will undergo during the next phase of things, which is likely to last forever.

Again, thanks for your book, Ben. It is the best thing I have read in many years. Keep doing what you're doing, and let me hear from you when you feel like writing.

Ever,

Jim

TO: HOWARD KAPLAN[139]

CC, 2 pp; Emory
Columbia, S.C.

February 25, 1987

Dear Howard, Carolyn, Herman, Shaye, and Everyone:

Here are the proofs, gone-over letter by letter, comma by comma. If I have missed anything it surely wasn't because I wasn't careful. I hope the fact that I have been able to get these pages back on schedule will make it possible for us to keep right to our time table, and that the publication date of June 5th will not have to be moved around. Let me know whatever I might be able to do, to keep us on track.[140]

About the proofs as I have edited them. The only thing that might cause difficulty is the use of the different type faces. I had originally intended for the heavy type to be used only in the left-hand side of the pages on which there is the double presentation: the Dark and Light format. On page 25, though, the heavy type is employed in a section which is <u>not</u> in the dark-light format. When I got to that part I figured that it might be a good idea to print all of the portions that deal with Cahill's introspection, his memories, his conjectures and so on, in this way, and after page 25 I made notations on the proofs that the heavy type should be used in these places. However, after reading through the whole book, I have decided that we should use the heavy type <u>only</u> on those pages that are split, and print the other places in regular type. I will leave the editorial decision to you. We could print <u>all</u> of the soliloquys, recollections, and so on, in the heavy type, or we could go back and change pages 25, 26, and most of 27, and then 28, 29, and 30 back into regular type, and, in keeping with this change in format, we could also print the little memory-flash on the bottom of page 40 and the top of page 41, now in italics, in regular type, and, if you like, to avoid confusion, we could have a little space between the last paragraph on page 40 and the little section that begins "Into a setting of scrub brush and a thin creek . . ." Again, I leave all this to you, and trust that you, readers as well as editors, will do what can be done to make the presentation as clear as possible.[141]

One other thing. The compositors have taken out a good many hyphens that were in the original typescript. I have gone through and put all these back in. This should be done because in a good many places the words do not make sense, or at any rate the same _kind_ of sense, without the hyphens. "That there" is not the same as "that-there," and in addition to missing out on the intended meaning it does away with the intonation of the red-neck vocabulary, which is crucial to the presentation of the characters involved. In other words, please _do_ give me back my hyphens! Hyphens, we need you!

Otherwise, the notations I have made on the page-proofs should be relatively easy to follow, but if there are any questions on any section or on any specific item please get right back to me, because I know exactly what I want in every place. My God, if there has ever been a writer in closer contact with his own words I'd sure like to shake his hand! Enormous labors, these! How _could_ I have written so much—and all so good, too! Well, we'll see what the others think.

Again, thank you—all of you—for your devoted and intelligent help on this enormous project. I stand ready to do whatever is desirable or possible to publicize and promote our book. Just let me know a little in advance and I'll be ready to go—wherever—and do what needs to be done. Everything is beginning.

Ever,

James Dickey

TO: HAROLD BLOOM[142]

RTL, 1 p; Emory
Columbia, S.C.

22 July 1987

Dear Harold:

I just have the book on my work which you edited,[143] and I wanted to take whatever time it takes to tell you how much I appreciate your trouble and intelligence in getting these things together and presenting them. There are some good, helpful pieces here, though surely the best comments are your own; though there are some points with which I could take issue in one or two of the other articles, there are none in yours. Again, you have my thanks for the work you have done in connection with work I have done. I hope the book will reach the readers I'd like it to have.

May I ask if you could give me news of Red's situation? I haven't heard anything from him since he was inquiring about my own brain surgery of last summer,[144] so that all that I have in the way of news is third and fourth hand. Whatever you could tell me about Red is very welcome, for I tend to worry more than most.

I hope all is well with you, your most beloved people and your work. Let me hear from you when you have the chance.

Ever,

James Dickey

P.S. Have you read my big new novel, <u>Alnilam</u>, yet? I'd be interested to know what you think, should you get round to it.

TO: EVAN CONNELL[145]

RTL, 1 p; Emory
Columbia, S.C.

2 October 1987

Dear Evan:

Thank you very much for your two books, which I have carried with me to many points on the compass (Rose!)[146] for the last couple of months, lost in admiration for your learning, and your ability to range around in history and connect the points.

I defer to no one in my admiration for your ability, but I <u>am</u> somewhat bothered by the anti-American propagandizing; say, on pages 89 & 90 of <u>Compass Rose</u>. If you wish to make these points—which are, maybe, quite legitimate—you need to bring a great deal more power to the language. As things are, a newspaper listing of these atrocities would be as effective as what you have.

But nobody likes to be told how to write, and if I have been forward, please forgive me. I say what I do because it seems to me that a dialogue has begun, and I had as soon it go on, at your own pleasure.

Again, thanks for the books. Believe me, I am with you.

Warmly,

James Dickey

TO: CHRISTOPHER DICKEY

RTL, 2 pp; Emory
Columbia, S.C.

20 November 1987

My dear Son:

I should have written sooner—as I should have written many letters to you over the years—but the recent events here have made it so that there has been no time for anything but anxiety and pain. My brother Tom is dying of cancer, and there seems to be no hope beyond a couple of months of life, which I hope will be relatively free from pain. Everything has been tried, including two weeks at Sloan-Kettering Cancer Institute in New York, but it was decided to send him back to Piedmont Hospital in Atlanta, since he would be closer to his people. The cancer has metastasized all over his body, and keeps going, as it will do. Some of the new stuff—Interleukin-2, mainly—seems to have the effect of keeping down some of the swelling, but all this is only an interim measure designed to ease the suffering, and maybe enable him to live a month or two longer. The doctors advised me not to go over there until he comes off the treatment, but then I will, and can let you know more in a week or so. It is a terrible thing, and the utter hopelessness is the worst of it. That, and the way the memory fills up with images of him when he was happy.[147]

I continue with various projects, and there will be some interesting news, which I hope you will like, coming out of New York in about two weeks.[148]

The screenplay for the film version of Alnilam is about half done, and seems to be going well. The director, John Guillermin,[149] seems very pleased, and tells me of various prospects as to location, actors, and so on, that he has in mind. But right now, the situation with Tom being what it is, I have little heart for my own efforts, and so push on by will alone, as I have had to do so many times in the past. I love my brother very much, and find that my main image of him is that extraordinary shot of him in your film,[150] where his laughter is lit by the blaze-up of powder he dug up from a war buried for a hundred years. That image is a wonderful emblem of Tom, and it took the eye and hand and imagination of a real artist to catch. That is one more thing I'd like to thank you for, among so many.

I think of you often, and worry that you may be in some danger or other. My only source of information is the press, and I read your material in Newsweek with the greatest interest and admiration. The public back here fears some cataclysmic happening down where you are,[151] and from where I stand it does seem more than likely. But of course you know a great deal more about that than I do, and for my part I can only read the newspapers—and Newsweek!—and hope that you will not be where the bad thing happens, if it does.

Let me hear from you whenever you have a chance to write. Do know how proud I am of you, and what great joy I take in your human qualities, and what you have done with them, and are doing. There is a scene in <u>Alnilam</u>—I am writing this part of the film now—where the image of an extraordinary young man, the most extraordinary I could imagine, comes up on the galvanized tin wall of a tool shed. There is no doubt as to the identity of that face.

All my love,

TO: WILLIAM WALLISCH[152]

RTL, 2 pp; Emory
Columbia, S.C.

13 January 1988

Dear Bill Wallisch:

Thanks indeed for both of your letters, and for the clipping about the Academy. Bill Styron never before looked forth on the world with such a face of genius![153]

I'm glad that arrangements for another visit have been going forward, and I'll do my best to come, when and if the invitation is tendered, even though we will be moving into pre-production on the film version of <u>Alnilam</u> about the time you mention. But if I can possibly arrange things, I'll come.

I'll be happy to meet with Allen McArtor, and any and everybody you'd like. Believe me I have plenty of ideas as to the "image" of modern aviation! One of the things I wanted most to do in <u>Alnilam</u> was to restore the sense of <u>bodily</u> flight to people: the feeling of being <u>carried</u> in the element they breathe, which is a sensation full of uncertainty, precarious balance, exhilaration, and above all, transgression. <u>That's</u> what I'm talking about!

I hope very much that I can come back out there, for my memory of the other visit is one of the best that time has given me. I can still see the deer—whole <u>herds</u> of them!—grazing at night on the campus. Some campus, I'd say!

My best to everyone out there, and particularly to the navigational instructors who helped me with <u>Alnilam</u>, sending me the Navigational Triangle for the date I requested, and the other things.

Let me hear from you again, when you have the chance. Your word is always good.

Ever,
James Dickey

JLD/kjk

TO: KAREN S. P. SCHEIDELER[154]

RTL, 2 pp; Emory
Columbia, S.C.

9 May 1988

Dear Ms. Scheideler:

I have waited a few days to answer your letter, for I have not been able to find a way of telling you how much I appreciate your writing, and the things you say about my novel. Of all the words in the seven hundred pages of Alnilam, I don't believe I could find any combination of them which would be adequate to express the nature of my reaction to your reaction, so I won't try. But please understand, from imagining the things I am not able to say, how pleased and grateful I am.

Yet there is more; I must say more. Authors, even if they don't publish much, or even if they are not very good, get plenty of mail, and a lot of it is gush, and much off the point of what he has been trying to say. People keep finding in his work things he never intended, and often these are the qualities for which he is praised. Being human, the poor writer usually doesn't disabuse his admirer. After all, he thinks, maybe I did mean something like that. Who can say? Or, who am I to say?

Your letter is not of that kind. What pleases me about it to an extent that it would be difficult for me to make clear to you, is that your affirmation of the novel is intelligent as well as heartfelt: the qualities you see in the book are the ones I most wanted to be seen. Your letter is worth more to me than all the approbation that the print and other media might give me. One of the best things about it is that it is not public but private, and by this I know that I have reached someone at the human depth where art operates.

I won't go on and on, for I am beginning to gush, myself, but will just thank you once more for your generosity, and your letter. If you should wish to communicate further, I'd like to know something of your life, your work, and your other interests. But such communication shall be as you wish, of course.

Sincerely yours,

P.S. I have just finished the screenplay for the film version of Alnilam, which it gives me great pleasure to hope you will go to see, when it comes out. That is, if we can get through the thousand road-blocks and barbed-wire entanglements that must be got through to make a movie; Hollywood has plenty of those in store for every writer. At any rate, John Guillermin is directing. He is a director who specializes in spectacular effects—The Towering Inferno is one of his, for example—

and I am hoping that the effects in <u>Alnilam</u> will be just spectacular <u>enough</u>, and no more. Well, we'll see.[155]

And again, thanks. And again, too.

JLD/kjk

TO: ANNA BALAKIAN[156]

CC, 2 pp; Emory
Columbia, S.C.

August 26, 1988

Dear Anna Balakian:

I am now in possession of your remarkable letter, and I must say from the very beginning of my answer how very deeply I am moved by your remarks on <u>Alnilam</u>. One is moved, but not always <u>moved</u> by what is said in regard to what one has written, because there is a degree of difference between people who are complimentary about the work, often for qualities that don't exist in it, and those who have grasped the work as the author wished it to be apprehended: for the reasons he hopes he has built into it. When a response like yours appears, what can the novelist do except to stammer that, though he has sometimes been understood rightly, he never has, <u>this</u> rightly? Again, I am grateful for your remarks, and the meticulousness with which you have gone through a very long book. There is no reading of it better than yours.

A couple of points. The hardest thing for me to project, to find a way to get into the story, particularly into the dialogue, was the fact that both Cahill and the girl, Hannah, are people who feel more than they are able to say. Both of them are very nearly illiterate, and I meant for their struggle toward a language which they cannot reach to have the power of making the reader wish to leap into the story and say for them what they themselves cannot find words for. Some of the passages of dialogue between them seems to me affecting in a way that the conversation of highly articulate characters, such as those in the novels of Aldous Huxley, for example, do not and cannot have. I have just finished the screenplay, and I believe that this struggle toward communication between the blind man and the sick—and perhaps dying—girl will have a depth of human emotion very rarely come upon in works of art. I say that <u>I</u> think this, but what others think of this part of the novel, and what the viewers of the screen version of it will think, is maybe another matter. Anyway, we'll see.

I can't make this the long letter I'd like to, for I have to get on yet another airplane. But do understand how extremely grateful I am for your extended and deep comments. <u>Alnilam</u> has found its truest reader. And if that one is yourself it needs no other. Again, thanks.

Please remember me to Nona, Peter, and the rest of your family, and those I met when I was among you at that remarkable occasion with Joyce Carol Oates and Ed Doctorow. That was among the best of human times; surely for me, it was; and remains.

And, yes, I see Jim Mann[157] often. In fact, I played tennis with him this morning—a savage shoot-out! It took us all morning to play one set—which he won in a tie-breaker! The boy shows promise!

Ever,

JD/bg

Dickey in the late 1980s

Dickey in April 1995

PART NINE

THE LAST WOLVERINE

September 1988–November 1996

Joseph Heller and Dickey, University of South Carolina,
September 1996

TLS, 3 pp;[2] Marc Jaffe

September 19, 1988

Dear Marc:

Thanks so much for your phone call, and for the news that you and Joe Kanon and Marley Russo (have I got her name right, at last? if not, do let me know)[3] will be able to come to the release party for <u>Wayfarer</u>, on October 6th. I don't know where the publisher will have me staying, but wherever it is my wife will be with me, and I will at last be able to get all of us together. As I say, I'll let you know more of the details as the time approaches.

Here is the opening of the novel. I understand that the word is usually <u>Thalassa</u>, but I have done a little research—not usually my strong point—and find that the word is spelled one way or the other according to which part of Greece the speaking person comes from. In Xenophon's original <u>Anabasis</u>, from which I took the idea, it is <u>Thalatta</u>, "the sea," and so at this time I am using this version not only because of these things but because I like the sound better, and because it is less predictable. It is not a major point with me, and for the right reasons, were they presented, I would be willing to change. But as of now the title is as I wish.

It may seem strange that I should send you just a couple of pages at this time. Someone like Trollope—or Mickey Spillane!—would be able to enclose several hundred pages, but that is not the way I work. At the beginning of things I am preoccupied with three points. The first of these is the style of the speaking voice, which in the case of a first-person narrator is all-important, and which you can get some idea of from the enclosed couple of pages. The second is the overall concept, and how it is to be implemented both as to the sequence of events, the transition between these, and the details pertaining to each. The third is what I want the overall impact to be. This latter is something like a cloud or an aura that comes out of and in a kind of way stands over everything that has been told. In connection with this latter, I intend for the audience to grow increasingly aware that the United States military, in its much-advertised

453

"war against the Axis," has released among the Japanese civilian population—almost all the men up to the age of 60 were in the armed services—a sociopath, a conscienceless murderer, a kind of Ted Bundy, who after a while does not even take into account that the people he kills are officially his enemies. Muldrow, in effect, has a license to kill, and it is unlimited; we wish to show this.

We also wish to show that his mind has the kind of ingenuity and self-justifying diabolism of certain people of this sort. Drawing at least partly on his upbringing in northern Alaska, on the Arctic Circle side of the Brooks range, he has an instinctive knowledge and mastery of camouflage, the use of color to make himself either invisible or the next thing to it. The sections of the novel are divided into episodes dealing with the color spectrum, beginning with red—the fire-bombing raid on Tokyo—and ending in white, as Muldrow reaches the northern tip of Hokkaido and sees the icebergs in the water, fulfilling what he has told someone in the first section of the novel: "For me, the ocean is not the ocean unless it's got ice in it."

I have spent the summer adjusting one part to the other. The transitions between one episode—and one color!—to the other have been hard to work out, but the whole thing is so fascinating, if I do say so myself, that whatever time I have had to put in on the story has only whetted my appetite for more. One of the main problems is not to become overly introspective, which is always a danger with me, as I suspect it is with most novelists, especially those who have written poetry. Muldrow must be able to say startling things, unexpected things, but he should not say them all the time. Again, this is one of the problems of adjustment, and of style.

So read these opening paragraphs and tell me what you think. Meanwhile, I will continue to work out the episodes, and their relation to each other. Your advice that Muldrow should not have had any kind of diary or log-book which the novel is purportedly dependent on either partially or exclusively, is the best advice I ever got from an editor; when Muldrow disappears into the white-out by the mere act of closing his eyes, it is the end of things, and no further explanations are either needed or forthcoming. I am in complete agreement.

I have just about completed the general plan, so that when Muldrow moves from one locality and one episode to the other it will seem natural as well as exciting. I warn you, some of the things that happen are very strange. I don't think there is anything like them in fiction.

But that is all to do, yet. Because I have put the time in as I have, this summer, though, the scenes will not have the effect of material scrappily thrown together, but will be, in that word beloved of writers—at least the good ones—organic. I do think they will; I sure do.

Let me hear from you when you have a chance, and we'll move along.

Ever,

Jim

JD/bg
encls.

TO: GORE VIDAL[4]

CC, 2 pp; Emory
Columbia, S.C.

December 14, 1988

Dear Gore Vidal:

I wished to write this letter for a number of reasons, but chief among these is the attention that you have paid in your last book, <u>At Home</u>,[5] to Frederic Prokosch. Like you, I have been strongly influenced by him, and since there has been no real attention to his work in all the years I can remember, I was especially pleased with what you had to say. Prokosch is an extremist of a very special sort, and in my opinion there should be that extreme. You can read passage after passage of his work and think that "this is the quintessence of a decadent romantic style," but decadent romanticism has its own virtues, and I defy anyone to read the passage on the zebras in <u>Storm and Echo</u>[6] without realizing that extremes are just that: places that ordinariness cannot reach, but which come back as observations from somewhere better than we are used to.

I have never met Prokosch, but he is an old man now, and I would like to give him whatever reaffirmation I may be capable of giving. If you have his address, or can let me know by what means I might be able to reach him, I will be glad to tell him what I am telling you.

I am sorry we have never met, for I admire your mind very much, in whatever form it chooses to exhibit itself. I make no real distinction between fact, fiction, history, reminiscence and fantasy, for the imagination inhabits them all. That is the place that Frederic Prokosch occupies: a kind of all-place. You yourself do the same, from Tarzan on up. As Whitman says, it all tastes good to me.

As I said earlier, I'm sorry we have never met, but there <u>was</u> one bit of a close thing, this being when you were on the phone with Jerry Hellman at a time when I was in his office, working on an aborted film script dear to his heart, by means of which Jerry hoped to project Delmore Schwartz into the Klondike gold rush. An admirable idea, I think all would agree. But Delmore was not destined to make the trek.

Anyway, I hope that we may meet, one day, and that we can talk about Prokosch and the other things that matter to us.

Let me hear from you when and if you have a moment, even if just for the information that this has reached you.

Sincerely,
James Dickey

JD/bg

TO: MARC JAFFE

TLS, 2 pp;[7] Marc Jaffe

December 21, 1988

Dear Marc:

Thank you so much for the letter, and for the things you say about the enterprise we are embarked on together.

Now that the promotional tour for <u>Wayfarer</u> is over, I am full into the novel, and have finished blocking-out the action. I have a consistent story, I think—one the likes of which has not yet appeared on earth—and am now working on the key scenes. If these big units are strong enough, I don't mind the time needed on the episodes that set them up. My problem here, as it has been with the two other novels I've done, is that I get so <u>into</u> the individual scenes that I just write on and on, until there are dozens of pages when there ought to be only three or four. I have a night gunnery scene, from Muldrow's position in the tail of the B-29, that is going to devastate anyone who reads it. It is a kind of mixture of actual gunnery and intuitive or metaphysical gunnery that I think you will be pleased with, and remember. And there is another episode in a kind of civilian-defense supply-cave which is also good, I think. And the night crossing from Honshu to Hokkaido is also suspenseful and unusual.

Although I don't usually do this, I am trying to research a little as I go along, though I usually like to turn the imagination loose on the subject without any reference to researched material; and then, if need be, go back and incorporate whatever I need from prior sources. But here, in the snow scenes, for example, I need to <u>know</u> a little more than I actually do know about the more desolate regions of Hokkaido, particularly the mountains in the northeast section, which in some respects are like the mountains of the Brooks Range in Alaska, where Muldrow grew up. Anyway, it is all coming together, and I am still letting imagination lead, for that is always best, with me. When you come down in January we'll go over all these things, and you can give me your ideas, which are always good, and always welcome.

I won't go on and on, now, about what I'm doing, but will get back to doing it.

I should have several hundred pages of fairly coherent manuscript by the time you come down here. The more I get into this story, the better I like it. There is a real possibility of a stark and unanswerable fable here, and that's the kind I like to write.

My best to you; and let me hear from you when you have a chance to write, or just when you want to.

Ever,

Jim

JD/bg

TO: MRS. PADDY SCHORB[8]

CC, 1 p; Emory

Columbia, S.C.

January 25, 1989

Dear Mrs. Schorb:

Thank you indeed for sending your husband's book, and for the things you say about my work; I'm sorry I'm late in answering.

I am much interested in your husband's approach to poetry, which seems highly individual—which I and Emerson and Wallace Stevens think is important and T. S. Eliot and C. S. Lewis don't, but the last two are wrong—and I am very happy to have access to it, and hope that you will continue to communicate with me and send whatever you would like me to see. I am very hard pressed at the present time, with seven books coming out and three movies, all in various stages of development, and these projects, plus teaching and traveling and looking after my people take up most of the available time. But I am always happy to drop everything—pretty nearly—when I make the acquaintance of a new poet as good as your husband, and I hope that you will let me thank you once more for your extreme generosity in sending me his words.

Believe me I understand your husband's state of mind, for it was my own for many years of labor at the bottom levels of college teaching, in the armed services, and for six years in American business houses. Such things tend to discourage one, but please tell your husband for me that he must not be downcast; that is for people who are hopeless because they lack talent, and that is not his case. Tell him I am much interested in his writing, and to go forward with it at all costs.

My best to you, and let me hear from you whenever you both have a moment, or would just like to communicate.

Best wishes,

James Dickey

JD/bg

TO: JAMES H. BILLINGTON[9]

CC, 2 pp; Emory
Columbia, S.C.

February 27, 1989

Dear Mr. Billington:

Thank you for your letter asking for my thoughts on the Laureateship, and I have been pondering these. The previous selections, Robert Penn Warren, Richard Wilbur and Howard Nemerov, have been good ones; as far as my personal feeling is concerned, they would be the ones I would have chosen.

As to where we go from here, I am not so sure. You ask for nominees, and after much consideration, I believe that the two best candidates are Karl Shapiro and Daniel Hoffman, with Anthony Hecht as a possible third.

You ask for a paragraph apiece about the two poets I have suggested, and I herewith offer these, though it must be understood that they are highly personal and inevitably prejudiced, and must not be seen as any kind of on-high judgment, subject to countermanding only by the Lord Himself. As I say, my opinions are one-sided, as must inevitably be the case with all us creatures this side of Olympus—or, in this case, Parnassus. For whatever they are worth, however, these are my opinions.

Karl Shapiro is an American poet of just under the first rank. Though he is not of the stature of Lowell or Roethke, he is still very good indeed. He is prolific and extremely opinionated, and this latter quality accounts for the fact that he is down-played in a good many circles, mainly by those whom he has attacked. But if there is anyone in American poetry who is completely his own man, it is he. The best of his poetry will stand up with anyone's, and his frightening honesty—even when I myself don't agree with him—is as refreshing as it is therapeutic. He is an old man now, but seems to be in good enough health, and could probably take on the post. Back in the forties he was Consultant, and therefore knows the Washington scene, and could operate there.

Daniel Hoffman is not so good a poet as Shapiro, though he is quite good. As to the characteristics that you cite in your second paragraph, those having to do with "an energetic spirit of the cause of literary education of young Americans, and even a certain entrepreneurial willingness to initiate projects that would call positive attention to the Laureateship," I think Hoffman should be given serious and entire consideration. He is the very soul of integrity, and his sense of responsibility toward others approaches the intimidating; it is positively dangerous to ask for a glass of water in Hoffman's presence, for if he overhears, you will be deluged with a swimming pool. I can't believe that over-generosity and an acute sense of responsibility are bad human traits, though, and I think that a poet and critic like Daniel Hoffman would answer well to a number of the considerations with which you are concerned.

If you'd like a third candidate, I would bring in Anthony Hecht, who is a very quiet, talented, devoted fellow, and has written some extraordinarily fine poems and translations. He is very low key; not as outspoken as Shapiro or as openly energetic as Hoffman, but he is a good presence to have on any scene, and in any capacity.

And, as Judge Roy Bean ("the Law West of the Pecos") used to say, "That's my rulin.'"

At least it is right now, but if you'd like to keep in touch I may have some further ideas later on. If you need these, or anything else from me, please don't hesitate to communicate, and I will do what I can.[10]

Sincerely yours,
James Dickey

JD/bg

TO: MICHAEL BLAIR[11]

CC, 2 pp; Emory
Columbia, S.C.

March 7, 1989

Dear Mike Blair:

Thanks so much for your letter and for the poem, which I like a lot. I'm delighted that the occasion went as well as you say; for my part I can tell you that I have seldom participated in a conference of disembodied voices that seemed to me so positive and so actually productive of gain as this one. Believe me, I wouldn't have missed it!

I will say this, too. Your students are extraordinarily lucky to study poetry with a real poet—which you definitely are—who can show them the workings of the imagination from the inside, and what happens when it is committed to paper. A student will get more from a working poet than from ten thousand scholars, for it is true, as Valery says, that the true poet is the one who makes poets out of his readers: the poets they would not have been, but for him.

And I'm glad you like wolves, too. If you have a VCR, you might want to get hold of the film I did about fifteen years ago for Warner's and NBC: Jack London's <u>Call of the Wild</u>. I did my own version of the story, though it is basically the same. We shot in the Yukon, in more or less the same setting Jack writes about, and at

Jackson Hole, Wyoming, and during the time I got to know some wolves pretty well. I was surprised at how large they are, and how friendly, once they are used to you. One of them, which (or whom?) I called Johnson, was a particular pal of mine, though he had teeth that must have been a half or three-quarters of an inch long. You and Mech and Barry Lopez and Boyce Rensberger[12] are quite right about the wolf: he has been much maligned. The male is a hard-working father, and has charge of instruction of the cubs. He is monogamous, too, which is rare these days!

But you know all this, I'm sure. The upshot of what I'm saying is that you do right to take the wolf for your total animal—as Jack London did himself, come to think of it (see my introduction to the Penguin edition of Call of the Wild).[13]

Well—enough, keep doing what you're doing, with your kids and with wolves, real or imaginary. And if I may I'd like to encourage your writing. Anyone who can have a wolf blink once after drinking black water, and trot off "into the dark east," can do anything. As I say, I await the results.

Write again when you feel like it. Meanwhile, remember me to all those from Orono that I met in mid-air last Wednesday. It was a great meeting, I say!

Cordially,
James Dickey

JD/bg

TO: MARC JAFFE

TLS, 2 pp;[14] Marc Jaffe

March 13, 1989

Dear Marc:

Thanks so much for the letter, and for the things you say about the pages I have done to date. I am plunging onward, and will have some more for you, when I get a reasonable chunk. The story goes forward so fast that some of the time I feel as though I'm taking dictation, and this might be some cause for alarm but for the fact that the things that keep happening are pretty much in line with my original idea. I plan to go on through to the end, at which time you and I can sit down and see what needs to be done, the second time around. Meanwhile I am reading some collateral material, and finding a good deal that I can use, though the actual Japanese feel is not definite enough; that will have to be put in later, and the whole structure built back around it. I want to give invention its fullest due, though, and will go with it through this draft, so as not to miss something inimitable because of a striving after fact.

As to your comments, yes I do think some version of the pages 79–80 might go earlier in the book; it would not be a hard change to make. I do intend, though, to have various images—or "visions"—of the Arctic crop up from time to time, as Muldrow reminds himself of what he is trying to do and where he is trying to go.

Again, you say that it might not be necessary to emphasize the danger of death in the event of capture, because the readers of the novel wouldn't know what the Japanese did with prisoners. It would seem to me that it should be stressed very strongly that as far as flyers were concerned the Japanese took no prisoners, and that every crew member knew this. If the Japanese routinely beheaded shot-down Allied aviators, what might they not do to one captured after such a fire-raid as the one on March 9th? Later in the novel Muldrow witnesses the execution of an American air crew member, and this will reiterate, I think, the danger he is in, even if the reader doesn't know it until this scene. But I want him to know it.

If you'll look at the skeletonized prospectus, and if you can make anything out of it, you'll see that I plan a scene in a monastery, probably Zen, where there is an English-speaking monk, or even one who is a Caucasian, perhaps even an American. From what I gather, the priests in those places, especially in the remote ones, as this one is, hardly knew there was a war going on. Nevertheless, it is this priest who betrays Muldrow, resulting in his capture, and—as I see it before I've written it!—one of the best scenes in the book.

In all this the matter of proportion is important. Here I have written 100 pages, and have barely gotten Muldrow clear of Tokyo! I could easily have done 100 more—or 200—about the same events, without knowing any more about what actually happened than I do now. A lot of what I have put down will be edited and changed, but we want to hold on to all versions, so that what is worthwhile is preserved intact, and things are not edited out just for the sake of editing. When we get the proportions we want, the novel will be finished.

But that's all in the doing, and I am hard at work in putting the stuff down that I am going to try to get the proportions to. As I say, I'm hard at work, and the thing is unfolding. We'll see what happens.

Great thanks and liking, from me.

Ever,

Jim

JD/bg

TO: JOHN LEHMANN[15]

CC, 2 pp; Emory
Columbia, S.C.

March 24, 1989

Dear John Lehmann:

I rarely write a letter like this, and since we haven't met, it may come as some-thing of an imposition on your time. But if you will accept from an American writer his deepest gratitude for your work in the field he himself has given his life into, the writer in question would be pleased. I have read your poems and your remarkable autobiography, In My Own Time,[16] over and over for years, and, though Stephen Spender lived through the same history and recorded some of the same events and his impressions of the same people, and was also for a semes-ter the occupant of my Chair at the University of South Carolina,[17] it is your account rather than his that I recommend to the students who want to gain a poet's eye-view of the period of world history which up to now seems to be the most important of all. Your effort during that time to keep creativity and the imagination alive is among the most positive and pro-human examples of courage, ingenuity, and faith that history can show: that history, or any history. I am not given to gush, so I hope you will understand what depth of concern and personal feeling lies behind what I say.

A couple of things. I am getting ready to film my second novel, Alnilam, with a British director, John Guillermin. My first book, Deliverance, I did with another director from there, John Boorman, but have no more plans to work with him. Guillermin, however, wants to project into the future, regardless of how we come out with Alnilam, and tells me he would like to do something with the involvement of British intellectuals with the Spanish War, particularly those who actually fought in it. I have suggested—and he is enthusiastic about—a film dealing with John Cornford and Julian Bell, about whom as a matter of fact I know little as yet, but would like to know more. As of now we only have a vague but simmering notion of what we want to do, but that we do have: that and the title, Cornford and Bell. The project is fairly far away, if indeed it ever materializes, but I thought, since you knew both of the protago-nists, you might venture to give an opinion as to whether you think the film might be an effective one: that is, if you think it might be effective under opti-mum conditions and with the maximum luck. If you have a moment, let me know your opinion; I'd appreciate it.

Also, was there ever made a kind of anthology of the various selections from your Orpheus series? If so, I'd like to get hold of it. I am using the second number now, which I acquired when I was in college 40 years ago, and have found the section where MacNeice[18] and the others discuss their approach to metaphor most stimulating for my students, and for myself.

One more aside, if I may. Since I mentioned <u>Alnilam</u> earlier, I should also tell you that the motivating figure, who never appears in the story, is based on the writings of Rollo Woolley,[19] which your autobiography put me on to. That's one more thing I thank you for, which I am glad to do. I was only able to locate two stories of Woolley's, the one you mention and another, published in <u>Horizon</u>, called "The Pupil," also about flying. Are there any others?

I won't go on and on, taking the time of someone I have never even met. But I did want you to know some of these things, for whatever they may be worth to you.

With best wishes,

James Dickey

JD/bg

TO: DON HIRSCH[20]

CC, 1 p; Emory
Columbia, S.C.

March 30, 1989

Dear Mr. Hirsch:

Thank you very much for your kind letter, and for the things you say about my work. In regard to <u>Alnilam</u>, I was most pleased with your comments, and particularly by the fact that you picked up, as though unerringly, on the exact nature of what I most wanted to convey. One of the points I intended in my depiction of Joel Cahill and his fanatical group is that, given certain conditions and a charismatic enough leader, there doesn't have to be a clearly defined goal; the followers will follow anyway, and do what the leader demands. That is why I left Joel's ultimate purpose deliberately vague, so that the Alnilam plot would be seen for what it is: an attempt to seize and generate power simply for the sake of the power itself.

Well, I won't go on and on, but simply thank you once more for your generosity in writing, and for sending along the strange letter from the Denver paper.[21] Ezra Pound once told me that in the end a man is judged by the quality of his enemies, and I can only hope that Mr. Willikers is of high enough calibre to confer this distinction. But somehow I doubt it!

Please accept my best wishes, and once again, my gratitude.

Sincerely,

James Dickey

JD/bg

TO: DEBORAH DICKEY[22]

CC, 2 pp; Emory
Columbia, S.C.

April 17, 1989

My dear girl:

Here is the $100 you asked for; please let me know if you want more. I also include inscribed books for Nancy and Karen, which I hope they will enjoy.

I completed a long questionnaire sent to me by Hazelden, and have tried my best to comply with their injunction that I be as honest in my facts, assessments, and opinions as I could. The people there seem to think that it is a matter of some importance that I do this, and if anything I say hurts your feelings or is offensive to you in any way, I hope I may be forgiven. But the shots I have called I have called as I see them; my opinion has been asked for, and the only opinion I have is mine, for what it may be worth. What I <u>hope</u> it is worth is that it constitute a positive element in your rehabilitation, as the Hazelden people assure me it will; and, as I say, I hope for that with all my gray-haired heart.

But remember this. There is nothing I can say or do that will contribute to your betterment so much as those turtles sleeping in the frozen mud up there. They are important because you <u>walked to see them</u>—that is, you got up and into your own physical body and travelled to where they were, and in your own way participated in what they were doing, and in their existence. You were therefore taking part in your own being as well as theirs, and that is the route clear of the Slough of Despond where you have been living most of your life. It is a far less creative place than the turtles' mud, and I hope that you—and I—can leave it behind forever.

Meanwhile, I have new ways of preoccupying Bronwen, and if she can go ahead and maintain her normal routine of school I think I can handle the home situation all right, with various treasure hunts, Mysteries, selected television programming, games, books, and other things. She is slowly understanding that the best thing that could happen to our family is for you to stay up there and complete your residence. In other words, she not only wants you back, but wants you here <u>as you can be</u>, without the strange and sickly dance of the endocrine glands brought on by drugs: that meaningless bombination in the Void of No Return. But I am sure that you get enough talk of this sort up there—though perhaps not put in such a peculiar way—so I will not add a fourth to the day's three lectures.

But <u>do</u> know that I miss you very much—every bit as much as Bronwen does—and that I look forward to the tenth of May as the greatest day since the creation of the earth—no; greater—and that the crown of life will be—for me—

when we look up together through the skylight at Litchfield and see the newest star come into view: that one will be ours, and from then on.

Let me know what you need, and what I may do.

Love,

JD/bg

encls.

TO: CHRISTOPHER DICKEY

TLS, 2 pp;[23] *Christopher Dickey*

May 3, 1989

Dear Chris:

Just a note to tell you that everything is going well here, and that there may be a real possibility that Debba and Bronnie and I can come over in August, if I can keep up-to-date on the various projects I am launched upon. There are so many things going on that I turn from one thing to another, and sometimes despair of ever finishing any of them. But one at a time they get done, and I am always start-ing something else, or, more likely two or three things. The more I do the more I see I can do, and I like to pick up on a challenge, particularly one I think up myself. Well, we'll see what comes of all this.

Meanwhile, I have just finished my 21st year of teaching at the University, and I am thinking about winding up this part of things in a year or so, and maybe moving down to the other place and working full time on my projects down there. I am undecided about this, for there are certain advantages in being in Columbia, and the kind of isolation I say I want in Litchfield might not be all that desirable, once I was committed to it. However, I don't have to decide that right now, and am presently enjoying the fact that I just turned in the final grades for this year, and so am free of all teaching duties until September, a good feeling if there ever was one.

I enclose a little poem I wrote for you after re-reading With the Contras.[24] It is maybe pretty slight, but at any rate I tried to get something said about the heat of the climate down there, which you so graphically and memorably describe, and also about the inter-connection between some of the good and bad elements of experience; in other words, if it weren't for the heat and the humidity we wouldn't have the butterflies—or, a possible parallel with the butterflies—the colorful way the people dress down there. Anyway, you can see what you think. Tell me if it's good enough to be printed in the new book, and I'll be guided accordingly.

I can't make this the long letter I'd like to, but will just close so as to get it in the mail. I love you a lot, and am proud of everything you do. Every father on earth ought to have a son he feels about as I do about you, and it's too bad that most of the others don't. As I say, too bad for them!

More love, and to Carol[25] also,

Dad

JD/bg

encls.

TO: DR. WILLIAM CHACE[26]

TLS (Xerox), 2 pp;[27] Emory

June 20, 1989

Dear President Chace:

Please allow me to comment briefly on the recent turn of events concerning the future of Wesleyan University Press,[28] and to use whatever influence I may have to urge you and the other involved parties to maintain and encourage the Press, financially and in any other possible manner.

As an American poet I owe the main body of my work, going back forty years, to Wesleyan. I left the Press in 1970 and went with a larger and more commercial publisher, largely because the company wanted to bring out a novel I was then beginning to write. In consequence of this arrangement, Doubleday published four books of my poems as well as the novel and two other books of literary criticism and reflection, but after some of this material appeared I began to be dissatisfied with the way in which my work, particularly the poetry, was being handled, and began to compare the treatment of the poetry by Doubleday with the verse I had previously published with Wesleyan; on the basis of such examination, I decided to bring my work back to Wesleyan.

The Press has never allowed any of my work to go out of print, and, since Wesleyan brought out the first book in 1962, this represents a remarkable act of fidelity and confidence—not to say courage—and one that the involved author would be foolish to ignore.

The Wesleyan poetry list is on all counts the most impressive and valuable that has ever been compiled in the English-speaking world. It is a remarkable achievement in the world of letters and that of the human spirit and imagination, and American literature would be dealt a very heavy blow indeed, were the Press to discontinue its production. At present I have two more books planned with Wesleyan, one of them a collection of new poems and the other a completed collected poems, to be called The Whole Motion.[29] This is the equivalent of saying that I place my entire career as a poet—that is, my life—in the hands of Wesleyan

University Press and its people, and if my return to the Press after having several other publishers does not constitute a kind of pledge of allegiance in itself, I should like at this time to insist that this is in fact its meaning.

Please let me know if I might be helpful in any manner concerning the well-being and continuation of the Press. Otherwise, I will attempt to do what I feel as my best service, which is to write the best poetry I can.

Let me hear from you on these matters, should you wish me to know about them at first hand.

Meanwhile, I remain,

Sincerely yours,
James Dickey

JD/bg
CC: Dr. Jeffrey Butler
    Dr. Nathan Brody
    Dr. Diane Goodrich
    Mr. John Ryden

TO: WALTER McDONALD[30]

TLS, 2 pp;[31] Walter McDonald

June 26, 1989

Dear Walter:

Well, that is a letter to justify thirty-seven years of uncertainty, a great deal of frustration, and so many drafts they'd make the final 800-page book look like some poet's slim first volume. There were many times I thought I would never finish <u>Alnilam</u>, and not only that I didn't have the key to it, but that there was <u>not</u> any key. But I went on, down one false trail after another, and ended up with what you read. I also ended up with the one book of mine of which I can truthfully say that I would not change a word. For better or worse, <u>Alnilam</u> is what I want to say, put in the way I want to say it. And your letter, fixing on the exact points I think are the key ones, is all the justification I could ever ask, for the outlay of time which has constituted so much of my life. Again, thanks, my old friend from the upper regions, from the air that only you and I and Joel—and one blind man— will ever know in its essence.

Meanwhile, I have finished the screenplay, and my director, John Guillermin— <u>The Towering Inferno</u>, <u>The Blue Max</u>—has agreed that it is what we want to film, to see come up on the screen shot by shot. We can't get started for a few months, when the cold weather sets in; John is finishing a film in Europe before we begin. However, I hear disturbing rumors that there has been some kind of personal tragedy in his family, and since he has already lost one son in an accident it may be that he is out of things, right now. I hope this isn't true, but I have no way of knowing, since he hasn't communicated for a couple of months. All I can really do is wait, and see. I'll keep you posted, if you like. There might be some way you could help in the production, if there ever should be one. As I say, I'll let you know.

Meanwhile, your own poetry is first-rate. It was always good—all those barbed-wire fences!—but the latest stuff is truly out of sight. There are few who can write about flying, as you know, but you are surely one of the best. During the time I was writing <u>Alnilam</u> I read through a lot of writers who dealt with the subject, as well as through a lot of old tech manuals, looking for a way to cut through the technical side of flying and get to the essence, the <u>feel</u> of the thing. St. Exupéry has some of this,[32] but is rather too rapt. A young RAF pilot named Rollo Woolley, who was killed after writing only two stories, has some of it, and oddly enough, T. E. (the Arabian) Lawrence[33] has some, in just a few paragraphs.

But you have most, and in the sequel to <u>Alnilam</u>, called <u>Crux</u>, your poems and your insights will surely be part of it; part of the Pacific night air war, where the issue becomes that between the U.S. Air Force and the <u>Alnilam</u> conspirators. I have already written a climactic scene that will blow the Universe's mind, and mine and yours along with it. But there is a novel to write around it, and that takes, as you know, those years I mentioned earlier, though thirty-seven more of them I haven't got, more's the pity.[34]

A question. Are you connected with the Press, there? I'm always looking for new outlets for the first books of my <u>really</u> good students, and if the Texas Tech Press prints poetry I might be able to send some distinctive stuff your way. Do let me know, and I'll be guided accordingly.

Meanwhile, my best, Wingman.

Ever,

Jim

JD/bg

TO: ALAN KEELE[35]

CC, 2 pp; Emory
Columbia, S.C.

June 27, 1989

Dear Alan Keele:

Thank you for your letter, and, yes, I have your kindly sent copy of the Rilke <u>Orpheus</u> Sonnets, with my statement appropriately displayed. I was happy to give it, because as it turns out it is exactly the statement I wanted to make, somewhere, about the territory which the translator inhabits.[36] I have been there myself, and I can vouch for the fact that the temptation to take liberties is all but overwhelming, especially in view of the fact that such poems as Pound's <u>Cathay</u> sequence <u>depend</u> on the liberties.

As to Rilke, almost every English-speaking poet with even a smattering of German has had a go at him. I am betting on yours and Leslie's[37] to be the best, by the evidence of what I have seen. A great many American poets are writing poems in what they <u>think</u> is Rilke's idiom, but none is really near. Lowell's Rilke sounds like Lowell, Jarrell's Rilke sounds like Jarrell, and so on. The British translators, like Leishman and Stephen Spender,[38] are hopeless. One of the better recent renditions is Stephen Mitchell's;[39] but yours and Leslie's is better, even.

Thanks so much for sending your try at one of the crucial <u>Elegies</u>. Believe me, I look for more.

I hope that you and Leslie will keep in touch, for there is good work going forward, and I will help.

Sincerely,
James Dickey

JD/bg

TO: LOUIS McKEE[40]

CC, 2 pp; Emory
Columbia, S.C.

June 29, 1989

Dear Louis McKee:

Thank you for your unexpected and very welcome letter, and for the things you say about my work. I am happy that your students like "The Sheep-Child," <u>Deliverance</u> and the other things, and I hope that you and they will like the work I am finishing now. There is a lot of it: seven books and three movies, some done and the others in various stages of development. It is all tough, but I enjoy such labors. Work is my recreation; I don't feel right in spending time just amusing myself, and since there is not a whole lot to amuse yourself with at the age of 66, I spend the time at the typewriter. So . . . you'll see all this later on, item by item, and I hope there will be something to interest you.

One point you bring up that I'd like some enlightenment on. I don't have any idea of what VISIONS is, but if they're printing poetry of mine without my knowledge I need to know about it.[41] "Eagles" came out a year or so ago in <u>American Poetry Review</u>,[42] but it has not yet appeared in a book, and this may cause some problems. Anyway, tell me what you know.

Yes, I had a very good friendship with John Logan. I met him first about 30 years ago when I went to read at Notre Dame in a snowstorm. Since that time I saw John on three or four other occasions, once in San Francisco and at least twice in Chicago, and couldn't help noting how fast he was going downhill on alcohol and promiscuity. He was a man of some talent, with a very real scholarly base, and what happened to him seems pathetic, if not absolutely tragic. He threw in with Robert Bly, a person of dictatorial mien and no talent who specializes in preying on others of no talent like Donald Hall, and writers who are talented but weak, like James Wright. However much Bly may have contributed to Logan's demise I don't really know, but I suspect somewhat.

But let me not close on such a sad yew-like note, but thank you once more for your kindness in writing. If you like, keep in touch, and tell me what your life is like.

Cordially,
James Dickey

JD/bg

TO: ALEX RICHARDSON[43]

CC, 1 p; Emory
Columbia, S.C.

June 30, 1989

Dear Alex:

Thanks for your letter, and for the poem, which is as good as you have done, or maybe a little better. Most of the physical detail is well-observed and strong, but you have one difficulty that you must do what you can to avoid. This is the tendency to dissolve the concrete details into abstraction, such as "the hollow basin of fulfillment," "ripples of experience," "the drowning pit of nourishment," and so on. One can see what you mean by these things, but they are not experienceable in the same sense that the "growths leading into open space" and other such insights are. Abstractions are not good for most poets, and they are less good for you than for other poets who use them. There is much merit in "Going to the Well," but it would be better without the generalizations, and without the let-down of the ending. You and your companion should be left "avoiding the worn paths": just <u>that</u>, without comment. Much more then comes through from what one might call the unwritten words of the poem: the implicit; suggestion.

But that's enough classroom palaver! Understand that I think of you often, and how proud of your progress I am. You have the ability to learn, to grow, and to pick up speed. The next few years should be very exciting for you, and I will surely be watching what you do.

With best wishes,
James Dickey

JD/bg

TO: WALLACE STEGNER[44]

CC, 2 pp; Emory
Columbia, S.C.

July 12, 1989

Dear Wallace:

I use your first name, presuming on no more than a handshake at the Institute and a life-long admiration for you and all your works; I hope this is all right.

I understand that you have just had an 80th birthday, which puts you about in the same range as Joe Allston when he went to Denmark,[45] and in honor of the occasion I went back and read all your works, at least the ones I have here, beginning with <u>On A Darkling Plain</u> (which, incidentally, holds up very well indeed, especially the parts dealing with the plains and their vistas), and I can assure you that this was a continuing delight which I plan to experience again, not waiting for such an auspicious occasion. I read the short stories as well as the novels, and found much to admire that I had not previously known, particularly "The Sweetness of the Twisted Apples" and "The Traveler," in which the description of the snow-fields in moonlight, with their peculiar kind of vividness of detail, is better than anything of its kind I have ever read, not excepting similar perspectives in the <u>Magic Mountain</u>, where Hans Castorp looks out on the Alps with nothing to do but sit in his outdoor reclining-chair and be sensitive. I discovered also your nature- and travel-writing, like the <u>Sound of Mountain Water</u>, which is just terrific, and brings back—better than it really was for me at the time—the periods I have spent in Colorado, Utah, and Idaho, as well as those in Arizona and New Mexico.

Well, I won't go on and on in this immoderate vein, but will just close with a couple of questions. Have you ever collected all your short stories in one book? You <u>must</u> do it! And all the books like <u>Mountain Water</u>, under one cover? I'd like to see you do that also; there should be plenty.[46]

And plenty good. So . . . accept this particular kind of homage from one who not only admires you extravagantly as a writer but who also feels that in your writing is communicated a friendship of the best kind I could have; better than I deserve, I can tell you.

Keep doing what you're doing, and I will be looking for it. And have a post-birthday drink for me—really, <u>with</u> me—there on Joe Allston's terrace, with the towhees.

Cordially,
James Dickey

JD/bg

TO: DIANE WOOD MIDDLEBROOK[47]

CC, 1 p; Emory
Columbia, S.C.

July 24, 1989

Dear Ms. Middlebrook:

Thank you for your letter, and for your remarks on my work; they were gracious indeed.

As to using some of the letters I wrote to poor Anne Sexton, I don't mind at all. I only saw her on a couple or three occasions, and, as you say, we wrote back and forth a few times. You may, however, want to correct one or two points, or add to what you already have. The occasion on which I spent the most time with Anne was at Syracuse University, where I had given a reading and then gone to bed, staying clear of the almost obligatory party that follows such affairs. I was stopping at the home of the college President, Dr. Piskor, and Anne woke me up over the phone to see if we could not meet for at least a little while. I got up and she came by, in a big black coat that looked like it had come from a gorilla, and we walked up and down the suburban road a few times, during which, as I remember, she told me about various episodes of her childhood, particularly in relation to her mother. I remember asking her what her maiden name was, and she told me it was Harvey. Have I got this right?

The last time I saw her was at Towson, Maryland, where I had lectured, and we lunched together and had a couple of drinks. At that time I remember she told me she had once caught her arm in a laundry mangle, though it seemed difficult to me to understand how this might be possible. Do you have documentation on this? Even if untrue, it is an interesting thing to invent, don't you think?

Well, I won't go on and on. I remember Anne with some affection, though her continual pushiness in literary circles was irksome to me, I'm afraid I must say. The only other person I have ever encountered who put such store on literary reputation and literary politicking was Robert Lowell, and, since she studied with him, maybe that came over as an influence. May she rest where she is now, and as they say happens to writers when they go to Heaven, may she have nothing to do for the rest of eternity but read favorable reviews.

Again, if there's anything else I can do to help out, I'll do my best to comply.

Sincerely yours,
James Dickey

JD/bg

TO: JOHN G. RYDEN[48]

CC, 1 p; Emory
Columbia, S.C.

July 26, 1989

Dear John Ryden:

As a follow-up to our telephone conversation, I tender this letter as an official acceptance of the position of Judge of the Yale Series of Younger Poets, and do so with a strong sense of the responsibility entailed. As I just said over the phone, the Series is the best of all gateways to the slopes of Parnassus for new American poets, and has been so since its beginning. In other words, as a poet who struggled hard to get onto those slopes years ago, I realize the importance of what I am being asked to do, and can say in response that I will do the best I can, given my abilities and orientation.

As to the immediate practical matters, I understand that I should keep the news of the appointment to myself until you have issued a press release, so as to be in keeping with your policies. I am happy to do this, and request only that you let me know when the announcement is to be made, and send me a copy of it.

Again, thank you so very much for the things you say about my work and my capacities. I hope to use these latter in the service of the new American poets, and can't think of a better thing I might do, or be asked to do. I will give it my best shot, I can tell you.

With best wishes,
James Dickey

JD/bg

TO: HARRY CROCKER[49]

RCC, 1 p; Emory
Columbia, S.C.

September 13, 1989

Dear Harry Crocker:

Thank you indeed for sending along Andrew Lytle's book,[50] which I have read with very great interest. I agree that the book is a major publishing event, and I will supply you with a comment if we can first do a couple of things that seem to me to be in order. First, I have known Andrew for years, and am acquainted with almost all of his work. Second, we have had a number of fallings-out, and on the basis of these he might not want my name on anything of his; anything at all. I was his assistant at the University of Florida, and without going into details, the first falling-out happened then, in 1956. A few years later he made me one of the editors of the <u>Sewanee Review</u>, where he was editor-in-chief, and after another misunderstanding I was kicked out of the position, much to the disgruntlement of both of us. Then, when I spoke at the inauguration of Jimmy Carter, I met up with Andrew again at a party and we told each other off in, as they say, no uncertain terms. All this does not bode well for my giving Andrew's book a recommendation. On the basis of the work itself, I would be glad to do so, for it is just as remarkable as you say it is. But considering these personal relations—and misunderstandings—over the years, I am not sure that any encomium from me is desirable. From my part it is, but it may not be from Andrew's point of view. If you want me to consider giving his book a quotation, I ask first that you send my name past Andrew for his approval or disapproval, and second that you let me know how this goes, so that I may be guided accordingly.

Do let me know how all this strikes you, but don't sit back and not pursue any of this, for I stand ready to back up Andrew's play—and yours—for both seem to me very much worth it.[51]

And if you want to send me some free books, you may make available Malcolm Muggeridge's <u>Chronicles of Wasted Time</u>, for I remember with favor a long series of telecasts he and I did a few years ago for the BBC. Also, I wouldn't mind having Seymour Cain's book on Gabriel Marcel and Robert Louis Stevenson's <u>Selected Essays</u>, if it wouldn't be too much trouble. I have followed your publishing effort ever since your early days in Chicago, when you published not only Joseph but Roy Campbell. Ask Mr. Regnery about this, for his memoirs, including reminiscences of Roy, are very good indeed; are not lost.[52]

I'll hold back on the Lytle quote until I hear from you.

With best wishes,

TO: JOANNA NEY[53]

CC, 1 p; Emory University
Columbia, S.C.

September 29, 1989

Dear Joanna:

What to say?

But we are united with Seymour,[54] and will be from now on, because we were that way when he was standing up and walking around with us, and riding the bus, or just leaning on a building as I took his picture, with his city behind him; you remember the occasion, and it is with you as it is with Debba and me.

I think your eulogy for him is just right; much better than anything I could have done. I am glad to have it, for it makes re-available for me your own feelings about Si, based on a much longer acquaintance with him than I was ever lucky enough to have.

Seymour's Nirvana and his Malebolge was the city. City literary politics—the old <u>Partisan Review</u> crowd that he always felt snubbed him—was not in the main either good for him or to him; on the other hand, the city was the fuel of his very dynamic dynamo of a talent, and of all the people who have ever written about New York, no one else has ever been able to get the malevolent and vital <u>rhythm</u> of the place like Seymour did, not only because he was a highly skilled and devoted literary man, but because he had something even better going: it was natural to him.

Again, I don't want to wind off into rhetoric, but just to tell you how hard hit I am by Seymour's death. The thought of not being able to talk to him again, ever, is more devastating to me than the hurricane that just went through here, and that blew away a lot of the Low Country to which Seymour had a perpetual invitation. He never accepted, though I had the impression he wanted to come, and would have, had his health permitted.

Please keep in touch, Joanna. Even from our very short acquaintance Debba and I care for you very much, and the solidity we have, the three, with Seymour and his memory and his work hold out a future that I dwell on with great positiveness and hope, amongst the untreasuring darkness of death. But <u>we</u> must treasure, and we will. The dead, and the living too!

Debba sends her love, and I mine.

Ever,

TO: PAULA GOFF[55]

CC, 1 p; Emory
Columbia, S.C.

November 13, 1989

Dear Paula:

Here is the book,[56] and I'd like you to take a good look at it. The publisher is very enthusiastic, but it is up to you and me to get the best poems between covers that we can.

You will notice that there are a good many accent-marks amongst the various poems. These should be kept. You will also notice, indicating various lines, the symbol M, which means that I would like there to be a space between the preceding line and the following; so as, as they say, to constitute "drama."

I hope you will go over everything very carefully, and give me your thoughts.

You will notice that the poems we did together constitute most of the book. But there are also poems which are more or less in my "old"—or narrative—style. We should isolate these, and perhaps give these poems a separate section. Let me know what you estimate.

But it is a wonderful book, I think! What we need to do is to present a format which will give the poems, as they unfold, an aspect of continuous delight, as the reader encounters them one by one. It may even be, as I think, of advantage to present the narrative poems, like "The Olympian," first. Tell me.

But I think not. I would like to have the reader encounter the "Later-phase Dickey" first, for better or worse. If he wants the more "traditional" Dickey he can find it in the middle of the book.

Do lean into this with me, and we will make something remarkable. As we have done, with, for example, Alnilam. And we will do again, as long as the Lord gives me the power to see lightning and hear thunder.

Ever,
James Dickey

TO: MARY BLY[57]

CC, 2 pp; Emory
Columbia, S.C.

January 19, 1990

Dear Mary Bly,

Thank you for your letter, and for listing the lines from the poems that your father wants to use. As I said, I will be happy to allow you to use these lines in the anthology your father is doing, which I will be very interested in seeing when it appears. You might want to check the next-to-last item as you list it, for I have written no poem called "Treebombing." It may be that you have in mind "The Firebombing," to which your father has, I am told, made reference in the past.

But that too is all right. It would help me if you could give me some notion of how these 173 lines will be used. I will be happy to waive my fee, but I would like some assurance that the quotation from my poems in <u>American Poetry: Wildness and Domesticity</u>, will not be used as material for a personal attack. My talk with your father the other day seemed to indicate that his intentions are otherwise, and that his anthology would deal with other matters than the personal. That seems to me to be the best course, but I would like to communicate as to this.[58]

You may assure your father that I miss the thirty years of friendship that we could have had. But you may also tell him that the end is not yet, and much is still possible on the positive rather than the negative side: that there can be good human time.

And as for yourself, Miss Mary Bly, I remember when you were born. At that time I had young children of my own, and, as I felt then, it seemed that my closest friends should also get into the Great Chain: not the great chain of buying, but the Great Chain of Being. By whatever circumstance, your father followed up, and you were the result. Never have I had such fine letters from a new father than from your own father to me, about you.

I am very happy you are working with him, and I hope to see you both on any conceivable occasion.

Again, thanks for your letter, and for the things you say. As I done said, the end is not yet, and may even be far off. We'll see, all of us.

With best wishes,
James Dickey

JD/jp

TO: GORDON VAN NESS[59]

CC, 1 p; Emory
Columbia, S.C.

January 24, 1990

Dear Van:

Thank you for your letter, and, again, for the things you say. I return the paper on my early notebooks that you sent Matt Bruccoli with just a few pencilled changes, indications of misspelled words, and so on. But on the whole I am most pleased, and look forward to your editing of these notebooks, and to reading back through the years to what I thought I was doing in those days. You can see how hard it was for me to articulate anything, but you can also see how hard I tried, and how I did not fool myself about what I was doing. I think that those who are interested in my work will enjoy seeing this part of the development of it, and I have gone from what was at first a mild interest in your project to a positive enthusiasm for it. So go ahead, and tell how the going goes.[60]

It is also wonderful news that you will be contributing to Bob Kirschten's new book.[61] I am also glad that Romy Heilen[62] is reading Puella. I met her briefly when she was here interviewing for a job she didn't get—they took on someone in Women's Studies, Black Studies, or something equally foolish urged on them, or demanded, by Affirmative Action—and I thought her very impressive. So . . . we'll see what happens.

The Eagle's Mile has just been copy-edited by the people at Wesleyan. I have sent back the manuscript as approved, and they have moved into the next stage, which is, I guess, to set type. But the management up there shifts with such bewildering rapidity that I hardly know to whom you should write for a look at the manuscript. My present editor has taken another job, so that the person for you to write is the incoming director, Eliza Childs. If Wesleyan has no objection to your looking over the book, I sure don't! If Wesleyan can't furnish you with a xerox, let me know, and I'll have one made for you down here.

Meanwhile, my best, as always. Things go well here, though there is always a sense of pressure. But I was born for combat, for the struggle, and would be lost without it. He who ever strives upward, Goethe says: Ah! Him can we save!

Ever,

TO: MARC JAFFE

TLS, 2 pp;[63] Marc Jaffe

February 27, 1990

Dear Marc:

Thank you so much for your letter, and for the things you say about Muldrow and his mysterious and violent way to the North.

Though he is moving, I have had to do what writing has been possible under the most terrible set of circumstances that the red universe has yet seen fit to contrive for me. A few months ago my wife's narcotic habit increased by geometrical proportions, so that there was not a day—or, especially, a night—when I knew where she was, what people she was among, or whether I and the child would ever see her again. She abandoned her family all but completely, and entered the dope culture at the very lowest point, where there are only pushers, pimps, whores, hit-men and other murderers, and the rest of an assortment that would made you think Dante was right in consigning all such to the eleventh circle of the Inferno, where everything is frozen solid with vice. There seemed to be nothing I could do, except to try to protect the child and keep her life going, move forward with the teaching as best I could, and write whenever I had a minute amongst all the pity and terror. But at last the situation became so unmanageable—and violent—that there was no choice but to have Deborah committed in order to save her life, for she was, most of the time, all but comatose with cocaine and heroin, usually in bizarre combinations. The people on the law end of things were all for prosecuting her, but as it turned out she was sent to a drug rehabilitation center for three weeks, at the end of which time she was remanded to my custody on a kind of work-release arrangement, whereby, if she falters again, and goes back to night-town, she will not be returned to treatment, but will go to prison. It is probably the case that such a threat constituted the only workable means of turning Deborah's head toward the light: toward <u>any</u> kind of light at all. She has been home a couple of weeks now, closely monitored by the courts, and seems to be making some progress toward rehabilitation, though, having been married to her for 13 years or so, I would not bet on what she will do, once the legal restrictions are removed. However, they obtain for the next six months, and for that time she will have to keep herself in line. I'm hoping that it all works out, for the little girl loves her very much, and wants her whole, as do I. We'll have to see, I guess, what the future gives us.

But despite all this, I have been moving the book; moving Muldrow. I have another hundred pages, written mainly late at night and just before dawn, but written. I have also revised the sequence of events, and now have what I think will give us a straight run out to the end. This is something I value as a novelist: the knowing what happens next, and what <u>that</u> leads to. As I say, I have the whole curve of the action now, just as I want it, and all I have to do is make the events happen, which is the easiest part for me, and the most characteristic of my kind of writing. Jill, who has been on vacation, is typing the pages I have done, and I can send them to you bit by bit as she completes them; or, if you like, I can wait till she does a hundred or so pages, and then hit you with the whole load at one time, if you like. Let me know, and I will be guided accordingly. If you get a return letter to me I can send along 25 pages immediately, and then follow with the others as Jill types them. Let me know how you'd like me to handle this, and we'll go forward. With Deborah balanced, however precariously, and with Jill back, I can work with a good deal more efficiency than I have been able to do in the last few months. And I can promise you one thing: <u>To the White Sea</u> will be published in 1991, as you suggest, no matter what the conditions are.[64] I am determined upon it, not only because of the obligation but because I am deep into the curve of the story, which I am convinced is one of the most remarkable ever conceived, and I want to play the string out to the end for its own sake, for Muldrow's sake, and the rest of us following him up there to those icebergs, that invisibility.

Let me say one thing more. You are the best editor I have ever had, by far, among a great many. I had rather cut off my own head with a dull razor than fail you in this way or any other; and you can be convinced that I will not. You are my rare unswerving company, and I will deliver what we both want, come what may.

My best, and let me hear.

Ever,

Jim

JD/jp

TO: DOUG CUMMING[65]

Spring 1990   *RTL (Xerox) and CC, 4 pp; Emory*
                                               Columbia, S.C.

Dear Doug Cumming,

You asked which Southern writers alive today will be read a hundred years from now, and I assume you'd like me to give reasons. I have of course not read all the works of living Southern writers, or, indeed, in some cases, any of them. On the other hand, I have some strongly definite opinions about the ones I have read, and on the basis of those I'm ready to wrestle with the Adversary, Time, catch-as-catch-can.

I am convinced, first of all, that Peter Taylor writes lasting fiction. It may be thought that only a few readers—all Southerners—would care to be involved in the complex tangle of relatives, customs, and small-town social nuances which Taylor fingers with such unerring assurance. Though a Southerner, I myself have not formerly been much interested in these associations, mores, family acceptances and ostracisms as they occur in the actual world, but Taylor's insight and penetration into the characters involved in them has made a total convert of me, even to the extent of causing me to look into the marital arrangements of my own ancestors, which I find also involve instances of well-to-do city forebears wedding poor and unexceptional people from the country; I can see the dilemma now, the drama, that I couldn't have before, and I count that a plus.

In the larger intent of his narratives, but mainly in their details, Taylor is closer to Chekhov than is any other American writer, I think: astonishingly creative, veracious, and memorable with particularities, usually domestic—matters of dress, furniture, food, cutlery, and plate—items ordinarily taken for granted, but having the unquestioned authority of things among which people live and die, that they pass on to living kin.

There is more. No less than Faulkner but in a gentler and subtler way, Taylor is a dramatist of social change, centering on the semi-rural small town as it is gradually influenced or enveloped by the city, and its customs and standards changed and then lost. He deals with the gradual leaving of the land which has taken place in his time: with all the sense of loss this entails, its irremediable pain, either sudden or slow and attritional, as people take jobs in cities—even in the North—families lose members in ways never before encountered, customs which have made life possible lose their meaning and power, and there is neither turning back nor escape.

As sure as Peter Taylor is in dealing with the intricacies of southern social conventions, this is only secondarily the reason he will continue to be read, or so I feel. The principal factor in his longevity will surely prove to be the delicate simplicity of his understanding: his ability to make people memorable, make them matter: to endow them with unforgettable individuality, so that the reader connects with them, as he does with the characters of Chekhov, above and beyond Middle Tennessee and Czarist Russia.

The quiet, uninsistent and steady voice of Wendell Berry will also be heard; it has resonance, echo. Berry's identification with the land is genuine, for he is a subsistence farmer, and participates bodily and daily in the birth-growth-decay-death-rebirth cycle, the turning of the seasons and the weathers, the unearthly beauty of the earth, its cantankerousness, its plants and creatures, minerals, liquids—its solaces, revenges, energies. His writings on ecology and agronomy are remarkable, and useful, not only as prophecies and warnings but as offering solutions that would surely turn out to be more than provisional, were they to be followed. But Berry's chief merit as a poet, and the fact that he seems at times to be the earth itself speaking with a human voice gives his word a vibration, a <u>fatedness</u>, beyond that attainable under any other conditions, or spoken by any other voice. When Adam and Eve looked back toward Paradise, past the angel with the sword, they understood what they had lost. When in a hundred years the inhabitants of the planet look back past the bulldozer to Wendell Berry's Kentucky, they will know the same thing.

Walker Percy will also survive, particularly in <u>The Moviegoer</u>,[66] a sad and hilarious novel about the misfortunes of young man trying to be dead-average in order to insulate himself from the pain of living a human life. It is surely among the most original novels ever written; through his highly personal approach to style and tone, Percy had given a new imaginative scope to whimsy, and done what would formerly have seemed impossible: provided whimsy with <u>bite</u>, satiric edge. Though he is a religious writer in the best sense, Percy does not preach; sacramentalism takes place in the interactions between people: between the unheroic hero, Binx Bolling, his idealistic aunt, his suicidally inclined cousin Kate, and his secretary, the strapping ex-drum-majorette from Eufala, Alabama, Sharon Kinkaid, whose walk across the office—"Her bottom is so beautiful that once as she crossed the room to the cooler I felt my eyes smart with tears of gratitude"—is immortal if time is.

These are my top three candidates to put up against the Adversary for the next hundred years, though there are also plenty of other Southern writers I like and could have talked about. I think another Kentucky poet and novelist, James Still, will carry Appalachia into the next century in good style, for example, and I also believe that Michael Shara's novel <u>The Killer Angels</u>[67] will endure, as the Civil War becomes, with added time, more and more mythological and mysterious, an heroic nightmare in which answers will forever be sought, and from which no one wishes to escape, or can.

Yours for the next hundred years,
and any bonus time beyond,
James Dickey

TO: WILLIAM H. PRITCHARD[68]

CC, 1 p; Emory
Columbia, S.C.

March 29, 1990

Dear Pritchard:

Thanks so much for sending along the Jarrell books. Your biography is very good indeed; Randall would have been pleased and I'm sure Mary is. I realize how difficult it must have been for you to deal with the question of suicide. As for myself, I don't doubt in the least that Randall killed himself; after all, he was down there at Chapel Hill at the Hand Clinic because he had already made one attempt. The hard thing is to figure out why a person with so many gifts should want to do such a thing, but that whole generation of poets—most or all of the best ones— were cases of self-destruction. Berryman, Randall, Win Scott, and Weldon Kees were actual suicides, and Roethke, Delmore, Lowell, Paul Goodman and Eliza-beth Bishop were virtual suicides from drink and the kind of living—or dying— they did. I knew them all—some pretty well and others only slightly—and their example is both exhilarating (temporarily) and dangerous (permanently). I think Randall's case was the saddest of the lot, with a possible competition—in that grim category—being Jim Agee, who in my opinion was the most talented of them all. Well, what to do? Read their work, I guess, is the only thing, for we will not see them any more, except in dreams, where, for me at least, they keep coming back, Randall with particular dimensionality, and with more meaning than the others.

Again, thanks so much for your considerateness. You are surely among the best biographers and critics around. What I'd like most is to see some original work of yours. After all, if Edmund Wilson can shut Mary McCarthy off in a room and tell her to write fiction, and have the result turn out as well as it did, I feel I can tell you the same thing, and get you to write poetry. Give it a shot. I would bet cold coin (also gold) on your ability to do it.

My best surely.

TO: JOHN LOGUE

CC, 2 pp; Emory
Columbia, S.C.

May 21, 1990

Dear John,

Thanks very much for your note, and for the things you say. But your comments on my work are not the main thing here.

The main thing is your poem. I have just been made judge of the Yale Series of Younger Poets, which gave James Agee birth, among others. But there is nothing in them to compare with your pages. This is not bullshit. Bullshit is not easy for me, for in matters of imagination, I must level. The ultimate tribute I could possibly make regarding your poem is that it draws me in, and makes me want to meddle with it, for the quality of imagination is high. As I say, that is the main thing. The skill is less, and there could be some cutting and rearranging, all in the service of <u>staging</u> the drama of which you write.

Believe me, I am astonished, and can do no less than urge you to write more poetry. If we can go back and forth on this thing, I would like to submit it either to <u>The New Yorker</u>, or, what might be better, to Dave Smith, who has just taken over the editorship of the <u>Southern Review</u>, out of Baton Rouge. If we can get rid of a certain sense of scatter, here, we can bind together a remarkable piece of rhetoric. Again, let me know if you'd like me to work and edit, to the best of my ability.[69]

But have no doubt that your imagination is remarkable. I have no axe to grind, but savor the imagination where I find it, in whatever form.

Do get back to me on this, and we will go somewhere with your work, either to <u>The New Yorker</u> or to Dave at Baton Rouge, or to the Arts of Kingdom Come, wherever she might be found.

Ever,

TO: CHRISTIANE JACOX KYLE[70]

CC, 3 pp; Emory
Columbia, S.C.

June 12, 1990

Dear Ms. Kyle,

I write in congratulation for your having been chosen the winner of the Yale Series of Younger Poets for this year. There were some unusually strong manuscripts in a variety of styles, but yours had a human dimension that the others did not even approach—many of them being long-winded reminiscences of childhood fishing trips or equally long recountings of love-hate family situations—never before have I encountered people with so many grandparents!—and a clarity that most of the others lacked. Yours is a very clear depth, and your dramatic sense, particularly in poems like the first one, is remarkable and completely convincing. I won't go on and on, but as judge of this contest for the first time, I want you to know that I am very happy indeed that you are the winner. And I would say this, also. Not only was your manuscript the best of the current batch, but except for a few rare exceptions—Robert Horan, whom Auden chose—none of the previous winners that I have read are as distinctive and memorable as you are. I thought you might like to know these things, so I pass them on, for what they might be worth to you.

The editors at Yale suggest that I might like to make some suggestions to you about your book, but I hesitate to do this, since you have chosen the work just as you wanted to present it.

However, I do have a couple of very slight suggestions, if I may make them. You might want to reconsider the title, for example. It is a good enough title as it stands, but there are many books of poems with similar names, and for this reason another might be preferable: something about human beings, among whom you move with such grace and imaginative understanding, rather than animals.

I like to look at all aspects of a book's appearance, and I am most interested in your name. I assume that Jacox is your maiden surname, but it is such an interesting word—sound—that I wonder if it might be possible for you to use it as a Christian name, and publish the book as Jacox Kyle. The chances are that for reasons of your own you would not want to do this, but I thought I would suggest it, because the possibility fascinates me, and I think the strangeness of the name, thus put, would not be lost on the possible audience, either, and might prove a real, though minor, sales factor. I do know that when I was on the Awards Board of the National Institute, and was given a number of poetry books to read, I read, first off, one by a poet named McKeel McBride, because I wanted to know—as quickly as possible!—what someone with a name like that would write! Turns out she was pretty good, too.[71]

But not so good as you. And I want to close by saying, just once more, how pleased I am with what you have done; how happy I am that you are my first choice, my first winner.

Cordially,
James Dickey
First Carolina Professor and
Poet in Residence
The University of South Carolina

TO: LYNN DOMINA[72]

CC, 1 p; Emory
Columbia, S.C.

July 9, 1990

Dear Ms. Domina,

I have just read your manuscript as a finalist in the Yale Series of Younger Poets competition. Though you didn't win, you had—and have—a very strong book, which should certainly be published. Of all the manuscripts that came in, yours comes closest to having elements of the truly tragic. Much of your work is searingly sad. Such emotions are very hard to convey, and your success in doing so is remarkable. I like to think you'd consider entering the contest again next year, if your book is not published—or to be published—elsewhere.

In keeping with the tenets of the Yale contest, I have sent your manuscript back to the authorities there, but should you have means to send me a bound-together copy I would be most pleased. And sign it, too, as a special favor. But that shall be as you wish, of course.

My congratulations on your work, and on the brilliant future you are sure to have.

Sincerely yours,
James Dickey
Judge, Yale Series of Younger Poets

TO: MICHAEL MUNGO[73]

TLS (Xerox), 2 pp;[74] Emory

December 14, 1990

Dear Michael,

In what looks like a transitional period at the University, I hope you don't mind my offering a suggestion at this particular time, though I am not a real academic, being more on the outside and operating not as a member of the massed troops of scholarship but rather as a kind of sharp-shooter or sniper, distantly connected to the army, but part of it just the same.

If we could institute a situation whereby the finalists for the job of President could become acquainted with the faculty, give the teachers a chance to know them at least a little, ask questions, and the other things that a personal connection could effect, the choice would be made under a very much more favorable atmosphere than if the search committee simply made a choice, according to whatever qualities they had decided upon as important, and in effect—as in fact—brought the new President in as one <u>imposed</u> on the University, no matter what. The members of the faculty I know—mainly limited to those on my floor—are restive about this, and feel that without at least <u>some</u> chance to evaluate the candidates, or at least know who they are, that they are in a position analogous to the early colonists of this country, who objected to "taxation without representation." I do think this is an important point, and I hope you will consider it. I love this University, and have given twenty-three years of my life to it; time that I will not get back. I want to see harmony here, because this can yet be a great institution, to which I am planning to give the rest of my years in order to prove. But we need more dialogue, and we need to know what choices there may be about the top-level and controlling interests, which you represent, and, as of right now, the people from whom will be chosen the new President. It is not absolutely essential that the faculty know the decision, but it is highly desirable that they feel themselves to be part of it.[75]

My best to you, as always. I hope you are continuing to write, and will let me see some of your things whenever you wish to send them along. But that shall be as you wish, of course.

Ever,
Jim

TO: WILLIAM JAY SMITH

December? 1990

RTL (draft), 1 p; Emory
Columbia, S.C.

Dear Bill,

Thanks so much for the card, the letter, and the things you say both about my comments on your work and on my own new book. And, yes, it was very nice to be reviewed adjoining you in the <u>New York Times</u>;[76] I can't think of a match-up I'd rather be part of. What I said about your book I meant, and mean.[77] As graceful as your poetry is, and as amiable as it is, it stays with you; the reader goes back to it. And I am glad to see that you have included some of my favorites, which were left out of <u>The Traveler's Tree</u>.[78] I should think that we have with this book just about everything, except for the poems you will do from now on, of which I hope there will be a great many.

By the way, have you gathered up your various critical pieces?[79] If not, I certainly think you should do so, for they are outstandingly helpful: amusing, penetrating and fair, all at the same time; and that is tough. I use a good many of your opinions in class, such as the reference to "the worm's ukelele," which you will remember is a quotation from the great metaphysical poet Jose Garcia Villa. I have never forgotten your comments on this line, the poem, and by implication all such pretentious and self-deluding "experimental" poets of the same ilk. By the way, I saw on TV a re-run of an old Clint Eastwood movie the other night, and there is a scene where Clint is holding an .03 Magnum to this comic gangster's head and telling him that he'd like to get rid of him and all others of his ilk. "Do you know what that means, you cretin?" asks Clint. "Yeah," says the gangster. "It's a big deer."

Good luck with your book, and with all your other writings. And let me know if there's anything else I can do to help your cause, which is one of the best of my time.

Ever,

TO: CHARLES GRENCH[80]

TLS (Xerox), 2 pp;[81] *Emory*

June 3, 1991

Dear Charles Grench:

I think we have made a good choice; I hope that by now you have had time to inform Mr. Samaras that this is, as they say, "his year."[82] I am having a copy made of the manuscript, which I will send you. Or I can keep the copy and send you the original if you prefer; just let me know.

As to the "few sentences to a paragraph" explaining why I chose this poet over the others, you may tell the Committee I said this:

> Nicholas Samaras' poems are unique in their orientation, and display a linguistic sense that should earn him a wide and discriminating audience. The most engaging quality of his work is his metaphysical internationalism, the note of the eternal exile who yet finds remarkable and life-enhancing particularities in the countries and peoples through which he passes. One assumes from his references to Greece that his closest affinity is to that ancient world, especially to the pastoral aspect of it. At his best he speaks with the voice of an inspired peasant, but one who believes in God with his very bone-marrow, no matter how much this bewilders him, hour after hour, day after day, place after place.
>
> Mr. Samaras understands from a completely individual viewpoint what the connection is between eternal things and the passing world. His book is

surely the best that has come under my scrutiny during my tenure as judge of the Yale contest, and I would put it up against any other book in the series, or indeed, against almost any written in recent years.

I hope this will do, and I hope I do not seem excessive in my affirmation. But believe me, I don't think time will be capable of proving this to be anything but the right choice; it seems to me that we are lucky.

I will send you along a copy of the manuscript—or the original—as soon as you tell me you have received this letter, and indicate which you want.

Meanwhile, my best. And thank all the "screeners" for me; their work and comments were a tremendous help. I hope they enjoyed reading the manuscripts as much as I did.

Ever,

James Dickey

P.S. I will write Samaras and others of the "Final Eight" as soon as I get word from you.

JD/pg

TO: MARC JAFFE

CC, 2 pp; Emory
Columbia, S.C.

August 1, 1991

Dear Marc:

I understand from Theron that you have only a hundred pages of the manuscript, so I enclose another typescript with those pages and an additional hundred, which as I judge should be about half of the whole thing. I feel I shouldn't go into the reasons for my delay, for fear that I might depress you with the details of a situation so disheartening, so endlessly complicated with legalities, with medical solutions that don't work, with lawyers, doctors, psychiatrists, policemen, judges, probation officers, and God knows who or what else, that to lay all this on you would be an extreme unkindness, so I won't.

I do want to say, though, that this maelstrom of misfortunes is not one in which a writer can sit down and do sustained work, and I, who more than most others am dependent on extreme isolation and concentration, have been at every turn deprived of the conditions in which I need to work. I have pushed forward when I could, though, and there are a hundred pages here that you haven't seen. Despite everything, the story has solidified in my mind, and now, due to necessity, I have found a way of working in which I can average ten pages of script a day, no matter whether an atomic bomb comes down my chimney. I should be able to hand you the rest by the end of August, or almost all of it, in any case.

I enclose a copy of <u>Partisan Review</u> with a section from the first part of the book;[83] the editors say it is causing a sensation, which I take to be a good sign. How do you feel about my publishing some other excerpts in magazines, like the swan sequence, maybe? I know little of the strategy of working up interest in a book by magazine appearances, but my other books have availed themselves of them in such places as <u>Esquire</u> and <u>The Atlantic</u>. Should we wait a while, or should we make available selections to the people asking for them? Do advise, and I will be guided accordingly.[84]

One or two other things. I enclose a little Japanese calligraphy figure which I think we might consider as the chief feature of the cover, for it is the emblem of snow. I can see it in white, with the rest of the cover red, since red is also associated with Japan—and, as Muldrow would tell you, with other things as well.[85]

My best, and let me know what you think of this last scene. It could have been more gruesome, but it is gruesome enough as it is is, and by downplaying the physical details I think it is made more effective.

Ever,
James Dickey

Enclosure
JD/pcg

TO: MARC JAFFE

CC, 2 pp; Emory

4620 Lelia's Court
Columbia, S.C. 29205
December 18, 1991

Dear Marc:

Please forgive the long silence, and the reasons underlying it. I am not one to make excuses, and there has never been one human obligation that I did not fulfill. But there are certain factors in the present situation that must be accounted for, and I outline them without any wish to burden you with the responsibility that is essentially mine.

I have pushed the manuscript forward until I have done all but the last two scenes, but the lack of competent professional help has kept me from having these xeroxed and sent in. I hope to rectify this as soon as possible, and will be sending large masses of paper with writing on it as soon as I can find some new method of getting them reproduced and sent. You can expect many pages soon.

Now I continue the outline of the situation. My director for the screen version of <u>Alnilam</u> wants a change in the basic story, which I am not prepared to give, and as matters stand at this time, I am willing to let the whole film go—including the various monetary inducements—rather than make any such changes as he suggests. Nevertheless, the matter must be handled, and these things drag out, with directors, producers, and the rest of the film-making paraphernalia.

That is one thing, and only one. Since I have a percentage of the film, it is a matter of considerable negotiation to get free and clear of my own story, but I believe I can do it without much more effort than has already gone into the situation.[86]

Next, my collected poems, the work of a lifetime upon which I must be expected to stand or fall, will be published in the spring, and there are a number of uncollected poems to which I must give my undivided attention as far as revision is concerned. I can do this a little at a time, I think, among the other commitments.[87]

But this is my problem. The main thing that we're faced with now is my wife's legal situation. If I were to tell you the full consequences of what is embroiled in her case with various allegations in different states, it would take a Clarence Darrow to figure it out; and I doubt that he would have much luck, either. Understand that this is purely personal, but in the human involvement it must matter. My situation is that of someone who must combine not only Laocoon, but all the snakes wrapped around him.

I understand your problem as my editor. No one could be more full of feeling for you, up there in the high-rise, trying to fend off these various people who are coming at us for a deadline. But I will not give down on one sentence of what I write, and you as my editor will understand what I mean when I say this. You have been the finest and the most patient friend that anyone could conceivably expect. But I can tell you, Marc, that you will get your book, and that all your worries about my performance will be dispelled. Understand me on this, and move with me a little longer. All my problems will be handled, and the book will be as we both wish.

I am deeply cognizant of your patience in the matter of this novel. But it will be worth it, I can tell you, a thousand times over. Hang on, as I have been hanging on, and the thing will happen. I am full of confidence and physical power, and that is what it takes to write.

Love,

TO: PAT CONROY[88]

Early 1993?   *RTL (draft), 2 pp; Emory*
                                                 Columbia, S.C.

Dear Pat,

I have your letter, and believe me I am deeply involved in every implication—down to the last and least one—of what you say. Without dwelling unduly on my own situation, which is that of a writer nearing seventy, and every day coming up against the possibility that all the things he has played his life on might very well have been wrong, it is gratifying indeed to get your paragraphs.

Understand me: there is no student of mine of whom I am more proud. And understand this also: the pride is not for the public acclaim, the novels, the movies, and all those things, but for a certain integrity of spirit that you showed from the beginning, and which I was sure would not be lost. There are few people who come into the classroom of a teacher and exhibit the twin characteristics of language-love and go-for-it that are yours by natural endowment. The Word is important to you—that fascination—and so is the power and terror of letting go: to see what happens, no matter what. All this is good, and can produce extraordinary things: as, in order to see, you need only to look at your own works.

This, though. You and I are both creatures of the Word. We want this word, rather than this word's second cousin twice removed. And that exclusiveness will save us, I do believe. Therefore, I want you to continue with your poetry, because if you and I hold that center of the creative wheel, nothing can violate us. If we submit honestly to the discipline of poetry in its mania to say the most possible thing that can be said by means of the human tongue, then everything we do partakes of that, and we'll draw energy and courage from it.

Now: I can only express extreme gratitude for your letter and for the things you say. Time is maybe getting fairly short for me, and the Dark Man may not be too far from paying me a visit. But I will say one thing, and make a promise. There will come a time before the Dark Visit in which you and I will sit down in the dead-low and middle of the night and talk as we have never talked before about the things that mean the most to us: the things we love—and those we hate: talk as the earth turns, till it come death or morning.

                                                          Ever,

TO: DON WILBER[89]

RTL (Xerox), 1 p;[90] *Emory*

November 3, 1993

Dear Mr. Wilber:

Thank you for your letter, and for the things you say about <u>To the White Sea</u>. I don't of course know what kind of officers you had in the outfit you were in or what their language might have been like, but in the 418th Night Fighter Squadron of the 5th Air Force our Commanding Officer, Bill Sellers, talked exactly like my Colonel in the book, if not with even a saltier tongue. In the movie version I may play the Colonel myself, as I did the sheriff in <u>Deliverance</u>, and I promise you his language will be plenty salty, as befits.

You and I have been in the same places, or some of them, like New Guinea, the Phillipines and the Ryukus. I was on Okinawa, flying out of Kadena and Yontan. I was never on Ie Shima, but even now I can see the exact shape of it as it came in on the radar. When we got that far, coming in from a raid on Japan, I knew we would get back to base; that is, would see the next day's mail. It was quite a war; and I plan to write more about it. The next will be a sequel to <u>Alnilam</u>, this one called <u>Crux</u>. By the way, you might like to read <u>Alnilam</u>, which is about the Training Command in the old days, but has two long sections about the war, one about a bomber squadron in Europe and the other in the Pacific, concerning one of the early raids on Rabaul.

Again, thanks for writing. And keep in touch, if you like. I have a second home at Pawley's Island, and spend as much time down there as I can. Maybe we can home in and meet, by means of a three-star fix on some bar or restaurant. I'd like that a lot, believe me.

Cordially,
James Dickey

JD/pcg

TO: DAVE SMITH[91]

TLS (Xerox), 1 p;[92] *Emory*

January 20, 1994

Dear Dave,

Thank you very much for your comments on the poem,[93] some of which were very helpful. I have had it re-typed to take care of the line-length problem and put into effect some of your suggestions, though not all. To take one example, in the fourth from last line you suggest "He can help you." But that is not fully what I intend: at this point in things, Bundy is helping, for he has taken over Tom's oxygen-starved consciousness and given it something to concentrate on until it fades away. In other words, I want something active here, something in process, ongoing. Again, I'd like to retain Bundy's execution in the manner I originally had it. You ask about the reference to his daughter reading to Tom about Bundy, and my emphasis is that, unknowingly, in my brother's dying brain, fixed on Bundy and his doings, the daughter becomes the last victim, or even a new victim. If I do say so myself, that seems a powerful paradox. Of course no harm can come to the daughter; it's all in the mind, the dying mind, taking and using—and being—what it can.

Look over this re-typed version and let me know if you have any further suggestions. If I were to comment individually on each of your comments, it would take much longer than either of us would like, so in the interests of your time and your deadline I return all materials to you. Let me know what you think as quickly as you can, and I will be guided accordingly. I must go to Italy on the 14th of February, and I'd like to help get this wrapped up before I go; that would be good.

Ever,

Jim

P.S. Have you accepted that South Bank invitation in London for this summer? I have also been invited, but haven't answered. If it is certain that you will be there, the fact constitutes a powerful incentive for me to accept. Again, let me know. Maybe we could "do the town." That would also be good!

TO: WILLIAM MAXWELL[94]

CC, 1 p; Emory
Columbia, S.C.

March 9, 1994

Dear Mr. Maxwell:

I have just re-read all your fiction as well as the essays and critical pieces I can find, and I want to offer you the foremost vote of confidence that can come out of the blue sky of South Carolina. I have known your work since I was a (belated) undergraduate at Vanderbilt, and it has always sustained and encouraged me, first as a beginning writer and then as one who picked up (some) momentum. I am now seventy-one, and can truthfully tell you that you have been the one writer I could always trust, and that the truth you made available to me was not only the truth of fact (as important as that is) but the truth of the imagination.

And there is more. You are an authentically <u>feeling</u> person, and this is a quality I have tried to get into my own work; whether or not I have always succeeded is a different matter. But I did want to let you know these things, for whatever might be in it for you.

The scene in <u>Time Will Darken It</u>[95] where the guy tells the other people how the man crawled into the carcass of a cow to keep from freezing to death is one of the great scenes in fiction. And if you think that my current novel, <u>To the White Sea</u>, does not bear a debt to this you would be wrong, and the world would be wrong.

Again, I hope you will accept my best wishes for your work and for your life. I will hope also that I'll see you on some future meeting of the Academy, where I can tell you what I say here, looking you right in the eye, as such things should be done.

Sincerely,
James Dickey

JD/pg

TO: CHARLIE BYRD[96]

RTL (Xerox), 1 p;[97] Emory

June 7, 1994

Dear Charlie:

I am so very sorry I missed your visit here, but I was out of town and there was no way I could make it back in time. But I have great hopes that we can get together later on, for I would surely love to jam with you. Although, I must add, whatever jamming I might be able to do at my level would not be much in comparison to yours. As I may have told you, I first came to your playing through my wife Maxine, years ago when I lived in Atlanta and was just getting serious about the guitar. She insisted on calling me away from the writing I was trying to do to come to the television to watch you and Herb Ellis play on the <u>Today Show</u>. Ellis is good, but he has nothing like your originality, and I became a convert on the spot. Then, when we moved to Los Angeles, I heard you play an evening at Shelly's Manhole, and was even more impressed. Years later I acquired your tapes from Guitarists' Workshop, and had great instruction from you. The tapes, including the Christmas songs, were difficult for a folk player not used to complicated chord formations, but, as I say, I got great learning, not only about the guitar, but about music in general, of which my knowledge is very sketchy. In addition to being the guitarist that you are, you are a very fine teacher, patient and helpful.

And I do thank you for everything. I am sure we will get together again, somewhere down the road. I have just learned that I can use the university airplane any time I want to go to Washington; so, since I have a good deal of business in Washington, that opens up a lot.

If you will keep in touch we can plan some things. I would like that a lot, believe me. Do write, when you can or when you want to. But that shall be as you wish, of course.[98]

With all best wishes,
James Dickey

JD/pg

TO: MARC JAFFE

RTL (Xerox), 2 pp; Emory
Columbia, S.C.

June 7, 1994

Dear Marc:

Thank you for your letter, and for the British paperback cover. Meanwhile, Martin Fletcher of the London office[99] has sent me an advance copy of their paperback,[100] which looks pretty good, I must say. The press in England has been better than any I have received on my other books brought out over there. I will be going to England the last of next month and will do some more promotion, at the direction of Martin and the other people in London. If you get any more copies of their paperback edition I'd appreciate your sending along ten or twelve to me here; I can use them.

I'm sorry I missed you in New York. I was pretty busy, with all the Academy stuff. I had a telephone message from you saying that you would call later, and I stayed in the hotel room my whole last afternoon—watching Clint Eastwood in The Outlaw Josie Wales, his best!—waiting for the call. Anyway, I am very sorry indeed I missed seeing you, but there will be other times, if luck is with us.

The James Dickey Reader sounds fine. There is a lot of material, going back fifty years, and I would like to see what somebody else might make of it. A good editor, if you yourself would like to pass it on, might be Brad Leithauser,[101] who gave us such a glowing review in the New Yorker. But there are a good number of other good candidates, and we should be able to pick and choose.[102]

I talked to Joe Cannon[103] at the Academy; he was at my table, wanting to talk about new novelistic projects. I told him that I had three ideas I wanted to pursue, but that I would take no advance, for I do not wish to be nailed into deadlines, and to take money for something I have not yet done. The advance would come later when the proposed work meets your approval; but only then.

I have three possibilities in mind. The first is called Lanyon's Stair,[104] which is about an artists colony in Cornwall. Into this comes, mainly on whim, a middle-aged American poet named Rabun, who is not at all sure of his vocation, but has been, as a professional, an engineer or doctor. Chiefly by a series of chance circumstances, he ends up in an artists' colony at St. Ives in Cornwall, impelled by the enthusiasm and artistic energy of a young sculptor named Peter Lanyon, who is about as equally divided with learning to sculpt in tin and flying gliders. Rabun himself is an ex-fighter pilot, and can fly anything on wings. The relationship between the two, plus the entry of the naive young girl who loves Lanyon and believes in his genius, and an older woman who has vague aspirations toward the arts but has mismanaged her life, and who connects, in a manner, with Rabun, will furnish the essential of the story. Lanyon's Stair is a thermal which carries the soaring craft upward, which Lanyon, in his youthful enthusiasm, wishes to find and use, see, and which kills him.

The next possibility is a sequel to Alnilam: this is the novel I wish most to write. It would concern the Pacific night air war in which the authority of the official US Air Force would be contravened by the underground force of the Alnilam movement. It would culminate in a show-down between military authority and the forces of the subversives, the Alnilam plotters, and result in the night hunt-down of one force by the other, all US aircraft trying to down the others.

The other book, called The Rising of Alphecca, would have to do with an old man, a widower and solitary householder, a retired CPA, who takes up astronomy, celestial navigation, as a hobby, and graduates as a rated navigator. As such he is offered a job on an old freighter, and, since there is nothing else of interest in his life, he takes it on, and the story is what happens to him as a result. A mutiny is involved, which depends on which star comes up, at what time. This time, it is the star Alphecca.[105]

TO: PAT CONROY

TL (Xerox), 2 pp;[106] *Emory*

April 8, 1996

Dear Pat:

I finally got the inscribed copy of <u>Beach Music</u> you had left with Bill Starr,[107] and I wanted to write and tell you how pleased I was, and am, that I could have befriended and been in any way beneficial to a writer of your caliber. This is indeed heartening; I feel, as they say on shipboard, that I haven't been sending with a dead key. Anyway, thanks again for the book, which I enjoyed very much; the emergency scene in the boat and its aftermath is particularly good. Again, thanks for your thoughtfulness.

And for your life and example. I only regret that I don't get to see more of you, so that we could sit and talk about the things that interest us. For example, Catherine Fry[108] has shown me the extraordinary jacket design for Jonathan Green's <u>Gullah Images</u>.[109] Since I have been living in South Carolina—and even before that, for I used to range up and down the Georgia coastal islands when I was a teenager—I have had a strong interest in the Gullah culture, but have never known much about the history or the real meaning of it, and for years have intended to inquire further. Their music is wonderful, and the <u>sound</u> of that strange language is enough to involve anyone who is fascinated with old things that are new to him.

My news is pretty good, except for the after-effects of the jaundice I contracted a year and a half ago. I am mending very slowly, but the attack was so catastrophic I lost eighty pounds in two weeks, and my system was so depleted that recovery, especially at my age, takes a lot of patience, as well as hard work. The main trouble is shortness of breath; my stamina was just about completely knocked out, and I have had to bring it back bit by bit, with much frustration and many set-backs and delays. But I will win out, yet. If I can get twenty minutes of real wind—matter-of-fact natural breath—I will have what I want. For this year, at least.

Meanwhile, the various projects are doing well. <u>To the White Sea</u> is going into production at Universal, and another story of mine called <u>The Sentence</u>—a film about a prison—has also been requested.[110] As a rule, I don't much like movie work, but I do it in order to keep some other person from messing up what I think is good enough not to be messed up. Well, we'll see.

A new book of my early journals, and the poems I wrote concurrently with them, will be out in a couple of weeks; I'll send you a copy on the publication date.[111]

I'd like to make this a longer letter, but will quit now to get it in the mail. Keep doing what you're doing, and include a letter to me somewhere in there.

Ever,

JD:cf

TO: JEANNE ZALESKY[112]

TLS (Xerox), 1 p;[113] Emory

April 12, 1996

Dear Ms. Zalesky:

Your letter is most welcome. I am happy that my work has reached you, and to know that you like "The Rain Guitar" and some of my other poems. The poem you single out is one of the very few literally every word of which is fact, except my interpretation, of course. I was in Winchester in 1962. It was beginning to rain a little, and I walked down a little way from the hotel to see the weir, which was charming. The one fellow fishing there was just, as I said, a veteran of Burma, and did have a wooden leg.

It is surprising how pleasant to talk about such violent things can be in a peace-time setting like that one. I recommend it to all veterans, and to anyone else.

Since you like my work as much as you say you do, I can tell you that there are a lot of new things coming out, including a movie made from my latest novel. See if you can get the book and read it: To the White Sea. Let me know what you think, if you're of a mind.

It was most generous of you to write, and I hope to hear from you again.

Sincerely yours,

James Dickey

JD:cf

TO: SAUL BELLOW

TL (Xerox), 1 p; Emory
Columbia, S.C.

April 22, 1996

Dear Bellow:

I have just been going through your It All Adds Up,[114] and it occurred to me that I should write and make clear my extreme gratitude for some of the things you say. It is good to have your own opinions as well as those coming from the characters in your novels, and very gratifying to see that you range around so widely in your reading as to include, for example, Greek poets like Seferis and Sikelianos. This is the kind of reading that I myself have been doing, especially in the last year and a half, when I have been more or less downed by jaundice and its long recovery; as a special favor to me, don't ever get it. Anyway, I feel that I have had a very good companion during this hard time, experiencing the word more or less at random, as I do, though reading different things.

You needn't bother to answer this; I just took the notion to write—again, at whim—for whatever it may be worth, and then to pass along.[115]

My best to you always, and to your work.

Sincerely,

JD:cf

TO: GRAY BANKS[116]

TL (Xerox), 1 p; Emory
Columbia, S.C.

April 29, 1996

Dear Mr. Banks:

Please forgive my belatedness in answering your letter, and acknowledging your kindness in sending me the tape and the various materials you included. I have been rather ill for the past year and a half, though, and that fact has made it impossible for me to handle all the correspondence that has come in. Your letter is unique, however, and I would like, here, to pay attention—more attention—to your passion, and your stand for Southern values. It is true that the Leviathan has won, is winning more and more with every new mill that locates among us. It is also true that we had and still to some extent have a way of life with more to recommend it than any yet instituted in the New World. But one thing is certain.

Once industry is in we can't throw it out. Once the city is instituted it will remain and grow, and the land and its traditions will die. Whatever preservation we may hope for will be only in music, in museums and a few books, for the stuff that is in Southern blood and at the heart of our region will in a few generations die out. The rest will be history—and history books. But you and I and a number of others have known what the South at its best was capable of being. The worst we know only too well, but amputations are supposed to cure the patient and not kill him. You and I can watch, and remember. And write. Remember what Faulkner, Agee, Walker Percy and others have done. They have proved what you and I know: that the South accomplished something that no other region or body of people could have done. That, too, is history.

I haven't played the tape you sent, but on looking at Samuel Barber's adaptation of Jim Agee's pieces I noticed that the one printed as a poem is actually a composite of several poems from his first book, Permit Me Voyage.[117] These lines are often given in this manner, but it is not as Jim would have them, which you can easily verify if you will refer to the book. Why Barber chose to do things in this way is not known to me, but I don't much like the setting of poems to music to begin with; Barber's gruesome rendition of Agee's rhapsody about Knoxville is a good case in point.[118]

Well, I won't go on and on, but will close to get this in the mail, with my gratitude and good wishes. Let me hear from you again, if you are of a mind, because I would like to keep up with such an impassioned and forthright mind. As I say, let me hear. But that shall be as you wish, of course.

Sincerely,

James Dickey

TO: RICHARD MILLER[119]

TLS (Xerox), 1 p; Emory
Columbia, S.C.

June 4, 1996

Dear Richard:

As we just finished discussing on the phone, I herewith present the new winner, Talvikki Ansel. I am glad to see that you are enthusiastic about the choice, for it was a difficult one. I am quite sure, however, that we have the right person, the right poems. I will depend on you and your staff to notify Mr.(?) Ansel, and I hope you will have him call me after you have announced the results to him/her.[120]

As I usually do, I plan to write Ansel and the other seven of my finalists and invite the non-winners to resubmit next year, for I want to set things up for you and the next judge as well as I can. If I were looking forward in time, or casting literary horoscopes, I should think that Mr. Evans will win next time around, and maybe Maxwell (in) the (next) year after that, if stronger manuscripts than those two do not come in. There is always a distinct possibility that this will happen, though, as it did in the case of Samaras—who came by here and visited, by the way, and is now teaching in Florida—and the prospect is perennially exciting. It has been so for me, and I hope it will be for the judges who follow me as well as, needless to say, for you as well. I don't believe a poetry judge has ever had a better editor, and I hope the fact that our relationship is no longer to be official will not in the least influence the ongoing friendship that has come to be. I won't go on and on in this immoderate vein, since I am not given to gush, but will hope that you will use a reading-between-the-lines intuition, which is always magical, to tell you the truth of such things.

Let me know if there is anything else I might do, for, as I say, I want my part of things to finish strong. Please tell the other readers of the manuscripts how much I appreciate their help, and I hope that at least some of them concur in my choices. One of these days I'll meet all of you, looking you right in the eyes, as should be done, and deliver (right word? Maybe) my gratitude.

Ever,

Jim

P.S.: Let me have the check as soon as possible, so that I may keep my records straight (and send my daughter through Choate).

TO: MICHAEL EVANS[121]

TL (Xerox), 1 p;[122] *Emory*

June 5, 1996

Dear Mr. Evans:

I have spent a good many hours with your manuscript, and, though in the final showdown it did not win this year, I can tell you that it ran very strongly indeed, and I would like here to ask (No! <u>Demand!</u>) that you resubmit next year. There will be another judge then, for I have been editor long enough, I feel, and after seven contests it seems to me that I should give someone else a chance to do the job. At any rate, I like your poems very much, and I wonder if it would be possible—since I must send all manuscripts back to Yale—for you to send me a copy of the poems I may keep for personal reasons. But that shall be as you wish, of course.

The Bligh material is most fruitful for you, I think. The poem as a whole does not seem to me to be completely successful, but the fact that you undertook it at all is encouraging. Bligh's voyage to Timor is one of the great chronicles of the sea, and you have immersed yourself in it to the extent that the reader feels as though his own life were involved in the weather, the attempts to get food, Bligh's sextant readings and the other details of those suffering and resourceful leagues. I like, also, that you take what amounts to a minimalist approach; this, at a time in which there is so <u>much</u> verbal run-off, so much indistinct volubility. You are very plainly your own man, and I like that, too.

So please <u>do</u> let the new judge see your work next year.[123] If and when you do send your poems to him I have only one suggestion, and it is that you consider changing the title, which belies the intent and feeling of the book. If it were me, I might think about using the line about Bligh at noon, taking the meridian-passage sight. I won't press this on you; only suggest.

If you can send a copy of your manuscript, also tell me something about yourself, and if possible enclose a photograph, for I like to have a sense of the physical presence of my finalists. I'd say there is some kind of mystique, or something, present in this. As my young daughter says, "It's just me."

Good luck, <u>Capitain</u>. Come back to us for your next landfall: not Timor but Yale.

Sincerely,
James Dickey

JD:cf

TO: SAUL BELLOW

TLS (Xerox), 1 p;[124] Emory

June 13, 1996

Dear Saul Bellow:

Thank you indeed for your letter, and for the things you say about <u>Deliverance</u>. It was written so long ago that, on re-reading it, I have not always been sure what I intended in certain places, but your remarks convince me that, in the case of the character Lewis, I actually got what I was driving at. In the movie version I was saddled with an actor who did not grasp the part as I conceived it. If Burt Reynolds is not dumber than an ox, he is not any smarter than one, either, and insisted on playing Lewis as an over-bearing bully, when the whole point is that the others follow him because of his mystiques, which they think may supply some of the answers they seek, only half-knowing that they do. Anyway, I thought we made at least a fairish try with the movie, and <u>did</u> follow the essential story, which doesn't happen in the case of most novels made into films.

By the way, a couple of years ago I saw on television your story, <u>Seize The Day</u>, which is a great favorite of mine; I have, ever since I first read it, wanted to find Tamkin and get counsel from him! I thought the film a very creditable try, and as evidence I adduce the fact that Robin Williams was pretty good in it, or so I thought. Ordinarily, I don't much like him, but I thought the scene with the adamant father was very moving, and as true to my version of your intent as could be got. By the way, did I not catch a glimpse of you in one of the hotel scenes? I could've sworn it.

I won't go on and on, but just acknowledge once more how grateful I am for your generous letter. And I am also very happy to know that you are moving among the fields and mountains of New England, as you describe them in your essay in <u>It All Adds Up</u>. If you like soft mountains you must come down here and see some of mine, at the tag end of Appalachia. I was born there, and I know a lot of good places. Once I was walking a trail and I came on a young man sitting on a rock writing, and said to myself, "He must be a poet! At last things are right!" I made bold to ask him what he was doing, certain, really, that he was working on his taxes or composing a protest letter to a newspaper, but he said, "I'm writing poetry," and I went on. Right is right.

Thanks again, and communicate when you like, or if you want to.

Cordially,

Jim D.

TO: TALVIKKI ANSEL

TL (Xerox), 2 pp;[125] *Emory*

June 14, 1996

Dear Ms. Ansel:

By now Richard Miller at Yale has told you that your manuscript is the new winner in the Yale Series competition. As its judge, I wish to congratulate you, and let you know that you have made an instant fan of me, though I must confess I was surprised at your gender. I don't believe I have ever encountered another Talvikki anywhere, so I hope I am not to be blamed for assuming that you were male. The main thing is, though, that you are a most interesting and good poet. I am now writing the Introduction to the book, and keep reading certain things over and over again. The title sequence is remarkable, and so is the suite about Caliban. You have a very strong sense of theme-and-development, and can take your chosen material through many changes, some of them quite unexpected. I like all this, and, as I said, I much admire your daring, the technical resourceful-ness of your poems, and your talent and <u>personality</u>, as they come through the words.

If I were asked to offer advice—which I have not been—I would suggest that you think again about the title of the book. In general, your titles are not as strik-ing and good as the poems that follow them. The overall title, <u>In Fragments, In Streams</u>, does not anywhere near convey the integratedness, the solidity, of your work, especially in the two main sequences. In fact, it is misleading, because it seems to imply a tentativeness, a fragmentariness that are far from the effect and feel of the poems. In my opinion you would do better to call the book after one of your other titles like "Conversation With The Sun Bittern" (or maybe just "The Sun Bittern"), or "Wolf Children," or even "Caliban." Or you could take one of your wonderful lines, or a portion of one, and use that: something like "Complete As Belief' or, (a title <u>I</u> would like, "Teatro Amazonas) or "The Second Owl" or "Chachalaca," or (from the Caliban sequence) "Sweet Breathers," or "Wood-Time, Dig-Time," or even "Should I Say Island?"[126]

Again, these are only suggestions, to be taken or rejected as you wish. And yet I have one more, which is that you might change "Inscrutable Pig" to "Kennings," which is (or, are) what the poem is about.[127]

Let me reiterate my confidence and delight. You are a sure-enough discovery, and have given me great pleasure. I'm glad you won.

Let me hear from you if and when you have time. And send me a photograph of yourself; I like to have a physical sense of the poet, if I can get it.

With best wishes and congratulations,
James Dickey

JD:cf

TO: ROBERT FAGLES[128]

RTL (Xerox), 1 p; Emory
Columbia, S.C.

July 10, 1996

Dear Bob:

I have your letter, and am glad to know that the quotation for your <u>Odyssey</u> pleases you.[129] Believe me, I mean what I say; if the public would read your

Homer it would be a better public. I don't at all agree with Auden that "poetry makes nothing happen." Poetry makes plenty happen; it can change your life. My whole existence has proceeded from one <u>word</u> in a poem, which I read in an anthology on Okinawa during the last weeks of the second War.[130] And good writing <u>about</u> poetry is wonderful, too. I remember that when I first read Mark Van Doren's essays on the <u>Iliad</u> and the <u>Odyssey</u> in his book <u>The Noble Voice</u>[131] I was again changed, for I had never read a critic—or commentator—write about poetry in such a way. Incidentally, have a look at what Van Doren says, for I'd like to know what you think. A good many people fault Mark, especially in regard to his opinions of Virgil, which are not high. Ward Briggs,[132] down here, argues with me (and Mark) all the time about this, and, again, I'd be pleased to have your opinion.

As to further poetry from me, I have a long suite of related poems called <u>Two Poems on the Survival of the Male Body</u>, but in my current jaundiced (literally) condition I have only a limited amount of energy to spend on poetry, though that is where I try to spend it. With luck I may be able to complete these in another year, but I can't promise you, or myself, anything at this time. I'll keep you posted, if you like.[133]

I would be delighted if you could come down here and spend some time. I live alone, and I could put you up. The location is pleasant enough, on a lake, and it is quiet here. Just the place to hear Achilles' sword banging on Hector's breastplate!

Write when you can, and tell me your news. Ward Briggs sends his best, and certainly you have mine.

Ever,

jd:mg

TO: RICHARD ROTH[134]

TL (Xerox), 3 pp;[135] Emory

23 July, 1996

Dear Richard:

Here are some comments, which I hope will prove of use either in the large or in the small, or, with luck, both. It is <u>necessary</u> that you know, and that you tell the Peoples,[136] that these observations and suggestions are offered in one connection only, and that is toward the making of as good a film as is possible. Emphasize that my intention is not to interfere, or to supersede the Peoples' screenplay in any way, but simply to be of whatever service I can in the furtherance of their already superior script.

Some large considerations:

I would very much like to have the sequence of Muldrow in the sewer pipe; we would do well—very well—not to miss this. If the Peoples feel that they can't do the movie this way, I offer to write the scene myself, but I do feel very strongly about it. It is of advantage for almost every reason. The free end of the pipe can be used as a kind of movie screen in itself, and some of Muldrow's "visions" of the Arctic might play there—including, in accordance with the unexpected, a white buffalo! or some white animal. We could also use this device for flashbacks—the cabin, the father, the red wall, the Kansas girl (mirror sequence?), or almost anything. Then, too, we could render the first explosion of the fire bomb raid by this means: the flash, the horrific impact on Muldrow's ears in this closed space, and so on. So, let's see what we can do about substituting this approach for the one currently in the script. Think about it; we must make a real decision here.

In the matter of proportion, it seems to me that some of the key scenes of the book are too short, and some of the less important ones are dwelt on at unnecessary length. For example, the duel with the old samurai should be worked for every bit of suspense there is in it, which is plenty. This part would do well to use long silences in which nothing at all happens; we just show the interior of the house, as in a still photograph. A good deal should be made of the sliding panels: we don't know which ones will open and close, and where: it should always be the unexpected one. We keep the viewer guessing, and see to it that he guesses wrong. This is a deadly and delicate game, played out in utter silence, and I would like us to raise the suspense to an unbearable level, and have the scene where Muldrow kills the samurai the most unexpected of all. Also, Muldrow's getting the bone splinters to sew with is important, and we should see him both getting the splinters and sewing with them. Gruesome but good. There could also be a hint of cannibalism.

As to the dialogue in general, it will be more effective if Muldrow speaks in much shorter communications than the screenplay indicates. He should never add anything to his basic statements to make them more personal, more human. In the Quonset hut he should not add the second sentence in statements like, "Suit yourself. No skin offa me." Again, when on page 8 the other gunner asks him about the stones in Muldrow's kit, Muldrow should just say something like, "Flints. (short pause) Fire." The point of these points on my part is that he never says anything that is not essential; if some of his statements are enigmatic, that is fine; it is in character.

Some details:

After the extremely good opening, in the matter dealing with the colonel's briefing, we should not have the briefing done out on the tarmac with the aircraft; such does not happen. It should take place in a briefing room, with maps, pointers, compass headings, and other flight paraphernalia.

From the preflight sequence I would be pleased to drop the material dealing with Major Sorbo. Everything he says about Muldrow we should see happen, or at least be given means by which the viewer can infer it. Nothing needs to be explained that action itself can show.

The part about the pinch-grip chin should <u>precede</u> the conversation with the other gunner about flints, and so on. The new gunner is more and more fascinated with Muldrow, and can't leave him alone. Yet—no one, not even Muldrow, can do a pinch-grip chin with one hand; two is plenty hard enough.

In the flight sequence Muldrow does not mutter to himself, as though he has a blood-vendetta against the Japanese. Quite the contrary: he has no more hatred toward the Japanese than he did, say, toward the Kansas girl. He is <u>indifferent</u>.

As to the Kansas girl herself, I think that somewhere in the first third of the movie we should get his early experience with her into the story: say, a brief shot of a room in Point Barrow where he watches her and her naked reflection in the mirror, thus seeing her from two sides at once (It's possible! And I <u>do</u> hope that this will give some <u>selected</u> people ideas!).

The log-train sequence should be longer, with Muldrow's "vision" of the Northern forest. At the first of this part he should listen to the rails, feel the wet trees, and so on. He should <u>drop onto</u> the train, as in the book, which coincides with his wish to fall on things from above.

The scene with the children and Muldrow when he does the string trick should be more as I have sent you in the enclosed version. For visual effects, as well as other things, there should be the business about the moon in the cat's cradle or Jacob's Ladder. The audience should believe that Muldrow is going to <u>murder</u> the children, and this would be graphically shown by having him put the string around one child's neck and the viewer's seeing the knot rise to the boy's throat and then fall, or lower, again.

In the scene with the American Zen monk we lose one of the best opportunities of all when we don't, when the monk says that "God is in every flake of snow falling on these temple stones" have Muldrow's reply that "No; the snow is in the snow." Also, it is important that the Japanese soldiers not break right in on Muldrow and the monk, for we must be aware that the monk <u>betrays</u> Muldrow, and not have the whole incident happen just out of the blue. In other words, the monk should not be present either when the soldiers capture Muldrow or when they take him away.

Earlier in the film I would like to put the part about Muldrow and the Eskimo boy looking into the heart of the glacier. It seems to me that this could be astonishingly effective. Among all the "visions" that Muldrow has, this could be the most memorable, as well as the most telling index to his character: the heart—even the beautiful and strange heart—of ice itself. This might be substituted for one or two of the shots of the hawk or the snowshoe hare.

At the end, emphasize the fact that the people who are shooting at Muldrow are not regular military, though there may be a soldier or two, looking rather unsoldierly, among them. This is a kind of posse consisting of all sorts, young and old. We should eliminate the sight of the hawk, though we may keep the sound of the hawk's <u>bell</u>. The very end should be a master shot of the members of the posse wandering aimlessly around, through the place where Muldrow has been, looking at the ground and at each other. One of them may pick up Muldrow's breadknife-sword and stare at it in bewilderment. A young person, or even a child, may glance up at the sound of the Hawk's bell. But mainly people are just seen wandering aimlessly about. There's no blood; only their tracks. The wind is blowing. We bring up the END credits, and maybe ring the hawk's bell one more time, faintly. A possibility here, picking up from the beginning VO: "When I tell you this, just say it came from a voice in the wind . . ." and ending with ". . . when the wind is from the north." I don't come out too forthrightly for the added VO; only a thought I had.

These remarks are what I have to say at this time, and are the main ones I would make at any time. Let me be sure I tell you, once again, that I bring them in for the possible good of the picture we are making. I would be more than happy if we could shoot the Peoples' script just as it is, and if these considerations may make it better, I would be even happier, my intent always being to raise from the excellent the better still.

Ever,

JD:cf

TO: ROBERT FAGLES

TLS (Xerox), 1 p;[137] *Emory*

August 14, 1996

Dear Bob:

Sorry to wait a few days before answering your good letter, but I have been busy with doctors and dentists and the beginning of school—not necessarily in that order—and have had my time pretty much taken up with mundane things. It is much better to think of Homer, of Mark Van Doren, and of your own abilities as a translator and poet. As to the latter, your inclination to do something with Virgil is a good one, despite what Mark says about him. As you know, there are certain things that he can do—or does, anyway—that Homer either can't do or doesn't want to do. Virgil is very introspective; his characters don't proclaim their intentions, their character, their lineage, their birthplace, and so on, at the top of their voices, as Homer's so magnificently do. Mark is right when he says that Aeneas' main condition is indecision, coupled with melancholy, and no one who has ever written can get this over better than he does. In Virgil the day is always overcast, it is always twilight, and the hero is torn between alternatives. Aeneas is thus much more "modern" than any of Homer's people, and that could give you something to go on, stressing his psychological difficulties and misgivings. And then, too, the language is so different. That would constitute quite a challenge, and would offer much. As greatly as I admire Robert Fitzgerald as a toiler in these vineyards, I don't think he is nearly as good as you are, and I want people to see this and know it. I used to tell Bob that his original verse is better than his translations, which it is; I think very highly of it, and suffer much at its neglect. The yield of his translation work is not on the level with yours at all. I haven't seen any original poetry by you, though I am sure there is some, so I can't say to you what I used to say to Bob: dig into yourself for a change, instead of into Homer and Virgil. He wouldn't listen to me, though, and consequently all his own poetry is in one depressingly slim volume—and some of this, too, is translation. So . . . knowing that I can't urge on you what I urged on Bob, and if you want my unsolicited advice—go ahead with Virgil. I'd like to see you deal fully with "the tears of things."

I won't go on and on, but just get this in the mail. Do translate Virgil and do come down here on any pretext at all, or none.

None except me. Me and Ward Briggs. We could have some good talk.

Ever,

Jim

TO: ELIZABETH SPENCER[138]

RTL (Xerox), 2 pp; Emory
Columbia, S.C.

October 7, 1996

Dear Elizabeth:

It is good indeed to hear from you, and to know that you connected with the people down in Shreveport. They give something called the Corrington Award, are very hospitable, and show you around Shreveport, where they insist on you eating all the crawfish that have been dredged out of the bayous the previous week—I think that I myself had at least two weeks' worth, which called for their dredging at night, but that was all right with them, because I went out in a pirogue and played Cajun music with them, with which they seemed to be familiar—

though not with my bluegrass variations! Only a little of this is true, except the part that might induce you to go down there and enjoy that place and those people; I guarantee you will, should you go.

Sure, I remember the old days on the Awards Committee, and Ginsberg trying to get Academy money for his queer cohorts and other crazies, and what we did to prevent it. I also recall Irving Howe's obtuse opposition to Shelby Foote's Civil War trilogy,[139] which I guarantee he had not read in full. I have, not once but twice, mainly because my brother, Tom, was the leading authority on Civil War projectiles, and I have gone over those battlefields with him and a metal-detector many times. Shelby is dead right on the terrain, as to the ones I have researched, and to have Howe dismiss that whole monumental work with a noncommittal "too many battles" I took as a personal affront, or at least partially did. That is too bad, because I liked Irving and otherwise thought he was a good chairman for our committee. Didn't you? Except, of course, for the fact that he didn't kick Ginsberg off, and one or two other oversights which I remembered then but have forgotten now.

Well, enough of committee work. I think we did some good, but it has long been time to turn back to our own fields, and this time I don't mean battlefields.

Know that I think of you often, and wish life had given me the chance to know you better. But what I do know is good indeed, and I hope you will continue writing, and writing to me. Though I am still struggling with the aftermath of jaundice and have some lung problems, I will be around for a while, yet. I hope to write more, for I have lots of plans. Right now I am making a movie of my last novel, To The White Sea; Universal is doing it. The screenplay is completed, and we are settling on a director and cast. I'll let you know what happens when the West Coast people tell me; sometimes they do, and sometimes they don't. But it will be a big production, no matter what. We have a good budget, and I hope we can get the most out of it. As I say, more later.

Keep writing to me, because, since I am on a life-support system, I can't move around as much as I'd like to, and mail means a lot. In my case, the sedentary life of a writer has become really sedentary, and I am driven back almost exclusively on the mind and imagination. And on friends, of whom I count you among the most valuable as well as most talented. You bet.

Ever,

JD:cf

TO: JOSEPH HELLER[140]

TL (Xerox), 1 p;[141] Emory

October 23, 1996

Dear Joe:

Thank you indeed for your letter, and for the things you say about <u>The White Sea</u>. Universal will do it as a movie, using the Coen brothers[142] and my original producer, Richard Roth. The screenplay I have is pretty good, though it needs some work, and from here we'll try to go on and make a good movie. But it's not done yet, and as you know there are so many kinds of things that can go wrong that one lives in a perpetual state of frustration. But all that is out of my hands, and I just wait for the people out there to tell me what they want me to know. I wonder if you had the same experience with <u>Catch-22</u>?[143] It is kind of coincidental, isn't it, that we both had films featuring Jon Voight? Well, I take that as a good sign.

And it is a good sign, also, that you and I were able to get together once more, though much too briefly. I have seldom met another writer with whom I have felt so at ease, and I look forward to seeing you at some time and place where we can sit down and talk about the things that matter to us. My mobility is limited right now, as you know, by my shortness-of-breath problem, but I hope to beat that one way or another, and then we can have another meeting; I like to think of it. Whenever you can, write and tell me how your life is going. It would be good indeed to hear from you; being more or less immobilized as I am, I feel about letters much as the overseas soldier does, and you know how <u>that</u> is. Letters—yes, always! But the <u>right</u> letter . . . !

Please accept my very best wishes, my old bombardier, and next time—next mission—we'll team up and drop 'em right down the pickle barrel! That's some barrel! Richard Hugo, an American poet I used to know, was also a bombardier, and he says that he was so inept that he couldn't even hit the Brenner Pass. Such inaccuracy! It's what all our wars need.

Ever,

TO: MARYROSE CARROLL[144]

RTL (Xerox), 1 p; Emory
Columbia, S.C.

November 15, 1996

Dear Maryrose:

Thank you very much for sending me the program of Paul's funeral service. If I had not been laid low myself I would have been right there, but in my lungs enough air could not be contained for a journey, and sometimes I think that there is not enough in the world for it, either. But I did want to tell you how gratifying it is to me that Paul spent his last years in my territory, the mountains of the South, where my father's people come from and my true roots are, and to imagine what surrounds Paul now that he is lying where he is. That is the true World, as it was made by something other than men. The trees and the creeks and the round rocks of them are as real as anything God could have given reality to, and the mountain <u>space</u> is real, and Paul is there with the things I am sure he had come to love.

As he may have told you, Paul and I first met in New York when we read at the Poetry Center of the YMHA in 1959. It was my first New York audience, and when I looked out and saw Norman Mailer in the first row and my venerable (new) editor at Scribner's, John Hall Wheelock, I felt that I was in the right place, and when I talked to Paul, a few minutes before the reading, I knew I was.

Over the years we met at various places, and I used to stay with him at his highrise on Lake Shore Drive in Chicago. One of these times was in connection with a reading, and Paul had a party. I stayed over the next day and it snowed, and I sat in a chair with my feet next to the window, drinking a martini and the snow falling a few inches from my feet, and I do sincerely believe that was the happiest I ever was in my life. <u>The</u> happiest.

I won't go on and on, but will just say once more how much Paul meant to me. He was as true a friend as I have ever had, and that matters. I hope you will continue to stay in touch, so that we may be with Paul on both sides of the shadow-line. One can do such things, as you know.

I can see Paul now, and feel the steadiness of his warmth and his imagination: something that was always there, and still is.

                                                            Ever,

NOTES

BEGINNINGS: AIR FORCE AND VANDERBILT,
MAY 1943–OCTOBER 1951

1. JD's mother.

2. From April through June 1943, JD began flight training and took classes, including English and physics, at High Point College, High Point, North Carolina.

3. Where JD and his fellow cadets were to be "classified."

4. JD's father, an Atlanta lawyer and real estate investor.

5. JD had attended Clemson Agricultural College in South Carolina during the fall semester 1942 before joining the Army Air Corps in early 1943. At Clemson he had played football under coach Frank Howard. A Xerographic copy of the essay described in this letter is at Emory University; the original essay has not been located.

6. JD's younger brother, who ran track in high school and, later, at Louisiana State University.

7. On letterhead printed with wings and "A/C Jim Dickey."

8. Refers to a speech in the 1935 MGM movie version of *Mutiny on the Bounty* starring Charles Laughton and Clark Gable.

9. World War II fighter-pilot ace.

10. On letterhead printed with wings and "A/C Jim Dickey."

11. From Aerial Gunnery School.

12. Maibelle Swift Dickey's mother had been born in Germany.

13. Peg Roney, an Atlanta girl.

14. Tom Dickey had been rejected for military service.

15. Jane Kirksey, a young widow.

16. Unidentified literary periodical.

17. New Guinea.

18. British poet (1901–57).

19. Earl R. Bradley of Morehead, Kentucky.

20. Perhaps Donald Armstrong of Buffalo, New York. JD celebrated Armstrong—who was not beheaded by the Japanese but instead died in a March 1945 plane crash—in "The Performance" (*Poetry*, July 1959).

21. JD's older sister.

22. Cartoon of JD as a slave driver.

23. British poet (1867–1900).

24. JD correctly identifies and quotes from Dowson's poem.

25. The title of this Dowson poem is "Impenitentia Ultima." JD accurately quotes its final stanza.

26. (1899–1954), editor and journalist whose patriotic poem was published in 1944.

27. JD skipped number 12.

28. JD wrote this letter between the atomic-bomb attacks on Hiroshima (6 August 1945) and Nagasaki (9 August); Japan offered surrender on 10 August.

29. Kathleen Winsor's *Forever Amber* (1944) was a best-selling historical novel; Delmore Schwartz's "Coriolanus and His Mother" is a narrative poem collected in his *In Dreams Begin Responsibilities* (1938); Thomas's collection of autobiographical stories is titled *Portrait of the Artist as a Young Dog* (1940).

30. JD enrolled at Vanderbilt University, Nashville, Tennessee, in the summer of 1946.

31. This draft of a story featuring Donald Armstrong apparently accompanied a now-lost letter to JD's mother.

32. British-born poet (1907–73).

33. Prof. Monroe K. Spears (1916–98), who taught JD at Vanderbilt, was an editor of *The Sewanee Review*. His "Late Auden: The Satirist as Lunatic Clergyman," which challenged judgments of poet-critic Randall Jarrell (1914–65), appeared in the Winter 1951 issue of *The Sewanee Review*.

34. Unpublished.

35. Maxine Dickey was pregnant with the Dickeys' first child.

36. Berryman (1914–72) published *The Dispossessed*, his second collection of poetry, in 1948.

37. Stephen Spender (1909–); the book is probably *World Within World*, the British poet's 1951 memoir.

38. From "Canto Amor," first published in *The Sewanee Review* (Winter 1947) and collected in Berryman's *The Dispossessed*.

39. JD's "Of Holy War" was published in the October 1951 issue of *Poetry*. None of his poetry appeared in either *Partisan Review* or *Hudson Review* until 1957.

40. This poem was not published. Gerard Manley Hopkins (1844–89), British experimental poet, was an early influence on JD.

41. Welsh poet (1914–53).

42. By Ezra Pound (1885–1972).

43. The book by the Spanish philosopher (1883–1955) was published in 1930.

44. British writer Christopher Isherwood (1904–86) and French writer André Malraux (1901–76).

45. Calhoun and Elizabeth Winton; Calhoun Winton had been a classmate of JD at Vanderbilt. Hall is unidentified.

46. In *The Literary Mind* (1969), Max Eastman reports Joyce's remark, "The de-

mand that I make of my reader is that he should devote his whole life to reading my works."

47. Enclosed in a 13 August 1951 letter.

48. RKO (1934).

49. JD is parodying the title of a popular 1949 movie, *A Letter to Three Wives*.

50. Poet Karl Shapiro (1913–) was then editor of *Poetry*.

51. Unpublished.

52. (1951).

53. Christopher Dickey, the Dickeys' first child, was born 31 August 1951.

APPRENTICESHIP:
AUGUST 1953–MARCH 1956

1. During the summer of 1953, JD was living with his parents in Atlanta, while Maxine and Christopher Dickey were staying with her mother in Nashville.

2. Doubleday editor Lee Barker, who rejected JD's novel, "Entrance to the Honeycomb," on which he had been working throughout the summer. The novel was not published.

3. MGM (1931).

4. *Lions and Shadows*, by Christopher Isherwood, was published in 1938; *The Barricades*, by Toynbee (1916–81), was published in 1943; *The Dark Thorn*, by Gardiner (1901–81), was published in 1946; *The Withered Branch*, by Savage (1917–), was published in 1950; and *Janus*, by Barker (1913–91), was published in 1935.

5. Chairman of the English Department, Mercer University, Macon, Georgia.

6. JD often exaggerated his military record.

7. By January 1954 JD had published one poem in *The Sewanee Review* and three poems in *Poetry*; he did not publish verse in *The Quarterly Review of Literature* until 1958. After Doubleday rejected "Entrance to the Honeycomb," JD began revising it as "The Casting," which was not completed.

8. (1902–95), poet and novelist who was then teaching in the writing program at the University of Florida, Gainesville.

9. Lytle had written to JD about a draft of "The Maze," the first part of "The Angel of the Maze," which was published in the June 1955 issue of *Poetry*.

10. JD had been awarded a *Sewanee Review* writing fellowship by a committee that included Spears, poet and critic Allen Tate (1899–1979), and drama theorist Francis Fergusson (1904–86).

11. Although the poem was first published in June 1955, JD did not collect "The Angel of the Maze" until *The Whole Motion* in 1992.

12. Anthology edited by Allen Tate in 1947. "The Guide" was a section of Lytle's work in progress, *The Velvet Horn*, published in 1957. *The Long Night* (1936) and *A Name for Evil* (1947) were two of his other novels.

13. Lytle's second novel, *At the Moon's Inn*, was published in 1941. No Lytle story about the conquest of Peru has been located in *The Sewanee Review*, although an excerpt from *At the Moon's Inn*—"A Fragment: How Nuno de Tovar Came To Cross the Ocean Sea"—was published in *Hika* (June 1939).

14. *The Craft of Fiction* (1921).

15. (1905–89), American poet and fiction writer whose work JD admired throughout his life.

16. The plot foreshadows that of *Alnilam*, which was published in 1987.

17. In an undated April 1954 letter Lytle told Dickey about a gangster's mistaking

him for a policeman in "that town thirty miles from Dallas" and about four detectives' questioning him as a possible criminal in St. Louis: "I don't know why it is I'm taken both for the obverse and reverse of the same thing, unless the artist is both criminal and preserver of order."

18. "The Image as Guide to Meaning in the Historical Novel," *The Sewanee Review* (Summer 1953).

19. *Poetry* (June 1953).

20. "The Angel of the Maze."

21. The Dickeys lived during the summer of 1954 with his parents in Atlanta. In June Maxine Dickey took the Dickeys' two-year-old son, Chris, to Nashville, where they were visiting with her mother.

22. Agee (1909–55), American poet, novelist, and film critic, whom JD called his favorite writer.

23. Putnam (1894–1948), an American poet admired by JD, was the author of *Trink* (1927) and *The Five Seasons* (1930).

24. Ezzard Charles fought Rocky Marciano for the heavyweight title on 19 June 1954 in Madison Square Garden. Charles lost in a fifteen-round decision; in his 17 September rematch with Marciano, Charles was knocked out in the eighth round.

25. Private club in Atlanta, originally for horsemen.

26. Two words omitted.

27. 1907 novel by British writer E. M. Forster (1879–1970).

28. Spender did not publish "The Angel of the Maze" in *Encounter,* nor did Lytle publish it in *The Sewanee Review;* the poem appeared in *Poetry.*

29. Novelist Caroline Gordon (1895–1981) was at that time married to Allen Tate.

30. (1907–88), literary critic.

31. These three poems are unidentified and not published under the titles listed here. "The Lemon Tree" may have been reworked as "Paestum," published in *Shenandoah* (Winter 1963) and collected in *The Whole Motion.*

32. Stories by James Joyce (1882–1941) and Stephen Crane (1871–1900).

33. JD's work was not published in *Botteghe Oscure.*

34. "The Ground of Killing" (October 1954).

35. In *The American,* James's 1877 novel.

36. Spender's "Archaic Head" appeared next to JD's "The Ground of Killing" in the October 1954 issue of *The Sewanee Review.*

37. JD was nearly twenty years old when he left college for the Army Air Corps.

38. JD reviewed Kazantzakis's *The Odyssey: A Modern Sequel* (1958) in the July–September 1959 issue of *The Sewanee Review.*

39. "The Sprinter's Mother," which appeared in *Shenandoah* (Spring 1955).

40. Drafts for this unpublished poem are at Emory University and at Vanderbilt University.

41. "His legs are sleeping among the works / Of the great lock of daylight: it is terrible . . ."

42. "The Confrontation of the Hero (April, 1945)," *The Sewanee Review* (July–September 1955); first collected in *The Whole Motion.*

43. Unlocated.

44. "The Confrontation of the Hero (April, 1945)."

45. Poet and anthologist who had been a schoolmate of JD at Vanderbilt University.

46. Applicants for college and university teaching positions in English and other languages and literatures are customarily interviewed at the annual meeting of the Modern Language Association.

47. "The Angel of the Maze."

48. Probably "The Sprinter's Sleep," first published in *The Yale Review* (September 1957).

49. (1907–88), surrealist poet.

50. Poet and translator Richard Wilbur (1921–) was in Italy on an American Academy of Arts and Letters Rome Fellowship.

51. Smith (1918–), poet and translator; Howes (1914–96).

52. (1916–), American poet and historian.

53. In the spring of 1955 Chester Gould's *Dick Tracy* comic strip included a story line about the "wild boy" twin sons of a millionaire health faddist. The boys periodically yell the phrase *Neki Hokey,* which a linguist in the strip says is "from a South Sea tribe and means almost anything—from joy to anger, from hello to farewell."

54. Louis, the "Brown Bomber," was heavyweight champion from 1937 to 1949; Olson was a middleweight and light-heavyweight boxer; Mel Patton was a track star.

55. JD's poem "The Vigils" was published in the *Beloit Poetry Journal* in Fall 1955; his work did not appear in the *Hudson Review* until Autumn 1957 or in *The Quarterly Review of Literature* until Winter 1958.

56. JD slightly misquotes this line from the last page of *The Great Gatsby.*

57. Poet Ezra Pound was incarcerated in St. Elizabeths Hospital, Washington, D.C., while it was being determined whether he was sane enough to stand trial for treason during World War II. Dickey visited and corresponded with Pound. Their letters, edited by Lee Bartlett and Hugh Witemeyer, were published in the Fall 1982 issue of *Paideuma.*

58. (1901–90).

59. Pound.

60. Sketch of Pound by Henri Gaudier-Brzeska.

61. Ernest Fenollosa (1853–1908), American scholar of Far Eastern art and poetry, whose work influenced Pound.

62. "Some of All of It," *The Sewanee Review* (April–June 1956).

63. Scottish poet W. S. Graham (1918–86).

64. Graham had been heavily influenced by Welsh poet Dylan Thomas.

65. Possibly "The Swimmer," *Partisan Review* (Spring 1957).

66. Unpublished.

67. Mrs. Pratt was pregnant.

68. British poet Basil Bunting (1900–85) published *Poems: 1950* with Cleaners' Press, Galveston, Texas, in 1950.

69. Pound's *ABC of Reading* was published in 1934. In Roman mythology Cerberus is the three-headed dog that guards the entrance to the infernal regions.

70. JD's reading of "The Father's Body" had offended this group; the poem was later published in *Poetry* (December 1956).

71. "The Swimmer" appeared in the Spring 1957 issue.

72. The quotation from Shakespeare's Sonnet 129 is "The expense of spirit in a waste of shame."

73. Prof. J. Hooper Wise.

74. Movie actor who appeared in Roman and Biblical epics.

75. *Hudson Review* published JD's "The Work of Art" in its Autumn 1957 issue, but *Botteghe Oscure* did not publish his poetry.

76. Smith's "Death of a Jazz Musician" appeared in the Winter 1956 *Partisan Review;* Howes's "Tea in the Garden" was published in the October 1955 *New World Writing.*

ADVERTISING AND MOONLIGHTING:
APRIL 1956–MAY 1961

1. JD had gone to New York City to begin training in the McCann-Erickson advertising agency.

2. Professor Wise.

3. Lytle had failed to support JD in the Pen Women's Club controversy.

4. Henry Rago (1915–69), editor of *Poetry*.

5. McCann-Erickson had just taken over the Atlanta-based Coca-Cola account.

6. One paragraph of seventy-five words omitted.

7. Lines from JD's "The Flight," which appeared in the Summer 1956 *Beloit Poetry Journal*.

8. Line 492 in Pound's *Canto 74* reads: "the sharp song with sun under its radiance."

9. Thomas had invented a place name, Llareggub, that could be read backwards. After his death the name was changed in *Under Milk Wood*.

10. "The First Morning of Cancer" appeared in the May 1957 issue of *Poetry*; "The Red Bow" was published in the October–December 1957 issue of *The Sewanee Review*.

11. Gotham Book Mart on Forty-seventh Street, owned and operated by Frances Steloff (1888–1989).

12. Last two sentences added in JD holograph.

13. (1900–64), poet and anthologist.

14. Her work was treated in JD's omnibus review "Some of All of It."

15. JD had proposed that a collection of his poetry be published by Phillips's Criterion imprint.

16. Poet Edwin Honig (1919–)

17. Thurairajah Tambimuttu (1915–83).

18. (1911–), American poet and translator.

19. Jarrell had reviewed Belitt's *Wilderness Stair* (1955) in *The Yale Review* (Autumn 1955).

20. (1927–), American poet.

21. "The Father's Body."

22. (1928–), American poet and anthologist. *New Poets of England and America*, edited by Hall, Robert Pack, and Louis Simpson, appeared in 1957; Dickey reviewed the influential anthology in *The Sewanee Review* (April–June 1958).

23. (1932–), British poet, whom Hall had met and encouraged at Oxford University.

24. (1929–), British poet.

25. Hall, Pack, and Simpson had included Wilbur, Merrill (1926–95), Hecht (1923–), and Merwin in *New Poets of England and America*.

26. British poet Philip Larkin (1922–85).

27. British poet Charles Tomlinson (1927–).

28. Dickey later claimed credit for the slogan "King Size Coke has more for you."

29. Co-editor of *Partisan Review*.

30. JD did not publish a book with Criterion.

31. Probably "From Babel to Byzantium," July–September 1957.

32. "The Swimmer."

33. "The First Morning of Cancer."

34. "To Be Edward Thomas."

35. "From Babel to Byzantium."

36. "The Red Bow," October–December 1957.

37. "The Work of Art."

38. Perhaps "The Sprinter's Sleep," published in September 1957.

39. Moss was poetry editor for *The New Yorker;* JD's first poem in *The New Yorker* was "Orpheus Before Hades," which did not appear until the 5 December 1959 issue.

40. JD's next poem to be published by *Partisan Review* was "Drowning With Others" in the Fall 1960 issue.

41. JD's appraisal of Charles Bell's *Delta Return* appeared in the omnibus review "Five Poets"; "An Exchange on *Delta Return*," letters between Humphries and JD, appeared in the March 1957 issue of *Poetry.*

42. "The Father's Body."

43. "The First Morning of Cancer."

44. JD was not given a prize by *Poetry* in 1957; the magazine's awards went to Sylvia Plath, Jay McPherson, Kenneth Rexroth, and Ben Belitt (for "Andaluz").

45. Humphries's *Green Armor on Green Ground* was reviewed by JD in "From Babel to Byzantium."

46. "To Be Edward Thomas."

47. "The Red Bow," October–December 1957.

48. "The Work of Art."

49. "The Sprinter's Sleep."

50. No JD poem with this title was published; he did not appear in *The Kenyon Review* until Autumn 1959.

51. No JD poems with these titles were published.

52. Philip Rahv (1908–73) was co-editor with William Phillips.

53. Grove Press did not publish a JD collection.

54. Lloyd Frankenberg (1907–75).

55. Unsubstantiated.

56. Belitt's five-part poem "Andaluz" was published in the November 1956 issue of *Poetry.*

57. Variations on this refrain appear in "Dover: Believing in Kings," which was published in the August 1958 issue of *Poetry.*

58. Poet John Crowe Ransom (1888–1974), editor of *The Kenyon Review,* did not publish a JD poem of this title.

59. A little magazine published by Pound admirers in Australia.

60. *Section: Rock-Drill 85-95 de los cantares* (1956).

61. See JD's "The Water-Bug's Mittens: Ezra Pound: What We Can Use," collected in *Night Hurdling.*

62. Literary critic and Pound specialist Hugh Kenner (1923–).

63. Pound endeavored to proselytize associates with his economic theories.

64. John Penrose Angold (1909–43), British poet and essayist who often wrote on economics.

65. (1900–35), French essayist and novelist.

66. British poet Robert Bhain Campbell (1911–40).

67. Berryman's 1957 lecture tour of India was sponsored by the United States Information Service.

68. JD's service was stateside during the Korean War. The Campbell book that he bought in Waco was *The Task* (1945), with a foreword by the poet Norman Rosten (1914–).

69. "Of the People and Their Parks" by Campbell.

70. Theodore Roethke (1908–63), whom JD identified as "The Greatest American Poet" in the November 1968 *Atlantic Monthly.*

71. (1904–), American poet and anthologist.

72. No evidence substantiates these claims.

73. Hall was then poetry editor for *The Paris Review*. JD's poetry first appeared in *The Paris Review* and *Virginia Quarterly Review* in 1960.

74. No Pound review of JD's work has been located.

75. American poet (1925–)

76. JD had reviewed Booth's *Letter from a Distant Land* (1957) in "In the Presence of Anthologies," *The Sewanee Review* (April–June 1958).

77. W. S. Graham.

78. By Graham.

79. Poet Howard Nemerov (1920–91).

80. "Dover: Believing in Kings."

81. Snodgrass (1926–) is not mentioned by JD in "In the Presence of Anthologies," though Snodgrass's work was represented in Hall, Pack, and Simpson's *New Poets of England and America*, a subject of JD's essay-review.

82. (1905–), American poet and reference-book editor.

83. "Among the Gods," *Botteghe Oscure*, Quaderno 15 (1955).

84. American poet (1911–79).

85. Robert Lowell (1917–77).

86. Kevin Dickey was born 18 August 1958.

87. (1927–80), American poet. In a 6 July 1958 letter, Wright angrily complained about JD's reviews of Philip Booth's and Wright's own work; he also enclosed a draft of his "A Note on Mr. James Dickey," which was intended for publication in *The Sewanee Review* but did not appear.

88. JD had mentioned Wright—"ploddingly 'sincere' (Wright)"—in "In the Presence of Anthologies."

89. "Dover: Believing in Kings."

90. JD published four poems in the Vanderbilt University literary magazine, *The Gadfly*, between 1947 and 1949; his first appearance in a national-circulation literary journal was "The Shark at the Window" in the April–June 1951 *Sewanee Review*.

91. American poet (1900–68).

92. W. S. Graham.

93. (1884–1960), French poet, fiction writer, and dramatist.

94. Saint-John Perse was the pseudonym of French poet Alexis Saint-Léger Léger (1887–1975).

95. *Understanding Poetry: An Anthology for College Students*, revised edition (1950).

96. Poet-critic Blackmur discussed Lawrence in *The Double Agent* (1935). Blackmur edited two collections of poems by John Wheelright (1897–1940).

97. (1896–1974), anti-modernist British poet.

98. Wright was then married to Eleutheria Kardules, who called herself "Liberty."

99. In JD holograph. JD sent Wright samples of his advertising copy.

100. JD is referring to "At the Executed Murderer's Grave," which was collected in Wright's 1959 volume, *Saint Judas*. "A Poem about George Doty in the Death House" had been collected in Wright's first book, *The Green Wall* (1957), Volume 53 of the Yale Series of Younger Poets.

101. (1929–), American poet, anthologist, and editor.

102. *René Char's Poetry* (Rome: Editions De Luca, 1956), in which Wright had an essay on and translations of Char.

103. A central idea of the New Criticism, which was the prevalent literary-critical school of the 1950s. One of the major theorists of the New Criticism was Cleanth Brooks (1906–94), whose *The Well Wrought Urn: Studies in the Structure of Poetry* (1947) drew its title from Donne's "The Canonization."

104. Unidentified; possibly a pseudonym.

105. (1900–47).

106. (1911–84).

107. JD's translation of "Heads" by Becker appeared in the *American Poetry Review* (March/April 1983); his translation of "L'Ange" by Emié appeared in *Translations by American Poets,* edited by Jean Garrigue (1970).

108. JD's first collection, *Into the Stone,* was published in *Poets of Today VII* (1960).

109. Published in *Beloit Poetry Review* (Summer 1958).

110. This work in progress anticipates *Alnilam.*

111. Unlocated.

112. Explaining that he kept a notebook of favorite poems, Wright had sent JD a copy of H. R. Hays's translation of verse by Chilean poet Pablo Neruda (1904–73).

113. JD exaggerated his athletic accomplishments.

114. Poet, teacher, and editor Carolyn Kizer (1925–).

115. American poet and art critic (1909–); Rodman's *Conversations with Artists* was published in 1957.

116. Poet (1926–) who taught at the University of Washington.

117. Probably an allusion to Kingsley Amis's popular 1954 novel.

118. "Propeller," collected in Booth's *The Islanders* (1961).

119. Booth retained his penultimate statement but revised his final one:

> It's curious, here,
> wondering at the magnitude of such work,
> to think how finally diminished
>
> the size will seem, in place, and of how
> submerged its ultimate function will be.
> But even now, as if geared to a far interior
> impulse, it churns the flat light: as far
> from here its cast will turn against time,
> and turn dark, and it will move the sea.

120. "Five Poets," *Poetry* (May 1959), and "A Gold-Mine of Consciousness," *Poetry* (April 1959).

121. "The Human Power," July–September 1959.

122. "The Other" appeared in the March 1959 issue.

123. Humphrey Chimpden Earwicker, a central figure in James Joyce's *Finnegans Wake.*

124. Cowley (1898–1989), an influential man of letters, was an editorial consultant at Viking Press. Viking did not publish JD's book.

125. JD did not win the Lamont Poetry Selection award sponsored by The Academy of American Poets. The 1959 prize went to Donald Justice's *The Summer Anniversaries.*

126. Wesleyan University Press is in Middletown, Connecticut.

127. (1930–).

128. A. Alvarez (1929–), British critic and memoirist.

129. The indictment against Pound had been revoked in April 1958, and he had returned to Italy.

130. Wright annotated JD's salary figure with the words "Jesus Christ!"

131. "At the Executed Murderer's Grave" was dedicated to J.L.D.

132. American poet (1923–82). Most of JD's letters to Hugo have not been located.

133. American poet (1918–93) who taught at Bowdoin College.

134. "The Other."

135. "The Vegetable King," April–June 1959.

136. Booth held a Guggenheim Fellowship in 1958–59.

137. "The Other."

138. This poem was first published four years later in *The Sewanee Review* (July–September 1963).

139. "The Call" (Winter 1959–60). The poem was later printed in *Drowning With Others* as the first part of "The Owl King."

140. Unlocated clipping.

141. A JD fabrication that he was fond of repeating.

142. Narrator in Vladimir Nabokov's *Lolita*.

143. July–September 1959 issue.

144. (1886–1978), American poet who was editing the *Poets of Today* series for Scribners.

145. JD did not publish poetry in *The Kenyon Review* until Autumn 1959 or in *Virginia Quarterly Review* until Spring 1960.

146. The eight JD poems published in the July 1959 issue of *Poetry* were "The Game," "The Landfall," "The Signs," "The Enclosure," "The Performance," "The String," "Below the Lighthouse," and "Into the Stone."

147. "Dover: Believing in Kings" had won the Union League Civic and Arts Foundation Prize from *Poetry* magazine in 1958.

148. "The First Morning of Cancer," "The Red Bow," and "Dover: Believing in Kings" were omitted from *Into the Stone*.

149. Baro's *Northwind and Other Poems* appeared with collections by Donald Finkel and Walter Stone in *Poets of Today VI*.

150. In a letter also dated 27 May 1959, Wheelock assured JD that *Into the Stone* would be included in *Poets of Today VII*, though Wheelock asked JD to keep this information confidential until after 1 August 1959.

151. *The Sewanee Review* (April–June 1959).

152. *Drowning with Others* was published by Wesleyan University Press in 1962.

153. JD first read at the Poetry Center of the 92nd Street YM-YWHA in March 1960.

154. "Marin," which Booth collected as "Sea-Change." John Marin (1870–1953) was an American painter.

155. Hall was a member of the editorial board for poetry at Wesleyan University Press.

156. Probably "Mindoro, 1944" published by the *Paris Review* in its Autumn–Winter 1960 issue.

157. When "The Snow" was collected in *A Roof of Tiger Lilies*, Hall no longer made the sun "protrude," his "vampire" was transformed to "an old man," and his line "The sun has gone back to bed" was changed to "The sun has withdrawn itself." Hall retained the lines "the weight of the sun / presses the snow / on the pane of my window."

158. JD's "The Signs" includes the lines: "My brain has glowed, / Before my son showed form, / To pick a son from the dead, // Alive with Apollo's shape. / That hope shed a man of light. / I could feel how a woman's womb / Would flash like a brain, with his image."

159. JD had spent three days in mid-November 1959 with Wright and poet/editor Robert Bly (1926–) in New York City.

160. Not published, although "Notes on the Decline of Outrage" appeared in a Doubleday Dolphin Book, *South*, edited by Louis D. Rubin Jr. and Robert D. Jacobs (1961).

161. *The Country of a Thousand Years of Peace and Other Poems*, Merrill's 1959 collection.

162. Bly.

163. Carroll (1927–96), poet, editor, and anthologist, wrote influential reviews of

Dickey's work. Mona Van Duyn (1921–) won a National Book Award for Poetry in 1971 and served as Library of Congress Poetry Consultant in 1992–93.

164. Wright had reviewed *Poets of Today VI;* Rainer Maria Rilke (translated by M. D. Herter Norton), *The Lay of the Love and Death of Cornet Christopher Rilke;* and Vladimir Nabokov, *Poems.*

165. In his 1938 poem "The Composer," Auden writes:

> All the others translate: the painter sketches
> A visible world to love or reject;
> Rummaging into his living, the poet fetches
> The images out that hurt and connect,
>
> From Life to Art by painstaking adaption,
> Relying on us to cover the rift;
> Only your notes are pure contraption,
> Only your song is an absolute gift.

166. Bly had founded a press and journal called *The Fifties,* which subsequently became *The Sixties* and *The Seventies.*

167. *Into the Stone.*

168. Harcourt, Brace and World did not publish *Drowning with Others.*

169. The poem appeared in the Fall 1960 issue.

170. *Virginia Quarterly Review* (Spring 1961).

171. Robert Payne, editor, *White Pony: An Anthology of Chinese Poetry from the Earliest Times to Present Day* (1947; reprinted 1960).

172. (1923–), American novelist and nonfiction writer.

173. (1923–87), poet, founder and co-editor of *Choice,* and poetry editor for *The Nation* and *The Critic.*

174. Wright reviewed *Into the Stone* in "Shelf of New Poets," *Poetry* (December 1961).

175. JD's review of books by Anne Sexton (1928–74), Galway Kinnell (1927–), and three other poets appeared in "Five First Books," *Poetry* (February 1961).

176. "The Movement of Fish" was published in the 7 October 1961 *New Yorker;* "Goodbye to Serpents" appeared in the 21 September 1963 *New Yorker;* "Don Yearwood's Death in a Flow of Wind" and "The Called Fox" were not published under these titles.

177. At this time both Wright and Berryman taught at the University of Minnesota; Bly was running *Sixties* magazine and the Sixties Press from his farm near Madison, Minnesota.

178. First published as "For Robert Bhain Campbell" in *The Whole Motion* (1992). Campbell died at the age of twenty-nine in December 1940.

179. JD's first quote comes from "Farewell to Miles": "(I hope you will be happier where you go / Than you or we were here, and learn to know / What satisfactions there are.)" The stanza he admires is from "New Year's Eve":

> I remember: white fine flour everywhere whirled
> Ceaselessly, wheels rolled, a slow thunder boomed,
> And there were snowy men in the mill-world
> With sparkling eyes, light hair uncombed,
> And one of them was humming an old song,
> Sack upon sack grew portly, until strong
> Arms moved them on, by pairs,
> And then the bell clanged and they ran like hares.

Both poems are collected in Berryman's *The Dispossessed* (1948).

180. "The Suspect in Poetry or Everyman as Detective," October–December 1960, included a review of *The Sense of Movement* by Gunn.

181. Herbert Francis, "Atlantan's Collected Poems: Defiance and a Vision," *Atlanta Journal and Atlanta Constitution* (18 September 1969).

182. "Drowning with Others" appeared in the Fall 1960 *Partisan Review*, "Between Two Prisoners" appeared in the Autumn 1960 *Yale Review*, "The Change" appeared in the Winter 1961 *Kenyon Review*, and "The Suspect in Poetry or Everyman as Detective" appeared in the October–December 1960 *Sewanee Review*.

183. (1917–93), poet and critic who taught at the University of Michigan, Ann Arbor.

184. Doubleday did not publish *Drowning with Others*.

185. Part IV of "American Monologues" in Squires's *Where the Compass Spins*.

186. George Seferis (1900–71) and Odysseas Elytis (1911–96) were important figures in the revival of Greek poetry during the 1930s.

187. The review was "From Babel to Byzantium," *The Sewanee Review* (July–September 1957).

188. "Lying in a Hammock at a Friend's Farm in Pine Island, Minnesota," *Paris Review* (Summer/Fall 1961); later retitled "Lying in a Hammock at William Duffy's Farm in Pine Island, Minnesota."

189. Daniel G. Hoffman, "Between New Voice and Old Master" (Autumn 1960).

190. The Dickey family was solidly middle class.

191. Two JD poems, "Via Appia" and "The Twin Falls," appeared in the Spring 1961 issue of *Choice*. "Adam in Winter" was published in *Choice*, 2 (1962).

192. JD titled the collection *Helmets*.

POET AND TEACHER:
JULY 1961–AUGUST 1964

1. JD slightly alters the last line of William Butler Yeats's "A Dialogue of Self and Soul": "Everything we look upon is blest."

2. JD quotes from Dylan Thomas's "Fern Hill."

3. JD quotes from Walt Whitman's "Song of Myself."

4. *Contemporary American Poetry*, edited by Hall (1962), included two JD poems: "Hunting Civil War Relics at Nimblewill Creek" and "The Performance."

5. Probably "An Airstrip in Essex, 1960," collected in *A Roof of Tiger Lilies* (1964).

6. Probably "Self-Portrait, as a Bear," collected in *A Roof of Tiger Lilies*.

7. In July 1961 *The Sewanee Review* did not list its editors, though JD was probably referring to Lytle. JD continued writing reviews for *The Sewanee Review* through the April–June 1964 issue.

8. (1917–), professor at Yale University.

9. *Drowning with Others*, which Hall had edited for Wesleyan.

10. At the University of Michigan, Ann Arbor, where Hall was teaching.

11. (1906–68), novelist and critic.

12. Smith was manager of the book department of the Yale Co-op.

13. American poet and critic Louis Simpson (1923–).

14. Published as *Helmets*.

15. Georg Trakl (1887–1914), Austrian lyrical poet, and Pablo Neruda.

16. The note following the signature is in JD holograph.

17. (1912–94), poet William Everson, who took the name Brother Antoninus when he became a lay brother in the Dominican order of the Roman Catholic Church. Antoninus was living in San Francisco during the early 1960s.

18. In its April–June 1961 and July–September 1961 issues, *The Sewanee Review* printed an exchange of letters between JD and Brother Antoninus concerning JD's October–December 1960 review of Antoninus's *The Crooked Lines of God.*

19. Critic Leslie Fiedler (1917–) had reviewed Brother Antoninus's *The Residual Years* in the August 1948 *Partisan Review.*

20. "The Stillness at the Center of the Target" (July–September 1962) included a section on Winters's *Collected Poems.*

21. "A Note on the Poetry of John Logan," *The Sewanee Review* (April–June 1962), in which JD praises the spirit of Logan's religious verse.

22. In "Experience in Image, Sound, and Rhythm" (*Saturday Review,* 12 May 1962) James Schevill identifies JD as a poetic mystic; Schevill does not use the phrase "the new mysticism," nor does he identify JD as a leader of this movement.

23. Address added in holograph by JD.

24. JD's translations were not published in *The Sixties.*

25. Bly's daughter.

26. Unlocated.

27. (1842–1910), American philosopher and psychologist.

28. JD did not write an essay on Hill's work.

29. At Wesleyan University Press.

30. Five JD poems—"The Call," "On the Hill Below the Lighthouse," "The Performance," "Trees and Cattle," and "Walking on Water"—had been reprinted in Hall and Pack's *New Poets of England and America: Second Selection* published in 1962 by Meridian, not Meredith.

31. (1917–94), American fiction writer.

32. (1908–97), poet whose *Antennas of Silence* JD had reviewed in the November 1956 issue of *Poetry.*

33. Logan reviewed *Drowning with Others* in the December 1962–January 1963 issue of *The Critic.*

34. Probably "Kudzu," 18 May 1963, and "The Scarred Girl," 1 June 1963; but could be "Bums, on Waking," 7 September 1963; "Goodbye to Serpents," 21 September 1963; "Cherrylog Road," 12 October 1963; "Breath," 9 November 1963; "The Driver," 7 December 1963; or "The Ice Skin," 28 December 1963, all of which appeared in *The New Yorker.*

35. Five JD poems—"At Darien Bridge, Georgia," "In the Marble Quarry," "The Dusk of Horses," "The Beholders," and "The Poisoned Man"—were published under the title "Poems of North and South Georgia" in the 1 December 1962 issue of *The New Yorker.*

36. No part of "The Deliverer," an early version of *Deliverance,* was published.

37. John Simon, "More Brass than Enduring," *Hudson Review* (August 1962), and Thom Gunn, "Things, Voices, Minds," *The Yale Review* (October 1962).

38. Hall's poem "The Stump" was published in *A Roof of Tiger Lilies* (1964); JD quotes from Roethke's "Big Wind," collected in his *The Lost Son and Other Poems* (1948).

39. *The Branch Will Not Break* (1963).

40. American poet (1925–).

41. In JD holograph. Radcliffe Squires had sent JD a typescript for his *The Major Themes of Robert Frost* (1963).

42. JD reviewed Conrad Aiken's *The Morning Song of Lord Zero* in the December 1963 issue of *Poetry;* the "chronicle" is "First and Last Things" published in the February 1964 issue.

43. In a 23 March 1963 letter to Rago, JD proposed using "Jesse Shields" or "Boyd Thornton" as his pseudonyms. He apparently abandoned this plan.

44. Rago's wife, an artist.

45. Probably *A Round of Applause* (1962) by Scottish poet Norman MacCaig (1910–96).

46. Rago's poetry collection, *A Sky of Late Summer,* appeared in 1963.

47. "A Folk-Singer of the Thirties," "The Being," and "Why in London the Blind Are Saviors" were published together in the August 1963 *Poetry.*

48. Seager's 1953 novel.

49. British writer Ford (1873–1939) whose novels included *The Good Soldier* (1915); American fiction writer Roth (1933–) whose first novella and stories, *Goodbye, Columbus* (1959), had won the National Book Award.

50. Poet William Stafford (1914–93).

51. Kizer.

52. In JD holograph.

53. Hall had won a Guggenheim Fellowship for 1963.

54. Willard Lockwood, Director of Wesleyan University Press.

55. The dedication to Maxine Dickey was retained; all of the poems listed in this paragraph were printed in *Helmets,* which had 84 pages of text numbered from "9" to "93."

56. The Emily Balch Prize was awarded by *Virginia Quarterly Review* to JD's poem in 1962.

57. Wesleyan abandoned its proposed 500-copy limit for first printings of its poetry volumes. The first printing for *Helmets* consisted of 1,000 clothbound and 2,000 paperbound copies.

58. Editor Donald Hutter.

59. Probably *A Roof of Tiger Lilies,* Hall's 1964 collection.

60. May have included "Reincarnation," which first appeared with "The Firebombing" in *Two Poems of the Air* (Portland: Centicore, 1964).

61. Not published under this title.

62. 18 May 1963 issue.

63. Hall had given the Dickey family a copy of his children's book *Andrew the Lion Farmer* (1959).

64. Note is in JD holograph.

65. An Atlanta friend of JD who was a partial model for Lewis Medlock in *Deliverance.*

66. No JD volumes with these titles were published.

67. "Reincarnation" was published in the 7 March 1964 *New Yorker* and collected as "Reincarnation (I)" in *Buckdancer's Choice* (1965).

68. This project did not develop.

69. Ken Kipnis, a Reed College student, from whom JD was taking guitar lessons.

70. "First and Last Things," February 1964. JD does not mention Squires's Frost book in his discussion of Jeffers's final collection.

71. Squires's book on the American novelist and poet (1906–89) was titled *Frederic Prokosch* (1964).

72. "The Lifeguard" had been published in the 5 August 1961 *New Yorker* and collected in *Drowning with Others.* When it was reprinted in *Poems 1957–1967,* JD did not emend the last line of the last stanza:

> I wash the black mud from my hands.
> On a light given off by the grave
> I kneel in the quick of the moon
> At the heart of a distant forest
> And hold in my arms a child
> Of water, water, water.

73. Hall remained on the Wesleyan University Press editorial board.

74. Hall, who had resigned as *Paris Review* poetry editor, had invited JD to take his place on the journal.

75. *Paris Review* editor—not the patriarch of the Massachusetts Kennedy clan.

76. George Plimpton (1927–), a founder of *Paris Review*.

77. JD did not serve as poetry editor of *Paris Review*.

78. JD is alluding to the Emily Dickinson poem that begins "A narrow Fellow in the Grass." Its final stanza reads:

> But never met this Fellow
> Attended or alone
> Without a tighter breathing
> And Zero at the Bone—

79. Boatwright was editor of *Shenandoah*.

80. *Shenandoah* (Winter 1964).

81. Probably "The Firebombing," *The New Yorker* (May 1964).

82. A member of the English faculty at the University of Virginia.

83. JD was listed as an Advisory Editor on the masthead of *Shenandoah*.

84. (1929–), poet and founder of The Jargon Society, a small press specializing in poetry, art, photography, and fine printing.

85. President John F. Kennedy was assassinated on 22 November 1963.

86. (1964).

87. Published as *Buckdancer's Choice* by Wesleyan University Press in 1965.

88. The calligrapher was Monica Moseley Pincus.

89. JD's longtime friend, an Atlantan who was a partial model for Lewis Medlock in *Deliverance*.

90. "If the Night Could Get Up & Walk," the first part of "Two Pastorals for Samuel Palmer at Shoreham, Kent," collected in *In England's Green &* (1962).

91. (1935–), American poet.

92. (1929–), poet, translator, and literary critic who became one of JD's important commentators; later editor of the James Dickey Poetry Series for the University of South Carolina Press.

93. "Five Poets" (March 1963).

94. Howard's translation of the work of French novelist Julien Gracq (1910–) had been published by Braziller in 1959.

95. Howard had concluded his assessment of *Drowning with Others* with the following statement: "Dickey is a poet of process, rather than presences, in his apprehension of nature, and at his Orphic extreme he finds notes that suggest only Heraclitus before him."

96. Hall's *A Roof of Tiger Lilies* was published in New York by Viking and in London by André Deutsch.

97. *The Suspect in Poetry* appeared in 1964.

98. JD did not undertake this book.

99. Jacques de Spoelberch.

100. (1924–), British poet and translator.

101. "Facing Africa," which had appeared in the April 1961 *Encounter,* was JD's only appearance in the magazine. The poem was reprinted in *Encounters: An Anthology from the First Ten Years of Encounter Magazine,* edited by Stephen Spender, Irving Kristol, and Melvin J. Lasky (1963).

102. *The Concise Encyclopedia of English and American Poets and Poetry,* edited by Hall and Spender (1963).

103. Poet Frederick Seidel (1936–). During 1964 X. J. Kennedy (1929–) was succeeded by Tom Clark (1941–) as *The Paris Review*'s poetry editor.

104. (1919–88), San Francisco poet associated with the Beats and the Black Mountain group.

105. *Poetry* (August 1963).

106. *The Sewanee Review* (July–September 1963).

107. "A Folk-Singer of the Thirties," *Poetry* (August 1963).

108. *Poetry* (August 1963).

109. "Hunting Civil War Relics at Nimblewill Creek," *The Sewanee Review* (January–March 1961).

110. *Poetry* (July 1959).

111. Although reincarnation is a pervasive theme of *Buckdancer's Choice*, "Reincarnations" was not the title of a separate section of the book.

112. JD rather unfavorably reviewed Duncan's collection in "The Stillness at the Center of the Target," July–September 1962.

113. Hollander had joined the English faculty at Yale and was also serving as poetry editor for *Partisan Review*.

114. JD had reviewed Hollander's *Movie-Going* in "Ways and Means," *Shenandoah* (Autumn 1963).

115. "To my right, / In a field of sunlight between two pines, / The droppings of last year's horses / Blaze up in golden stones." These lines come from Wright's "Lying in a Hammock at William Duffy's Farm in Pine Island, Minnesota," originally published in *The Paris Review* (Summer/Fall 1961) and collected in *The Branch Will Not Break* (1963).

116. Bader was then directing the Hopwood Contests sponsored by the University of Michigan at Ann Arbor. During 1964 JD and Henry Rago served as the poetry judges.

117. All contestants for Hopwood Awards used pseudonyms. The winners for 1964 were:

Major Contest

Meryl S. Johnson (Ruth Kline)—$1,000

J. Michael Yates (R. F. McGurk)—$1,000

Trim Bissell (St. B)—$700

William D. Perkins (Leslie Dickerson)—$700

Minor Contest

Lynne Knight (Rebecca Keith)—$500

Albert J. Ammerman (Jean Bodin)—$500

118. American poet (1923–97).

119. JD did not review Levertov's *O Taste and See* (1964) or any other of her collections.

120. "The Stump," "Wells," "Assassin," " 'Internal and External Forms,' " and "The Grave, the Mine."

121. Louis Simpson won a 1964 Pulitzer Prize for his collection *At the End of the Open Road* (Wesleyan University Press, 1963).

122. *The Suspect in Poetry.*

123. Duncan's "Oriented by Instinct by Stars" appeared in the November 1964 issue of *Poetry.*

124. "The Fiend," *Partisan Review* (Spring 1965).

125. (1930–75), editor of *Critique* who was a member of the English Department at the University of Minnesota.

126. Allen Tate and Robert Kent were both in the English Department at the University of Minnesota.

127. "James Dickey and Other Good Poets," *Minnesota Review* (Summer 1963).

128. "Leonardo da Vinci," *The Renaissance:* "For the way to perfection is through a series of disgusts. . . ."

129. Probably "The Step-Son." See 28 February 1969 letter to James and Barbara Reiss.

130. Published in the April 1967 *Atlantic Monthly* as "May Day Sermon to the Women of Gilmer County by a Lady Preacher Leaving the Baptist Church" and collected in *Poems 1957–1967* as "May Day Sermon to the Women of Gilmer County, Georgia, by a Woman Preacher Leaving the Baptist Church."

131. Levertov was then on the editorial board of the Wesleyan poetry series.

132. Unlocated.

133. This project did not develop.

134. "Reincarnation," which was collected as "Reincarnation (II)" in *Poems 1957–1967.*

135. JD habitually exaggerated his athletic achievements.

136. Hilary Corke (1921–), a British poet and mineralogist.

137. Maxine, Christopher, and Kevin Dickey were visiting her mother in Nashville before the family's departure for California.

138. Robert Lescher was JD's first agent.

139. Maibelle Swift Dickey was an heir to the family-owned S.S.S. tonic company. Tucker Wayne & Co. was the Atlanta advertising agency that represented S.S.S., and Robert Schaefer was one of Tucker Wayne's executives. In 1963 JD had suggested that the agency use "Get that young blood feeling" to advertise the tonic. When the slogan became part of the S.S.S. campaign, JD asked to be paid, but he was not compensated for his idea.

140. Both *Two Poems of the Air* and *Helmets* were reviewed by X. J. Kennedy in "Joys, Griefs and 'All Things Innocent, Hapless, Forsaken,' " *New York Times Book Review* (23 August 1964).

141. King.

142. The Chattooga River in northeastern Georgia was a model for the Cahulawassee River in *Deliverance.*

MIDSTREAM:
SEPTEMBER 1964–JUNE 1968

1. Seager was awarded a Guggenheim Fellowship for 1966.

2. Seager's biography of Theodore Roethke, *The Glass House,* to which Beatrice Roethke raised objections, was published in 1968.

3. Seager's daughter.

4. Working title for Howard's 1967 collection, *The Damages.*

5. JD reviewed *Final Solutions* by Frederick Seidel in "First and Last Things," *Poetry* (February 1964).

6. Goldfinger was the title villain in the Ian Fleming novel (1959) and movie (1964).

7. Howard's translation of Jules Renard's *Natural Histories* was published by Horizon in 1966.

8. Published as *Untitled Subjects* in 1969.

9. Snodgrass, "In Praise of Robert Lowell" (3 December 1964).

10. Snodgrass, "The Last Poems of Theodore Roethke," *The New York Review of Books* (8 October 1964).

11. "Slave Quarters," which was published in the 14 August 1965 issue of *The New Yorker,* was revised for *Buckdancer's Choice.* JD had sent Wesleyan the typescript for the book in late 1964.

12. Bly published several collections with Harper & Row.

13. (1903–), American poet. Ghiselin's work was not published by Harper & Row.

14. "Barnstorming for Poetry," *New York Times Book Review*. The movie project did not develop.

15. Levertov.

16. The poems JD sent are no longer with his letter.

17. *Buckdancer's Choice* printed the version of "The Shark's Parlor" that appeared in the 30 January 1965 *New Yorker*.

18. "Dust" was published in *The Bulletin* [Sydney, Australia], 8 May 1965. Levertov did not accept the poem for *The Nation*.

19. Levertov's 1964 collection, *O Taste and See*, was not nominated for the National Book Award in Poetry. Nominees in the category included Ben Belitt, John Berryman, Jean Garrigue, Galway Kinnell, Robert Lowell, William Meredith, Theodore Roethke, and JD. Roethke won for *The Far Field*.

20. Levertov was married to novelist Mitchell Goodman.

21. *A Roof of Tiger Lilies*.

22. Levertov accepted "The Birthday Dream" for *The Nation* (27 September 1965).

23. William Rogers, *Wise Men Fish Here: The Story of Frances Steloff and the Gotham Book Mart* (1965).

24. *Vision and Rhetoric: Studies in Modern Poetry* (1960).

25. British poet (1912–).

26. This story-cycle by the American poet and fiction writer (1892–1944) was published in 1931.

27. JD wrote about the journals and diaries of W. N. P. Barbellion (Bruce Cummings, 1889–1919) in the January 1973 issue of *Mademoiselle*. In a Summer 1975 survey published in *Antaeus*, he chose *The Journal of a Disappointed Man* as one of the unjustly neglected books of the twentieth century.

28. Philip Lyman, manager of the Gotham Book Mart. This note is in JD holograph.

29. In JD holograph.

30. *The Suspect in Poetry*, which was published in boards (thin cardboard) and in paper wrappers, did not go into a second printing.

31. In "A Way to Say What a Man Can See" (13 February 1965), Robert D. Spector dismisses JD's *The Suspect in Poetry* and praises many of the poets JD attacks, including John Ciardi (1916–86).

32. These two words added in JD holograph.

33. *The New Yorker* (24 February 1962).

34. *The New Yorker* (12 October 1963).

35. No anthology edited by Jarrell was published; he was struck by an automobile and died on 14 October 1965.

36. Jarrell's poem had appeared in *Virginia Quarterly Review* (Spring 1965).

37. JD was visiting with his parents in Atlanta before teaching for a month at the University of Wisconsin, Milwaukee. Maxine Dickey and the two children had remained in Northridge.

38. Essays by JD on Christopher Smart, Gerard Manley Hopkins, Matthew Arnold, Francis Thompson, and William Carlos Williams appeared in *Master Poems of the English Language*, edited by Oscar Williams (1966).

39. Director Bill Hale planned to make a movie, *The Celebration*, based on JD's poem of that title. Mel Sloan collaborated with JD on the screenplay, but the project did not develop.

40. This reference is to guitar playing.

41. Michael Allin, a student at San Fernando Valley State College, had become a close friend of the Dickey family.

42. Widow of Theodore Roethke, who had died on 1 August 1963.

43. JD's "Theodore Roethke" had appeared in the November 1964 issue.

44. Kizer.

45. (1923–); literary critic who was then English Department Chairman at Hollins College. Rubin had offered JD a teaching position at Hollins for the 1966–67 academic year.

46. This sentence and closing are in JD holograph. Rubin was editor of the *Hollins Critic*.

47. Editor at Houghton Mifflin.

48. Paul Brooks, Editor in Chief of the General Books Division, Houghton Mifflin.

49. JD served as poet in residence at the University of Wisconsin, Madison, February–March 1966.

50. On 19 November Spoelberch replied: "As for my unpronounceable name, think of a spool of thread and a bear with a de before it, and you not only have the name licked but also correctly pronounced."

51. (1903–82) Librarian of Congress; in a 23 December 1965 letter, Mumford had offered JD appointment as Consultant in Poetry to the Library of Congress beginning in September 1966.

52. Roy P. Basler, Director of the Reference Division, Library of Congress.

53. JD had unfavorably reviewed Sexton's *To Bedlam and Part Way Back* (1960) in *Poetry* (February 1961) and *All My Pretty Ones* (1962) in the *New York Times Book Review*, 28 April 1963. The two poets first met in December 1965 following a JD reading at Syracuse University.

54. Howard had sent JD a prepublication text of "On James Dickey," which was published in the Summer 1966 *Partisan Review*.

55. The Melville Cane Award for *Buckdancer's Choice*.

56. Howard was awarded a Guggenheim Fellowship in 1966.

57. Of the Lordly & Dame lecture agency.

58. In JD holograph with arrow pointing toward address.

59. This remark is usually attributed to Samuel Goldwyn.

60. On "Knickerbocker on the Lake" letterhead.

61. JD was again teaching a summer class at the University of Wisconsin, Milwaukee.

62. *The Suspect in Poetry* was not reprinted.

63. Librarian, Springbrook High School, Silver Spring, Maryland.

64. Seager's first wife.

65. JD's review-essay—which was also a memoir of Seager—was published by *The Atlantic Monthly* as "The Greatest American Poet" in November 1968.

66. "May Day Sermon."

67. Seager did not review JD's collection.

68. A former student whom Seager married in 1968.

69. Honorary Consultants in American Letters for 1967–68 included Conrad Aiken (beginning July 1, 1968), Katherine Garrison Chapin, JD (beginning July 1, 1968), Richard Eberhart, Ralph Ellison, MacKinlay Kantor, Marianne Moore, Howard Nemerov, Katherine Anne Porter, Robert Penn Warren, John Hall Wheelock, and Reed Whittemore.

70. British poet (1878–1967) who had served since 1930 as England's Poet Laureate.

71. Five of JD's poems—"Blood," "Diabetes," "Venom," "The Cancer Match," and "Pine: Taste, Touch and Sight"—were published in the June 1969 issue of *Poetry*.

72. Berry (1934–) had reviewed *Helmets* in the November 1964 issue of *Poetry*. JD's review of Hazel's *Poems 1951–1961* appeared in *The Sewanee Review* (April–June 1964). Berry's letter of response to JD's review was printed in the July–September 1964 *Sewanee Review*.

73. Donald W. Baker's review appeared in the March 1968 issue.

74. Benedikt (1935–) did not write about JD's work, but Lieberman (1935–) became one of JD's principal commentators.

75. American poet born in Germany (1924–).

76. Christopher Dickey was in France under the sponsorship of Schoolboys Abroad.

77. Henry de Montherlant (1896–1972), French novelist, dramatist, and essayist.

78. Terry Miller had property in West Virginia where he and JD hunted.

79. Val Syerson, Maxine Dickey's father.

80. The quotation from Wolfe's novella " 'I Have a Thing to Tell You' " reads: "Something has spoken to me in the night, burning the tapers of the waning year; something has spoken in the night; and told me I shall die, I know not where."

81. The quotation is from Blake's *Notebook* (published in facsimile in 1973).

82. *Babel to Byzantium: Poets and Poetry Now,* published by Farrar, Straus and Giroux in 1968.

83. Bly had protested Farrar, Straus and Giroux's publication of *Babel to Byzantium* because the volume reprinted material first collected in *The Suspect in Poetry,* which was still in print.

84. Arthel Lane "Doc" Watson (1923–), well-known folk guitarist.

85. "The Lord in the Air," *The New Yorker* (19 October 1968).

86. These lines were revised before the poem was published in the November 1968 *Harper's Magazine.*

87. "The Worldly Mystic," *Hudson Review* (Autumn 1967).

88. Davidson (1857–1909) was a British poet. JD quotes the final lines of "A Ballad in Blank Verse of the Making of a Poet" collected in his *Ballads & Songs* (1898).

89. This word is in JD holograph.

90. (1904–72), British poet, who succeeded Masefield as England's Poet Laureate.

91. Editor of *South Florida Review,* a campus publication of the University of South Florida. Jaworski had asked Dickey for poems and for a statement to use in publicity material for Dickey's impending campus visit.

92. Dr. Martin Luther King Jr. had been assassinated in Memphis, Tennessee.

93. No *Choice* review of *Poems 1957–1967* has been located.

94. Senator Robert F. Kennedy, a presidential candidate, had been assassinated in Los Angeles.

UNIVERSITY OF SOUTH CAROLINA AND *DELIVERANCE:*
SEPTEMBER 1968–JUNE 1970

1. (1897–1970), American poet.

2. The Dickeys moved to Columbia, S.C., in August 1968 in preparation for his joining the University of South Carolina faculty as poet-in-residence and Professor of English the following January. During the Fall term he fulfilled contractual obligations to deliver the Franklin Foundation Lectures at the Georgia Institute of Technology in Atlanta and in December 1968 spent two weeks teaching at Washington University in St. Louis.

3. JD was a member of the panel to award the Pulitzer Prize for Poetry for 1968. The award that year was presented to *Of Being Numerous* by George Oppen (1908–84).

4. Wilbur was on the editorial board for the Wesleyan University Press poetry series.

5. *The Eye-Beaters, Blood, Victory, Madness, Buckhead and Mercy.*

6. JD had enduring regard for Warren, and they became warm friends.

7. The second part of "Diabetes," *Poetry* (June 1969). "Under Buzzards" was dedicated to Warren.

8. The contract, dated 11 November 1968, for two works—*The Eye-Beaters, Blood, Victory, Madness, Buckhead and Mercy* and *The Indian Maiden*—included a $25,000 advance. "The Indian Maiden," projected as a book-length poem, was not published and does not survive in draft.

9. JD was apparently misdiagnosed; he was subsequently assured that he did not have diabetes.

10. Of the Department of Modern Languages, Southeastern Massachusetts Technological Institute.

11. "Boutlare" is a secretarial mistranscription for French poet Charles-Pierre Baudelaire (1821–67). Other writers mentioned here include André Frénaud (1907–93), French poet; Richard Dehmel (1863–1920), German poet; Gottfried Benn (1886–1956), German poet and essayist; and Günter Eich (1902–72), German poet and writer of radio plays.

12. Of the English Department, Miami University, Oxford, Ohio. The Reisses had recorded and edited the material published by Doubleday as *Self-Interviews* in 1970.

13. In a 2 June 1924 letter, American poet Robinson (1869–1935) wrote: "I have also been reading the Old Testament, a most bloodthirsty and perilous book for the young. Jehovah is beyond a doubt the worst character in fiction." *Selected Letters of Edwin Arlington Robinson*, introduction by Ridgely Torrence (1940).

14. *Falling* was first printed as the final section of *Poems 1957–1967*.

15. Unpublished; drafts for this poem are at Washington University Libraries.

16. JD's literary agent.

17. (1910–85), poet and translator; Boylston Professor of Rhetoric at Harvard University.

18. "A Memoir," *The Collected Short Prose of James Agee,* edited by Fitzgerald (1968).

19. Macdonald (1906–82) was a journalist and literary critic.

20. Dudley Fitts (1903–68), who had been Fitzgerald's teacher at Choate, was his cotranslator of plays by Euripides and Sophocles.

21. Fitzgerald and his wife, Sally Fitzgerald, had been friends of O'Connor's (1925–64) and were editing posthumous collections of her work.

22. (1919–), Professor of Modern English Literature at University College, London.

23. In the letters section of the December 1968 *Atlantic Monthly* Kermode and such other writers as Howard Nemerov, W. D. Snodgrass, Stanley Kunitz, Robert Bly, Denise Levertov, William Stafford, Kenneth Burke, Malcolm Cowley, and X. J. Kennedy mostly admired JD's essay but also disagreed with his characterization of Roethke as America's greatest poet. A letter from Beatrice Roethke denied JD's contention that she had interfered with Allan Seager's writing of his Roethke biography and objected to JD's portrayal of Roethke's character. Kermode's letter read in part: "I don't think Theodore Roethke was the greatest American poet, but I like James Dickey's way of talking about him, . . . and the passage about lying and poetry is well done. It *is* possible to talk sense about poetry and poets without using the dialect of the graduate school, . . . and it will have to be our business to see that the thousands of critics we are turning out of the schools understand this."

24. One of the quotations from Blake that Kermode used as an epigraph for *Romantic Image* read: "If the Spectator could enter into these Images in his Imagination, approaching them on the Fiery Chariot of his Contemplative Thought . . . or could make a Friend & Companion of one of these Images of wonder . . . then would he arise from his Grave, then would he meet the Lord in the Air & then he would be happy." JD's poem "The Lord in the Air" appeared in *The New Yorker,* 19 October 1968.

25. *Wallace Stevens* appeared in 1960, *Puzzles and Epiphanies* in 1962, *The Sense of an Ending* in 1967, and *Continuities* in 1968.

26. Secretarial mistyping for George Santayana (1863–1952), Harvard poet and aesthetician.

27. British poet (1867–1900).

28. The story's title is "The Dying of Francis Donne."

29. Vladimir Nabokov (1899–1977), Russian-born American writer.

30. Unlocated.

31. Managing Editor, *Playboy.*

32. Paul Carroll's interview with Beat poet Ginsberg (1926–97) appeared in the April 1969 *Playboy.*

33. Robie Macauley (1919–95) was fiction editor at *Playboy.* No JD fiction appeared in *Playboy.*

34. (1906–), American poet and man of letters, with whom JD had a warm friendship.

35. (1970). JD did not provide a statement for the dust jacket, but he did write a foreword, "The Total Act," for the 1991 third printing.

36. *The Seamless Web* was dedicated to American novelist Josephine Herbst (1892–1969).

37. Published in 1966.

38. (1908–77), literary biographer and critic, who was a professor of English at the University of California, Berkeley.

39. A collection of essays that appeared in 1968.

40. Schorer's biography had been published in 1961.

41. A member of the Department of German and Russian at Oberlin College. Friebert had invited JD to contribute poetry to a new literary journal called *Field.* In his letter he listed potential contributors and invited JD to be photographed with other writers in a field of bathtubs.

42. The sense of the sentence requires "I do not have a good deal of regard for them."

43. JD refers to poets Gary Snyder (1930–), William Stafford, Robert Bly, W. S. Merwin, Adrienne Rich (1929–), Günter Eich, Karl Krolow (1915–), Pedro Salinas (1891–1951), Donald Hall, Louis Simpson, James Wright, and Ian Hamilton Finlay (1925–).

44. Secretarial mistyping of *crises.*

45. (1901–87), American novelist and essayist.

46. (1962).

47. American fiction writer Katherine Anne Porter, British fiction writer and playwright W. Somerset Maugham (1874–1965), and American literary critic Edmund Wilson.

48. Born in 1894, Cummings had died on 3 September 1962. JD introduced him at a February 1962 reading at the Poetry Center, 92nd Street YM-YWHA.

49. *Good-bye Wisconsin* (1928).

50. (1904–79), literary critic and English Professor at Columbia University. *Selected Letters of E. E. Cummings,* edited by Dupee and George Stade, was published in 1969; Dupee's "*The King of the Cats*" and *Other Remarks on Writers and Writing* had been published in 1965.

51. "Memories of James Agee" was collected in "*The King of the Cats*" *and Other Remarks on Writers and Writing.*

52. (1894–1977), poet, novelist, and critic. His E. A. Robinson biography, *Where the Light Falls,* had been published in 1965. Smith had written JD about his review of Louis O. Coxe's *Edwin Arlington Robinson: The Life of Poetry* (*New York Times Book Review,* 18 May 1969), in which JD or Coxe had failed to credit Smith with the phrase "Wrecked Empire" in describing the Robinson family. Smith also invited JD to submit a poem—which would meet Smith's "quantitative standard of greatness"—to be treated in a revised edition of his

Pattern and Variation. This projected revised edition of *Pattern and Variation* did not appear.

53. "The Sheep Child" was first published in the *Atlantic Monthly* (August 1966).

54. Writer Elizabeth Janeway (1913–), who was married to economist Eliot Janeway (1913–93), had been, like JD, a supporter of Senator Eugene McCarthy in the 1968 presidential campaign. The Democratic nomination went to Vice President Hubert Humphrey who was defeated in the general election by Republican Richard Nixon.

55. Senator Vance Hartke, Democrat from Indiana.

56. (1909–), American poet, art critic, and travel writer.

57. (1927–), avant-garde American poet.

58. No book with this title was published. JD's essay "The Self as Agent" was published in *The Great Ideas Today 1968* by Encyclopaedia Britannica in 1968 and was collected by JD in *Sorties,* as was "The Greatest American Poet: Theodore Roethke."

59. Jorge Luis Borges (1899–1986) was an Argentinian short-story writer and poet.

60. Octavio Paz (1914–98), Mexican poet and critic; in 1990 he won the Nobel Prize for Literature.

61. Yevgeny Yevtushenko (1933–), Russian poet.

62. Andrey Voznesensky (1933–), Russian poet.

63. Ponge (1899–1988), Bonnefoy (1923–), Enzensberger (1929–), Eugenio Montale, Giuseppe Ungaretti, Salvatore Quasimodo, Umberto Saba (1883–1957), Cernuda (1902–63), and Aleixandre (1898–1984).

64. Rodman did not produce an anthology of world poetry after 1949, though his travel memoir, *South America of the Poets,* appeared in 1970.

65. Rodman's *Death of the Hero* (1964) treated the death of Sir Frederick Banting, the discoverer of insulin.

66. (1919–), American fiction writer and member of the Brown University faculty.

67. No statement by JD appears on the dust jacket of Cassill's 1968 novel *La vie passionée of Rodney Buckthorne.*

68. Cassill recalled, in a 15 December 1998 letter to Matthew J. Bruccoli:

> About Tiny Alice and her cry: Within the year before I was with my friends in Utah, I had seen a Broadway play with the titillating title *Tiny Alice.* The subject matter included the attempt of some lesbians to bring out a woman who had heretofore been straight. At the denouement of one act (or scene) this woman is grabbed from behind as she passes through a doorway and, being so taken, emits a piercing yowl, obviously intended to be a submissive orgasmic yielding to the assault. I remember it as a bit of highly effective theater. During the weeks after I saw and heard this, I used to emit it on a few selective occasions with memorable effect. I don't remember just when Peter and Jim may have heard me let go. Surely some time when I was drinking with them or traversing the corridor of the dormitory we shared.
>
> To tell the truth it was a hair raising shriek. Like the war cry of Menelaus maybe? Surely it offended as many people as it entertained.

69. JD recalled his Utah writers' conference experiences in "Open Letter to the Open World About Verlin Cassill," *December: A Magazine of the Arts and Opinion,* 23, nos. 1/2 (1981).

70. *Walking to Sleep: New Poems and Translations* (1969).

71. The 1970 Pulitzer Prize for a volume of poetry published in 1969 went to Richard Howard's *Untitled Subjects.*

72. Walsh's review of collections by Wilbur, Daniel Berrigan, Anne Sexton, Tom

Clark, Edgar Simmons, and Adrien Stoutenburg appeared in the 27 July 1969 *Washington Post Book World*.

73. Tom Clark; popular poet McKuen (1933–).

74. "Dodwells Road (*Cummington, Massachusetts*)"—Part III of "Running."

75. Son of critic Leslie Fiedler. Eric Fiedler had sent JD a mimeographed manifesto on green paper.

76. This book was not published.

77. Mike Steen's *A Look at Tennessee Williams*, which included reminiscences of and tributes to the playwright, had been published in 1969.

78. Editor, *Esquire*.

79. Heavyweight champion who had changed his name to Muhammad Ali in 1964 when he became a Black Muslim. In 1967 he was stripped of his title when he refused induction into the U.S. Army. The statement that JD signed, along with 104 other well-known people, read, "We believe that Muhammad Ali, Heavyweight Champion of the World, should be allowed to defend his title." It appeared in the November 1969 *Esquire*.

80. One of the fiction editors at *Esquire*.

81. Arnold Gingrich (1903–76), editor in chief of *Esquire*.

82. JD's statement in "The Challenge of the Seventies" (*Esquire*, December 1969) includes this declaration: "The greatest challenge America faces in the Seventies—or any other time—is to find a way to create a valid emotional life for people."

83. *Esquire* did not print a pre-publication excerpt from *Deliverance*.

84. Victoria J. White, an undergraduate at the University of North Carolina, Chapel Hill, who had asked JD to read and comment on her poetry. She apparently did not reply to JD's letter.

85. Designer at Houghton Mifflin, who was working on the *Deliverance* jacket.

86. The final jacket for the first American edition was credited to Paul Bacon Studios. It had a stylized blue eye in a round green peephole covered by black, leaf-shaped silhouettes; the title and author's name were in the same green as the peephole.

87. (1937–), American poet then living in Greenwich Village.

88. Bly had published his attack on JD's poetry in "*Buckdancer's Choice* [The Collapse of James Dickey]," *The Sixties* (Spring 1967).

89. (1922–89), professor at Columbia University and author of *Voyager: A Life of Hart Crane* (1969).

90. Simpson's review appeared in the 13 July 1969 *Washington Post Book World*.

91. Associate Director of Information, Freedoms Foundation at Valley Forge, Pennsylvania.

92. "Looking for the Buckhead Boys," *Atlantic Monthly* (October 1969).

93. A drugstore mentioned in the poem.

94. The *Atlantic Monthly* did not publish a letter from Mason.

95. Lowell had agreed to appear in Encyclopaedia Britannica's documentary movie on JD, *Lord, Let Me Die But Not Die Out* (1970).

96. The movie version of *Deliverance*, with a screenplay by JD, was made by Warner Brothers in 1972. It was directed by John Boorman and featured Jon Voight as Ed Gentry, Burt Reynolds as Lewis Medlock, Ronny Cox as Drew Ballinger, and Ned Beatty as Bobby Trippe. JD played a cameo role as the Southern sheriff.

97. An Atlanta friend of JD and King.

98. King did not serve as a hired consultant for the movie.

99. Unlocated.

100. (1928–), poet who was also poetry editor for the *Atlantic Monthly* and director of Atlantic Monthly Press.

101. (1970). JD's statement read: "Peter Davison's quiet, deep poems are among the

best being written. Any thoughtful reader will certainly be moved by his clear, unpretentious writing, his imaginative participation in life, his passionate balance."

102. Robert Manning. "Two Days in September" appeared in the February 1970 issue.

103. L. E. Sissman (1928–76), poet and advertising executive.

104. Of Westbury, New York.

105. Frank O'Connor (1903–66), Irish short-story writer.

106. Part of *Lord, Let Me Die But Not Die Out* was filmed in Lowell's apartment.

107. JD had asked Lowell to be his literary executor.

108. Widow of poet Winfield Townley Scott (1910–68), whose *Exiles and Fabrications* had been published in 1961.

109. (1928–), literary critic and professor at the College of William and Mary.

110. A collection of essays published in 1961.

111. In the July–September 1959 issue of *The Sewanee Review*.

112. (1927–), vice president and editor in chief of Hallmark Cards.

113. Donaldson's *Poet in America: Winfield Townley Scott* appeared in 1972.

114. (1969).

115. JD was beginning work on what became *Sorties*.

116. (1907–73), publisher and editor of *The American Scholar*.

117. Power's novel was published in 1950.

118. (1929–), professor at SUNY, Stony Brook, and Kafka scholar.

119. (1887–1959), British poet, essayist, and translator of Kafka.

120. Manager of Public Relations, Hallmark Cards Incorporated, Kansas City. JD had agreed to serve as a national judge for the Kansas City Poetry Contests, which awarded Hallmark Honor Prizes. He was paid $50 for judging the entries.

121. *The Eye-Beaters.*

122. The title of Williams's 1966 anthology is *Master Poems of the English Language.*

123. "Theodore Roethke: The Greatest American Poet," *Atlantic Monthly* (November 1968).

124. *Deliverance* appeared on the best-seller lists of the *New York Times* for twenty-six weeks between 12 April and 4 October 1970. Between 24 April and 14 June the novel reached third place, its highest ranking.

125. "Exchanges" took the form of a dialogue with early twentieth-century poet American Joseph Trumbull Stickney (1874–1904); the poem was published in *Harvard Bulletin* (6 July 1970) and reprinted in the *Atlantic Monthly* (September 1970).

126. Edward Dahlberg (1900–77), American fiction writer.

127. The collection of aphorisms was published as *Reasons of the Heart* (1965).

128. "An Exchange of Letters, Edward Dahlberg and Herbert Read," edited by Reginald C. Terry, *The Malahat Review* (January 1969).

129. JD's letters to Bunting are unlocated.

130. On 8 August 1969 Polanski's wife, actress Sharon Tate, and four other people had been murdered at the Polanskis' Bel Air mansion by members of Charles Manson's cult.

131. Probably *An Ear in Bartram's Tree* (1969).

132. JD's statement was not published by *Esquire*.

133. Williams was in England.

134. (1929–92), writer whose best-known book is *A Fan's Notes* (1968).

135. JD's statement appeared on the back cover of the Pocket paperback: "Written with brilliance and insight. . . . No one who has ever read it can forget it."

136. A movie version of *A Fan's Notes* was produced in 1972 by Coquihala Films, a Canadian subsidiary of Warner Brothers. Exley did not write the screenplay.

137. (1969) by Philip Roth.

138. (1921–), American poet and editor.

139. *The Voice That Is Great Within Us: American Poetry of the Twentieth Century* (1970). The anthology includes four poems by JD: "The Movement of Fish," "Fence Wire," "The Driver," and "The Celebration."

140. *Appendix A* was published in 1963 and *After the Stranger: Imaginary Dialogues with Camus* in 1965.

141. The dust jacket of Carruth's anthology carried endorsements from Karl Shapiro, Wendell Berry, Adrienne Rich, and William Stafford. It did not print a statement by JD.

142. "Root-light, or the Lawyer's Daughter," *The New Yorker* (8 November 1969).

143. JD had been commissioned by *Life* magazine to cover the lift-off of Apollo 7 from Cape Kennedy. His essay "A Poet Witnesses a Bold Mission" appeared in the 1 November 1968 issue. Two JD poems inspired by the Apollo missions were published in *Life* during 1969: "For the First Manned Moon Orbit" in the 10 January issue, and "The Moon Ground" in the 4 July issue. Both were later collected in *Eye-Beaters*. The Apollo 11 astronauts were Neil A. Armstrong, Edwin E. Aldrin Jr., and Michael Collins.

144. Wright had married Edith Anne Runk in 1967.

145. Bly.

146. Student at the Portsmouth Priory School, Portsmouth, Rhode Island, and son of William F. Buckley Jr. (1925–), conservative commentator and editor of *The National Review* (1925–).

147. During the October 1968 lift-off of Apollo 7.

148. "In Memory of W. B. Yeats" (1939).

149. Buckley occasionally broadcast *Firing Line* from Columbia, South Carolina.

150. The mother of William F. Buckley Jr. maintained a home in Camden, South Carolina.

151. Christopher Dickey had married Susan Tuckerman; their son, James Bayard Tuckerman Dickey—called "Tucky"—was born in the summer of 1970.

152. (1920–93), liberal commentator and literary critic.

153. "Tribute to an American Poet," June 1970.

154. "Edwin Arlington Robinson: The Many Truths," JD's introduction to Zabel's *Selected Poems of Edwin Arlington Robinson* (1965), was collected in *Babel to Byzantium*.

155. Howe had published his *Thomas Hardy* in 1967.

156. Howe reviewed Carlos Baker's *Hemingway: A Life Story* in the May 1969 *Harper's*.

157. *Self-Interviews*.

158. Carruth did not publish a collection of his reviews.

159. Carruth's assessment of *Wodwo* (1967) by Hughes (1930–98) appeared in the September 1968 issue.

160. Carruth did not publish a large collection of his poems at this time.

161. "Camden Town" was in the Spring 1970 issue.

162. World War II training plane.

163. (1910–), American poet, fiction writer, and composer.

164. Daniel Halpern (1945–), editor in chief of The Ecco Press.

165. (1923–), composer.

166. (1954).

167. (1949).

168. (1898–1981), British novelist, travel writer, and memoirist.

169. Halpern published the first issue of *Antaeus* in 1970.

170. Nothing by JD appeared in either *Partisan Review* or *Modern Occasions* during 1970.

171. Lewis Mumford was awarded the 1970 Gold Medal for achievement in Belles Lettres.

172. " 'Resurrection for a Little While,' " 23 March 1970.

173. *The Eye-Beaters.*

174. Kallman (1921–75), Simic (1938–), and Taylor (1920–) all had books published in Howard's Braziller Poetry Series.

175. JD served as *Esquire* poetry editor from January 1971 through August 1977.

176. A. R. Ammons (1926–), American poet.

CELEBRITY:
JULY 1970–NOVEMBER 1980

1. (1934–), novelist, who was fiction editor for *Esquire.*

2. See JD's 23 March 1963 letter to Henry Rago. No poetry by Jesse Shields is in the *Esquire* files at the Lilly Library, Indiana University.

3. (1908–).

4. JD holograph note in margin: "(yes; it is)." Mary Cantwell was an editor at *Mademoiselle.*

5. "The Poet Tries to Make a Kind of Order: A 'Self-Interview' with James Dickey" (September 1970). Cantwell's memoir *Speaking with Strangers* (1998) includes material on JD.

6. This paragraph is in JD holograph.

7. Vice president at Warner Brothers.

8. For *Deliverance.*

9. Screenwriter.

10. Geoffrey Norman, "*Playboy* Interview: James Dickey" (November 1973).

11. No excerpts from the screenplay were printed in magazines; JD's complete screenplay was published in 1982.

12. Unidentified; JD adds in holograph "will send later—".

13. Sorrells's "The Amputation" was published in the January 1971 issue; Berryman's "Washington in Love" and "Tampa Stomp" appeared in the April 1971 issue, and his "The Form" appeared in the May 1971 issue.

14. Unidentified.

15. Poet and member of the English faculty at the University of Illinois, Urbana-Champaign. His *Achievement of James Dickey: A Comprehensive Selection of His Poems with a Critical Introduction* was published in 1968.

16. Daniel Alpert, Dean of the Graduate College, University of Illinois, Urbana-Champaign.

17. Lieberman's *Unassigned Frequencies: American Poetry in Review (1964–77)* appeared in 1977.

18. Editor of *Yale Review.*

19. Boorman (1933–) produced and directed *Deliverance.* He received Golden Globe and Academy Award nominations as best director of 1973, JD was nominated in the screenwriting category for the Golden Globe, and the movie was nominated for both awards in the Best Motion Picture category.

20. The book described here was published as *Sorties* in 1971.

21. This project developed into *Alnilam* published in 1987.

22. Published as *Stolen Apples* in 1971. Anthony Kahn received credit as JD's co-translator.

23. The second paragraph was published in Harold T. P. Hayes's "Editor's Notes" column, *Esquire* (January 1971), 162.

24. No poem by Richard Howard was published by *Esquire* in 1971.

25. On letterhead printed with JD's name and home address.

26. No review of *Self-Interviews* appeared in the *New York Times* or in the *New York Times Book Review.*

27. For *Untitled Subjects.*

28. (1905–78), writer best known for her light verse.

29. Howard acted on JD's recommendation in *Preferences: 51 American Poets Choose Poems From Their Own Work and From the Past* (1974).

30. Corman (1924–) founded the journal *Origin;* Shiffert (1916–) was highly influenced by Japanese and Chinese poetry.

31. Heavyweight boxing contender, whose 26 October 1970 championship fight with Muhammad Ali in Atlanta was stopped in the third round to save Quarry from further punishment. He never won the title.

32. 1935 novel, which JD probably read in the Armed Services Edition.

33. No poetry by Prokosch was published by *Esquire* during the 1970s.

34. "A Poem for Breakfast" by Holloway (1920–) was published in the April 1971 *Esquire.* Brotherson has not been identified.

35. *Esquire* published "The Title of the Poet" by Robert Graves (1895–1985) in the March 1972 issue.

36. An omnibus review by Barton Midwood in the December 1970 *Esquire* described *Deliverance* as "a diagrammatic metaphor for the homosexual psyche" and attacked the novel for its "idiotic" characters and plotting: "How much longer can the author carry on like this?"

37. "Bimini," an excerpt from *Islands in the Stream* (1970), was published in the October 1970 *Esquire.*

38. "Swimming Last Summer" by Pastan (1932–) was published in the April 1971 issue.

39. These four lines are in JD holograph.

40. Of Columbus, Ohio.

41. (1934–), American poet.

42. On letterhead printed with JD's name and home address.

43. No poem by Strand appeared in *Esquire* during the 1970s.

44. "dm'd (Bollingen!)" inserted in JD holograph.

45. Donald Gallup, librarian at Yale University.

46. Mona Van Duyn and Richard Wilbur were awarded the Bollingen Prize in 1971.

47. On letterhead printed with JD's name and home address.

48. Wright's *Collected Poems* was published by Wesleyan in 1971. JD's statement read: "James Wright is one of the few authentic visionary poets writing today. Unlike many others, James Wright's visions are authentic, profound, and beautiful. Moreover, even among visionaries he is rare, for he is a visionary not with an unearthly or heavenly vision, but a human vision. He is a seer with astonishing compassion for human beings. We are lucky to have James Wright among us."

49. JD took no legal action against Bly.

50. "Old Dog in the Ruins of the Graves at Arles" appeared in the February 1971 *Esquire.*

51. On letterhead printed with JD's name and home address.

52. Williams's letter apparently supported Midwood's attack on *Deliverance.* The letter was not printed in *Esquire.*

53. Editor at *Time* magazine.

54. Kurt Vonnegut Jr. (1922–), American fiction writer whose best-selling *Slaughterhouse-Five* had been published in 1969.

55. Willie Morris (1934–99), Mississippi writer and editor of *Harper's*, who was a friend of JD's.

56. JD did not remain on the wagon.

57. *Deliverance*, Saul Bellow's *Mr. Sammler's Planet*, Shirley Hazzard's *The Bay of Noon*, John Updike's *Bech: A Book*, and Eudora Welty's *Losing Battles* were nominated for the 1971 National Book Award for fiction; *Mr. Sammler's Planet* won.

58. Martin's novel was not published.

59. Early title for *Alnilam*.

60. "For the Death of Vince Lombardi," *Esquire* (September 1971).

61. (1924–97), author of *Home from the Hill* (1958).

62. Frazier retained the heavyweight championship in a unanimous fifteen-round decision.

63. (1938–), American fiction writer and poet.

64. On letterhead printed with JD's name and home address.

65. Oates's 1970 collection, *Love and Its Derangements: Poems*. This book was not dedicated to JD. He makes the common error of confusing the words *dedication* and *inscription*.

66. Volume of connected stories that was charged with obscenity when initially published in 1946.

67. On letterhead printed with JD's name and home address.

68. No poems by Johnson appeared in *Esquire* during JD's tenure as poetry editor.

69. Probably *The Loco Logodaedalist in Situ* published in London in 1972.

70. (1925–94), British novelist and biographer identified with the "Angry Young Men" movement in England. His introduction appeared in Williams's *Lines About Hills Above Lakes* (1964).

71. On letterhead printed with JD's name and home address.

72. Burnshaw chose the title *In the Terrified Radiance* for his 1972 book.

73. Theater producer, who was Chairman of the Awards Advisory Committee for the National Book Awards Committee.

74. *Sorties* was one of ten nominees in the Arts and Letters category.

75. Bly had won the 1968 National Book Award in Poetry for *The Light Around the Body*, which attacked American political and social institutions and the country's involvement in the Vietnam War. Ginsberg, one of the five jurors on the 1971 poetry committee, had denounced the choice of the winner, Mona Van Duyn's *To See, To Take*, as "ignominious, insensitive and mediocre."

76. The judges for the National Book Award in Arts and Letters for 1971 were Burnshaw, Frederick Morgan, and John Lahr; see JD's 8 September 1971 letter to Burnshaw.

77. On letterhead printed with JD's name and home address.

78. Frederick Morgan (1922–), poet and founder of *Hudson Review*.

79. Theater critic John Lahr (1941–), who had published *Notes on a Cowardly Lion: The Biography of Bert Lahr*, about his father, in 1969.

80. Wayne received his only Academy Award for his performance in this 1969 movie.

81. See "Dear Committee" by Ginsberg and "Dear Allen" by Howard, *New York Times Book Review* (4 April 1971).

82. On letterhead for the *Deliverance* movie.

83. Poems by Philip Dacey (1939–) appeared in the March and June 1972 issues. *Esquire* did not publish verse by John Betjeman (1906–84), who was named British Poet Laureate in 1972.

84. Lish had proposed that photographer Scott Turner take pictures of the "top ten U.S. poets" for which JD would provide accompanying paragraphs explaining his own

poetic superiority in each case. Among the poets Lish suggested were Robert Lowell, Robert Duncan, Robert Creeley, Gary Snyder, J. V. Cunningham, Allen Ginsberg, Galway Kinnell, Alan Dugan, and Howard Nemerov.

85. Harold T. P. Hayes.

86. JD was godfather to Lish's infant son, Atticus.

87. In JD holograph.

88. Statement and list in JD holograph.

89. Richard Jefferies (1848–87), *The Story of My Heart: An Autobiography* (1891).

90. E. B. White (1899–1985), essayist associated with *The New Yorker.*

91. Jason Epstein (1928–), vice president at Random House and director of the left-wing *New York Review of Books.*

92. The column to which JD refers has not been identified.

93. On letterhead printed with JD's name and home address.

94. Anatole Broyard's review of *Sorties* appeared in the 17 December 1971 issue of the *New York Times.* An equally dismissive review by David Kalstone appeared in the 23 January 1972 *New York Times Book Review.*

95. "The Son, the Cave, and the Burning Bush," *The Young American Poets,* edited by Paul Carroll (1968).

96. William Heyen's review of *Sorties* and *Straw for the Fire: From the Notebooks of Theodore Roethke* was published in *The Saturday Review* (11 March 1972); Janeway's brief notice of *Sorties* appeared in her *Cosmopolitan* book column (February 1972). No review by Margaret Manning has been located in *The Boston Globe.*

97. Thomas R. Goethals, a classics professor and author of the novel *Chain of Command* (1955).

98. Edwin Seaver, Burnshaw's editor at Braziller.

99. (1971).

100. No poetry by Hill appeared in *Esquire* during the 1970s.

101. On letterhead printed with JD's name and home address.

102. Burnshaw had reported to JD that Morgan, his fellow judge on the National Book Awards Arts and Letters panel, was supporting John Simon's *Movies into Films* (1971) and B. H. Haggin's *Fact and Symbol* (1971).

103. The National Book Committee announced the finalists in each NBA category on 26 March and the winners on 11 April. Charles Rosen's *The Classical Style: Haydn, Mozart, Beethoven* received the award in the Arts and Letters category.

104. This anthology project, based on Burnshaw's theories in *The Seamless Web,* did not develop.

105. The poem dedicated to JD was "Not to Bereave . . . ," collected in *In the Terrified Radiance.* No poem by Burnshaw appeared in *Esquire* while JD was its poetry editor.

106. JD was inducted into the National Institute of Arts and Letters on 17 May 1972.

107. On letterhead printed with JD's name and home address.

108. A portrait of JD with his life mask was used as cover art for the February 1976 issue of *Esquire,* in which "Cahill Is Blind," the prepublication excerpt from *Alnilam* described here, was published.

109. *The Zodiac,* which was not published until 1976.

110. Rural retreat of the private Bohemian Club to which members may invite guests.

111. "Escape Artist" by H. A. Phrydas was published in the September 1975 issue of *Esquire.*

112. "Rattlesnake Country" appeared as the only poem in the December 1973 *Esquire.*

113. Tate.

114. Warren was married to fiction writer Eleanor Clark (1913–96).

115. On letterhead printed with JD's name and home address.

116. The last part of the poem reads:

> I remember
> The need to enter the night-lake and swim out toward
> The distant moonset. Remember
> The blue-tattered flick of white flame at the rock-hole
> In the instant before I lifted up
> My eyes to the high sky that shivered in its hot whiteness.
> And sometimes—at dawn usually—I remember the cry on the mountain.
>
> All I can do is to offer my testimony.

117. This collection was published in 1979 as *The Strength of Fields*.

118. JD is quoting a line from "Children," by Henry Wadsworth Longfellow (1807–82).

119. On letterhead printed with JD's name and home address.

120. Eliot's poem was published on 5 November 1922 in the American little magazine *Dial*, which helped make the poet's reputation and also relieved some of his financial difficulties.

121. None of these magazines published *The Zodiac*.

122. *Mademoiselle* did not print *The Zodiac*. The poem was first published as a book, in limited and trade editions, during the fall of 1976.

123. On letterhead printed with JD's name and home address.

124. JD wrote the screenplay for *The Call of the Wild*; the television series did not develop.

125. Burnshaw's *Mirages: Travel Notes in the Promised Land* (1977) was dedicated to JD.

126. The line from Lowell's "To Allen Tate 2. 1960's," collected in *History* (1973), reads: " 'I don't know whether to call you my son or my brother.' "

127. Signature and last line are in JD holograph.

128. Editor in chief of Holt, Rinehart and Winston.

129. Wallace had asked JD for a blurb for *Robert Frost: The Later Years* by Lawrance Thompson and R. H. Winnick. An excerpt from JD's November 1966 *Atlantic Monthly* review of Thompson's *Robert Frost: The Early Years* was printed on the back jacket of the Thompson/Winnick biography: "Dr. Thompson's authoritative and loving book . . . has, or should have, the effect of leading us all into a private place—the grave of judgment, or the beginning of it—where we ponder long and long the nature 'of life and art,' their connections and interconnections, and the appalling risk, the cost in lives and minds not only of putting rhythmical symbols of ink on a white page, but of encountering, of reading them as well."

130. *Three on the Tower: The Lives and Works of Ezra Pound, T. S. Eliot, and William Carlos Williams* (1975).

131. Robert Lowell died of a heart attack on 12 September 1977.

132. Editor, *Next* magazine. JD's list, along with those of eight others, appeared in the Preview Issue of *Next* (1979).

133. *Broca's Brain: Reflections on the Romance of Science* (1979).

134. (1935–), poet and faculty member at Duke University.

135. Applewhite's 1980 collection was titled *Following Gravity*.

136. American poet (1936–) and faculty member at the University of North Carolina, Greensboro.

137. American poet (1925–) who spent most of his career at the University of North Carolina, Greensboro.

138. On letterhead printed with JD's name and home address.

139. Son of Malcolm Cowley, Robert Cowley was then an editor at Random House.

140. Floyd C. Watkins and John T. Hiers, editors, *Robert Penn Warren Talking: Interviews, 1950–1978* (1980).

141. Washington University in St. Louis had purchased JD's papers between 1968 and 1970; Emory University acquired large JD collections in 1993 and 1998. Warren's papers went to Yale University.

142. Warren's 1953 verse drama was published in revised version in 1979.

143. Published in book form in 1969.

144. Maxine Dickey had died 28 October 1976. Section VII of *Audubon: A Vision* (1969)—"Tell Me a Story"—reads:

[A]

Long ago, in Kentucky, I, a boy, stood
By a dirt road, in first dark, and heard
The great geese hoot northward.

I could not see them, there being no moon
And the stars sparse. I heard them.

I did not know what was happening in my heart.

It was the season before the elderberry blooms,
Therefore they were going north.

The sound was passing northward.

[B]

Tell me a story.

In this century, and moment, of mania,
Tell me a story.

Make it a story of great distances, and starlight.

The name of the story will be Time,
But you must not pronounce its name.

Tell me a story of deep delight.

145. Hugo was then teaching at the University of Montana, Missoula. After Hugo's death in 1982, JD wrote a tribute to him published in the 1983 issue of *Corona.*

146. On 26 April 1968 JD had read selections from his poetry at the American Embassy, London, under sponsorship of the Cultural Affairs Office of the American Embassy and the British publisher of *Poems 1957–1967,* Rapp & Whiting.

147. Hugo's lectures and essays on poetry published by Norton in 1979. He read at the University of South Carolina in November 1980.

148. JD's joke involved serial killer Theodore Bundy.

149. On 18 May 1980, the volcano Mount St. Helens in Washington had erupted, killing sixty people.

150. JD had married Deborah Dodson, one of his students, on 30 December 1976.

151. On letterhead printed with JD's name and home address.

152. German poet (1887–1912).

153. (1924–), German-American poet and translator. His translation of "Judas" appears in *Modern German Poetry: 1910–1960,* edited by Hamburger and Christopher Middleton (1962).

154. JD is quoting from his own version of "Judas," collected in his *Head-Deep in Strange Sounds: Free-Flight Improvisations from the UnEnglish.*

155. "The Surround."

156. Poet Rukeyser died on 12 February 1980 at the age of sixty-seven.

157. Young Adult Librarian at West Dade Regional Library in Miami, Florida.

158. (1922–89), essayist and social commentator.

159. James Laughlin (1914–97), founder of New Directions press.

160. Miller's *The Books in My Life* was published in 1952. Dwight Macdonald's assessment in the January–February 1953 issue of *Partisan Review* said, ". . . his recent books aren't literary productions at all but rather tape-recordings of the garrulities of a mildly intoxicated, mildly intelligent, mildly genial old fellow in a bar."

161. American fiction writer (1924–84). Although the two writers were not close friends, JD provided Capote's memorial tribute that was read at the American Academy and Institute of Arts and Letters and published in the Academy's *Proceedings*. The tribute included a poem, "To Be Done in Winter by Those Surviving Truman Capote."

162. "I shan't be gone long.—You come too," is a repeated line in Frost's poem "The Pasture." Capote did not read at the University of South Carolina.

163. On letterhead printed with JD's name and home address.

164. *Being Here: Poetry 1977–1980* (1980).

165. "Robert Penn Warren's Courage" (August 1980). This review was collected as "The Weathered Hand and Silent Space" in *Night Hurdling*.

166. "Foreword," *Dictionary of Literary Biography, Volume Five,* edited by Donald J. Greiner (1980). In his foreword Dickey writes, "What Seymour Krim says of Thomas Wolfe's readers is doubly true of those who have encountered Roethke: 'There is nothing we will not give to the person who can show us the undiscovered world within ourselves, for most of us are unaware of the possibilities we hold.' " Krim's 1961 book, *Views of a Nearsighted Cannoneer,* had been republished in an enlarged edition in 1968.

167. (1918–80).

168. *A Piece of Lettuce* was published in 1964; *Conversions* was published in 1971.

169. (1966).

170. Writers at *Time* magazine.

171. In his 25 August 1980 *Time* essay, "America Needs a Poet Laureate, Maybe," Morrow had facetiously suggested that poet-laureate candidates run on tickets with presidential candidates and that JD fit better on a ticket with Lyndon Johnson than with Jimmy Carter.

172. Of El Paso, Texas.

173. "The Lifeguard."

MAN OF LETTERS:

JANUARY 1981–AUGUST 1988

1. (1949–), poet who was working on his Ph.D. at Florida State University and whose first collection, *Shooting Rats at the Bibb County Dump,* was published in 1980.

2. On letterhead printed with JD's name and home address.

3. JD says in *Self-Interviews* that British fiction writer Lowry (1909–57) was so fascinated by the work of the Norwegian poet Grieg (1902–43) that Lowry traveled to Norway to meet Grieg. JD uses the anecdote to support his contention that one should not disassociate the poem from the poet.

4. (1936–), journalist and fiction writer.

5. On letterhead printed with JD's name and home address.

6. *Too Old to Cry,* Hemphill's 1981 collection of newspaper columns, included "The Late Karl Wallenda."

7. Frady (1940–) had published *Billy Graham* in 1979 and *Southerners* in 1980; Crews (1935–) had published a collection of nonfiction pieces, *Blood and Grits*, in 1979.

8. (1931–); Wolfe's account of the Apollo astronauts, *The Right Stuff*, had been published in 1979.

9. JD inserts in holograph the words "excuse grammar here!"

10. (1915–), American novelist who had won the Nobel Prize for Literature in 1976.

11. Hellman's credits as a producer included *The World of Henry Orient* (1964), *Midnight Cowboy* (1969), *The Day of the Locust* (1975), and *Coming Home* (1978).

12. American poet (1913–66). Bellow's *Humboldt's Gift* was published in 1975.

13. On letterhead printed with JD's name and home address.

14. Harriet Wasserman of Russell & Volkening, Inc.; James Atlas, author of *Delmore Schwartz: The Life of an American Poet* (1977).

15. JD quotes from Schwartz's "The Ballad of the Children of the Czar," collected in his *Summer Knowledge: New and Selected Poems, 1938–1958* (1959).

16. Pierre Berton's *Klondike Fever* (1958), Jack Hope's *Yukon* (1976), and Keith Tryck's *Yukon Passage* (1980).

17. JD produced a first-draft treatment for "Klondike," which is now at Emory University along with several notebooks with transcriptions of JD-Hellman conferences on the movie and substantial correspondence between the writer and the producer/director.

18. On letterhead printed with JD's name and home address.

19. Burnshaw novel published by Horizon in 1981. JD's dust jacket statement reads:

> It would be hard to say with sufficient conviction and eloquence how important a work *The Refusers* is. It focuses and dramatizes an almost unbelievable amount of history crucial not only to the survival of humanity but to the meaning of it. And if this meaning remains a mystery, it is one that gives off an unignorable light.
>
> It may be that the eternal seeker for the revelation of Jewishness is "no more than my father's brother who tried / To turn time inside out looking for ancestors"; or that "we have always been led to a void at the end of a maze / By the wrong questions." It may also be that the meaning resides in the blank silence of the desert out of which a God is invented from the heat's trembling mirror itself. . . . The reader can choose, for as in all mysteries there are many possibilities.
>
> But once he has encountered *The Refusers*, he himself cannot refuse: to participate, to be moved and shaken, to draw conclusions from the oldest questions, for with this dark and radiant book he is involved in nothing less than the enigma of history, life and himself.
>
> A tremendous, vital piece of work.

20. Bronwen Elaine Dickey was born 17 May 1981.

21. On letterhead printed with JD's name and home address.

22. Published by Louisiana State University Press in 1981.

23. On letterhead printed with JD's name and home address.

24. As a journalist for the *Washington Post*.

25. Howard was translating Charles Baudelaire's *Les Fleurs du Mal*, which was published in 1983 and won the 1984 American Book Award for translation.

26. Campbell's translation was published in 1952; Edna St. Vincent Millay and George Dillon's translation appeared in 1936.

27. In *The Voyage and Other Versions of Poems by Baudelaire* (1968).

28. (1951–), poet and member of faculty at Colgate University.

29. Balakian's father had died.

30. Balakian was co-founder and co-editor of *Graham House Review,* which published "Deborah and Deirdre as Drunk Bridesmaids Foot-Racing at Daybreak" and "Summons" in its Spring 1982 issue.

31. Nona Balakian (1919–91), associate editor of the *New York Times Book Review* and literary critic.

32. (1958–), editor of *MSS* and wife of novelist John Gardner (1933–82).

33. Poems from *Puella*—"From Time" and "Deborah as Scion" ("With Rose at Cemetery" and "In Lace and Whale Bone")—were published in the Spring 1981 *MSS,* edited by Gardner and Rosenberg.

34. Unpublished.

35. 1948.

36. 1947; revised edition, 1951.

37. Edited by Edmund Wilson in 1948.

38. Six poems—"Deborah in Mountain Sound: Bell, Glacier, Rose," "Ray-Flowers I," "Ray-Flowers II," "Doorstep, Lightning, Waif-Dreaming," "Deborah in Ancient Lingerie, in Thin Oak Over Creek," and "The Lode"—appeared in the Winter 1982 *Kenyon Review,* which was then edited by Ronald Sharp and Frederick Turner.

39. On letterhead printed with JD's name and home address.

40. JD, Warren, and Gerald Stern were judges for the 1981 William Carlos Williams Award sponsored by the Poetry Society of America. They presented the award to Ghiselin for his *Windrose: Poems, 1929–1979* (1980).

41. Assistant Director and Executive Editor, Louisiana State University Press.

42. On letterhead printed with JD's name and home address.

43. Stuart's *Common Ground* was published by Louisiana State University Press in 1982.

44. Louisiana State University Press did not publish Cotterill's typescript; her collection *The Hive Burning* was published by Sleeping Bird Press in 1983.

45. Louisiana State University Press published *Durations: Poems* by Scott in 1984 and three collections by Applewhite in the 1980s: *Foreseeing the Journey* (1983), *Ode to the Chinaberry Tree and Other Poems* (1986), and *Lessons in Soaring* (1989).

46. On letterhead printed with JD's name and home address.

47. Seamus Heaney (1939–), 1995 winner of the Nobel Prize in Literature.

48. Edgar Finley Shannon Jr., Professor of English and former President of the University of Virginia. Bottoms remained at Georgia State University.

49. On letterhead printed with JD's name and home address.

50. John Lugar, who had worked as assistant producer on the movie *Coma* (MGM, 1978) and associate producer on the movie *Looker* (Warner Brothers, 1981).

51. JD wrote a preliminary treatment for a screenplay of Seager's novel, but the project did not develop.

52. East of the South is unidentified, but a collection of Lish's short stories, *What I Know So Far,* was published in 1984 by Holt, Rinehart, and Winston.

53. Abrahams was an editor at Holt, Rinehart, and Winston, the publisher of Lish's novel, *Dear Mr. Capote* (1983).

54. Abrahams and Stansky had edited *The Unknown Orwell* in 1972 and *Orwell: The Transformation* in 1979. Their *Journey to the Frontier* had appeared in 1966.

55. Poet (1925–) whose collection *Monolithos: Poems, 1962 and 1982* was published in 1982; his *Views of Jeopardy* was published in 1962.

56. Fiction writer Kay Boyle (1902–92).

57. JD's statement reads: "These are poems that seem to have been not so much written but fired at the reader, with deadly aim and intent. Yet when he recovers from the

shock, he finds that his heart has flowered and his mind deepened, for the imagination of Jack Gilbert is astonishing, uncompromising, and totally memorable."

58. *Alnilam.*

59. On letterhead printed with JD's name and home address.

60. A reference to the custom of army recruits being paid a small sum at the time of enlistment.

61. Writer Milton Klonsky (1921–81), whose death Krim had reported in his 8 December 1981 letter to JD.

62. The dust jacket statement attributed to JD reads: "Hart Crane's 'the fury of the street' is one of the great phrases of our literature since Baudelaire, when, in the 'ant-swarming city,' 'the ghost in broad daylight plucks you by the sleeve.' Michael Seide has caught and articulated this fury, has made it lament and scream and sing: has bodied forth the city-sensibility at its most naked and creative. His vision is all-out, and his language matches it. I have read no more powerful and releasing book in years."

63. Unlocated.

64. (1938–), North Carolina poet whose *Walking Out* had been published in 1975 and whose *Nettles* would appear in 1983.

65. Atwood (1939–), Oliver (1935–), Stoutenburg (1916–82). JD wrote a foreword for Stoutenburg's posthumously published *Land of Superior Mirages* (1986).

66. *Puella.*

67. Thomas N. Walters (1935–83), North Carolina writer and editor, who had cancer.

68. On letterhead printed with JD's name and home address.

69. Doc Watson.

70. According to those who heard him, JD's desire to play the guitar exceeded his proficiency.

71. Newsletter of the Academy of American Poets.

72. Gardner (1915–81).

73. (1921–79); Simmons's *Osiris at the Roller Derby,* with a foreword by JD, was published in 1983.

74. Bottoms did not review *Puella.*

75. *Night Hurdling* was published in October 1983, not October 1982.

76. Allin's poem—about how the motifs of saloons turned drinking in them into journeys—was not published by *Shenandoah.*

77. Published by Bruccoli Clark Layman, not Harcourt Brace.

78. *Amicus Journal* (Summer 1982).

79. Dolly Langdon, "James Dickey's Wife, Deborah, Says Deliverance Is Escape from Her Poet Husband's Shadow," *People* (30 August 1982).

80. *Two Poets, Two Friends.*

81. Leslie Bates, then JD's secretary.

82. Warren dedicated "Chief Joseph of the Nez Perce" to JD.

83. On letterhead printed with JD's name and home address.

84. In a 26 March 1982 letter to JD, Hellman had expressed reservations about JD's first-draft treatment for "Klondike":

> But the concerns I have been expressing regarding the lack of a clear line of character development . . . and the fact that we have still not successfully gone to the mat with the very basic issue of STORY . . . [have] combined to leave me feeling that perhaps we must alter the focus of our next efforts.
>
> For in spite of all the wonderful texture that exists in details, the sum total is, in my judgment, finally neither sufficiently dramatic nor sufficiently involving. . . .

In point of fact, it often seems we are relying on the uniqueness of the terrain and the larger events to cover over the fact that we really don't yet have an adequately well-developed or carefully thought-out story.

By the fall of 1982 the project had been abandoned.

85. Bookie Binkley sued JD for the return of the advance and won his case in court.

86. Burnshaw was not elected to the National Institute of Arts and Letters.

87. In his 13 July 1982 letter to JD, Burnshaw mentioned that he had not received honorary degrees, nor had he been elected to the "Boston-centered Academy of the Arts."

88. Elie Wiesel (1928–), survivor of and writer about the Holocaust; Vendler (1933–), literary critic.

89. (1879–1955), American modernist poet.

90. *Atlantic High: A Celebration* (1982), which Buckley inscribed for but did not dedicate to JD.

91. During the early 1980s JD took a correspondence course in navigation.

92. Balakian reviewed *Puella* in "Poets of Empathy," *The Literary Review* (Fall 1983).

93. (1942–), American poet and member of the faculty at Louisiana State University.

94. (1928–), American literary critic.

95. All of these titles were changed before the poems were collected in *Puella*.

96. Editor and publisher of *AB Bookman's Weekly*.

97. These books were not recovered.

98. On letterhead printed with JD's name and home address.

99. (1892–1982), American poet, playwright, and public servant; Winnick's *Letters of Archibald MacLeish, 1907–1982* was published in 1983.

100. MacLeish's "Dry Tortugas" appeared in the 1 February 1939 issue of *Vogue*.

101. Van Doren (1894–1972), literary critic and Columbia University faculty member. *The Dialogues of Archibald MacLeish and Mark Van Doren*, edited by Warren V. Bush, was published in 1964.

102. Winnick's *Archibald MacLeish: An American Life* was published in 1992.

103. One of JD's former University of South Carolina students who had been admitted to the Writers' Workshop at the University of Iowa.

104. On letterhead printed with JD's name and home address.

105. Poets Stanley Plumly (1939–) and Marvin Bell (1937–) were on the staff of the Writers' Workshop in 1983.

106. Leggett (1917–), a novelist, was in 1983 Director of the Writers' Workshop; his 1974 book was a dual biography of Ross Lockridge Jr. (1914–48) and Thomas Heggen (1919–49), writers who committed suicide after producing best-selling novels.

107. In 1953 German mystic Eugen Herrigel (1884–1955) had published a book that was translated and published in English as *Zen in the Art of Archery*.

108. These six words are in JD holograph. Jacobs (1946–) published a collection of poetry, *Our Eyes, Like Walls*, in 1981.

109. (1916–), poet, member of the Princeton University faculty, and editor of *The Quarterly Review of Literature*.

110. On letterhead printed with JD's name and address.

111. Weiss's 1982 critical book.

112. The University of South Carolina hosted a four-day birthday celebration for JD in February 1983.

113. Poet and reviewer living in Bronxville, New York.

114. On letterhead printed with JD's name and home address.

115. "Business and Poetry," *Hudson Review* (Spring 1983).

116. Editor at W. W. Norton.

117. *Making Certain It Goes On: The Collected Poems of Richard Hugo* was published by Norton in 1984.

118. "Be dust myself pretty soon; not now" is the final line of Berryman's "Note to Wang Wei," first collected in *His Thought Made Pockets & the Plane Buckt* (1958).

119. On letterhead printed with JD's name and home address.

120. From *Alnilam;* published as "Blind Snow, Warm Water" in the 50th-Anniversary Issue (1984) of *Partisan Review.*

121. JD's former secretary who became one of his editors at Doubleday.

122. *The Paris Review* did not publish a prepublication excerpt from the novel.

123. Executive editor at Doubleday.

124. O'Neill, a Doubleday editor.

125. Doubleday editor.

126. Doubleday declined this project; the book was published by Oxmoor House as *Wayfarer* in 1988.

127. This volume was not published.

128. *Bronwen, the Traw, and the Shape-Shifter* appeared in September 1986.

129. The Sunfish is ten feet long.

130. On letterhead printed with JD's name and home address.

131. The typescript for *Alnilam.*

132. Quotations from Lucretius and Hume appear as epigraphs for the novel.

> And next I will speak of the air which is changed over its whole body every hour in countless ways. For whatever ebbs from things, is all borne always into the great sea of air; and unless it in return were to give back bodies to things and to recruit them as they ebb, all things ere now would have been dissolved and changed into air. —Lucretius

> May I not clearly and distinctly conceive that a body, falling from the clouds, and which, in all other respects, resembles snow, has yet the taste of salt or feeling of fire? —Hume

> Where am I, or what? From what causes do I derive my existence, and to what condition do I return? Whose favour shall I court, and whose anger must I dread? What beings surround me? —Hume

133. Wouk (1915–) wrote the 1954 play, *The Caine Mutiny Court-Martial,* which was drawn from his 1951 novel, *The Caine Mutiny.*

134. JD's grandson, Tucky, was attending St. George's School in Newport, Rhode Island.

135. On letterhead printed with JD's name and home address.

136. JD encouraged his grandson to call him Fun Man. Beneath his holograph signature, JD drew an arrow, under which he wrote "slightly crookèd (can be straightened!)".

137. On letterhead printed with JD's name and home address.

138. *Possessions: New and Selected Poems, 1928–1985* (1986).

139. Doubleday editor.

140. The novel was published on 5 June.

141. In the published book, the bold-face type was used only on the split pages.

142. (1930–), literary critic and Sterling Professor of Humanities at Yale University.

143. *James Dickey* was a 1987 volume in the Chelsea House Modern Critical Views Series edited by Bloom.

144. Warren was struggling with bone cancer; JD underwent surgery for a subarachnoid hemorrhage resulting from an injury.

145. (1924–); author of the novel *Mrs. Bridge* (1959) and of a biography of General George Armstrong Custer, *Son of the Morning Star* (1984), Connell had written an influential review of *Deliverance* for the 22 March 1970 *New York Times Book Review.*

146. An allusion to Connell's 1973 collection of poetry, *Points for a Compass Rose.*

147. Tom Dickey died on 10 December 1987 at the age of sixty-two.

148. On 4 December 1987 JD was inducted into the fifty-member American Academy of Arts and Letters. He occupied Chair 15, previously held by scholar Wilbur Cross, painter Raphael Soyer, and novelist John Steinbeck.

149. (1925–), a director of large-budget movies with spectacular special effects; his movies include *The Towering Inferno* (1974) and the 1976 remake of *King Kong.*

150. Christopher Dickey's 1976 documentary, *War Under the Pinestraw,* about Tom Dickey's pursuit of Civil War relics.

151. Central America.

152. Executive at NEF, Inc., in Colorado Springs, who was helping arrange a reading engagement for JD at the Air Force Academy.

153. Wallisch had sent JD a clipping from the Colorado Springs *Gazette Telegraph,* in which captions on photographs of JD and Styron had been reversed.

154. A reader from Bronxville, New York, who had, in her 21 April letter, praised *Alnilam* for its focusing on senses other than sight and for its "deeply challenging story and theme."

155. This movie was not made.

156. (1916–97), comparative literature professor at New York University, who, responding to *Alnilam,* praised JD for his representation of the blinded as opposed to blind man, for his ability to convey the sensations of flight, and for his "virtuosity of imagery . . . totally original and unbeatable." She was, however, critical of the profane language in the novel.

157. A former student of JD's at the University of South Carolina.

THE LAST WOLVERINE: SEPTEMBER 1988–NOVEMBER 1996

1. Editor at Houghton Mifflin; *To The White Sea* was published in 1993 by Houghton Mifflin as "A Marc Jaffe book."

2. On letterhead printed with JD's name and home address.

3. Joe Kanon and Marley Rusoff were editors at Houghton Mifflin.

4. (1925–), American novelist and essayist.

5. *At Home: Essays, 1982–1988* was published in 1988.

6. Prokosch's 1948 novel.

7. On letterhead printed with JD's name and home address.

8. A Mooresville, North Carolina, resident, who had sent JD a copy of her husband's book of poetry and requested a note of encouragement.

9. Librarian of Congress.

10. Howard Nemerov served a second term as Poet Laureate and was succeeded in 1990 by Mark Strand.

11. High-school teacher in Orono, Maine, who had arranged a teleconference with JD for his students.

12. L. David Mech (1937–), Barry Lopez (1945–), and Boyce Rensberger (1942–) wrote books about nature.

13. *The Call of the Wild, White Fang, and Other Stories,* edited by Andrew Sinclair, was published in 1981.

14. On letterhead printed with JD's name and home address.

15. English poetry editor who, as his secretary informed JD, had died in 1987.

16. (1969).

17. Spender had been visiting poet in residence while JD was on leave.

18. Louis MacNeice (1907–63), British poet and dramatist.

19. Wooley died at the age of twenty-three during World War II. Lehmann had published his story "The Search" in *New Writing and Daylight* in 1943.

20. Hirsch, a writer who was living in New Orleans, wrote JD a fan letter about *Alnilam.*

21. Hirsch had enclosed a letter/manifesto, purportedly by Gus Willikers but actually by Hirsch himself, that had been printed in a Denver magazine.

22. Mrs. Dickey was undergoing treatment for drug and alcohol addiction at Hazelden Center in Center City, Minnesota.

23. Printed on letterhead with JD's name and home address.

24. Christopher Dickey's 1985 book. The poem to which JD refers is "To the Butterflies," collected in *The Eagle's Mile.*

25. Christopher Dickey had married Carol Salvatore in 1980.

26. President, Wesleyan University, Middletown, Connecticut.

27. On letterhead printed with JD's name and home address.

28. It had been proposed that Wesleyan University Press merge with the University Press of New England in Hanover, New Hampshire. The merger went into effect on January 1, 1990.

29. *The Eagle's Mile* (1990) and *The Whole Motion* (1992) were published by Wesleyan University Press/University Press of New England.

30. Poet and former Air Force pilot who was on the faculty of Texas Technical University in Lubbock.

31. On letterhead printed with JD's name and home address.

32. French aviator and writer Antoine de Saint-Exupéry (1900–44).

33. (1888–1935).

34. The novel was not completed. Twenty-nine pages of corrected typescript are in the James Dickey Collection at Emory University.

35. Professor in the Honors Program at Brigham Young University.

36. Dickey's dust-jacket statement reads: "Between one language and another there exists for poetry a kind of creative limbo which can be inhabited by anyone. The real translator operates there at his peril, but with resourcefulness and daring. Norris and Keele give us not only accurate translations, but work that contains that 'x-quality,' without which the poetry would not be poetry." *The Sonnets to Orpheus,* translated by Keele and Norris, was published in 1989 by Camden House.

37. Leslie Norris, Keele's co-translator on the Rilke volume.

38. J. B. Leishman and Stephen Spender had, together and separately, translated several Rilke volumes.

39. Mitchell's *The Selected Poetry of Rainer Maria Rilke* had been published by Random House in 1982.

40. Teacher at Father Judge High School, Philadelphia.

41. McKee had mentioned that a journal called *Visions* had reprinted JD's poem "Eagles."

42. In the March/April 1987 issue.

43. Former student of JD at the University of South Carolina.

44. (1909–93), American novelist and nonfiction writer.

45. A recurring character in Stegner's fiction.

46. *Collected Stories of Wallace Stegner* was published in 1990.

47. Member of the Stanford University English Department and biographer of Anne Sexton.

48. Director, Yale University Press.

49. Editor at Henry Regnery Publishing Company.

50. *From Eden to Babylon: The Social and Political Essays of Andrew Nelson Lytle,* edited by M. E. Bradford, was published by Regnery in 1990.

51. No JD statement appeared on the dust jacket of Lytle's 1990 collection.

52. Regnery's *Memoirs of a Dissident Publisher* was published by Harcourt Brace Jovanovich in 1979.

53. Friend of Seymour Krim who was helping to organize his memorial service.

54. Krim had committed suicide on 30 August 1998.

55. A former student of JD at the University of South Carolina, Goff sometimes worked as his typist and editorial assistant.

56. Typescript for *The Eagle's Mile.*

57. Robert Bly's daughter was helping him clear permissions for a forthcoming book.

58. In her 2 March 1990 reply, Mary Bly explained that her father's book was a collection of his earlier essays, including a shortened version of his "On James Dickey," which quoted from and attacked JD's work, including "The Firebombing."

59. A former student of JD at the University of South Carolina and member of the English faculty at Longwood College.

60. Published as *Striking In: The Early Notebooks of James Dickey* in 1996.

61. *Critical Essays on James Dickey,* edited by Robert Kirschten (1994).

62. Romy Heylen, a Belgian scholar who wrote an essay on *The Zodiac,* taught at the University of South Carolina for four years.

63. On letterhead printed with JD's name and home address.

64. Publication of the novel was delayed until 1993.

65. Features Editor at *Southpoint: The Metropolitan Monthly* in Atlanta. JD's letter was not published because the magazine ceased publication in June 1990.

66. (1961).

67. Shaara's novel was published in 1974.

68. English Department faculty member at Amherst College whose biography, *Randall Jarrell: A Literary Life,* was published in 1990.

69. No poem by John Logue was published in *The New Yorker* or *The Southern Review* in 1990 or 1991.

70. Of Spokane, Washington. Her *Bears Dancing in the Northern Air* was published in the Yale Series of Younger Poets in 1991.

71. JD's suggestions for title and byline changes were not acted on.

72. Of Joliet, Illinois.

73. Chairman, Board of Trustees, University of South Carolina.

74. On letterhead printed with JD's name and home address.

75. John M. Palms, President of Georgia State University, was named President of the University of South Carolina.

76. JD's *The Eagle's Mile* and Smith's *Collected Poems, 1939–1989* (1990) were reviewed together by Herbert Mitgang in the 27 October 1990 *New York Times.*

77. JD provided a dust jacket statement for Smith's collection:
Grace, a highly personal and responsible relation to form, and effortless and natural imagination combine in William Jay Smith's poems to create an atmosphere which is a valuable, liveable space. When wit is added, as it often is, his art becomes inimitable indeed. No one should miss these poems.

78. (1980).

79. Smith did not assemble a collection of his criticism.

80. Executive Director of Yale University Press with whom JD worked as the judge for the Yale Series of Younger Poets.

81. On letterhead printed with JD's name and home address.

82. Nicholas Samaras's *Hands of the Saddlemaker* was published in the Yale Series of Younger Poets in 1992.

83. "The Promised Fire" appeared in *Partisan Review,* volume 63, number 3 (1991).

84. Another excerpt from *To the White Sea,* "Outfitting," appeared in the October 1992 *Southern Review.*

85. The Houghton Mifflin edition of the novel used a gold Japanese calligraphy figure on a red circle as part of the dust jacket art.

86. The project did not develop further.

87. *The Whole Motion,* published by Wesleyan University Press/The University Press of New England in 1992, included twenty-five previously uncollected poems from JD's early career.

88. (1945–), novelist and former student of JD.

89. Of Hilton Head Island, South Carolina.

90. On letterhead printed with JD's name and home address.

91. Poet and editor of *The Southern Review.*

92. On letterhead printed with JD's name and home address.

93. "Last Hours" appeared in the Autumn 1994 issue of *The Southern Review.*

94. (1908–), novelist and fiction editor at *The New Yorker.*

95. Maxwell's 1948 novel.

96. Prominent guitarist.

97. On letterhead printed with JD's name and home address.

98. Last two sentences in JD holograph.

99. Editor at Simon & Schuster, UK.

100. Of *To the White Sea.*

101. American poet and fiction writer (1943–). His review of *To the White Sea* appeared in the 27 September 1993 issue of *The New Yorker.*

102. Willie Morris was selected to edit the volume but subsequently withdrew and was replaced by Henry Hart.

103. Probably misspelling of Joe Kanon, executive at Houghton Mifflin.

104. JD did not begin work on this novel.

105. JD did not begin work on this novel.

106. On letterhead printed with JD's name and home address.

107. The Cultural Affairs Editor of *The State* newspaper, Columbia, South Carolina, had delivered Conroy's 1995 novel to JD.

108. Director, University of South Carolina Press.

109. Conroy provided a foreword to this book, published by the University of South Carolina Press in 1996.

110. This screenplay was not produced.

111. *Striking In.*

112. A high-school senior from Marietta, Georgia, who had written JD to praise his poetry.

113. On letterhead printed with JD's name and home address.

114. A 1994 collection of essays by Bellow.

115. In his 27 May reply, the Nobel Laureate praised *Deliverance.*

116. Of Summerville, South Carolina.

117. (1934).

118. Barber (1910–81), American composer. His *Knoxville: Summer of 1915*, Op. 24, was first performed in 1948.

119. Editor, Yale Series of Younger Poets.

120. Ms. Ansel lived in Menlo Park, California.

121. Of McGaheysville, Virginia; finalist in the 1996 Yale Series of Younger Poets competition.

122. On letterhead printed with JD's name and home address.

123. W. S. Merwin, JD's successor as judge for the Yale Series of Younger Poets, found no entry worthy of the award in 1997.

124. On letterhead printed with JD's name and home address.

125. On letterhead printed with JD's name and home address.

126. Ansel retitled her collection *My Shining Archipelago* for its publication as the 1997 Yale Series of Younger Poets winner.

127. Ansel retained the title "Inscrutable Pig" for her poem.

128. Member of the Comparative Literature faculty at Princeton University and translator of *The Odyssey*.

129. JD's statement read: "To re-create a world where everything is living, down to the chairs and table-linens, is very nearly as difficult as to create it. Fagles does this with triumphant assurance; every arrowhead flashes lightning, every bush burns: Homer is with us."

130. JD claimed that he embraced poetry on Okinawa at the end of the war after reading lines from poet Joseph Trumbull Stickney: "Thou art divine, thou livest,—as of old / Apollo springing naked to the light, / And all his island shivered into flowers." The word that inspired him was *shivered*.

131. (1946).

132. Professor of Classics at the University of South Carolina and close friend of JD.

133. These poems were unfinished at the time of JD's death.

134. Producer whose movies include *Blue Velvet* (1986), *In Country* (1989), and *Havana* (1990).

135. On letterhead printed with JD's name and home address.

136. David and Janet Peoples, who had written the screenplay for *To the White Sea*.

137. On letterhead printed with JD's name and home address.

138. (1921–), American novelist living in Chapel Hill, North Carolina.

139. Novelist and historian Foote (1916–) had published the individual volumes of his *The Civil War: A Narrative* in 1958, 1964, and 1973.

140. JD and novelist Heller (1923–) had met at the University of South Carolina World War II conference in 1994 and again, in September 1996, at the university's F. Scott Fitzgerald Centenary Celebration, for which Heller delivered the keynote address.

141. On letterhead printed with JD's name and home address.

142. Joel and Ethan Coen, producer/director/writer team whose movies include *Raising Arizona* (1987), *Miller's Crossing* (1990), and *Fargo* (1996). As of late 1999, the Coen/Universal option on *To the White Sea* was still in effect.

143. The movie version of *Catch-22*, directed by Mike Nichols, was released in 1970.

144. Widow of poet and editor Paul Carroll.

INDEX

Page numbers in *italics* refer to illustrations. Only works by Dickey are indexed: his poems and essays are enclosed in quotation marks; his book-length works are in *italics*.

A NOTE ON THE TYPE

This book was set in Minion, a typeface produced by the Adobe Corporation specifically for the Macintosh personal computer, and released in 1990. Designed by Robert Slimbach, Minion combines the classic characteristics of old-style faces with the full complement of weights required for modern typesetting.

Composed by North Market Street Graphics,
Lancaster, Pennsylvania

Printed and bound by Quebecor Printing,
Martinsburg, West Virginia

Designed by Cassandra J. Pappas

Matthew J. Bruccoli, Dickey's friend and colleague for nearly thirty years, is the Jefferies Professor of English at the University of South Carolina. He and Judith S. Baughman have jointly edited the letters of Vladimir Nabokov and F. Scott Fitzgerald.

With 20 photographs

Jacket photograph by Timothy Galfas
Jacket design by Chip Kidd

Alfred A. Knopf, Publisher, New York

www.randomhouse.com

11/99